ArtScroll Halachah Series®

Rabbi Nosson Scherman / Rabbi Meir Zlotowitz
General Editors

NISHMAT

Published by
Mesorah Publications, ltd

AVRAHAM

VOLUME II: YOREH DEAH

Medical Halachah for doctors, nurses, health-care personnel and patients

Translated From The Hebrew *Nishmat Avraham*
by its author
ABRAHAM S. ABRAHAM M.D., FRCP

FIRST EDITION
First Impression . . . January 2003

Published and Distributed by
MESORAH PUBLICATIONS, Ltd.
4401 Second Avenue
Brooklyn, New York 11232

Distributed in Europe by
LEHMANNS
Unit E, Viking Industrial Park
Rolling Mill Road
Jarrow, Tyne & Wear NE32 3DP
England

Distributed in Australia & New Zealand by
GOLDS WORLD OF JUDAICA
3-13 William Street
Balaclava, Melbourne 3183
Victoria Australia

Distributed in Israel by
SIFRIATI / A. GITLER — BOOKS
6 Hayarkon Street
Bnei Brak 51127

Distributed in South Africa by
KOLLEL BOOKSHOP
Shop 8A Norwood Hypermarket
Norwood 2196, Johannesburg, South Africa

THE ARTSCROLL SERIES ®
NISHMAT AVRAHAM
VOL. 2 — YOREH DEAH
© Copyright 2003, by MESORAH PUBLICATIONS, Ltd.
4401 Second Avenue / Brooklyn, N.Y. 11232 / (718) 921-9000 / www.artscroll.com

---

No part of this book may be reproduced
in any form *without* **written** *permission from the copyright holder,*
except by a reviewer who wishes to quote brief passages
in connection with a review written for inclusion
in magazines or newspapers.

THE RIGHTS OF THE COPYRIGHT HOLDER WILL BE STRICTLY ENFORCED.

ISBN: 1-57819-712-0
(hard cover only)

Printed in the United States of America by Noble Book Press Corp.
Bound by Sefercraft Quality Bookbinders, Ltd., Brooklyn, N.Y.

This book is dedicated
to the memory of
my dear parents z"l

אדוני אבי מורי ועט"ר
ר' אלידהו ב"ר נחמיה ז"ל
נפטר ח' אלול תשכ"א

ואמי מורתי ועט"ר
מרת חנה כתון בת רחל ז"ל
נפטרה י"ט אייר תשי"ד

ת.נ.צ.ב.ה.

Mesorah Heritage Foundation *and*
The Association of Orthodox Jewish Scientists
express their gratitude to the following
physicians of the Syrian Jewish community of Brooklyn
for their vision and generosity
in helping bring this monumental work
to the English-speaking public.

RABBI ELIE ABADIE, MD
in memory of his father Rabbi Abraham Abadie

RICHARD V. GRAZI, MD
in honor of his wife Leslie and children Sally, Joseph, Ariel, Rebecca,
Evan and Tamar

VICTOR M. GRAZI, MD
in honor of my wife Joanne and children Paulette, Simone, and Maurice

MARTIN (MORDECHAI) GROSSMAN, MD
in memory of Tzvi Hersch Grossman and David H. Tawil
Me'Eli Hacohen

ALBERT MATALON, MD
in honor of my wife, Rochelle, "my inspiration"

ROBERT MATALON, MD
in honor of my wife, Barbara, from whom I derive moral strength
and clarity of purpose

STANLEY S. SCHREM, MD
in honor of my wife Lynn, "whom I cherish"

INTRODUCTION

It is with a heart full of gratitude that I thank *Hashem* for His great kindness in giving me the merit to complete this English *Yoreh Deah* section of my Hebrew *Nishmat Avraham*. May it be His will that this volume will serve, in some small way, to glorify His Torah in showing how *halachic* problems and questions which modern medical concepts and discoveries bring in their wake are solved by the *poskim* of today based on the words of our Sages.

ArtScroll Mesorah Publications, founded by Rabbis Meir Zlotowitz and Nosson Scherman, has become a household word throughout the Jewish world and I am proud to have them publish my book. Rabbi Avrohom Biderman, who coordinated this work, and Mrs Mindy Stern, who meticulously proofread the book, are a pleasure and honor to know and work with. Mr Shmuel Blitz, the ArtScroll coordinator in Jerusalem, kept everything running smoothly and efficiently, and Professor Yaakov Petroff edited the book with great skill and understanding of the *halachic* intricacies involved. To all of them and the many others of the ArtScroll family who have had a share in the production of this book, my gratitude and thanks.

My sincere thanks to my colleagues, Dr. Robert Matalon and his son, Dr. Albert Matalon, for their continued support of this project. It is through their initiative that the Physicians of the Syrian community of Brooklyn have come together to generously allow the translation of *Nishmat Avraham* to become a reality.

My sincere thanks also to the anonymous donors who have helped this project. May *Hashem* reward and bless them all.

This book could not have been written without the help of my wife, Sylvia. Her constant encouragement, ideas and advice, repeated proofreading and wise comments have made the book what it is. May *Hashem* shower His blessings upon her for a long life of health and happiness.

I pray to *Hashem* that I will be privileged to finish the third and final volume of this translation and that my books merit to glorify His Name and spread His Torah throughout the Jewish world.

Abraham S. Abraham, MD, FRCP
Jerusalem

כסלו תשס"ג / November 2002

Bob and Susie Schulman

Our dear friends, Drs. Robert (Bob) Schulman and his wife Susie, remain the backbone of this publication. As with volume 1 of this series, their constant encouragement and interest has been instrumental in bringing this volume to publication. May *Hashem* grant them much happiness and good health for many more years with lots of *nachas* from their families, children and grandchildren.

ABOUT THE BOOK

This volume is a translation and collation of the *Yoreh Deah* section of the *Shulchan Aruch* and *Nishmat Avraham*, taken from volumes two, four and five of my Hebrew *Nishmat Avraham*. In addition there has been updating of material and a complete rewriting of some parts.

This volume, partly because of the subject matter and partly because of the need for an understanding and appreciation of many basic but intricate concepts and ideas in *halachah*, posed many problems. The main one, by far, was to decide what to translate and what to omit; not everything that appears in the *Shulchan Aruch* or in the Hebrew *Nishmat Avraham* has been translated. Therefore, no *halachic* decision should be made on the basis of what I have written here. All the more so, a decision must not be made on the basis of what I have *not* written here. This translation has not been written to serve as a quick do-it-yourself *halachic* handbook to replace a *posek*, but rather to make the reader aware of a problem that he or she may not have realized exists, so that it can be put to a *posek* for his decision.

Names of authors or their books, and words and phrases requiring explanation appear in the *Nishmat Avraham* section in italics, and are to be found in the Glossary. There, Hebrew and medical words and phrases are explained; authors' names, and where possible, dates of death are given, so as to give the reader an idea of the era in which they lived.

FOOD FOR THOUGHT

The *Rambam* writes:[1] It is fitting to ponder the Laws of our Holy Torah and to delve into their meaning to the best of our ability. But, if one does not find a reason for — or does not understand — something, it must not lessen its importance in his eyes. One can never reach the understanding of the Almighty and attempting to do so will cause you harm; nor must one think of the Torah in the same way that one thinks of secular matters. See how strict the Torah is with the Laws of wrongful use of that which has been sanctified. Sticks and stones, earth and ashes, become truly sanctified once a human being has dedicated them to the Master of the Universe, even if only by the spoken word, and one who desecrates such sanctity, even if only unintentionally, has transgressed, and must bring a sacrificial offering. How much more so may we not transgress and belittle the commandments that were given to us by the Almighty, just because we do not fully understand their meaning.

A PRESCRIPTION FOR THE PATIENT

The *Rambam* writes:[2] Take the roots of *Shabbat*, of praise and thanksgiving, of joy and trust; remove from them the seeds of grief and worry; take the flower brimming with knowledge and good sense, the roots of patience and satisfaction. Grind them all in a mortar of lowliness and cook them all in a vessel of humility; knead them with sweet words and dissolve them in the waters of grace and loving-kindness. Give the despairing patient two scoops morning and evening together with three scoops of the waters of explanation, having first cleansed it all of the refuse of anger and over-strictness and mixed it with a concentrated mixture of the acceptance of the wishes of *Hashem*, the Master to Whom all praise and thanksgiving is due. Give it to the patient to drink in a vessel of praise to the Almighty and he will be comfortable and calmed.

1. סוף הלכות מעילה
2. הקדמה לספר הנמצא שמיוחס להרמב"ם מובא בספר "רבי משה בן מימון" של הרב י.ל. מימון ז"ל עמ' קן

CONTENTS

Siman refers to the *Siman* of the *Shulchan Aruch*

CHAPTER 1
THE LAWS OF RITUAL SLAUGHTER

Siman 1	Who is permitted or not permitted to slaughter / A deaf-mute / Someone who suffers from "drop attacks" / A *shoteh* / Doubt regarding the status of a *shochet* / A *ger* / A deaf person / A dumb person / One whose hands tremble or are unsteady / One who is ill / Slaughtering while sitting / A blind person / Wearing glasses / A blind person and his obligation to perform *mitzvot*	2
Siman 19	Saying a blessing or performing a *mitzvah* in an unclean place / Bed-bound patient	8
Siman 28	Covering the blood spilt during slaughtering / Research in animals / Research and experimentation in humans — the patient, the healthy volunteer, one who is unable to give consent, placebo controlled trials, research on *Shabbat* and *Yom Tov*	9

CHAPTER 2
THE LAWS OF *TREIFOT*

Siman 29	*Treifot* in a bird or animal / The concept of *treifah* in humans / Setting aside Sabbath laws for a *treifah* / Sacrificing a *treifah* to save others / The *HaGomel* blessing	13

CHAPTER 3
THE LAWS CONCERNING BLOOD

Siman 66	Consuming the blood of animals, fowl or fish / Sucking a bleeding wound / Sucking a bleeding wound on *Shabbat*	16

CHAPTER 4
THE LAWS OF SALTING MEAT

Siman 69 — The ritual salting of meat / A patient who is on a strict salt-free diet / Using sugar / Dietetic salt / The minimum time during which the salt must remain on the meat / If salt is completely forbidden to the patient — 18

CHAPTER 5
THE LAWS OF THAT WHICH COMES FORTH FROM A LIVING CREATURE

Siman 81 — Nursing a baby by a mother who eats forbidden food / Receiving a blood transfusion from one who eats forbidden foods / Hospitalizing a *shoteh* who will be fed forbidden foods / A *seriously ill* patient who will eat more forbidden food than he needs for his cure / Mentally handicapped children — giving them up for foster care, adoption or placing them in an institution / Eating food mistakenly pronounced *kosher* / Does the Torah commandment: "You shall not deviate from what they tell you" refer to the Sages of all generations? / Reward for bringing up a handicapped child / Facilitated communication — 21

CHAPTER 6
LAWS CONCERNING WORMS

Siman 84 — An epileptic — a *seriously ill* person / Treatment with forbidden *foods* / Forbidden food that has undergone a chemical change / Medication made from forbidden food / Gelatine capsules — 29

CHAPTER 7
THE LAWS CONCERNING MEAT WITH MILK

Siman 87 — Eating or having benefit from meat with milk / Feeding research animals with it / Eating fish with milk — 32

Siman 89 — How much does a patient need to wait to have milk after eating meat / Does he need to annul a vow / A praiseworthy custom has the force of a vow / Annulling it / Waiting to have milk after chewing meat for a baby / Kashering false teeth / What temperature is

	yad soledet / Feeding via a naso-gastric tube or gastrostomy / Clear meat soup for a patient	34

CHAPTER 8
FOOD COOKED BY NON-JEWS

Siman 116	Drug abuse / Source in Rashi's comment	41
Siman 117	Using soap made from forbidden animal fat	42

CHAPTER 9
THE *KASHERING* OF UTENSILS

Siman 120	Utensils made by or bought from a non-Jew / Obligation to immerse them in a *mikveh* / Food cooked in a vessel that was not immersed / Patient in hospital	44

CHAPTER 10
WINE THAT HAS BEEN USED FOR LIBATION

Siman 123	Forbidden food or wine for a *non-seriously ill* patient / *Non-seriously ill* patient who may become *seriously ill* / *Stam yenam* for *Kiddush* and *Havdalah* / Saying the blessings when eating forbidden food / Fulfilling a *mitzvah* with forbidden food / Why did the Israelites not eat *matzah* made from *chadash* when they entered *Eretz Yisrael* / The skin of Paschal lambs that became mixed together and a wart found on one of them / A Jew who willfully and publicly desecrates the Sabbath / Using wine touched by him for *Kiddush* and *Havdalah* / Boiled wine / Pasteurized wine	46

CHAPTER 11
THE LAWS CONCERNING IDOLATRY

Siman 150	Danger to life and *marit ha'ayin* / Martyrdom and the three cardinal sins / Committing a sin which is only an offshoot of one of the three cardinal sins / A bedridden patient and prayer when there is a crucifix or statue opposite him	52
Siman 151	Praising an idolater doctor or nurse for their skills	53
Siman 155	Non-Jewish doctor / Treatment that carries a high risk / Definition of *chayei sha'ah* and *chayei olam* / Pa-	

tient refuses to risk his *chayei sha'ah* / When may one not treat a suffering patient / Transplantation of a mechanical heart / Bypass surgery / Inability to restart the heart / When did the patient die / *Non-seriously ill* patient and surgery / Moving a *gosses* / Risk of side-effects of medications / Plastic surgery / Rejoining an amputated finger on *Shabbat* / Minimizing injury and danger to the patient / Procedures performed by students and residents / Circumcising for the first time / Missionary hospital / Miracle springs and baths / Deriving benefit from *kila'im* / *Non-seriously ill* patient and Rabbinically forbidden food / Tablets, capsules and lozenges made from forbidden food / Rabbinically forbidden foods on *Pesach* / Eating less than a *measure* / Rabbinically forbidden work on *Shabbat* or *Yom Tov* / Food cooked by a non-Jew / Moving or eating that which is *muktzeh* / Danger to a limb / Patient who has brought his illness on himself / Food forbidden by the Torah / Unconventional treatment / Giving charity for the purpose of unconventional treatment / Using charity money for other *mitzvot*   54

Siman 157   Source for setting aside Torah law for *pikuach nefesh* / Gynecological examination by a male doctor / Setting aside Torah law when there is only danger to a limb / Robbing to save life / Shaming another publicly to save life / Perverting justice to save life / Undergoing suffering to save life / Inciting another to sin to save life / Putting a stumbling block before the blind / Being a recipient for a heart transplant   73

CHAPTER 12
THE LAWS OF INTEREST

Siman 160   Borrowing with interest to save life   83

Siman 176   Renting out medical instruments   84

CHAPTER 13
LAWS CONCERNING THE STATUTES OF IDOLATERS

Siman 178   Cloaks worn at a graduation ceremony and *shatnez*   85

CHAPTER 14
LAWS CONCERNING BELIEF IN OMENS

Siman 179   Faith in *Hashem* / Patient visiting one who practices divinations or sorcery / Going to an astrologer / The use of hypnosis in medicine / Psychotherapy / Uttering a charm to save life / Elective surgery on *Shabbat* combined with acute surgery / Reciting verses from the Torah for a cure / Reciting Psalms for a patient / Studying Torah to cure one's soul / Using an amulet / Copper bracelet   86

CHAPTER 15
LAWS CONCERNING TATTOOING

Siman 180   Tattooing / Writing on one's skin   91

CHAPTER 16
THE LAWS OF SHAVING

Siman 181   Shaving off *pe'ot*   93

CHAPTER 17
LAWS FORBIDDING ONE TO DRESS LIKE THE OPPOSITE SEX

Siman 182   Shaving body hair for a medical reason / Shaving the hair of the armpits or crotch / Dyeing one's hair black / Removing a blemish / The wearing of a wig or toupee by a male / Is it considered a head covering with regard to saying blessings   94

CHAPTER 18
THE LAWS OF *NIDDAH*

Introduction   Reproductive organs of a woman / The menstrual cycle / The *Rambam's* description of the anatomy   98

Siman 183   Definition of the *niddah* state / Ovulatory bleeding   100

Siman 187   Bleeding due to an inflammation, injury or growth in the *uterus* or *birth canal* / Non-Jewish doctor / Fibroids (*myomas*) / Accepting medical opinion / A non-observant Jewish doctor   100

Siman 188	Uterine prolapse / Bleeding after a *hysterectomy* / Bleeding during surgery	106
Siman 189	Menstruation during breast feeding / Defining the beginning of pregnancy / *Sonography* (*ultrasound*) to determine the sex of the fetus	107
Siman 190	The laws of a *ketem* (bloodstain) / Using dipsticks to ascertain whether the stain is blood / After the menopause / Wearing colored underwear	109
Siman 191	Hematuria (passing blood while urinating) / A *ketem* that is found on toilet paper / Nylon cloth / Bladder infection	111
Siman 193	Hymeneal blood / Postponing the menstrual period of a virgin bride / Medication for the purpose / Surgical removal of the *hymen* / minor gynecological surgery	114
Siman 194	Childbirth and the laws of *niddah* / Breakage of water / *Petichat hakever* / Cessation of contractions and *niddah* / *Cervical incompetence* during pregnancy / Dilatation of the *cervix* during labor / *Tumat ledah* / Ectopic pregnancy / Instrumentation of the *uterus* and *petichat hakever* / Instrumentation / *Hysterosalpingography* / Tubal patency / *Hysteroscopy* / Pap smear / Cervical culture / Intrauterine device and bleeding / D and C / Definition of birth / Induction of labor / Elective Caesarian section / Before *Shabbat*	117
Siman 195	When one's wife is a *niddah* / Guiding her blind husband in the street when she is a *niddah* / Putting *tefillin* on her husband who is unable to do so himself / Helping a person who is paralyzed / Passing a baby from one to another / Carrying a baby carriage (pram) together / Presence of the husband when his wife is giving birth / Holding her hand / Psychologic stress / Caring for her ill husband / Treating one's wife when she is a *niddah* / Rubbing ointment into his wife's skin / Putting in eyedrops / Helping his paralyzed wife / Drawing blood and giving injections / Treatment of the opposite sex / Learning medicine or a paramedical profession in the first instance / Forbidden sexual relationships / An unmarried girl	125

Siman 196	The *niddah* period and the ritual of purification / Short menstrual cycle and pregnancy / Douching / Use of vaginal suppositories and *hefsek taharah* / Use of a diaphragm and *hefsek taharah* / Birth control pills / Uterine pessary and *hefsek taharah* / Going out on *Shabbat* while wearing a pessary / Intrauterine device / Using absorbent cotton as an examination cloth / Difficulty in self-examination / Virgin bride and self-examination / Blind woman / Showing the examination cloth to her husband / May he rule in these matters / A woman who is a deaf-mute / Surgery for a cervical laceration / Artificial insemination	136
Siman 197	Immersion in a *mikveh* when her husband is medically prohibited to have *coitus* / When she is medically prohibited to have *coitus*	143
Siman 198	Immersion in a *mikveh* and *chatzizah* / Absorbent-cotton plug in the ear / A woman who has been forbidden to allow water to enter her eyes / Glass eye / Contact lenses / Salve on the eyelid / Scab on a wound / Dried blood / Peeling skin / Band-aid (adhesive tape) / Intravenous catheter (PICC) / Hickman catheter / Removing a band-aid and pulling out hair on Shabbat / Bandage / Plaster cast / Sutures / Blood that is still incompletely dry / Ointment / Dirt under a fingernail / Teeth / Permanent filling / Temporary filling / Dentures and crowns / Loose tooth / Fixed orthodontic appliance (brace) / Sutured gum / *Beit hasetarim* / Intrauterine device / *Pessary* / *Colostomy* / *Ileostomy* / Urinary catheter / Peritoneal dialysis / *Gastrostomy* and *jejunostomy* / *Nephrostomy* / *Cholecystostomy* / Absorbent cotton in the ear / Perforated eardrum / *Tracheostomy* / Paralysis / The woman who oversees the immersion and weak eyesight	144

CHAPTER 19
LAWS OF VOWS

Siman 214	Definition and annulment / A patient who usually fasts between *Rosh Hashanah* and *Yom Kippur* / A woman who is too ill to go to the synagogue to hear the *shofar*	160

Siman 228	One who became weak as a result of fasting / Vowed to go and live in *Eretz Yisrael* / Is there a mitzvah to visit *Eretz Yisrael* / Took a vow when in trouble	161
Siman 232	Vow taken under duress / Took a vow at the request of his dying wife	163
Siman 234	Nullifying a vow taken by his wife to have treatment to conceive	164

CHAPTER 20
LAWS OF OATHS

Siman 238	The difference between a vow and an oath / The oath taken by the Jewish nation at Mount Sinai	165

CHAPTER 21
HONORING PARENTS

Siman 240	A sick father who demands food that is medically forbidden to him / A father who demands that his son tell him the nature of his illness / Obligation to look after a sick parent / A blind person's obligation to stand up before his parent / A mentally deranged parent / Tying him down / Finding someone else to look after him / Professional care / The reward for honoring parents	166
Siman 241	Drawing blood from a parent / Giving injections / Paying for medical expenses / Injuring a parent / A doctor who causes harm to his patient / Extracting a parent's tooth / Bathing a parent and rubbing in ointment into a part of the body that is usually covered / A *ger* and his obligation to his non-Jewish parents	169

CHAPTER 22
THE LAWS OF HONORING A TORAH SCHOLAR

Siman 244	Standing up in the bus and offering him one's seat / If one is ill and cannot remain standing	174

CHAPTER 23
THE LAWS OF TORAH STUDY

Siman 245	How big should a class of children be / Mentally

	handicapped children / Forcing a community to pay for a teacher / The obligation of a mentally handicapped child to keep *mitzvot* / How and what should he be taught	175
Siman 246	Who is obligated to learn Torah / Equvalent to all the *mitzvot* / Is it greater than saving life / Submitting a research project in Medical-*Halachah* for a prize or to further one's career	177

CHAPTER 24
THE LAWS OF CHARITY

Siman 249	Money given so that a child can have private surgery rather than one covered by state insurance; will it be considered as charity / Money given so that a patient can have surgery abroad	180
Siman 252	Putting oneself into possible danger to save someone who is in certain danger / Triage / Who takes precedence / Leaving one patient to attend to another / Taking a machine from one patient to give to another / Giving precedence to a *Cohen* / The concept of "in turn" in *Halachah* / The right to be seen "in turn" in the doctor's office / Giving precedence to a Torah scholar / Sacrificing one's life for another / Heart transplant from a *treifah* or *gosses* / Kidney transplant from a *gosses* / Priorities when there is no *pikuach nefesh*	181

CHAPTER 25
THE LAWS OF *BRIT MILAH* (CIRCUMCISION)

Siman 260	Should the father do the *brit* / A father who is blind / Child born after artificial insemination (AIH) / In-vitro fertilization	188
Siman 261	The use of anesthesia for a *brit*	189
Siman 262	Clotting factors and circumcision / A sick baby / A baby who is a *treifah* / A baby who has been given a life span of months / Performing a postponed *brit* on a Thursday or Friday / Perfoming a postponed *brit* before *Yom Tov* / Waiting seven full days after recovery	

from illness / Waiting seven days before perfoming other minor surgery / Recovering from fever / Recovering from a generalized illness / Anemia / Heart disease / The definition of fever / Fever due to dehydration / When does the counting of the seven days begin / A baby who needed to be put in an incubator / Localized illness / Hare-lip / Cleft palate / Congenital dislocation of hip / Fractured leg / Painful eyes / Inflamed eye / Blockage of a tear duct / Low birth weight / Forceps delivery / *Epispadias* and *hypospadias* / If the *mohel* brought in *Shabbat* early / Very painful eyes / *Makkah* on the back of the hand or foot / *Androgynous* and *tumtum* / How is the moment of birth defined — 191

Siman 263 The jaundiced baby / Pathological and physiological jaundice / *Rav Auerbach zt"l's* ruling / The red baby / Hemophilia / Using laser to perform the *brit* / Naming the baby when the *brit* is postponed / A baby who is born circumcised / *Hatafat dam brit* / Why is *hatafat dam brit* more dangerous than drawing blood from a baby / A baby who dies before he is circumcised / Circumcision before burial / Burying a *nefel* on *Yom Tov* / Naming such a baby — 203

Siman 264 A *mohel* whose hands shake or who has poor eyesight / *Brit* takes precedence over a burial / Father is an *onen* / How is a *brit* performed / Freeing the foreskin before the *brit* / Using a Magen clamp / *Periah* / Surgical circumcision by a non-Jew or Jew / *Metzizah* / Using a pipette / Fear of AIDS or hepatitis — 214

Siman 265 A *hatafat dam brit* or *periah* that had to be postponed / *Metzizah* on a public fast day / *Yom Kippur* and *Tishah B'Av* — 221

Siman 266 Performing a postponed *brit* on the second day of *Yom Tov* / Defining the moment of birth / The definition of *bein hashemashot* (twilight) / *Brit* following Caesarian section / Second day of *Yom Tov* / The sign of a premature baby / Baby born after eight months of gestation — 223

CHAPTER 26
THE LAWS OF *GERIM* (PROSELYTES)

***Siman* 268** — Conversion if circumcision will be dangerous / Became *seriously ill* after the *brit* / Circumcision on a Thursday or Friday — 229

CHAPTER 27
THE LAWS CONCERNING THE *MEZUZAH*

***Siman* 286** — *Mezuzahs* on doorposts of rooms used by medical staff or patients / Using a urinal or bedpan / Covering the *mezuzah* / Does an elevator require a *mezuzah* — 230

CHAPTER 28
THE LAWS OF *ORLAH*

***Siman* 294** — Can *orlah* fruit be used medicinally — 234

CHAPTER 29
THE LAWS OF *PIDYON HABEN*

***Siman* 305** — Redemption of a firstborn son / A father who is a deaf-mute / Siamese twins / Which comes first, a *brit* that was postponed until the thirty-first day or the *pidyon haben* / Redemption without circumcision / If the baby is still in an incubator / A baby who was given a prognosis of a few days but lived more than thirty-one days / Is such a baby a *nefel* / Mourning for him / A baby who is born a *treifah* / Mourning a baby who was killed before he was thirty-one days old / A baby who is a *treifah* / A baby who is a *gosses* / A baby born after a previous miscarriage / A baby born by Caesarian section / Defining the moment of birth / Born by Caesarian section and the fast of the firstborn / Ectopic pregnancy / Forceps delivery / Delivery by vacuum — 236

CHAPTER 30
THE LAWS OF *CHALLAH*

***Siman* 322** — Introduction to the Laws of *challah* / The hospitalized patient — 245

Siman 328   A blind person — separating *terumah* and *challah*   245

CHAPTER 31
THE LAWS OF *TERUMOT* AND *MA'ASROT*

Siman 331   Introduction / Medications made from the produce of *Eretz Yisrael* / *Shemittah* produce and medications / Using corn (maize) to make tablets / Seriously ill patient whose only available food is either *terumah* or *tevel* / Separating tithes from someone else's food / Nullifying the *terumah* by putting it back / Untithed *matzah* on *seder* night / A deaf or dumb person / A blind person / A drunk or blind person and *ma'aser* / Hospital personnel and patients / Separating *tithes* or *challah* on *Shabbat* or *Yom Tov* / The "stipulation" / Setting aside of *challah* / Tithing fruit grown and packed in *Eretz Yisrael*, in the Diaspora   247

CHAPTER 32
THE LAWS OF *BIKUR CHOLIM*, MEDICINE, THE DYING PATIENT AND THE *GOSSES*

Siman 335   The *mitzvah* of *bikur cholim* / Its source / Its purpose / Hinted in the Torah / Is it a Torah or Rabbinic *mitzvah* / Using one's body, soul and money to perform the *mitzvah* / The *non-seriously ill* patient / Visiting after three days / Performing the *mitzvah* even if the patient is asleep / Whom to visit, the rich patient or the poor one / Visiting a patient of the opposite sex / A *Cohen* and *tumat met* / A *Cohen* visiting a relative in the hospital / Doubtful *tumah* in a public place / *Sof tumah latseit* / The *Cohen* transgresses two negative commandments / Taking away one sixtieth of the patient's disease / Giving unnecessary advice / Visiting an enemy / Sitting in an appropriately serious manner / The *Shechinah* is above the patient's head / Sitting at the head of the patient's bed / Which hours of the day should one visit / Telephoning to ask about the patient / Praying for the patient's recovery / Praying for one's parents or *Rav* / One who does not pray for the patient / The patient's prayer for himself / Praying for the patient to die / Praying for the patient in his presence / In which language should one pray / Including the patient in the prayer for the other sick of Israel / *Ger*, praying for a parent / Praying on *Shabbat* / Visiting a patient with diarrhea / Visiting a patient with infectious disease / Treating a patient with infectious disease / Obligation to do so / Attending to a patient of the opposite sex / Asking the Rav to pray for the patient's recovery / Praying in the synagogue / The power of prayer / Visiting the sick or comforting mourners   254

INTRODUCTION TO Siman 336
Verapo Yerapei / The *permission* to heal / How can we heal one whom *Hashem* has smitten / Medicine is an uncertain science / Charging for treatment / The *obligation* to heal / Depending on miracles / Treatment by *Hashem* and by man / *Hashavat Aveidah* (returning lost property — the person's lost health) / The *Rambam's* view / The *Ramban's* view / Preventive treatment / External and internal disease / Cures in Nature / Everything is from *Hashem* / The doctor is merely His messenger / Protecting oneself from disease / The *non-seriously ill* patient / Medications of the Talmud   269

Siman 336   The real Doctor is the *Shechinah* / A patient must realize that the true cure comes from *Hashem* / The study of medicine / Studying medicine on *Shabbat* / The *Rambam's* recipe for all patients / *Mitzvah* to treat / Preventive medicine / Is the doctor obligated to answer every call / When the doctor is eating or sleeping / The martyrdom of Rabban Shimon ben Gamliel and Rebbe Yishmael / Delaying justice / Consultation with colleagues / "The best of doctors to Hell" / The doctor and pride / The prescribing of medications by pharmacists / Laymen advising patients / Permission to treat from a professional body / Unintentional harm to a patient / The difference between a surgeon and a physician / The injection of the wrong drug / A doctor who caused harm as a result of negligence / Obligation to reprove him / Obligation to report him / Telling the patient or family

/ Negligence by inactivity / Is the doctor liable for exile / Taking payment for treatment / Payment for his trouble / Refraining from other employment (*sechar batalah*) / *Rabbanim* taking payment for services / The doctor who refuses to treat a patient who cannot afford to pay / Charging for issuing a death certificate / Fees for work done on *Shabbat* / Charging a high fee / The obligation of the patient to pay the doctor — 278

Siman 337 The seven family members for whom one is obligated to mourn / Telling a patient that a family member has died / Lying to him about the deceased / How does a mourner visit a patient / Does the patient need to sit *shivah* when he recovers / Tearing the patient's garment / Speaking in the presence of an unconscious patient / The death of an unrelated person / Observing the *halachot* of mourning if they will harm his health — 294

Siman 338 The dying patient / Confession of sins / Confessing on *Shabbat* / Seriously ill patient and confession / Who should confess / Telling a patient that he is *dangerously ill* / Telling a patient that he has cancer / Telling him he has advanced disease of the heart or lungs / Giving a definitive prognosis / The confession of a dying person — 297

Siman 339 The *gosses* / Definition / Hastening his death / Setting aside Sabbath laws for him / Defining death / Crushed brain / The *Chatam Sofer's* definition / Brain death / Anatomy and physiology / Blood supply / The history of brain death / Harvard criteria / Presidential commission / *Apnea* test / Tests for cerebral blood flow / What is current medical opinion of brain death / Is it universally accepted / Evidence against total brain death in brain-dead patients / Physiological decapitation / How many of these tests are done / In what percentage of donors are these tests done / How long have brain-dead patients lived / Pregnant brain-dead women / Voices against brain death in the medical world / The *Halachah* / The ruling of the Chief Rabbinate of Israel / *Rav Auerbach zt"l's* view / The sheep experiment /

Did *Rav Auerbach zt"l* and *Rav Waldenberg shlita* change their decision / *Rav Eliashiv shlita's* view / *Rav Waldenberg shlita's* view / The view of other *Gedolei HaDor* / *Rav Feinstein zt"l's* view / Summary / The name game / Chronic vegetative state / *Anencephalic* infants / Touching a *gosses* / A *Cohen* and a *gosses* / What may be done to or for a *gosses* / Moving a *gosses* to save the life of a *seriously ill patient* / Euthanasia / *Rav Auerbach zt"l's* view / The patient with ALS / *Rav Eliashiv shlita's* view / The patient with ALS / *Rav Waldenberg shlita's* view / *Rav Feinstein zt"l's* view / Summary / Differentiating between DNR and DNT / Conclusion / The living will / Moving a *gosses* / The inhabitants of Luz / The elderly woman who was tired of living / Removing an impediment to dying / A dying patient must not be left alone / A *Cohen* must leave the room / A doctor who is a *Cohen* / The martyrdom of Rebbe Yishmael / Artificial respiration - source in *Chazal* / Intubation — source in *Chazal*   300

CHAPTER 33
THE LAWS OF *KERI'AH*

Siman 340 Who is obligated / A blind person / Doctors and other caregivers and *keri'ah* / *Shabbat* and *Yom Tov*   330

CHAPTER 34
THE LAWS OF *ANINUT*

Siman 341 Performimg a *mitzvah* in the presence of a corpse / Putting *tefillin* on a patient in the presence of a corpse / *loeg larash*   332

CHAPTER 35
THE LAWS OF MOURNING

Siman 345 A person who committed suicide / Definition of suicide in *Halachah* / Psychiatric illness / The obligation to prevent a suicide / Setting aside Sabbath laws for an attempted suicide / *Birkat HaGomel*   334

Siman 349 Autopsies (postmortem) in *Halachah* / For the pur-

	pose of learning medicine / What are the *halachic* problems / To save life / Biopsy on *Shabbat* / A person who has donated or sold his body to science / Autopsy on an aborted fetus / Watching an autopsy / Postmortem needle biopsy / Practicing intubation / To save a limb / Corneal transplant / Skin graft from a skin bank / Bone transplant / Non-Jewish corpse / Removal of a pacemaker from a corpse / Transplantation from a corpse / Cornea / Skin / Transplantation from a live donor / Is one permitted, obligated or forbidden to put his life in danger to save another / Donating: blood, bone marrow, stem cells, kidney, bone / Human experimentation	335
Siman 362	Burying a limb that was amputated during life / Having benefit from it / Having benefit from flesh removed during life	348
Siman 364	Accidental death and burial of the blood that was spilled / Death in childbirth / Death during surgery	349
Siman 369	The *Cohen* and ritual defilement by a corpse / The prohibition nowadays / The *Ra'avad's* opinion / A *Cohen* and the study of medicine / Is there an obligation to study medicine / The *Cohen* who nevertheless studies medicine / The *Cohen* who is a doctor, nurse or other caregiver / Limb, or part of one, that was amputated from a living person / Rejoining a *Cohen's* finger that has become severed / Rejoining a severed finger on *Shabbat*	350
Siman 370	A person who is decapitated / If it were possible, would it be a *mitzvah* to bring him back to life / Broken neck / How did Elijah (who was a *Cohen*) revive the dead boy / Is there a *mitzvah* to revive the dead / May a *Cohen* enter the room of a *gosses* to treat him / May a *Cohen* examine a deceased to confirm death	354
Siman 371	Tumah entering via a common stairwell or corridor / May a *Cohen* force a family to remove their deceased relative out of the building / A *Cohen* who is a minor	356
Siman 372	The *halachah* concerning the rooms in a hospital	

	when there is a corpse in one of them / A corpse in one apartment and a *Cohen* in another in the same buiding / May the *Cohen* living in one apartment go out to perform a *mitzvah* when there is a corpse in another / Moving a corpse on *Shabbat* / The *Cohen* as a patient / *Non-seriously ill Cohen* — difference between hospitals in Israel and in the Diaspora / *Seriously ill Cohen* / A hospitalized *Cohen* / Attending a hospital clinic	357
Siman 373	A *Cohen* undergoing surgery that will disqualify him from service in the Temple / Non-seriously ill Cohen requiring surgery / *Mitzvah* for a *Cohen* to defile himself to a close relative / Who are these relatives / Is he obligated to do so or only permitted / Is this so on *Shabbat* as well / Causing a baby *Cohen* to become defiled / A sick *Cohen* in the same house as a corpse / Being under the same roof as a severed limb or part of one / A deceased relative whose body is incomplete	362
Siman 374	Mourning for a baby born after only eight months of gestation / Premature baby who was in an incubator / Mourning for a baby born prematurely / *Pidyon Ha-Ben* for a baby born prematurely	366
Siman 376	Does a mourner stand before one whom he must so honor	367
Siman 380	A doctor who is in mourning / Visiting a patient during the (doctor's) *shivah* week / Taking a fee for his services / Taking something from a house of mourning / Taking a fee from a house of mourning	367
Siman 381	A woman in mourning who has given birth — washing herself	369
Siman 382	A person in mourning who has a wound on his foot — wearing shoes	369
Siman 384	Patient in mourning and the blessing of *HaGomel* / Mourner, studying medicine	369
Siman 385	Wishing a new mother *mazal tov* when she is in mourning / Wishing a mourner *shalom*	370

Siman 396	A *seriously ill* patient and *keri'ah*	370
Siman 397	Yahrzeit / One who was seen alive before sunset and found dead after nightfall / Date of death unknown	371
Siman 402	Informing of the death of a relative / A hospitalized patient who died on *Shabbat* / How should the relatives be told / One must not lie	373
Glossary of Hebrew Terms		377
Glossary of Medical Terms		385
Bibliography		389
Index		399
About the Author		430

NISHMAT AVRAHAM

CHAPTER 1
The Laws of Ritual Slaughter

SIMAN 1
WHO ARE PERMITTED TO SLAUGHTER

§5 One may not allow (A)a deaf-mute, (B)a *shoteh* — one who

NISHMAT AVRAHAM

SIMAN 1

(A) a deaf-mute. It would appear that this also applies to one who had been healthy but later became a deaf-mute, and this is the ruling of the *Bach*.[1]

The *Darchei Teshuvah*[2] writes that slaughter by a *shochet* (ritual slaughterer) who suffers from epileptic attacks once every few months is valid without question. Since he is an expert and is proficient in examining his knife,[3] and since his attacks are infrequent, one need not have any qualms about his *shechitah*. However the *shochet* should be stringent with himself and have another examine his knife at least twice weekly. When he feels that an attack is due he must have someone else supervise him while slaughtering; he is believed if he says that he was careful to have done this.[4]

A *shochet* who suffers occasionally from "drop attacks" (when, without prior warning, he falls suddenly to the ground and lies unmoving for a very short while before being able to get up and return to his normal self) should cease to slaughter but continue to receive a stipend from the community.[5] It is forbidden for such a person to slaughter unless someone who can discern if he is not fully in control of his senses supervises him throughout the act of slaughtering.[6] On the other hand, there is an opinion that he should not be allowed to slaughter at all even if he maintains that he is perfectly well and even if another supervises while he slaughters.[7]

(B) a *shoteh*. The examples given by the *Shulchan Aruch* are not meant to be exclusive. Rather anything that he does in a bizarre and uncontrolled manner makes him a *shoteh*; *Chazal*[8] only gave the above indications as examples. The *Da'at Torah*[9] writes that *Chazal* mention one who speaks normally but nevertheless, the presence of these signs would

---

trachea is not torn by any irregularity in any part of the knife that came into contact with it during the *shechitah*. The person who examines the knife is known as a *bodek*.

4. שו״ת צמח צדק החדשות חיו״ד סי׳ ח
5. שו״ת אבני צדק חיו״ד סי׳ א
6. שו״ת אמרי בינה סי׳ ה
7. שו״ת טוב טעם ודעת תליתאי סי׳ כח
8. חגיגה ג ע״ב
9. ס״ק מ. וראה שם בס״ק מג

1. ש״ך ס״ק כב
See *Nishmat Avraham*, vol. 1 *Orach Chaim*, Siman 55B, p. 26.

2. ס״ק קמג

3. The *shechitah* knife must be meticulously examined along its edge as well as on either side of the knife edge, both with the fingernail and with the tip of the finger, to make sure that it is absolutely sharp and without flaw along the entire edge. Only then can one be sure that the bird or animal is killed immediately by the razor-sharp edge and that its esophagus or

SIMAN 1: WHO ARE PERMITTED TO SLAUGHTER / §5

goes out alone at night, tears his clothes, sleeps in a graveyard or loses whatever he is given, even if he only does one of the above but does so in a bizarre fashion — or a child who is unable to master the act, to perform ritual slaughter. Even if a responsible adult supervises him, (C)he is not allowed to slaughter. However, if he did slaughter while a responsible adult supervised, the animal is considered ritually slaughtered.

GLOSS: *There are those who are stringent about giving a license to anyone younger than eighteen years of age, for it is only then that he is considered responsible enough* (D)*to take care when slaughtering.*

NISHMAT AVRAHAM

prove him a *shoteh* in the eyes of the *Halachah*. However if he speaks incoherently and in an insane manner there is no need for any further proof that he is a *shoteh*.[10] One who alternates between periods of sanity and insanity is judged according to his state at the time he performs a particular act such as *shechitah*.[11] If a *shoteh* is completely cured, is capable of examining the *shechitah* knife and is familiar with the views of the *rishonim* and *acharonim* on the subject of *shechitah*, he may be appointed as the community *shochet*.[12]

See also *Nishmat Avraham*, vol. 1 *Orach Chaim*, Siman 55B, p. 26 regarding the status of a *shoteh*.

(C) he is not allowed. The *Darchei Teshuvah*[13] asks whether in every instance where the *Shulchan Aruch* rules concerning a definite deaf-mute, *shoteh*, minor or blind person that something is not permissible, would it be permissible to ask him to do so should there be a doubt as to whether he belonged to one of these categories or not? For example, can we ask him to slaughter if there is a doubt whether he is still a minor, or whether he is a *shoteh*; or if there is a doubt whether one whose eyesight is affected by disease or old age will be able to see clearly while slaughtering? The *Darchei Teshuvah* leaves the question open.

(D) to take care. The *Ba'er Heitev*[14] cites a view that one should not slaughter over the age of eighty and notes that the *Bach* writes that this must be decided individually since one who is weak may not slaughter even if he is only aged fifty. The *Pitchei Teshuvah*[15] writes that nowadays, since people are weaker it should be made a rule that one who has reached the age of seventy should not be allowed to slaughter even though he is still capable of examining the *shechitah* knife. Nor can one depend on the *shochet's* opinion of himself, since he may claim that he is as good as ever, but, in fact, is unaware of the deterioration in his capabilities.[16]

---

10. מובא בדרכ"ת ס"ק קנב

11. ראה אהע"ז סימן קכא סעיף ג וחו"מ סימן רלה סעיף כא

12. שו"ת צמח צדק החדשות סי' ח מובא בדרכי תשובה ס"ק קמד

13. ס"ק קנט בשם ספר תוספת ירושלים - ולא הכריע לדינא

14. ס"ק כז בשם הבית יעקב

15. ס"ק יב

16. דרכ"ת ס"ק קעג

§6 One who is (E)deaf but not dumb may not slaughter since he cannot hear the blessing said before slaughtering. However if he did slaughter even when alone, the meat is *kosher*.

§7 One who is only (F)dumb but can hear may slaughter if he is an expert and someone else says the blessing for him.

───────── NISHMAT AVRAHAM ─────────

(E) deaf. This ruling that the meat would still be *kosher* is only if he was born healthy and later became deaf; but if he was born deaf the *shechitah* would not be valid even if he could speak.[17] The *Rambam*[18] writes that one who is born completely deaf will not be able to speak either, since he cannot hear at all. *Rav Shlomo Zalman Auerbach zt"l* told me that it would appear from this comment of the *Rambam* that the *Shulchan Aruch* refers only to one who later became deaf.

The *Rambam* there notes that one who later becomes deaf may separate tithes. *Rebbe Akiva Eiger*[19] questions this ruling and the *Mishnah Rishonah*[20] maintains that there must be a printer's error in this ruling. Indeed the *Rambam* himself rules[21] that if he had separated tithes his action takes force, although if he has as yet not separated the tithes, he may not do so. This "printer's error" was in fact a mistranslation from the *Rambam's* original Arabic and the translation of *Rav Kapach zt"l* is: He may not separate tithes.

(F) dumb. The *Darchei Teshuvah*[22] writes that if one who is dumb has slaughtered, the meat is not *kosher* unless he has first been examined and pronounced completely sane. The inability to speak may of itself cause him to become unstable and it is immaterial whether he was dumb at birth or only became so later.[23]

Since all Israel are responsible for one another, the general rule regarding a blessing said before doing a *mitzvah* is that it may be said for another who is about to do the *mitzvah* even though the person saying the blessing will not do the *mitzvah* or has already completed it. For example, a person who will be putting on *tefillin* later or who has already done so may say the blessing for another who is about to do so but is unable to say it. In contrast, *birkat hanehenin* — a blessing said before one enjoys something, such as food or drink — may be said only by the person who will have the enjoyment. One may include another in his blessing only if he also must say the same blessing on that which he is about to enjoy. Thus one may say the blessing *shehakol* to include another person only if both are about to eat or drink that which requires the blessing of *shehakol*. As to the blessing said before slaughtering, the *Taz*[24] rules that another may say the blessing even if he will not also slaughter since it is a blessing of praise and acknowledgement as with *birkat erusin*. However the *Kaf HaChaim*[25] quotes a long list of *poskim* who rule that if the other person did not also slaughter, even though he transgressed and said the blessing for the dumb person,

───────────────────

17. דרכ"ת שם ס"ק קעד בשם יריעות שלמה
18. פי' המשניות תרומות פ"א מ"ב ועיין שם ברע"ב
19. תוס' רעק"א שם
20. שם
21. הל' תרומות פ"ד ה"ד
22. ס"ק קפ בשם השמלה חדשה
23. תבואת שור ס"ק נז
24. ס"ק יז
25. ס"ק קסד

SIMAN 1: WHO ARE PERMITTED TO SLAUGHTER / §6, 7, 8

§8 One who is completely intoxicated is likened *halachically* (G)to a *shoteh*; if he is not completely intoxicated, he may slaughter.

GLOSS: *There is an opinion that one who is drunk may not slaughter since he may sever the esophagus or trachea of the bird or animal* (H)*by exerting pressure with the knife as opposed to cutting with it.*

NISHMAT AVRAHAM

the latter may not slaughter.[26] It would appear that these two rulings depend on how the blessing over the *shechitah* is defined. If it is considered a *mitzvah* in itself, it is then a *birkat hamitzvah* and may be said by another with the intention to include the *shochet*. On the other hand, if the act of *shechitah* is not considered a *mitzvah* in itself but only a requirement should one wish to eat meat, then the blessing would be a *birkat hanehenin* and may be said only by the *shochet*. The *Chatam Sofer*[27] writes that it is universally accepted that *shechitah* is a *mitzvah* in itself.

There is an additional *mitzvah*, applicable only to the slaughter of birds and non-domesticated kosher animals, such as deer, that part of the blood is spilled and covered with earth.[28] If a dumb person has slaughtered one of these, he is now obligated to do this *mitzvah* and someone else may say the blessing for this *mitzvah* for him.[29]

(G) to a *shoteh*. One who is elderly or one whose hands tremble either because of weakness or because he naturally has unsteady hands, will, in most cases, sever the *esophagus* or *trachea* by pressure rather than by cutting it. Even if he says he is certain that he did not use pressure, he is not believed since it is very probable that he did.[30] See above **D** that the *Pitchei Teshuvah* states that one who has reached the age of seventy may not slaughter. However the *Teshuvah MeAhavah*[31] writes that this is a mere stringency and is not mentioned by other *poskim*. On the contrary, generally speaking, so long as a person is strong and is proficient in examining the knife, his slaughtering is *kosher* even if he is one hundred years old. If he is not sufficiently proficient in examining the knife, then even if he is only thirty years old, the *shechitah* is not valid.

(H) by exerting pressure. One who is ill may not slaughter for he is *halachically* considered a *shoteh* in this respect.[32] *Rav Auerbach zt"l* told me that an ill person in this context is compared to an old man who feels that he is weak, cannot control his actions and who is not clear in his thoughts as a result of illness. The *Igrot Moshe*[33] also writes that this *halachah* concerns one who has an illness affecting his whole body, such as a fever. However if he is only ill in part of his body, for example, in his *gastro-intestinal tract*, there is no need to take this into consideration.

26. עיין שם בס"ק קסח שכותב דמ"מ נראה דאם כבר בירך האחר וכיון להוציא את האלם והאלם גם כן כיון עליו לצאת בזה, יש לסמוך על הט"ז משום ספק ברכות להקל ואין לעשות ברכה לבטלה

27. שו"ת, או"ח סי' נה. וראה שם טעם המחלוקת לדעתו

28. יו"ד סי' כח

29. דרכ"ת ס"ק קפא

30. באר היטב סוס"ק לב בשם הסמ"ג מ"ע סג ד"ה דרסה

31. שו"ת, ח"א סי' קיח

32. מנחת יוסף ח"א סי' א סע' כ - הראה לי הגרש"ז אויערבאך זצ"ל

33. שו"ת, יו"ד ח"א סי' ב

§9 (I)One who is blind should not slaughter unless another supervises him. If he did slaughter on his own the *shechitah* is valid.

NISHMAT AVRAHAM

The *Ba'er Heitev*[34] writes that one must be cautioned not to slaughter while sitting, as this position will bring him to use pressure while cutting. Thus one who is confined to a chair because of illness or a broken leg may not slaughter. However if he did slaughter while sitting the *Pri Chadash* rules that the *shechitah* is valid.[35] The *Darchei Teshuvah*,[36] however, writes that the custom in Jerusalem and in Izmir is to permit slaughtering while sitting[37] and this is also the opinion of the *Zivchei Tzedek*.[38] But, writes the *Darchei Teshuvah*, in our country we are stringent not to permit *shechitah* while sitting. This is also the opinion of the *Pri Megadim*.[39] However, he adds that if the *shochet* did slaughter while sitting, one should not be stringent if otherwise the loss concurred will be great; if the *shochet* is certain that he did not use any pressure, one may permit the meat even if the loss is not great. The *Tuv Ta'am VeDa'at*[40] differentiates between slaughtering fowl or cattle. With cattle it is difficult to slaughter without using pressure; with fowl, since he takes it entirely in his hand, there is no difference whether he stands or sits. Therefore if it is essential that a person who is confined to a chair slaughters, he may be permitted to slaughter fowl. *Rav Auerbach zt''l* concurred with this ruling. The *Tuv Ta'am VeDa'at* adds that this stringency should only be applied to one who slaughters while sitting and not to one who must lean while slaughtering.[41]

(I) One who is blind. The *Shach*[42] quotes the *Or Zarua* that it is forbidden to eat meat slaughtered by one who was born blind. However, the *Darchei Moshe*, commenting on this ruling of the *Or Zarua*, writes that other *poskim* do not make this distinction between one who became blind and one who is blind from birth. One who is only blind in one eye, however, is considered like anyone else with regard to *shechitah*.[43]

If, however, one has weak eyesight, the *Darchei Teshuvah*[44] writes that it is controversial whether he may or may not be a *shochet* or *bodek* (the one responsible for examining the cutting edge of the knife to make sure it has no flaws, see ref. 3). If his vision is corrected with lenses then he may slaughter. The *Tuv Ta'am VeDa'at*,[45] on the other hand, is unsure of this *halachah* since the *Magen Avraham*[46] writes that one may not search for *chametz* through a glass window. However the *Da'at Torah*[47] disagrees and rules that one not need be stringent in this matter

---

34. סי׳ כד ס״ק ג בשם הכנה״ג הגהות ב״י אות כ
35. וכ״כ בה״י וראה גם במג״א סי׳ ח ס״ק ב
36. סי׳ כד ס״ק לא
37. ומ״מ הברכה בעמידה אם אפשר, כדין ברכות המצוות ועיין בחכמת שלמה או״ח סי׳ ח סע׳ א - כתב לי מו״ר הגרי״י נויבירט שליט״א
38. ס״ק יג, שכותב דמנהג עיר בגדאד ששוחטים מיושב ואין פוצה פה
39. סי׳ כד ס״ד ס״ק ה. וראה בכף החיים ס״ק כד שמוסיף, שמא שכותב הזבחי צדק הנ״ל מדובר בעופות אבל בבהמות לא שמענו ולא ראינו ששוחטים מיושב
40. שו״ת, תליתאי סי׳ פז
41. וראה גם בשו״ת אג״מ יו״ד ח״א סי׳ ב
42. ס״ק לו
43. דרכ״ת ס״ק קצד
44. ס״ק קצג
45. שו״ת, תליתאי סי׳ פה
46. או״ח סי׳ תלג ס״ק ד
47. כאן ס״ק נ

SIMAN 1: WHO ARE PERMITTED TO SLAUGHTER / §9

--- NISHMAT AVRAHAM ---

and this is also the opinion of the *Shevut Yaakov*.[48] *Rav Neuwirth shlita* wrote to me commenting that the *Magen Avraham* is speaking about dark glass whereas spectacles are of clear glass. *Rav Ovadiah Yosef shlita*[49] wrote to me that *Rav Neuwirth shlita's* comment was in keeping with that of the *Da'at Kedoshim* who wrote that the *Magen Avraham's* ruling was based on the unclear glass of his time and one could act leniently in our days (with regard to searching for *chametz* through glass). The *Da'at Torah*,[50] based on this, rules that one may slaughter at night by the light of a lamp since the clear glass magnifies the amount of light, and this is also the ruling of the *Yad Yitzchak*.[51] In any case, *Rav Yosef shlita* writes that glass cannot be compared to spectacles which are specially made to improve the wearer's vision; he also refers to what he wrote in *Yabia Omer*.[52]

THE BLIND PERSON'S OBLIGATION TO PERFORM *MITZVOT*. According to Rebbe Yehudah[53] the Torah exempts a blind person from all *mitzvot*. The *Minchat Chinuch*[54] and the *Chida*[55] both quote the *Sefer HaMachriya*[56] who appears to believe that this exemption includes negative commandments. However the *Rosh*[57] writes that a blind person is obligated Rabbinically to perform all the *mitzvot*, unlike a woman who is exempt (from positive Torah *mitzvot* connected with time). This is because he is a man and besides, if he is exempted from all *mitzvot*, he would be like a gentile. A woman, however, is obligated to perform positive *mitzvot* unconnected with time and is forbidden to transgress negative *mitzvot*. The *Chida*[58] writes that it would appear that when the *Rosh* writes that "he would be like a gentile," he refers to positive *mitzvot* which he has to actively perform, such as putting on *tefillin*, reciting the *Shema* and *Shemoneh Esrei* and affixing a *mezuzah* to his door. If he does not perform them he would be like a gentile. However negative *mitzvot* are passive and not transgressing them does not make him like a gentile. The *Chida* also deduces that when the *Rosh* writes that a woman "is forbidden to set aside negative *mitzvot*" he also, like the *Sefer HaMachriya*, rules that a blind person, unlike a woman who is not blind, has no obligation with respect to the negative *mitzvot*. The *Korban Netanel*[59] edits the statement of the *Rosh* leaving out the words "and is forbidden to set aside negative *mitzvot*." However the *Yam Shel Shlomo*[60] quotes the *Rosh* in full. The *Chida*[61] adds that there is no proof that the *Rosh* rules like the *Sefer HaMachriya*, explaining that the *Rosh* means that the blind person is not culpable for not keeping the *mitzvot*. The *Rosh* elsewhere[62] writes that although Rebbe Yehudah ruled that the Torah exempts a blind person from all *mitzvot*, nevertheless he is Rabbinically obligated to perform them like any seeing person. And, although a woman is exempted, even Rabbinically, from all positive *mitzvot* connected to time, nevertheless she still has many *mitzvot* that she is obligated to perform. Not so the blind

---

48. שו"ת ח"א סי' קבו
49. בהערות לנשמת אברהם כרך ב יו"ד עמ' רפט
50. דעת תורה יו"ד סי' יא סע' ג
51. שו"ת, ח"ג סי' רעו
52. שו"ת יביע אומר ח"ד חאו"ח סי' מ
53. ב"ק פז ע"א
54. מצוה ב
55. מחזיק ברכה או"ח סי' נג ס"ק ה
56. לרבינו ישעיה, סי' עח
57. קדושין פ"א סי' מט
58. פתח עינים על ב"ק שם
59. על הרא"ש קדושין שם ס"ק ט
60. קדושין פ"ק סי' סד
61. מחזיק ברכה שם
62. שו"ת, כלל ד סי' כא

SIMAN 19
THE LAWS CONCERNING THE BLESSING BEFORE SLAUGHTERING

§1 Before slaughtering one says the blessing: Who has sanctified us and commanded us about slaughtering. If he slaughtered without saying the blessing the *shechitah* is still valid.

GLOSS: *If he slaughtered in a slaughterhouse, which is unclean, he should say the blessing* (A)*a distance of four cubits away before*

---NISHMAT AVRAHAM---

person; should he be exempted from all *mitzvot*, both by Torah and by Rabbinic law, he would be like a gentile who has no relationship whatsoever to our Torah. Hence the Sages obligated him to perform all the *mitzvot*. All of this only expounds Rebbe Yehudah's ruling, but according to the Sages who disagree with him, Torah law obligates him to keep all the *mitzvot*.

Tosafot[63] also write that although according to Rebbe Yehudah the Torah exempts him from performing all *mitzvot*, nevertheless the Sages obligated him to perform them; this is also the opinion of the *Beit Yosef*.[64]

Rabbeinu Yerucham,[65] however, rules like the *Sefer HaMachriya* that the blind person is exempt from all commandments. The *Radbaz*,[66] however, writes that *Rabbeinu Yerucham* stands alone in this ruling; the *Beit Yosef*[67] also expresses surprise at his ruling. However in later generations, the *Yavetz*[68] and the *Noda BiYehudah*[69] both rule that a blind person is exempt even from negative commandments, and the *Chida*[70] quotes an early *Tosafot*[71] who also rule like the *Sefer HaMachriya*. The *Da'at Torah*[72] proves from a *Yerushalmi* that, in Rebbe Yehudah's opinion, a blind person is exempt even from negative commandments.

However, the *Chida*[73] writes that it is not plausible that this is so; it cannot be that if he were to desecrate the Sabbath, eat *chametz* on *Pesach* or eat on *Yom Kippur*, he would not be guilty of transgression. But his exemption is to be compared to that of an *onen* who is exempt from positive commandments but bound by negative ones. This is also the opinion of the *Maharatz Chayot*,[74] *Rebbe Akiva Eiger*[75] and the *Pri Megadim*.[76]

See *Nishmat Avraham*, vol. 1 *Orach Chaim*, for further *halachot* concerning a blind person.

SIMAN 19

(A) a distance of four *cubits* away. The *Darchei Teshuvah*[1] writes that one sees from this *Rama* that the blessing may not be said in an unclean place, but the *shechitah* may be carried out there. But how can the positive *mitzvah* of *shechitah* be

---

63. ב"ק פז ע"א ד"ה וכן
64. או"ח סוסי' תעג
65. ריש נתיב יג
66. שו"ת, ח"א סי' נט וח"ב סי' לט
67. או"ח סוסי' תעג
68. שו"ת ח"א סי' עה
69. שו"ת, תנינא או"ח סי' קיב
70. עין זוכר מערכת ס אות כ
71. תוספות קמא לתלמיד רבינו פרץ
72. או"ח סי' נג סע' יד
73. פתח עינים על ב"ק פז ע"א
74. ב"ק שם
75. חידושיו כאן ובשו"ת סי' קסט
76. פתיחה כוללת ח"ב ס"ק לג וח"ג ס"ק כט
1. ס"ק כא בשם ספר עקרי הד"ט סי' ה אות טו

entering the slaughterhouse; he must not speak until after he has slaughtered.

SIMAN 28

THE LAWS CONCERNING COVERING THE BLOOD SPILT DURING *SHECHITAH*

§16 **One who slaughters** (*a fowl or animal part of whose spilt blood must be covered — author*) **for a patient on *Shabbat*,** (A)**may not cover the blood even if there is already a spade dug**

NISHMAT AVRAHAM
---

carried out in unclean surroundings? The *Chida* writes that one may not perform the *mitzvah* of *lulav* in a unclean place, as the *Zohar* writes that the performance of a *mitzvah* must only be in a place that is clean. The *Darchei Teshuvah* concludes that the *Rama*, unlike the *Chida*, rules that it is not forbidden to concentrate on the performance of a *mitzvah* in unclean surroundings. What is forbidden is to think of words of Torah or to think of the words of a blessing in such surroundings. The *Zohar* also only refers to performing the *mitzvah* in the best possible manner and not that one should refrain from performing the *mitzvah* if there is no choice. The *Darchei Teshuvah* continues that he believes the *Chida* also only specifically forbade performing the *mitzvah* of *lulav* in unclean surroundings since it is an obligatory *mitzvah* and brings appeasement from *Hashem*.[2] Neither of these apply to *shechitah* and the *Chida* would also permit *shechitah* in an unclean place. The *Elef HaMagen*[3] writes that a Jew in an unclean prison cell may not pray or say blessings; he may nevertheless, under these forced circumstances, listen to the *shofar* (and perform other positive commandments such as putting on *tefillin*) without saying or thinking of the blessing.

In view of the above, a bed-bound patient whose room is either unclean or has a bad smell may perform a positive commandment such as the *mitzvot* of *tefillin* or *lulav*, if the time for doing these *mitzvot* would pass before the room is cleaned. However he must not think of the blessings concerned with the *mitzvah*.[4] If later the room is cleaned and there is still time to do the *mitzvah*, for example putting on *tefillin*, he should put them on again, this time with the blessing.[5] (See also *Nishmat Avraham*, vol. 1 *Orach Chaim*, Siman 62A, 85A,B and 588A.)

Rav Auerbach zt"l told me that under these forced conditions a bed-bound patient may put on *tefillin* with the thought that this is the Will of *Hashem*.

SIMAN 28

(A) may not cover. The *Taz*[1] writes that even though this is only Rabbinically forbidden we do not say that since he slaughtered with permission he may also cover the blood (as on *Yom Tov*[2]). The

---

2. וכמ"ש הריטב"א המיוחס להרשב"א בסוכה ריש פרק לולב הגזול.
3. על המטה אפרים סי' תקפח ס"ק א.
4. הגר"ע יוסף שליט"א בשו"ת יביע אומר ח"ו יו"ד סי' כט וכן עיין בדבריו המובאים בנשמת אברהם כרך א או"ח עמ' שלו אות יג. הגרש"ז אויערבאך זצ"ל מובא

4. בנשמת אברהם שם סי' תקפח הערה א.
הגרא"י ולדינברג שליט"א שם עמ' שמב אות יב.
5. או"ח סי' תקפח סע' ב בביה"ל ד"ה שמע.
1. ס"ק יג וכותב שכ"כ הר"ן ריש פרק כיסוי הדם.
2. ראה פרטי דינים באו"ח סי' תצח סע' יד.

into the earth. After *Shabbat*, if the stain of the blood is still visible, he should cover it.

§18 One who slaughters, even if (B)only for the blood, is obligated to cover the spilt blood. If, however, he does not ritually slaughter the fowl he need not cover the spilt blood.

— NISHMAT AVRAHAM —

reason is that the Sages wished to distinguish between *Yom Tov*, when one may slaughter to have fresh meat, and *Shabbat*, when one is basically forbidden to slaughter. Hence, on *Shabbat* they only permitted the slaughter which is necessary for the (*seriously ill*) patient but not the covering of the blood. See also *Nishmat Avraham*, vol. 1 *Orach Chaim*, Siman 328 (14A), p. 200. The *Darchei Teshuvah*[3] writes that this *halachah* is not commonly needed today, for fresh meat can always be gotten from neighbors and friends. See *Nishmat Avraham*, vol. 1 *Orach Chaim*, Siman 318A references 6 and 7, p. 170.

(B) only for the blood. ANIMAL RESEARCH. The Torah[4] commands us to help the donkey of an enemy which has collapsed under its heavy load. *Chazal*[5] learned from this that it is forbidden by the Torah to cause suffering to an animal.[6] The *Rama*[7] qualifies this by ruling that whatever is done for a medical or other purpose does not carry this prohibition. Hence it is permissible to pluck feathers from a live goose and one need not worry about causing pain; however it is customary to avoid this since it makes one cruel. The *Noda BiYehudah*,[8] discuss-

ing hunting, writes that whatever is done for man's use does not transgress this prohibition; moreover, the prohibition applies only if one causes an animal suffering and then leaves it to continue suffering without killing it. The *Otsar HaPoskim*,[9] however, quotes the *Imrei Shefer*[10] that the *Rama* only meant to permit causing suffering when it was essential, for instance for a medical purpose, but not for monetary gain. Also it is not certain that one may carry out medical experiments on animals since the benefit is only a possibility. The *Shevut Yaakov*[11] was asked whether poisonous substances could be fed to animals to learn about their reactions and thus one would be able to treat humans, and he consented. He added that the question asked was not the same as the *Rama's* example of plucking feathers from a live goose, for there the pain was inflicted immediately. In the case in question, the animals do not have any pain at the time they are given the poison to drink and their later suffering is an indirect consequence. The *Chelkat Yaakov*[12] disagrees with the *Imrei Shefer's* ruling stating that the *Gemara*[13] writes that one may castrate a cock by removing its comb,

---

3. ס"ק קטו
4. שמות כג:ה
5. שבת קכח ע"א וב"מ לב ע"ב
6. כך פסקו הגאונים, הרי"ף (עיין נמ"י ב"מ לב ע"ב) והרא"ש שם פ"ב סי' כט. וראה בכסף משנה הל' רוצח פי"ג ה"ט שכן דעתו של הרמב"ם (וראה בביאור הגר"א חו"מ סי' ערב ס"ק יא), וכ"כ הרמב"ם בפי' המשניות ביצה פ"ג מ"ד ובמורה נבוכים ח"ג פי"ז. שו"ע או"ח סי' שה סע' ח ו-ט. חו"מ סי' ערב סע' ט. וראה בשו"ת יביע אומר ח"ט או"ח סי' ל שלומד משם סע' ה שגם לדעת מרן צב"ח מן התורה. וראה גם בשו"ע הרב שם סע' כט
7. אהע"ז סי' ה סע' יד. וראה שם בביאור הגר"א ס"ק מ
8. תניינא יו"ד סי' י מובא בפ"ת יו"ד כאן ס"ק י
9. אהע"ז סי' ה ס"ק פז
10. סי' לד
11. שו"ת, ח"ג סי' עא
12. שו"ת, ח"א סי' ל
13. שבת קי ע"ב

NISHMAT AVRAHAM

even if only for monetary gain. The *Chelkat Yaakov* concludes that it is certainly permissible to perform medical or scientific experi-ments on animals even if it causes them suffering. However one should desist, as an act of piety, to avoid becoming cruel. The *Seridei Eish*[14] disagrees with the *Chelkat Yaakov* writing that although in essence his ruling is correct, there is no need for pious behavior since one may only be stringent with oneself but not when it affects others. And how can one say that avoiding the suffering of animals is more important than the suffering of patients whom he might be able to help? This is somewhat similar to what the *Tosafot* write.[15] Doctors must therefore be permitted to conduct animal experiments without hesitation. The *Chatam Sofer*[16] also rules that whatever is done for the needs of man, for his honor or to avoid monetary loss, is not included in the prohibition of causing suffering to animals. This is also the ruling of the *Shevut Yaakov*,[17] the *Binyan Tzion*[18] and the *Tzitz Eliezer*.[19] It should, however, be obvious that wherever possible the suffering must be avoided or kept to the absolute minimum necessary. When the experiment is completed, if the animals are still in pain they should be killed as quickly as possible.

It is forbidden to kill any living thing without reason.[20]

RESEARCH AND EXPERIMENTATION ON HUMAN BEINGS. This may be divided into five different areas for discussion: (1) where the patient undergoes experimental treatment; (2) healthy volunteers; (3) those who are unable to give their consent such as children and the mentally disabled; (4) *placebo* controlled trials; (5) research on *Shabbat* and *Yom Tov*.

(1) THE PATIENT. The *seriously ill* patient — see below Siman 155B, p. 55. The *non-seriously ill* patient — see below Siman 155B(3), p. 59.

(2) THE HEALTHY VOLUNTEER. Where the volunteer will certainly come to no harm, this is not only permitted but is praiseworthy. If, however, there is any risk involved, *halachic* guidance must be sought for there is a controversy between the *Talmud Yerushalmi* and *Talmud Bavli* as to whether one is permitted to put himself into possible danger to save another who is in certain danger.[21] The *poskim* of our generation rule this is permitted (but not obligatory), if the patient to be saved is present at the time, the chances of saving the patient are great, and the risk of the volunteer dying is small. But, as far as volunteering for an experiment is concerned, one may do so only if the injury is small, for example, giving a small blood sample and certainly if there is no injury at all. However, if the risk of injury is not small, and certainly if there is a possible danger, one may not volunteer for such a procedure and neither may the doctor conduct such research. If, however, the *seriously ill* patient is present and may be saved by the experiment, one may volunteer even if there is a slight risk involved. Rav Auerbach zt"l agreed with this.

(3) UNABLE TO GIVE CONSENT. A child for this purpose is defined as a boy under the age of thirteen and a girl under the age of twelve.

If such a patient will not suffer from the

---

14. שו"ת, ח"ג סי' ז מובא בשו"ת חלקת יעקב ח"א סי' לא. וראייתו מהתוס' ע"ז יא ע"א ד"ה עוקרין

15. ע"ז יא ע"א ד"ה עוקרין

16. חידושיו על שבת קנד ע"ב ובב"מ לב ע"ב

17. שו"ת, ח"ג סי' עא

18. שו"ת, סי' קח

19. שו"ת ציץ אליעזר חי"ד סי' סח. וראה גם באיסור והיתר סי' נט סע' לו ועיין שם בור זהב ס"ק יז וכן בשו"ת תרומת הדשן פסקים וכתבים סי' קה

20. רד"ק על יהושע יא:ט. חינוך מצוה קפו. שאלת יעב"ץ ח"א סי' קי

21. ראה בשו"ע חו"מ סי' תכו בסמ"ע ס"ק ב ובפ"ת ס"ק ב

research: One may send a specimen of his body fluids (urine, feces or sputum) for laboratory examination. If a specimen of his blood needs to be examined for diagnosis or treatment, one is permitted to take a little extra at the same time for research purposes (see below *Rav Eliashiv shlita's* opinion). If the patient will suffer a little from the research: One may use him for the research if the results will help him and the pain or suffering involved is small. However, if the research will cause him pain or suffering without any benefit to him and only other patients will benefit, he may not be used.[22] If there is a slight risk involved in the research, but the benefits to him will be much greater, he may be used, since every treatment carries with it some risk. If, however, the risk is great and, certainly, if only another, but not he himself, will benefit from the research, it is forbidden. In such a situation parental consent is not acceptable. If the patient is *seriously ill*, he may undergo experimental treatment which is risky, if he would certainly die without this therapy and the treatment has a chance, however small, of curing him. See below Siman 155B, p. 55.

Rav Auerbach zt"l wrote to me that if it is impossible to explain to a *seriously ill* patient regarding the use of an experimental or dangerous procedure which has a good chance of curing him but could, on the other hand, curtail his life, it would possibly be permitted to depend on the consent of the family. This is provided that one knows for certain that their only concern is the patient. I would add that in any case, one should give much thought before deciding; all the specialists involved should be consulted and a final decision should be given by a recognized *posek*.

Rav Auerbach zt"l wrote to me that he agreed with all of the above and added that it would permitted to amputate a child's finger to save his life. When asked by *Rav Neuwirth shlita* whether parental consent was necessary, he answered that they have no ownership rights over him. A father has no ownership rights over his young daughter, although he may choose a husband for her. *Rav Eliashiv shlita* also told me that one may not use a boy below the age of thirteen (or a girl below the age of twelve) for research despite parental consent. He added that he disagreed with what I had written above (with *Rav Auerbach zt"l's* consent) regarding taking blood for research at the same time that blood was drawn for diagnosis or treatment. In his opinion one could not draw blood from a sick child over and above what was need for his treatment.

(4) PLACEBO CONTROLLED TRIALS. In these trials, half the group is given the experimental drug whereas the other half is given a *placebo* which is indistinguishable from the experimental drug. Neither the patient nor the doctors involved in the trial know what a given patient is getting since all medications are coded. Such a trial is permissible provided that: (a) The patient gives his full consent after being fully informed of the possible risks and that he may be put into one or other group randomly. (b) All patients, regardless of which group they will belong to, will continue to receive the medication they were getting until now. The experimental drug or *placebo* is merely added to their present treatment.

(5) RESEARCH ON *SHABBAT* AND *YOM TOV*. The *Shemirat Shabbat KeHilchatah*[23] rules that a doctor may give experimental treatment on *Shabbat* (or *Yom Tov*) to a *seriously ill* patient, even if the results of such treatment are doubtful,

---

22. ראה בנשמת אברהם כרך ד חו"מ סי' רמג ס"ק א (עמ' קצט) מה שכתב לי הגרש"ז אויערבאך זצ"ל

23. פ"מ סע' לו

CHAPTER 2
The Laws of Treifot

SIMAN 29
THE EIGHT TYPES OF *TREIFOT* AND THEIR SIGNS

§1 There are eight types of (A)*treifot*: A bird or animal that:

──────── NISHMAT AVRAHAM ────────

and even if Torah laws are set aside for this purpose. Regarding the *placebo*-controlled trial, Sabbath laws of Torah force may not be set aside, for one does not know if this particular patient is getting the experimental drug. For one may not set aside Sabbath laws needlessly for one patient to perhaps save another's life later on. This situation is not to be compared to the one in which *Rav Auerbach zt"l* ruled[24] that one may set aside Sabbath laws for a premature baby with severe congenital defects who will certainly not live for thirty days, despite the fact that by strict *halachic* criteria, Sabbath laws may not be set aside for a baby who is a *nefel*. The reason in that situation is different. For in a hospital setting, one must set aside even Torah law for him since not all the other doctors and nurses involved will know to differentiate between one very sick baby and another in the future. This may lead later to a lackadaisical approach to another sick baby who in fact may respond to treatment. *Rav Neuwirth shlita* agreed with this.

May a Jew set aside Rabbinic laws on *Shabbat* or may he ask a non-Jew to set aside Sabbath laws for the purposes of research? *Rav Neuwirth shlita* wrote to me that although it is doubtful whether the patient is receiving the experimental drug or only the *placebo*, the *Halachah* is more lenient with regard to asking a non-Jew to do whatever is necessary. This is because, in any case, someone may benefit from the trial, be it this patient or another.

See *Nishmat Avraham*, vol. 1 *Orach Chaim*, Siman 448A and 468A regarding research on *Pesach*, and Siman 532A regarding research on *Chol HaMoed*.[25]

SIMAN 29

(A) *treifot*: A bird or animal with one of these *treifot* will not live for more than twelve months[1] and may not be eaten (see *Nishmat Avraham*, vol. 1 *Orach Chaim*, Siman 328 (6A), p. 192). If such a bird or animal nevertheless lives for more than twelve months it still may not be eaten.[2]

Does the concept of *treifah* apply to humans? The *Ramban* and *Rashba*[3] write that the *treifot* enumerated in animals do not apply to humans. However, if one's leg is torn off above the knee he is considered a *treifah*, and if untreated, will not live.[4] The *Rambam*[5] widens this to include any

────

24. See *Nishmat Avraham*, vol. 1 *Orach Chaim*, Siman 330Q, p. 228.

25. וראה בע"ז בגמ' ותוס' ד"ה לאפוקי. יו"ד סי' קנח סע' א ברמ"א, ט"ז ונקוה"כ. שו"ת יחוה דעת ח"ב סי' יד

1. חולין מב ע"א

2. רמ"א יו"ד סי' נז סע' יח ועיין שם בש"ך ס"ק מח

3. יבמות קכ ע"ב

4. ראה בית שמואל אהע"ז סי' יז ס"ק צז

5. הל' גרושין פי"ג הט"ז

(1) was mauled by a beast of prey, (2) has a perforated internal organ, (3) was born missing an organ or part of one, (4) one of its organs or part of one was removed during life, (5) has most of the flesh enveloping the stomach torn, (6) fell from a height, (7) has a severed spinal cord or trachea, or (8) has a majority of its bones broken.

NISHMAT AVRAHAM

limb which, if torn off, will lead to death. The *Maggid Mishneh*,[6] quoting the *Yerushalmi*, the *Ramban* and the *Rashba*, writes that a person who is a *treifah* will not live for twelve months. *Tosafot*[7] quote *Rabbeinu Tam* that an animal becomes a *treifah* if the inner of the two membranes enveloping its brain is pierced whereas a human becomes so only if part of his skull is also missing. The *Tosafot* attribute this difference to the fact that the inner membrane in man is much stronger. However with regard to the other signs of *treifah* there is no difference between an animal and man. It is possible though that this difference of opinion between *Rabbeinu Tam* and *Tosafot* applies only to the reason that makes an animal or man a *treifah*. Both agree, however, that a *treifah*, whether an animal or man, will not live for more than twelve months.[8] This is also the opinion of many *acharonim*.[9] On the other hand, the *Tosafot*,[10] the *Hagahot Mordechai*[11] and the *Kesef Mishneh*[12] write that a person who is a *treifah* does live for more than twelve months and the *Kesef Mishneh* is quoted by the *Beit Shmuel*.[13]

The *Chazon Ish*[14] writes that the important difference between man and animals is that a man who is a *treifah* can be treated whereas an animal cannot. Thus the *Gemara's*[15] opinion that a man who is a *treifah* will not live more than twelve months is relevant only if he is left untreated. It is common knowledge that a person who is operated on his gastro-intestinal tract can live a full life, unlike an animal that is a *treifah* because of a hole in his gastro-intestinal tract. Even if medical opinion today says that a particular form of *treifah* cannot be cured, one cannot depend on this since it may only be a question of time before a cure will be found. *Chazal*, because of their purity of spirit, were given the Heavenly power to define what is a *treifah*. This was at the giving of the Torah and remains the *halachah* for all time. Their definition of what is a *treifah* was Heaven ordained at that time and included all instances for which *Hashem* has not yet disclosed the cure to man. The *treifot* defined then remain so for all time (*unless they can be treated*). In addition, continues the *Chazon Ish*, this change in our times is probably not only

---

6. שם
7. חולין מב ע"ב ד"ה ואמר רב יהודה. וראה גם תוס' עירובין ז ע"א ד"ה כגון בשם ת"י כ"י. תוס' גיטין נו ע"ב ד"ה וניקר ובכורות לו ע"א ד"ה כדי
8. עיין בחולין נז ע"א שהדבר תלוי במחלוקת תנאים אם אדם טריפה חי י"ב חי או לא
9. פרי חדש יו"ד סי' לא ס"ק ז, ספר ברכת הזבח דף עח ושו"ת פנים מאירות ח"א סי' מח (ודלא כהכסף משנה הל' גרושין פי"ג הט"ז), ב"ש אהע"ז סי' יז ס"ק צ. וראה גם בשו"ת צמח צדק החדשות סי' עה פלתי יו"ד סי' לא
10. תוס' בשם ר"ת וזבחים קטו ע"א ד"ה דילמא
11. הגהת מרדכי ריש פ"ג דחולין בשם תוס' שאנ"ץ
12. על הרמב"ם הל' גירושין פי"ג הט"ז
13. אהע"ז סי' יז ס"' צ
14. הל' אישות סי' כז ס"ק ג
15. יבמות קכ ע"ב

SIMAN 29: THE EIGHT TYPES OF *TREIFOT* AND THEIR SIGNS / §1   ❏   15

---NISHMAT AVRAHAM---

due to the discovery of new medications but also to a change in our bodies; for example, the amounts removed in bloodletting of the earlier generations would be life threatening if removed in our day. There are also differences in climate and other matters of nature today.[16] It is also possible that operations that are successfully carried out today would not have helped in earlier times.

It would appear that the *Chazon Ish's* statement that the definition of a *treifah* in man is dependent on whether a cure is available or not, was in fact enunciated by the *Rambam*.[17] He wrote that every man is considered complete and killing him carries the death penalty (in the days of the *Sanhedrin*), unless it is known for certain that he was a *treifah* and the doctors declare that he cannot be cured.

The subject is discussed at length in the *Otsar HaPoskim*.[18]

Sabbath laws are set aside for a person who is a *treifah* and is *seriously ill*, the same as for anyone else.[19] If an enemy demands a scapegoat of a member of a group who will be slain by them, in order to allow the others to go free, one may not sacrifice a *treifah* to save the life of others who are not *treifot*.[20]

One who is a *treifah* and whose life is saved, but remains a *treifah* because of his illness, should say the *HaGomel* blessing; however he should do so without mentioning *Hashem's* Name or Kingship.[21] The *Tzitz Eliezer*,[22] however, disagrees and rules that he should say the blessing with *Hashem's* Name and Kingship. On the contrary, if he were told not to say the blessing in the usual manner, he will think that he has an incurable illness. Therefore, if he were to ask whether he should say the blessing it is best that he is answered in the affirmative.

Regarding the *pidyon haben* of a child who is a *treifah* see below Siman 305C.

---

16. עיין ברמ"א אהע"ז סי' קנו סע' ד ובשו"ת יביע אומר ח"ג אהע"ז סי' א

17. הל' רוצח פ"ב ה"ח. וראה במאמרו של הגר"מ פיינשטיין זצ"ל במוריה אלול תשד"מ עמ' נה

18. סי' יז ס"ק רסח (ב) עמ' לט-מ

19. שו"ת אחיעזר ח"ג סי' סה ס"ק יד. ספר פתח דביר סי' קצט ס"ק ט ובסי' שכט ס"ק ו ושו"ת ציץ אליעזר ח"י סי' כה פכ"ז. וראה גם במ"ב סי' שכט סע' ד בביה"ל ד"ה אלא

20. שו"ת נודע ביהודה תנינא חו"מ סי' נט. שו"ת תורת חסד אהע"ז סי' מב ס"ק ז. שו"ת ציץ אליעזר ח"ט סי' יז פ"ו. וע"ע במנחת חינוך מצוה רצו ומצוה תר

21. ספר פתח הדביר ח"ב סי' ריט אות ג, מובא גם בשדי חמד אסיפת דינים מערכת ברכות סי' ב סע' יב

22. שו"ת, ח"י סי' כה פכ"ז

CHAPTER 3
The Laws Concerning Blood

SIMAN 66
FOOD WHICH IS FORBIDDEN BECAUSE OF BLOOD

§10 It is forbidden for one to suck [A]his own blood because of *marit ha'ayin*. Therefore if one bites into bread and blood from his teeth is visible on the bread it must be scraped off. Blood that remains between his teeth may be sucked in and swallowed.

GLOSS: *Since the Torah does not forbid the blood of fish or humans, it is not forbidden (even by Rabbinic rule) if it is mixed and not visible.*

---NISHMAT AVRAHAM---

SIMAN 66

(A) his own blood. It is forbidden by Torah law to consume the blood of all animals or fowl.[1] The blood of fish is permitted by Torah law but forbidden by Rabbinic law because of *marit ha'ayin*[2] (the onlooker may believe that he is drinking the blood of an animal); the same applies to human blood.

Is one permitted to suck blood from a bleeding finger? The *Darchei Teshuvah*[3] writes that this depends on the two conflicting views of *Rashi* and *Tosafot*.[4] According to *Rashi* one is only permitted to swallow blood that is between his teeth because it is not visible to an onlooker; he would therefore forbid one to suck blood from a bleeding finger. *Tosafot*, on the other hand, permit one to swallow blood that is between one's teeth since it is obviously human blood; he would therefore permit one to suck blood from a bleeding finger. The *Darchei Teshuvah* does not come to a decision as to the *halachah*. The *Orach Mishor*,[5] however, rules that if the finger is obviously bleeding it would be permitted to suck it. The *Hafla'ah*[6] writes that since the blood is sucked directly from the finger or during a *brit milah*, it may be swallowed. Since this blood is not visible to an onlooker there is no possibility that he may think that the blood swallowed is that of an animal. However, he concludes that further study is needed. The *Nachal Eshkol*[7] rules that since it is obvious that the blood is coming from the finger it would be permitted to suck it. On the other hand, the *Knesset HaGedolah*[8] rules that the Rabbinic prohibition includes sucking blood that is ob-

---

1. ויקרא ז:כו. דברים יב:טז. יו״ד כאן סע׳ א
2. יו״ד כאן סע׳ ט
3. ס״ק סח
4. רש״י כתובות ס ע״א ד״ה וחילופא. תוס׳ כריתות כא ע״ב ד״ה דכוותה
5. ס״ק ה
6. על כתובות שם ד״ה בגמ׳
7. ח״ג סי׳ כה ס״ק יט
8. הגהות ב״י סוף סי׳ סו

SIMAN 66: FOOD WHICH IS FORBIDDEN BECAUSE OF BLOOD / §10   17

---NISHMAT AVRAHAM---

viously human. The *Darchei Teshuvah*, having quoted all of the above, writes that according to the *Knesset HaGedolah* it would be permissible to suck the blood if it is then spat out.[9]

What if it is *Shabbat*? See *Nishmat Avraham*, vol. 1 *Orach Chaim*, Siman 328 (48B), p. 215) where I quoted the *Mishnah Berurah*[10] that it is forbidden by Torah law to suck blood from a wound on *Shabbat*. This includes blood from between the teeth or from bleeding gums. However in the latter case, the *Shulchan Aruch HaRav*[11] rules that this is only Rabbinically forbidden,[12] while the *Magen Avraham*[13] writes that it is also possibly forbidden by Torah law because it may be considered the *melachah* of "causing a wound."

---

9. וראה בהגהות יד אברהם על היו"ד כאן
10. סי' שכח סוס"ק קמז
11. סי' שכח סע' נד
12. שם ס"ק נג
13. שם סוס"ק נג

CHAPTER 4
The Laws of Salting Meat

SIMAN 69
THE LAWS OF SALTING AND RINSING MEAT

§3 One should not use (A)salt as fine as flour nor salt so coarse that it falls off the meat (*if, however, the only salt available is as fine as flour, it may be used*).

NISHMAT AVRAHAM

SIMAN 69

(A) salt. After *shechitah* the meat must be soaked in water for thirty minutes and then rinsed well;[1] it is then salted to cover all of its external and internal surfaces,[2] allowing the blood to drain away from it. It is thus left for an hour and then rinsed again well before it can be cooked.[3] *Rav Auerbach zt"l* wrote to me that according to many *poskim*, if the meat was not soaked and rinsed first, so that blood was visible on it and it is then salted or cooked, the meat is forbidden to be eaten by Torah law.[4] As to the blood of such meat that remains below the surface and was cooked, there is a controversy whether it is forbidden by Torah or Rabbinic law, depending on their interpretation of the *Gemara*.[5] There are those who rule that, by eating it, one transgresses a Torah commandment that carries with it the punishment of *karet*,[6] while others rule that it is forbidden only by Rabbinic law.[7]

Is a patient who is on a strict salt-free diet permitted to use sugar instead of salt to "salt" his meat? The medical problem is not so much the salt (sodium chloride) as salt but the sodium from which he is medically restricted. The *Halachot Ketanot*[8] and the *Ikerei HaDat*[9] both rule that there is no difference between salt and sugar in this context. The *Da'at Torah*[10] writes that if sugar is used, the meat would at least not be forbidden by Torah law.

However the majority of *acharonim* dis-

---

1. רמ"א כאן סע' א
2. כאן סע' ד
3. כאן סע' ו ברמ"א
4. איסור עשה. וכן הובא בדרכ"ת סי' סו ס"ק ה בשם שו"ת הרי"ם מגור יו"ד סי' ז ושו"ת נפש חיה יו"ד סי' ה
5. במנחות כא ע"א
6. רש"י חולין קט ע"א במשנה ד"ה הלב וקב ע"א ד"ה הקפה, חידושי הר"ן חולין קב ע"א, הרמב"ם הל' מאכ"א פ"ו ה"י לדעת הבי"י סי' פז ועיין שם בש"ך ס"ק טו, שו"ת הרדב"ז ח"א סי' קצט, כו"פ ריש סי' פז
7. תוס' חולין שם ד"ה הלב וקב ע"א ד"ה הקפה וקיא ע"א

ד"ה דם, הרא"ש חולין פ"ח סי' כז וסי' לג, הרשב"א תורת האדם בית נ שער ג מובא בטור סוסי' עו, ספר התרומות סי' נו, הרא"ה בבדק הבית סי' עו, תורת חטאת כלל א דין ז, ט"ז סי' סט ס"ק כד, ש"ך סי' סט ס"ק מבו-עו סי' ע ס"ק מטו וסי' עו ס"ק כד והפר"ח סי' סט ס"ק א. וראה גם בשו"ת חת"ס יו"ד סי' ע

8. שו"ת, ח"א סי' ריח
9. או"ח סי' יד אות לו
10. כאן, כמו בדם שמלחו ובישלו דאינו עובר עליו משום דאינו ראוי להקרבה, והרי בעירב דבר פסול למזבח וה"ה הסוכר. וראה גם בשו"ת שואל ומשיב מהד"ק סי' קמב

§6 After salting, the salt should remain on the meat for (B)about twenty minutes.

GLOSS: *One may depend on this ruling under extenuating circumstances; it is also the ruling if honoring guests is involved or if it is necessary for Shabbat. Otherwise the custom is to have the salt remain on the meat for an hour, and one should not change this.*

NISHMAT AVRAHAM

agree and rule that meat that is cooked after "salting" with sugar is forbidden.[11]

According to many *poskim*,[12] however, it would be permitted to salt meat for such a patient using dietetic salt composed of ammonium chloride instead of sodium chloride. Potassium chloride may also be used if the patient's medical condition warrants or permits it. Both of these are salts and cannot be compared to sugar. However there are those who disagree.[13] Such a patient must, however, be under strict medical and biochemical supervision.

(B) about twenty minutes. The *Shach*[14] writes that this means eighteen minutes and this is also the ruling of the *Mechaber*.[15] However the *Pri Chadash*[16] writes that the *Rambam*, *Rashi* and the *Rav MiBartinura* all rule that the lapse of time should be exactly twenty-four minutes.[17] The *Magen Avraham*[18] also writes that it should be twenty-four minutes[19] and that this is also the ruling of the *Maharil*. The *Darchei Teshuvah*[20] writes that one may not be lenient regarding this and it is also the ruling of the *Chayei Adam*.[21] The *Mishnah Berurah*[22] writes that the lapse of time is twenty-four minutes or at least twenty-three minutes and otherwise the meat may not be eaten; this is also the ruling of the *Shemirat Shabbat KeHilchatah*.[23]

However the *Chazon Ish*,[24] after quoting the *Mishnah Berurah*, writes that taking into consideration the opinion of the *Gra*, one may permit meat upon which the salt has remained for eighteen minutes to be eaten. Certainly for a patient one may have the salt remain on the meat for only

---

11. ערוגת הבושם יו"ד כאן ס"ק יז, היד יהודה כאן ס"ק צז, שו"ת דברי חיים מצאנו ח"א יו"ד סי' כה, מהר"ש ענגיל ח"ג סי' קכא ס"ק ב, שו"ת הר צבי יו"ד סי' סו, הגר"ח פלאגי בשו"ת רוח חיים יו"ד סי' סט ס"ק ה, ובנו בשו"ת יפה ללב ח"ג יו"ד סי' סט ס"ק א, הבן איש חי שנה ב פ' טהרות סע' כב ובשו"ת רב פעלים ח"ב יו"ד סי' ד, שו"ת חסד לאברהם תאומים יו"ד סי' לב, שו"ת יביע אומר ח"ד יו"ד סי' ב, ושו"ת ציץ אליעזר ח"ט ט"ו לה חי"א סי' עז וחי"ב סי' נב. וראה גם בדרכ"ת כאן ס"ק שכח ובכף החיים כאן ס"ק שכב, שו"ת אבני נזר או"ח סי' תקלב, שו"ת טוב טעם ודעת מהד"ק ס"י קיא שו"ת כתב סופר יו"ד סי' לו, שו"ת שואל ומשיב מהד"ק ח"א סי' קמב ו-קמג ושו"ת תירוש ויצהר סי' קעח

12. שמירת שבת כהלכתה פמ"ס סע' פז, נועם ח"י עמ' קף וחט"ז קונטרס הרפואה עמ' ג. וראה בספר מזון כשר מן החי עמ' 434

13. שו"ת תירוש ויצהר סי' ריח בשם אסיפת אגודת הרבנים וחברי ועד הרבנים בקרלבאד - הראה לי גיסי הנכבד ר' דוב אריה הלוי היל שליט"א

14. ס"ק כה
15. או"ח סי' תנט סע' ב
16. כאן ס"ק כו
17. וראה גם בחק יעקב סי' תנט ס"ק י וכרתי כאן ס"ק יז
18. או"ח סי' תנט ס"ק ג
19. לאותם המחשבים מהנץ החמה עד שקיעתה
20. ס"ק קט
21. כלל ל סע' ט
22. סי' תנט ס"ק טו וביה"ל ד"ה הוי
23. פ"מ סע' פז. וראיתי ששתי הדעות מובאות בחת"ס שו"ת או"ח סי' פ ואה"ע ח"א סי' סג פסק שמהלך מיל הוא עשרים וארבע דקות, אמנם בהגהותיו על האו"ח סי' פט על המג"א ס"ק ב, בשו"ת ח"ו סי' טז ובתורת משה על שביעי של פסח ד"ה ותען להם מרים מובא שמהלך מיל הוא שמונה עשרה דקות, רצ"ע
24. או"ח סי' קכג אות א

―――― NISHMAT AVRAHAM ――――

eighteen minutes. *Rav Waldenberg shlita*[25] also rules that one may act leniently where a patient is concerned and may have the salt remain on the meat for eighteen minutes only.

If, however, the patient is not allowed by his doctor to salt his meat at all, he should either use the other salts mentioned above **A**, or else scald the meat by putting it into water that is boiling on the fire (having first soaked it in water for thirty minutes and rinsed it well);[26] he should use utensils specially set aside for this purpose.[27]

---

25. לב אברהם ח"א עמ' כא ושו"ת ציץ אליעזר חי"ב סי' נב. ח"ב יו"ד סי' כו

26. שמירת שבת כהלכתה פ"מ סע' פז. שו"ת שבט הלוי

27. שמירת שבת כהלכתה שם בשם הגרש"ז אויערבאך זצ"ל

CHAPTER 5
The Laws of That Which Comes Forth From a Living Creature

SIMAN 81
WHATEVER COMES FROM THE UNCLEAN IS ALSO UNCLEAN

§7 **GLOSS:** *Although the mother's milk of a non-Jewess is permissible for a Jewish infant, nevertheless, where possible a baby should not nurse from her since her milk will dull the sensitivities of the heart and produce a mean nature. Similarly a nursing woman, even a Jewess,* (A)*should not eat whatever is halachically*

NISHMAT AVRAHAM

SIMAN 81

INTRODUCTION. Mother's milk is directly related to the diet of the mother and reflects that diet. Since Jews are prohibited from eating certain foods, Jewish babies are affected by milk coming from someone who eats food prohibited to a Jew. As the *Maharal*[1] explains, the reason that forbidden foods have this effect on the Jew is not because they are inherently bad; it is only because *Hashem* forbade them to us that they cause spiritual harm to the Jew who eats of them. And the *Pri Chadash*[2] writes that since his generation are not careful to prevent young children from eating forbidden foods (although they are not required by *Halachah* to do so), most of these children will become wicked later in life. These are the insolent ones of the generation who have no fear whatsoever of Heaven and who are unwilling to be admonished to change their wicked ways.

(A) should not eat. The *Taz*[3] and the *Shach*[4] both write that even if the woman is permitted to eat the forbidden food because she is *seriously ill*, she must nevertheless not nurse the child. The *Tosafot*,[5] quoting a *Midrash,* write that milk can cleanse and milk can defile, for example Antoninus (the Roman ruler) who was nursed by *Rebbe*'s mother, later converted to Judaism, undergoing circumcision.[6] The *Darchei Teshuvah*[7] quotes the *Shul-*

---

1. תפארת ישראל פ״ח
2. ס״ק כו
3. ס״ק יב
4. ס״ק כה
5. ע״ז י ע״ב תוסד״ה אמר. ועיין בילקוט שמעוני ישעיה תכט: ואף רשעי ישראל וצדיקי עכו״ם שנשתיירו בגיהנם עונים ואומרים אמן מתוך גיהנם וכו׳ שנא׳ כהניך ילבשו צדק וחסידיך ירננו, כהניך אלו צדיקי אומות העולם שהם כהנים להקב״ה בעה״ז כגון אנטונינוס וחביריו. וחסידיך, אלו רשעי ישראל שנקראו חסדים וכו׳
6. וראה בתוס׳ חגיגה טו ע״א ד״ה שובו וע״ז י ע״ב ד״ה אמר, הגהות אשרי על הרא״ש ריש פ״ב דע״ז, ריטב״א על ע״ז כו ע״א ד״ה ולעניו, רש״י סוטה יב ע״ב ד״ה דבר טמא, ורשב״א על יבמות קיד ע״א מובא גם בר״ן ע״ז כו ע״א לגבי התנא אחר
7. ס״ק צא

forbidden; (B)*even a child should not do so, for it will spiritually harm him in later years.*

---NISHMAT AVRAHAM---

chan Aruch HaRav[8] that there is no difference in this context between food that is *halachically* forbidden in and of itself (such as bacon), and food that is only forbidden at certain times (for example *chametz* during *Pesach*). A child who has reached the stage of some understanding should not be allowed to eat any of these forbidden foods, but one need not prevent a younger child from eating them.[9] The *Darchei Teshuvah* adds that although this differentiation between a younger child and one with some understanding is *halachically* true, one should still prevent a younger child from eating forbidden food, for fear that it will dull the sensitivities of his heart. The *Shach*[10] writes that this includes foods that are only Rabbinically forbidden.

The *Ramban*[11] writes that the Torah illuminates our eyes in the secrets of procreation. It has forbidden some animals, some birds and some fish since they are not beneficial to health and besides which, also harm the soul, and this is the meaning of what the Torah writes:[12] "Lest you become defiled through them."[13]

The *Chelkat Yaakov*[14] was asked to give a ruling regarding a great, Heaven-fearing Rav, who was suffering greatly and required a blood transfusion. Was it necessary to ascertain that the blood was only donated by people who did not eat forbidden foods which would dull the heart and produce a mean nature? The *Chelkat Yaakov* answered that although

the situation is similar to that stated by the *Rama*, nevertheless one should not act strictly. One who requires a blood transfusion is defined as being *seriously ill* or at least possibly *seriously ill* and therefore does not need to wait for blood that has been donated by someone who is of good conduct (*being observant of the mitzvot — author*). Even if one would say that, as an act of piety, one should act strictly despite the possible danger, it is not at all certain that a blood transfusion from a person who eats forbidden foods will give rise to these bad attributes. For the *poskim* only speak of this when such food is taken orally, and when discussing things which are abstruse and beyond logic, perhaps such a distinction may be drawn although logically we may not think so. Since it is not something we can be sure of it would appear that one should not be strict about it. The *mitzvah* of: "Live by them"[15] (the Laws of the Torah), and not die because of them[16] will guard him and prevent insensitivity of his heart and the development of a mean nature.

(B) even a child. The *Chatam Sofer*[17] writes that although by strict law it is permissible to hospitalize a child who is a *shoteh* for prolonged treatment in a hospital where he will only be fed forbidden foods, nevertheless our predecessors have warned us that these foods in childhood will dull the sensitivities of the heart and produce a mean nature. Therefore, rules the *Chatam Sofer*, it is better for him to

---

8. או"ח סי' שמג סע' י
9. שו"ע הרב שם סע' ג
10. ס"ק כו
11. דרשות, תורת השם תמימה
12. ויקרא יא:מג. וראה גם בפירושו על ויקרא יא:יג
13. כתוב ונטמתם חסר א' לומר שהן מטמטמות הלב
14. שו"ת ח"ב סי' מ
15. ויקרא יח:ה
16. Only the three cardinal sins (idolatry, murder and forbidden sexual relationships) demand martyrdom.
17. שו"ת או"ח סי' פג

SIMAN 81: WHATEVER COMES FROM THE UNCLEAN IS UNCLEAN / §7

NISHMAT AVRAHAM

remain a *shoteh* all his life rather than be considered wicked before *Hashem*, even fleetingly.[18] The *Maharam Shick*[19] rules similarly regarding the admission of a blind child to a school for the blind for many years. *Rav Auerbach zt"l* wrote to me that it is obvious that the *Chatam Sofer* did not mean that one must act strictly with one who is a real *shoteh* for whom the possibility of a cure is very slim. His ruling refers to one who is mentally retarded only. The *Maharam Shick* also refers only to a blind girl who requires admission to the school to learn a trade to make her self-sufficient and not because it may be possible to cure her.

The *Igrot Moshe*[20] was asked about someone whose eleven-year-old daughter was born a *shoteh* and for whom there is no cure. Is it permissible to put her into a home run by the state where she will be given forbidden foods? *Rav Moshe Feinstein zt"l* answered that the *Chatam Sofer* was discussing a child who was not a true *shoteh* but only a child of low intelligence. In a school with specially trained teachers such children are educated to reach higher levels of understanding. It is possible that such a child who is not a *shoteh* but merely of very low intelligence would be obligated to keep the *mitzvot*. However, if the girl fits the definition of a true *shoteh*, age will not alter anything. Even when she becomes of age she will still be exempt from *mitzvot*. However the *Chatam Sofer*, who was unsure whether the child was a real *shoteh* or only one of low intelligence, ruled strictly that he should be removed from the hospital before he became obligated to perform *mitzvot*. For a true *shoteh*, however, there is no *halachic* reason to differentiate between a child and an adult. The *Chatam Sofer* also considered the bad effect the forbidden foods eaten in childhood would have on him later in life, since his training would make him obligated to keep the *mitzvot*. In the case in question, the girl was a true *shoteh* who would never become obligated to keep *mitzvot* and even if the forbidden foods that she ate would dull the sensitivities of her heart, she would not be considered wicked before *Hashem* and therefore there is no need to be strict.

Rav Waldenberg shlita[21] was asked about a girl who was of low intelligence and childlike in her behavior. He ruled that it is certainly forbidden to admit her to an institution where she would be fed forbidden foods and should she already be in one, it would be obligatory to take her out to prevent her from eating such foods. What should be done if she had been admitted to an institution which had served kosher food, but later, because of their high costs, the owner decided to give the cheaper non-kosher foods instead? *Rav Waldenberg shlita* writes that the obligation of her brother-in-law to remove her in such a case is no different from that of any other Jew. Moreover, the *Chatam Sofer*,[22] who ruled that one is forbidden to admit his eighteen-year-old epileptic daughter to an institution where she would be given non-kosher food, also ruled that the father was not responsible for the maintenance or treatment of a daughter who was eighteen years old; the obligation for this lay with the community. Similarly, in the case in question the responsibility of removing the girl from the institution and placing her in one where she would be given kosher food lay with the community and its leaders.

---

18. וראה בתוס׳ שבת יב ע״ב ד״ה הרבי, חגיגה טו ע״ב ד״ה אם וחולין ה ע״ב ד״ה צדיקים

19. שו״ת או״ח סי׳ קסג

20. שו״ת, או״ח ח״ב סי׳ פח

21. שו״ת ציץ אליעזר חי״ד סי׳ סט

22. שו״ת, יו״ד סי׳ עו

NISHMAT AVRAHAM

The *Melamed LeHo'il*[23] writes that if the food is only Rabbinically forbidden, it would be permitted to admit a *shoteh* to such an institution; however his discussion only relates to the issue of supplying forbidden food and not to the problem of dulling the sensitivities of the heart.

The *Pri Megadim*[24] forbids one to actively give forbidden food, even to a *shoteh*. And although the *Shivat Tzion*[25] ruled that one may do so, the *Petach Ha-Devir*[26] agreed with the *Pri Megadim* and quoted the *Chikrei Lev* [27] in support.[28]

The *Igrot Moshe*[29] discusses the case of a patient who was seriously ill with brain disease. The only place where he could be cured would not allow any food to be brought in and he would have to eat non-kosher food although this was not necessary for his cure. Although there was no doubt that this is permitted, nevertheless this only applies to one who is observant and will eat what he is told he must eat. However it is forbidden to admit to such a place one who is not careful to avoid non-kosher food and who will eat to satisfy his desires even if the food is non-kosher and unnecessary for his cure. Although the negative commandment: "Do not place a stumbling block before a blind person,"[30] is set aside if necessary to save life, and therefore it should be permitted to bring him there for admission, since it is the only place where his life may be saved, nevertheless it is forbidden. This is because the patient would be forbidden to admit himself to an institution even if this would mean that he would die from his untreated disease, were he to know that he would be unable to withstand his desires there and would set aside other negative commandments. The threat to life does not set aside one's desires to sin [see the *Kesef Mishneh* (*Sanhedrin* 20:3)]. Commandments are set aside only in the context of a threat to life when there is no other choice and when the circumstances force one to set them aside, but not when they are set aside because one desires and enjoys doing so. Therefore one may not permit a patient who will eat non-kosher foods because he desires and enjoys them, although they are not part of his cure, to enter an institution where he will do so. And others are therefore also forbidden to admit him there.

I found difficulty understanding the proof that *Rav Moshe Feinstein zt"l* brought from the *Kesef Mishneh*. The situation discussed by the *Kesef Mishneh* concerns forbidden relationships that are not set aside even to save life. Eating forbidden food is permitted to save life. And, even if one eats them unnecessarily and is punishable for each olive's size of food that he eats, is he obligated to give up his life rather than avoiding doing so? Nor does what the *Mishnah Berurah*[31] writes seem relevant here. He says that one is not permitted to set out in a caravan if he knows that he will certainly have to set aside Sabbath laws because of danger.

---

sin, irregardless of whether the sinner knows or does not know that he is about to sin, provided that without this help he could not have sinned. The classical case is that of a Nazarite (who is forbidden to drink wine) who asks that a bottle of wine on the other side of a river be passed to him. The person doing so will have transgressed this negative commandment whether the Nazarite is aware or not that he is forbidden to drink wine.

31. סי' רמח ס"ק כו

23. שו"ת ח"ב סי' לא
24. או"ח סי' רסו מ"ז ס"ק ד ובפתיחה כללית ריש חלק ב
25. סי' ד
26. ח"ד סי' שמג אות ז
27. שו"ת, או"ח סי' עד ואהע"ז סי' כד
28. מובא בשדי חמד מערכת חית כלל קסו. וראה גם בשו"ת ציץ אליעזר חי"ד סי' סט
29. שו"ת, יו"ד ח"ב סי' נט
30. ויקרא יט:יד, לפני עור
The above verse also includes aiding someone to

SIMAN 81: WHATEVER COMES FROM THE UNCLEAN IS UNCLEAN / §7

NISHMAT AVRAHAM

And that there are those who, having nevertheless set out, endanger themselves a little rather than set aside Sabbath laws, so that their setting out will not retrospectively be considered a sin. However this is not to be compared to the situation being discussed here. The *Mishnah Berurah* discusses one who set out for personal reasons. (If he set out to perform a *mitzvah* he may not be prevented from doing so even if he set out during the three days prior to *Shabbat*.[32]) In our case the patient who is *seriously ill* is permitted to enter the hospital even though he knows that he will have to eat non-kosher food which is not part of his cure.

Rav Auerbach zt"l explained *Rav Feinstein zt"l's* reasoning to me: The Torah permitted the setting aside of its laws in order to save Jewish life but did not permit saving his life, if he would later definitely set aside its laws. *Rav Auerbach zt"l* subsequently wrote to me that he finds this ruling surprising for it is certainly permitted to set aside the *Shabbat* to save the life of one who eats non-kosher food or who constantly sins even when the consequences are *karet*. If he were drowning it is a *mitzvah* to save him and one may not cut off the finger of a Jew to prevent him from setting aside a negative commandment. One does not need to fear that he who causes another to sin is worse than one who kills him. Perhaps the reason is that with all sins (apart from the three cardinal ones) one hopes that he will repent and be forgiven. (*Author's explanation: Allowing or facilitating someone to sin is possibly a worse category of sin than that of a murderer. By saving a sinner's life or even by not harming him to prevent him sinning, one is not considered as one who causes another to sin.*) However *Rav Elchanan Wasserman zt"l*[33] also has the same opinion (as the *Igrot Moshe*). *Rav Auerbach zt"l* refers to what he wrote at length in *Minchat Shlomo*.[34]

(1) THE MENTALLY HANDICAPPED CHILD. Most children with Down syndrome may be brought, by early special education, to a level where they would be obligated to learn Torah and keep *mitzvot*. Because of the many problems involved in the fairly common practice of giving these — and children with other types of congenital disabling syndromes — to adoption soon after birth, *Rav Neuwirth shlita* and I went to see *Rav Shlomo Zalman Auerbach zt"l* and received the following answers to our questions:

1. These children may not be given up for adoption even to a religious family or institution since they, with their pure souls,[35] deserve parental love and a warm home the same as any other child. Only if the parents are unable or incapable of caring for them and must give them up to receive the special care that they need, they should be given to foster parents or to an institution; but the parents must continue to visit them regularly so as not to break the natural bond between them. Only if this is also impossible are the parents permitted to give up the child for adoption. In all cases, the child must be placed only where there is an atmosphere of Torah and *mitzvot*.

2. It is forbidden to place such a child within a family or institution that is irreligious, for he will then be given non-kosher food. If, however, it is certain that he cannot be educated and will remain an absolute *shoteh* all his life, it would be permitted.

3. It is even more forbidden to place him with non-Jews, even if he is so handicapped mentally that it is certain that he will never become obligated to learn Torah and keep *mitzvot*. For, said the

---

32. שם ברמ"א סע' ד
33. קובץ הערות סי' כג אות ג
34. ח"א סי' ז סע' ד
35. ראה לב אברהם ח"ב פי"א

CHAPTER 5: THAT WHICH COMES FROM A LIVING CREATURE

NISHMAT AVRAHAM

Rav zt"l: How is it possible to allow a Jewish child to be given to non-Jews who will bring him up, to all intents and purposes, as a non-Jew, finally to be buried among them?

4. To abandon a mentally handicapped child in the hospital for the authorities to place is also forbidden for the above reasons.

Rav Auerbach zt"l wrote to me adding that if looking after such a child at home will be at the expense of the other, healthy, children in the family, it would possibly be permissible to give him up for adoption to a religious family.

One may ask: Why is it permissible to place a complete *shoteh* in a place where he will be fed non-kosher food? Why are we not afraid that this will dull the sensitivities of the heart of the child who has a pure soul? Both *Rav Auerbach zt"l* and *Rav Eliashiv shlita* told me that dulling of the heart only applies when there is a present transgression of *Halachah*. A complete *shoteh* who will never become obligated to keep *mitzvot* also does not transgress by eating non-kosher food. He is like one who must eat non-kosher food as the only means of saving his life, who does not transgress but performs a *mitzvah* by eating.[36] A proselyte may reach the spiritual heights of a *Tanna*; although as a non-Jew he ate non-kosher foods, he did so when he was permitted to eat these foods and he does not at that time suffer a dulling of the sensitivities of the heart. [However, an infant, though he does not have any obligation to keep *mitzvot*, should not normally be given forbidden food, because his heart will become dulled, since he will be obligated to keep *mitzvot* when he comes of age.[37]]

The *Ran*[38] writes that even if one ate food that was non-kosher but that was mistakenly pronounced kosher by the *Sanhedrin*, his soul will not be harmed. (Whether the commandment:[39] "You shall not deviate from what they tell you," also applies to the Sages of all the generations following the dissolution of *Sanhedrin* will possibly depend on the controversy between the *Chinuch* and the *Chayei Adam* on the one hand, and the *Rambam* and *Ramban* on the other.[40])

Some eight years ago, *Rav Neuwirth shlita* wrote an open letter to parents of handicapped children and the following are excerpts from it: These children live as Jews, each at his own level of capability, for *Hashem* does not demand from a person more than he is capable of. And who knows whose reward will be greater in the World of Truth, they who do what they are capable of doing or we. For who can say that he is complete in body and soul? Surely we must fear the Day of Judgment. Furthermore, we do not find any difference with respect to *Shabbat* between one Jew and another. Although it is certain that even a child whose body is shattered and who will not live long enough to honor the sanctity of future Sabbaths, nevertheless Sabbath laws are set aside for him even though the reasoning

---

36. ולכאורה קשה מהרמ"א כאן, איזה עבירה יש בשתיית חלב של גויה? ורצ"ל שמטעמים סגוליים יש כאן צד עבירה ולכן מטמטם את לב התינוק - מו"ר הגרי"י נויבירט שליט"א

37. כשאין ברירה אחרת
See also what I wrote in *Nishmat Avraham*, vol. 1 *Orach Chaim,* Siman 328 (14A), p. 200, in the name of the *Tzitz Eliezer*.

38. דרשות יא ד"ה ואני סובר

39. דברים י"ז:י"א

40. לדעת החינוך מצוה תצה העובר על דברי חכמים ותקנתם בכל דור ודור עובר על לאו דאורייתא של לא תסור אך חולק עליו המנ"ח שם ס"ק ג וראה שם בהערה א ו-ג (הוצאת מכון ירושלים) שכן דעת הרמב"ן בספר המצוות שורש ראשון. ובדעת הרמב"ם נחלקו המנ"ח והגרי"פ פערלא, ראה שם בהערה ג. והחיי אדם כלל קכז סע' א כותב כהחינוך. וראה גם בתורה תמימה דברים יז אות מז ו-נט

SIMAN 81: WHATEVER COMES FROM THE UNCLEAN IS UNCLEAN / §7

NISHMAT AVRAHAM

"desecrate this *Shabbat* so that he may keep others" does not apply to him.[41] Sabbath laws are set aside even if he is too young to confess his sins before he dies. Thus we have before us a Jewish soul whose parents also witnessed the Revelation on Mount Sinai and who is therefore a full-fledged Jew. Thus, even though the *shoteh* is unaware of what he is doing, nevertheless his performance of a *halachically* required act is more acceptable than if it is done by a non-Jew.[42] Moreover, a Jewish child who dies before the age of eight days is circumcised at the graveside so that he may be mercifully remembered by Heaven and be brought back to life at the Resurrection.[43] In short, one who is born a Jew is a Jew in every way, even if Heaven has decreed that he be disabled in body and mind. *Chazal*, commenting on the verse:[44] "And I returned and saw etc. and behold, the tears of the oppressed and they had no comforts," tell us:[45] Rebbe Yehudah says: These are the children who are put aside in this world etc., but who will stand up in the company of the righteous in the World to Come. *Rav Wosner shlita* explains "children who are put aside" to mean those unfortunate children, disabled in body or mind, who were not accepted into society but were hidden at home to waste away, leading lives devoid of content; in the future they will stand with the righteous. It is told that the *Vilna Gaon's* daughter, who died a few days before her wedding, came to him in a dream some days later and said: Had you known what merit you gained for having accepted Heaven's decree, you would have danced at my funeral more than you would have done at my wedding. This is what *Chazal* referred to in expounding the verse:[46] "Be silent before *Hashem*, await Him expectantly": If *Hashem* afflicts you with suffering do not rebel against it; instead accept it joyfully.[47]

Rav Neuwirth shlita adds that he wishes to include the *halachot* that he merited to hear from his teacher, the *Gaon Rav Shlomo Zalman Auerbach zt"l*:

1. It is not permissible to leave a baby in a hospital for the authorities to place him unless one knows that he will be taken into a family that keeps the *mitzvot* and eats kosher food. God forbid abandoning him to non-Jews so that when he dies, he will do so with a cross on his body.

2. The best option of all is that the parents take home this Heaven-sent gift, a gift and not a burden. However this may not necessarily be a permanent arrangement, for the parents, for all sorts of reasons, may be unable to keep him at home. Before such a decision is reached a *posek* who is familiar with these problems must be consulted. In any case, it is not permitted to place him where he might be fed non-kosher food. For although the *Chatam Sofer*[48] attempts to find a reason why such an alternative arrangement might be permissible (until the age of adulthood, but no more), nevertheless he concludes that it would be preferable that he remains a *shoteh* all his life rather than be considered wicked before *Hashem* even for a short while.

And *Rav Neuwirth shlita* concludes: I would suggest that you read the Chapter "Belief and Consolation" in the work *Yalkut Lekach Tov* from page 118 onwards, from which you will realize that what you

---

41. או"ח סי' של סע' ז ושמירת שבת כהלכתה פל"ו הערה כד
42. ראה ביו"ד סי' ב סע' א ושם סי' א סע' ה
43. יו"ד סי' רסג סע' ה
44. קהלת ד:א
45. ילקוט שמעוני קהלת רמז תתקסט
46. תהלים לז:ז
47. ילקוט שמעוני תהלים רמז תשבט
48. שו"ת או"ח סי' פג

are doing brings satisfaction to our Father in Heaven; for it is impossible to measure the greatness of your reward. *Hashem* be with you.

Rav Eliashiv shlita told me that even if there is a chance that the child will only reach a small level of understanding, enough to appreciate what money is and how to look after it,[49] he may not be placed in an environment where he will be fed non-kosher food (as ruled by the *Chatam Sofer*). Even more so, he may not be given up to non-Jews for adoption.

Rav Moshe Feinstein zt"l[50] writes, regarding a complete *shoteh*, that although he had written in a previous *responsum*[51] (quoted above reference 29), that by strict Jewish law (theoretically) one may not forbid his placement in a government institution, nevertheless, in practice one may not do so unless it is impossible to look after such a child at home and there is no Jewish home willing to care for him.

I would like to call the reader's attention to the *Gemara*[52] which explains why Rebbe Yosi the son of Rebbe Elazar (the son of Rebbe Shimon bar Yochai) was not allowed to be buried at his father's side in the cave where Rebbe Shimon was buried. A Heavenly voice was heard saying that not because Rebbe Elazar was greater than Rebbe Yosi, but because Rebbe Elazar hid and suffered together with his father Rebbe Shimon bar Yochai in the cave (for thirteen years to escape the wrath of the Romans[53]), whereas Rebbe Yosi did not. Who therefore can measure the merits and rewards of parents who bring up — with all its accompanying pain and problems — a child, severely disabled in his mind but pure in soul, who has been given into their care by the Compassionate One, our Father in Heaven.

(2) FACILITATED COMMUNICATION. There are claims that computers can be used to communicate with children who are disabled in mind or intelligence (facilitated communication). Many famous scientists have conducted scientific experiments on the subject to decide whether there is objective evidence that this is true. Their verdict is that there is no evidence to verify this claim.[54]

Rav Neuwirth shlita wrote to me regarding *Rav Auerbach zt"l's* view on the matter. He wrote that with regard to the subject of facilitated communication in which claims are made that these children have the power to contact the next world, I was present when my teacher and master *Rav Shlomo Zalman Auerbach zt"l* was asked about this phenomenon. At first he showed great interest in the matter. However, later, when they wished to bring such children before him he said that he did not attach too much truth to the matter and did not want to be spoken to on the matter and also that these children should not be brought to him. The *Rav shlita* concludes that he later spoke to *Rav Auerbach zt"l's* son Reb Baruch *zt"l* who confirmed this.

See also Siman 245A below, p. 175 and *Nishmat Avraham,* vol. 1 *Orach Chaim,* Siman 55A and B and Siman 618B, pp. 26 and 310.

---

49. ראה גיטין סד ע"ב א"ר יהודה א"ר אסי, צרור ווזרקו אגוז ונוטלו
50. עם התורה מהדורא ב חוברת ב עמ' י
51. ר.ראה גם בשו"ת אג"מ יו"ד ח"ב סי' נט ואו"ח ח"ב סי'
52. ב"מ פה ע"א
53. שבת לג ע"ב
54. אסיא חוברת נז, עמ' 9 תשנ"ז

CHAPTER 6
Laws Concerning Worms

SIMAN 84
THE LAWS CONCERNING *SHERATZIM* FOUND IN WATER, FRUIT, FLOUR AND CHEESE

§17 A (A)*sheretz* that has been burnt may be eaten for its medic-

---NISHMAT AVRAHAM---

SIMAN 84

(A) *sheretz* that has been burnt. The *Taz*[1] quotes the *Maharshal* who rules that an epileptic is considered to be in the category of the *seriously ill* since he has an internal disease. It is therefore permissible to give him food containing burnt *sheratzim* if its medical efficacy is proven; otherwise it is forbidden to do so. The *Chatam Sofer*[2] writes that although one may prove from a *responsum* of the *Rosh*[3] that an epileptic is not considered to be one who is *seriously ill*, nevertheless where there is doubt as to whether his status is that of a *seriously ill* patient or not, one rules leniently and considers him to be *seriously ill*. One may therefore depend on this ruling of the *Maharshal* and feed him that which is forbidden if its medical efficacy has been proven. This is also the ruling of the *Issur VeHeter*,[4] the *Aruch HaShulchan*[5] and *Rav Waldenberg shlita*.[6]

The *Pri Megadim*[7] quotes the above *Taz* that Torah law may be set aside to give a treatment whose efficacy has been proven; if its efficacy has not been proven it is forbidden to be used. However if a non-Jew mixed the forbidden food with more than sixty parts of kosher food, thus nullifying it, it may be eaten even though in its unmixed state it was forbidden by Torah law. The law forbidding one to mix a non-kosher substance with sixty parts of kosher food to nullify it and thus permit it to be eaten, also does not apply since it is a non-Jew who does so. The *Knesset HaGedolah*[8] even writes, in the name of the *Mordechai*,[9] that a *sheretz* that has been burnt to dust may be eaten although a healthy person should be careful not to do so, and this is also the ruling of the *Issur VeHeter*[10] and the *Yam Shel Shlomo*.[11] This supports the ruling of the *Mechaber* that eating a burnt *sheretz* is permitted for a medical reason only but a healthy person is not permitted to eat it. However, continues the *Pri Megadim*, the *Minchat Yaakov*[12] expresses suprise at the *Beit Yosef* (the *Mechaber*) since the

---

1. ס״ק כד בשם המהרש״ל שהעתיק בשם תשובת ר״י
2. שו״ת יו״ד סי׳ עו ואעה״ז ח״א סי׳ קטו מובא גם בפ״ת ס״ק יג
3. כלל מב
4. כלל נט סע׳ לה
5. סע׳ צה
6. לב אברהם ח״א עמ׳ כ. שו״ת ציץ אליעזר חי״ג סי׳ לה
7. מ״ז ס״ק כד (ויש שם ט״ס, וצ״ל כד במקום כג)
8. הגהות ב״י אות קיא
9. פסחים פ״ב סי׳ תקמה
10. הארוך כלל לב דין ט
11. חולין פרק אלו טרפות סי׳ קכו
12. כלל מו אות ט

inal value, since it is (B)considered to be merely dust.

---NISHMAT AVRAHAM---

Mordechai, the *Yam shel Shlomo* and the *Issur VeHeter* rule that one may not burn a *sheretz* to give to a healthy person to eat since he would be nullifying that which is forbidden so as to eat it. One may deduce from this that if it is already burnt it would be permissible even to one who is healthy.

See also below Siman 155F(6), p. 68 regarding the permissibility of treatment with that which is normally forbidden.

(B) considered to be merely dust. The *Darchei Teshuvah*[13] quotes the *Ramatz*[14] who was asked: If a *sheretz* that is burnt is considered merely dust why should the *Shulchan Aruch* only permit it to be eaten for medicinal purposes? He replied that the *Shulchan Aruch* is referring to a *sheretz* that was not completely burnt; if it was completely burnt to fine ashes it can certainly be eaten even if not for its medicinal value. The *Zer Zahav*[15] quotes a *responsum* of the *Rashba*[16] who writes that if what is forbidden is so completely destroyed that it would be like mere dust, it would not be forbidden at all. The *Chok Yaakov*[17] also quotes this *responsum*. This would also appear to be the opinion of the *Or Zarua*,[18] quoted by the *Shach*[19] and the *Pri Chadash*.[20] The *Darchei Teshuvah* quoted above also adds that it is permissible to destroy a forbid-

den creature and this would not be included in the prohibition of nullifying that which is forbidden in order to eat it. However the *Yad Avraham*[21] permits eating a *sheretz* that was completely burnt only for its medicinal powers for otherwise it would be considered to have the status of food (*achshevei*).

Rabbeinu Yonah[22] permits musk (a substance found in a pouch of a particular deer) to be eaten, for although it comes from blood which is forbidden, nevertheless it has now been changed into something else.[23]

The *Achiezer*[24] permits a patient to eat that which is forbidden provided it has first undergone a chemical change such that it is no longer edible; even if it is still edible to animals though not fit for human consumption, it is no longer prohibited. This is also the opinion of the *Chavot Da'at*[25] who writes that even if it is reconstructed and sweetened so that it once again becomes edible to humans, it is permitted since the forbidden food no longer exists, having been changed to mere dust. Although it is now edible, its prohibition does not return.[26] However, the *Sha'agat Aryeh*[27] forbids it for a *non-seriously ill* patient.

The *Tzitz Eliezer*[28] permits a *non-seriously ill* patient to take a medicine pre-

---

13. ס״ק קצה
14. יו״ד סי׳ ל אות ו
15. על האו״ה כלל נט ס״ק יד
16. מובא בב״י או״ח סוסי׳ תמו
17. או״ח שם ס״ק מו
18. פרק אלו טרפות סי׳ תלו
19. סי׳ סו ס״ק ד. כל זה מחזור זהב
20. מים חיים סי׳ ו
21. יו״ד סי׳ קנה סע׳ ג
22. מובא ברא״ש, ברכות פ״ו סי׳ לה
23. וראה גם בשו״ת הרדב״ז סי׳ תתקעט (ח״ג סי׳ תקמח)
24. שו״ת ח״ג סי׳ לא ויו״ד סי׳ יא ס״ק ה
25. יו״ד סי׳ קג בביאורים ס״ק א. וראה בשו״ת חלקת יואב סי׳ יא ובשו״ת שבט הלוי ח״ב סי׳ לח
26. וראה בשו״ת האלף לך שלמה יו״ד סי׳ רב שמתיר לחולה שאין בו סכנה לשתות שומן דגים טמאים. וראה גם בש״ך סי׳ רלט ס״ק כ. וראה בשו״ת יביע אומר ח״ב חיו״ד סי׳ יב ובשמירת שבת כהלכתה פ״מ סע׳ פו
27. שו״ת, סי׳ עה
28. שו״ת, ח״ו סי׳ טז וח״י סי׳ לב אות ח

SIMAN 84: SHERATZIM FOUND IN FOOD / §17

― NISHMAT AVRAHAM ―

scribed by a physician even if it originates from that which is forbidden.[29] He also[30] permits capsules made from gelatine to be swallowed by a *non-seriously ill* patient and does not require them to be opened so that only the powder contained in them be swallowed.[31] See also Siman 155F below, p. 65.

---

29. וראה גם בזבחי צדק סי' פד ס"ק קלו וכף החיים כאן

30. ח"י סי' כה פרק כ ס"ק ב וכן הגר"י אברמסקי זצ"ל

מודפס בשו"ת ציץ אליעזר ח"ד בהתחלת הספר

31. וראה גם בשערים מצויינים בהלכה סי' מז ס"ק ה

CHAPTER 7
The Laws Concerning Meat With Milk

SIMAN 87

TO WHICH MEAT DOES THE *HALACHAH* OF MEAT WITH MILK APPLY AND THE DEFINITION OF COOKING

§1 The Torah tells us — three times — not to cook a baby goat in its mother's milk: once to forbid cooking them together, once to forbid eating this mixture, and once to forbid (A)having any benefit from it. The injunction not to eat them (after cooking them together) was couched in terms of cooking to tell us that the Torah only forbids meat with milk to be eaten if the meat and milk were cooked together. However, it is Rabbinically forbidden in any case *(one may benefit from meat with milk which were mixed together without cooking since this is not forbidden by the Torah)*.

──────────── NISHMAT AVRAHAM ────────────

SIMAN 87

(A) having any benefit. The three injunctions mentioned in the *Shulchan Aruch* are separate and independent of each other and each on its own is forbidden by Torah law. See also §3 below. Therefore, a doctor who keeps animals for research must be careful not to give them food containing meat and milk that were cooked together (for example, from cans) even if it was cooked by non-Jews. Although the *Dagul MeRevavah*[1] rules that one may benefit from meat (from a kosher animal) which was not ritually slaughtered that was cooked with milk to avoid monetary loss, the *Pri Megadim*,[2] *Chida*,[3] *Chatam Sofer*,[4] *Gilyon Maharsha*,[5] *Aruch HaShulchan*,[6] *Pitchei Teshuvah*,[7] *Chavot Da'at*,[8] *Zivchei Tzedek*[9] and *Ben Ish Chai*[10] all forbid this.[11] See also §3 below.

---

1. סע׳ ג ולומד זה מדברי הרמב״ם פי׳ המשניות כריתות פ״ג מ״ד
2. פתיחה להלכות בשר וחלב ד״ה עוד אדבר, וכן במ״ז ס״ק ב
3. מחזיק ברכה כאן ס״ק טו
4. שו״ת, יו״ד סי׳ צב
5. סע׳ ג כאן
6. סע׳ יב
7. ס״ק ו
8. סי׳ צד בביאורים ס״ק ד
9. ס״ק יג
10. שנה ב פ׳ בהעלותך סע׳ ה
11. וראה גם בדרכי תשובה ס״ק לא

§3

This *halachah* only applies to meat from a kosher (B)domesticated animal with milk from a kosher animal. Meat from a kosher animal with milk from a non-kosher one or meat from a non-kosher animal and milk from a kosher one may be cooked together and benefit derived from them. Meat from a non-domesticated (kosher) animal or bird may also be cooked with milk even from a kosher animal and one may also benefit from the mixture; eating anything of the mixture, however, is Rabbinically forbidden. (C)Fish and (kosher) locusts cooked with milk are not forbidden under this *halachah*, even Rabbinically.

NISHMAT AVRAHAM

(B) domesticated animal. Such as cattle or sheep as opposed to non-domesticated kosher animals such as deer.

(C) Fish. The *Shach*[12] quotes the *Levush* that one should not eat fish with milk because it is a hazard to one's health and this is the ruling of the *Beit Yosef*.[13] (*Rabbeinu Bachya*[14] also forbids one to eat fish with cheese.) The *Shach*, however, continues that although the *Levush* based his ruling on the *Beit Yosef*, there must be some (printer's[15]) error in the *Beit Yosef* for it is only fish and meat that may not be eaten together because it is a hazard to health.[16] There has never been any problem with eating fish with milk and, on the contrary, it is an everyday occurrence to eat fish cooked with milk. The *Darchei Moshe* also expressed his reservations on this *Beit Yosef* as did the *Be'er Sheva* and other *acharonim*, concludes the *Shach*.

However, the *Pitchei Teshuvah*[17] supports the ruling of the *Levush* that it is forbidden to eat fish and milk and writes that this is accepted medical opinion. This is also the view of the *Pri Megadim*[18] quoting the *Bahag*. Nevertheless, the *Pitchei Teshuvah* concludes that nowadays, since everyone cooks fish with milk, it is permitted for "many have made light of it (that it is a health hazard) and *Hashem* guards simpletons."[19] The *Chatam Sofer*[20] writes that since the *Rambam*, who was a great scholar, both in medicine and in the natural sciences, omitted this from his rulings, we must assume that he researched the subject and found that nature had changed in this context. And the *Shiurei Knesset HaGedolah* explains that although the *Beit Yosef* wrote that fish with milk is dangerous, he based this on medical opinion that since meat and fish together is dangerous, so too must this be true for fish and milk. This however is not so, concludes the *Chatam Sofer*, and we rely on the *Rambam*, the great physician.[21]

---

12. ס"ק ה
13. או"ח סי' קעג
14. פ' משפטים כג:יט
15. ראה טז ס"ק ג
16. וכן ביו"ד סי' קטז סע' ב
17. ס"ק ט
18. מ"ז ס"ק ג
19. יבמות עב ע"א
20. שו"ת, יו"ד סי' קא
21. וראה בתוס' סופ"ק דמו"ק

SIMAN 89
THE PROHIBITION OF EATING CHEESE AFTER MEAT

§1 One must wait ⁽ᴬ⁾six hours after eating meat from any animal or bird before eating cheese. Even if one waits this

--- NISHMAT AVRAHAM ---

The *Kaf HaChaim*[22] writes that although climatic conditions are different in different places, as are the constitutions of people from different parts of the world, nevertheless that which is dangerous is more serious than that which is forbidden, and one must therefore forbid fish with milk. However fish with butter is permitted. On the other hand, the *Aruch HaShulchan*[23] writes that since fish with milk is considered a delicacy throughout the world one may eat it without fear, adding that even the *Beit Yosef* did not bring his ruling in the *Shulchan Aruch*.

Rav Ovadia Yosef shlita wrote to me[24] that *Rav Yitzchak Lampronti*, who was also a famous doctor, wrote in his *Pachad Yitzchak*[25] that there really is a danger of a severe and even fatal illness if one drinks milk and immediately after eats fish, or drinks milk after eating fish. And, writes the *Pachad Yitzchak*, although I know of no danger in eating fish with cheese or butter, since the *Beit Yosef* wrote that fish and milk is dangerous, one should avoid doing so. *Rav Yosef shlita* quotes other *poskim* who feel the same and concludes that this is the custom among Sephardim and Jews of Middle Eastern origin, in accordance with the rulings of the *Zivchei Tzedek*[26] and the *Ben Ish Chai*.[27] However, concludes *Rav Yosef shlita*, one may be lenient with fish and butter as he has written in a *responsum*.[28] See also what I wrote regarding the concept that "nature has changed" in *Nishmat Avraham*, vol. 1 *Orach Chaim*, Siman 4C and Siman 330 reference 73, pp. 5 and 229.

SIMAN 89

(A) six hours. The *Chatam Sofer*[1] writes that even one with a minor illness need not wait more than an hour after eating meat in order to drink whey (the supernatant water of milk) as a medicine. He waits an hour after *birkat hamazon* and then drinks as much as necessary. The *Aruch HaShulchan*[2] writes that if his doctor so prescribes, he may even drink milk after waiting an hour and washing out his mouth. This is also the opinion of the *Chochmat Adam*,[3] the *Zivchei Tzedek*,[4] the *Ben Ish Chai*[5] and the *Kaf HaChaim*.[6] This is also the ruling of *Rav Ovadia Yosef shlita*[7] with regard to

---

22. ס"ק כד
23. סע' טו
24. הערות על נשמת אברהם כרך ב חיו"ד עמ' רצ
25. מערכת ב דף סט ע"א
26. סי' פז ס"ק יח
27. שו"ת רב פעלים ח"ב חיו"ד סי' י
28. שו"ת יחוה דעת ח"ו סי' מח. וראה גם בפרישה ס"ק ט

1. שו"ת, יו"ד סי' עג מובא גם בפ"ת ס"ק ג. אגב, יש דעות ששש שעות לאו דוקא אלא ה"ה חמש שעות ועוד, עיין ברמב"ם הל' מאכ"א פ"ט הכ"ח שכותב "כמו שש שעות" וכ"כ המאירי במגן אבות הענין התשיעי: אנו מחמירים עד

2. סע' ז
3. כלל מ סע' יג
4. סע' יא
5. שנה ב פ' שלח לך סע' יא
6. ס"ק כא
7. שו"ת יחוה דעת ח"ג סי' נח

SIMAN 89: PROHIBITION OF CHEESE AFTER MEAT / §1

NISHMAT AVRAHAM

one who has a minor illness, a woman within thirty days of giving birth who is unwell, or a woman who is breast-feeding and does not have enough milk.

Does such a patient need to annul a vow if until now he had waited six hours between meat and cheese products? If he had done so because he followed the ruling of the *Mechaber* whose opinion is that this is the *halachah*, he does not need to annul a vow. This is because he waited six hours when he was healthy by force of *halachah* and not just as a praiseworthy custom. Had he waited six hours because he considered it a praiseworthy custom, it would have had the force of a vow. Now that he is ill and will have to break his custom, the question arises whether he must have this so-to-speak vow annulled. This question applies to all situations in which a person accepted upon himself a praiseworthy custom which he now needs to break because of the force of circumstances. The *Mechaber*[8] and the *Shach*[9] both rule that, in all such situations, he needs an annulment.[10] However the *Magen Avraham*[11] rules that there is no need to have an annulment. The *Dagul MeRevavah*[12] disagrees with the *Shach* and writes that even the *Mechaber* does not rule strictly in all cases. Only if the patient wishes to permanently break his previous custom and to continue with the new one of waiting only an hour, does he need to have his "vow" annulled. Applying the *Dagul MeRevavah's* ruling to eating a diary meal after a meat meal, if he intends to wait an hour only when ill but to return to his previous custom of waiting six hours when he recovers his health, he does not require to have his "vow" annulled. This, in the opinion of the *Dagul MeRevavah*, is also the ruling of the *Magen Avraham*. Both the *Mishnah Berurah*[13] and the *Yabia Omer*[14] write that all would agree that if he cannot find anyone to annul his vow, he may act leniently under such stressful conditions.

However, *Rav Shlomo Zalman Auerbach zt"l* writes[15] that if one fasts on the eve of *Rosh Hashanah* and the eve of *Yom Kippur* but does not want this custom to take on the force of a vow, his wish is effective. Although he does not intend that such a custom should have the force of a vow, the Torah gives it the force of a vow. However, if he proclaimed specifically beforehand that this custom was not to have the force of a vow, why should his wish not be effective? This also applies to one who, at the beginning of the year, proclaims that he does not wish any praiseworthy custom that he will take upon himself to have the force of a vow. Therefore, in my opinion, writes the *Rav zt"l*, if one takes upon himself a practice in a general fashion without using the phrase-ology of a vow, it is as if he has specifically proclaimed that it is not to be a vow. According to this ruling by *Rav Auerbach zt"l*, I thought that in the case we are discussing, he would also not require the annulment of a vow; the conflicting views of the *poskim* above would only apply to one who had not made such a statement before the New Year. However the *Rav zt"l* told me that this case is different in that we are discussing a praiseworthy custom that many have accepted upon themselves and not just the patient in question. Thus the discussion above between the *poskim* as to whether he does or does not require his vow to be annulled still stands.

---

8. יו״ד סי׳ ריד סע׳ א
9. שם ס״ק ב
10. וראה גם במ״ב סי׳ רלח ס״ק ה
11. סי׳ תקפא ס״ק יב
12. יו״ד שם
13. שעה״צ סי׳ תקפא ס״ק לג
14. שו״ת יביע אומר ח״ב סי׳ ל אות ו
15. ספר זכרון ע״ש הרב עמרם בלוי זצ״ל

time, meat remaining between the teeth must first be removed. **(B)One who chews meat to give to a baby must also wait this time before eating cheese.**

───────── NISHMAT AVRAHAM ─────────

(B) One who chews. There are two different reasons given by the *rishonim* as to why it is Rabbinically forbidden to have dairy products after meat. The *Tur*[16] writes that this is because the meat exudes fat during digestion and, as a result, its taste remains for a long time. The *Rambam*,[17] on the other hand, writes that the prohibition is because of meat that may have remained between the teeth. When one chews meat (for a baby) but does not swallow it, the *Taz*[18] and *Shach*[19] write that according to *Rashi* one would not have to wait to have milk whereas according to the reason given by the *Rambam* one would have to wait. The accepted ruling is to act strictly, taking both reasons into account. However, *Rebbe Akiva Eiger*[20] deduces from the language of the *Rama* that one acts strictly only if he has eaten the meat. Since there are those who permit milk immediately, there is no need to wait six hours after chewing meat for a baby. The *Pri Megadim*[21] writes that it would appear that if one chews a food for a baby, containing meat fat but not meat, he would not have to wait according to both reasons. Since he did not eat the food the reason given by *Rashi* does not apply, and, since he did not chew meat, neither does the reason of the *Rambam*. Nevertheless we do not differentiate between one circumstance and another, and one must act strictly and wait six hours. The Jewish nation is holy and one must not make a breach in "walls" erected to prevent transgressing Torah law.

This is also the ruling of the *Chida*,[22] the *Pitchei Teshuvah*[23] and the *Zivchei Tzedek*.[24] All that has been said applies only to one who chews. However if one only tastes the food, spitting it out immediately, everyone would agree that he does not have to wait. Even if he put a piece of meat into his mouth and spat it out whole immediately, he need not wait; and certainly if he tasted a fatty food and spat it out.[25]

FALSE TEETH. As to the need to *kasher* them between meat and dairy meals, the *Kaf HaChaim*[26] writes that one need not act strictly since they are made of a hard and smooth material, which, like glass, neither absorbs nor emits the taste of anything. Besides, food and drink that one puts into one's mouth are usually from a *keli sheni* and are below the temperaure of *yad soledet* (hot enough to recoil from). Nevertheless, he adds that it is fitting for anyone who is Heaven-fearing to have separate dentures for meat and milk. Certainly it is fitting that one have new dentures made specially for *Pesach*[27] and there are those who are careful to do so. However, see Siman 105 §2

---

16. טור כאן. וראה בט"ז ס"ק א וש"ך ס"ק ב. ודעת הערוה"ש כאן סע' ד והפמ"ג מ"ז ס"ק א שזה גם דעת רש"י, חולין קה ע"א
17. הל' מאכלות אסורות פ"ט הכ"ח
18. ס"ק א
19. ס"ק ב
20. חי' רעק"א על השו"ע
21. מ"ז ס"ק א
22. שיורי ברכה ס"ק יב
23. ס"ק א
24. ס"ק ד
25. כף החיים ס"ק ד. וכ"כ הזבחי צדק ס"ק ה
26. ס"ק כב. וכ"כ הדרכ"ת ס"ק יא
27. See *Nishmat Avraham*, vol. 1 *Orach Chaim*, Siman 451A, p. 254 regarding the *kashering* of dentures for *Pesach*.

SIMAN 89: PROHIBITION OF CHEESE AFTER MEAT / §1

GLOSS: *If he did find meat between his teeth he must wash his mouth after removing the meat and before eating cheese. There is an opinion that one need not wait six hours but it is sufficient that he end his meal and recite birkat hamazon provided he cleans and rinses his mouth. The accepted custom in these countries is to wait one hour after eating meat before eating cheese. However, he must recite birkat hamazon after his meat meal, for in the opinion of those who rule leniently, only then may he eat cheese since it is now a separate meal. If he did not recite birkat hamazon, he may not eat cheese even if he has waited an hour. It does not make a difference if he waits the hour before or after reciting birkat hamazon. If he finds meat between his teeth an hour later, he must remove it. Although there is an opinion that one may not recite birkat hamazon so as to eat cheese, people have not accepted it. There are those who are meticulous about waiting six hours between meat and cheese and this is how one should act.*

NISHMAT AVRAHAM

that heat less than *yad soledet* does not lead to the absorption or emission of the taste of food into anything else. Since one certainly cannot eat food that is *yad soledet*, his dentures will neither absorb nor emit any taste of food. Therefore, concludes the *Kaf HaChaim*, it would be sufficient *halachically* if he washed them between eating meat and dairy products; this would certainly be true if the dentures are made of material that does not absorb or emit. One who cannot afford separate dentures may rely on this.

The *Maharsham*[28] also rules that one may be lenient regarding the use of the same dentures for meat and dairy products. However, regarding *Pesach,* since there are *poskim* who rule strictly with regard to *keli sheni* and even if the *chametz* is cold, one should nevertheless act strictly and pour hot water over the dentures before *Pesach*. Rav Ovadia Yosef[29] also rules leniently regarding the use of the same dentures for meat and milk.

Rav Auerbach *zt"l*, however, wrote to me that people do eat food hot enough to cause a transfer of tastes; that the upper plate of the dentures is often made partly of silver or gold and that many have teeth capped with gold (*these materials are not like glass; they absorb and emit taste — author*). Moreover, we eat solid pieces of food, which, according to many *poskim*, have the *halachah* of a *keli rishon*. All of these points should lead one to think that dentures need *kashering* between meat and milk. Nevertheless the main reason why one may act leniently is because the natural heat within the mouth spoils and impairs the taste of that which is absorbed; and even after a short space of time the absorbed taste is considered as being twenty-four hours old. Besides, *Chazal* only ruled strictly with regard to eating actual meat and milk and did not at all worry about the taste of the food that is absorbed into the dentures.

---

28. שו"ת חו"א סי' קצו   29. שו"ת יביע אומר ח"ג או"ח סי' כד

NISHMAT AVRAHAM

Incidentally, *Rav Auerbach zt"l*[30] deduced that up to 45°C there is no need to fear that food or drink have the *halachic* status of "hot" even in Torah law. The *Gemara*[31] tells us that it is unanimously accepted that an animal's throat is considered "cold" before the end of the slaughtering process. And, nowhere do the *poskim* differentiate between the knife used for slaughtering an animal or a bird; in both cases the knife does not absorb anything of the taste (of the meat or the blood). It is known that the body temperature of healthy pigeons and of turtledoves is 45°C and even then we rule that the throat is considered "cold" and that the knife does not absorb anything. The temperature of a duck is close to 45°C and can rise to at least 47°C when it is ill. From this we can definitely deduce that up to this temperature one need not fear that food or drink is considered to be "hot." The *Rav zt"l* told me that this thought came to him when he was sitting by Dr. Wallach *zt"l* (*the founder and first director of the Shaare Zedek Hospital in Jerusalem*). The latter excused himself to go to tend to a sick cow with a temperature of about 42°C (at the time cows were kept on the ground floor of the hospital so that fresh milk was always available for the patients who were on the first floor).

FEEDING BY NASO-GASTRIC TUBE OR GASTROSTOMY. May a patient who must be fed artificially in this way be given meat and dairy products together or one immediately after the other, if they had not been cooked together? The question only concerns the prohibition of eating. The prohibition of having benefit from such a mixture does not apply since they were not cooked together.[32] The question here is whether the definition of eating applies to one who eats without his throat deriving pleasure from the food. Rebbe Yochanan and Reish Lakish argue about this in the *Gemara*.[33] Rebbe Yochanan felt that the definition of eating depends on the throat deriving pleasure from the food; Reish Lakish felt that it was sufficient if his intestines benefited from it. The *Rambam*[34] rules that one is liable for having eaten that which is forbidden, even if his throat did not derive any pleasure; for example, if he ate meat and milk that was cooked together mixed with something bitter. However the *Achiezer*[35] writes that although those foods which Torah law forbids one to derive any benefit from, such as meat cooked with milk, carry culpability even when they are eaten in an unusual fashion (for example, when mixed with something bitter), this is not because Rebbe Yochanan would agree that benefit to the intestines alone is sufficient. Rather, the reason is because the Torah does not use the word eating when forbidding us to derive benefit from them. Therefore the condition that food be eaten in the normal manner does not apply. However there is still an element of pleasure to the throat sufficient to make him culpable. Rebbe Yochanan's ruling requiring benefit to one's throat before one is culpable of eating the forbidden food applies universally throughout the Torah to include even those foods that carry culpability when taken in an abnormal manner. One may deduce from this *Achiezer* that the *Rambam's* ruling that one is still culpable for eating meat cooked with milk in an unusual manner (such as when mixed with something bitter), would not apply to this

---

30. נועם כרך ו תשכ"ג עמ' שיד. וראה במנחת שלמה ח"א סי' צא אות ח
31. חולין ח ע"ב. וראה גם ביו"ד סי' י סע' ב ובש"ך שם
32. יו"ד סי' פו סע' א וסע' ג, ט"ז ש"ך וראה גם בבאיר היטב שם
33. חולין קג ע"ב
34. הל' יסודי התורה פ"ה ה"ח
35. שו"ת, ח"ג סי' סא

§3

It is permitted to eat (C)a cheese dish after eating a meat dish. One may, if one so wishes, wash his hands between the two (*according to some he must wash his hands*). However, if he wishes to eat cheese after eating a meat dish or to eat

--- NISHMAT AVRAHAM ---

question. For since the meat and milk were not cooked together, the prohibition is Rabbinic only, and since the food does not touch his throat, this is not considered eating at all. Thus, the *Maharsham*[36] writes that even according to the ruling of the *Sha'agat Aryeh*[37] that one is culpable on *Yom Kippur* for eating something in an unusual manner, if the food does not pass his mouth it is not considered eating at all. The *Machazeh Avraham*[38] also ruled regarding one whose esophagus was burnt and the doctors fed him through a tube in his stomach, that there is no prohibition to feed him thus on *Yom Kippur*. This is also the ruling of the *Ketav Sofer*[39] and the *Chelkat Yaakov*.[40] And, although the *Minchat Chinuch*[41] and the *Chatam Sofer*[42] both rule that regarding *Yom Kippur*, the benefit of his intestines is enough to make him culpable, the *Achiezer* (quoted above) explains that this is only if his throat also had pleasure from the food. Without his throat having pleasure he has not eaten *halachically*. This is also the opinion of the *Eglei Tal*.[43]

In conclusion, it would appear therefore that such a patient may be fed with cold meat and dairy products mixed together (provided they have not been cooked together) or one after the other through his *naso-gastric tube* or *gastrostomy*. This is the ruling of *Rav Waldenberg shlita*.[44]

Regarding the blessing before and after eating or drinking in this manner, see *Nishmat Avraham*, vol. 1 *Orach Chaim*, Siman 210 A, p. 91.

(C) a cheese dish after eating a meat dish. "Cheese dish" and "meat dish" refer to foods that contain neither meat nor cheese that were cooked in a clean pot that was also used for cooking milk or for cooking meat, and this "neutral" food therefore absorbed the milk or meat taste from the pot.[45]

The *Taz*[46] quotes the *Beit Yosef*[47] that clear soup made with meat in it has the same *halachah* as meat itself. However, *Rabbeinu Yonah*[48] rules that the clear soup itself is considered only a food made in a meat pot. Thick soup is considered meat. The *Birkei Yosef*[49] and the *Zivchei Tzedek*[50] both rule that even if one drank clear meat soup one may not eat cheese afterwards and it is the custom to act strictly according to both the *Mechaber* and the *Rama*. However taking into account what I wrote in §1 regarding a patient, even one with only a *minor illness*, it should certainly be permitted to act leniently and allow him to drink milk after waiting an hour. *Rav Auerbach zt"l* concurred with this.

---

36. שו"ת, ח"א סי' קכג ו-קכד
37. שו"ת, סי' עה ו-עו
38. שו"ת, או"ח סי' קכט
39. שו"ת, או"ח סי' צו
40. שו"ת, ח"ג סי' סח
41. מצוה שיג ס"ק ב
42. שו"ת, או"ח סי' קכו
43. מלאכת טוחן ס"ק סב(ב). וראה גם בארחות חיים סי' תריב סע' א ואחיעזר ח"ג סי' לא סוס"ק ד
44. שו"ת ציץ אליעזר חי"ד סי' ע
45. חולין קה ע"ב בתוס' בשם ר"ת. ראה באר הגולה
46. ס"ק ה
47. או"ח סי' קעג בשם הגהות מיימוני
48. ברכות מ ע"ב ד"ה לא שנו
49. שיורי ברכה ס"ק ל
50. סע' לב

meat after a cheese dish, he must wash his hands between the two.

GLOSS: *There is no difference halachically between meat and its fat. It is customary now to act strictly and not eat cheese after a dish made from meat just as one does not eat cheese after eating meat. However if there is no meat in the food which was only cooked in a pot generally used for cooking meat, cheese may be eaten afterwards and there is no custom to act strictly in this case. It is also accepted that one may eat meat after eating a dish made from cheese or milk; however one must wash one's hands between the two meals. Even if he does not intend to eat meat itself — only a meat dish after a cheese dish, he must wash his hands if he touched the food with his bare hands. If the waiter touched the food with his bare hands, he does not need to wash his hands since this is only required of those who are eating.*

CHAPTER 8
Food Cooked by Non-Jews

SIMAN 116
THE PROHIBITION AGAINST FOOD OR DRINK THAT WAS LEFT UNCOVERED

§5 GLOSS: *One must be careful to avoid anything that* (A)*may lead to danger, for this is more serious than committing a Torah transgression. One must be even more careful of that which is only probably dangerous than that which is a probable sin by Torah law.*

NISHMAT AVRAHAM

SIMAN 116

(A) may lead to danger. NARCOTIC DRUGS. *Chazal* have already said that one who puts himself into danger saying: "What business is it of others if I endanger myself?" or one who does not take care to avoid danger, commits a serious sin.[1] *Rav Auerbach zt"l* told me that the taking of narcotics in any shape or form is included in this injunction.

Rav Moshe Feinstein zt"l[2] writes concerning taking marijuana (hashish) that this is obviously forbidden by Torah law on several counts. It damages and destroys the body. Even though there may be those who apparently are, to a large extent, unaffected physically by it, nevertheless their intellect is affected so that their ability to function mentally is affected. This is even worse than a damaged body, for not only will it prevent the person from studying Torah as he should, but it will also prevent him from praying and performing *mitzvot*. For if one prays or performs a *mitzvah* without the clear mind and thought required, it is as if he had neither prayed nor performed the *mitzvah*. Besides, it creates a pathological desire for things, far greater than the natural desire for food and the like which are required for one's well-being. There are those who will be unable to contain or fight this desire and this is, in itself, a severe transgression. For the abnormal desire for good food, even though it is kosher, is the sin of the wayward son.[3] How much more serious is it that he brings upon himself this abnormal desire for that which is not a necessity. One may add the fact that, like the wayward son, he will come to steal and murder to satisfy his desires (see *Sanhedrin* 68b). And, his parents will surely grieve, and he will thus transgress the *mitzvah* of honoring one's parents. He will also transgress the positive commandment to be holy[4] as the

---

1. ומכין אותו מכת מרדות - רמב"ם הל' רוצח פי"א ה"ה. וראה בשו"ת נודע ביהודה תניינא יו"ד סי' י הובא בפ"ת יו"ד סי' כה ס"ק י
2. שו"ת אג"מ יו"ד ח"ג סי' לה
3. בן סורר ומורה - דברים כא:יח
4. ויקרא יט:ב

SIMAN 117
ONE MAY NOT BUY AND SELL THAT WHICH IS FORBIDDEN

§1 One may not trade in anything which may not be eaten by Torah Law, even if one is permitted to benefit from it (*nor may one use it as security for a loan or even buy it for his non-Jewish workers to eat*), except for (A)fat which the Torah

---NISHMAT AVRAHAM---

Ramban explains;[5] this, in turn, will lead to many other sins. In short, concludes the *Rav zt"l*, it is clear and obvious that this is one of the more serious sins and every effort must be made to remove this contamination from the children of Israel.

Incidentally, although drug abuse has been known from time immemorial, the internationally accepted definition of addiction was formulated only in 1950 and defines it as a combination of the obligation to use the drug, to obtain it by any means and a dependency on it. It is interesting to note that *Rashi*[6] some 900 years ago wrote that one should not take narcotics since it will become a fixed habit, you will always seek it and you will waste much money.

See *Nishmat Avraham*, vol. 1 *Orach Chaim*, Siman 503A for a discussion on smoking, and Chapter 155B regarding the importance of looking after one's health.

SIMAN 117

(A) **fat.** Animal fat from an animal which has not been ritually slaughtered or from a non-kosher animal may not be eaten by Torah law; some of the fats from a slaughtered animal are also forbidden. Is it permitted to use soap made from animal fat (which is forbidden to be eaten)? For although the soap is not eaten there is a concept in *Halachah* that "anointing is like drinking." This means that if one rubs something into his skin it is as if he has drunk the substance. The *Vilna Gaon*,[1] following the ruling of many of the great *poskim*, rules that soap (made from fat that is forbidden to be eaten) may not be used since it is then considered to have been consumed. In his opinion this is at the very least a Rabbinic prohibition. This is unlike the ruling of *Rabbeinu Tam*[2] and those who rule like him, who permit it completely. The *Mishnah Berurah*[3] points out that the custom all over the world is to use soap made from non-kosher animal fat and only a few who are meticulous in their attention to *mitzvot* take care not to use it. If, however, soap which is not made from fat is available, one must certainly take into account those who rule strictly. See the *Rambam*[4] who rules that in all situations anointing is like drinking.

However, *Rabbeinu Tam*[5] and others rule that the concept of "anointing is like drinking" only applies to *Yom Kippur* and does not apply to fat or grease which is not even Rabbinically forbidden in other cir-

---

ס"ק יז

2. נדה לב ע"א ד"ה וכשמן, יומא עז ע"א ד"ה דתנן
3. ביה"ל סי' שכו סע' י ד"ה בשאר
4. הל' מעשר פי"ג הט"ז
5. תוספות יומא עז ע"א ד"ה דתנן בשם רבינו תם

5. שם
6. פסחים קיג ע"א
I am grateful to my brother-in-law Rav Moshe Turetsky *zt"l* for showing me this reference.
1. ביאור הגר"א על או"ח סי' שכו סע' י ויו"ד סי' קנה

SIMAN 117: NOT TO BUY AND SELL FORBIDDEN ITEMS / §1

(*Leviticus* 7:24) **permits one to use. If a trapper happens to catch a wild animal, or a bird or fish of a sort that is forbidden to eat** (*similarly one who happens to have that which is either treifah or a neveilah in his home*), **he is permitted to sell them, provided he did not plan to catch them.**

GLOSS: *He must sell them immediately and not leave them to fatten before selling them. If a non-Jew owes him money he may take non-kosher food from him in lieu, so as not to forfeit the debt owed to him. It is forbidden to sell to a non-Jew meat from an animal which has not been slaughtered in the guise of slaughtered meat.*

Everything which is only Rabbinically forbidden to be eaten may be bought and sold.

NISHMAT AVRAHAM

cumstances.[6] The *Nekudot HaKesef*[7] quotes the *Rashba*[8] that even a patient who is *not seriously ill* may anoint himself with the fat or grease of pigs. Nevertheless this is forbidden to one who is healthy. This is also the opinion of the *Semag*.[9] The *Darchei Teshuvah*[10] quotes the *Pri Chadash* that everyone permits the use of soap made from fat since the fat is now spoiled and no longer edible. The *Aruch HaShulchan*[11] also writes that since the fat in the soap is no longer edible even to an animal, a healthy person may also use it and this is the custom in all Israel. The *Kaf HaChaim*[12] also permits such soap to be used by the healthy. The *Darchei Teshuvah*, however, concludes that nowadays since soap made from non-fat ingredients is available for the same price, one should certainly use it. This is also the conclusion of *Rav Ovadia Yosef shlita*.[13]

---

6. עיין שבת פ"ט מ"ד
7. יו"ד סוף סי' קיז
8. מובא בב"י ריש סי' קכג
9. הל' שבת דף כא ריש פ"ב
10. כאן ס"ק לג
11. כאן סע' כט
12. או"ח סי' שבו ס"ק מה ויו"ד כאן ס"ק טו ו-יז
13. שו"ת יחוה דעת ח"ד סי' מג

CHAPTER 9
The Kashering of Utensils

SIMAN 120
LAWS CONCERNING THE IMMERSION OF UTENSILS IN A *MIKVEH*

§16 If one forgot to immerse a vessel before *Shabbat* or *Yom Tov*, he should give it to a non-Jew as a present, then borrow it from him. He may then use it.

GLOSS: *This is what he should do even on a weekday if there is no mikveh available. If he transgressed and used the vessel before immersing it, the food that was placed in it* (A)*does not become forbidden. He must still immerse the vessel afterwards.*

NISHMAT AVRAHAM

SIMAN 120

❧ Utensils made by or bought from a non-Jew, even if new, must be immersed in a *mikveh* before they may be used. This includes all utensils that will be used for food or drink, if they are made of metal or glass, or earthenware coated internally with metal or glass.[1] However utensils that are borrowed or rented from a non-Jew may be used without immersion.[2]

(A) does not become forbidden. Although food cooked in a vessel that was not immersed is permitted, the *poskim* discuss whether one may cook in such a vessel.[3] The *Issur VeHeter*,[4] the *Shulchan Aruch*[5] and the *Pri Chadash*[6] forbid it. The *Tevilat Keilim*[7] writes that *Rav Moshe Feinstein zt"l*[8] rules that when a Jew buys a vessel from a non-Jew, either to eat from it or to rent it out for this purpose, he is obligated to immerse it. On the other hand, the *Aruch HaShulchan*[9] and *Darchei Teshuvah*[10] write that it is common practice that such vessels are rented for festive meals and the *Minchat Yitzchak*[11] rules that one may drink at a Jewish kiosk or hotel from such a vessel.[12] *Rav Ovadiah Yosef shlita*[13] also permits one to drink at a Jewish kiosk or restaurant even if he knows for certain that the utensils have not been immersed.[14]

The *Tevilat Keilim*[15] writes that *Rav*

---

1. שו"ע כאן סע' א. וראה בספר טבילת כלים במבוא פ"ב בשם האבני נזר יו"ד סי' קו, וראה שם פ"א פרטי דינים
2. שו"ע כאן סע' ח
3. טבילת כלים פ"ג סע' יד
4. כלל נח דין פט
5. כאן סע' ח
6. ס"ק כב
7. הערה כד
8. הובא במאסף לתורה והוראה חוברת ב עמ' 20
9. סע' מה
10. ס"ק ע
11. שו"ת, ח"א סי' מד
12. וראה בשו"ת טוב טעם ודעת מהדו"ג ח"ב סי' כב
13. שו"ת יחוה דעת ח"ד סי' מד
14. ולא כפי שהובא בשמו בטבילת כלים שם
15. שם

SIMAN 120: IMMERSION OF UTENSILS IN A MIKVEH / §16

—————————————— NISHMAT AVRAHAM ——————————————

Auerbach zt"l ruled that if the vessel was not immersed, one may act leniently since the prohibition against using a vessel that has not been immersed is only a Rabbinic law; therefore if he cannot immerse the vessel, he may use it if he requires it urgently. *Rav Auerbach zt"l* wrote to me adding that *Chazal* forbade one to use such a vessel so as to put pressure upon him to immerse it; thus when such an option is not available at the time, the vessel may be used.

The above discussion concerns one who is healthy. *Rav Auerbach zt"l* told me that a patient in a Jewish hospital is permitted to eat and drink, even if he knows for certain that the utensils have not been immersed.

CHAPTER 10
Wine That Has Been Used for Libation

SIMAN 123
SOME OF THE LAWS CONCERNING SUCH WINE

§2 (A)**A *non-seriously ill* patient** may not (for medicinal purposes) bathe in wine that was made or handled by a non-Jew.

---NISHMAT AVRAHAM---

SIMAN 123

~§ Torah law forbids one to drink or benefit from wine if some of it was poured out in a libation before an idol. The *Mechaber*[1] rules that *Chazal* forbade us to benefit even from *stam yenam* (wine made or touched by a non-Jew); the *Rama* permits this. Both forbid drinking such wine.[2]

(A) A *non-seriously ill* patient. The *Beit Yosef*[3] quotes the *Rashba* who writes that he could not find any grounds for leniency for a *non-seriously ill* patient to eat or drink anything that is forbidden even by Rabbinic law, except for eating kosher food that was cooked by a non-Jew. Since a non-Jew may attend to all the needs of a *non-seriously ill* patient on *Shabbat*, this includes cooking for the patient. Thus, to give him *stam yenam* to drink would be forbidden. This is also the ruling of the *Rama*.[4] However, in a *responsum*,[5] the *Rama* writes that in certain circumstances the *posek* may use his discretion to allow a *non-seriously ill* patient to drink *stam yenam* since this is not more serious nowadays than other decrees of *Chazal*. Nevertheless this is only limited to a patient who takes to bed and who craves for wine that is necessary for his cure; "the heart knows if what one does is for a legitimate purpose or out of perverseness."[6] If he can walk about with a stick but only feels a little out of sorts he is not considered to be ill. But, concludes the *Rama*, he who acts strictly will be blessed. However the *Nishmat Adam*[7] writes that since he has already proven that this *responsum* of the *Rama* is contrary to all the *rishonim* — the *Rashba*, the *Ra'ah* and the *Ran* — who rule that all forbidden food, even food that is *muktzeh* (with the exception of kosher food that was cooked by a non-Jew), is forbidden to a *non-seriously ill* patient, this unsigned *responsum* must be a forgery.[8] The *Rivash*[9] also writes that it is forbidden for a *non-seriously ill* patient to drink *stam yenam*. See also the

---

1. שו"ע כאן סע' א
2. שם
3. כאן ד"ה כתב הרשב"א
4. סי' קנה סע' ג. וראה שם בבאר הגולה
5. שו"ת סי' קכד (בדפוס האמבורג, והושמט בדפוס אמשטרדם), הובא במג"א סי' שכח ס"ק ט. וראה שם בנתיב חיים
6. והלב יודע אם לעקל או לעקלקלות: תוספתא שביעית פ"ג מ"ה. ירושלמי שם פ"ד סוף ה"א. לעקלקלות, לעבור על דת - רש"י סנהדרין כו ע"א
7. הל' שבת כלל סט ס"ק ג
8. וכותב הנשמת אדם שם שהיא תשובה גנובה שנכתבה ע"י איזה תלמיד שהניחה בין כתבי הרמ"א, ע"ש רקע המעשה
9. שו"ת, סי' רנה

SIMAN 123: LAWS CONCERNING SUCH WINE / §2

NISHMAT AVRAHAM

Machatzit HaShekel,[10] *Ikerei HaDat*,[11] *Orchot Chaim*[12] and *Darchei Teshuvah*[13] on this subject. On the other hand, the *Sdei Chemed*[14] quotes two great sages[15] of the era who reject the *Nishmat Adam's* reservations regarding the *Rama's responsum* and rule that the accepted custom is to permit *stam yenam* for a *non-seriously ill* patient if kosher wine is unavailable. The *Sdei Chemed* also reaches the same conclusion. However, since the *rishonim* mentioned above rule strictly and so do the *Mechaber* and the *Rama* himself,[16] one cannot rule leniently.[17]

As for a *non-seriously ill patient* who may become *seriously ill*, the *Nishmat Adam*[18] writes that if kosher wine is unavailable he may drink *stam yenam* if his doctors say that he needs to drink wine for his cure. However if he does so merely to strengthen himself and certainly if only because he enjoys it, all would agree that it is forbidden, and this is also the ruling of the *Shach*.[19] The *Chochmat Adam*[20] wonders whether it would be permissible to have a *seriously ill* patient drink normally forbidden wine by deluding him into thinking it is kosher wine, if he wishes to act strictly in accordance with the ruling of the *Rivash*[21] that even *stam yenam* falls into the category of being an offshoot of idol worship and one must suffer martyrdom rather than drink it. He concludes that the patient should be told that, in his situation, the majority of *poskim* permit *stam yenam* nowadays [see also Siman 155F(5)(i) below p. 68].

THE USE OF *STAM YENAM* FOR *KIDDUSH* AND *HAVDALAH*. *Rav Chaim Palaggi*[22] quotes the *Chesed Le-Avraham*[23] as being unsure whether a *seriously ill patient* who is permitted to drink *stam yenam* may use it for *Kiddush*. The *Tiferet Yisrael*[24] writes that although one may not recite *Kiddush* on *stam yenam*, for this is not a blessing but an insult, nevertheless when a *seriously ill patient* drinks such wine he must say the blessing *borei peri hagafen*. Since the wine nourishes and is palatable to him he must say the blessing in the same way as a *seriously ill patient* who must drink wine on *Yom Kippur* has to say the blessing of *borei peri hagafen*. And, although one could differentiate between the two situations, nevertheless here also the wine is permitted to him and, on the contrary, it is a *mitzvah* for him to drink it. He is no worse than a *seriously ill patient* who must eat on *Yom Kippur* and must recite *birkat hamazon*. Rav Auerbach zt"l wrote to me that it is not clear from the *Tiferet Yisrael* whether he may recite *Kiddush* on *stam yenam* for it is possible that he only needs to say the blessing *borei peri hagafen* (but not the blessing of *Kiddush*) when he drinks it for his cure, like one who eats pork because he is *seriously ill*. See also *Nishmat Avraham*, vol. 1 *Orach Chaim*, Siman 196A, p. 86.

The *Halachot Ketanot*[25] and the *Ba'er Heitev*[26] both write that the *Be'er Esek*

---

10. או"ח סי' שבח ס"ק ט
11. יו"ד סי' טו אות ט
12. סי' שבח ס"ק טו
13. סי' קנה ס"ק כג
14. סוף מערכת יין נסך
15. הגאון הגדול הרב יוסף זכריה שטעהרין והג"ר משה טייטלבוים בשו"ת השיב משה
16. סוסי' קנה
17. וראה גם בשו"ת מהרש"ם ח"ד סי' קלו וכן בדעת תורה או"ח סי' שבח סוסע' יד
18. הל' שבת כלל סט ס"ק ג
19. סי' קנה ס"ק י
20. כלל פח סע' ב
21. שו"ת, סי' רנה ו-רנו
22. ספר רוח חיים חיו"ד סי' קנה סע' ג, מובא בשדי חמד מערכת יין נסך ד"ה וכל זה
23. סי' כד
24. ברכות פ"ו ס"ק ד
25. שו"ת, ח"א סי' י
26. או"ח סי' רעב ס"ק ב

ruled that one who drinks *stam yenam* may say the blessing *borei peri hagafen* and recite *Kiddush* and *Havdalah* over it. It is enough that he is committing a transgression by drinking such wine; surely he should not commit two by drinking it without a blessing. However, the *Halachot Ketanot* comments that in the view of his teachers, predecessors and in his own opinion, this is not a blessing but an insult. The *Yavetz*,[27] *Mahari Assad*[28] and the *Birkei Yosef*[29] all rule like the *Halachot Ketanot*. Rav Auerbach zt"l wrote to me pointing out that the discussion concerned one who is healthy and not a patient.

Although the *Shulchan Aruch*[30] rules that a *seriously ill patient* who eats forbidden food (*even if it is forbidden by Torah law*[31]) must make the appropriate blessings over it, this applies only to *birkat hanehenin* and *berachah acharonah*; it does not apply to *birkat hamitzvot*. Thus rules the *Yeshuot Yaakov*[32] citing the *Yerushalmi* quoted by *Tosafot*.[33] The *Yerushalmi* wonders why the Children of Israel did not eat *matzot* made from *chadash* wheat (*which they found in the granaries*) at the *seder* meal when they entered the Land of Israel. [The *halachah* is that the five species of grain (wheat, spelt, barley, oats and rye) which were planted before *Pesach* may not be eaten until after the *Omer* sacrifice was brought on the second day of *Pesach*.[34]] For there is a general rule that a positive commandment overrides a negative commandment that stands in its way, and here we have a positive Torah commandment to eat *matzot* at the *seder* service and a negative Torah commandment forbidding one to eat *chadash*. Thus the Israelites should have been permitted to eat *matzot* at the *seder* service even though they were made from wheat which was *chadash*. Moreover, the Torah permitted the Israelites to eat non-kosher food taken as spoils of war in the fourteen years during which they were conquering the Land of Israel and dividing it between the Tribes.[35] From this the *Yeshuot Yaakov* argues that although non-kosher food taken as spoils of war was permitted, nevertheless it could not be used to fulfill a *mitzvah*.

The *Gemara*[36] rules that if the skins of five *Paschal* lambs became mixed together and a wart was found on one of them (*disqualifying the lamb from becoming a sacrifice*), the meat of all five lambs may not be eaten (*as a Paschal sacrifice*), since the meat of the disqualified lamb cannot be identified. The *Chavot Da'at*[37] questions why this should be so. Since four of the lambs qualify as kosher sacrifices, one should be permitted to eat the fifth lamb since forbidden food that inadvertently became mixed with a majority of identical looking, kosher food, such that it cannot be identified, is considered null and void and the entire mix may be eaten.[38] To this the *Oneg Yom Tov*[39] answers that although the non-kosher food may be eaten, this is only because the prohibiton against eating it falls away. However it

---

27. שו"ת ח"א סי' מה
28. שו"ת, או"ח סי' קס
29. או"ח סי' קצו ס"ק ג
30. או"ח סי' קצו סע' ב וסי' רד סע' ט
31. מ"ב סי' קצו ס"ק ה
32. סי' רעב ס"ק ב. וראה ברמב"ם, ראב"ד וכ"מ הל' ברכות פ"א הי"ט. או"ח סי' קצו סע' א. כף החיים ס"ק ד ומ"ב ס"ק ד שם. קרבן נתנאל, פסחים פ"ב סי' יח ס"ק ק. שו"ת ציץ אליעזר חי"ד סי' מא

אות ה
33. קדושין לח ע"א ד"ה אקרוב
34. או"ח סי' תפט סע' י ויו"ד סי' רצג סע' א
35. חולין יז ע"א
36. פסחים פח ע"ב
37. שו"ת חות דעת סי' קא
38. יו"ד סי' קט סע' א   See there for details.
39. שו"ת, או"ח סי' ד

SIMAN 123: LAWS CONCERNING SUCH WINE / §2

NISHMAT AVRAHAM

cannot attain any special status that the kosher food has, and thus cannot attain the special status of a kosher sacrifice that the other lambs have. Similarly, although *stam yenam* is permitted to a *seriously ill patient*, it cannot attain a status to allow one to perform a *mitzvah* with it. It would appear from this argument that although a *seriously ill patient* may eat forbidden food for his cure and must say the appropriate *berachah rishonah* and *acharonah*, he would not be permitted to fulfill a *mitzvah* with it. However, Rav Auerbach zt"l wrote to me that this is not so. For the *Oneg Yom Tov's* intention was to point out that when kosher food is in the majority, it only removes the prohibition from the non-kosher food; it cannot however give to the non-kosher food the status that it itself has. However in the situation of a *seriously ill patient* who is permitted to drink the *stam yenam*, he should be permitted to use it for *Kiddush*. However, since the *acharonim* have stated that its use for a *mitzvah* is abhorrent, it cannot be used for *Kiddush*.[40] However, the Rav zt"l concludes that this ruling is not obvious and clear.

See also the *Minchat Elazar*,[41] *Yesodei Yeshurun*[42] and *Yabia Omer*.[43]

Rav Neuwirth shlita wrote to me questioning the need for the above discussion among the *poskim* as to whether one may recite *Kiddush* on such wine. Since the *seriously ill patient* is only permitted to drink *stam yenam* for his health, what does making *Kiddush* have to do with his cure?

I wondered whether the discussion was regarding a patient who needed to drink *stam yenam* for his health at a time when he was also obligated to recite *Kiddush*. One must also add that the discussion only applies when kosher wine is not available and he also does not have bread available (or is unable to eat bread) on which he can recite *Kiddush*. Rav Auerbach zt"l wrote to me that I had already quoted the *Chesed LeAvraham* (ref. 23) who specifically refers to a *seriously ill patient* who needs to drink *stam yenam*. This certainly refers to a situation where the wine is required for a cure and it is in this context that the *Chesed LeAvraham* rules that he may also recite *Kiddush* over it.

A person who willfully and publicly desecrates *Shabbat* is, in certain respects, *halachically* compared to a non-Jew.[44] See also *Nishmat Avraham*, vol. 1 *Orach Chaim*, Siman 328 (2B), p. 185.[45]

May one who is healthy use wine that has been touched by such a Jew for *Kiddush* or *Havdalah*? The *Bahag*,[46] *Rashba*,[47] *Or Zarua*,[48] *HaEshkol*,[49] *Rivash*,[50] *Tashbetz*,[51] *Minchat Yitzchak*[52] and *Igrot*

---

40. Nullifying non-kosher food does not declare that it is now kosher but that it may be eaten because it is nullified. However when a patient is permitted to drink *stam yenam* we are saying that for him it is kosher (it has lost its non-kosher status). Once it is kosher, one would have thought that it should be treated like any kosher wine and may therefore be used for *Kiddush*. However this argument is not true for since its use for a *mitzvah* is abhorrent, it cannot be used for *Kiddush*.

41. שו"ת, ח"ב סי' יח וח"ג סי' כג.
42. ח"ג עמ' רכו.
43. שו"ת, ח"א יו"ד סי' יא אות כג.
44. ראה שו"ת חלקת יעקב ח"א סי' מה. שו"ת יעב"ץ ח"א סי' ל. שו"ת בית יצחק יו"ד קו"א להלכות טרפות סי' כג. חזו"א יו"ד סי' ב ס"ק טז ו-כח ושו"ת ציץ אליעזר ח"ח סי' טו פ"ה ופ"ו וח"ט סי' ח פ"ב אות ח
45. ראה גם בנשמת אברהם כרך א או"ח סי' שכח ס"ק ו
46. בה"ג שחיטת חולין קבו ע"ד
47. מובא בב"י יו"ד סי' קיט ד"ה החשוד
48. ח"א סוסי' שסו
49. ספר האשכול ח"ג עמ' קנא
50. שו"ת, סי' ד מובא גם בב"י שם
51. שו"ת, ח"ג סי' שיב
52. שו"ת, ח"ג סי' כו אות ד

§3 (B)Boiled wine that has been touched by a non-Jew is permitted. It is considered boiled for this purpose when it has started to simmer.

NISHMAT AVRAHAM

Moshe[53] all rule that the wine has a status of *stam yenam* and cannot be drunk.[54] However, the *Binyan Tzion*[55] writes that in our day most such Jews either think that there is nothing wrong in desecrating the Sabbath or do not appreciate that there is such a concept as the Sabbath. They may be compared to a Jew who has been brought up among non-Jews to believe he is a non-Jew and are therefore not to be considered as apostates. Therefore, although there as those who act strictly, and treat wine touched by these sinners like *stam yenam*, nevertheless those who act leniently have a basis upon which to rest their decision. However, if it is known that the person is aware of the laws of *Shabbat* but still dares to desecrate it publicly, he is certainly to be considered an apostate and his touch makes wine forbidden. This is also the view taken by the *Mahari Assad*, [56] the *She'elat Yavetz*,[57] the *Beit Yitzchak*,[58] the *Sdei Chemed*,[59] the *Maharsham*,[60] the *Melamed Le-Ho'il*,[61] the *Chelkat Yaakov*[62] and the *Yabia Omer*.[63]

The prohibition of using *stam yenam* does not apply to wine that has been boiled (see below §3).[64] Therefore, a hospitalized patient, duty physician, nurse or health worker who will be making *Kiddush* or *Havdalah*, must put the wine in a safe place until needed, or use previously boiled wine.[65]

(B) Boiled wine. What is the *halachah* regarding pasteurized wine? *Rav Shlomo Zalman Auerbach zt"l*[66] writes that the *Shulchan Aruch* rules that wine is considered boiled to meet the requirements of this *halachah* once it has started to simmer and, from the *Gra's* comment, it would appear that it does not need to boil until it bubbles. Therefore many are accustomed not to worry about a non-Jew touching pasteurized grape juice. Nevertheless there are strong doubts regarding this lenient view comparing pasteurization to the definition of boiling by the *Talmud* and the *poskim*. For the *Rashba*, *Meiri* and others interpret this *halachah* to apply to boiling proper, strong enough to cause immediate evaporation and loss of the alcohol, and to change the taste and appearance of the wine.[67] Pasteurization, on the other hand, is done in closed pipes and neither the appearance nor the

---

53. שו"ת, יו"ד ח"א סי' מו
54. וראה בלבושי מרדכי ח"א או"ח סי' קיא ומהד"ת או"ח סי' ט. ועל אף שפשטות השו"ע או"ח סי' שפה סע' ג משמע שאפילו אינו מחלל שבת אלא באיסור דרבנן, הרי הוא כעכו"ם, מ"מ כותב הפ"ת יו"ד סי' ב ס"ק ח וכן המ"ב שם ס"ק ה, שזה רק לענין ביטול רשות
55. שו"ת החדשות סי' כג
56. שו"ת, יו"ד סי' נ
57. ח"א סי' ל
58. שו"ת, יו"ד קו"א להלכות טרפות סי' כט ובאהע"ז ח"ב סי' סב
59. מערכת מ כלל פו
60. שו"ת, ח"א סי' קכא. וראה גם בח"ב סי' קנו ובדעת תורה יו"ד סי' ב ס"ק ל
61. שו"ת, ח"א סי' כט
62. שו"ת, ח"א סי' עו
63. שו"ת, ח"א יו"ד סי' יא ועיין שם בס"ק כא
64. ועיין בש"ך ס"ק ז שהמבושל אינו מצוי כל כך ובמילתא דלא שכיחא לא גזרו
65. שמירת שבת כהלכתה פמ"ז סע' יט
66. הנאמן, גליון נה תשרי תשמ"ב. מנחת שלמה ח"א סי' ד
67. כתב לי הגאון זצ"ל להוסיף

SIMAN 123: LAWS CONCERNING SUCH WINE / §3

---NISHMAT AVRAHAM---

taste of the wine changes. What then is the basis for this leniency? The *Rav zt"l* concludes that he does not know on what basis one can be lenient and depend on pasteurization — which is only meant to sterilize the wine — and consider it as being equivalent to boiling. There is no change in the appearance, smell or taste, the total volume of wine remains the same and it is generally known as wine and not as boiled wine. Besides, such wine is commonplace and easily obtainable (and the edict of *Chazal* regarding *stam yenam* applies to all easily available wine). Therefore, continues *Rav Auerbach zt"l*, one must be careful and strict to make sure that such wine or grape juice is not handled by non-Jews or by those who are *halachically* compared to them. *Rav Ovadia Yosef shlita* wrote to me[68] that he certainly agreed with this ruling of *Rav Auerbach zt"l*. However, if one has no choice, since pasteurized wine has certainly reached the boiling point, it may be permitted since this is the opinion of the *Geonim*.

---

68. הערה על נשמת אברהם כרך ב יו"ד עמ' רצ. וכן העלה בהערתו על הכף החיים יו"ד סי' קיח ס"ק ז

CHAPTER 11
The Laws Concerning Idolatry

SIMAN 150
ONE MUST DISTANCE ONESELF FROM THEIR WAYS AND NOT BOW BEFORE THEM

§3 One may not drink from water fountains fashioned in the shape of faces which stand before idols, since when he puts his mouth to theirs to drink, it appears as if he is kissing idols.

GLOSS: *There are those who say that what is forbidden only because of* (A)*marit ha'ayin, such as in this halachah, is permitted should he be in danger of dying of thirst. Martyrdom is not required in such a case.*

---NISHMAT AVRAHAM---

SIMAN 150

(A) ***marit ha'ayin***. The *Ran*[1] discusses whether he is forbidden to drink from such a fountain if he is in danger of his life and if no one saw him doing so. He concludes that he would be forbidden to drink from such a fountain unless it is certain that he would otherwise die, because he would not find water elsewhere to drink in time. The *Gra*,[2] however, disagrees and writes that the *Rashba* and *Tur* also do not accept this interpretation of the *Ran*, but rule that he is forbidden to drink even if he were to otherwise die of thirst. In addition, the *Gra* aduces from a *Gemara* that the more stringent position is the correct one. The *Gemara*[3] tells us of a person who became infatuated with a woman to the point of becoming dangerously ill. However the Sages would not permit him to even speak to her across a curtain to save his life, although this only involves a Rabbinic prohibition. Idol worship and illicit relationships both require martyrdom if that is the only way to avoid them. Both cases discussed here involve Rabbinic prohibitions only — in the instance of idol worship there is no actual idol worship, only *marit ha'ayin;* and in the one involving an illicit relationship there is no act prohibited by the Torah, he would only speak across a separating curtain. The *Gra* deduces that just as the latter was forbidden so is the former.

The *Mekor Mayim Chaim*,[4] on the other hand, writes that since drinking from the fountain does not involve actual idol worship, but only gives the appearance of being so, it would possibly not be included in the *mitzvah* of martyrdom. He dis-

---

1. על ע"ז יב ע"א (דף ג ע"ב בדפי הרי"ף). יומא פב ע"א (דף ג ע"ב בדפי הרי"ף)
2. על היו"ד כאן ס"ק ד
3. סנהדרין עה ע"א
4. בהגהות כאן

SIMAN 151
IT IS FORBIDDEN FOR A JEW TO SELL THAT WHICH IS NECESSARY FOR IDOL WORSHIP

§14 It is forbidden to praise an idolater. Even to say how handsome he looks is forbidden, and more so (A)to praise his deeds or sayings. However, if the intention when praising him is to thank *Hashem* for having created a handsome being, it is permitted.

─── NISHMAT AVRAHAM ───

agrees with the proof of the *Gra*. For the *Gemara* describes a situation where he became ill because of his own wrongful desires for an illicit relationship and *Chazal* therefore decreed that he should die rather than commit even the smallest measure of sin (see the *Gemara* for details). In the case discussed here, however, the person is about to die of thirst and wishes to drink to save himself, albeit in a way that would cause unfounded suspicion of idolatry in the eyes of others.

The *Ran*[5] writes that with the three cardinal sins (idolatry, murder and illicit relationships) even when there is no death penalty involved but only a negative commandment (which is only an offshoot of one of them[6]) there is a *mitzvah* of martyrdom. As proof, the *Ran* cites the above *Gemara*. The *Tosefet Yom HaKippurim*[7] questions the proof. The case discussed in the *Gemara* refers to one whose illness was brought on by sin and therefore he should die rather than be permitted to do anything that is an offshoot of the sin of illicit relationships. On the other hand, if he were forced to commit a sin which is only an offshoot of one of the three cardinal sins, why should he be obligated to submit to martyrdom? The *Radbaz*[8] also rules that in such a case he would not be obligated to submit to martyrdom. However, the *Mishneh LaMelech*[9] replies quoting a *Yerushalmi* (quoted by the *Ran*[10]) that even where the sin does not involve the death penalty and is not the cause of his illness (as in the situation discussed here), he is obligated to submit to martyrdom.

A bedridden patient in a room with crucifixes or statues must not therefore bow during the *Shemoneh Esrei* prayer if he faces them — see *Nishmat Avraham*, vol. 1 *Orach Chaim*, Siman 94G, p. 60.

SIMAN 151

(A) to praise his deeds. The *Rambam*[1] writes that the source of this is the Torah's[2] injunction regarding the seven Canaanite nations: "You shall not show them favor." And although the *Torah Temimah*[3] writes that this injunction applies to idolaters only, the plain meaning in the *Talmud* and *poskim* does not ap-

---

5. יומא פב ע״א (דף ג ע״ב בדפי הרי״ף).
6. רמ״א יו״ד סי׳ קנז סע׳ א. וראה בקובץ שיעורים קונטרס דברי סופרים סי׳ א ס״ק כח בשם שו״ת הריב״ש סי׳ רנה דאפשר שגם האיסור דרבנן שבהן הוא מכלל אביזרייהו
7. על יומא פב ע״א ד״ה כתב הר״ן
8. שו״ת, סי׳ אלף עו (ח״ד סי׳ ב)
9. הל׳ איס״ב פי״ז ה״ז
10. על פסחים כה ע״א (דף ה בדפי הרי״ף ד״ה בכל)
1. הל׳ עכו״ם פ״י ה״ד וספר המצוות לא תעשה מצוה נ
2. דברים ז:ב
3. דברים שם

CHAPTER 11: LAWS CONCERNING IDOLATRY

SIMAN 155
MAY ONE BE TREATED BY AN IDOLATER

§1 One may not receive treatment from an idolater for any injury or disease **(A)**which is so dangerous that Sabbath laws could be set aside for the purpose. However, if he is a recognized specialist, it is permitted. If he is not, one may not receive treatment from him even if

--- NISHMAT AVRAHAM ---

pear to be so.[4] I wondered, therefore, why it is common practice to praise their deeds and inventions in the fields of medicine, science, etc. Would it be forbidden for a patient to praise the good treatment that he received from a doctor, nurse or hospital? On the contrary, we find that Rebbe Yehudah praised the deeds of the Romans for having built marketplaces, bridges and baths.[5] However the *Gra*[6] writes that Rebbe Yehudah only meant to say that it is better to be under their rule than that of another nation, whereas Rebbe Shimon bar Yochai believed that even this was forbidden. Nevertheless the *Rambam*[7] praises Aristotle saying that his knowledge is just short of those who eventually reach the heights of prophecy. Similarly, the *Tiferet Yisrael*[8] praises the efforts of non-Jewish researchers at length. On the other hand, the *Igrot Moshe*[9] rules that an idolater may not be praised even if he deserves it.

Rav Auerbach zt"l told me (basing his opinion on the *Shach*[10]) that if a Jew is to benefit from this, it is permitted, but each situation must be judged on its own. The *Chida*,[11] quoting the *Rashba*, the *Ramban* and the *Ran*,[12] and the *Shoel U'Meshiv*[13] also rule that where one derives benefit, the injunction: "You shall not show them favor," does not apply. Rav Waldenberg shlita[14] wrote to me that the injunction only applies to idolaters and that this is the ruling of the *Rambam*,[15] the *Chinuch*,[16] the *Meiri*[17] and the *Rashba*.[18] Certainly in a case where their deeds are beneficial medically or in other fields it is good to praise them. However, Rav Auerbach zt"l wrote to me asking why this is different from allowing even a non-idolater to live in Israel, since both are derived from the same Torah verse.[19]

SIMAN 155

(A) which is so dangerous. In our days every qualified doctor is considered a specialist in this context and one may go to a non-Jewish doctor who is more

---

4. ועיין בב"י חו"מ סי' רמט שאפילו ישמעאלים במשמע, ורק לאפוקי גר תושב, ומובא כאן בבאר היטב ס"ק יד. וכן נפסק להלכה בשו"ע שם סע' ב. ובשו"ע של הדרכי תשובה הגירסא היא אסור לספר בשבחן של נכרים. ועיין בנשמת אברהם כרך ב יו"ד סי' קנד ס"ק ב
5. שבת לג ע"ב
6. חידושי הגר"א שם
7. שו"ת פאר הדור סי' קמג
8. אבות סופ"ג בבועז
9. שו"ת, או"ח ח"ב סוסי' נא
10. כאן ס"ק יג
11. מחזיק ברכה, או"ח סי' רנד ס"ק ג
12. גיטין לח ע"ב
13. שו"ת, תניינא ח"ב סוסי' עז
14. שו"ת ציץ אליעזר חט"ו סי' מז
15. ספר המצות, לא תעשה נ
16. מצוה תכו
17. ע"ז כ ע"א
18. שו"ת, ח"א סי' ח
19. שו"ע כאן סע' ז ו-ח

SIMAN 155: MAY ONE BE TREATED BY AN IDOLATER / §1

there is a possibility that the disease may be fatal. However, if he would (B)certainly die, he may go to him for treatment for, in such a case, there is no fear that one's life may be shortened by the treatment. If, however,

---
NISHMAT AVRAHAM

specialized and knowledgeable in the field than a Jewish one.[1] The *Chida*[2] and other *acharonim*[3] write that since no one can practice medicine without having received a license from the authorities, every doctor is considered a specialist in the context of this *halachah*.

(B) certainly die. The *Gilyon Maharsha*[4] was asked regarding a patient who was told that if treated with certain drugs he would be cured but there was also the possibility that he would die immediately. On the other hand, if left untreated he would certainly die later. He wrote that the patient may take the treatment, basing his ruling on the above *Shulchan Aruch*.

What is the source for this *halachah* that in a situation where a patient will certainly die of his untreated disease within a short time, one may treat him so long as there is a possibility of cure even if, on the other hand, the treatment could shorten his life? We are told[5] that the capital city of Shomron in Israel was besieged in the time of King Yehoram and the prophet Elisha, resulting in a terrible famine. Four lepers who sat at the city gate discussed their serious situation: Why should we sit here until we die? If we enter the city we will die of starvation and if we remain here we will also die. Let us go and surrender to the enemy; if they let us live we will live, and if they put us to death we will die. They took this chance and came to the enemy camp only to find that *Hashem* had caused the enemy to flee for their lives, leaving everything behind. Rebbe Yochanan[6] learns from this episode that one who is in a critical situation which if untreated could cause his death, is permitted to undergo treatment which may cure him but may also kill him immediately. The *Gemara* asks whether he is permitted to sacrifice his *chayei sha'ah* (the short time he has to live if untreated) and take the risk of dying much sooner as the result of the treatment. The *Gemara* answers that from the above episode we learn that one may indeed risk losing his *chayei sha'ah* in order to gain *chayei olam* (*in this context — his full life span — author*).

Rav Moshe Feinstein zt"l[7] asks an interesting question. How is it possible, he asks, that we should learn a Torah *halachah* from these four unlearned lepers whom Rebbe Yochanan elsewhere[8] tells us were Gehazi and his sons, and Gehazi has no share in the World to Come?[9] *Rav Shlomo Zalman Auerbach zt"l* wrote to me that it would seem that there is no hint that they did anything that they should not have done by going to the enemy

---

1. שו"ע כאן ואו"ח סי' תריח סע' א. ש"ך ס"ק ב. או"ה כלל נט סע' ז. תוספת שבת או"ח סי' שכח ס"ק יג
2. שיורי ברכה או"ח סי' שכח ס"ק א
3. שו"ת פנים מאירות ח"א סי' יב. שו"ת שבות יעקב ח"ב סי' עו. וראה גם בתפארת ישראל ע"ז פ"ב ס"ק ו וכף החיים או"ח סי' שכח ס"ק מח ו-נו. וראה בשו"ת חת"ס או"ח סי' עו מובא גם בפ"ת כאן
4. הגה על השו"ע כאן
5. מלכים ב:ז-ז
6. See *Rashi's* explanation. ע"ז כז ע"ב
7. שו"ת אג"מ יו"ד ח"ג סי' לו
8. סנהדרין צ ע"א
9. סוטה מז ע"א

─── NISHMAT AVRAHAM ───

camp. Besides, Gehazi's name is not mentioned in the entire episode; it only says that the salvation came through the lepers. Therefore, we may learn from them. Incidentally the *Yerushalmi*[10] describes Gehazi as a stalwart in Torah.

A specialist physician asked the *Shevut Yaakov*[11] regarding a patient who would, according to all his doctors, die within a day or two. However there was one more treatment available which might cure him of his illness. But, it was also possible that if the treatment failed he would die immediately or within an hour or two. May one give him this treatment or do we fear for his *chayei sha'ah* and therefore should desist from doing anything? The *Shevut Yaakov* answered that if there was a possibility that he would be completely cured by this treatment, one certainly must not consider his *chayei sha'ah*. However, before taking this decision the doctor should consider the situation carefully and consult with other doctors in the city; the decision must then be taken according to a two-thirds majority. The Rav of the city must also approve the final decision.

The *Achiezer*[12] was asked about a patient who, specialists had said, had only six months to live. If he would be operated on, it was possible he would live a normal life span. However the operation was very risky and there was a greater chance of him dying earlier. He replied that from the above *Gemara* one could deduce that where he would otherwise certainly die, we do not fear for his *chaye sha'ah*, if there is a remote possibility that he can be cured and his doctors had despaired of any other possibility. One, must however, receive permission from the *Beit Din* and operate only after much thought and consultation with the best specialists.

The *Darchei Teshuvah*[13] quotes a *Tashbetz* who was asked about a year old baby with a hernia. Occasionally when the baby cried, part of his intestines would descend into the hernia and endanger his life. The doctors were unanimous that there was no other treatment except surgery which, however, was risky and could lead to his death. However, each day the baby was in danger of dying should part of his intestines descend into the hernial sac and could not be put back into the abdomen. He replied that it was already an established *halachah* to permit this. This is also the opinion of the *Binyan Tzion*,[14] *Beit Meir*,[15] *Da'at Torah*,[16] *Yad HaLevi*,[17] *Rav Unterman zt"l*[18] and the *Tzitz Eliezer*.[19]

What is the definition of *chayei sha'ah* (a short life expectancy), and when does it become *chayei olam* (a normal life expectancy)? The *Darchei Teshuvah*[20] quotes the *Chochmat Shlomo* who asked the question, arguing that if one would define *chaye sha'ah* as someone who would die within the next year or two, what would be the definiton of *chayei olam*? Everyone must die sometime, so what is the difference between one year, two or a hundred? It is also difficult to say that only if he dies from the present illness is it considered *chayei sha'ah* but if he were to die from another illness it would not be; what does it matter which illness it is? He concludes that since a *treifah* animal will die from

---

10. סנהדרין פ"י ה"ב
11. שו"ת, ח"ג סי' עה, מובא גם בפ"ת יו"ד סי' שלט ס"ק א
12. שו"ת, ח"ב סי' טז אות ו
13. כאן ס"ק ב
14. שו"ת, ח"א סי' קיא
15. יו"ד סי' שלט סע' א
16. או"ח סי' שכח סע' י
17. שו"ת, ח"א יו"ד סי' רז
18. נועם כרך יג עמ' ה
19. שו"ת, ח"ד סי' יג וח"י סי' כה פי"ז
20. כאן ס"ק ו

SIMAN 155: MAY ONE BE TREATED BY AN IDOLATER / §1

NISHMAT AVRAHAM

its fault within twelve months, this proves that if the patient would die within twelve months of his illness, this would be considered *chayei sha'ah*. If, however, he would die only after twelve months this would be considered *chayei olam*.

What if the patient refuses the treatment offered because he fears for his *chayei sha'ah*? It would appear that the *Sefer HaChaim*[21] rules that he is not obligated to agree to risk his *chayei sha'ah* (i.e. risk his short life expectancy for the possibility of a normal one). However, the *Lev Aryeh*[22] writes that it is debatable whether the *Gemara's* ruling that one need not consider one's *chayei sha'ah* means that the patient is permitted to risk it for a cure. It may only mean that if he dies he is not considered as if he has committed suicide and the doctor is not considered a murderer. However if he fears for his *chayei sha'ah* and does not wish to take the risk, this is also permitted. Or, do we say that he must take the risk and save himself since the Torah commands: "And you shall live by them"? On the contrary, if he does not consent to having the treatment, is it considered as if he has committed suicide? The *Lev Aryeh* thinks that it would appear from the wording of the *Gemara* that "one may take the treatment" and not that "one is obligated to take the treatment," that the choice is left to him and he is not obligated to risk his *chayei sha'ah*. However one could argue that where the offer of treatment is based on a balanced opinion and even more so on a majority view, he is obligated to accept the treatment and the doctor must treat him. *Rav Auerbach zt"l* wrote to me commenting that if the treatment is *halachically* permitted, the patient would be obligated to have it.

A fifty-year-old diabetic with major complications of his disease was admitted with infected gangrene of his remaining leg. He had severe atherosclerotic disease of his extremities with a history of repeated infections and the other leg had already been amputated for a similar reason. He was blind in both eyes. On admission he had a high fever and severe pain in his leg. Treatment with antibiotics was started but consultation between the medical and surgical teams led to the decision that only amputation of his remaining leg could possibly save his life. He would surely die within a few days from his infection; surgery could save his life, but, in his poor medical state, could also result in his death on the operating table. We were not offering him a cure of his underlying disease but were merely treating one complication. The patient refused surgery; he was frightened of undergoing surgery with the accompanying pain and suffering. Above all, he did not wish to live, alone, blind in both eyes and with no legs. I asked *Rav Auerbach zt"l* what the *halachah* would be? He ruled that, in this case, one should not operate against the patient's will or even attempt to persuade the patient to have surgery. The surgery was major and risky, and would only add to the patient's suffering without any hope of a normal life expectancy.

And thus *Rav Auerbach zt"l*[23] writes: There are many who struggle with this problem; those who believe that just as it is obligatory to set aside Sabbath laws to prolong a patient's *chayei sha'ah* so it is obligatory to force a patient to accept such treatment since he has no rights over his body to concede even a minute of his life. It would appear that if the patient has much pain and suffering, even only severe mental anguish, food and oxygen must be given to him even against his will. On the

---

21. או"ח סי' שכח
22. שו"ת ח"ב סי' לה
23. ספר הלכה ורפואה ח"ב עמ' קלא. שו"ת מנחת שלמה ח"א סי' צא אות כד

other hand, one may desist from giving him treatment that will cause him additional suffering if that is the patient's wish. However, if the patient is Heaven fearing and is not confused, it would be very desirable to explain to him that one more hour of repentance in this world is better than all of the World to Come. The *Gemara*[24] tells us that it is a "privilege" to suffer for seven years rather than to die quickly.

See also Siman 28B (5), p. 12 above.

(1) **TRANSPLANTATION OF A MECHANICAL HEART.** So long as such a procedure is still experimental, it would be forbidden for a patient to undergo such a procedure or for a surgeon to perform it. In the near future when, with *Hashem's* help, such a procedure having proven to be successful, will lengthen the life of a patient without question, it would be permitted for a patient who otherwise has a short life expectancy to undergo such an operation just as he might undergo any other common open heart surgery. *Rav Auerbach zt"l* agreed with this. I write this because of a *responsum*[25] I saw that forbids such a procedure since the patient is "killed" when his heart is removed preparatory to transplanting a mechanical one. This opinion is difficult to understand, for in every open heart procedure, although the heart is not removed from the patient's body, it is nevertheless stopped completely, the circulation to the rest of the body being maintained by a mechanical "heart" to which the patient is attached. I do not know of any *posek* who objects to this type of surgery,[26] nor do I see any difference between stopping the heart during open-heart surgery and removing it prior to its replacement with a mechanical heart.[27] This is the ruling of the *Lev Aryeh*,[28] and *Rav Auerbach zt"l* concurred.[29]

(2) **BYPASS SURGERY.** At the close of bypass surgery on the heart, the patient's heart is warmed and blood is allowed once again to flow through it. The circulation of blood to the body is, however, still maintained through the bypass machine (effectively an external, artificial heart through which the patient's blood circulates, bypassing his heart) which is only disconnected when the heart has again started beating regularly and is efficiently pumping blood throughout the body. Occasionally, the heart fibrillates and has to be electrically shocked before it will resume its normal rhythm and pumping action. What would happen if the heart does not return to its normal state and remains incapable of pumping blood despite all efforts to get it started? In this rare circumstance, after all efforts to resuscitate the heart have failed, the bypass machine is disconnected from the patient and he is pronounced dead. Is the act of disconnecting the artificial pump from the patient an act of taking a life, for until now he had been considered alive? Or, is he *halachically* considered to have died retroactively at the beginning of the operation when he was connected to the bypass machine and his heart was stopped by the surgeon so that he could work on it? *The Tzitz*

---

24. סוטה כ ע"א

25. שו"ת דברי מנחם סי' כז. וראה בספר רפואה לאור ההלכה ח"ב עמ' קכב

26. ועיין במאמרו של הגר"מ הרשלר זצ"ל תורה שבעל פה תשמ"ג עמ' צט

27. ראה בשו"ע סי' מ סע' ה שכותב: ניטל הלב בין ביד בין מחמת חולי טריפה. ולפי הרמב"ם הל' רוצח פ"ב ה"ח שכותב לגבי טריפה: ויאמרו הרופאים שמכה זו אין

לה תעלה באדם ובה ימות וכן', עכ"ל, וכן לפי החזו"א, יו"ד סי' ה ס"ק ג, שכותב דבזמן הזה הרבה טריפות אפשר לרפאותם וכן החוש מעיד עכ"ל, רואים אנו שאם הוא חי אח"כ ע"י טיפול, הוברר הדבר שחי היה כל הזמן ולא היה לא דין מת לעולם, והסכים אתי הגרש"ז אויערבאך זצ"ל

28. שו"ת, ח"ב סי' לו

29. שו"ת ציץ אליעזר חט"ז. וראה מה שכתב הגרא"י ולדינברג שליט"א באסיא אלול תשד"ם עמ' 10 סי' כד

SIMAN 155: MAY ONE BE TREATED BY AN IDOLATER / §1

NISHMAT AVRAHAM

Eliezer[30] writes that it would seem to him that *halachically* the patient dies when efforts at resuscitation fail. Otherwise it would appear as if the surgeon who stopped the patient's heart at the beginning of the operation has taken a life. *Rav Auerbach zt"l* wrote to me that the patient is considered alive throughout the operation and Sabbath laws are set aside for him when necessary. However, when it finally becomes evident that after the operation it would be impossible to disconnect him from the bypass machine — since the heart could not be restarted — it seems reasonable to assume that the patient died when the heart was stopped at the beginning of the operation. But it is also possible that he died during the operation. In any case, at the stage when all attempts at resuscitation fail, he is considered as certainly dead and may be disconnected from the bypass machine.

(3) A *NON-SERIOUSLY ILL* PATIENT. Is a patient, who is suffering from his illness, permitted to undergo surgery that inevitably puts his life at risk? The *She'arim Metzuyanim BaHalachah*[31] writes that it is commonplace for patients to undergo surgery even in a situation which is not life threatening. One must say that since he is suffering he is permitted to undergo treatment that will stop it.[32] Moreover, even if there is no suffering he is permitted to undergo surgery to be cured just as bloodletting was carried out in the times of the Talmud.[33] See also *Tosafot*[34] and *Ramban*.[35] *Rav Auerbach zt"l* wrote to me commenting that it is possible that any procedure that has become acceptable to people comes under the saying of our Sages:[36] Nowadays *Hashem* watches over the simple.[37]

However, the *Yavetz*[38] writes complaining that there are those who choose to put themselves into possible danger of their lives in order to cure themselves of severe suffering. They permit a stone to be removed from their bladder or *ever* and gravel from their kidney which cause great pain and suffering. They permit themselves to undergo these procedures since many times they are indeed saved; however they should fear for themselves, for so long as there is no danger with the pain, they are wrong to do so. Even on a weekday one may not put himself into possible danger of life. Although many have done so and been saved, many others have died because of the operation. Thus, concludes the *Yavetz*, it is not at all permitted to have such surgery, even on a weekday. *Rav Auerbach zt"l* wrote to me that it would appear, on the face of it, that the *Tosafot*[39] also rule like this since they did not answer their question by saying that the verse was intended to permit such a case. [*Tosafot* ask: Why does the *Torah*[40] *use a double phrase "verapo yerapei" for "And he shall surely heal"? They answer that the Torah tells us by this phraseology that not only do we have its permission to treat injuries caused by man, but we may also treat Heaven-sent diseases, and that this does not mean that we are nullifying a Heavenly decree. Rav Auerbach zt"l comments that the Tosafot could have answered that it is to tell us that one may put oneself into possible danger even to cure a*

---

30. שו״ת, חי״ז סי׳ יא
31. סי׳ קצ ס״ק ד
32. וכותב: כעין שכתבו התוס׳ נזיר נט ע״א ד״ה והא
33. שבת קכט ע״א
34. כתובות לג ע״ב ד״ה אילמלי
35. על בראשית לב:כו
36. יבמות עב ע״א
37. תהלים קטז:ו
38. מור וקציעה סי׳ שכח
39. ב״ק פה ע״א ד״ה שניתנה
40. שמות כא:יט

NISHMAT AVRAHAM

non-fatal disease. Since the Tosafot do not do so it would seem that they do not think that we have permission to do so — author.]

On the other hand, we see that although one may not move a *gosses* since any movement may hasten his death,[41] nevertheless one may move him to safety to save him from being burnt in a fire.[42] Since one's only thought is to help the *gosses* who will certainly be terrified of being burnt to death, this is permissible. Although there is a possibility that one may hasten his death by moving him, one may nevertheless do so to prevent suffering since one's whole thought is to save him. See also the *Chazon Ish*[43] who discusses whether one may perform an action which will save many who are in danger of their lives, but will simultaneously cause the death of one uninvolved bystander.

One may ask how it is permitted, then, to prescribe any medication for a patient. Every drug has side effects, and some may be dangerous or even fatal. However the *Ramban*[44] writes regarding a son treating his father that one need not fear that the patient may die as a result of the treatment. For the Torah commanded us to treat and there is no treatment that does not carry any danger, for that which may cure one can kill another. This shows that when the Torah permitted doctors to treat patients, it took into consideration that there is no treatment without danger; nevertheless, it is a *mitzvah* to treat patients. It would appear, therefore, that if the patient consents, and the treatment has a good chance of success, it would be permitted to treat him even if there may be a small risk of a dangerous side effect.[45]

(4) PLASTIC SURGERY. Is one permitted to undergo surgery, injuring one's body in the process, where the reason for doing so is not to cure that which is causing physical suffering? In addition, is one permitted to put himself into danger (through anesthesia and surgery) for this purpose? Thus, is plastic surgery permissible if disfigurement makes it difficult to find a spouse or causes marital problems? The *Minchat Yitzchak*[46] was asked whether plastic surgery can be done to repair or improve one's looks or correct a limb that was disfigured at birth or in an accident. He answered that the *Rambam*[47] only forbids causing injury when the purpose is to harm, and refers the questioner to the *Mahari Assad*[48] and to a *responsum* of his own.[49] However, as to the danger involved, he writes that although the patient is certainly suffering and troubled by his disfigurement, and should be considered as one who is ill, nevertheless he is not *seriously ill*. He concludes that the matter needs further thought.[50]

The *Tzitz Eliezer*[51] forbids one to undergo plastic surgery in the absence of disease or pain, when the purpose is only to enhance a part of the body. He writes that it was not for this purpose that the Torah gave permission to heal and one may not allow a surgeon to injure him (*by the act of surgery*) for this purpose nor is

---

41. יו"ד סי' שלט סע' א

42. ספר חסידים סי' תשכד. חי' רעק"א יו"ד סי' שלט סע' א

43. יו"ד סי' סט

44. תורת האדם ענין הסכנה, מובא בב"י יו"ד סי' רמא ד"ה ומ"ש

45. וראה גם בשו"ת ציץ אליעזר ח"י סי' כה פי"ז

46. שו"ת, ח"ו סי' קה אות ב

47. הל' חובל ומזיק פ"ה ה"א

48. שו"ת, חיו"ד סי' רמט

49. שו"ת, מנחת יצחק ח"א סי' לו אות ד

50. וראה גם שם ח"א סי' כח אות ב

51. שו"ת, חי"א סוסי' מא

וחי"א סי' מב

SIMAN 155: MAY ONE BE TREATED BY AN IDOLATER / §1

— NISHMAT AVRAHAM —

the surgeon permitted to do so. And we should know and believe that there is no artist like *Hashem* and everyone was given the physical form best suited to him. The *Ramban*,[52] in discussing why it is permitted to injure a patient as part of his treatment, writes that the reason is the *mitzvah* to love your friend as yourself. He does not mention the *mitzvah* of returning a lost object, in this case the patient's good health, that he himself later quotes (*in the context of treatment without physical injury*). This leads the *Tzitz Eliezer* to say that the *mitzvah* of returning a lost object does not apply where injury to the patient (*an operation*) is necessary to cure him. On the contrary, the injury itself is a loss to the patient and not a return of something that was lost. Thus the *Ramban* found an alternative *mitzvah*, that of loving your friend as yourself. However this excludes injury for the purpose of beautifying the body where there is no loss to return, only injury to change what is present. In addition to this, concludes the *Tzitz Eliezer*, one may certainly not put oneself into any danger, however slight, for such a purpose.

On the other hand, the *Chelkat Yaakov*[53] permitted a young girl to undergo plastic surgery to straighten and reduce the size of her nose although she submits to bodily injury. Regarding the problem of putting herself into possible danger from the procedure, he first quotes the *Avnei Nezer*[54] who forbids a child to undergo surgery to straighten out a crooked leg because of the danger or possible danger of the procedure. The *Chelkat Yaakov* disagrees with his ruling, quoting the *Ramban*[55] who writes that no one would practice medicine because of the fear of making a genuine but fatal mistake. Since a doctor is permitted to treat patients and performs a *mitzvah* in so doing, he need not fear. As long as he acts in an acceptable fashion whatever he does is a meritorious act, for *Hashem* commanded him to render treatment, and any mistake on his part was genuine. The *Ramban* continues that bloodletting, which also carries serious side effects, was permitted, although it would appear from the *Gemara*[56] that this was done to keep healthy and not because one was *seriously* or *possibly seriously ill*. The *Chelkat Yaakov* adds that it is commonly accepted practice for people to undergo surgery of their internal organs, such as the intestines or lungs, although according to the *Halachah* a hole made in these organs makes the patient a *treifah*. But they depend on the *Tosafot*[57] who state that since man is not ruled by the stars and therefore will respond to treatment, he does not automatically become a *treifah*. We see that the vast majority of patients are cured by these procedures. Besides, patients who are not in any danger from their illness or at the most suffer from an illness which threatens a limb submit themselves to surgery. Moreover, every pregnancy carries a risk. Would we dream of saying that a woman is not to marry and have children because of the risk?[58] But this is the lot of a woman and the natural way of the world and since everyone takes these risks we say: "*Hashem* watches over the simple."[59]

The *Igrot Moshe*[60] was also asked whether a young girl could undergo plastic surgery to make her look more beautiful

---

52. תורת האדם מובא גם בב"י סי' רמא וגם בקצרה בנמו"י בסוף פ"ט דסנהדרין
53. שו"ת, ח"ג סי' יא
54. שו"ת, יו"ד סי' שכא
55. תורת האדם ענין הסכנה, מובא גם בב"י יו"ד סי' רמא
56. שבת קכט ע"א וע"ב
57. חולין מב ע"ב ד"ה ואמר
58. See below, p. 124, the *Igrot Moshe*.
59. תהלים קטז:ו
60. שו"ת, חו"מ ח"ב סי' סו

NISHMAT AVRAHAM

so that she could more easily find a husband. He answered quoting the *Rambam*[61] who only forbids causing injury when the purpose is to harm. This prohibition does not apply here since the purpose of the injury is to beautify her. The *Gemara*[62] does not ask if one is permitted to let blood from another, only whether one may do so to one's father. We may deduce from this that when the injury is part of the treatment it is permissible; it is forbidden only when done with the specific purpose of injuring one's fellow. Therefore, surgery would be permitted for the good of a person, even if it does not treat an illness. Therefore since the operation is for the girl's good and not in order to cause her harm, it is permitted. This is also the view of the *She'arim Metzuyanim BaHalachah*[63] and *Rav Jakobovits zt"l*.[64]

Rav Auerbach zt"l wrote to me (*in response to those who forbid plastic surgery*) about a person whose arm or finger had been traumatically amputated, who had been treated so that he was no longer in danger of his life. If there was a possibility of rejoining his amputated limb by surgery and under general anesthesia, what should be done? On *Shabbat* or *Yom Tov* this would not be permitted since there was only *danger to a limb* and one could not set aside Torah law for this. But on a weekday this would certainly be permitted since the surgery would not be considered an injury but a repair and treatment to save the limb. Why then should it be forbidden for someone to undergo plastic surgery in order to look normal? The *Rav zt"l*, in a *responsum*,[65] writes that if the plastic surgery is done to prevent suffering and shame caused by a defect in his looks (for instance a nose which is very abnormal) this would be permitted based on the *Tosafot*[66] and the *Gemara*,[67] since the purpose is to remove a blemish. However if the only reason is for beauty, this is not permitted.

(5) MINIMIZING THE INJURY AND THE DANGER. May one treat a patient, if someone else is present who can do the same procedure with less pain or danger to the patient? *Rav Waldenberg shlita*[68] writes that without doubt it is forbidden for a doctor in training to perform surgery when the patient is under general anesthesia. He will take longer to do the operation than an expert and the patient will be under general anesthesia longer, thus increasing the risk. If as a result the patient dies or suffers serious injury, the doctor in training will be held liable both by the laws of Heaven and those of the Sanhedrin. *Rav Auerbach zt"l*, however, wrote to me that where there are not enough non-Jewish doctors, if Jews do not train as doctors, who will practice medicine? Therefore if the patient does not demand that an expert do the surgery, we assume that he does not mind. *Rav Waldenberg shlita*[69] also notes that medical students take blood from patients and cause them unnecessary injury because of their inexperience. He rules that this is certainly not permitted, unless there is no one with more experience to do so and taking the blood is necessary for the patient. This would include a situation where the more expert person is busy with a more urgent case. However one may possibly permit this if it is not certain that the student will indeed cause more injury, for then there is no intention to

---

61. הל' חובל ומזיק פ"ה ה"א
62. סנהדרין פד ע"ב
63. סי' קצ ס"ק ד
64. נועם כרך ו עמ' רעג
65. מנחת שלמה תנינא סי' פו אות ג
66. יבמות מח ע"א ד"ה לא
67. נזיר נט ע"ב
68. שו"ת ציץ אליעזר חי"ד סי' פד ו-פה
69. שם סי' לה

SIMAN 155: MAY ONE BE TREATED BY AN IDOLATER / §1

NISHMAT AVRAHAM

cause harm, nor is it certain that he will indeed do so. In any case the patient must be asked for his consent. *Rav Auerbach zt"l* wrote to me in response that a lack of intention to do harm only applies to actions between man and Heaven but not to injury to one's fellow man. Thus it is forbidden to throw a stone into a public thoroughfare although he does not intend to harm anyone and although it is not certain that he will do harm. The *Gemara*[70] forbids one to treat one's father because of the fear that he might injure him in the process. It is possible that the injury to a parent is considered somewhat as an instance of laws between man and his fellow (and not just between man and Heaven). Although there is no intention to harm and it is by no means certain that he will, nevertheless it is forbidden. The *Rav zt"l* added that since this (medical students drawing blood) is the practice in hospitals, the patient realizes this before his admission and there is therefore no need to ask his permission. And indeed the doctors are busy seeing and treating patients and will find it difficult to also find the time to take blood. On the contrary, since the students or paramedics take blood the doctors have more time to do what only they have the right to do.

I asked *Rav Waldenberg shlita* how his ruling fits with the ruling of the *Shulchan Aruch*[71] that one who has never circumcised a baby may not do his first circumcision on *Shabbat*, for if he did not carry out the circumcision properly he will have desecrated the Sabbath. However if he has done a circumcision once, he may circumcise a baby on *Shabbat* even if he is its father. It would appear from this ruling that he is permitted to do a circumcision, for the first time, on a weekday although an expert *mohel* is present at the time (*and can perform the circumcision*), and the second time, even on *Shabbat*. The *Rav shlita*[72] answered me that the *Shulchan Aruch* is not discussing a case where he will certainly not do a proper circumcision, only that he might do so. Moreover, since there is no danger in taking blood, this is permitted by a student if the patient consents. With circumcision which is dangerous, the *Chida*[73] rules that one who is circumcising a baby for the first time may not do so even on a weekday without an expert *mohel* supervising. If such supervision is not available the circumcision must be postponed until it is, even if the father is willing for it to be done without supervision. In addition, the *mitzvah* of circumcision was given to us in spite of there being some small danger attached to it. The *Gemara*[74] expounds the verse:[75] "Because for Your sake we are killed all the time," to refer to the *mitzvah* of circumcision, and *Rashi* explains: For occasionally it is fatal. [*Rav Auerbach zt"l* wrote to me that this (*the permission to take the slight risk present in every circumcision — author*) only refers to whatever is needed to perform the *mitzvah*, but not to

---

70. סנהדרין פד ע"ב. וראה בירואים עמוד החמישי שכולל מכה אביו ואמו סי' קעז (נט) באיסורים שאדם עושה בהם רע לשמים ולבריות וכן בחינך מצוה לג שכתב: משרשי המצוה זו (כיבוד או"א) שראוי לו לאדם שיכיר ויגמול חסד למי שעשה עמו טובה וכו'. וכשיקבע זאת המידה בנפשו יעלה ממנה להכיר טובת הקל ברוך הוא, שהוא סיבתו וסיבת כל אבותיו עד אדם הראשון, ושהוציאו לאויר העולם וסיפק צרכו כל ימיו, והעמידו על מתכונתו ושלימות אבריו, ונתן בו נפש יודעת ומשכלת, שאלולי הנפש שחננו הקל יהיה כסוס כפרד אין הבין, ויערוך במחשבתו כמה וכמה ראוי לו להזהר בעבודתו ברוך הוא, עכ"ל. וכן עיין ברמב"ן שמות כ:יב. חזקוני שם. ספורנו שם: כי אמנם ענין אלו החמשה דברות הוא כולו אומר כבוד לקל יתברך. כלי יקר: במצוה זו חתם חמשה דברות ראשונות המדברים בכבוד המקום ברוך הוא וכו'.

71. יו"ד סי' רסו סע' ו

72. שו"ת ציץ אליעזר חי"ד סי' לו

73. שו"ת חיים שאל ח"א סי' נח ו-נט

74. גיטין נז ע"ב

75. תהלים מד:כג

(C)he will treat him in the name of his idol, one may not go to him even if the disease is certainly fatal if it is not treated.

§2 A patient is forbidden to (D)use water for cure if this is offered to him by an idolater in the name of an idol.

§3 If the patient is *dangerously ill*, he may eat anything for a cure that would be forbidden for a healthy person, even if he takes it in the normal way. If he is *not seriously ill* he may only take them in an unusual manner, except for the produce of a (E)vineyard sown with a mixture of seeds, and meat and milk cooked together which are forbidden even if taken in an unusual manner. Only a *seriously ill* patient may eat these for his cure.

NISHMAT AVRAHAM

cause needless suffering. Therefore it would seem that (*the novice is permitted to do a circumcision — author*) only because of the other reasons.] See also the *Shevut Yaakov*[76] and the *Maharam Shick*.[77] The *Chacham Zvi*[78] explains that one is considered an expert after one circumcision because, since he can cause great damage and even death, he would not practice circumcision if he were not sure of himself. *Rav Waldenberg shlita* concludes, that, in our case, the student must be supervised many times to be certain that he does not cause unnecessary injury.

(C) he will treat him in the name of his idol. The *Darchei Teshuvah*[79] writes that this applies nowadays to missionaries who use every opportunity to seek to convert Jews. *Rav Auerbach zt"l* ruled that it is forbidden to be treated in a missionary hospital for fear of being influenced by them.

(D) use water. Baths and springs for which miraculous religious powers are claimed are not defined *halachically* as idols[80] since they are a part of the earth.[81] Although the idolater believes that it is the idol that has miraculous powers and praises it for them, *Rav Auerbach zt"l* told me that it would not be forbidden to use them if the reason was to benefit from their special composition and concentration of minerals. It is, however, certainly forbidden to use them if the patient thinks that the cure comes because of the influence of the idol.

(E) vineyard sown with a mixture of seeds. The Torah[82] forbids one to sow grapes together with vegetables or grain or to sow vegetables or grain in a vineyard (*kila'im*). If this was done one may neither eat nor have any benefit from the produce. For further details see the *Rambam*.[83]

---

76. שו"ת, ח"ג סי' כה
77. שו"ת, או"ח סי' קנא
78. שו"ת, סי' סט
79. ס"ק ט בשם הדיני דחיי לאוין מ"ה דף מט ע"ג. וראה שם מה שכותב על יש"ו. וראה גם בבאר היטב כאן ס"ק ד
80. עיין יו"ד סימן קמה סע' א
81. ש"ך שם ס"ק ב
82. דברים כב:ט
83. הל' כלאים פ"ה ו-פ"ז

SIMAN 155: MAY ONE BE TREATED BY AN IDOLATER / §2, 3

GLOSS: *There are those who rule that food from which it is only* (F)*Rabbinically forbidden to derive benefit may be used as a*

NISHMAT AVRAHAM

(F) Rabbinically forbidden to derive benefit. The *Shach*[84] writes that he must not eat or drink it and the *Rama* states this opinion later in this section. However if he eats it in an unusual manner, the *rishonim*[85] permit it.

A NON-SERIOUSLY ILL PATIENT AND RABBINICALLY FORBIDDEN FOOD. The *Ketav Sofer*[86] compares the transgression of eating on *Yom Kippur* to eating foods forbidden by the Torah. He writes that a *non-seriously ill* patient may eat a forbidden food as a cure if he eats it in an unusual manner or if he mixes it with something bitter, so that he does not enjoy the taste. This is true whether the food is only forbidden to be eaten or even if it is forbidden to have any benefit from it. If he does not need the food for a cure but only to strengthen him, he should act strictly and not eat it, even in an unusual manner, since by eating it he gives it importance (*achshevei*). On the other hand, since eating it in an unusual manner is only a Rabbinic transgression, one may act leniently if necessary. The *Sha'agat Aryeh*,[87] however, writes that even food or drink that are not fit to be eaten are forbidden to a *non-seriouslly ill* patient on *Yom Kippur* even if they are taken as a cure, and this is true also for everything that is forbidden by the Torah.

One must also differentiate between eating food that is forbidden, and using it for a cure (without eating it) which is permitted for the *non-seriously* ill.[88]

The *Radbaz*[89] permits a *non-seriously ill* patient to eat all Rabbinically forbidden food. He writes that one may differentiate between transgressing Rabbinic laws of *Shabbat* and other Rabbinic laws, for we see that food cooked by a non-Jew is permitted for him. However the *Rashba*[90] writes that a *non-seriously ill* patient is not permitted to eat Rabbinically forbidden food. Rabbinic decrees are not always comparable, whether on *Yom Tov*, on *Shabbat* or on a weekday. Thus there are many things forbidden by Rabbinic decree (*shevut*) which are sometimes permitted in order to perform a *mitzvah*, for example asking a non-Jew to draw up legal documents on *Shabbat* finalizing the purchase from him of land in Israel. On the other hand, our Sages have, in other instances, insisted on their decree being kept even if it would result in the abrogation of a *mitzvah* carrying the penalty of *karet*. Thus we cannot use the permission given to set aside one specific *shevut* to do so for another. Only where we have specific permission by our Sages to set aside a given *shevut* may we do so; if there is no such permission given specifically by them, we may not. Thus, concludes the *Rashba*, although they have forbidden us to ask a non-Jew to do anything on *Shabbat* that we ourselves may not, they have permitted it for a patient. This does not mean than we can permit him to drink *stam yenam* or to eat or drink other Rabbinically forbidden foods. See also the *Mishnah*

---

84. ס"ק יד
85. המרדכי והאגודה, פסחים ריש פרק כל שעה
86. שו"ת, או"ח סי' קיא
87. שו"ת, סי' עד-עו
88. ש"ך כאן ס"ק יד
89. שו"ת, סי' אלף עו (ח"ד סי' ב)
90. שו"ת הרשב"א המיוחסות סי' קכז (כותב השם הגדולים ערך הרשב"א: ונודע דתשובות המיוחסות להרמב"ן הם מהרשב"א וכמ"ש מרן בית יוסף בהקדמתו). וראה במ"מ הל' שבת פ"ו ה"ט. ובאגלי טל מלאכת טוחן סע" יו ס"ק ו ובהגה ס"ק ו

NISHMAT AVRAHAM

Berurah[91] in this context.

In another *responsum*, the *Rashba*[92] writes that he could not find any way to permit a *non-seriously ill* patient to eat or drink any forbidden food or fluid even if it is only Rabbinically forbidden, except for kosher food cooked by a non-Jew on *Shabbat* (*even though it, too, is normally forbidden*). However *stam yenam* or the fat surrounding the inner sinew of an animal's thigh, which is Rabbinically forbidden, may not be given to such a patient. Food cooked by a non-Jew on *Shabbat* is permitted because it is a less serious transgression and a Jew may not cook for such a patient on *Shabbat*. The *Rashba*[93] stresses that kosher food cooked by a non-Jew is only permitted for a *non-seriously ill* patient on *Shabbat* and becomes forbidden again immediately after *Shabbat* or even on *Shabbat* if the patient is cured. The *Rivash*[94] also forbids such a patient to eat or drink anything that is Rabbinically forbidden including *stam yenam*. This is also the ruling of the *Ran*.[95] The *Nishmat Adam*[96] also rules that Rabbinically forbidden food or drink is forbidden to a *non-seriously ill* patient. And the *Pri Megadim*[97] writes that it is known that a *non-seriously ill* patient may be fed Rabbinically forbidden food (*if he eats it in an unusual manner*). If, however, there are two different sorts of such food available, the one which involves a lesser degree of prohibition is given to him (as with Torah forbidden foods; see *Nishmat Avraham*, vol. 1 *Orach Chaim*, Siman 618 §9). The *Mishnah Berurah*[98] also rules like the *Shulchan Aruch* here that a *non-seriously ill* patient may not eat or drink Rabbinically forbidden foods (see also the end of Siman 84 above).

Tablets or capsules made from forbidden food, which are swallowed, may be taken by a *non-seriously ill* patient, but not if they are lozenges that are sucked.[99] See also Siman 84B above regarding medication containing forbidden products and capsules made of gelatine.[100]

Rav Auerbach zt"l wrote to me that he was unsure as to which type of patient this *halachah* applies to. On the one hand, treatment on *Shabbat* is permitted for a *non-seriously ill* patient or for a patient who is suffering (*in his whole body*), and perhaps the same would apply here. However it is also possible that one cannot extrapolate from the laws of *Shabbat*, for *Chazal* did not permit Rabbinic law to be set aside unless the patient was really ill (*a non-seriously ill patient as opposed to one who is merely uncomfortable or is only suffering mildly*). In our case, the *Mishneh LaMelech*[101] explains that the *Tosafot* [102] rule that as long as the Rabbinically forbidden food is taken in an unusual manner, it is permitted even for one who is healthy. Although we do not accept this ruling for one who is healthy, nevertheless it is possible that it would be correct for someone who is suffering only mildly, for example, one who has trouble sleeping or who has a mild headache.

---

91. סי׳ שז ס״ק כא
92. מובא בב״י יו״ד סי׳ קכג ד״ה כתב הרשב״א
93. מובא בט״ז יו״ד סי׳ קכב ס״ק טו
94. שו״ת, סי׳ רנה מובא גם בדרכי משה כאן ס״ק ג
95. פסחים ריש פ״ב ד״ה וראיתמי שכתב וע״ז פ״ב ד״ה דרך הנאתן. וראה גם בחידושיו על ע״ז כח ע״א
96. הל׳ שבת כלל סט ס״ק ג ד״ה ועוד ראיה ברורה
97. או״ח סי׳ שכח א״א ס״ק יא
98. סי׳ שכח ס״ק סג
99. שמירת שבת כהלכתה פ״מ פה
100. וראה בשו״ת האלף לך שלמה יו״ד סי׳ רב שמתיר לחולה שאין בו סכנה לשתות שומן דגים טמאים. וראה גם בש״ך סי׳ רלט ס״ק כ. וראה בשו״ת יביע אומר ח״ב חיו״ד סי׳ יב ובשמירת שבת כהלכתה פ״מ סע׳ פו
101. הל׳ יסוה״ת פ״ה ה״ח ד״ה וראיתי
102. פסחים כט ע״א סוד״ה אין פודין (השני)

SIMAN 155: MAY ONE BE TREATED BY AN IDOLATER / §2, 3

NISHMAT AVRAHAM

1. Foods which are Rabbinically forbidden on *Pesach*. The accepted *halachah* is that *chametz* is not nullified even in a mixture of one part in a thousand.[103] This is in contrast to the opinion of the *She'iltot*[104] that *chametz* becomes nullified in a mixture of one part to sixty like any other forbidden food. *Rabbeinu Tam*[105] also rules like him. The *Mishnah Berurah*[106] writes that if there are many other reasons to permit such a mixture (of one part of *chametz* to sixty) one may depend on the ruling of the *She'iltot*.[107] The *Shoel U'Meshiv*[108] was asked regarding an incident in a hospital where water was taken from an urn that had been used during the rest of the year for *chametz* and was put into utensils used on *Pesach*. He replied that since a tiny amount of *chametz* (*that is in a mixture containing more than sixty parts to one of chametz*) is only forbidden Rabbinically, a *non-seriously ill* patient is permitted to eat Rabbinically forbidden foods. And, although the *Shulchan Aruch* discusses Rabbinic prohibitions which are not founded on Torah law, and *chametz* is forbidden by Torah law (*before it was mixed*), nevertheless, since the amount is so small and the *She'iltot* and *Rabbeinu Tam* permit it, it may be permitted in a hospital.

One may not eat nor have any benefit from *chametz* that was in a Jew's possession during *Pesach*.[109] Many *poskim*[110] forbid even a *non-seriously ill* patient to eat it after *Pesach* although they allow him to have benefit from it. The *Mishnah Berurah*[111] writes that one may be treated with such *chametz* and Rav Neuwirth *shlita* told me that this includes eating it for a cure.

2. *Stam Yenam*. See Siman 123A above.

3. Food that is unfit for consumption or whose composition has been changed. See Siman 84B above.

4. Eating less than the *measure* required to transgress. The *Elef Lecha Shlomo*[112] discusses the question of a *non-seriously ill* patient eating less than a *measure* of food. He writes that, given a choice, it is better for him to eat less than a *measure* of food that is forbidden by the Torah rather than to eat a full *measure* of Rabbinically forbidden food.[113] However the *Yabia Omer*[114] disagrees, quoting the *Maggid Mishneh*[115] and the *Mishneh LaMelech*[116] who both rule that eating less than a *measure* of forbidden food is forbidden by the Torah (*even though not punishable by* the *Sanhedrin*)[117] and this is more serious than eating that which is Rabbinically forbidden. The *Chinuch*,[118] however, writes that a patient, although not fully *seriously ill*, may be given less than a *measure* of food forbidden by the Torah if he is weak. And the *Minchat Chinuch*[119]

---

103. או"ח סי' תמז סע' א
104. שאילתות פ' צו סי' פ, מובא גם בתוס' פסחים ל ע"א ד"ה אמר רבא
105. שו"ת ר"ת סי' מח סע' ט. וראה במעדני שמואל סי' קיז ס"ק טז
106. סי' תמז ס"ק ב
107. ראה בשו"ת ציץ אליעזר חי"ז סי' כג בנוגע לשתית מי-כנרת בפסח כשמרובים יושבים ואוכלים חמץ על שפת ימה ומשליכים חמץ הנשאר להם אל תוך המים. וכן תשובתו של הגר"ע יוסף שליט"א בשבילי ההלכה ניסן תשמ"ח עמ' 5
108. שו"ת, תליתאה ח"ג סוסי' מא
109. או"ח סי' תמח סע' ג
110. שו"ת שאגת אריה סי' עה בשם הר"ן. חק יעקב סי' תסו ס"ק א. כף החיים שם ס"ק ח
111. שעה"צ שם ס"ק ד
112. שו"ת, יו"ד סי' רב. וכן עיין בש"ך סי' רלט ס"ק כ
113. וראה גם בשו"ת ציץ אליעזר ח"ו סי' טז ודרכ"ת כאן ס"ק יח
114. שו"ת, ח"ב חיו"ד סי' יב
115. הל' שביתת עשור פ"ב ה"ג
116. הל' יסודי"ת פ"ה ה"ח ד"ה ודע שעדיין אני נבוך
117. יומא עב ע"א מחלוקת רבי יוחנן וריש לקיש, והלכה כר' יוחנן
118. מצוה שיג
119. שם

NISHMAT AVRAHAM

comments that it would appear that the *Chinuch* permits a *seriously ill* patient to eat a full *measure* of forbidden food and a *non-seriously ill* patient less than a *measure* of such food. The *Minchat Chinuch*, however, disagrees with this ruling, pointing out that Torah law may not be set aside for a *non-seriously ill* patient, and, indeed, he may not even be given Rabbinically forbidden food to eat. The *Yabia Omer* explains this very difficult ruling of the *Chinuch* by saying that when the *Chinuch* wrote "not fully *seriously ill*" he nevertheless meant that he was somewhat *seriously ill*.

5. Rabbinically forbidden work. For example, asking a non-Jew to cook food on *Shabbat*. One must differentiate between a Jew doing work himself on *Shabbat* or *Yom Tov*, but in an indirect fashion, and asking a non-Jew to do it (which he will do in the usual manner). This includes even Torah forbidden *melachot* such as cooking, but in both instances the prohibition (doing the work in an indirect fashion or asking a non-Jew to do it) is Rabbinic. The *Chayei Adam*[120] rules that whenever a Jew is permitted to do the *melachah* in an indirect fashion, he may do so even if a non-Jew is present and could be asked. See *Nishmat Avraham*, vol. 1 *Orach Chaim*, Siman 328(17e) for a discussion as to which is more serious, a Jew doing the *melachah* himself on *Shabbat* or *Yom Tov*, but in an indirect fashion, or asking a non-Jew to do it. One must also remember that there is a discussion whether a Jew may do work forbidden by the Torah in an indirect manner for a *non-seriously ill* patient [ibid. 328(17c), p. 203].

(i) *Shabbat*. A non-Jew may be asked to cook on *Shabbat* for a *non-seriously ill* patient.[121] See also *Nishmat Avraham*, vol. 1 *Orach Chaim*, Siman 318A. The *Pri Megadim*[122] asks why this should be permitted when a *non-seriously ill* person is forbidden to eat any Rabbinically forbidden food. He answers that we must differentiate between food that is itself forbidden and food that is forbidden for an extraneous reason. Here, the food itself is kosher, and it is forbidden only because it was cooked by a non-Jew, and this is why it is permitted to a *non-seriously ill* patient. Why, then, asks the *Pri Megadim* rhetorically, is he forbidden to drink *stam yenam*? He answers, quoting the *Beit Yosef* who in turn quotes the *Ran*, that *Chazal* did not wish to be stricter with food cooked by a non-Jew on *Shabbat* than with the *melachot* which a non-Jew may be asked to do for a *non-seriously ill* patient. Another reason given is that since a Jew may not cook on *Shabbat* for such a patient, the reason that food cooked by a non-Jew was forbidden by *Chazal* does not apply.[123]

(ii) *Weekday*. Food cooked by a non-Jew is forbidden to a *non-seriously ill* patient even if food cooked by a Jew was unavailable at the time.[124]

6. That which is forbidden for an extraneous reason. Things that are usually permitted may be forbidden at certain times, for example *muktzeh*. The *poskim* discuss whether they would be permissible to a *non-seriously ill* patient. Thus *Rebbe Akiva Eiger*[125] was unsure whether such a patient would be permitted to eat fruit, needed for his health, if the only fruit available had fallen from a tree on *Shabbat*. The *Pitchei*

---

120. מובא במ"ב סי' שכח ס"ק נא
121. או"ח שיו סע' יו ברמ"א
122. או"ח סי' שכח א"א ס"ק יא
123. משום חתנות. ראה בב"י או"ח סוסי' שכח אות יט ד"ה כתב רבינו ירוחם בשם הר"ן בשם הרא"ה

(בדק הבית)
124. ראה בט"ז או"ח סי' שכח ס"ק ו ופמ"ג שם א"א ס"ק יא. וראה גם ביו"ד שם סע' טו ברמ"א ט"ז ונקוה"כ. ובמ"ב סי' שכח ס"ק סג
125. שו"ת, סי' ה

SIMAN 155: MAY ONE BE TREATED BY AN IDOLATER / §2, 3

NISHMAT AVRAHAM

Teshuvah,[126] quoting him, explains that the question is whether this fruit is like any other food forbidden by our Sages (as the *Rama* rules here) or whether, since the fruit itself is permissible but because it became available for use only after Sabbath began, it is considered like anything else forbidden by the Sages on *Shabbat*, but permitted for a *non-seriously ill* patient. He concludes that *Rebbe Akiva Eiger*, basing his decision on a *Tosafot*,[127] rules that the fruit is permissible. However, the *She'arim Metzuyanim BaHalachah*[128] quotes the *Lechem Shlomo*[129] who interprets the *responsum* of *Rebbe Akiva Eiger* as forbidding such fruit to a *non-seriously ill* patient. The *Chayei Adam*[130] and the *Ketsot HaShulchan*[131] also rule that whatever is *muktzeh* is forbidden to a *non-seriously ill* patient. The *Magen Avraham*[132] writes that a child who requires something for his health is categorized as a *non-seriously ill* patient, and may be fed *muktzeh*. The *Yeshuot Yaakov*[133] deduces from this that a *non-seriously ill* patient is permitted to eat that which is *muktzeh*. And, although the *Rama* forbids a *non-seriously ill* patient to eat Rabbinically forbidden foods, this only applies to foods which are inherently forbidden, such as *stam yenam*. However food that is kosher but forbidden for an extraneous reason, such as *Shabbat*, is permitted.

Rav Auerbach zt"l wrote to me that nevertheless, if one cooked for a *seriously ill* patient on *Shabbat*, the food would be forbidden to a *non-seriously ill* patient even though the food is forbidden because of the time element — *Shabbat*, and not because it is inherently forbidden. This is to avoid more food than is necessary being cooked for the *seriously ill* patient, so as to have enough for the *non-seriously ill* patient as well. See *Shulchan Aruch Orach Chaim,* Siman 318:2.

As to moving something that is *muktzeh* for a *non-seriously ill* patient, we can deduce from *Rashi*[134] that it may be moved only in an indirect manner; the *Magen Avraham* rules according to this opinion.[135] *Rashi* refers to carrying a child clutching a stone (*muktzeh*) within a court-yard and who would become ill if it is taken away from him. *Rashi* explains that it is permitted for the father to carry him since the stone itself is carried in an indirect manner. However, in *Rashi's* example, the *muktzeh* is not needed for a *non-seriously ill* patient, for if it were, it could be moved directly and the *Magen Avraham*[136] says as much. Thus medication may be moved for a *non-seriously ill* patient who needs it and this is the ruling of the *Kalkelet Shabbat*,[137] who quotes the above *Magen Avraham* that it is permissible to feed *muktzeh* by hand to a *non-seriously ill* patient if there is no alternative. See also *Nishmat Avraham*, vol. 1 *Orach Chaim,* Siman 321C.

The *Shemirat Shabbat KeHilchatah*[138] rules that a *non-seriously ill* patient may move and eat that which is *muktzeh* — for example, food cooked by a non-Jew on *Shabbat* and fruit that fell from a tree on *Shabbat* — if indeed there is no alter-

---

126. כאן ס"ק ח
127. שבת צה ע"א ד"ה והרודה
128. סי' צא ס"ק ט
129. או"ח סי' נו
130. כלל סט סע' טז
131. סי' קלד בבדה"ש סוס"ק ז
132. סי' שכח ס"ק טו
133. סוסי' שט
134. שבת קמא ע"ב ד"ה בתינוק
135. סי' שט ס"ק א
136. סי' שכח ס"ק טו
137. סוף כללי מוקצה "זה הכלל בכל פרטי מוקצה" אות ג (ד)
138. פל"ג סע' ו

cure even for (G)*a non-seriously ill patient provided he does not eat or drink it since he is not seriously ill. In each case, this must only*

---NISHMAT AVRAHAM---

native to be obtained. Not only the patient, but anyone else may also move the *muktzeh* for him, but not more than is necessary for the patient. One may move a lamp, including an electric lamp, to see what the patient needs; one must move an oil or kerosene lamp with care so as not to shake the oil or kerosene that is inside. Where possible he should do all of this in an indirect manner.[139] The *Rav shlita* told me that he based his ruling on that of the *Chazon Ish*[140] who permits a *non-seriously ill* patient to eat that which is *muktzeh* and *Rav Auerbach zt"l*[141] also writes that fruit that fell from a tree may be eaten by a *non-seriously ill* patient, since, unlike food that was cooked on *Shabbat*, it fell passively and not as a result of a direct action by anyone.

7. Danger to a limb. The *Pitchei Teshuvah*[142] writes that the ruling of the *Rama* that a patient may not eat or drink that which is Rabbinically forbidden, only applies to a *non-seriously ill* patient. However if the patient is in danger of losing a limb, he may eat or drink such forbidden food. This is also the ruling of the *Pri Megadim*.[143]

(G) a *non-seriously ill* patient. The *Orchot Chaim*[144] and the *Darchei Teshuvah*[145] both write[146] that one may not set aside even Rabbinic laws on *Shabbat* for a patient who has brought his illness upon himself, for example, by eating food that he knew would make him ill. However if one becomes *seriously ill*, Sabbath laws may be set aside for him. *Rav Auerbach zt"l* wrote to me that this ruling needs further elucidation, since the *Gemara*[147] rules that one may not commit even a Rabbinic transgression to save another from a Torah sin that he commited willfully on *Shabbat* and which carries the death penalty. However it could be that the *Gemara* rules strictly because he deserves his punishment for having willfully desecrated the Sabbath. Here, however, he did not sin but put himself into a dangerous situation. The *Shemirat Shabbat KeHilchatah*[148] writes that if he did something before *Shabbat* that leads to having to set aside Sabbath laws for him, even though what he did was wrong, nevertheless now that he is in danger, Sabbath laws must be set aside.[149] However the *Mishnah Berurah*[150] writes that it is forbidden for one to set out on a journey early in the week knowing that he will have to set aside Sabbath laws. The *Chochmat Shlomo*[151] also rules that where one endangered himself willfully, Sabbath laws are not set aside to save his life. The *Kovetz He'arot*[152] writes that at first sight this ruling is surprising for, on the contrary, it is forbidden to act strictly in a life-threatening situation. However he explains that it is wrong to think that one may sin to save life; the proper way of

---

139. סי׳ שכח מ״ב ס״ק נח
140. חזו״א או״ח סי׳ מד ס״ק ה
141. מנחת שלמה ח״ב מהד״ת סי׳ כג
142. כאן ס״ק ח
143. או״ח סי׳ שכח מש״ז ס״ק ז
144. או״ח סי׳ שכח ס״ק יט
145. כאן ס״ק כא

146. שניהם בשם החקר הלכה ח״ב דף ו
147. שבת ד ע״א
148. פל״ב הערה צו
149. ראה בשעה״צ סי׳ שלא ס״ק יז
150. סי׳ רמח ס״ק כו
151. או״ח שלט
152. על יבמות סי׳ כג ס״ק ג

SIMAN 155: MAY ONE BE TREATED BY AN IDOLATER / §2, 3

be at the advice of experts or the cure must be one **(H)** *of known efficacy. If the patient can be cured without the use of forbidden food, he should not be treated with it, although he may have*

---NISHMAT AVRAHAM---

seeing it is that in a life-threatening situation, what is forbidden is set aside and there is no sin. However he may not transgress and put himself in a life-threatening situation which would demand that Sabbath laws be set aside. For then he is seen as sinning retroactively and, in such a case, Sabbath laws are not set aside, even to save a life. *Rav Auerbach zt"l*,[153] however, writes that this ruling of the *Kovetz He'arot* is surprising for were he to act strictly and, as a result, die, his setting out on the journey will have caused his death. If it is forbidden to set out lest Sabbath laws will have to be set aside because of a life-threatening situation, surely it would be forbidden if it were to cause his death. Thus he merely exchanges setting aside Sabbath laws in a life-threatening situation for the greater sin of causing his own death. True, *Chazal* forbade him to set out on a journey that would lead to the desecration of the Sabbath, but the latter would certainly be permitted if, otherwise, this would lead to danger and cause his death.

(H) of known efficacy. The *Taz*[154] quotes the *Maharshal*,[155] permitting a *seriously ill* patient to eat a food forbidden by the Torah only if its efficacy has been proven. This is also the ruling of the *Hagahot Maimoniot*,[156] the *Magen Avraham*,[157] and the *Shulchan Aruch HaRav*.[158] However the *Pri Megadim*[159] asks why only something of proven efficacy should be permitted. This would be true for a *non-seriously ill* patient, but for one who is *seriously ill*, even what is only a possible cure is permitted. The *Tosefet Yom HaKippurim*[160] also writes that it appears from *Rashi* that forbidden food is not permitted unless it would certainly cure. He asks why we should not give him the forbidden food if it may cure him. If the desecration of *Shabbat*, which is very serious, is permitted for a possibly *seriously ill* patient, why should other laws, which are less serious, not be set aside? He rules that one must differentiate between a medication that has been accepted rationally as being possibly efficacious and one that is given as a charm (as in *Rashi's* example). The *Darchei Teshuvah*[161] discusses the issue at length. See also *Nishmat Avraham*, vol. 1 *Orach Chaim,* Siman 301L, p. 150 regarding the use of charms.

The *Tehillah LeDavid*[162] disagrees with the *Pri Megadim*, for the *Issur VeHeter*[163] writes that even a *seriously ill* patient may take forbidden food as medication only if its efficacy has been proven. The *Tehillah LeDavid* goes on to say that we define "known efficacy" as something that most people would want to take for their disease; however if they are in doubt, it would be forbidden. However when the *Rama* writes "experts

---

153. מוריה סיון תשל"א עמ' לב. מנחת שלמה ח"א סי' ז אות ד
154. יו"ד סי' פד ס"ק כד
155. בתשובה וכן בסוף פרק אלו טרפות
156. פי"ד ממאכ"א
157. סי' שכח ס"ק א
158. שם סע' ב
159. סי' שכח א"א ס"ק א
160. יומא פג ע"א ד"ה מי שנשכו כלב שוטה
161. ס"ק ל
162. סי' שכח ס"ק ב
163. כלל נט סע' לה

NISHMAT AVRAHAM

must have accepted" he means even if there is doubt. The *Da'at Torah*,[164] however, writes that the *Gemara* (that *Rashi* refers to) is discussing a cure that has not been prescribed by a doctor but by a non-medical idolater. This is why the *Issur VeHeter* did not permit it. If, however, the medication had been generally recognized, he would have permitted it since all medication is permitted for a *seriously ill* patient even if it is made from foods which, if eaten by the healthy, carry serious penalties, even though the patient may only possibly be *seriously ill* or the medication only possibly efficacious. The *Zer Zahav*[165] shows that in the *Rambam's*[166] opinion even medication which will not completely cure him but will only ease his suffering, is permitted.

UNCONVENTIONAL TREATMENT.

A patient with widespread cancer who is beyond any further treatment for his disease wishes to undergo unconventional treatment. There is no evidence that this "treatment" is at all effective and the costs are exorbitant. Is one obligated to try to convince the patient not to do so or, on the contrary, is it forbidden to do so, for then one takes away his last hope from him? What if he cannot afford the costs? Is there an obligation on his family, friends or the community to give him charity for the purpose? *Rav Neuwirth shlita* answered me that it is forbidden to try to persuade him not to go for this would remove his last hope. On the other hand there is no obligation to give him charity for the purpose. *Rav Auerbach zt"l* agreed with this and added that a private individual is not obligated to give him charity and if he does so it may not be deducted from the charity that he is obligated to give from his earnings. Moreover, those who are responsible for public charity funds are forbidden to give him monies from their fund.

Rav Eliashiv shlita told me that if one thought that the psychological effect on the patient of receiving this treatment would be such that he would live a little longer, one would be obligated to give him charity money, even if the treatment itself has no effect whatsoever on the disease. If there will be no such effect, he is not obligated to give him any charity money.

Rav Auerbach zt"l told me that one would be permitted to give a little of his charity money as a *chesed* to calm the patient's soul.

Rav Neuwirth shlita questioned the above ruling of *Rav Auerbach zt"l* (that charity money may not be used for this purpose), quoting the *Ahavat Chesed*[167] that one must give charity from money set aside for charity even to prevent despair. For the *Ahavat Chesed* writes that the *acharonim*[168] rule that one may use money he has set aside for charity to provide for a wedding if he did not have other funds available for the purpose. Similarly he may use these monies to pay for the privilege of being a *sandak* or to write Torah books that can be lent out to others. He may also use the books himself provided he writes on them that they were bought from charity money so that his heirs will not mistakenly believe that the books belong to them. However, the *Pitchei Teshuvah* quotes the *Chatam Sofer* who writes that the *Maharil* and the *Rama* both rule that charity money from one's earnings may be used only for the poor and not for other *mitzvot*. It would seem, however, continues the *Ahavat Chesed*, that it would be permissible if the money is given for a circumcision when

---

164. כאן
165. הגה על האיסור והיתר ס"ק טו
166. פיהמ"ש יומא פ"ח
167. פי"ט ס"ק ב
168. עיין ש"ך יו"ד סי' רמט ס"ק ג

to [I]*wait a little while before kosher food is obtained, as long as there is no danger in doing so.*

SIMAN 157
WHEN IS MARTYRDOM OBLIGATORY

§1 If one is told that he will be killed unless he transgresses a Torah law, he may transgress [A]any Torah law to save his

---

NISHMAT AVRAHAM

the father lacks funds, for a wedding for a poor couple, or for books which are to be used by those who otherwise would not be able to afford them. One may even use the money to buy the privilege of being called up to the reading of the Torah, if he knows that the money donated will be distributed to the poor.[169]

The *Shevut Yaakov*[170] writes that the *Shach* and *Taz* (references 168 and 169) have both ruled that monies earmarked for charity cannot be used for *mitzvot* such as providing for a circumcision, marriage or buying Torah books, which are not concerned directly with the poor. Only if those *mitzvot* will not be performed because of poverty would one be allowed to use his charity money for this purpose. This is also the opinion of the *Be'er Sheva*.[171] As to using charity money for *mitzvot*, such as buying candles for the synagogue, the *Pnei Yehoshua*[172] permits it but the *Taz* permits this only if at the time that he bought the *mitzvah*, he did so with the intention of paying from his charity money.

(I) **wait a little while.** The *Gra*[173] writes that this rule of the *Rama* refers even to one who is *seriously ill* and it ap-

plies to all that is forbidden. The *Nishmat Adam*[174] rules that this is also true for a *non-seriously ill* patient who must be given something that is Rabbinically forbidden, as treatment. If he knows that should he wait he will be able to acquire an alternative one that is permitted, he must wait.

SIMAN 157

(A) any Torah law. The *Chatam Sofer*[1] writes that our Sages learned[2] from the Torah verse:[3] "And you shall keep My decrees and laws which man shall carry out and by which he shall live," that in a life-threatening situation all Torah laws may be set aside excluding the three cardinal sins.[4] However, he wonders about this exclusion. For the verse from which our Sages derived the ruling that one can save one's life by transgression is written in juxtaposition to the verses forbidding illicit relationships. Why then does the ruling not apply to illicit relations? *Rav Waldenberg shlita*[5] wrote to me to answer the *Chatam Sofer's* question as follows: The verse in question is a general commandment that we observe *Hashem's* decrees and laws. Since it is an all-embracing commandment, there really

---

169. עיין ט"ז שם ס"ק א
170. שו"ת, ח"ב סי' פה
171. שו"ת, סי' מא
172. שו"ת, סי' ב
173. כאן ס"ק כד
174. הל' שבת כלל סט ס"ק ג ד"ה מה ששאל

1. תורת משה פ' אחרי
2. יומא פה ע"ב
3. ויקרא יח:ה
4. פסחים כה ע"א ושו"ע כאן
5. בהערותיו על נשמת אברהם כרך ב יו"ד עמ' רצג ובשו"ת צי"ץ אליעזר חי"ז סי' לב

life, except for the three cardinal sins: idolatry, (B)illicit sexual relationships and murder. He may set aside all the other Torah commandments if his life is threatened in private. But he may, if he so wishes, act strictly and give up his life if the reason for the threat is specifically anti-religious.

GLOSS: *If he can buy his life with everything he possesses, he must do so rather than set aside any negative Torah commandment. Although our Sages have said that if one is in a position to protest*

─────────────── NISHMAT AVRAHAM ───────────────

is no question as to why it is written in the context of illicit relationships. For there are examples, such as those mentioned by *Tosafot*[6] where there is no obligation to suffer martyrdom since a positive action is not involved. That being so, the ruling that one need not give up one's life for other Torah laws can be written even in the context of illicit relationships. See reference 5 for *Rav Waldenberg shlita's* further comments.

(B) illicit sexual relationships (*gilui arayot*). This includes transgressing negative commandments where the punishment is not death (or *karet*) (see *Rama*), such as forbidden bodily contacts. The *Darchei Teshuvah*[7] discusses the permissibility of gynecological examination by a male doctor. He quotes the fact that *rishonim* and *acharonim* have extensively discussed the ruling regarding a woman who has bleeding or spotting immediately following coitus with her husband (see Siman 187 below). The discussion revolves around whether one may depend on the opinion of doctors who say that the blood comes from her *prozdor* and not from her *uterus* (for blood that comes from the *prozdor* does not make her a *niddah*). None of these *poskim* raised the possibility that

she should not be permitted to subject herself to a gynecological examination. The *Noda BiYehudah*[8] discusses a case where the doctor inserts an intrauterine ring and the *Noda BiYehudah* does not say that it should be forbidden because of *gilui arayot*. The *Darchei Teshuvah* writes that one must say that this is permitted because neither the doctor nor the woman is doing this for sexual pleasure but for a medical reason. The doctor is only concerned with his professional work and there is therefore no fear of *gilui arayot*. He notes that the *Binyan Tzion*[9] was asked whether a doctor could be the obstetrician for his brother's wife even though other Jewish and non-Jewish obstetricians were available. He replied that a Jew could be the obstetrician for another's wife even if non-Jewish obstetricians were available and therefore the doctor could be the obstetrician for his brother's wife. We depend on the ruling of the *Shach*[10] who permits a doctor to take a married woman's pulse, since bodily contact is only forbidden if done for sexual pleasure. Since he is only concerned with his professional work, bodily contact, in the context of his work, is not forbidden. The *Atsei Arazim, Kreiti U'Pleiti* and the

───────────────

6. תוס׳ יומא פב ע״א ד״ה מה, יבמות נג ע״ב ד״ה אין וסנהדרין עד ע״ב ד״ה והא

7. ס״ק ח

8. שו״ת, קמא חיו״ד סי׳ סז

9. שו״ת, ח״א סי׳ עה

10. יו״ד סי׳ קצה ס״ק כ

SIMAN 157: WHEN IS MARTYDOM OBLIGATORY / §1

against another's sinning and does not do so he is held culpable for the same sin, however, if there is even (C)*a possible risk to his life he does not need to protest or spend money to prevent the other from sinning.*

On the other hand, if he would have to set aside Torah law publicly, that is, before ten Jews, and the reason for the threat is anti-religious, he must choose martyrdom (*even if all that is demanded of him is to wear his shoelaces as the idolaters do*). **However, if the reason for the threat is only to satisfy the pleasures of the idolater, he may set aside a Torah law (unless the three cardinal sins are involved). If there is a general anti-religious edict** (*specifically against Jews*) **he must choose martyrdom even if the issue is only about shoelaces.**

GLOSS: *This is only if the demand was to abrogate a negative Torah commandment. If, however, the edict was not to keep a positive Torah commandment on pain of death, he need not keep the commandment. But if the circumstances of the time were such that martyrdom was preferable, he may choose martyrdom and keep the positive commandment.*

Regarding the (D)**three cardinal sins: idolatry, illicit sexual**

─────────────── NISHMAT AVRAHAM ───────────────

Sidrei Taharah all agree with this ruling of the *Shach*.[11] For further discussion see Siman 195 below.

(C) a possible risk to his life. DANGER TO A LIMB. The *Shach*,[12] referring to a *responsum* of the *Rivash*[13] and to the *Shulchan Aruch*,[14] asks whether such a situation should be compared to a risk to one's life or to one's money. He decides that it should be compared to a risk to one's life and one may therefore act leniently and all Torah laws (unless any of the three cardinal sins are involved) may be set aside in a situation of danger to a limb even though there is no danger to life. The *Pri Megadim*[15] adds that *Shabbat* is the exception to this rule and Torah law may not be set aside unless there is danger to life. See *Nishmat Avraham*, vol. 1 *Orach Chaim*, Siman 328 (17C and D).

(D) three cardinal sins. Are these three sins the only ones in which transgression is always forbidden and martyrdom is required? Let us look at some other possibilities:

(1) ROBBING TO SAVE LIFE. The *Gemara* [16] relates an incident when King David and his troops were surrounded by

───────────────────────────────

11. אך הבית שמואל אהע"ז סי' כ ס"ק א חולק על הש"ך
12. ס"ק ג
13. שו"ת ריב"ש סי' שבו (צ"ל שפז)
14. או"ח סי' שכח סע' יז
15. פמ"ג סי' שכח מש"ז ס"ק ז. הגרש"ז אויערבאך זצ"ל בשמירת שבת כהלכתה פל"ג הערה יז*. שו"ת ציץ אליעזר חי"ג סי' צ
16. ב"ק ס ע"ב

CHAPTER 11: LAWS CONCERNING IDOLATRY

relationships and murder, he must choose martyrdom even if the demand is that he sin in private, or if the idolater only demands it to satisfy his own pleasures.

GLOSS: *With all the prohibitions connected with the cardinal sins of idolatry, illicit sexual relationships and murder, even if only a negative commandment, not carrying the death penalty, but an offshoot of one of them, is involved, one must choose martyrdom.*

--- NISHMAT AVRAHAM ---

the Philistines who were hiding behind sheaves of barley. King David questioned whether he could set fire to the sheaves, belonging to a Jewish non-combatant, thus saving himself and his men. Is it permitted to save oneself at the expense of another's possessions? The *Sanhedrin* replied that a private individual may not save himself by destroying another's possessions. However, as the king, King David was permitted to do so. *Rashi*[17] rules that it is forbidden to save one's life at the expense of another's property. However the *Igrot Moshe*[18] explains *Rashi's* ruling differently from the way it is usually understood, namely, that one may not save oneself by destroying another's possessions. He writes that the usual way that *Rashi* is understood, that this is a general rule for all life-threatening situations, is untenable (*see, however, below the view of the Binyan Tzion — reference 36*). One must say either that the danger to King David and his soldiers was very small, or else, he was certain that only by acting strictly would he be granted *Hashem's* salvation.

Similarly, the *Gemara*[19] relates the story of a saintly man who was *seriously* ill and told by the doctors that his only hope was to drink milk directly from a goat's udders, which he did. The Sages came to visit him but, on seeing the goat tied to the foot of his bed, turned around and left, proclaiming that they could not visit someone who had an "armed robber" in his house. (*Rashi* explains that the Sages forbade one to rear goats in the Land of Israel, since they pasture in fields belonging to others and thus their owner robs many.) They looked into his deeds and found that he had never transgressed except in this. He, too, proclaimed before he died that he had not transgressed any sin except this one when he had acted against an edict of the Sages. The *Meiri*[20] comments that we see that although one may set aside negative laws to save life, an edict that was enacted to prevent public robbery may not be transgressed. The *acharonim*[21] question this ruling of the *Meiri* for what the saintly man did was only to save his life and it is difficult to rule strictly where a life is at stake. The Sages who departed from him probably did so because they did not realize that he needed the goat for his cure. The *Sdei Chemed*[22] explains that it is not possible

---

17. ד"ה ויצילה

18. שו"ת, יו"ד ח"א סי' ריד. וראה בנחל אשכול על ספר האשכול הל' מילה סי' לו עמ' 119 שמסביר את רש"י בדרך אחרת

19. ב"ק פ ע"א

20. שם ומבוא גם בשיטה מקובצת

21. השירי קרבן על הירושלמי סוטה פ"ט ה"י. החיד"א בפתח עינים על מס' תמורה טו ע"ב. הבן איש חי ובן יהוידע על ב"ק פ ע"א. וראה גם בעירובין כא ע"ב שאמר ר' עקיבא: מוטב שאמות מיתת עצמי ולא אעבור על דברי חברי. וראה בשבת קלד ע"א ופסחים נא ע"ב תוסד"ה אני

22. מערכת האלף סוף אור"ק טז

SIMAN 157: WHEN IS MARTYDOM OBLIGATORY / §1   77

─────────────── NISHMAT AVRAHAM ───────────────

that the *Meiri* would disagree with all the *rishonim* who rule that one may save life at the expense of another's possessions provided that one later pays for the damage caused. However the case of the goat was different since they pasture in different fields at will and it becomes impossible to assess the damage they have caused or to whom compensation is owing. Since it is impossible for the man to pay for the damage he caused another in saving his life, the *Meiri* ruled strictly.

The *Ra'avad*[23] asks: One who flees from a would-be killer to save his life and causes damage to another's property in the process is liable unless the property damaged belongs to the would-be killer. Why? Because the threat to his life did not come from the owner of property that he damaged. Similarly if he got lost in a vineyard, he may cut his way out, but is liable for the damage caused. Yehoshua, when he conquered the Land of Israel and divided it up among the People of Israel, did so with a number of conditions. One of these was that one may cut one's way out of a vineyard if he was lost and in danger of his life, provided he paid for the damage. If so, why did King David not know that he could burn the sheaves if he paid for them afterwards? And if he did not know, surely the *Sanhedrin* would have known. Why did they say that it was forbidden to others but only permitted to him as king? One must therefore say that their reply was that for him as king of Israel it was permitted even without paying for the damage. From this we learn, concludes the *Ra'avad,* that one may save his own life at the expense of another's property, with or without his permission,

provided he pays for it afterwards.

Basing himself on the *Ra'avad*, the *Zecher Simchah*[24] writes that *Rashi* also meant that the *Gemara's* question was only about saving one's life without paying for the damages caused to another.

However, *Tosafot*[25] specifically write that King David's question was whether he would be liable for burning the sheaves in order to save his life and the lives of his soldiers. This is also the way that the *Rosh*,[26] the *Ra'avad*[27] and the *Ramban*[28] interpret the *Gemara*. And the *Yam Shel Shlomo*[29] writes that on the contrary, if one does not save himself for fear of the damage he will cause to another's property in the process, he will be held liable for his life.

The *Rashba*,[30] contrary to *Rashi* and *Tosafot*, writes that it should be so obvious that one may save one's life and not need to pay for damages caused to another's property in the process, that it need not be written. For imagine one who is dying of thirst in the desert and finds a flask of water belonging to another, should he die of thirst and not drink? How can he be considered a thief if the owner would be obligated to give him the water without charge to save his life? Even where Rebbe Akiva disagrees with Ben Petura[31] (see *Nishmat Avraham*, vol. 1 *Orach Chaim*, Siman 329B, page 218) this is only in a situation where two people are dying of thirst and there is only one flask of water which is insufficient to save both of them. Then Rebbe Akiva rules that the owner of the water need not share it with his fellow sufferer because one's own life comes before that of another. If, however, there is no danger to oneself, he is obligated to

---

23. מובא בשיטה מקובצת ב"ק קיז ע"ב
24. שו"ת, סי' רלה
25. ב"ק ס ע"ב ד"ה מהו
26. שם
27. מובא בשיטה מקובצת ב"ק פא ע"ב ד"ה מפסג ועולה
28. ב"ק במלחמות סוף פ"י ד"ה ועוד דברי הרי"ף
29. ב"ק פו סי' כז
30. שו"ת הרשב"א ח"ד סי' יז
31. ב"מ סב ע"א

NISHMAT AVRAHAM

share his water with another. How then can taking the water without permission be called robbery? As to the *Gemara* concerning one who is lost among vineyards, the *Rashba*[32] writes that Yehoshua's edict was that he may cut his way through to save his life without paying for damages. For since the law anyway is that he may do so but has to pay, there was no need for making a special edict to the effect that he may cut his way out and pay.

This controversy is not only to be found in the *rishonim* but exists among *Amora'im* and even *Tanna'im*. The *Gemara*[33] states that Rav Chisda (an *Amora*) reported that Rebbe Meir (a *Tanna*) rules that witnesses who were threatened with death if they did not sign a false document should choose martyrdom rather than sign to a falsehood. Rava (an *Amora*) said to Rav Chisda that if they were to ask him he would rule that they should sign rather than be killed, for nothing stands in the way of saving life except transgressing the prohibitions of idolatry, forbidden sexual relationships or murder. The *Ramban*[34] writes that there is another version: Rav Chisda says in the name of Rebbe Meir that they should choose martyrdom rather than sign. For although there is a *Tanna* who says that only three cardinal sins stand before the saving of life, Rebbe Meir adds a fourth — robbery. And, finally, the *Yerushalmi*[35] also states that not only if he is commanded to kill another must he choose martyrdom rather than comply, but the same would apply if he were commanded to rob him.

The *Binyan Tzion*,[36] dealing at length with the problem, disagrees with the explanation of the *Tosafot* and *Rosh*, and sides with the ruling of *Rashi* that one may not save one's life at the expense of another's property even if he will recompense him afterwards. This is also the ruling of the *Shoel U'Meshiv*[37] and the *D'var Yehoshua*.[38]

The *Binyan Tzion* draws support for his ruling from a *Gemara*.[39] Rebbe Yehudah and Rebbe Yosi were traveling together. Rebbe Yehudah was seized by an attack of *bulimos* and forced a nearby shepherd to give him his bread. Rebbe Yosi exclaimed: Why did you force him to give you his bread? When they reached the city, Rebbe Yosi was seized with a similar attack. All the citizens surrounded him with plates of honey and other sweet foods. Rebbe Yehudah exclaimed: I forced a shepherd and you forced a whole city! The *Binyan Tzion* asks why Rebbe Yosi complained to Rebbe Yehudah? All he did was to save his life? Therefore one must say that Rebbe Yehudah ruled like the *Tanna* with whom Rebbe Meir disagreed (see above in the name of the *Ramban* — reference 34) whereas Rebbe Yosi ruled like Rebbe Meir that one may not rob to save one's life. This is why he protested that forcefully taking bread from the shepherd was robbery, and forbidden. This led to Rebbe Yehudah's exclamation when Rebbe Yosi was given food by the citizens; he meant that just as in Rebbe Yosi's case there was no robbery for they gave him food willingly, so too, in his own case this was not considered robbery for what he did was *halachically* correct. Since the

---

32. מובא בשיטה מקובצת ב"ק פא ע"ב ד"ה מפסג ועולה
33. כתובות יט ע"א. וראה בריטב"א שם יח ע"ב ד"ה ובתוספות. והעיר לי ר' יונה עמנואל ז"ל משו"ת חת"ס חו"מ סי' א ד"ה ראה וד"ה ואיידי - ראה בהמעין ניסן תש"מ כרך כ גליון ג עמ' 53
34. מובא בשיטה מקובצת שם
35. ע"ז פ"ב ה"ב
36. שו"ת, סי' קסז ו-קסח
37. שו"ת, מהד"ק ח"ב סי' קעד
38. שו"ת, ח"ג סי' כד
39. יומא פג ע"ב

SIMAN 157: WHEN IS MARTYDOM OBLIGATORY / §1

NISHMAT AVRAHAM

general rule is that in any controversy between Rebbe Yehudah and Rebbe Yosi, the *halachah* is like Rebbe Yosi,[40] *Rashi* ruled like Rebbe Yosi, and particularly since Rebbe Meir also rules the same.

The *Maharam Shick*[41] disagrees with the *Binyan Tzion* and rules like the *Tosafot* and *Rosh*, and this is also the ruling of the *Tosefet Yom HaKippurim*,[42] *Chatam Sofer*,[43] *Sdei Chemed*[44] and *Maharsham*.[45]

And the *Shulchan Aruch*[46] rules: Although he is in danger of his life and needs to rob another to save his life, he may not do so unless he intends to pay him. And this is also the ruling of the *Sema*,[47] the *Gra*,[48] *Shulchan Aruch HaRav*[49] and *Aruch HaShulchan*.[50]

(2) SHAMING ANOTHER PUBLICLY. The Torah[51] tells us: "You shall reprove your fellow and do not bear a sin because of him." From this verse *Chazal*[52] learn that one may not reprove another in a way that will shame him. *Chazal*[53] also tell us that if one shames another publicly, it is as if he has killed him and will have no share in the World to Come. From the story of Yehudah and Tamar[54] *Chazal*[55] learn that it is better to throw oneself into a fiery furnace rather than shame another publicly (Yehudah had ruled that Tamar was to be burned for adultery, yet she did not publicly disclose that Yehudah was the father of her expected children.)

Tosafot[56] rule that one may not shame another publicly even if he would lose his life as a result. The reason it is not counted among the three cardinal sins is because, unlike them, it is not specifically stated in the Torah but derived by *Chazal* from a verse. *Rabbeinu Yonah*[57] rules that it is a negative commandment that is an offshoot of the sin of murder and, like the sin of murder, demands martyrdom. On the other hand, the *Meiri*[58] says that *Chazal*'s statement that it is better to throw oneself into a fiery furnace rather than shame another publicly is an eloquent comment (to indicate a moral stance) and is not a *halachic* pronouncement. The *Rambam*[59] also does not cite this statement of *Chazal* in his *Yad HaChazakah*.

The *Binyan Tzion*[60] writes that this *halachah* is hinted at by the *Rama* here, when he rules that one must choose martyrdom rather than transgress any prohibitions which are offshoots of the cardinal sins of idolatry, illicit sexual relationships or murder, even those for which there is no death penalty. For the only example we have of a negative commandment which does not carry the death penalty but which is an offshoot of murder, is the shaming of another publicly. And

---

40. עירובין מו ע״ב
41. שו״ת, יו״ד סי׳ שמז
42. יומא פב ע״ב ד״ה ואם אומרים
43. שו״ת, יו״ד סי׳ שיט ד״ה ולא עוד
44. מערכת האלף או״ק טז
45. שו״ת, ח״ה סי׳ נד
46. חו״מ סי׳ שנט סע׳ ד
47. שם ס״ק י
48. שם ס״ק ד
49. הל׳ גזילה וגניבה סע׳ ב
50. שם סע׳ ג
51. ויקרא יט:יז
52. ערכין טז ע״ב. רמב״ם הל׳ דעות פ״ו ה״ח
53. ב״מ נח ע״ב. רמב״ם הל׳ חובל ומזיק פ״ג ה״ז
54. בראשית לח:כה
55. ברכות מג ע״ב. סוטה י ע״ב
56. סוטה שם ד״ה נוח
57. שערי תשובה שער ג סי׳ קלט
58. סוטה שם
59. אנציקלופדיה תלמודית כרך ט ערך הלבנת פנים הערה 45
60. שו״ת, סי׳ קעג בשם הקול הרמ״ז על הירושלמי פ״ב דפאה. וכ״כ הפרי חדש בספרו מים חיים וכן מביא היד מלאכי בשם הרדב״ז, הכנסת הגדולה והלחם יהודה - כל זה מהבניין ציון

NISHMAT AVRAHAM

although the *Binyan Tzion* notes that we have a general rule that a *Midrash* cannot be the source of a *halachah,* this is only if a *Gemara* contradicts the *Midrash*.[61]

The *Shoel U'Meshiv*[62] also writes that one should suffer martyrdom rather than shame another publicly for it is akin to murder. However, since it is only akin to murder and not murder, *Chazal* did not obligate him to suffer martyrdom, but only permitted him to do so. Thus he will not be liable for committing suicide by needlessly sacrificing himself. However the *Yabia Omer*[63] rules that one is *halachically* obligated to suffer martyrdom rather than shame another publicly. He writes that the *Pri Chadash*[64] also rules like the *Tosafot* (reference 56) that shaming another publicly is a cardinal sin and obligates martyrdom. See also the *Pnei Yehoshua*[65] who discusses whether he is permitted to, or obligated to, suffer martyrdom.

Rav Shlomo Zalman Auerbach zt"l[66] writes that one may not save one's life by shaming another. However, if someone is attempting to destroy another's property or to cut off his limb, just as one may not desecrate *Shabbat* to save the person's property or even to save his limb (*when there is no danger to his life*), similarly one may not desecrate Shabbat to save him from being shamed. For the laws of *Shabbat* may be set aside only for one whose life is in danger. However according to the *Kappot Temarim*[67] who rules that one may save one's life at the expense of another's limb, it would also be permitted to shame him for the same purpose. However all this is only if the idolater specifically wants him to shame another or be killed. However, if the idolater threatens him with his life, and he finds a way of saving himself by shaming another publicly, it is possible that he must not do so but rather allow himself to be killed (see E below).[68]

(3) PERVERTING JUSTICE AND INCITING ANOTHER TO SIN. These are possible examples of other transgressions that may or may not be allowed even to save one's life. See what I have written[69] (including comments from *Rav Auerbach zt"l* and *Rav Waldenberg shlita* and *Reb Yonah Emanuel z"l* [70]) about perverting justice to save one's life. See, too,[69] a comment from Rav Professor Yehudah Levi *shlita* about causing another to sin, since *Chazal*[71] have said that if one incites another to sin it is worse than if he kills him (see Siman 160 below).

(4) UNDERGOING SUFFERING TO SAVE LIFE. Is one obligated to suffer to save the life of another and, if so, to what extent? The *Magen Avraham*[72] writes that it appears from the *Gemara*[73] that one is obligated to undergo suffering to save another's life. The *Ha'amek She'elah,*[74]

---

61. וכ"כ החיד"א במחזיק ברכה קונטרס אחרון לסי' נא בשם רבינו תם. הפ"ת אהע"ז סי' קיט ס"ק ה. שו"ת שבות יעקב ח"ב סי' קעה והשדי חמד מערכת האל"ף סי' צה. וראה גם בתוס' פסחים כח ע"ב ד"ה אבל וברכות יח ע"א ד"ה למחר. ויש חולקים - תיו"ט ברכות פ"ד מ"ד (וראה שם בתוס' רעק"א וראשון לציון שחולקים עליו) ושו"ת נו"ב מהד"ת יו"ד סי' קסא

62. דברי שאול על יו"ד סי' שמה סע' ב

63. שו"ת, ח"ו יו"ד סי' יג אות יב

64. מים חיים הל' יסודה"ת פ"ה ה"ב

65. על ב"מ שם

66. מנחת שלמה ח"א סי' ז עמ' נה

67. תוספת יום הכפורים יומא פב ע"ב ד"ה ואם אומרים

68. וראה שם שדן אם מותר לחלל שבת באיסור דרבנן או באיסור תורה בשב ועל תעשה משום כבוד הבריות

69. המעיין טבת תש"מ כרך כ גליון ב עמ' 25

70. לפי הערתו של העורך הנכבד ר' יונה עמנואל זצ"ל שם ניסן תש"מ עמ' 51

71. ספרי תצא פיסקא רנ"ב. הגרי"פ פערלא ז"ל על ספר המצות לרבינו סעדיה גאון, עשה כח ד"ה אלא דאכתי

72. סי' קנו

73. שבת לג ע"ב

74. פ' שלח סי' קכט אות ד

SIMAN 157: WHEN IS MARTYDOM OBLIGATORY / §1

NISHMAT AVRAHAM
---

quoting another *Gemara*,[75] writes that one is certainly obligated to undergo whatever suffering is necessary in order to save the life of another and this is also the view of the *Zer Zahav*.[76] See also the *Encyclopedia Talmudit*.[77]

However this is not a universally accepted ruling. The *Yavetz*[78] writes that there is no obligation to suffer to save another's life. Just as one must choose martyrdom rather than give up another to be tortured, all the more so one is not obligated to give oneself up to be tortured to save another's life. He writes[79] that in this matter being killed or tortured or even giving up of wealth, are one and the same. This is also the ruling of the *Taz*[80] who deduces from the *Gemara*[81] that torture is worse than death. See also the *Chochmat Shlomo*[82] who discusses whether one is obligated to save the life of another if he were to be shamed in the process or even if he must only take a lot of trouble to do so. However *Rav Auerbach zt"l*[83] expresses great surprise at this, for how can one compare one's own shame to shaming someone else.

The *Shulchan Aruch*[84] quotes two opinions in a situation where the *Beit Din* have decided on how much food a divorced, nursing mother must be given monthly by her ex-husband, and she wishes to eat more or more expensive food. There are those who say[85] that he cannot refuse on the grounds that the infant may be endangered, for her suffering takes precedence. And there are those who say[86] that he may refuse, for the life of the infant takes precedence over her suffering. The *Chelkat Mechokek*[87] and the *Beit Shmuel*[88] both express suprise at the first opinion. For why should one think that her suffering be given precedence over the possible danger to the infant? On the other hand, if her life would also be possibly endangered, who would disagree with the first opinion? According to the generally accepted rule[89] that when the *Shulchan Aruch* refers to two opinions, and prefaces each with "there are those who say" he rules like the second, we see that one is obligated to undergo suffering, if this is necessary to save the life of another.

However, *Rav Shlomo Zalman Auerbach zt"l*[90] wrote to me disagreeing with my last statement, for the slight suffering of one who would be denied eating more cannot be compared to the great suffering of one undergoing torture. He added that for a specific *seriously ill* patient, one is certainly permitted to undergo even great suffering, for example donating a kidney, to save him [*assuming that there is no danger to the life of the donor — author's note;* see Siman 28B(2) above]. See also Siman 28B(2) above regarding volunteering for medical experiments involving suffering.

---

75. סנהדרין עג ע"א
76. על האו"ה כלל נט ס"ק כא
77. כרך י ערך הצלת נפשות עמ' שנ
78. מגדל עוז באבן בוחן פנה א אות פג
79. שם אות עד
80. כאן ס"ק ח
81. כתובות לג ע"ב
82. חו"מ סי' תכו סע' א
83. שו"ת מנחת שלמה ח"א סי' ז אות ד סוד"ה ומדי
84. אהע"ז סי' פ סע' יב - הראה לי מו"ר הגרי"י נויבירט שליט"א
85. דעת הרמב"ם הל' אישות פכ"א הי"א
86. דעת הטור שם
87. שם ס"ק כב
88. שם ס"ק טו
89. כף החיים או"ח סי' יג ס"ק ז. שדי חמד כללי הפוסקים סי' יג ס"ק יד בשם הש"ך, כנסת הגדולה, אליה רבה, נחפה בכסף, יד מלאכי וברכ"י (או"ח סי' נח ס"ק ו וסי' מ ס"ק ב). וראה בשו"ת יביע אומר ח"ח או"ח סי' מב אות ב וחו"מ סוסי' ד
90. המעין ניסן תש"מ כרך כ גליון ג עמ' 49

But when the commandment involved is (E)not to place a stumbling block before one who is blind, he may set it aside to save life.

NISHMAT AVRAHAM

(E) not to place a stumbling block before one who is blind. This is interpreted not only as physical blindness. It includes causing another to sin, for example, if the idolater forces him to lend something to be used for idolatry.[91] *Rav Auerbach zt"l* told me that one must differentiate between two different situations. If what he is being compelled to do is itself the cause of the danger to his life, he may set aside the negative commandment: "Do not place a stumbling block." If, on the other hand, he is already in a situation that is life threatening and, to save his life, he does something that will indirectly lead to the death of another, this is forbidden. Thus here in Israel, a patient whose life can be saved only by a heart transplant, cannot present himself for the procedure, since the surgeon will take a heart from a donor who is *halachically* considered a *gosses*. This is more serious than the negative commandment: "Do not place a stumbling block," for here he comes voluntarily to the surgeon, thus indirectly causing the death of the donor. For further details and discussion, see Siman 339B 5(b) (page 307) below.

---

91. ש"ך ס"ק יא. וראה מה שכתב לי הגרש"ז אויערבאך זצ"ל בנשמת אברהם כרך ב יו"ד סי' קנז ס"ק ה

CHAPTER 12
The Laws of Interest

SIMAN 160
THE SEVERITY OF THE SIN OF INTEREST AND HOW MUCH ONE MUST TAKE CARE TO AVOID IT

§22 One may (A)borrow on interest to save life.

─── NISHMAT AVRAHAM ───

SIMAN 160

(A) borrow on interest. The *Taz*[1] writes that the *Shulchan Aruch* takes his ruling from a *Tosafot*.[2] The source of this ruling is a *Midrash*[3] that Ovadiah borrowed money on interest from Yehoram the son of King Ahab to feed the one hundred prophets that he had hidden in caves to escape the wrath of the king.[4] The *Taz* points out that the *Shulchan Aruch* refers to a case where a loan cannot be obtained except from a Jew who demands interest. To save a life one may take a loan from him with interest. However, the lender is certainly committing a sin for taking interest since he is not saving a life. On the contrary, he is obligated to give an interest-free loan to save life, fulfilling the verse,[5] "You shall not stand (aside) while your fellow's blood is shed." Yehoram was an idolater and one does not learn from him. Thus there was no reason for the *Shulchan Aruch* to have written this *halachah*. For the lender is certainly committing a transgression whereas it is obvious that the borrower is permitted to do so, for nothing stands in the way of saving life (except the three cardinal sins). *Rav Auerbach zt"l*[6] writes that what is so obvious to the *Taz*, that one may borrow on interest to save life even though he transgresses the prohibition, "Do not place a stumbling block before a blind person,"[7] requires further study. (*Both the lender and the borrower are forbidden by Torah law to take or give interest. By paying interest on the loan, Ovadiah caused Yehoram to commit the sin of taking interest, although he himself was permitted to borrow with interest to save life — author's note.*) For one who causes another to sin is worse than one who kills.[8] Why then is it permitted to cause him to transgress the sin of taking interest which the verse[9] compares to murder, for which his death will be everlasting and he will not be resurrected?[10] Why should this be permitted to possibly save a life from a death which is only temporary? Since one may not sin to save another from sin, how then may

---

1. ס"ק כא
2. ע"ז כו ע"ב ד"ה אני
3. שמות רבה לא:ד
4. מלכים א יח:ד
5. ויקרא יט:טז
6. מנחת שלמה ח"א סי' ז אות ד ד"ה גם
7. ויקרא יט:יד
8. מדרש רבה פרשת פינחס כא:ד. תנחומא שם ד. ילקוט שמעוני שם רמז תשעג
9. יחזקאל יח:יג. וראה ב"מ סא ע"ב
10. ילקוט שמעוני יחזקאל סוסי' שעה

SIMAN 176
WHICH TYPE OF RENTING IS PERMITTED AND WHICH IS NOT

§3 One is permitted to rent out a copper utensil and take money for its rental and (A)for the depreciation of its weight.

NISHMAT AVRAHAM

one directly cause another to sin? However it would seem that in such a case one may say, "Let him (the lender) stew in his own juice."[11] We do not have to worry for the lender, for it is he who kills himself through eternity. The question is about transgressing the negative commandment of "Do not place a stumbling block" only, and we are permitted to set this aside to save life as with any other Torah precept. The *Rav zt"l* concludes that he was pleased to see later that the *Sha'ar Mishpat*[12] used the same argument to answer the *Taz's* question.[13] The *Rav zt"l* agreed with me that if later he could avoid paying the interest he is obligated to do so, paying back only the money borrowed.

SIMAN 176

(A) for the depreciation. Although one may not rent out one's money (*which is what lending money at interest is — author*), if the borrower needs it to study its appearance or to show it to others and will return the same coins, this is permissible. The *Taz*[1] points out that if the borrower is permitted to spend the money and takes responsibility for its loss, it is considered a loan and therefore taking money for its rental is interest and forbidden. However the owner may rent out utensils which will be returned and take money for their depreciation. Since the rental is not for the loan but for their use, the money pays for their depreciation and does not abrogate the *halachah* of taking interest even though the borrower takes responsibility for their loss. Therefore utensils made of gold or silver, which do not depreciate with use, may not be rented out if the borrower takes responsibility for their loss. Medical instruments may be rented out although the borrower takes responsibility for their loss. Since these instruments depreciate with use, the rental money is not considered interest.[2]

---

11. הלעיטהו לרשע וימות - ב"ק סט ע"א וכן במשניות ירושלמי מעשר שני פ"ה ה"א. וראה בחזו"א דמאי סי' ח או"ק ט שהוא לישנא בעלמא שאינך זקוק למעשהו ולשקוד על הצלתו. ועיין בש"ך יו"ד סי' קנא ס"ק ו דגול מרבבה וגליון מהרש"א שם. ולכאורה צ"ע מהשו"ע יו"ד סי' שג סע' א ברמ"א ומהמ"ב סי' שמו בשעה"צ ס"ק ח. וראה בספר נפש חיה של הרב ראובן מרגליות זצ"ל על או"ח סי' קסט סע' ב

12. בשער דעה על יו"ד כאן וראה גם בשו"ת אג"מ יו"ד ח"ג הל' רבית סי' קס הערה יז ושו"ת שבט הלוי ח"ב סי' סט

13. וראה גם בשו"ת אג"מ יו"ד ח"ג הערות על הל' רבית בסוף הספר סי' קס הערה יז

1. ס"ק א

2. שמעתי ממו"ר הגרי"י נויבירט שליט"א

CHAPTER 13

Laws Concerning the Statutes of Idolaters

SIMAN 178
ONE MAY NOT DRESS IN THE STYLE OF IDOLATERS

§1 **One may not follow the statutes of idolaters. Thus one may not wear clothes that mark one as an idolater.**
GLOSS: *However, when something serves a useful purpose, like the special dress which a doctor wears to mark him as a doctor, one may wear it. Similarly, clothes worn as* (A)*a mark of honor or for some other such reason, are permitted.*

NISHMAT AVRAHAM

SIMAN 178

(A) a mark of honor. One may not, however, wear it if there is a possiblity that it contains a mixture of linen and wool (*shatnez*).[1] Thus, when receiving an MD (or any other) degree, if a special cloak is worn at the graduation ceremony, one must make certain that it is free of *shatnez*.

---
1. ויקרא יט:יט. דברים כב:יא

CHAPTER 14
Laws Concerning Belief in Omens

SIMAN 179
ONE MAY NOT PRACTICE SORCERY, DIVINATION OR ASTROLOGY

§1 **One may not go to astrologers or to those who cast lots.**
GLOSS: *For the Torah says:* (A)*"You shall be wholehearted with Hashem." All the more so is it forbidden to go to one who* (B)*practices divination, reads omens or practices sorcery.*

--- NISHMAT AVRAHAM ---

SIMAN 179

(A) "You shall be wholehearted with Hashem."[1] And *Rashi* comments: You should follow *Hashem* with perfect faith, put your hope in Him, do not investigate the future but accept your fate wholeheartedly. Then you will be with Him and become His portion.

(B) practices divination. The *Shach*,[2] quoting the *Maharshal*, writes that it is forbidden for a patient to go to one who practices divination or sorcery, unless there is danger to life. Even if he was at the risk of losing a limb (without danger to life) he may not do so. This is also the ruling of the *Bach*.[3] And the *Beit Yosef*, quoting the *Zohar*, writes that it is a serious sin, even if he is ill, to go to a sorcerer. This ruling of the *Shulchan Aruch* applies even if the sorcerer is a non-Jew.[4]

The *Ba'er Heitev*[5] writes that since there is no true sorcery nowadays and the Torah only forbade the sorcery of those days, it is not forbidden to go and ask of such people (non-Jews[6]) regarding the fate of a patient. The *Pitchei Teshuvah*[7] pleads the cause of those who have become accustomed to permit themselves to seek out non-Jewish sorcerers to ask them about a patient. Although the *Zohar* (quoted above) rules that this is a serious sin, this follows the ruling of Rebbe Shimon bar Yochai[8] (its author) that a non-Jew is also forbidden by the Torah to practice sorcery. However, since the *halachah* is that they are not forbidden, the Jew who goes to them only transgresses the prohibition of *amirah lenochri* and he does not fulfill "You shall be wholehearted with *Hashem*." Thus, for a patient, and particularly if he is *seriously ill*, it is possible that this is permitted. Nevertheless, one who values his soul should stay away from them.

However the *Radbaz*[9] rules that even a

---

1. דברים יח:יג
2. ס"ק א
3. בסוף הסימן כאן
4. מנחת חינוך מצוה תקיב ס"ק ג
5. ס"ק א
6. כתב לי מו"ר הגרי"י נויבירט שליט"א
7. ס"ק ב בשם השו"ת משכנות יעקב סי' לט
8. סנה' נו ע"ב
9. שו"ת, ח"א סי' תפה

§7 If one is running away from snakes and scorpions, one may (C)utter a charm so that they not harm him.

---NISHMAT AVRAHAM---

seriously ill patient is not permitted to go to them since all of these laws are negative commandments that are offshoots of idolatry. One may not learn from what the *Ramban* wrote that the Torah forbids only the act of sorcery but does not relate to one who seeks out a sorcerer, and therefore a Jew who goes to a non-Jewish sorcerer only abrogates "You shall be wholehearted with *Hashem*," similar to one who goes to an astrologer.[10] For what the *Ramban* meant was only that the seeker would not be setting aside a negative commandment but not that it was permissible, and this also seems to be what the *Rivash* writes.[11]

HYPNOSIS IN MEDICINE. The *Igrot Moshe*[12] writes that neither he nor *Rav Henkin* (*zt"l*) think that hypnosis should be forbidden for it has no connection with sorcery. However one must be concerned lest the doctor, if he is suspect of violating Torah law, will suggest to the patient, under hypnosis, to set aside a Torah law. If the patient then does so, he will not be judged as having done so unwillingly for he consulted the doctor of his own free will. If, however, the doctor is observant, or in a situation where the fear of being told to set aside a negative commandment or not to perform a positive one is unfounded, one may undergo treatment by hypnosis. This ruling includes a *non-seriously ill* patient. Nor is there need to fear that one belittles one's self, for where there is no alternative one may belittle and shame himself as stated in the *Gemara*.[13]

PSYCHOTHERAPY. The *Igrot Moshe*[14] rules that one may not go to a non-religious doctor for psychotherapy. Since treatment is not by medication but by conversation to diagnose and treat the patient by advising him how to behave and conduct himself, one must certainly be aware that he may be advised to do something which is against Torah law, or even to do something which negates the very basis of Torah or laws concerning modesty and chastity. With regard to a sick child, if the doctor is a specialist and promises the parents that he will not speak to the child of matters negating Torah law and belief, one may possibly accept his word. Therefore, if a religious psychotherapist is not available, the parents may take their child to a non-religious one, on condition that he promises not to speak to the child of matters concerning Torah and religious beliefs.

(C) utter a charm. The *Taz*[15] writes that since nothing stands in the way of saving life, if the only way one can save oneself is by transgression, he may do so. Thus in this situation, since by transgressing the negative commandment of uttering a charm[16] he can save himself, it is permitted. The *Atsei Levonah*[17] asks rhetorically why the *Taz* must tell us this, for surely it is obvious that it is permissible to transgress a negative commandment to save life. He answers that the *Taz*'s intention was to tell us that even

---

10. פסחים קיג ע"ב עיין שם ברשב"ם
11. שו"ת, סי' צב
12. שו"ת, יו"ד ח"ג סי' מד
13. סנה' כו ע"ב
14. שו"ת, יו"ד ח"ב סי' נז
15. ס"ק ד
16. דברים יח:יא
17. הגהה על השו"ע כאן

NISHMAT AVRAHAM

when one of the three cardinal sins which demand martyrdom is involved, he may transgress unless the idolater wishes to make him sin. However, if the idolater has no intention of forcing him to sin, but has decreed an edict which carries with it danger to the life of a Jew, and another Jew can save him only by setting aside a Torah law, for example, as Esther did to save the Jews,[18] it is permitted and does not require martyrdom. Similarly, it is permitted to utter a charm to save one's life, although he does so voluntarily and not because he is being forced to do so on pain of death. This is contrary to the ruling of the *Shach*.[19] However he wonders whether such a proposition holds true only with regard to *gilui arayot* — as with the example of Esther — but not with regard to idolatry and murder. With regard to idolatry and murder perhaps, one must suffer martyrdom rather than save himself.

The *Darchei Teshuvah*,[20] however, expresses surprise that the *Atsei Levonah* should have written what he did, for the *Gemara* and *poskim* all rule that one may not set aside any one of the three cardinal sins even in a situation of danger to life. Rav Auerbach zt"l wrote to me that although what the *Atsei Levonah* wrote is certainly surprising, nevertheless he believes that when the *Gemara*[21] says that Esther only transgressed the sin of *gilui arayot* passively, it was only because what she did was public knowledge. Were it not for her being entirely passive, she would have been obligated to suffer martyrdom even to avoid tying her shoelaces the way idolaters do (see above Siman 157 §1).

The *Binyan Tzion*[22] also asks why the *Taz* had to use the ruling of the *Shulchan Aruch* here as a source for the *halachah* that Torah laws are set aside to save life, since there is a *Mishnah*[23] which says that one who has an attack of *bulimos* (an acute, life-threatening hunger) may eat forbidden food and that one may use *orlah* fruit (from which one is forbidden to have any benefit) to save life.[24] The *Binyan Tzion* answers that those sources only refer to one who is already dangerously ill, but the *Shulchan Aruch* here rules that one may set aside Torah law even for a situation where he may possibly be bitten, becoming *seriously ill* as a result.

Following the ruling of the *Binyan Tzion*, what would the *halachah* be regarding one who has a date set for elective surgery under general anesthesia in the future, but becomes acutely *seriously ill* on *Shabbat* with an entirely different disease requiring urgent lifesaving surgery, under general anesthesia on *Shabbat*? When the acute surgery has been completed, and while he is still under the anesthetic, may he have the elective surgery done as well? By having both operations done now, on *Shabbat*, he will be saved the risks of a second general anesthetic at a later date for the elective surgery (this assumes that the anesthetist is sure that the risks of the two general anesthetics at different times is greater than one prolonged anesthetic for the two operations together). Since the laws of *Shabbat* are set aside not only for a life-threatening situation that is present, but also to prevent such a situation in the future, it would appear that it would be permitted for the patient to undergo both operations on *Shabbat*. Rav Neuwirth shlita agreed with this conclusion. However, Rav Auerbach zt"l wrote to me that even if

---

18. וכתב לי מו"ר הגרי"י נויבירט שליטא: קצת קשה, התם הוה קרקע עולם
19. ס"ק ט
20. כאן ס"ק כט
21. פסחים כה ע"ב
22. שו"ת החדשות, סי' קסט
23. יומא פג ע"א
24. סנה' עד ע"ב

§9 One may not [D]recite a verse from the Scriptures over a baby who is injured nor may one place a Torah scroll on him.

NISHMAT AVRAHAM

it were true that having the two operations together would reduce the anesthetic risk slightly, nevertheless one needs to weigh carefully if this slight reduction in risk would permit one to set aside Sabbath laws. See also *Nishmat Avraham*, vol. 1 *Orach Chaim*, Siman 321C whether a *seriously ill* or *non-seriously ill* patient taking medication for his illness on *Shabbat* may also take medication for a concomitant lesser illness.

(D) recite a verse. The *Taz*[25] writes that the Torah was not given to us to cure physical ailments but to cure spiritual ones. However a healthy person who only needs to be protected from becoming ill may use the words of the Torah for this purpose. This is why the *Shema* is recited before sleeping to protect him during the night. However it is also obvious that if the baby was seriously injured, one may use the words of the Torah as a cure.

The *Gemara*[26] tells us that Rebbe Yehoshua ben Levi would recite certain Psalms before retiring for the night. The *Gemara* asks how could he do this when he himself had ruled that one may not use verses of the Scriptures for a cure. The *Gemara* answers that since he did it to protect himself, it is permitted. But, if one has a wound or injury he is forbidden to whisper verses of the Scriptures over it. The *Gemara* asks: Is it only forbidden? Surely we have already learned that one who does so has no share in the World to Come. The *Gemara* answers in Rebbe Yochanan's name that that is only if he spits[27] before mentioning *Hashem's* Name (as was customary then as part of the charm). *Tosafot*[28] ask that the *Gemara*[29] elsewhere writes that verses may be said over one who has a high fever, and answer that it concerns a case of a life-threatening situation.

As to reciting Psalms for a patient, the *Chinuch* writes that this cannot be compared to uttering a charm. Although *Chazal* have ruled that one may not use words of the Torah as a cure, when one says Psalms it arouses the soul to seek *Hashem's* protection, to put one's entire trust in Him, fix the fear of *Hashem* in his heart and place all one's dependence on His loving-kindness and goodness. This awakening of his soul will lead to his protection. This is what the *Gemara* (quoted above) answered that since Rebbe Yehoshua ben Levi did it to protect himself, it is permitted. It meant that the Torah does not forbid one to recite Scriptural verses if he does so to arouse his soul so that the merit of doing so will stand by him and protect him.[30]

The *Maharsha*[31] has a profound explanation of the subject. He writes that just as there is a cure for physical illness, there is a cure for a spiritual one. For *Chazal*[32] tell us that the antidote to the evil inclination is the Torah. And, although one may not use the Torah to cure, one may use it to protect. Yet the *Gemara*[33] tells us that one who has a

---

25. ס"ק ח
26. שבועות טו ע"ב
27. This was the way incantations were said, first spitting and then saying the incantation (*Rashi, Sanhedrin* 101a).
28. שם ד"ה אסור
29. שבת סז ע"א
30. מצוה תקיב
31. שבת שם
32. קדושין ל ע"ב
33. עירובין נד ע"א

§12 One may use an ⁽ᴱ⁾amulet for a cure even though it has *Hashem's* Names written on it.

──────── NISHMAT AVRAHAM ────────

headache should delve into Torah and he will be cured. One must say that learning cures the soul and this surely will lead of necessity to a cure of the body and this is permitted. Only if he recites verses over a wound to cure it, without any intention of purifying his soul, is it forbidden.

If one looks carefully at the words of the *Gemara*, continues the *Maharsha*, it says that one who has a headache should "delve into Torah." It does not say "delve into the words of the Torah" — the conclusion of the blessing over the Torah which we say each morning. This means that even if he is too ill to speak, delving into Torah in his thoughts or by doing something that concerns Torah, will cure his soul and of necessity it will effect a cure for his headache. See also *Nishmat Avraham*, vol. 1 *Orach Chaim*, Siman 288A.

(E) amulet for a cure. See *Nishmat Avraham*, vol. 1 *Orach Chaim*, Siman 301L regarding wearing a copper bracelet on *Shabbat* and also for a discussion regarding the use of charms.

CHAPTER 15
Laws Concerning Tattooing

SIMAN 180
THE PROHIBITION OF TATTOOING

§1 (A)Tattooing involves scratching the skin and filling the scratch with blue dye or special ink or any color that leaves a permanent mark.

─── NISHMAT AVRAHAM ───

SIMAN 180

(A) **Tattooing.** The *Mishnah*[1] rules that if one writes without scratching the skin underneath or scratches the skin without filling the scratch with color he is not liable; he is liable only if he both scratches the skin and fills it with color. And the *Rambam*[2] writes, based on this *Mishnah,* that he is not liable; only if he both scratches the skin and fills the scratch with a color is he liable. What if one writes on his skin such as doctors commonly do, writing telephone numbers on the palm of their hands when paper is not available or when they are in a rush? Is this permissible or is there a Rabbinic transgression in doing so? For the *Mishnah* and the *Rambam* says of one who writes without scratching the skin underneath that he is not liable (or that he is exempt), intimating that he is liable by Rabbinic law. Moreover, *Tosafot*[3] write: He has not transgressed Torah law but he has transgressed Rabbinic law.[4]

The *Rambam*[5] rules that one who cuts off his beard with scissors (as opposed to shaving it off with a razor) is exempt from punishment (the *Mishnah*[6] writes: He is only liable by Torah law if he shaves off his beard with a razor). The *Kesef Mishneh*[7] comments that by writing "exempt" it would appear that the *Rambam* rules that this is by Torah law only, but it would still be forbidden by Rabbinic law (*this is the usual meaning of "exempt" — author's note*). But, the *Kesef Mishnah* concludes that the *Rambam* merely followed the wording of the *Mishneh* writing exempt instead of permitted without being precise, but the *halachah* is that this is permissible. One may therefore say that both the *Mishnah* and the *Rambam* quoted above may not necessarily mean that it is not permissible by Rabbinic law to write on one's skin, as is often done.

The *Minchat Chinuch,*[8] however, writes that it is uncertain from the wording of the *Rambam* whether writing or scratching alone is Rabbinically forbidden or not. From the fact that he writes exempt it would appear that one who does so transgresses Rabbinic law although

---

1. מכות פ״ג מ״ו
2. עכו״ם פי״ב הי״א
3. גיטין כ ע״ב ד״ה בכתובת
4. וראה בבית שמואל אהע״ז סי' קכד ס״ק טז ובתפארת ישראל מכות פ״ג מ״ו ס״ק מה
5. עכו״ם פי״ב ה״ז
6. מכות פ״ג מ״ה
7. על הרמב״ם שם
8. מצוה רנג ס״ק א

NISHMAT AVRAHAM

the *Kesef Mishneh* believes that it is permissible without any transgression. On the other hand, *Tosafot* write that there is a Rabbinic transgression and the *Beit Shmuel* also writes that even if he only writes without scratching he has transgressed Rabbinic law. However, Rabbinic law only forbids writing that is permanently indelible, but if he merely uses ink to write on his body he does not transgress any law.

Rav Kanievsky shlita[9] concludes that both the *Rosh* and the *Meiri* rule that there is no transgression in writing without scratching or vice versa. And although *Tosafot* appear to rule that this is a Rabbinic transgression and so does the *Beit Shmuel*, nevertheless both the *Chatam Sofer*[10] and *Dina DeChayei*[11] write that there are many *acharonim*[12] who rule leniently. Even then, this controversy is only with regard to one who scratches but does not write. However regarding one who writes without scratching there is no proof that this is Rabbinically forbidden at all. On the other hand, the *Minchat Chinuch*, *Sefer Kovetz* and *Dina DeChayei* all write that in the opinion of *Tosafot* there is a Rabbinic transgression. Therefore if one wishes to act leniently and write on his skin writing that is temporary, there are those on whose ruling he can depend. And the *acharonim* have already written that the present day custom is to act leniently.

The *Shevet HaLevi*[13] writes that the words of the *Minchat Chinuch* are surprising for if one looks at what the *Tosafot Ha-Rosh* writes, one will see that there is only a Rabbinic transgression if one scratches his skin without filling the area with ink. There is no mention of writing without scratching. The *Beit Shmuel* also only refers to writing without filling with ink, meaning scratching without filling with ink; that is Rabbinically forbidden. But writing without scratching is not mentioned and the language of the *Gemara* (*Gittin* 20b) is "wrote and scratched."

Finally, since the *Shulchan Aruch* and *Rama*, the *Chochmat Adam*,[14] *Kitzur Shulchan Aruch*[15] and *Ben Ish Chai*[16] all do not mention writing alone on the skin without scratching, it would seem that writing alone does not involve any transgression.

Rav Shlomo Zalman Auerbach zt"l told me that one may write on one's skin with a pen. Doing so does not involve any transgression of even a Rabbinic prohibition for since he intends to erase it soon, the writing is not permanent. One may not, of course, apply this ruling to writing on *Shabbat*. See *Nishmat Avraham*, vol. 1 *Orach Chaim*, Siman 340D.

---

9. פתשגן הכתב סי׳ יח
10. על גיטין שם
11. על הסמ"ג ל"ת סא
12. ספר משנת חכמים סי׳ נז ביבין ושמועה אות א. תופעות ראם בדברי היראים סי׳ שלח וספר הקובץ
13. שו"ת, ח"ג סי׳ קיא אות א
14. כלל פט סע׳ יא
15. סי׳ קסט סע׳ א
16. שנה ב פ׳ מסעי סע׳ טו

CHAPTER 16
The Laws of Shaving

SIMAN 181
IT IS FORBIDDEN TO SHAVE OFF ONE'S *PE'OT*

§4 If the person whose *pe'ot* are being shaved (A)helps in the process by moving his head to make it easier for the person doing the shaving, he is also guilty of transgressing a negative commandment. Even if he does not help in any way, it is forbidden to have his *pe'ot* shaved off. Therefore he may not have his *pe'ot* shaved even by a non-Jew.

---NISHMAT AVRAHAM---

SIMAN 181

(A) helps in the process. Rav Auerbach zt"l wrote to me that the *Shulchan Aruch* means that he will be liable to *malkot* if, at the time that he is being shaved, he moves his head to help the person who is shaving him. However, even by presenting himself to be shaved he transgresses a negative commandment, al-though he is not liable to *malkot* if he does not do anything active to help at the time. Thus a woman who presents herself to a gynecologist to have an abortion which is not sanctioned by *Halachah* will also transgress a negative commandment, although she is under general anesthesia at the time the baby is killed. See *Nishmat Avraham*, vol. 1 *Orach Chaim*, Siman 656A.

CHAPTER 17
Laws Forbidding One to Dress Like the Opposite Sex

SIMAN 182
THE LAW THAT A MAN NOT DRESS AS A WOMAN: WHAT IS FORBIDDEN

§2 There are those who (A)permit one to also shave the hair of his armpits and of his crotch if he shaves all the hair of his body from head to foot.

§6 A man is forbidden to pluck out even one white hair from among the black ones because of the negative commandment that a man may not dress as a woman. Similarly a man (B)may not dye even one white hair black.

NISHMAT AVRAHAM
SIMAN 182

(A) permit one. The Torah[1] commands us that a woman shall not dress as a man and neither shall a man dress as a woman.

The *Shach*,[2] commenting on the person discussed by the *Shulchan Aruch*, writes that he surely shaves all his body hair for a medical reason for if it were done in order to beautify himself he would, on the contrary, have made himself unsightly. The *Darchei Teshuvah*[3] writes that one is not permitted to shave off all his hair except for a medical reason and that the *Shulchan Aruch* did not consider it necessary to state this. For since it makes one unsightly, no one will do so if it is not medically required. However the *Rif* and *Rambam* forbid this even for a medical reason unless he is *seriously ill*. This *Darchei Teshuvah* is difficult to understand. For the *Rambam*[4] and the *Shulchan Aruch*[5] write that shaving the armpits and crotch is only forbidden in a country where only women do so, for then it is as if he wishes to look like a woman. This is also what the *Kesef Mishneh* writes quoting the *Rif*. It would appear that it is permitted for a *non-seriously ill* patient and perhaps even for a patient with a minor illness.

(B) may not dye even one white hair. Rav Neuwirth shlita asked Rav Auerbach zt"l about a twenty-year-old bachelor whose hair (both that of his head and beard) had turned white (not because of any medical condition) and who was ashamed to be seen in public. Would

---
1. דברים כב:ה
2. ס"ק ה
3. ס"ק ה
4. הל' עכו"ם פי"ב ה"ט
5. כאן סע' א

NISHMAT AVRAHAM

he be permitted to dye his hair black? The *Rav zt"l* answered that he would be permitted to do so, for white hair in a young person would be considered a blemish and it is not forbidden to remove a blemish. His one proviso was that he must tell a prospective wife that his hair is dyed.

The *Gemara*[6] states one may scrape off crusts of feces or crusts of a wound if it causes him suffering; he may not however do so to make himself attractive. *Rashi* explains that the reason is the negative commandment forbidding a man to dress like a woman (*therefore anything that a man does to make himself attractive is, according to this opinion, forbidden — author's note*). *Tosafot* comment that even if he is only ashamed to go out in public, this is permitted, for surely there is no greater suffering than this. The *Rama* quotes this *Tosafot* in the *Darchei Moshe*[7] and in the *Shulchan Aruch*.[8]

However there is great controversy among the *acharonim* on the subject and as to the interpretation of this *Tosafot*. The discussion revolves around the case of a young man half of whose hair and beard had turned white. The *Minchat Yitzchak*[9] writes that most *poskim*[10] forbid him to dye his hair black. However there are those who permit it.[11] He himself was asked whether a yeshivah student who had a patch of white hair among the black which grew out of a mole and made him look ugly could blacken this white hair or remove the mole surgically. The *Minchat Yitzchak* ruled that this was certainly a blemish and there is no negative commandment to forbid its removal. This was the ruling of the *Levushei Mordechai*[12] about a man who had red blotches on his face who asked whether he could have them removed medically. He reasoned that this was not to be compared with dyeing hair since hair naturally changes to white with age. But, just as one may wash one's face every morning to honor his Maker,[13] all the more so would it be permitted to remove dirt or blotches. One merely removes what is extraneous to one's body without changing his body. And, even to dye his white hairs to look like the other hairs in his beard should be permitted according to the reasoning of the *Levushei Mordechai*. However, the *Minchat Yitzchak* concludes that since even young people may have white hair,[14] dyeing it would not be permitted.

The *Sdei Chemed* writes: Who can rule leniently to abrogate a negative commandment of the Torah? How can we equate what *Tosafot* write regarding scraping off the crusts of a wound with dyeing one's hair? *Tosafot* write that even if his intention is to make himself attractive, if he does so in honor of his Maker it is permitted. That only applies to scraping off crusts of feces or crusts of a wound for they are loathsome to others. However

---

6. שבת ע"ב.
7. יו"ד סי' קנו.
8. שם סע' ב.
9. שו"ת, ח"ו סי' פא בשם השערים מצויינים בהלכה סי' קע"א ס"ק א.
10. שו"ת שואל ומשיב מהד"ק ח"א סי' רי (עיין שם שכותב: מי שרוצה לסמוך על רוב הפוסקים שהם רובא דמינכרא דלא ס"ל כהרמב"ם, פ"ב מעכו"ם ה"ו, וא"כ אינו רק איסור מדרבנן ויוכל לסמוך בזה, עכ"ל). שו"ת מהר"י אשכנזי חיו"ד סי' יט. שו"ת דברי חיים ח"ב יו"ד סי' סב. שו"ת מהר"ם שיק חיו"ד סי' קעב ו-קעג.
11. שו"ת מנחת אלעזר ח"ד סי' כג (להלכה ולא למעשה). שו"ת אבני זכרון ח"ג סי' לט (כל זמן שאין מתלבנים השערות בטבע). ספר מנחת פתים יו"ד סי' קפב. שו"ת בית היוצר יו"ד סי' מה (מתיר ע"י עכו"ם והוא לא יסייע כלל).
12. שו"ת, ח"א סי' ק
13. שבת נ ע"ב. רמב"ם הל' תפלה פ"ד ה"ג. מג"א סי' ד ס"ק א
14. פי' המשניות להרמב"ם סו"פ א דברכות

he may not remove the crusts merely to make himself more attractive. How much more so does this apply when his appearance is not loathsome to others but merely a subject of wonder and strangeness. How can others staring at him be compared to a medical need; he is not loathsome to them as is one whose face has crusts of feces or crusts of wounds. Moreover, removing crusts from one's face is only Rabbinically forbidden. Dyeing one's hair is forbidden by the Torah. How can one be lenient?[15]

The *Maharsham*[16] also forbade a thirty-year-old man in a similar situation to dye his hair. He ruled that *Tosafot* only permitted a Rabbinic law to be set aside if a situation causes suffering. Torah law may not be set aside to prevent suffering. This ruling he based on a *Magen Avraham*[17] who forbids one to wear leather shoes on *Yom Kippur* even when among non-Jews (who will laugh and make fun of him) since there is an opinion that this is forbidden by the Torah. Wearing leather shoes is forbidden only if he wears them for pleasure and one is permitted to wash off mud from his body on *Yom Kippur* since he is not washing for pleasure. Nevertheless, wearing leather shoes on *Yom Kippur* to avoid become a laughingstock is forbidden. This is also the opinion of the *Shevet HaLevi*[18] based on the fact that most *poskim* forbid it.

Many *poskim*, however, rule leniently. The *Levush Mordechai*[19] (not to be confused with the *Levushei Mordechai* quoted above) permits a young man who looks older than his age, because of the white in his beard, to dye it so that he can find a job.

The *Seridei Eish*[20] also discusses the question at length and concludes that dyeing one's hairs should be permitted according to everyone, if he does not do it to make himself attractive, but for a practical reason.[21] Furthermore, many *rishonim* have permitted one to wear a woman's clothes, shave his armpits or look in a mirror, in order to prevent suffering and shame, or as protection from injury or cold. Similarly, it is permitted to dye one's white hairs if they cause him financial loss or shame. For the basis of the negative commandment is the wish to adorn oneself with a woman's ornaments. Where this is not the reason there is no transgression.

The *Chelkat Yaakov*[22] also writes that he would have wished to permit a young man to dye his hair since the Torah only forbade it if the purpose is to make oneself attractive. However, he writes, it is difficult to rule contrary to the rulings of the *Maharam Shick* and the *Divrei Chaim* (see reference 10).

The *Igrot Moshe*[23] writes that if the reason for dyeing one's hair is not to make himself attractive but to make it easier to find a job (provided he knows that he is indeed capable of working like a young man) this is permitted. He notes that the *Taz*[24] and *Shach*,[25] quoting the *Bach*, rule that one may wear a woman's clothes to protect oneself against heat or cold so long as it does not make him look like a woman. The *Tzitz Eliezer*[26] also permits a young man with white hair to dye it black

---

15. מערכת הלמד כלל קטו ד"ה ולא ילבש בשם השו"ת מהרי"י אשכנזי חיו"ד סי' יט
16. שו"ת, ח"ב סי' רמג
17. סוסי' תריד
18. שו"ת, ח"ג סי' קיא אות ג וח"ו סי' קיח אות ג
19. שו"ת, סי' כד
20. שו"ת, ח"ב סי' פא
21. כותב: כמו שהוכחנו שלסמ"ג ולר"ת הדבר מפורש בנזיר נט ע"א
22. שו"ת, ח"ב סי' עז
23. שו"ת, יו"ד ח"ב סי' סא
24. יו"ד סי' קפב ס"ק ד
25. שם ס"ק ז
26. שו"ת, חכ"ב סי' יד ס"ק ד

SIMAN 182: A MAN MAY NOT DRESS AS A WOMAN / §6

NISHMAT AVRAHAM

so that he can find work.[27]

After *Rav Auerbach zt"l* saw all of the above he repeated what he had said before (see above) that the ruling is straightforward since the negative commandment, "A man shall not wear," does not apply here, for the question is the removal of a blemish and this is permitted. Similarly, with regard to a young man who had hair growing between his eyebrows, he ruled that this was a blemish and could be removed. He noted that *Tosafot*[28] write that whatever comes naturally with age is not a blemish even in youth and one might think that this would apply also in the case of white hairs in a young person. However in people's eyes this is considered a blemish and an abnormality, and cause for shame. Anything that is accepted as being a defect is certainly considered a blemish.[29]

WIG OR TOUPEE IN A MAN. Is this considered a head covering or is he obligated to wear a hat or *kippah* as well? The *Mishnah Berurah*[30] writes that one must do so because of *marit ha'ayin* although there are those who rule leniently. And the *Ba'er Heitev*[31] writes that because of *marit ha'ayin* one should wear a hat or *kippah* if possible. The *Sh'lah HaKadosh*[32] writes that although there is no *marit ha'ayin*, since most people wear wigs (*in his time — author*), nevertheless it is customary to act strictly when mentioning *Hashem's* Name and this is how one should act. The *Pachad Yitzchak*[33] writes that it is forbidden to sit in the synagogue or to put on *tefillin* while wearing a wig without a head covering for it (bareheadedness in a place of worship) is a transgression of adopting a custom of non-Jews. He also writes[34] that if one sits with a wig but without a head covering it is as if he sits bareheaded. If he does so in the synagogue or house of learning or while reciting *birkat hamazon* or putting on *tefillin*, he is like one who follows the customs of non-Jews. The *Chida*[35] also writes that although a wig is considered a head covering, the custom is not to say blessings without a hat. *Rebbe Akiva Eiger*[36] writes that it is possible that one must act strictly when mentioning *Hashem's* Name but one may walk wearing a wig without any other head covering and there is no *marit ha'ayin*. The *Levushei Mordechai*[37] writes that there is no transgression of the negative commandment, "A man shall not wear ... ," but it is certainly forbidden to say a blessing wearing a wig alone because of *marit ha'ayin*.

With regard to wearing *tefillin*, see *Nishmat Avraham*, vol. 1 *Orach Chaim*, Siman 27D, p. 13.

---

27. וראה בשערים מצויינים בהלכה סי׳ קעא ס״ק א
28. בכורות לז ע״א ד״ה מה ומדובר שם במום לגבי כהן
29. ראה בשו״ת חות יאיר סי׳ רב
30. סי׳ ב סוס״ק יב
31. שם ס״ק ו ובשם העולת תמיד
32. בסידורו, מובא בשערים מצויימים בהלכה סי׳ ד
33. אות כמה חציף
34. אות פירוקא
35. שו״ת חיים שאל ח״ב סי׳ לה
36. הגהות על או״ח סי׳ צא סע׳ ד
37. שו״ת, מהד״ת סי׳ קח
ס״ק ה

INTRODUCTION TO THE LAWS OF *NIDDAH*

ℰ§ The laws of *niddah* are very complicated and intricate and only those that are concerned with medical problems and situations will be discussed. In all cases, competent medical opinion must be obtained and presented to a Rav who will decide whether the woman is a *niddah* or not.

THE REPRODUCTIVE ORGANS IN A WOMAN. The *uterus* (womb) is a hollow pear-shaped highly muscular organ lying behind the bladder and in front of the *rectum*. Its inner lining (the *endometrium*), rich in blood vessels, is shed during *menstruation* — see below. The lower part of the *uterus* (the neck of the pear), the *cervix*, opens into the *prozdor* (*vagina*), part of it protruding into the anterior wall of the canal so that the closed dome of the *prozdor* lies above the opening of the *cervix* and completely encloses its lower end. The lower end of the *prozdor* opens into the *vulva* and its entrance is partially closed by the *hymen* in the virgin. The *fallopian tubes* open at the top two corners of the *uterus* (the broad base of the pear), each extending towards the *ovary* on its side. The *ovaries* are not attached to the *fallopian tubes* but are suspended nearby. The end of each tube flares into a funnel shape for the egg to fall into when released from the *ovary*. When a woman lies flat on her back her bladder opens into the *vulva* at its top end and the opening of the *prozdor* lies below it. Below and behind the opening into the *prozdor* and outside the *vulva* is the opening into the *rectum*, the *anus*. The *cervical canal* is very narrow — about three millimeters in diameter — opening slightly more during *menstruation* and much, much more before childbirth. During a gynecological examination the doctor inserts two fingers into the *prozdor* and can feel the *cervical* opening at the upper end of the *prozdor*. He cannot pass even one finger into the *cervical canal*. Before childbirth, when the *cervical canal* is much wider, he can reach its internal opening (into the *uterus*) and feel the head of the fetus. The *Chatam Sofer*[1] already wrote that the examining finger can only reach the external opening of the *uterus* and cannot be introduced into the *cervical canal* until it opens naturally. The *cervical canal* is usually closed by the juxtaposition of its walls, opening at the time of *menstruation*. This natural opening of the *cervical canal* is called *petichat hakever* (the opening of the *uterus*). This is also described by the *Maharsham*[2] and the *Minchat Yitzchak*.[3]

THE MENSTRUAL CYCLE. *Menstruation* is the shedding of the lining of the *uterus* (the *endometrium*) accompanied by bleeding and occurs in approximately monthly cycles. Each *ovary* contains many hundreds of thousands of *follicles* (fluid-filled cavities each with an egg embedded in its wall). Under the influence of different hormones a single *follicle* grows and the *endometrium* thickens and its blood vessels increase both in number and in length. The growing *follicle* finally ruptures through the wall of the *ovary* releasing its egg into the *fallopian tube* — *ovulation*. The egg travels down the tube and into the *uterus* and the ruptured *follicle* closes, forming a *corpus luteum* which secrets increasing quantities of the hormone progesterone. This hormone is responsible for the slight rise in body temperature at the time of *ovulation*; the elevated temperature remains until *menstruation*. This phase, from *ovulation*

---

1. שו"ת, יו"ד סי' קעט
2. שו"ת, ח"ב סי' מ
3. שו"ת, ח"ג סי' פד

to *menstruation*, lasts fourteen days. After fourteen days, the *follicle* degenerates, resulting in the breakdown of the thickened *endometrium* and bleeding — *menstruation*, and the beginning of a new menstrual cycle. If the egg is fertilized, the *corpus luteum* begins to produce a hormone — human chorionic gonadotrophin. Pregnancy tests are based on detecting increased levels of this hormone. *Rav Auerbach zt"l* wrote to me that any uterine bleeding will make the woman a *niddah* whether this happens on the day she is born or at a ripe old age and whether or not the above changes are present. The bleeding is not attributed to other factors (*unless there is a known pathological cause in the uterus from which the bleeding originates — author's note*) and when she purifies herself in the *mikveh* she does so saying the blessing.

The life of an egg, after its release from the follicle, is between six and twenty-four hours, whereas the life of a sperm is about three days.

The *Rambam*,[4] basing himself on the *Mishnah* and *Gemara*,[5] writes that a woman becomes ritually impure when *uterine* blood enters the *prozdor* although it has not exteriorized and is still confined within her body. He notes that *Chazal* have used metaphorical language for the reproductive organs of a woman. They called the womb the source, for it is the source of the blood of *niddah*. It is also called the chamber since it is deep within her body. The neck of the womb is the area that closes tight during pregnancy to hold the fetus within the womb and opens wide during birth; it is called the corridor, for it leads to the entrance of the womb. Above the corridor and the womb are the two *ovaries*. The tubes in which the eggs mature are called the attic. And a hole opens from the attic to the roof of the corridor and is called the "lul." During *coitus* the *ever* enters the corridor and reaches above the "lul." The *Maggid Mishneh* comments on this passage: Our teacher explained their anatomy in keeping with his expertise in surgery.

Many have written discussing, commenting and explaining this *Rambam*, but nevertheless there remain problems in matching his description to our present-day knowledge of anatomy. It would appear that he includes both the *cervix* and the *prozdor* in what he calls the corridor. Indeed, *Rav Auerbach zt"l*[6] writes that in the *Rambam's* time the doctors included the *prozdor* and the *cervix* under the same name. One could say that by "lul" the *Rambam* refers to the *cervical* opening in the top of the *prozdor* (the attic), hence his statement that the *ever* enters the corridor (the *vaginal* portion of the corridor) and reaches to above the "lul" during *coitus*. However, the difficulty in understanding what he means when he writes "the attic is the tubes in which the eggs mature" remains. And his statement that "a hole opens from the attic to the roof of the corridor and is called the 'lul'" is also most difficult. For we know that the *fallopian tubes* (what the *Rambam* calls the attic) do not open into the *prozdor*. However *Rabbeinu Chananel* writes that the attic is the bladder and lies closer to the *prozdor* than the *uterus*. This being so, "lul" must refer to the opening of the bladder (the *urethra*). This would explain the *Gemara's*[7] statement that the "lul" opens from the attic (the bladder) to the corridor (assuming that the corridor also includes the *vulva* into which both the *urethra* and the *prozdor* open[8]). It nevertheless

---

4. הל' איסו"ב פ"ה ה"ב-ה"ד

5. נדה יז ע"ב ו-מ ע"א

6. קונטרס בעניני נדה בסוף ספר אמרי אברהם ס"ק לח

7. נדה יז ע"ב

8. הגרמ"מ כשר זצ"ל, נועם כרך ח תשכ"ה עמ' רצג. וראה מה שכתב הרב ד"ר מרדכי הלפרין שליט"א, אסיא חוברת סא-סב ניסן תשנ"ח עמ' 106 הערה 17

CHAPTER 18

The Laws of Niddah

SIMAN 183
A WOMAN WHO SEES A DROP OF BLOOD NEEDS TO WAIT SEVEN CLEAN DAYS

§1 A woman who has [A]uterine bleeding becomes a *niddah*. Even if she sees only a tiny spot of blood she must wait seven clean days before immersing herself in a *mikveh*.

SIMAN 187
A WOMAN WHO BLEEDS AS A RESULT OF *COITUS*

§1 A woman who bleeds immediately following *coitus* on three successive occasions is forbidden to have further

---
NISHMAT AVRAHAM
---

remains difficult to understand the *Rambam*.[9]

A woman only becomes a *niddah* as a result of uterine bleeding and not when the source of the bleeding is the *prozdor*.[10]

SIMAN 183

INTRODUCTION. A woman becomes a *niddah* if she has any uterine bleeding, no matter how minute and irregardless of whether this is part of her regular *menstruation* or not. This state begins from the moment blood leaves her *uterus* to enter the *prozdor* even if it is not yet visible outside her body. She remains in her *niddah* state until she has undergone a process of ritual purification, culminating in immersion in a *mikveh*. During the whole of this period, no matter how long it lasts, she is prohibited to her husband. The prohibition includes any physical contact.

(A) uterine bleeding. There are women who bleed at the time of *ovulation*. As explained above (see menstrual cycle), *ovulation* occurs when an *ovarian follicle* ruptures through the wall of the *ovary* releasing its egg, together with some fluid from the ruptured follicle and blood, into the *fallopian tube*. At the same time there is a fall in the blood level of the hormone estrogen which itself can cause *uterine* bleeding and this is the accepted reason today for the bleeding. Both *Rav Auerbach zt"l* and *Rav Eliashiv shlita* told me that since it is medically accepted that this is *uterine* bleeding and not blood from the *follicle*, she becomes a *niddah*.

---

9. וראה גם במאירי על נדה שם. סדרי טהרה סי' קצד ס"ק כו. חת"ס, חידושיו על נדה יח ע"א ד"ה כאן וחזו"א יו"ד סי' קסז. ולרש"י פירוש אחר, ראה - אסיא חוברת סג-סד כסלו תשנ"ט עמ' 169

10. מדכתיב (ויקרא כ:יח) והיא גלתה את מקור דמיה ולמדרו חז"ל (נדה מא ע"ב) שאינה טמאה אלא בדם הבא מהמקור - ש"ך סי' קפג ס"ק א

relations with her husband and must be divorced. If the same occurs with a second husband, she becomes forbidden to him and must be divorced. If she marries a third time, and again bleeds immediately following *coitus* on three successive occasions, she is forbidden to have further relations with her husband. She must be divorced and cannot marry again until the cause of her bleeding is determined (*see below* §8 — *author*).

§5 However, if she has a (A)*makkah* in her uterus one may ascribe the bleeding to it.

GLOSS: *This applies only to a woman who has a fixed, unchanging menstrual cycle. However if her cycle is not fixed she can ascribe her bleeding to the makkah only if she is* (B)*certain that it*

NISHMAT AVRAHAM

SIMAN 187

(A) *makkah* in her uterus. A *makkah* is any form of inflammation, injury or growth in the *uterus* or *prozdor* from which a woman bleeds. The *Shach*,[1] quoting the *Bach*, writes that this does not mean that the bleeding comes from just any part of the *uterus* but that it comes from the *makkah* itself. Therefore if the bleeding is uterine, there must be evidence that there is a *makkah* there from which the blood originates. The *Chavot Da'at*[2] writes that only if she feels that the blood is coming from her *uterus* must she know that there is a *makkah* in her *uterus*. However, if there is no such feeling, bleeding may be attributed to the *makkah*. The *Pitchei Teshuvah*[3] writes that even if the *makkah* is in her *uterus*, nevertheless (when not expecting her menses) the bleeding does not make her a *niddah* as it may be ascribed to the *makkah*, and this is also the ruling of the *Shach*[4] and the *Chavot Da'at*. Rav Auerbach *zt"l* wrote to me that she only becomes a *niddah* when bleeding is a natural phenomenon. Thus, although the *makkah* bleeds from the very same blood vessels that bleed during *menstruation* she does not become a *niddah*. Bleeding due to the opening of the *uterus*, however, makes her a *niddah* even if it was opened by an external force (and not that it opened naturally) such as an instrument. See, however, below Siman 194A (cessation of contractions, p. 118) and D, p. 120.

(B) certain that it is the source of the bleeding. The *Ba'er Heitev*[5] writes that one may depend on a non-Jewish doctor who says that bleeding a few days after she purified herself in a *mikveh* (midcycle) is due to a *uterine makkah*, and she may cohabit with her husband. The *Pitchei Teshuvah*[6] quotes a series of *poskim* who discuss this issue. The *Chatam Sofer*,[7] however, writes that *Chazal* did not give credence regarding a known *makkah* to doctors who say that it is respon-

---

1. ס"ק יז
2. ס"ק ד
3. ס"ק כב בשם מהר"ם מלובלין סי' קיא
4. ס"ק יט
5. ס"ק יז בשם שו"ת ש"י שאלה סה ושו"ת פני יהושע סי' לב ו-לד
6. ס"ק ל
7. שו"ת, יו"ד סי' קעג

is the source of the bleeding. In any case just (C)before her expected period or thirty days from the previous period she may not ascribe bleeding to the makkah, for if so she will never become ritually impure. Staining, however, is always ascribed to the makkah.

NISHMAT AVRAHAM
---

sible for a discharge with reddish hairs. They are believed only in the context of a threat to life, and then only to the extent that their opinion makes it a possible threat to life (*this is enough to allow the setting aside of Torah law on Shabbat and on Yom Kippur — author*). However since such a discharge is a known phenomenon, *Chazal*[8] have ruled that the hairs may be immersed in water to determine if they indeed contain blood or not. Without this medical evidence, *Chazal* would not have depended on this test. See below **D,** p. 103.

The *Shach*[9] writes that even if at the time she bleeds she does not feel that the blood comes from the *makkah,* she still does not become a *niddah*. However, the *Chazon Ish*[10] rules that only with regard to a woman who bleeds as a result of *coitus* do we attribute such bleeding to her *makkah*. But, as far as the impurity of *niddah* is concerned, we do not rule leniently and attribute the bleeding to a *makkah,* but rule that she must wait seven clean days and immerse herself in a *mikveh*. If, however, it is known that her *makkah* bleeds, we attribute the bleeding to the *makkah* even with regard to the laws of *niddah*. Thus she does not need to immerse herself in a *mikveh* and remains in her previous established state of purity.

(C) before her expected period. *FIBROIDS (MYOMAS).* These are benign tumors, some of which lie just beneath the *endometrium* and intrude into the uterine cavity. They are rich in blood vessels and may cause prolonged or excessively heavy *menstruation (menorrhagia),* or uncommonly, bleeding during the cycle, such that the patient can never have the opportunity to prepare herself for immersion in a *mikveh*. Most *fibroids* cause no symptoms and the reason why some cause disproportionate bleeding is not clear but may be due to both abnormal vessels and an increase in the number of vessels.[11] If after she has been to the *mikveh* she has spotting or bleeding before she is due for her next period, and it can be shown that the bleeding is confined to the fibroids with no bleeding from the rest of the endometrium, the question arises whether the bleeding can be considered to be from a *makkah* and she will remain permissible to her husband until before her next expected period, or not.

The *Chazon Ish*[12] discusses the case of a woman who, according to her doctor, has "blisters" in her *uterus*. She bleeds profusely at the beginning of *menstruation* after which the bleeding decreases but never stops completely for a period of time sufficient for her to purify herself in a *mikveh*. Based on a *Rambam*[13] and *Rashba*[14] (quoted by the *Beit Yosef*) and a *Taz*,[15] he rules leniently that she should wait the number of days of her usual menstrual period plus another seven days. This, on condition that after she has immersed herself in a *mikveh,* her bleeding is still only minimal and not profuse. Another condition is that it is known that the

---

8. נדה כב ע"ב
9. ס"ק כד
10. חזו"א יו"ד סי' פב ס"ק ב וראה שם סי' פא
11. Lancet 357:293, '01
12. יו"ד סי' פא
13. הל' איסו"ב פ"ד ה"כ
14. תוה"א בית ז שער ד ובחי' לנדה סו ע"א
15. סי' קפח ס"ק ה

§8

If she wishes to be cured she must seek medical assistance before she has seen blood on three successive occasions following *coitus*. For, after seeing blood on three successive occasions, there are those who are unsure whether it is permitted to (D)depend on medical opinion (that she has been cured) and therefore permitted to her husband. However, there is an opinion that if a Jewish doctor tells her that she is cured she is permitted to her husband.

NISHMAT AVRAHAM

makkah causing her bleeding began while she was between periods and ritually clean, or that she was, at least, able to purify herself once after the *makkah* began. The *Chazon Ish* continues that since the "blisters" in her *uterus* bleed even at the time of her period, we attribute the bleeding to her *makkah*. Even though the menstrual blood passes via the blisters, we say that the blood is from the *makkah* and not menstrual blood, for if we say it is, then the whole concept of a bleeding *makkah* (*which does not make her a niddah*) falls away. However, he concludes that this does not include bleeding at the time of her expected period, for otherwise she will never become a *niddah* and this also cannot be.

The *Tzitz Eliezer*,[16] basing himself on a *responsum* of the *D'var Shmuel*[17] and on the *Chazon Ish*, rules that a woman with *fibroids* that bleed (when the rest of the *uterus* does not) does not become a *niddah*. The *D'var Shmuel* writes that a uterine abscess, tumor or vascular growth[18] is defined as a *makkah*. The *Shevet HaLevi*[19] writes that if she has a *makkah* in her uterus (which the doctor can see) that is known to bleed, we rule leniently if the bleeding is not at the time of menstruation. On the other hand, the *Cheshev HaEphod*[20] rules that she is a *niddah*. Rav Auerbach *zt"l* told me that bleeding from fibroids do not make a woman a *niddah* provided the bleeding is not at the time of her expected period. *Rav Neuwirth shlita* wrote to me, also ruling that she is not a *niddah* so long as she does not bleed close to the expected time of her periods. However since the details will vary from one patient to the next, in each and every case a *posek* must be consulted after the medical details have been verified.

(D) depend on medical opinion. Rebbe Elazar the son of Rebbe Tzadok[21] tells us of two questions that his father asked the Sages in Yavneh. A woman had a red scab-like discharge and turned to his father who turned to the Sages who then spoke to the doctors about it. The doctors replied that she had an internal *makkah* that was the source of her discharge, and that she should put the discharge into water; if it dissolved she would be ritually impure (since it must be blood) (*It is unclear whether the doctors suggested the test or whether the Sages demanded it — author's note*). And again, a woman had a red hair-like discharge. She turned to Rebbe Tzadok who turned to the Sages who then spoke to the doctors. They replied that she had an internal growth which was the source of her discharge, and that she should put the discharge into

---

16. שו"ת, חי"ז סי' לו
17. שו"ת דבר שמואל סי' עא
18. "מורסות שומים או טחורים" בלשון המחבר
19. שיעורי שבט הלוי סי' קפז סע' ה ס"ק א ו-ב
20. שו"ת, ח"ב סי' קכח
21. נדה כב ע"ב

water; if it dissolved she would be ritually impure.

The *Rosh*[22] asked the *Rashba*: If the discharge comes from a *makkah*, why is she impure? For the *Gemara*[23] concludes that a woman who bleeds from a *makkah* in her uterus remains ritually pure. (Unfortunately we do not know what the *Rashba* replied.[24]) The *Tosfot HaRosh* writes: Not that the doctors were certain that she had an internal *makkah*, for if so, even if the discharge dissolved in water, proving that it was blood, she would be ritually pure. But the doctors were uncertain and only said that perhaps she had an internal *makkah*; if the discharge dissolved in water it was menstrual blood (and she did not have a *makkah*) and she was a *niddah*. This is also the opinion of the *Maharik*.[25]

The *Chatam Sofer*[26] quotes the *Rosh* who says that however you look at it there is a problem. If the Sages believed the doctors, why then demand the water test? And, if they did not believe them, why ask them? The *Chatam Sofer* adds that we cannot compare this situation to that of a life-threatening situation on *Shabbat* or *Yom Kippur* for, in such an instance, if their opinion causes any doubt, that is sufficient for Sabbath and *Yom Kippur* laws to be set aside. Here, however, one needs to be completely certain before saying that the blood is not menstrual. See also above **B**.

Maran, the *Beit Yosef*,[27] writes that the doctors said the discharge was certainly due to an internal *makkah* or growth because it is unusual for a woman to have a scab-like or hair-like discharge. Therefore, even if the woman does not feel the *makkah* or the growth, the doctors are believed. The *Rama*[28] expresses surprise at the ruling of the *Beit Yosef* for the *Gemara* specifically rules that we do not depend exclusively on the opinion of the doctors but demand the water test as well. However, *Maran*, in his *Bedek HaBayit* (later additions to the *Beit Yosef*) adds that this (the doctors' opinion) applies only if the discharge did not dissolve after being immersed in tepid water for twenty-four hours. It would appear that the *Rama* had only the original version of the *Beit Yosef* before him, without the additional notes of the *Bedek HaBayit*.

The *Kreiti U'Pleiti*[29] also discusses the *Rosh's* question. He concludes that one must accept medical opinion as being certain only for an external *makkah*, for example a fractured arm or a wound, since these can be seen and the doctor understands their nature. This is not so with internal organs which the doctor cannot see. Here they will use their intellect and imagination and weigh the possibilities; and many have fallen victims and died as a result.[30] Such situations require much composure and patience and many other such traits to avoid mistakes, otherwise the outcome may be fatal.

Rav Kook zt"l[31] writes that what the doctors say can only be accepted as possibilities and not as certainties. They themselves cannot be certain, for there are times when one or many of them establish

---

22. שו"ת הרא"ש כלל ב סי' יח
23. נדה טז ע"א
24. ראה שו"ת מהרש"ם ח"א סי' יג ודעת תורה כאן. שו"ת חכם צבי סי' מו וחכמת בצלאל (פתחי נדה) כאן
25. שו"ת סי' קנט
26. שו"ת, יו"ד סי' קנח ו-קעה ואהע"ז ח"ב סי' סא
27. יו"ד סי' קצא סוד"ה כתב הר"ן
28. דרכי משה ס"ק ד
29. סי' קפח ס"ק ה
30. כי רבים חללים הפילה ועצומים כל הרוגיה, משלי ז:כו
This is a play on the verse, "For she has caused many to fall as corpses and the numbers of those she has slain is great."
31. דעת כהן סי' קמ

SIMAN 187: A WOMAN WHO BLEEDS AFTER COITUS / §8

NISHMAT AVRAHAM

an axiom in medicine (and this is so for all fields of knowledge) and many accept it as being true. But then a later generation decides, after investigation, that it was nonsense. What one builds another destroys and all their words are merely conjecture and possibilities so that everything they say is questionable. But we depend on them to rule leniently with regard to *Shabbat* and *Yom Kippur* because all negative commandments are set aside even for a possible life-threatening situation. There is no need to bring proof that the words of the doctors are only conjecture for they themselves say so; wretched is the dough whose baker testifies against it.

The *Da'at Torah*,[32] quoting the *Mei Niddah*,[33] writes that Jewish doctors today who desecrate the Sabbath have the same standing as idolatrous doctors and one cannot depend on them. However, if the woman (who bleeds following *coitus*) was also examined with an instrument (see the *Shulchan Aruch* here §2), then we may depend on the diagnosis that the bleeding was from a *makkah* and even her first husband need not divorce her (see *Shulchan Aruch* here §1). See also the *Chatam Sofer*[34] who cast doubts on the credibility of doctors in his time. The *Panim Meirot*[35] also says that we do not depend on the opinion of doctors. For he notes that the *Gemara*[36] asks how the *Sanhedrin* can inflict the death penalty on a convicted murderer, since the victim may have been a *treifah*. It answers that since most people are not in the category of *treifah*, we assume that the victim is part of that majority of most people and the death penalty may be carried out. He also wonders why the *Gemara* should raise the issue of the victim possibly being a *treifah*. Perhaps the doctors had known him and diagnosed him as not being a *treifah*, but sound and healthy. He therefore concludes that this shows that we cannot rely on a doctor's diagnosis and this allows the *Gemara* to wonder whether the victim was possibly a *treifah* and give the answer it does — that most people do not fall into the category of *treifah*.

Rav Neuwirth *shlita* questioned this deduction of the *Panim Meirot*. For even if we say that the doctors can diagnose someone as a *treifah*, the opposite is not true. They can never be sure that a person is not, for as the *Gemara* (reference 36) says, no examination can verify that someone is not a *treifah*. Rav Auerbach *zt"l* wrote to me, answering that the *Panim Meirot's* intention was to show from the *Gemara* that (regardless as to whether a doctor can give an absolutely definite opinion) we do not rely on a doctor who says that he knows the patient and says he is completely sound and healthy.

The *Maharsham*[37] writes that many authors say that from the two episodes described above (with Rebbe Elazar the son of Rebbe Tzadok), we learn that we do not depend on medical opinion, for the Sages demanded that the discharge be tested to see if it dissolved in water. The Rav of Karlin, author of the *Mishkenot Yaakov*,[38] was of the opinion that there was a printing error with regard to these two episodes and the words "put it into water, etc." were in fact part of a previous statement in the *Gemara*. As proof of this we see that these words are not included

---

32. דעת תורה כאן
33. קונטרוס אחרון מהד"ת
34. חידושיו על ע"ז לא ע"ב
35. שו"ת ח"א סי' יב
36. חולין יב ע"א
37. שו"ת מהרש"ם ח"א סי' יג בשם ספר מנחת עני בשם מהר"ח מוולאזין ומהר"י מקארלין
38. מובא במהרש"ם בשם המנחת עני ששאל את המהר"י מקארלין

SIMAN 188
THE LAWS CONCERNING
THE DIFFERENT HUES OF BLOOD

§3 A woman who has a (A)uterine prolapse and flesh-like pieces fall into her *prozdor* remains ritually clean.

---NISHMAT AVRAHAM---

in the *Tosefta's* and the *Yerushalmi's* description of the two episodes, and this was also reported in the name of *Reb Chaim of Volozhin*. The *Gra*, however, upheld the version we have in the *Gemara*.

The *Aruch HaShulchan*[39] writes that the Torah permitted doctors to heal, and bleeding after *coitus* is a disease for which there must be a cure. Therefore, if the woman stops bleeding after being treated it is as if the Torah believes the doctor when he claims that she has been cured. And, we do not differentiate between a Jewish and non-Jewish doctor; if he is a trained doctor we accept his opinion.[40]

The *Maharsham*[41] also writes that nowadays Jewish doctors who desecrate *Shabbat* publicly have lost their credibility. However, if two doctors independently give the same diagnosis, they are believed since they would not wish to jeopardize their name and, most importantly, since there is corroborative evidence that the diagnosis is correct. Many other *acharonim*[42] also discuss the subject.

SIMAN 188

(A) uterine prolapse. However, if she bleeds she is a *niddah*.[1] After the menopause, however, if there is a possiblity that there is a *makkah* and this is confirmed medically, for example, if a ring was put into the *prozdor* to support the *uterus* (*and the bleeding could be from the prozdor — author*), she would be considered clean.[2]

HYSTERECTOMY. After total *hysterectomy*, when the *uterus* and *cervix* are removed, any bleeding must come from the *prozdor* and she is therefore clean. If, however, she was a *niddah* before surgery she remains so until she has counted seven (clean) days and immersed herself in a *mikveh*.[3] However *Rav Neuwirth shlita* told me that she does not need to count seven clean days, for the bleeding now is no longer *uterine*. If a total of seven days have passed since the operation (or a total of seven days including the clean days she had before the operation) she may immerse herself in a *mikveh*. If, however, she had a *subtotal hysterectomy* where only

---

39. סע' סח
40. דלא מרע אומנתו
41. שו"ת, ח"א סי' יג. וראה שם סי' כד, כה ו-קיד וח"ב סי' עב
42. שו"ת אמרי יושר ח"א סי' קס. שו"ת מהר"ש ענגיל ח"ז סי' יב. שו"ת בית יצחק ח"א סי' ה. עיקרי הד"ט סי' כא ס"ק א ו-ח. טהרת ישראל סע' קי. שו"ת שבות יעקב ח"א סי' סה. שו"ת מהר"ם שיק יו"ד סי' קנה ו-רמג. שו"ת דברי חיים יו"ד ח"א סוסי' לא וח"ב סי' עו. שדי חמד מערכת יוהכ"פ סי' ג. דרכי תשובה כאן ס"ק צח. פתחי תשובה כאן ס"ק ל. שו"ת היכל יצחק אהע"ז ח"א סי' ח. שו"ת משפטי עוזיאל מהד"ת יו"ד ח"א סי' כו. שו"ת הר

צבי יו"ד סי' קמט. שו"ת מנחת יצחק ח"א סי' קכה ס"ק ו וסי' קכז ס"ק ב, ח"ג סי' כו ס"ק א וסי' קמה, ח"ד סי' קיט וח"ה סי' יא ס"ק ה. שמירת שבת כהלכתה פ"מ הערה א
1. ש"ך ס"ק ח. נו"ב מהד"ק סי' נח ומהד"ת סי' פט ו-קיד. חוות דעת בחידושים ס"ק ח. שו"ת יד יצחק ח"א סי' פב. ועיין גם בחזו"א יו"ד סי' פא
2. נו"ב מהד"ק סי' נה ומהד"ת סי' קיד. וראה גם בשו"ת יד יצחק ח"א סי' קעח ודרכי תשובה ס"ק לז
3. שו"ת זקן אהרן ח"ב סי' נ. שו"ת מהר"ש ענגיל ח"ו סי' יב. שו"ת הר צבי יו"ד סי' קמז. שו"ת חלקת יעקב ח"ג סי' יד. שו"ת מנחת יצחק ח"א סי' קכה ו-קכו. שו"ת שבט הלוי יו"ד סי' צ. וראה גם שם סי' קכב

GLOSS: *Even if she bleeds she remains clean so long as the pieces remain in her prozdor. We attribute the bleeding to the flesh-like pieces since we know that she has a prolapse and the bleeding is the result of a makkah.*

If, however, the piece is a large one she is *temei'ah* even if she does not see any blood, for it is ^(B)impossible for her uterus to open without bleeding. This is so even with a very early abortion when the fetus is as yet unformed.

SIMAN 189
THE LAWS CONCERNING WOMEN WHO HAVE FIXED MENSTRUAL PATTERNS AND THOSE WHO DO NOT

§33 After the first three months of pregnancy and ^(A)during the twenty-four months of breast-feeding, a woman does not establish a fixed menstrual cycle even if she has mis-

---NISHMAT AVRAHAM---

the majority of the body of the *uterus* is removed but part of the lower body together with the *cervix* is left in place, all the laws of *niddah* will apply.

What about the bleeding via the *prozdor* during surgery? Whether the *hysterectomy* is done via an abdominal approach or via the *prozdor*, the surgeon does not introduce an instrument into the cavity of the *uterus* nor does he cut into the *uterus* or *cervix*. All the surgery is done outside the body of the *uterus*, freeing it from surrounding structures. In the *prozdor* the surgery frees the *cervix* so that the whole *uterus* together with the *cervix* is removed as one piece. The *prozdor* is then sutured at the site where the *cervix* was removed. It would seem therefore that all bleeding via the *prozdor*, both during and following surgery is from the *prozdor* and, if the woman was ritually clean before surgery, she remains clean.[4] However, *Rav Auerbach zt"l* wrote to me: I used to think that a woman following a *hysterectomy* is re-

quired to immerse herself and say the blessing. But, even though I now know that I erred, nevertheless, I still think that it would be best for her to immerse herself in a *mikveh*, but she should do so without saying the blessing. (*The Rav zt"l ruled strictly for fear that the handling of the uterus during surgery might lead to bleeding from the endometrium even if only minimally — author.*)

(B) impossible for her uterus to open without bleeding. See below Siman 194D, p. 120.

SIMAN 189

(A) during the twenty-four months of breast-feeding. *Rav Auerbach zt"l* told me that nowadays it is rare for a new mother to stop *menstruating* for twenty-four months after giving birth even if she breast-feeds for that time, and this is even certainly so for a woman who miscarries. Therefore, since she might bleed on the thirtieth day of her cycle and establish a

---

4. וראה שו״ת חלקת יעקב ח״ג סי׳ יד. שו״ת הר צבי יו״ד סי׳ קמז

carried or stops breast-feeding. She is considered to have ceased menstruating throughout her pregnancy and during the twenty-four months of lactation.

§34 Once her (B)pregnancy is obvious to others, and during breast-feeding, she does not need to worry about her previous periods and is permitted to her husband.

———————————— NISHMAT AVRAHAM ————————————

new *menstrual* cycle, we must act strictly and be concerned that she might bleed at those times.

(B) pregnancy is obvious. When do we define a woman as being pregnant and assume that she has stopped *menstruating*? The *Gemara*[1] says that this applies when she is three months into the pregnancy and this is also the ruling of the *Shulchan Aruch*, §33 of this Siman. The *Ma'adanei Yom Tov*,[2] quoting the *Rashba*, writes that the reason is that at three months, when she is visibly pregnant, but not before, her head and body feel heavy to her and she is like a sick person and stops *menstruating*. The *Divrei Chamudot*[3] quotes the *Beit Yosef* that this means three full months. *Rebbe Akiva Eiger*[4] writes that even if women stop menstruating and their bodies change as soon as they become pregnant, nevertheless the *halachah* that they do not need to worry about menstruating only applies after three months of pregnancy. For the *Shulchan Aruch*[5] writes "when she is visibly pregnant" and there is no hint in the writings of the *acharonim* that this *halachah* applies even before this stage.

The *Avnei Nezer*,[6] on the other hand, also rules like *Rebbe Akiva Eiger*. And the *Sidrei Taharah*[7] writes that we require the pregnancy to be visible for this *halachah*, because only then does she feel that her head and body are heavy to her and not because we need to have evidence that she is pregnant.

The *Shevet HaLevi*[8] and the *Machazeh Eliyahu*[9] also rule that we require a full three months of pregnancy and Heaven forbid that these particular laws of *niddah* be set aside before then.

However, *Rav Eider shlita*[10] quotes *Rav Moshe Feinstein zt"l* as ruling that nowadays if tests show that she is pregnant we say that these changes in her body have taken place, even before three months. *Rav Feinstein zt"l*[11] writes that *Rebbe Akiva Eiger* apparently forgot momentarily that both the *Bach* and the *Noda BiYehudah* rule leniently even when grave *halachot* are in question. And this is certainly so if she did not examine herself or feel anything at the expected time of her period, for the prohibition is only Rabbinic. *Rav Eider shlita* also writes that *Rav Feinstein zt"l* ruled that a gynecologic examination is also sufficient to define her as pregnant for the purposes of this

1. נדה ח ע"ב
2. על הרא"ש נדה פ"א סע' ג ס"ק ס
3. שם ס"ק ה. וע"ע בדרכ"ת ס"ק קכז. ועיין בדעת תורה כאן
4. שו"ת סי' קכח
5. כאן סע' לג וסי' קץ סע' נב
6. שו"ת, יו"ד סי' רלח ס"ק ג
7. סי' קצד ס"ק ז
8. שו"ת, ח"ג סי' קיד
9. שו"ת מחזה אליהו סי' קה. וראה שם שהוא שליט"א לומד מדברי החת"ס יו"ד סי' קסט, דגם בזמן חז"ל רוב מעוברות לא ראו דמים בשלושה חודשים הראשונים של עיבורן, ולא כהגרעק"א שהשתנו הטבעים בנשי דידן
10. ספר הל' נדה ח"א עמ' 18 הערה פה
11. שו"ת אג"מ יו"ד ח"ג סי' נב

SIMAN 190
LAWS CONCERNING STAINING AND EXAMINATION

§1 A woman becomes a *niddah* by Torah law only if she feels that she has bled. *Chazal,* however, decreed that she is a *niddah* even if she only found a (A)*ketem* (*bloodstain*) on her

---NISHMAT AVRAHAM---

halachah, for things have changed today.[12]

In another *responsum*[13] Rav Feinstein zt"l rules that before her pregnancy is visible she must examine herself at the expected time of her period. After this, if there is no bleeding she must examine herself each day and also before *coitus.* If, however, she forgot to examine herself on an occasion, she is permitted to her husband. However if she forgot to examine herself at the expected time of her period, or on the thirtieth day of her cycle, she is forbidden to her husband until she does so. See the *responsum* for further details.

Rav Neuwirth *shlita* wrote to me adding that this *halachah* only applies if she *menstruated* once during her pregnancy. If she did not — and nowadays an established, fixed *menstrual* cycle is rare — there is no need for her to worry that she might bleed, for how will she know from which day she should start counting to reach the thirtieth day? She need only worry that she might bleed on the thirtieth day following a period, but not from a missed period. One wonders, he writes, why the *acharonim* discussed at such length something that has no practical significance. On the other hand, we do know that there are women who may have regular *menstrual* cycles throughout their pregnancy. Rav Auerbach zt"l wrote

to me that if a woman did *menstruate* once during pregnancy, there are those who rule strictly[14] that she needs to worry about the possiblity of bleeding on the thirtieth day even after three months of pregnancy.

Incidentally, is a woman permitted to undergo *sonography (ultrasound)* to learn what the sex of the fetus is? The *Midrash*[15] enumerates seven things which are hidden from man, one of them being the sex of the fetus. The *Yefei To'ar*[16] gives two reasons for this: This knowledge may grieve the parents throughout the pregnancy if the sex of the baby is not of their choice; if they wish for a boy and discover that this is indeed the sex of the fetus, it will diminish their joy at the birth and the mother will not have the full reward for her labor pains. On the other hand, the *Gemara*[17] also enumerates the seven things that are hidden from man but the sex of the fetus is not one of them. Rav Neuwirth *shlita* told me that it would be preferable not to undergo *sonography* for this purpose.

SIMAN 190

(A) *ketem* (**bloodstain**). A *ketem* makes a woman a *niddah* only if the blood has come from her uterus. However there are occasions when the staining on her underwear may not be blood but some reddish coloring, for example, nail polish

---

12. וראה בשו"ת באר משה ח"א סי' מח
13. שם בסוף ספר הל' נדה
14. כוסת שאינו קבוע - שו"ע הרב ס"ק קטו וחוות דעת ס"ק לז
15. מדרש רבה בראשית פרשה סה סי' יב
16. שם
17. פסחים נד ע"ב

body or clothes without feeling that she had bled, and even if, on examining herself, the examination cloth is clean. She will require a *hefseik taharah* (*after waiting a preliminary minimum of five days — author*), **which means she must examine herself to make sure she is clean, count seven clean days after this, and then immerse herself in a *mikveh*.**

§18 **Since a *ketem* only makes a woman a *niddah* Rabbinically, we rule leniently and attribute it to any extraneous factor if possible. But this is only if it is found on her garment. If, however, it is found on her body, we assume that it comes from her *uterus* (B)unless she has a wound on some other part of her body and blood from it could have stained her body.**

---NISHMAT AVRAHAM---

or a reddish stain from a red garment which has been washed together with it. May one use special tablets or papers ("dipsticks") to establish whether there is any blood in the stain or not? The *Tzitz Eliezer*[1] rules that one may never depend on this test for a ruling. However, *Rav Neuwirth shlita* wrote to me that if the *posek* was in doubt as to whether this was blood or merely coloring, he may utilize the test, if it is known to be accurate, and accept both a positive (the stain was indeed blood) or negative result. This is also true, not only in the case of a *ketem* which makes her Rabbinically a *niddah*, but even when she examined herself and found a stain on the examining cloth, in which case she may be a *niddah* by Torah law. *Rav Auerbach zt"l* told me that the only acceptable ruling is one which is made by a *posek* on the basis of what he sees. However, in a situation where the *posek* is in doubt, he may use this test to resolve his doubt. This is certainly so with regard to a doubtful *ketem* found on her body or garment when she is in midcycle, since *Chazal*[2] ruled leniently in many instances.[3]

(B) unless she has a wound. The *Rashba*[4] was asked about an elderly woman well past her menopause who found a *ketem*. She was known, however, to have *hemorrhoids* that bled occasionally. He ruled that the *ketem* could be attributed to the *hemorrhoids* provided they bled on being wiped. Not only in her case, but every woman who has *hemorrhoids* that bleed on being wiped could attribute a *ketem* to them. See also the *acharonim*[5] who discuss this situation.

Rav Auerbach zt"l wrote to me pointing out that I should write that it is advisable for a woman to wear colored underwear (during the days when she is permitted to her husband) for *Rebbe Akiva Eiger*[6] rules that a *ketem* found on colored underwear

---

1. שו"ת, חי"ג סי' פא ס"ק ג
2. ראה סע' יח כאן
3. וראה גם חי' רעק"א על סע' כג
4. שו"ת, ח"ה סי' חן
5. שו"ת רב פעלים ח"ג יו"ד סי' יג. טהרת ישראל סע' צו ו-צח. וראה גם ט"ז ס"ק כג. פ"ת ס"ק לט ודרכ"ת ס"ק קנד
6. שו"ת, מהד"ת סי' לד

SIMAN 191
THE LAW CONCERNING A WOMAN WHO PASSED BLOOD IN HER URINE

§1 If a woman (A)passed blood while urinating she remains ritually clean whether she did so standing or sitting. Even if she had a *hargashah* she need not worry since it is due to her urine. Urine does not come from her uterus and the blood is from a *makkah* in her bladder or kidney.

NISHMAT AVRAHAM

does not make her a *niddah*. [See the *Shulchan Aruch*[7] and *acharonim*[8] on this subject. And, although the *Chatam Sofer*[9] wrote that one may not rule leniently with regard to colored underwear, the *Shevet Ha-Levi*[10] wrote that the accepted opinion is of the *poskim* who disagree with him, and the *Chazon Ish*[11] also rules leniently – author.] *Rav Ovadiah Yosef shlita*[12] wrote to me pointing out that he had ruled[13] leniently on this matter, and he added a further list of *poskim* who had ruled leniently.

SIMAN 191

(A) passed blood while urinating (*hematuria*). *Rav Eider shlita*,[1] quoting *Rav Feinstein zt"l*, writes that if a woman finds blood within the lavatory bowl or in the water, she is a *niddah*, no matter how small the amount, unless she is known to have a *makkah*. In a *responsum*,[2] *Rav Feinstein zt"l* writes that she is certainly a *niddah*. And, if the blood is on the seat above the hollow part of the bowl (and it was known to be clean before she sat on it), it must have come from her body and presumably from the *uterus* unless it is certain that she had no *hargashah* at all. If it came with the urine the blood would have been within the bowl. Since it is not, it must have come either before or after she started urinating. Even if there was no *hargashah* she is a *niddah* Rabbinically. *Rav Neuwirth shlita* wrote to me that she would be permitted to her husband provided that this did not occur close to an expected period. *Rav Ovadiah Yosef shlita*,[3] basing himself on the view of *Maran* here, writes that a woman who passed blood in her urine is permitted to her husband.

If, after urinating, a woman finds blood on wiping herself she is a *niddah*, either by Torah or Rabbinic law, depending on whether she wiped herself immediately after urinating or not; see Siman 190 §51. This is the view of the *Chavot Da'at*[4] and *Rav Feinstein zt"l*.[5] The *Shulchan Aruch*[6]

---

7. כאן סע׳ י

8. ברכ״י שם. שו״ת תשובה מאהבה ח״א סי׳ קסג. שו״ת מהרש״ם ח״א סי׳ פא. חזו״א סי׳ פט ס״ק ד ושו״ת שבט הלוי ח״א סי׳ פז. וע״ע פ״ת ס״ק כא. שו״ת חת״ס סי׳ קסא מובא בפ״ת ובשו״ת מנחת יצחק ח״ד סי׳ קיח אות ג שמחמירים

9. שם

10. שם

11. שם

12. הערה על נשמת אברהם כרך ב יו״ד עמ׳ רצא

13. שו״ת יביע אומר ח״ג יו״ד סי׳ י

1. ספר הל׳ נדה ח״א עמ׳ 28 הערה קכו

2. שם בסוף הספר, אות יג

3. שו״ת יביע אומר ח״ו יו״ד סי׳ טו או״ד

4. סי׳ קפג חידושים ס״ק ב

5. ספר הל׳ נדה שם. וראה גם בשערים מצויינים בהלכה סי׳ קנג ס״ק ז

6. סי׳ קצ סע׳ י. וראה שם סע׳ נא שמבואר שם דאם שהתה יותר מכדי שיעור בדיקה מהטלת המי רגלים עד הקינוח, טהורה מדאורייתא

CHAPTER 18: LAWS OF NIDDAH

GLOSS: *There are those who rule strictly in certain circumstances, if she once happened to see blood during urinating. However, if*

NISHMAT AVRAHAM
---

rules that a *ketem* that is found on an object that cannot become *tamei* (*halachically* impure) does not make the woman a *niddah*. What then is the *halachah* regarding paper? The *Pitchei Teshuvah*,[7] quoting the *Noda BiYehudah*,[8] writes that our paper has the same *halachah* as felt and does become *tamei*. The *Noda BiYehudah*[9] quotes a great *posek* who questioned his ruling, for the *Rambam*[10] specifically writes that paper does not become *tamei*. This *posek* said that it cannot be compared to felt because paper is a new entity; it has taken on a new face and is now unlike the matter from which it is derived. He replies that there is a difference between our paper and the paper used by previous generations. Ours is made from rags or crushed plants, and has the same *halachah* as felt. The paper then was made from leaves and barks of trees which were smoothed out and prepared as paper, and cannot become *tamei*. It is to such paper that the *Rambam* referred.

The *Chatam Sofer*[11] also rules that a *ketem* found on paper makes a woman a *niddah*. The *Sidrei Taharah*,[12] on the other hand, writes that there is no difference between the paper used by *Chazal* and ours. For, although our paper comes from linen, the linen has been ground and has taken on a new face. However, the *Chochmat Adam*[13] disagrees with the *Sidrei Taharah* and rules that paper can become *tamei*.[14]

The *Igrot Moshe*[15] writes that since toilet paper is soft and not washable and therefore cannot be used again and certainly not if soiled with blood, it cannot become *tamei*. He agrees with the *Sidrei Taharah's* ruling but differs with him about the reason. The controversy among the *poskim* was regarding hard paper that was not rendered useless after being used once, and this certainly does not apply to toilet paper which is used for wiping. Similarly, he writes elsewhere[16] that blood found on toilet paper and tissues, which are thin, does not have the *halachah* of a *ketem*; that the discussion by the *Chatam Sofer* and the *Chochmat Adam* was with respect to thick paper that can be used many times, and not our thin paper which is completely useless after being used once. From this ruling of the *Igrot Moshe* one can deduce that where the question of *niddah* is Rabbinic (that is, she did not wipe herself immediately, see Siman 190 §51), after wiping herself with toilet paper, she would be considered ritually clean.

However, *Rav Neuwirth shlita* wrote to me that if upon wiping herself, she introduced some of the paper within the *prozdor*, she would certainly be a *niddah*, for the blood found on that part would not be a *ketem* but rather blood found during a self-examination. This would be so even if she used toilet paper and even if she did not wipe herself immediately after urinating. Even if she was certain that she only

---

7. סי' קצ ס"ק יח
8. שו"ת, תניינא סי' קה
9. שו"ת שיבת ציון סי' לט
10. הל' כלים פ"ב ה"א
11. שו"ת, ח"ו סי' פא
12. ס"ק יט
13. כלל קיג סע' ח. וכנראה שגירסא אחרת היתה להפ"ת ולהחת"ס
14. וראה גם בחזו"א יו"ד סי' פט ס"ק ב ו-ג
15. שו"ת, יו"ד ח"ג סי' נג
16. בתשובות בסוף ספר הל' נדה אות יד

SIMAN 191: BLOOD IN HER URINE / §1

she is accustomed to seeing blood in her urine and (B)*feels pain while urinating, she is in all cases not a niddah.*

--- NISHMAT AVRAHAM ---

wiped herself externally, and did so a little while after urinating, many *poskim* would still rule strictly and treat it as if it were a self-examination. However, the *Shevet HaLevi*[17] writes that there is no need for her to look at the paper with which she had wiped herself. *Rav Neuwirth shlita* also wrote to me that she should wipe herself and throw away the paper without looking at it.

Rav Auerbach zt"l agreed with *Rav Neuwirth shlita* and wrote to me adding that according to the *Noda BiYehudah*[18] even the slight introduction of the examination cloth (or paper) into the beginning of the *prozdor* would make it a self-examination and, if blood were found, she would be a *niddah*. However, if there was great need, one may rule leniently.

In all cases, immediate medical advice should be sought for it is easy to determine from a subsequent urine sample whether she is having *hematuria* or not, and a *posek* must then be consulted.[19]

With regard to using a nylon cloth, the *Minchat Yitzchak*[20] writes that there is no such thing as a garment that one wears that cannot become *tamei*. For though there is debate among the *poskim* as to whether paper can or cannot become *tamei*, all would agree that even paper can become *tamei* if it is worn as a garment.

See the *Taharat Yisrael*[21] and especially the *Maharsham*.[22] Thus a nylon garment could also become *tamei* and blood found on it will have the status of a *ketem*. However the *Igrot Moshe*[23] writes that since nylon is made from oil which comes from the depths of the earth, it certainly cannot become *tamei* even by Rabbinic law; it is like earthenware. It therefore follows that blood found on it does not have the status of a *ketem*.

(B) feels pain while urinating. The *Cheshev HaEphod*[24] was asked about a pregnant woman who felt pain while urinating (and whose urine contained blood). She had been diagnosed as having a bladder infection. He ruled that she did not need to examine herself and was ritually clean. He based his ruling on the *Panim Meirot*[25] who writes that an elderly woman with a similar story is ritually clean and need not examine herself. Blood in the urine has the status of a *ketem* and the *halachah* of *ketem* does not apply to an elderly woman. True, the *Sidrei Taharah*[26] expressed surprise at this statement of the *Panim Meirot*, for the *Shulchan Aruch*[27] rules that the *halachah* of *ketem* does apply to an elderly woman.[28] However, the *Cheshev Ha-Ephod* writes that the *Gaon of Tshubin* agreed with him.[29]

---

17. שיעורי שבט הלוי סי' קצ סע"י ס"ק ג ד"ה ומ"מ
18. שו"ת, סי' מו
19. שיעורי שבט הלוי סיכום הלכות כאן ס"ק ו. וראה בט"ז סי' קצ סע"ק כג
20. שו"ת, ח"ד סי' קיח
21. בבאר יצחק סי' קצ אות קיא
22. שו"ת, ח"א סי' ב
23. שו"ת, יו"ד ח"ג סי' נג
24. שו"ת, ח"א סי' קכו
25. שו"ת, ח"א סי' ס
26. סי' קצ ס"ק צה. וראה גם בפ"ת סי' קצא ס"ק ב
27. סי' קצ סע' נב
28. וכותב החשב האפוד: ושמעתי פעם מפי הגאון מטשעבין שבשו"ת מהרי"א הלוי סי' ס יישב דברי הפנים מאירות בטו"ט. וראה שם בחשב האפוד שמעתיק את המהרי"א הלוי בעניין זה
29. עיין בשו"ת שבט הלוי ח"ה סי' קכג שמחמיר באשה שיש לה כאב באיזור הכליה וראתה דם בעת עשיית צרכיה

SIMAN 193
HYMENEAL BLOOD

§1 When a bridegroom consummates his marriage to a (A)virgin bride, he completes this act of *mitzvah*, then

---
NISHMAT AVRAHAM

SIMAN 193

(A) virgin bride. *Rav Auerbach zt"l* wrote to me that if a bride-to-be is worried lest she have a period and be a *niddah* on her wedding night it would seem reasonable to have her take tablets which postpone the menstrual period and rely on them. For generally, though fear itself can postpone a menstrual period,[1] nevertheless a woman experiencing fear is forbidden to her husband at the time of her expected period. This is because it is possible that if she forgets her fear she may then bleed, or that she may forget her fear during *coitus*. But now that tablets are available that have been proven to postpone menstruation, one may permit a woman who is taking these tablets to be with her husband even during the night or the day preceding the expected first day of her period. Similarly, she would be permitted to him on the day or night following, provided she examines herself and confirms that there was no bleeding. The *Radbaz*[2] specifically permits a woman to her husband if she is taking medication to postpone her menstruation even though in his time the effect of the medication was not certain. However one must be certain that the tablets taken today completely prevent menstruation without even the tiniest amount of spotting.

In a series of *responsa*[3] discussing a woman who is taking tablets to prevent pregnancy, *Rav Moshe Feinstein zt"l* warns: One should know that there are women who bleed a little while taking these tablets. Therefore, during the whole of the twenty days that she takes the tablets during the first month, she should wear white underwear and, in addition, wear a pad. She should also examine herself every day towards evening. She should not bathe but take showers.

Rav Neuwirth shlita also told me that a bride who takes tablets before her wedding day needs to examine herself every day.[4]

Ideally, a bride-to-be should not take any medication to prevent her being *temei'ah* on her wedding night. Rather she should put her trust in Heaven and work out her dates as best she can. However, if she is extremely nervous and feels she must take medication, there are two forms of treatment that are available: either (1) taking combined estrogen/progesterone tablets or (2) taking progesterone-only tablets.

(1) Combination tablets. There are two possibilities: (a) The bride starts taking them about six weeks before her wedding date and stops some twenty days or so before the wedding night. This would

---

1. סי' קפד סע' ח
2. שו"ת, ח"ה סי' קלו
3. שו"ת אג"מ אהע"ז ח"ד סי' עב, ח"ב סי' יז וח"ג סי' כד. וראה גם שם ח"א סי' סה
4. ולא הבינותי, למה אין כאן דין של כתם (כשמדובר שאין לה שום הרגשה)? תלבש בגדי צבעונים כפסק השו"ע והרמ"א סי' קצ סע' י ולא תצטרך לחשוש? וראה

בחזו"א יו"ד סי' פט, שו"ת ציץ אליעזר ח"י סי' כג ושיעורי שבט הלוי סי' קצ ס"ק ה ו-ז. וצ"ל שחזו"ל לא גזרו על כתמים כי היה אז במה לתלות לקולא, אך כאן אדרבא, היא לוקחת כדורים שבמקרים לא מועטים גורמים לדימום ולכן אם היא רואה דם יש לה דין נדה. וראה להלן מה שכתבתי בשם מו"ר הגרי"י נויבירט שליט"א

SIMAN 193: HYMENEAL BLOOD / §1

separates himself from her. (B)She is now a *niddah*, even if she examines herself and does not find blood.

― NISHMAT AVRAHAM ―

then induce "withdrawal bleeding" within a day or so, giving her sufficient time to undergo the process of ritual purification and immersion in a *mikveh* before her wedding night. However, withdrawal bleeding does not always come as planned and, particularly in young women, it may be delayed by as much as a week or two. (b) The bride takes "high-dose" combination tablets until after the marriage has been consummated.

(2) Progesterone-only tablets. If she has a period twenty days or more before the wedding she should take them for two weeks before the wedding and until after the marriage has been consummated. If, on the other hand, she has a period within twenty days before the wedding, there is no need for medication for she then has enough time to undergo the purification process and immerse in a *mikveh*. But, if she is still very nervous, the tablets may be taken for a week before the wedding and until after the marriage has been consummated.

I have consulted with religious colleagues both here in Israel and in the United States and there is no consensus of opinion among them; each claims that the method, other than the one he uses, causes spotting.

Rav Neuwirth shlita told me that although a bride cannot examine herself properly because of her *hymen*, and therefore may have minimal bleeding close to her wedding which will go unnoticed, *Chazal* have not demanded that she examine herself as a married woman does. If she is ritually clean during the seven clean days, she is permitted to her husband. However, this only applies when nature is allowed to take its usual course. However, once she interferes with this by taking tablets, if she now has spotting as a consequence and misses seeing it because of her inability to examine herself properly, she will be *temei'ah*, albeit unknowingly.

Therefore, in each case, expert gynecological advice should be sought in good time and the approval of a *posek* must then be obtained.

(B) She is now a *niddah*. What is the *halachah* regarding a bride whose *hymen* is so fibrous and tough that surgery is required before she can have relations with her husband? The *Shach*[5] quotes the *Rosh* who discusses why a bride is a *niddah* after *hymeneal* bleeding (which is obviously not *uterine*). The *Rosh* writes that it appears that the reason for this strict ruling is not because of the fear that there is *uterine* bleeding as well as bleeding from the torn *hymen*. It is because this *mitzvah* is performed by every bridegroom and not every one of them can differentiate between whether she sees blood or not. Besides, the newly married husband may not be able to conquer his emotions. Therefore *Chazal* have decreed an unchanging rule for all circumstances. The *Cheshev HaEphod*[6] comments that the reason given by the *Rosh* applies only to bleeding as a consequence of *coitus*. However bleeding following surgery on the *hymen* is not different from the blood of any other *makkah*. Thus, at first sight, she should not be considered a *niddah* after such surgery. However, the *Cheshev HaEphod* says that the *Maharsham*[7] ruled that even after surgery she is a *niddah*. One must therefore assume that the

---

5. סי׳ קצ ס״ק ג
6. שו״ת, ח״ב סי׳ קיז
7. שו״ת, ח״א סי׳ רי

NISHMAT AVRAHAM

Maharsham believes that after *Chazal* decreed that *hymeneal* bleeding following *coitus* makes her a *niddah*, we do not differentiate between one cause of bleeding and another.[8]

However, the *Binyan Tzion*,[9] quoting *Rav Natronai Gaon*,[10] writes that *Chazal* were concerned that *hymeneal* bleeding might also cause *uterine* bleeding and make her a *niddah*.[11] In another *responsum*[12] the *Binyan Tzion* quotes *Rav Hai Gaon* who also writes that *hymeneal* bleeding causes the *uterus* to bleed as well, since the first time a woman has *coitus* she shudders and trembles inwardly and this brings about *uterine* bleeding. For it is written that the queen (Esther) shuddered greatly when she heard that Mordechai had put on sackcloth and ashes,[13] and the *Gemara*[14] says that she became a *niddah* as a result. Therefore a bride must undergo the process of purification and immersion after the first *coitus*.[15] The *Binyan Tzion* concludes that we see that the *Geonim* wrote explicitly that the decree of *Chazal* regarding *hymeneal* bleeding rested on their concern of possible accompanying *uterine* bleeding; had their *responsa* been available to the *Rosh*, he surely would not have written as he did. The *Shevet HaLevi*[16] and the *Tzitz Eliezer*[17] also rule strictly.

The *Igrot Moshe*,[18] on the other hand, writes that a bride is permitted to her husband following *hymeneal* surgery for the blood is from a *makkah* and she is not required to immerse herself in a *mikveh*. *Chazal* decreed that she is a *niddah* only following the first *coitus* but not following surgery. The *Minchat Yitzchak*,[19] however, wrote to him asking him to reevaluate the problem for he, the *Minchat Yitzchak*, thought that one should rule strictly like the *Geonim* and the *Maharsham*; and the *Mahari Shtief*[20] also rules strictly.

I found difficulty in understanding the reasoning behind the strict ruling. For, as explained in my introduction, the *hymen* is a membrane, situated at the *vulva*, that partially covers the entrance to the *prozdor*. In most cases where the bridegroom has difficulty in penetrating the *hymeneal* opening into the *prozdor*, the doctor merely enlarges the opening a little; in rarer cases he may have to cut away some of the *hymen*. How does this cause such shuddering that *uterine* bleeding is induced? And, if this is so, why then does a woman not become unclean after all minor gynecological surgery?

Rav Ovadiah Yosef shlita[21] writes that this strict ruling applies only to the first *coitus* and not to surgery of the hymen. *Rav Auerbach zt"l* also told me that one may rule leniently like the *Igrot Moshe* adding, in a letter to me, that were we to rule strictly because of shuddering, then we would also need to do so for any surgery in that area.

---

8. וראה גם בדרכי תשובה כאן ס"ק טו ועקרי הדת יו"ד סי' כא ס"ק י
9. שו"ת, סי' סט
10. שו"ת הגאונים סי' קסה
11. אי אפשר לבא דם בתולים בלא צחצוחי זיבה
12. סי' קסח
13. אסתר ד:ד
14. מגילה טו ע"א
15. כתב: ותטבול במים חיים. וראה ברש"י סנהדרין פז ע"א ד"ה הלכות אחד עשר (ועיין שם ברש"ש) ובבכורות נה ע"ב ד"ה מקוה ובספר הפרדס הל' נדה
16. שו"ת, ח"ה סי' קיט
17. שו"ת, ח"י סי' כה פי"ב
18. שו"ת, יו"ד ח"א סי' פז
19. שו"ת, ח"ד סי' נח
20. שו"ת, סי' קלא
21. שו"ת יביע אומר ח"ד סי' י

פס' בשמחת חתן וכו'. וכ"כ בספר חסידים סי' תקט. אך עיין ברש"י שבת סה ע"ב ד"ה שמא, נדרים מ ע"ב ד"ה ועביד ומו"ק ה ע"א ד"ה מרגילין ובהגהות הב"ח שם. ועיין ברמב"ן סו"פ מצורע. חת"ס על נדרים שם ושו"ת שואל ומשיב תליתאי ח"ב סי' צב. שאלתות פ' אחרי סי' צו ובהעמ' שאלה שם ס"ק יב

SIMAN 194
THE LAWS CONCERNING
CHILDBIRTH AND MISCARRIAGE

§1 A woman [A]following childbirth is ritually unclean like a *niddah* whether she gives birth to a live baby, a stillborn

───────────── NISHMAT AVRAHAM ─────────────

Following the surgery, if she bleeds after the first *coitus*, then she is considered a *niddah* like any other bride following the first *coitus*. However, if she does not bleed after the first *coitus*, she is not a *niddah*[22] (a bride following the first *coitus* is a *niddah* whether she bleeds or not — *Shulchan Aruch*).[23]

SIMAN 194
(A) following childbirth. At what stage does she fall into the category of one who has given birth and become ritually unclean? The *Shulchan Aruch*[1] defines childbirth (or labor), with regard to setting aside Sabbath laws, from the time she crouches to give birth, when bleeding is obvious, or when she is unable to walk without aid. The *Sidrei Taharah*[2] writes that these signs are not exclusive and her husband must avoid physical contact with her from the time she has regular contractions and asks for the midwife. *Petichat hakever* (the opening of the *cervix* which makes her ritually unclean) is not caused by her crouching to give birth but rather it is because she is close enough to childbirth to be put on the special bed used for giving birth that we are concerned that this may occur.

(1) BREAKAGE OF WATER. If this happens during contractions, Sabbath laws may be set aside for her as necessary.[3] If she examines herself and does not find blood, she is not a *niddah*. The *Teshuvah MeAhavah*,[4] quoting the *Noda BiYehudah*, writes that if there is no discharge, or there is a thin discharge (that does not require a large opening of the *cervix*) or a watery discharge, she is not unclean since, under these circumstances, there can be *petichat hakever* without *uterine* bleeding. I also heard this from *Rav Auerbach zt"l*.[5] *Rav Neuwirth shlita* also told me that if she examines herself and does not find blood she is not unclean.

It is also well known that some women have a breakage of water during their pregnancy, without any contractions, and, a multiparous woman may have a two-finger opening of her *cervix* (normally open about three millimeters only) a month or two before she gives birth. With regard to both these cases, *Rav Neuwirth shlita* told me that we follow the ruling of the *Noda BiYehuda* to the *Teshuvah MeAhavah* and she is not considered unclean.

The *Torat HaShelamim*[6] also writes that a woman who is known not to menstruate during pregnancy and breastfeeding is not unclean, even if there is *petichat hakever*. The *Sidrei Taharah*[7] agrees with the *Torat HaShelamim*. And this is also the ruling of many *acharo-*

───────────────

1. או"ח סי' של סע' ג
2. כאן ס"ק כה
3. שמירת שבת כהלכתה פל"ו סע' ט
4. שו"ת, ח"א סי' קטז
5. וכ"כ הגאון זצ"ל בתשובה בספר מראה כהן עמ' קפד שאלה ו
6. סי' קצ ס"ק ב
7. שם ס"ק ג

22. שו"ת אג"מ, מנחת יצחק וביע אומר שם
23. והמהר"י שטייף מסתפק בדבר משום לא פלוג. וראה גם בדרכי תשובה כאן ס"ק כה

NISHMAT AVRAHAM

nim,[8] although others disagree.[9] The *Chazon Ish*[10] writes that there is no disagreement between the two groups; each has a different situation in mind.

(2) MUCUS PLUG. The discharge of a blood-tinged mucus plug precedes the onset of labor by hours or days. Normally, only a few drops of blood escape with the mucus plug; more substantial bleeding is suggestive of an abnormal cause.[11] *Rav Neuwirth shlita* told me that even if the plug does not appear to be blood-tinged, she is a *niddah*.[12]

(3) CESSATION OF CONTRACTIONS. The *Pitchei Teshuvah*,[13] quoting the *Noda BiYehudah*,[14] writes that when *Chazal*[15] said that there cannot be *petichat hakever* without *uterine* bleeding, they did not differentiate between a natural opening of the *cervix* or one that is caused by the insertion of an instrument[16] by a doctor. They also did not differentiate between a young woman (who still *menstruates*) and an elderly woman after her menopause; a pregnant woman or one who is breast-feeding. In all circumstances, there cannot be *petichat hakever* without *uterine* bleeding. The *Noda BiYehudah*[17] also writes that when they said there cannot be *petichat hakever* without *uterine* bleeding, this was only if there was a discharge of something solid from the *uterus*, for example a fetus or some solid material which was thicker than a straw. However if there is no discharge at all or only a discharge of something that is very thin or fluid, there can be *petichat hakever* without *uterine* bleeding. If this were not so, how can there then be such a concept as *uterine* bleeding which does not make her unclean. Surely there must have been some opening of the *cervix*?

The *Pitchei Teshuvah*[18] notes that the *Nachalat Shivah* says that a pregnant woman whose labor and contractions have stopped is unclean for there must have been some opening of the *cervix*. The *Chavot Da'at*[19] also quotes the *Nachalat Shivah* that a woman who reaches the stage that she is put on the special bed to give birth, but whose labor and contractions cease, becomes unclean and will require ritual purification, for at this stage there is *petichat hakever* and there cannot be *petichat hakever* without uterine bleeding. However, the *Chavot Da'at* himself disagrees with this ruling. For at the end of this Siman (§14), the *Shulchan Aruch* rules that following Caesarian section, if she only bleeds via the abdominal wall and not through her *cervix* she is not unclean (*this possibility does not exist today — author*). The *Chavot Da'at* asks how can she not be a *niddah* according to the reasoning of the *Nachalat Shivah*. Surely

---

8. חכמת אדם כלל קיג סע' ב. שו"ע הרב סי' קצ סע' ב. ערוה"ש שם סע' יג. גליון המהרש"א שם והיעב"ץ ח"ב סי' ה מובא בפת"ש שם ס"ק ז
9. רעק"א חידושיו שם. שו"ת נודע ביהודה תניינא סי' קב. שו"ת חת"ס סי' קסח
10. סי' פט ס"ק א ע"ש טעמו
11. Williams Obstetrics, 21st edition, p. 252
12. ובשעורי שבט הלוי עמ' רמה כותב: פקק הרחם שיוצא לפני הלידה, יש לחוש עליו משום פתיחת הקבר, ויעשה שאילת חכם
13. כאן ס"ק ד
14. שו"ת, תניינא יו"ד סי' סו"ס קב
15. נדה כא ע"ב וכן נפסק להלכה סי' קפח סע' ג
16. אמנם כתב הנו"ב "כגון שהרופא הכניס אצבעו או איזה כלי ופתח פי המקור" אך כבר כתב עליו בבינת אדם סי' כג דמ"ש כגון שהרופא הכניס אצבעו, אגב שיטפיה כ"כ ולא דק וכו' וראה גם בשו"ת חת"ס סי' קעט שכתב דהן אשה הבודקת את עצמה בחורין וסדקין והן המילדת שבדקה, לעולם לא יגוע בפתיחת הקבר שהוא המקור וכו' ובשום אופן אינה יכולה להכניס אצבעה לפנים עד שתפתח בטבע. וכ"כ השו"ת חסד לאברהם תאומים תניינא יו"ד סי' מו. שו"ת מהרש"ם ח"ב סי' מ. שו"ת אבני נזר יו"ד סי' רכד ושו"ת אג"מ אור"ח ח"ג סי' ק. וראה גם בדרכ"ת כאן ס"ק יט
17. בשו"ת תשובה מאהבה ח"א סי' קטז
18. ס"ק ח בשם הבה"ט של הרב מהרי"ט שהביא בשם תשובת נחלת שבעה סי' ט
19. כאן

SIMAN 194: CHILDBIRTH AND MISCARRIAGE / §1

or even after a miscarriage, and even if she (B)does not see any blood.

---NISHMAT AVRAHAM---

she had been put on the special bed. The ruling that there cannot be *petichat hakever* without uterine bleeding applies only if she discharged something that forced the *uterus* to open. Only then do we say that this cannot be without some uterine bleeding. But, if the *uterus* opens without discharging anything (when her contractions ceased), then there is no uterine bleeding and she is not unclean. The *Teshuvah MeAhavah*[20] also disagrees with the *Nachalat Shivah*. In his view she is not a *niddah* and, he writes that the *Noda BiYehudah* agreed with his ruling. This is also the opinion of the *Chatam Sofer*.[21]

(4) INCOMPETENCE OF THE CERVIX DURING PREGNANCY. One of the causes of miscarriage is incompetence of the *cervix* which begins to dilate during pregnancy. This may be treated by *cervical cerclage* (suturing the *cervix*) to keep it closed until labor. The procedure will cause bleeding from the *cervix*. Rav Auerbach zt"l told me that this is categorized as bleeding from a *makkah* and the woman is not a *niddah*. This ruling, he added, does not contradict his ruling regarding injection of material into the *uterus* under pressure (see below, **D (3) - Tubal patency**). In that procedure an instrument is inserted into the uterus. If this is done close to an expected menstrual period, the procedure itself may bring on early menstruation. However *cervical cerclage* does not involve opening the cer-

vix; on the contrary, the purpose is to close it. Thus there is no fear of menstrual bleeding and she is not a *niddah*.

(5) DILATATION OF THE CERVIX DURING LABOR. Rav Neuwirth shlita told me that even if the doctor or midwife found that there was dilatation of the *cervix* on examination, she is not a *niddah* so long as she herself did not feel the *cervix* opening or did not find evidence of bleeding. Rav Auerbach zt"l agreed with this and wrote to me that this is because we know that it is the fetus which is causing the *cervix* to open. However, the *Igrot Moshe*[22] writes that perhaps one should act strictly following the ruling of the *Chavot Da'at*[23] that she should nevertheless examine herself. If, however, she did not do so, she need not act strictly. The *Igrot Moshe* continues that if there was cervical dilatation preparatory to childbirth but childbirth was delayed by some hours or even a day, one must act strictly following the ruling of the *Sidrei Taharah*.[24] However *Rav Ovadiah Yosef shlita*[25] rules leniently.

(B) does not see any blood. Following childbirth, or miscarriage forty days or more after conception, a woman is *temei'ah* both because of uterine bleeding (*niddah*[26]) and because of childbirth — *tumat ledah* even if there is no bleeding. The difference between the two is in Torah law only; nowadays she is *temei'ah* regardless.

The *Gemara*[27] speaks of a "dry child-

---

20. שו"ת, ח"א סי' קיד
21. שו"ת, סי' קעט
22. שו"ת, יו"ד ח"ב סי' עו
23. ס"ק א
24. ס"ק כה. ועיין בטהרת הבית ח"ב עמ' נ-נב
25. טהרת הבית ח"ב עמ' נ-נד
26. כותב השו"ע כאן: עכשיו בזמן הזה כל היולדות חשובות יולדות בזוב וצריכות לספור ז' נקיים. לכן כתבתי שהיא גם טמאה טומאת נדה בכל אשה נדה היום שצריכה ז' נקיים משום חומרת זיבה. וראה בשיעורי שבט הלוי סי' קצד ס"ק א
27. נדה מב ע"ב

§2

A woman who ^(C)miscarries within forty days from conception need not consider the fetus *(that is, it does not make her temeiah because of childbirth — author)*, **but she must be concerned and, even though she does not see any bleeding, she becomes a *niddah*.**

GLOSS: *For there ^(D)cannot be petichat hakever without uterine bleeding.*

───────────── NISHMAT AVRAHAM ─────────────

birth," that is, childbirth without bleeding for example when the head of the baby has entered the *prozdor* (see §10 below). Rashi explains that although the head of the fetus is still within the *prozdor* the woman is considered to have given birth and is ritually unclean because of childbirth (*tumat ledah*[28]). How does this concept fit in with the axiom that there cannot be *petichat hakever* without *uterine* bleeding (see also below §2)? The *Kesef Mishneh*[29] writes that although the *Rambam*[30] does not accept this axiom of Rebbe Yehudah (and rules like the *Tanna* who disagrees with Rebbe Yehudah[31]) that there cannot be *petichat hakever* without *uterine* bleeding, nevertheless in this case he rules that she is unclean like a *niddah* even though she did not find any evidence of bleeding. For, the passage in the Torah (reference 28 above) says she is *temei'ah* as a result of childbirth whether she sees blood or not.[32]

(C) miscarries. ECTOPIC PREGNANCY. Occasionally a pregnancy occurs outside the womb, for example within a *fallopian tube*. Such a situation is life threatening for the mother and suitable treatment, medical or surgical, must be given to abort the fetus. *Rav Auerbach zt"l* wrote to me that the *halachot* of a woman who has given birth (*tumat ledah*) do not apply to her even if the diagnosis is made forty or more days after conception, but if she bled via the *uterus* she is a *niddah*, and this is also the ruling of the *Shevet HaLevi*.[33] *Rav Neuwirth shlita* told me that a boy born after such a pregnancy (if he is a firstborn) must have a *Pidyon HaBen*, and *Rav Auerbach zt"l* added that the *Pidyon HaBen* be performed with the blessing.

(D) cannot be *petichat hakever*. The *Noda BiYehudah*[34] writes that when *Chazal*[35] said that there cannot be *petichat hakever* without uterine bleeding, they did not differentiate between a natural opening of the cervix or an opening caused by the insertion of an instrument by a doctor. The *Chazon Ish*[36] asks what the basis for this statement of the *Noda BiYehudah* is. He notes that the *Gra*[37] agreed with the *Noda BiYehudah* that there is indeed no difference between the *uterus* opening naturally or through an external cause. However, he concludes that in practice, the matter requires thought.[38]

---

28. ויקרא יב:ב
29. ריש פ"י מהלכות איסו"ב
30. שם פ"ה הי"ג
31. פסק כת"ק דרבי יהודה נדה כא ע"ב. ועיין בתוס' כריתות י ע"א ד"ה קמ"ל בשם השאלתות. וכן ברש"י ריש פ' תזריע
32. עיין בהגהות מיימוניות שם
33. שו"ת, ח"ח סי' רלט
34. שו"ת, תניינא יו"ד סו"ס קב
35. נדה כא ע"ב וכן נפסק להלכה סי' קפח סע' ג
36. יו"ד הל' נדה סי' פג
37. סי' קפח ס"ק כג
38. וראה גם בשו"ת אבני נזר יו"ד סי' רכד

NISHMAT AVRAHAM

(1) INSTRUMENTATION. If an instrument is introduced into the *prozdor* but cannot, because of its size, be introduced into the *cervical canal* and *uterus*, the woman is ritually clean even if there was blood on the instrument or she found blood immediately afterwards. The bleeding is from the *prozdor* and does not make her a *niddah*. This is so only on condition that the examination was performed in midcycle or at least a few days before her expected period and she had the status of ritual purity beforehand.[39] This is the ruling of the *Beit Yitzchak*,[40] the *Atsei Ha-Levanon*,[41] the *Maharsham*[42] and the *Tzitz Eliezer*.[43]

There is no consensus, however, among the *poskim* regarding bleeding after an instrument is passed into the *cervical canal*. There are those,[44] including Rav Auerbach zt"l, who rule strictly because there may have been a *petichat hakever* during the examination, but many others[45] rule leniently.[46]

If the instrument was passed into the *uterus*, the *Igrot Moshe*[47] writes that even if she does not find blood on examination and the doctor, even if he is an observant Jew, tells her that there was no bleeding, she is nevertheless *temei'ah*. For it is impossible to be certain that she did not bleed a single drop and the gynecologist missed it. However this is only if the instrument opened the cervix to the diameter of a *pikak*. If it did not, one may rule leniently as long as she did not see blood, and she need not examine herself. The *Igrot Moshe*[48] writes that the diameter of a *pikak* is about three-quarters of an inch (about nineteen millimeters).[49]

(2) X-RAY OF THE *UTERUS* AND *FALLOPIAN TUBES* WITH CONTRAST MEDIUM (*HYSTEROSALPINGOGRAPHY*). This procedure is done soon after the last day of *menstruation* (to avoid radiation during pregnancy) and is carried out as follows: The *cervix* is held firmly by a *tenaculum* (a type of forceps) placed on the outside of the canal within the *prozdor*. This will cause minimal bleeding from the outer wall of the *cervix* and will not make the patient *temei'ah*. A thin instrument, less than three millimeters in diameter, is then passed through the *cervical canal* into the *uterus*. Contrast (radio-opaque) fluid is injected via the instrument to fill the *uterus* which can then be X-rayed. Although this may also cause bleeding due to the instrument scraping the inner wall of the *cervical canal*, the bleeding is from a *makkah* and will not make the patient a *niddah*. Rav

---

39. עיין בשו"ת אג"מ או"ח ח"ג סי' ק
40. שו"ת, יו"ד ח"ב סי' יד
41. סי' נ, מובא בשערים מצויינים בהלכה סי' קנג סוס"ק טז
42. שו"ת, ח"ד סי' קמו
43. שו"ת, ח"י סי' כה פי"א
44. שו"ת בית יצחק יו"ד ח"ב סי' יד ושו"ת שאילת שלום מהד"ק סי' נט, מובא בשערים מצויינים בהלכה סי' קנג סוס"ק טז
45. שו"ת עונג יו"ט סי' פד. שו"ת דברי מלכיאל ח"ב סי' נו וח"ג סי' סא. סדרי טהרה כאן סע' ט. מנחת שי סי' נד. שו"ת מהרש"ם ח"ד סי' קמה ושו"ת מלמד להועיל יו"ד סי' סה
46. וראה גם בדרכ"ת כאן ס"ק יט. שו"ת הר צבי יו"ד סי' קנב ושו"ת מנחת יצחק ח"ג סי' פד
47. שו"ת, או"ח ח"ג סי' ק
48. שם. וראה גם שם יו"ד ח"א סי' ו-פט ובדברות משה על ב"ק סי' טז ענף ט

49. Generally, the cervical canal is closed but can easily be opened to a diameter of 3 millimeters. Most procedures are done using instruments of 3-7 millimeters. There are occasions when a 12-millimeter-diameter instrument is passed into the uterus (for the procedure of dilatation and curettage), but to do this general anesthesia is required and the cervical canal is gradually enlarged by passing instruments of increasing diameter into it. A 20-millimeter instrument is passed only to evacuate a dead fetus. The *Halachos Niddah* (page 7 note 33) also questions this ruling.

NISHMAT AVRAHAM

Neuwirth shlita agreed with this. The *Igrot Moshe*[50] writes that as long as the instrument is less than three-quarters of an inch in diameter (see reference 49), the doctor is believed if he says that any bleeding is due to the instrument rubbing against the wall of the *cervix* since she was known to be clean beforehand. See, however, *Rav Auerbach zt"l's* ruling in the next paragraph.

(3) TUBAL PATENCY. Insufflation of the *fallopian tubes* is rarely performed today. However a ruling of *Rav Auerbach zt"l* in this context has important implications. When it was in vogue, a thin tube was inserted into the *uterus* (via the *cervical canal*) and air or contrast fluid injected under pressure into the *uterus* in an attempt to force open a blocked tube and facilitate pregnancy. The procedure was done at a time when she could have relations with her husband and become pregnant before the blockage recurred. As above (2), the procedure led to bleeding both from the *prozdor* and from the *uterus* and was due to a *makkah*. However, *Rav Auerbach zt"l* wrote to me that even if the doctor certainly scratched the inner wall of the *cervix* and the bleeding is therefore from a *makkah*, nevertheless if the procedure was done close to her next period, it would be best to rule strictly. For the very introduction of an instrument into the *uterine* cavity could cause her to menstruate prematurely. She would then be possibly *temei'ah* if there is indeed bleeding. *Rav Neuwirth shlita* wrote to me commenting that if this is so she should be *temei'ah* even if she did not find evidence of bleeding, since it could be that she did bleed a little but this was obscured by the contrast material used during the procedure. *Rav Auerbach zt"l* wrote to me in reply that one should not act strictly if there was no evidence of bleeding.[51]

(4) HYSTEROSCOPY. A thin instrument is inserted into the *uterus* allowing the gynecologist to view the inside of the *uterus*, take biopsies or do minor procedures such as *polypectomy* (removal of polyps). The procedure is carried out after the end of menstruation, that is during the counting of the seven clean days before immersion in a *mikveh*, and leads to *uterine* bleeding. *Rav Neuwirth shlita* told me that the bleeding is from a *makkah* and does not affect the counting of the seven clean days.

(5) PAP. SMEAR. This procedure involves the taking of samples from the *prozdor* and the outer wall of the *cervix* (by abrasion) and from the *cervical canal* by rotating a brush inserted within it. The patient may experience a little bleeding. According to the *Igrot Moshe*[52] she retains her clean status, even if samples were taken from inside the uterus, but according to *Rav Auerbach zt"l*, if the samples were taken from the uterus close to an expected period, it would be best to rule strictly.

(6) CERVICAL CULTURE. The *cervical canal* is swabbed to screen for infectious agents and the abrasion may cause bleeding. The same *halachic* controversy mentioned with a *hysterosalpingography* and *Pap. smear* will be present here (see above).

The *Pap. smear* and *cervical* culture should both be done, if possible, just before the next expected period, thus avoiding a *halachic* problem.

(7) INTRAUTERINE DEVICE (IUD). Bleeding caused during the insertion of the device is due to the use of a *tenaculum* to hold the *cervix* steady, but may also

---

50. שו"ת, או"ח ח"ג סי' ק
51. וראה שו"ת חשב האפוד ח"ב סי' ז ובחזו"א סוף ספר זכרון שאול (הגר"ש ברזם ז"ל) ח"א
52. שו"ת, או"ח ח"ג סי' ק

SIMAN 194: CHILDBIRTH AND MISCARRIAGE / §2

NISHMAT AVRAHAM

come from the *uterus*. The same *halachic* controversy mentioned with a *hysterosalpingography* and a *Pap. smear* will be present here (see above). If there is bleeding or spotting after its insertion, there are gynecologists who believe that this is due to a local irritative effect of the IUD.[53] This bleeding would therefore be from a *makkah* and she should be permitted to her husband. However others have told me that it is impossible to be certain that the bleeding is not due to hormonal disturbances.[54] Because of this uncertainty, *Rav Neuwirth shlita* rules that she is *temei'ah* and this is also the ruling of the *Igrot Moshe*.[55] After the insertion, even if there was no bleeding, it would be wise for her to examine herself daily for a month to be sure that the device is not causing spotting. On the other hand, *Rav Ovadiah Yosef*[56] rules that bleeding at a time other than that of her expected period is from a *makkah* and she is ritually clean. If the IUD releases a hormone (progesterone) any bleeding or spotting must be attributed to this and she will be *temei'ah* according to all opinions.

Rav Auerbach zt"l wrote to me that when the device is removed she must act strictly because of the possibility of *petichat hakever*. According to the gynecologists there is always some spotting at the time of removal. The presence of the device does not prevent her from undergoing the process of purification and immersion in a *mikveh*.[57]

I asked *Rav Auerbach zt"l* what the *halachah* would be concerning a woman who is two months after childbirth and is breast-feeding. An IUD had been inserted on the ruling of a *posek*. Would she still be clean even if she had *uterine* bleeding? Since she is breast-feeding she will not be menstruating and, in addition, the bleeding is due to a *makkah* (the insertion of a foreign body into the *uterus*)? Or, since nowadays not every woman who is breast-feeding stops menstruating, she will be a *niddah*? *Rav Auerbach zt"l* wrote to me that she will be a *niddah*. However it would be better if the device is inserted while she is still *temei'ah* as a result of childbirth.

I also asked *Rav Auerbach zt"l* what the *halachah* would be for a woman who already has an IUD and who is breast-feeding, and who finds blood on self-examination. A woman with an IUD who bleeds is a *niddah*, but in this case she is breast-feeding. May one assume that the bleeding is due to a *makkah* [because of the presence (as opposed to the insertion) of a foreign body in her *uterus*] or do we not differentiate and she is a *niddah*? The *Rav zt"l* told me that she is a *niddah* even though there is no *petichat hakever*.

(8) DILATATION AND CURRETAGE (D & C). This procedure is carried out under general anesthesia and the *cervix* dilated to 7-9 mm. so that the currete can be inserted into the *uterus*. The procedure is used to determine the cause of and treat *menorrhagia* and other forms of abnormal bleeding and to remove an incomplete miscarriage. Since the patient will be a *niddah* anyway, the procedure itself will be irrelevant as far as this is concerned.

---

53. אסיא חוברת סג-סד כסלו תשנ"ט עמ' 138-147

54. ראה באסיא חוברת ב ניסן תשל"ג עמ' 19 וחוברת כט סיון תשמ"א עמ' 15

55. שו"ת, אהע"ז ח"ג סי' כא

56. טהרת הבית ח"א עמ' רנג

57. שו"ת ציץ אליעזר ח"י סי' כה פ"י וחי"א סי' סג. שו"ת מנחת יצחק ח"ו סי' פז וראה שם שכותב שקשה להן לטהר עצמן כי שכיחי בה הרבה כתמים. ויש להזהר בכל אלה, בכל אשה ואשה לפי מזגה

§10 Birth is defined as the moment that (E)the baby's forehead leaves the *prozdor* even if it is still within the vulva.

---NISHMAT AVRAHAM---

(E) the baby's forehead. The *Shach*[58] writes that both the *Tur* and the *Beit Yosef* write "most of the forehead." Elsewhere, the *Shach*[59] also writes that we see from the *Shulchan Aruch*[60] that once the forehead has appeared it is as if the whole head has appeared, and this is also the opinion of the *Levush*, the *Sema*[61] and the *Perishah*.[62] The *Tur* also writes that if the baby was a breech delivery he is considered born when most of the body has emerged. These definitions are of importance in defining when a *brit milah* should be performed and will be discussed later — Siman 262:4 and 266:8. For a definition of the moment of birth, see Siman 305E below.

INDUCTION OF LABOR. The *Igrot Moshe*[63] writes that the practice of arranging a convenient date with the obstetrician to induce the delivery of the baby is forbidden, even though this will be done by medication only and not by Caesarian section. It is only permitted in a situation where the woman is having a difficult labor and her life is in danger. Although she will not undergo surgery and the date of childbirth will be brought on artificially by medication only, it is better for the fetus to remain in its mother's womb until it is born spontaneously. Even if the doctors think that there is no benefit to the fetus by remaining inside the mother's womb, nevertheless one must remember that childbirth causes suffering and is life threatening and should not be brought on artificially even though the danger will be exactly the same as when she gives birth spontaneously. Therefore it is forbidden to induce delivery unless there would otherwise be danger to life. In any case, the *Igrot Moshe* explains, he believes that there is a more compelling reason to forbid this. Although it is commonly accepted, as stated above, that childbirth is dangerous, this is not true. For, since Hashem created the world for man to be fruitful and multiply, He surely created it so that procreation would be a blessing and not a danger. *Hashem* decreed that procreation is a positive commandment and it is unreasonable to think that He would command a woman to endanger herself so that a man can fulfill the positive commandment of procreation. Moreover, since this commandment is not incumbent upon women, we certainly cannot say that a woman is permitted to endanger herself. Therefore we must conclude that there is no danger whatsoever in pregnancy and childbirth; that is, *Hashem* has given His assurance to this.[64] Although women do die during childbirth, this is because of some other offense, as the *Mishnah* (*Shabbat* 31b) states. This promise of *Hashem* is only operative for spontaneous childbirth at its natural time, for it is then that *Hashem* gave His promise at Creation that she would not endanger herself, along with the positive commandment to procreate.

Rav Auerbach zt"l wrote to me that according to this explanation of the *Igrot Moshe*, it may be possible to permit a

---

58. ס"ק י
59. יו"ד סי' יד ס"ק א
60. חו"מ סי' רעז
61. שם ס"ק ו
62. כאן. וראה גם בסדרי טהרה ס"ק כו
63. שו"ת, יו"ד ח"ב סי' עד
64. See, however, *Shulchan Aruch Orach Chaim*, Siman 330 §1 and §3 and *Nishmat Avraham*, vol. 1 *Orach Chaim*, Siman 330F.

SIMAN 195
WHAT IS FORBIDDEN WHEN ONE'S WIFE IS A *NIDDAH*

§2 A husband may (A)not touch his wife when she is a *niddah*,

─────────── NISHMAT AVRAHAM ───────────

pregnant woman not to fast on *Tishah B'Av* even in her ninth month, if there was a possibility that it would induce childbirth before its time. However this would not be a reason for her to eat on *Yom Kippur*.

The *Shevet HaLevi*[65] also rules like the *Igrot Moshe*, although he disagrees with his thesis. *Rav Ovadiah Yosef shlita*[66] also rules that one should not induce childbirth unless it would be dangerous for the mother to continue her pregnancy and quotes the *Ari z"l* who also forbade this. *Rav Neuwirth shlita* also told me that childbirth should not be induced as long as there is no danger to the mother or the fetus in not doing so.

The *Igrot Moshe* also discusses the question of a woman who previously underwent a Caesarian section because of a small pelvis and who now requires a second Caesarian section for the same reason. The doctors advise her not to wait until labor starts but to book a date for the surgery according to when they think she will have reached term. He rules that she should not do this, since, whenever there is surgery, there is some danger and injury, and this must not be imposed before its time, even though she will undergo the same suffering and face the same danger a day or two later. Therefore she should wait and only have the Caesarian section when she starts labor and the doctors say that surgery can no longer be delayed. If, however, the doctors say that it would be dangerous for her to wait, she may have the Caesarian section at that time, but she should not arrange a predetermined date for the operation.

The *Shemirat Shabbat KeHilchatah*[67] notes that although one may not do anything from Wednesday onwards that will lead to the need to set aside Sabbath laws to save life, this does not apply to a pregnant woman at term who has not yet started to have contractions.[68] It would certainly be permissible to induce labor, even though she will possibly deliver on *Shabbat*, if the doctor says that her life or that of the baby may otherwise be endangered.[69]

SIMAN 195

(A) not touch his wife. The *Darchei Teshuvah*[1] writes concerning one who became blind as a result of disease and for whom it was dangerous to go out into a public thoroughfare to work. Since he was totally blind and would not be able to prevent himself from falling over obstacles in the street, he asked whether his wife could hold him and guide him when she is a *niddah*. He replied that even if her hands were covered (*for example, she wore a glove — author*) it would be forbidden; however if they both held on to different ends of a stick or piece of cloth, this would be permitted, but only if it was absolutely necessary. *Rav Auerbach zt"l* [2] wrote to me that if the woman saw that her husband was about to fall or bump into something, she could pull him away by holding

---

See *Nishmat Avraham*, vol. 1 *Orach Chaim*, Siman 248A. 69.

65. שו"ת, ח"ו יו"ד סי' קכח
66. ספר טהרת הבית ח"ב עמ' נד
67. פל"ב סע' לג
68. הערה צח

1. ס"ק ז בשם שו"ת פרי השדה ח"ג סי' קיט
2. לב אברהם ח"ב פ"ז סע' ט

not even her little finger. He may (B)**not pass anything directly to her nor receive anything directly from her lest he touch her bare skin** (*similarly it is forbidden for husband and wife to throw anything from one to the other*).

NISHMAT AVRAHAM
---

his clothes. If necessary she could even pull him away by holding onto him himself. He later told me that this would only be permissible if he needed to go out or went to perform a *mitzvah* such as going to pray or to study Torah. However it would not be permitted to go for an unnecessary walk should there be a chance that a situation would arise which would result in his *niddah* wife touching him. See also the *Rama*.[3] *Rav Auerbach zt"l* added that the same *halachah* would apply if the wife were blind.[4]

The *Be'er Moshe*[5] permits a wife who is a *niddah* to put *tefillin*[6] on her sick husband who is unable to do so himself and has no one else to put them on him, provided she wears gloves. This is only permissible if he would otherwise not be able to perform the *mitzvah* of *tefillin* that day. He bases his ruling on the *Shach*[7] who permits contact between a husband and his *niddah* wife so long as it is not done out of affection.[8] *Rav Auerbach zt"l* agreed with me that one could add the extra reason that he was an ill person and therefore too weak to consider sinning with his wife. However he added that this would apply only to one who is really ill and wholly weak and if there is no other possiblity for him to perform the *mitzvah* without her help. And, even if he is not generally ill and weak throughout his body but paralyzed, it would probably be permitted so that he could perform a *mitzvah*, provided there really is no other alternative.[9]

A man and his *niddah* wife may together help a paralyzed patient to sit, stand and walk if they hold him, one on one side and one on the other.[10]

(B) not pass anything directly. The *Pitchei Teshuvah*[11] writes that the *Tashbetz*[12] permits a husband to take a baby from his *niddah* wife's arms since there is a concept that "a living person carries himself." (See *Nishmat Avraham*, vol. 1 *Orach Chaim*, Siman 308A.) Therefore she does not really do anything since it is the baby who moves from her arms to his. The *Aruch HaShulchan*[13] expresses surprise at this ruling asking what relevance this concept has to the *halachot* of *niddah*.[14] The *Shevet HaLevi*[15] writes that one may not rely on this ruling, for the *Tashbetz* seems to follow his ruling that the husband and his *niddah* wife may throw an object from one to the other. However, since we rule that this is forbidden (see *Rama* here), the same would apply in taking a baby from his *niddah* wife (*or vice versa — author*) even if we do use the concept of "a living person carries himself."

---

3. כאן סע' טו
4. וראה גם בשו"ת ציץ אליעזר חי"ב סי' נח
5. שו"ת, ח"ד סי' ו
6. See *Nishmat Avraham*, vol. 1 *Orach Chaim*, Siman 27, p. 11.
7. ס"ק כ
8. ש"ך כאן ס"ק יט. ט"ז יו"ד סי' שלה ס"ק ה
9. וראה בדרכ"ת ס"ק מט ולהלן סי' שלה ס"ק כה. לקט הקמח החדש סי' כז ס"ק טו. סוגה בשושנים פל"ו סע' כה
10. שו"ת מנחת יצחק ח"ז סי' סט
11. ס"ק ג
12. שו"ת, ח"ג סי' נח וסי' רל, מובא גם בברכ"י
13. סע' ה
14. כמ"ש המג"א סי' שח ס"ק ע ו-עא. וראה גם בדרכי תשובה ס"ק ט
15. שו"ת, ח"ב סי' צב

§7 (C)He should not look even at her heel (*and certainly not*) at parts of her body that are usually covered (*he may, however, look at those parts of her body that are usually uncovered even if doing so gives him pleasure*).

─────────────── NISHMAT AVRAHAM ───────────────

The *Tzitz Eliezer*[16] permits a husband to help his *niddah* wife carry a baby carriage (pram) up and down the stairs since it is difficult to always find someone else to help. It would be even better if one of them wore gloves and stood one at the head and the other at the foot of the baby carriage. However, *Rav Auerbach zt"l* wrote to me that it would be correct to act strictly (this does not contradict his ruling above regarding the blind husband for there the *Rav zt"l* ruled leniently only in a situation where she saw that he was about to fall, and to prevent injury). *Rav Neuwirth shlita* also drew my attention to the *Chayei Adam*,[17] and the *Igrot Moshe*[18] [that both (would) also forbid it].

(C) He should not look. Is the husband permitted to be present when his wife gives birth? The *Igrot Moshe*[19] writes that he does not see any prohibition to this even if there is no necessity. However it is forbidden for him to look at the birth process for he is forbidden to look at those parts of her body that are usually covered, when she is a *niddah*. Moreover, he is forbidden to look at her private parts even when she is not a *niddah*. Nor may he view the birth process in a mirror. However, if he is careful not to look there is no prohibition. *Rav Auerbach zt"l* told me that in principle, there is no prohibition for a husband to be present when his wife gives birth, if he is careful not to look at those parts of her body that are normally covered and especially her private parts, and he certainly may not touch her. Nevertheless it is not in good taste to do so and is even somewhat repugnant. However if she really is afraid then it would certainly be permitted for him to be there. The *Minchat Yitzchak*[20] writes that he forbids the husband to be present unless his not being there would possibly add to her danger, for if it would be permitted at all times, it would lead to the setting aside of prohibitions.

He[21] was also asked about a woman who was due to give birth and who suffered from a nervous state. She was fearful of labor pains and wished that her husband be present and hold her hand. *Rav Grossnas zt"l* who raised the question wondered whether this could be permitted if a piece of cloth separated their hands. Since there would be no direct contact, it should be permitted even in a *non-seriously ill* patient. Moreover, in this situation, the ruling of the *Rama* who permits a husband to care for his wife if there is no alternative (see §17) might be applied, for here it is as if there is no alternative. However, *Rav Weiss zt"l* replies that one may not permit this even if the husband wore gloves, unless there is a question of *pikuach nefesh* (*over and above the danger due to labor and childbirth — author*). This would only occur where severe mental distress might lead to *pikuach nefesh*. But since women are often highly imaginative, it may be that her imagination heightens her fears and this

---

16. שו"ת, חי"ב סי' נח
17. כלל קל בדיני סדר בקצרה ס"ק ז
18. שו"ת, יו"ד ח"ב סי' עה
19. שו"ת, שם
20. שו"ת, ח"ח סי' ל אות ב
21. שו"ת מנחת יצחק ח"ה סי' כו

§15 (D)If he is ill and there is no one to care for him apart from his wife who is a *niddah*, she may care for him. However,

─────────── NISHMAT AVRAHAM ───────────

leads to her request and not severe mental distress.[22]

I find this argument difficult to understand. The *Biur Halachah*[23] writes that one does not require expert opinion as one does in determining the danger of fasting on *Yom Kippur*; for it is likelier that a woman in childbirth might become *dangerously ill* from fear that she is not being adequately treated than a patient suffering from hunger. However, *Rav Auerbach zt"l* told me that the two situations (holding the hand of a wife who is about to give birth who is *temei'ah*, as against turning on the light in the room for a blind woman in labor — see *Nishmat Avraham*, vol. 1 *Orach Chaim*, Siman 330D and E) are not comparable. It is accepted and known that there are situations — when a blind person (*who is seriously ill — author*) is a patient or someone who says he is having pain in his heart — which can cause severe mental stress. In such cases, Torah Sabbath laws are set aside for even the slightest possibility of danger to life. But, when they wish to be reassured, in situations that are not known and accepted, because of the convention of a modern outlook, then setting aside even Rabbinic law is prohibited. For example, we do not play a musical instrument on *Shabbat* in order to calm a patient. Therefore, *Rav Auerbach zt"l* concludes that the husband is not permitted to touch her even with gloves or through a cloth unless there is a real fear that she is so anxious that she may become severely distressed if her request is not granted.

It is interesting to note that the *Yerushalmi*[24] already discussed the influence of psychological stress on a person and his disease. Rav Huna in the name of Rebbe Elazar ben Yaakov explained the verse,[25] "*Hashem* will remove all illness from you," as referring to one's thoughts, for Rebbe Eliezer also explained the verse,[26] "He will put an iron yoke on your neck," as referring to one's thoughts. The *Korban HaEidah*[27] explains that the *Yerushalmi* means that all illness is dependent on one's worrisome thoughts such as the fear of the enemy, and other (worrisome thoughts) which are a result of losses. These thoughts will not leave him until his dying day. Similarly, the *Pnei Moshe*[28] explains the *Yerushalmi* to mean one's thoughts and worries which are constantly with him.

The *Ran*[29] writes that there is little doubt that in such times one must search to cure the soul before searching for a cure for the body. For King David said,[30] "*Hashem*, heal my soul for I have sinned against You," meaning that during illness I pray for my soul and it is for that that I strive and not for a cure for my body. However, *Rav Auerbach zt"l* wrote to me that the *Ran* meant to say that there is no suffering without preceding sin and therefore one must first cure himself of his sins; he does not relate to a person who may be psychologically ill.

(D) If he is ill. The *Rosh*[31] writes that if one is ill and his *niddah* wife is the only

---

22. וראה בשו"ת הרי בשמים מהדו"ת סי' קפט
23. סי' של סע' א ד"ה נר
24. שבת פי"ד ה"ג
25. דברים ז:טו
26. דברים כח:מח
27. ירושלמי שם ד"ה זה רעיון
28. ירושלמי שם ד"ה זה רעיון
29. דרשות, הדרוש הששי ד"ה ולפעמים
30. תהלים מא:ה
31. שו"ת, כלל בט סי' ג

she must **(E)**be as careful as she possibly can not to wash his face, hands and legs or prepare his bed in his presence.

§16 A husband may not touch his **(F)**wife who is ill and is a

---NISHMAT AVRAHAM---

one to care for him, she may do so, but she must be as careful as she possibly can not to wash his face, hands and legs or prepare his bed in his presence. Since there is no one else available, it is not possible that she not take care of him. *Rav Auerbach zt"l* wrote to me that it would appear from this that she may serve all his needs and not only those concerned with his healing.

The *Beit Yosef* comments on this *Rosh* that so long as there is someone else to serve him, even if with difficulty, she is not permitted to serve him at all. The *Terumat HaDeshen*[32] writes that she may serve him without touching him (his bare skin) and may help him sit up, lie down or support him, since these are not actions that are necessarily done out of affection. Since he is ill and weak, we do not fear that he may sin with her. This is also the ruling of the *Shach*[33] and the *Ben Ish Chai*.[34] The *Ben Ish Chai* also quotes the *Radbaz*[35] who points out that the *Terumat HaDeshen* only allowed her to take care of her husband if no one else is available, otherwise she must hire someone to care for her husband rather than do so herself. *Rav Auerbach zt"l* told me that she is forbidden to care for her husband if she can hire someone else to do so. In any case, writes the *Darchei Teshuvah*,[36] when she does care for him she must do whatever she can in a manner different

from the usual (*as a constant reminder that she is a niddah — author*). And, if the husband is not really ill but just feels unwell or has some mild pain, the *Darchei Teshuvah*[37] writes that she may not care for him, to avoid a possibility that he may transgress.

(E) be as careful as she possibly can. The *Darchei Teshuvah*[38] writes that one may deduce from this that if she is unable to do so and must wash his face or prepare his bed in his presence, she may do so.

(F) wife who is ill and is a *niddah*. The *Beit Yosef*[39] writes that if she is *seriously ill*, and there are no other doctors available, it appears somewhat from a *responsum* of the *Ramban*[40] that it is permitted because of *pikuach nefesh*. However, this is in keeping with his ruling that touching a *niddah* is only Rabbinically forbidden. On the other hand, the *Rambam*[41] rules that this is forbidden by the Torah. If so, perhaps even in a situation of *pikuach nefesh* it should be forbidden, for the sin of physical contact is an offshoot of the sin of illicit sexual relationships (see the *Rama*, Siman 157:1 above); the *halachah* needs further study.

The *Shach*,[42] quoting this *Beit Yosef*, comments that this is also the ruling of the *Levush*. But, he feels that the *halachah* does not appear to be so. For even the *Rambam* does not rule that physical

---

32. שו"ת, סי' רנב
33. ס"ק יט
34. שו"ת רב פעלים ח"ג יו"ד סי' יב
35. שו"ת, אלף עו (ח"ד סי' ב)
36. ס"ק נ בשם המקור חיים ס"ק טו
37. ס"ק מט בשם המקור חיים ס"ק נח
38. ס"ק נא בשם המקור חיים ס"ק נד
39. כאן
40. שו"ת, סי' קכו
41. הל' איסו"ב פכ"א ה"א
42. ס"ק כ

niddah in order to care for her, for example, to sit her up or lie her down or support her (*there are those who say that if there is no one else to care for her, he may do whatever is necessary and this is the custom, if there is a great need for it*).

─────────── NISHMAT AVRAHAM ───────────

contact is forbidden by the Torah unless this is done as an act of affection and a prelude to *coitus;* see Siman 157:10 above. But it is not so here (the contact between them is for the purpose of treating her), and he notes that it is common practice that Jewish doctors take the pulse of female patients, even if they are married or non-Jewish, even if non-Jewish doctors are available. They also have physical contact in other medical examinations. The *Shach* writes that the matter is clear. For, although the *Rama* (Siman 157:10) appears to rule like the *Rambam*, here he permits taking her pulse. However, if the illness is not life threatening, the husband is forbidden to take the pulse of his *niddah* wife in accordance with the ruling of the *Ramban* in his *responsum* and the *Rama*.[43]

The *Beit Shmuel*[44] and the *Torat Ha-Shelamim*,[45] however, both disagree with this ruling of the *Shach* and rule that the husband is not permitted to take his wife's pulse when she is a *niddah*, even if she is *seriously ill*.

The *Pitchei Teshuvah*[46] refers to one who writes that he saw *poskim* who permitted the husband to feel his wife's pulse through a cloth.

The *Radbaz*,[47] in discussing this subject, writes that he permits the husband to take her pulse even if she is *non-seriously ill* if there is no other alternative. This is also the ruling of many *acharonim*.[48]

The *Aruch HaShulchan*[49] says that the controversy between the *Beit Yosef* and the *Rama* only concerns a *non-seriously ill* patient. But if she is *seriously ill* the *Beit Yosef* agrees that the husband may take her pulse. *Rav Waldenberg shlita*[50] wrote to me that he agrees with the reasoning of the *Aruch HaShulchan* that although the *Beit Yosef* writes that perhaps according to the *Rambam's* ruling the husband may not treat his wife who is a *niddah* even in a life-threatening situation, when he wrote his definitive ruling in the *Shulchan Aruch* he permits it, following the ruling of the *Ramban* and the *Radbaz*. And, to strengthen the view of the *Aruch HaShulchan*, *Rav Waldenberg shlita* quotes from the well-known *Sephardi gaon*, the author of the *Zera Emet*,[51] who also writes in the same vein that this is why the *Beit Yosef* writes "perhaps" and concludes "needs further study." For he

───────────

43. ועיין בש"ך סי' קנו ס"ק י שכותב דמשמע דאף הרמב"ם לא קאמר אלא כשעושה חבוק ונשוק דרך חיבת ביאה, וראיה מהאמוראים שהיו מחבקים ומנשקים לבנותיהם, וכ"כ מהר"י ליאון וכן משמע מלשון הרמב"ם שכתב דרך תאוה וכו' הרי זה לוקה, וכ"כ הסמ"ג, לאוין קכו, והכתר תורה. אלמא אינו לוקה אלא בדרך תאוה וחיבת ביאה, וזה דלא כהב"י בסוף סי' קצה

44. אהע"ז סי' כ ס"ק א
45. כאן ס"ק טו
46. ס"ק יז בשם המקור חיים ס"ק סא
47. שו"ת, אלף עו (ח"ד סי' ב)
48. שו"ת חות יאיר סי' קפב. הפלתי כאן סע' ו. הגר"א ס"ק כא. כנה"ג כאן. סדרי טהרה ס"ק כד. חוות דעת ס"ק יג. שו"ת נודע ביהודה תניינא יו"ד סי' קכב. טהרת ישראל ס"ק מה ו-מו. חכמת אדם כלל קטו סע' יא ו-יב. קיצור שו"ע סי' קנג סע' יד. שו"ת חלקת יעקב ח"ב סי' יח. שו"ת אג"מ אהע"ז ח"ב סי' יד. מקור הלכה על שבת ח"ב סי' יז אות ד ושו"ת שבט הלוי ח"ב סי' קמג. וראה באוצר הפוסקים אהע"ז סי' כ ס"ק ג
49. סע' כו ו-כז
50. הערות על נשמת אברהם כרך ב יו"ד עמ' רצד. שו"ת ציץ אליעזר חי"ז סי' לב
51. ח"ג חיו"ד סי' קטז

§17 If her husband is a physician, he may not take her pulse.

GLOSS: *Following on from what I wrote that the custom is to permit a husband to care for his wife where necessary, it would certainly be permitted for him to take her pulse if there is no other physician to do so, if it is necessary and she is seriously ill.*

─────────── NISHMAT AVRAHAM ───────────

did not think that the *Rambam* meant that such physical contact would really be an offshoot of the sin of illicit sexual relationships; only that the Torah forbade it as a preventative measure to *coitus*. Thus, in a life-threatening situation this Torah commandment (forbidding physical contact) could be set aside. This is why the *Shulchan Aruch* only describes the wife as "ill" and not that she is *seriously ill*. The *Zera Emet* concludes that even if the *Beit Yosef* was uncertain about the *Rambam's* opinion in this situation, in his *Shulchan Aruch* he permitted it even according to the *Rambam*. Rav Waldenberg shlita concludes that we have a strong basis of many great *poskim* who permit the doctor to treat his *niddah* wife in a life-threatening situation even for the *Sephardim* who always rule according to *Maran* the *Beit Yosef*.

Rav Palaggi zt"l[52] writes that if the husband can hire a woman to care for his *niddah* wife, he must do so. However if he does not have the means, or such help is not available, he may care for her himself since he has no choice. The *Ben Ish Chai*[53] was asked about a wife who was a *niddah* caring for her husband. In his reply, after quoting *Maran*, he also quotes the *Radbaz* (above) regarding the husband caring for his *niddah* wife. Since he quoted this *Radbaz*, which does not concern the situation he was asked about, it would seem that he rules like him. Elsewhere, the *Ben Ish Chai*[54] writes that although the *Beit Yosef* ruled that it is possible that a doctor may not take his wife's pulse when she is a *niddah* even if she is *seriously ill*, nevertheless, if one is asked, one should rule that this is permitted. It is not an act which must be avoided even to the point of martyrdom, for *Maran* also only ruled thus if it is possible. I found this difficult to understand for *Maran* in the *Shulchan Aruch* ruled categorically that it is forbidden. Rav Auerbach zt"l wrote to me that the *Shulchan Aruch*, however, did not write that this falls into the category of an act which requires martyrdom; it is the *Gra* who adds that it is forbidden even if there is *pikuach nefesh*. Rav Ovadiah Yosef shlita told me that he also rules leniently.[55] Later, he wrote to me,[56] referring me to what he had written at length in *Taharat HaBayit*,[57] and his conclusion is[58] that a doctor may treat his *niddah* wife who is *seriously ill* if there is no other expert available who can do so as competently. He should be as careful as possible not to touch her bare skin but to use gloves.[59]

Rav Ovadiah Yosef shlita[60] also writes that if the husband must rub ointment into his *niddah* wife's skin, he may do so in a life-threatening situation. Thus, in a

---

52. ספר רוח חיים סי' קצה ס"ק ז, מובא גם בדרכ"ת ס"ק נג
53. שו"ת רב פעלים ח"ג יו"ד סי' יב
54. ספר תורה לשמה להבן איש חי, שאלה תצד
55. וראה בשו"ת יביע אומר ח"ו יו"ד סי' טו אות ג
56. הערה על נשמת אברהם ח"ד עמ' רכו
57. ח"ב עמ' ריח
58. שם עמ' רכה
59. וראה בשדי חמד מערכת חתן וכלה אות יב ד"ה קריבה
60. טהרת הבית ח"ב עמ' רכה

situation where she may develop pressure sores, or already has them, and no one else is available to treat her, he may do so. The *Rav shlita*[61] also permits a husband to raise or lower the head of a hospital bed either by hand or electrically, even if she is *not seriously ill,* since he does not touch her.[62]

Rav Auerbach zt"l writes[63] that a husband may not treat his *niddah* wife as long as he can find someone else to do so, even if he must pay for the service. On the other hand, continues the *Rav zt"l,* if a woman who is a *niddah* is suffering from diarrhea, neither her husband nor another man may tend to her needs (*if this involves bodily contact,* see Siman 335 §10 — author) even if she is *seriously ill,* and her husband must hire a woman to tend to her needs.

A husband may put drops into his *niddah* wife's eyes, if she cannot do so herself and there is no one else to do so, since he only touches her with the dropper. However, if he must touch her to keep her eyes open, he should wear gloves.[64]

A woman who is recovering from a *hemiplegia* (paralysis of one half of her body), and manages to walk and do almost everything for herself without aid, may nevertheless require help in certain things such as tying her shoelaces and buttoning her clothes which she cannot do with one hand. Her husband may do these things for her even when she is a *niddah* since there is no alternative and he does not touch her directly.[65]

It would appear that it is forbidden for a husband to care for his *niddah* wife, even in a situation where there is no *yichud* and therefore no possibility of sin, for once this is forbidden, we do not differentiate between one situation and another. This would appear to be the opinion of the *Har Tzvi*[66] and the *Minchat Yitzchak*[67] for the latter does not permit a husband to hold the hands of his wife during childbirth even though there are others in the room. *Rav Ovadiah Yosef shlita*[68] and *Rav Neuwirth shlita* both agreed with this.

May a doctor draw blood or give injections to his *niddah* wife? The *Darchei Teshuvah*[69] permits this if there is no alternative.[70] This ruling would also apply to a nurse or female doctor who is a *niddah*, drawing blood from her husband.

Finally, the *Darchei Moshe*[71] writes that he found a *gloss* on the *Mordechai*[72] which states that those who abstain from touching their *niddah* wives even though they are ill, are pious fools.[73]

In summary, according to most *poskim*, a doctor may, in most situations (see above reference 63), treat his *niddah* wife if she is *seriously ill* and there is no one else available to do so.

(1) TREATMENT OF THE OPPOSITE SEX. I quoted the *Shach* (above reference 42) that it is common practice for Jewish doctors to take the pulse of female patients, even if they are married or non-Jewish, and even if non-Jewish doctors are available. They also make physical contact with them in other medical examinations. Which is the more serious problem, treating a woman who is married or

---

61. שם עמ' רכו
62. וכן פוסקים השיעורי שבט הלוי סי' קצה סע' טו אות ד והשו"ת באר משה ח"ד סי' עד
63. מנחת שלמה תנינא סי' לח
64. שו"ת בית שערים יו"ד ח"ב סי' רעד
65. שו"ת קנה בושם יו"ד סי' צב
66. שו"ת, יו"ד סי' קנד
67. שו"ת, ח"ה סי' כז
68. טהרת הבית שם עמ' רכו
69. ס"ק נז בשם הרדב"ז הובא גם בכנה"ג
70. ראה גם בחכמת אדם כלל קטז סע' יב
71. כאן ס"ק ו
72. שלטי הגבורים על המרדכי שבת סט ע"ב אות ה בשם הר"ם
73. ראה גם בבדי השולחן יו"ד סי' קפז ביאורים ד"ה אף וכו' בשם הבית מאיר

NISHMAT AVRAHAM

treating one's own *niddah* wife? The *Sidrei Taharah*[74] writes that by Torah law whatever is forbidden because of *gilui arayot* is certainly more serious when another's wife is concerned rather than his own wife when she is a *niddah* even though he is on familiar terms with her (because she is his wife). However the *Torat HaShelamim*[75] and the *Machatzit HaShekel*[76] disagree, writing that perhaps the problem is less serious with another woman than with his own *niddah* wife. The *Pnei Yehoshua*[77] writes that it certainly appears that merely touching a woman is not forbidden by the Torah and is not mentioned with respect to other *arayot*. He points out that the *Rambam*[78] only writes that one may not touch one's wife when she is a *niddah* to prevent him from sinning with her. This shows that touching one's wife who is a *niddah* is more serious than touching other *arayot*.

The *Mishnah Berurah*[79] writes that an unmarried girl who is a *niddah* is included in the prohibition of *gilui arayot* and young girls are assumed to be in a state of *niddah* from the time of their *menarche*.[80]

The *Darchei Teshuvah*[81] comments that many of the great *rishonim* and *acharonim* discussed whether one may or may not depend on medical opinion with regard to a woman who bleeds following *coitus* (see Siman 187 above). None of them even mentions that a woman is forbidden to go to a doctor and allow him to perform a gynecological examination because of the sin of *gilui arayot*. In a like vein, the *Noda BiYehudah*[82] discusses the case of a woman who had a ring put into her (*uterus*) *prozdor* by the doctor without mentioning that perhaps there is a sin involved if a doctor — Jew or gentile — does so. The *Darchei Teshuvah* assumes from this that since both the doctor and the patient's intentions are purely medical, and the doctor is busy with his professional duties, there is no fear at all for the sin of *gilui arayot*; and that it is also an everyday occurrence that women who have a medical problem go to a doctor who performs a gynecological examination, looking at her sexual parts and inserting a finger into her *prozdor* before giving her medication. No one has forbidden this because of *gilui arayot*. He notes that the *Binyan Tzion* [83] was asked whether a doctor may deliver his sister-in-law in childbirth even if there are other competent doctors, both Jew and gentile, available. He replied that although it would seem, at first sight, that a Jewish doctor may not deliver a married woman, even one who is unrelated to him, this is without doubt permitted. Nevertheless, the *Binyan Tzion* feels that a Heaven-fearing doctor should distance himself from this if another doctor is available, since in any case it is repugnant and may bring him to sinful thoughts. However those who are accustomed to act leniently in such cases have on whom to depend. And it is obvious, according to the opinion of the *Shach*, that there is no difference between an unrelated married woman and his sister-in-law.

Obviously much is dependent on the person and his self-control. *Tosafot*[84]

---

74. ס"ק כד
75. ס"ק טו
76. ס"ק כ
77. שו"ת, ח"ב סי' מד
78. איסו"ב פי"א הי"ט
79. סי' עה ס"ק יז
80. וראה מה שהעיר הגרא"י וולדינברג שליט"א עלי בנשמת אברהם כרך ב יו"ד עמ' רצה ושו"ת ציץ אליעזר חי"ז סי' לב
81. סי' קנז ס"ק ח
82. שו"ת, מהד"ק יו"ד סי' סז
83. שו"ת, ח"א סי' עה
84. קדושין פב ע"א ד"ה הכל. וראה גם בתוס' שבת יג ע"א ד"ה ופליגא

―――――――― NISHMAT AVRAHAM ――――――――

write that we accept that women can assist us since it is done for platonic reasons. The *Ritva*[85] writes that the *halachah* depends on a man's perception of himself. If he fears that because of his inclinations and impure thoughts he should put himself at a distance, he should do so; moreover, he would be forbidden to even look at her colorful attire.[86] On the other hand, if he knows that his inclinations are well-controlled and he has no sinful thoughts, he may speak to, and look at, a married woman and ask after her health. That is why Rebbe Yochanan,[87] Rebbe (Ami) Abahu,[88] Rav Adda bar Ahavah[89] and other Sages acted as they did since they knew that they had no need to fear that they would have impure thoughts. Nevertheless, only a very pious person who knows himself may act leniently as did the Sages mentioned. Happy is the one who can control his inclinations and whose whole labor and profession is in the Torah.[90]

The *Gemara*[91] recounts the ways of the physician Abba Umna, whom a *Bat Kol* (voice from Heaven) greeted with *Shalom* every day, but only greeted the Sage Abaye every Sabbath eve. The *Gemara* asks, what were his deeds (that he should be so honored)? And answers, that when he had to *phlebotomize* (perform bloodletting), he treated men and women separately (in the interests of modesty — *Rashi*). In addition, he had a special garment with a scalpel already inserted into it (which he gave the female patient to wear so that he would not have to look at her bared arm — *Rashi*).

If we assume that a doctor treating a patient is busy with his professional duties,[92] the same should hold true for a male doctor, nurse or technician who needs to treat a female patient. *Rav Auerbach zt"l* told me that a man may learn a medical or paramedical profession, since they involve *pikuach nefesh*. However each person must decide for himself if he will be able to control his inclinations and work in an objective manner. *Rav Neuwirth shlita* told me that it would be best, if possible, for him to be married before he embarks on such a course of studies.[93] See also Siman 335 below.

(2) UNMARRIED GIRL. The sin of *gilui arayot* covers having *coitus* or even physical contact with close relatives of the opposite sex, another's spouse, a woman who is a *niddah* — be she one's own wife or a single girl — sodomy and bestiality. Both partners are equally guilty and with all, *coitus* carries, at the least, the penalty of *karet*;[94] in some instances, *coitus* also carries the death penalty.[95] In addition, physical contact is also forbidden with all the women mentioned.[96] If a man is forced to have *coitus* with one of his close relatives, another's wife or to commit sodomy, on pain of death, *Halachah* demands martyrdom (see Siman 157:1 above).[97]

―――――――――――――――――――――

85. קדושין שם - הראה לי הגרא"י ולדינברג שליט"א, והובא בפ"ת אהע"ז סי' כא ס"ק ג
86. ע"ז כ ע"ב
87. ברכות כ ע"א. ב"מ פד ע"א
88. כתובות יז ע"א
89. שם
90. וראה בתוס' סוכה מז ע"ב ד"ה כהן בשם הירושלמי
91. תענית כא ע"ב
92. המושג שבמלאכתו הוא עוסק אנו מוצאים בגמ' ב"מ צא ע"א. גם במאירי שכותב על המשנה בסוף קדושין: כל שעסקיו עם הנשים לא יתייחד עם הנשים - ר"ל אפילו
אותו שמתעסק במלאכת נשים שהיה לנו לומר בעבידתיה טריד
93. שיהא פת בסלו, ראה בקדושין שם. וראה גם בשמות רבה פט"ז ס"ק ב על הפסוק משכו וקחו לכם. שו"ת הרשב"א ח"א סי' אלף קפה. הבן איש חי בספרו עוד יוסף חי פ' משפטים סע' כב.
94. הל' איסו"ב פ"א ה"ז והל' שגגות פ"א ה"ד
95. הל' איסו"ב שם ה"ד-ה"ו
96. ראה באהע"ז סי' כא
97. אנציקלופדיה תלמודית ערך יהרג ואל יעבור עמ' עב

SIMAN 195: WHEN ONE'S WIFE IS A NIDDAH / §17

NISHMAT AVRAHAM

Is martyrdom also demanded with regard to a *niddah* even if she is a single girl? I wrote above (reference 79) that the *Chafetz Chaim* in his *Mishnah Berurah* rules that an unmarried girl who is a *niddah* (and nowadays all girls after the menarche are assumed to be in that state) is included in the prohibition of *gilui arayot*. However *Rav Waldenberg shlita*[98] wrote to me disagreeing and quoting a number of *acharonim*[99] who rule that although all the *halachot* of *niddah* apply to her, the prohibitions concerning her do not fall into the category requiring martyrdom (see Siman 157 above). He suggests that perhaps the *Mishnah Berurah* also only wrote this with regard to the prohibition of hearing her sing (the subject under discussion), but not to include her in the category of prohibited relations which require martyrdom.[100] *Rav Auerbach zt"l* also wrote to me that although in matters of *gilui arayot* two witnesses are required to confirm the facts, only one witness would be required in matters involving an unmarried *niddah*; the prohibitions with respect to her are like the prohibitions against eating blood and forbidden fats. In a like manner, the prohibitions with respect to her do not fall into the category of prohibitions which must not be broken even if martyrdom is required. However, with regard to the *halachot* of *yichud* it is possible that *yichud* with an unmarried *niddah* is forbidden by Torah law.

The *Chafetz Chaim*[101] writes that even a wife who is a *niddah* is included in the prohibition of *arayot* as specifically written in the Torah, *Gemara* and *poskim*; and that the prohibitions of *arayot* not only refer to *coitus*, but also include hugging and kissing of any woman who is in the category of *arayot* or a *niddah* (single or married), and all demand martyrdom. Anything that is forbidden because it is an offshoot of one of the three cardinal sins — idolatry, forbidden sexual relationships and murder — even though it is only a negative commandment that does not carry the death penalty, requires martyrdom.

Besides the above, the *Chafetz Chaim* writes[102] that people should know, and this is common knowledge to every learned person, that a *niddah* (single or married) is included in the prohibition of *arayot* which is one of the three cardinal sins that demand martyrdom. In a letter co-signed with *Rav Chaim Ozer Grodzinsky zt"l*, the *Chafetz Chaim* writes:[103] Take to heart my brethren the seriousness of the sin of *niddah* for it is included in the prohibitions demanding martyrdom. Again, he writes there[104] that a woman who is a *niddah*, who has not purified herself according to the demands of *Halachah*, is prohibited in exactly the same way as *arayot* and more seriously than other negative commandments of the Torah which, though punishable by *karet*, do not demand martyrdom. And elsewhere the *Chafetz Chaim* writes[105] that even if an idolator forcibly demands that one have *coitus* with a *niddah* on pain of death, he must accept martyrdom rather than agree, for the sin is equivalent to the

---

98. הערה על נשמת אברהם כרך ב יו"ד עמ' רצה. שו"ת ציץ אליעזר חי"ז סי' לב. וראה גם שם ח"י סי' מ פ"א ופ"ה וחט"ז סי' ע

99. שו"ת פני יהושע ח"ב אהע"ז סי' מד. מהרש"ם בספר נחל ברית, קונטרס דברי שלום שבסוף הספר אות לט. הגרי"א ז"ל מקאוונה בספר מור ואהלות בקונטרס אוהל ארץ נוד

100. עוד כותב הגרא"י ולדינברג שליט"א: וראיה לכך שכותב שם דגם קול זמר פנויה נכרית היא גם כן בכלל ערוה והרי הבא על הכותית דרך זנות פוסק הרמב"ם פי"ב מאיסו"ב ה"ב דרך מכין אותו מכת מרדות מדברי סופרים

101. טהרת ישראל פ"ד וכן בספר נדחי ישראל סופי"ט

102. ספר בית ישראל פ"ג סע' ד

103. אגרות ומאמרי החפץ חיים על טהרת המשפחה בישראל אות טו

104. שם מאמר לחיזוק יסודי התורה אות יז

105. ספר המצוות הקצר, לא תעשה קלב

SIMAN 196
THE LAWS CONCERNING THE WEARING OF WHITE UNDERGARMENTS AND HER SELF-EXAMINATION

§1 The seven-clean-days period starts the day after she stops

---NISHMAT AVRAHAM---

sin of idolatry.

It would appear that the *Chafetz Chaim* follows the ruling of the *Gra*[106] that a husband may not treat his *niddah* wife, if this involves physical contact even if she is *seriously ill*. See also the *Pitchei Teshuvah*.[107] However, *Rav Auerbach zt"l* wrote to me that there is no certain proof that the *Gra* includes a *niddah* in the prohibition of *arayot*, since *kiddushin* is possible with a *niddah* and her prohibition is only temporary (*this is distinct from the prohibition of arayot where kiddushin do not take effect — author*).

Rav Waldenberg shlita[108] wrote to me again that even if we accept that the *Chafetz Chaim* in his writings did include *niddah* in terms of *Halachah*, and did not write the way he did only to encourage people to keep this serious *mitzvah* (for he did not bring any sources for his statements), nevertheless with all respect, it is not enough to challenge the rulings of other great *poskim*, early and late. He concludes: I have based my ruling on them (as written above).[109]

SIMAN 196

◆§ **INTRODUCTION.** A woman becomes a *niddah* when she has uterine bleeding, no matter how minute; she is immediately forbidden to her husband. In order to purify herself she must first count a minimum of five consecutive days even if she has stopped bleeding before then.[1] At the end of these five days or on any subsequent day that she stops bleeding, she performs a self-examination known as the *hefsek taharah*[2] to verify that there is no more bleeding or staining. This examination is performed at the end of her *menstrual* period, that is at the end of the fifth day from the start of her period or, if she is still bleeding then, at the end of any other subsequent day when the bleeding has stopped. The examination consists of her inserting a clean white piece of cloth deep into her *prozdor* before sunset and moving it slowly and carefully within all crevices and folds. If the cloth is completely clean, she then inserts another similar cloth into her *prozdor*, leaving it there from before sunset to nightfall; this is the *moch dachuk*.[3] If this is clean, she changes to clean prechecked undergarments and sleeps on a prechecked white bedsheet for the next seven days.[4] During these seven consecutive[5] days (which start on the day following the day of *hefsek taharah*) she must examine herself in the morning and late afternoon of each day to be certain that there is no bleeding or staining; these are the seven clean days.[6] Finally, she immerses herself in a *mikveh*. This is the ritual of purification following her being a *niddah*, in general terms only. It does not cover

---

106. יו"ד סי' קצה ס"ק ב
107. ראה גם בפ"ת שם ס"ק טו
108. שו"ת ציץ אליעזר ח"כ סי' לו
109. ראה באנציקלופדיה תלמודית ערך יהרג ואל יעבור הערה 221 - 222

1. כאן סע' יא ברמ"א. אך לפי המחבר די בארבע ימים
וכן פוסק השו"ת יביע אומר ח"ה יו"ד סי' יז
2. כאן סע' א
3. כאן סע' ב
4. כאן סע' ג
5. כאן סע' י
6. כאן סע' ד

menstruating and these are its rules: If she only **(A)bleeds for two or three days and then stops** (*in practice this is a minimum of five days, see §11 — author*), **she examines herself the day she stops, before sunset, to mark the cessation in purity** (*this is the custom but, even if she realized that she had only examined herself in the morning and found that she was clean, this is sufficient*). **Everyone should always teach** (*that they should act strictly*) **his family that a woman on the day on which she conducts the examinaton, should wedge an examination cloth tightly into the *prozdor* before sunset and leave it there until after nightfall, thus verifying beyond all doubt that she is clean.**

§4 **(B)She should examine herself twice a day, every day of the seven clean days, once in the morning and again close to sunset.**

--- NISHMAT AVRAHAM ---

many other essential details which a woman must learn and understand thoroughly in order to avoid the possibility of cohabitating with her husband while she is still a *niddah*.

(A) bleeds for two or three days. As explained in my Introduction to the *Halachot* of *Niddah* (preceding Siman 183), the usual *menstrual* cycle is about twenty-eight days. *Ovulation* always takes place fourteen days before the start of the next period. Therefore, when a woman has immersed herself in a *mikveh* and is permitted to her husband, it is, in the vast majority of cases, around the time of *ovulation* and therefore the optimum time for pregnancy. However, if she has a short *menstrual* cycle, *ovulation* may have already taken place some days before she is permitted to her husband. Since the life span of the egg is about six to twenty-four hours only, the chances of her ever becoming pregnant become drastically reduced. Many *responsa* [7] have been written concerning this problem. However, since nowadays medication is available to lengthen her cycle (without lengthening the days of bleeding) and thus postpone *ovulation*, this *halachic* problem no longer exists. Similarly, a woman who has prolonged bleeding and therefore cannot immerse herself in a *mikveh* until after the time of *ovulation*, can also be treated to postpone *ovulation* until the time when she is permitted to her husband.

The *Igrot Moshe*[8] writes that a woman who was medically forbidden to have *coitus* with her husband may not take those days into consideration when counting the five obligatory days before she can make a *hefsek taharah*.

(B) She should examine herself. If a woman must douche herself for medical reasons, during the seven clean days, need she worry lest she has washed away

---

7. שו"ת דברי מלכיאל ח"ה סי' קב. שו"ת אג"מ יו"ד ח"ב סי' פד. שו"ת דובב מישרים ח"א סי' ח. שו"ת מנחת יצחק ח"ג סי' פה. שו"ת הר צבי יו"ד סי' קנו. ועיין גם בערוה"ש כאן סע' מ
8. ספר הל' נדה בתשובות אות כא. וראה שם לגבי יוהכ"פ, ט' באב וימי אבלות

traces of bleeding without her being aware of it? The *Igrot Moshe*[9] writes that she should douche herself on the first and seventh days in the morning after she has examined herself. During the intermediary days if she can do the same easily, she should do so. If, however, it is difficult for her to do so in the morning she may, in the intermediary days, douche herself at night (and not worry that her examination the next morning will not be valid since she may have washed away blood that was present after nightfall before the douching). If, medically, she must douche herself at night, even on the first day, she may, in these circumstances, do so. And although in another *responsum*, the *Igrot Moshe*[10] writes that she is forbidden to douche herself on the first and seventh days before her examination, in yet a third *responsum*[11] he explains the apparent contradiction; the first *responsum* dealt with most women while the second dealt with a woman with special problems. Many *acharonim*[12] permit douching even on the first day, after her examination.

1. VAGINAL SUPPOSITORY.
The *Igrot Moshe*[13] rules that a woman who needs to insert suppositories every day may do so after she has performed the *hefsek taharah* examination and examined herself once on the following day (the first of the seven clean days). On the seventh she should not insert the suppository so that she may (perform an examination on the seventh day and) have the two required examinations (one on the first and one on the seventh).

2. DIAPHRAGM.
This device is self-inserted into the *prozdor* and closes off the entrance to the *cervical canal*, thus preventing the entry of sperm. It may only be used with permission from a *posek*. What is the *halachah* if the woman forgot to remove the device when she carried out her *hefsek taharah* and during the whole seven clean days? The *Har Tzvi*[14] rules that after she removes the diaphragm she must repeat the *hefsek taharah* and count a further seven clean days before immersing herself in a *mikveh*.

Rav Moshe Feinstein zt"l[15] writes that blood found on a diaphragm removed some hours after *coitus* does not have the status of a *ketem* and the woman is a *niddah* no matter how small the stain. However, one must ascertain whether she possibly scratched herself internally with her nails when she inserted or removed the diaphragm. If such a possibility exists, she is not a *niddah* even if spots of blood are found on it.

3. BIRTH CONTROL PILLS.
Rav Neuwirth shlita told me that a woman who is taking birth control pills (after she was permitted to do so by a *posek*) should examine herself twice daily, morning and evening (before sunset) during the first month after starting to take them, lest there is breakthrough bleeding which will make her a *niddah*. If she does not find any evidence of bleeding during this month, she need not examine herself again while she is taking them. However, if she did bleed, she must continue to examine herself until there are two whole months without bleeding while she is still taking the pills.[16] Whether or not there is bleeding, during the first month she is

---

9. שו"ת, יו"ד ח"א סי' צד
10. שם יו"ד ח"ב סי' עא
11. שם יו"ד ח"ג סי' נו
12. שו"ת מהרש"ם ח"ב סי' מ. שו"ת דברי מלכיאל ח"ג סי' סא. שו"ת מהר"ש ענגיל ח"ו סי' צז. שו"ת חלקת יעקב ח"ב סי' פז. ושו"ת יביע אומר ח"ה יו"ד סי' טז אות ה. וראה גם בשו"ת לבושי מרדכי יו"ד סי' קכג
13. שו"ת, או"ח ח"ד סי' קה
14. שו"ת, יו"ד סי' קנה
15. ספ' הל' נדה בתשובות אות טז
16. וראה גם בשו"ת אג"מ אהע"ז ח"ג סי' כד

NISHMAT AVRAHAM

forbidden to her husband on the day of her expected period and on the thirtieth day after her last period, for it is not certain that she will not bleed on these two days. This is also the ruling of the *Shevet HaLevi*.[17]

4. UTERINE PESSARY. This device is sometimes inserted to support a prolapsed *uterus,* usually in older women and, rarely, in younger women. The *Zichron Yosef*[18] writes that the presence of the pessary should not interfere with her examinations including the *hefsek taharah* and her use of a *moch*. On the other hand, the *Sidrei Taharah*[19] writes that she should remove the pessary for the *hefsek taharah,* and the *Binyan Tzion*[20] requires that it be removed at least for the *hefsek taharah* and the first day of the seven clean days. The *Aruch HaShulchan*[21] writes that if she can remove it for the *hefsek taharah*, she certainly should do so. If it would be dangerous to do so, she may nevertheless examine herself deep into the *prozdor* leaving the cloth there from before sunset to after nightfall. This must be done for the *hefsek taharah* and once during the seven days. The other days she examines herself as best she can. This is also the opinion of the *Taharat Yisrael*.[22] The *Avnei Nezer*[23] rules that one may be lenient only if she does not usually bleed more than seven days and now too, with the device, does not bleed more than seven days.[24]

The *Cheshev HaEphod*[25] writes that if she cannot remove the pessary, she may examine herself as usual since the pessary will not be considered a *chatzitzah* for the purposes of the examination. He bases his ruling on the opinion of the *Chelkat Yoav*[26] that whatever is incorporated into the body for seven days is considered a permanent part of it. This is also the ruling of *Rav Neuwirth shlita*. Rav Auerbach *zt"l* wrote to me that it would appear that the *Cheshev HaEphod* rules that just as this is not considered a *chatzizah* (with respect to immersion in a *mikveh*) so it is not a *chatzizah* for the examination. Thus, although it may prevent the exit of blood, this does not preclude the examination.

5. SHABBAT. Although there is a controversy whether a woman may[27] or may not[28] go out on *Shabbat* into a *public domain* with a *moch dachuk*, it would probably be permitted for her to go out with a pessary. This is because the pessary is worn for a medical purpose; see *Orach Chaim* Siman 310:22 and the *Cheshev HaEphod*.[29] *Rav Neuwirth shlita* agreed with this.

6. INTRAUTERINE DEVICE (IUD). See Siman 194D above. Its presence does not interfere with the counting of the seven clean days.[30] However it may cause spotting and some women may find it difficult to ever be able to complete the process of purification before immersion.

---

17. שו"ת, ח"ד סי' צט אות ט. אך עיין בשו"ת מנחת יצחק ח"א סי' קכו שמשמע מדבריו שהוא מתיר אחרי בדיקה
18. יו"ד סי' י
19. כאן ס"ק כג ד"ה וראיתי
20. שו"ת, סי' עא
21. כאן סע' כט
22. כאן סע' מו
23. שו"ת, יו"ד סי' רנה ו-רנו
24. וראה גם בשו"ת נודע ביהודה קמא סי' סד ותנייגא סי' קלה. שו"ת רעק"א סי' ס. שו"ת חת"ס סי' קצב. דרכ"ת כאן ס"ק סג וחזו"א יו"ד סי' צב ס"ק כד ו-כה
25. שו"ת, ח"ב סי' קיח
26. שו"ת, ח"א סי' ל
27. הגרש"ז אויערבאך זצ"ל מובא בשמירת שבת כהלכתה פי"ח הערה פו והשו"ת ציץ אליעזר ח"י סי' יג אות ו
28. שו"ת תשורת שי סי' שיט. שו"ת מנחת יצחק ח"ד סי' כח אות ט וח"ה סי' לו. שו"ת אג"מ יו"ד ח"ג סי' מז. שו"ת שבט הלוי ח"ב סי' ס ושו"ת חשב האפוד ח"ב סי' קב
29. שו"ת, ח"ב סוסי' קב
30. שו"ת ציץ אליעזר ח"י סי' כה פ"י וחזי"א סי' סג. שו"ת מנחת יצחק ח"ו סי' פז.

§6

All of these examinations, whether for the *hefsek taharah* or during the seven days, must be made with a white linen cloth or (C)absorbent cotton or clean white, soft cotton cloth. It must be introduced deeply into the *prozdor* as far as the finger can reach and into all the crevices and folds. She then examines the cloth to see whether there is any reddish discoloration. It is not sufficient if she merely inserts it a little to wipe herself. Even if she finds it (D)too difficult to insert it deeply, she must nevertheless do so for at least the *hefsek taharah* and the first day.

GLOSS: *If she did not do so for the examination on the first day she should do so once during the remaining days. However, if she did not, inadvertently, examine herself as far as the finger can reach, but only examined herself well in the crevices and folds as far inside the prozdor as she can, this is sufficient.*

NISHMAT AVRAHAM

(C) cotton wool. *Rav Neuwirth shlita* wrote to me that one may not use absorbent cotton for examination for a number of reasons: A tiny spot may be absorbed into the absorbent cotton and missed; there is a serious possibility that a strand of absorbent cotton with blood may stick to the wall of the *prozdor* and be left behind; since it is difficult to introduce it internally, the area will only be wiped superficially and a proper examination has not been performed.

(D) too difficult to insert it deeply. The *Aruch HaShulchan*[31] and the *Chochmat Adam*[32] rule that it is sufficient for a woman who has difficulty examining herself because of a *makkah* (laceration or other painful wound) in her *prozdor*, to examine herself for the *hefsek taharah* and once more during the seven days. This is also the ruling of the *Igrot Moshe*.[33] If the examination is too painful, she may dampen the examination cloth.[34]

A virgin bride in preparation for her wedding should be taught that it is sufficient if she inserts the examination cloth gently, only as far as she can,[35] or, alternatively, put in a narrow *moch* gently as far as she can and leave it there until after nightfall.[36] In both situations she must take the utmost care not to tear the *hymen* by forcing the examination cloth into the *prozdor*. Any bleeding that may result will be very problematic and will require the ruling of a *posek*.

---

31. כאן סע׳ כו וראה גם שם בסע׳ ל. וכן ראה בשו״ת שבות יעקב סי׳ לו. סדרי טהרה ס״ק טו. שו״ת חת״ס יו״ד סי׳ קמד ו-קמה. חו״ד חידושים סי׳ קפז ס״ק יז ובאורים סי׳ קצו ס״ק ג, הובא בפ״ת סי׳ קפז ס״ק לב

32. כלל קיז סע׳ יב

33. שו״ת, יו״ד ח״ב סי׳ סט וראה גם ח״ג סי׳ נו אות ג

34. שו״ת מהרש״ם ח״א סי׳ קמו

35. ב״ח סי׳ קצב סד״ה עבר. חכמת אדם כלל קטו סע׳ ב. סדרה טהרה ס״ק כג. וכן שמעתי ממו״ר הגרי״י נויבירט שליט״א

36. הגר״מ פיינשטיין זצ״ל הלכות נדה להג״ש איידר עמ׳ 67 באמצע ס״ק קו

SIMAN 196 / §6, 7, 8

§7 A (E)blind woman examines herself and shows the cloth to a friend.

§8 A woman who is either mute but can hear or deaf but can speak is no different from one who speaks and hears. But if she is (F)a deaf-mute or a *shoteh* or has become mentally

───────────── NISHMAT AVRAHAM ─────────────

(E) blind woman. May she show the cloth to her husband? (If she fears that he will rule strictly whenever there is the slightest doubt in his mind, or if the sight of the stains may be repugnant to him, it would be better for her to show the cloth to a friend.[37]) The *Shach*[38] rules that she may do so. The *Chochmat Adam*[39] also permits a husband to decide questions concerning the stains on an examination cloth, but not questions concerning her immersion in a *mikveh*. He explains[40] that although in both situations she is a *niddah*, nevertheless the examination cloth reflects only a temporary state since she does not always find blood stains on the cloth; therefore one may allow even her husband to decide. On the other hand, she is a confirmed *niddah* until she immerses herself in a *mikveh* and the ruling must therefore come from someone who is not subjectively involved. This is also the ruling of the *Darchei Teshuvah*.[41] On the other hand, the *Chavot Yair*[42] and the *Mahari Assad*[43] rule that he may even rule on questions concerning her immersion. Many *acharonim*[44] agree with the ruling of the *Shach*. And the *Chazon Ish*[45] writes that the sin of taking bribes is not a matter of rational law but of an edict, for the Torah did not forbid a Rav to rule for himself. He may rule as to whether his own chicken or animal is *treifah* even though he is poor and his sustenance depends on his decision. Similarly, he may rule for himself on a question of *chametz* that was not sold before *Pesach* even if the sum involved is very great. Moreover, if he does rule leniently and someone casts aspersions on his ruling, this man is numbered among those who cast doubts on the integrity of their Rav. Since we are certain that our *Chachamim* are above such lowly traits, it is only those who are themselves lacking any understanding and intelligence who do not appreciate the greatness of a wise man.

Rav Neuwirth shlita wrote to me pointing out that this discussion only concerns *halachot* that require a ruling by deduction. A *halachah* that is specifically stated in the *Shulchan Aruch* and *poskim* is not considered to be a ruling that requires a *posek*, and anyone, even a husband, may rule on such matters, see *Siman* 242:9.[46]

(F) a deaf-mute. *Rav Moshe Feinstein zt"l*[47] writes that although nowadays male and female deaf-mutes can be educated to understand as well as normal people, nevertheless the *halachah* concerning them does not change. They remain exempt from performing *mitzvot*

---

37. ראה תוס' נדה כ ע"ב ד"ה כל יומא. וכ"כ הטהרת ישראל סי' קפח סע' כא
38. סי' קפח ס"ק ז
39. כלל קט סע' ו ומובא גם בפ"ת ס"ק ו
40. בינת אדם שם סע' ג
41. סי' קפח ס"ק כד. וראה גם בדעת תורה שם סע' ב
42. שו"ת, סי' קכב
43. שו"ת, יו"ד סי' קפז
44. בית שערים יו"ד סי' מד. שו"ת מהר"ם שיק יו"ד סי' ל. שו"ת מהרש"ם ח"ד סי' יא ודעת תורה סי' יח ס"ק מד. ערוה"ש סי' קפח סע' כב. שו"ת יביע אומר ח"ו יו"ד סי' יח. ושו"ת שבט הלוי ח"ה סי' קנו אות ז
45. אמונה ובטחון פ"ג סי' ל. וע"ע ביו"ד סי' שיב סע' ב
46. וראה גם בסי' רמב סע' יב ובפ"ת שם ס"ק ה
47. ספר הלכות נדה בתשובה בסוף הספר אות כה

unbalanced because of disease, she must be examined by another woman to establish her menstrual cycle so as to permit her to her husband. Once her cycle has been established she is considered to be like any other woman. If a regular cycle cannot be established she must abstain from *coitus* every thirty days and is examined by a normal woman.

§10 The seven clean days must be consecutive without any evidence of bleeding. If she does see blood, even at the end of the seventh day, the count is annulled and she must perform a *hefsek taharah* and recount another seven clean days.

GLOSS: *If there is a* (G)*makkah on her body that she knows bleeds, she may ascribe a ketem to it regardless of the size of the stain.*

§11 If a woman (H)discharges semen during the seven days, she loses that day.

──────── NISHMAT AVRAHAM ────────

and one may not depend on their judgment just as one may not depend on their written word. Even a previously normal person who has become a deaf-mute and who is taught to write, does not return to his previous *halachic* status, if he lost his ability to write when he became a deaf-mute. He remains a deaf-mute *halachically*. *Rav Auerbach zt"l* wrote to me that I should see what *Rav Scheinberg shlita*[48] wrote and what he had added in that article. See *Nishmat Avraham*, vol. 1 *Orach Chaim,* Siman 38H and 55A,B.

(G) *makkah* on her body. The *Shevet HaLevi*[49] describes a case of a woman who had surgery because of a *cervical* laceration on the fifth day of her seven clean days. This was followed by bleeding for some days. She asked if she could immerse herself at the end of her original seven days and attribute the interim bleeding to the *makkah* (surgery) in accordance with what she had been told by her doctor. He replied that she must definitely count a further seven clean days. For, although she could certainly attribute the bleeding to the surgery, while she was hospitalized she certainly would not have thought about the seven clean days. Such an absence of awareness of the seven days would annul the count,[50] particularly since the bleeding from the surgery will cause her to completely put the matter of clean white underwear out of her mind. This will certainly annul the previous count and she is required to start counting all over again.[51]

(H) discharges semen. The basis of this *halachah* is too intricate and complicated for the purposes of this book and the

---

48. מוריה תמוז תשמ"ב

49. שו"ת, יו"ד ח"א סי' עג

50. וכותב שפשיטא דנחוש לדברי התשובה מעיל צדקה

שהובאו בפ"ת כאן ס"ק ג

51. וראה גם שם ח"ג סי' קבג, ח"ו סי' קלט אות א ושיעורי שבט הלוי סי' קצו סע' ב ס"ק ב. וראה גם בחכמת אדם כלל קיז סע' יג

SIMAN 197
SHE MAY NOT IMMERSE HERSELF IN A *MIKVEH* DURING THE DAYTIME

§2 If her husband is in town, it is a (A)*mitzvah* for her to immerse herself in a *mikveh* at the right time so as not to defer the *mitzvah* of procreation even for one night.

── NISHMAT AVRAHAM ──

reader should refer to those books that deal with the basic understanding of the laws of *niddah* for a full explanation of the concepts involved.

Rav Neuwirth shlita told me that a woman who undergoes artificial insemination with her husband's semen during the seven clean days (after she has been permitted to do so by a *posek*), must add a further four days to her count in case there is a discharge of semen. Since the procedure is done during the day, the question raised by the *Rama* of a mistake because of *coitus* during twilight does not arise. This is akin to the *halachah* of *coitus* on the wedding night. Here also, since the possibility of *coitus* during twilight is not present, even according to the *Rama* the *hefsek taharah* can be done on the fourth day towards evening.[52]

SIMAN 197

(A) *mitzvah*. Rav Shlomo Kluger zt"l[1] discusses the case of a man who has been warned by his doctors not to have *coitus* since it will harm him. Should his wife immerse herself in a *mikveh* so as to enable other physical contact with her husband, and if so, should she say the blessing? He answers that if she immerses herself with the thought that she is purifying herself from her *niddah* state, she should say the blessing. However she is certainly not obligated to immerse herself just to permit other physical contact, for her obligation to immerse herself exists only if her husband can fulfill his marital obligation. Also it would be better for her not to immerse herself if there is another who can see to his needs, for if she does immerse herself, he may not be able to restrain himself and he would thus endanger himself.

It would appear from this that if it is the wife who has a medical reason preventing her from having *coitus* she should not immerse herself, for it will be even more difficult for her husband to restrain himself (see Siman 195:16 above). However the *Shevet HaLevi*[2] writes that if she cannot have *coitus* with her husband for whatever reason, it is still a *mitzvah* for her to immerse herself so as to permit other physical contact. And, in his opinion, even though they cannot cohabit, it would seem that she should immerse herself, for she nevertheless has obligations to her husband aside from what is involved with *coitus*. However, since Rav Shlomo Kluger zt"l wrote that although she is permitted to immerse herself there is no obligation involved, this requires further study.[3]

Rav Zilberstein shlita,[4] quoting Rav

---

52. ראה בטהרת ישראל סי' קצג בבאר יצחק ס"ק יב

1. קנאת סופרים בקונטרס ההשמטות לספרו שיירי טהרה סי' קצט סי' סד

2. שו"ת, ח"ב (יו"ד) סי' קא

3. ראה גם בערוה"ש סי' קפד סע' מג

4. עת ללדת סוף קונטרס הערות עמ' נו

SIMAN 198
THE LAWS OF IMMERSION AND *CHATZIZAH*

§1 She must immerse all parts of her body simultaneously. Therefore there must not be (A)anything, however small, on her body, that stands between her and the water. If it is

──────── NISHMAT AVRAHAM ────────

Eliashiv shlita and *Rav Wosner shlita* (author of the *Shevet HaLevi*), writes that only if her husband is absolutely certain that physical contact alone will not arouse him to have an emission, is she permitted to immerse herself; if he is not certain, she should not immerse herself.

Rav Auerbach zt"l wrote to me that if coitus is not to be allowed for some time, it is better for her to immerse herself since there are those who fear that otherwise there may be a problem of *yichud* (see the *Maharsham*).[5] [*The Maharsham* discusses the problem of a healthy woman who refuses to immerse herself in a mikveh, and writes that it is clear to him that *yichud* for her with her husband is forbidden, for the Ve-Shav HaCohen writes that a woman with open cuts (which prevent her ritually preparing herself for immersion) who may be curable, is nevertheless forbidden to be secluded with her husband. This can be seen from the Gemara (Ketubot 63b) which rules that a woman who refuses to cohabit with her husband is fined by having a fixed sum deducted each week from her ketubah, including the days when she is *niddah* and coitus is forbidden. She is not like an ordinary *niddah* for that is a situation which the husband knows to be temporary. For even though it is possible that she will relent, as of the moment her husband can only see her refusal as a permanent one.[6] The Torah only permits *yichud* with a *niddah*, because, as Tosafot write (Sanhedrin 37a), she will soon be able to ritually purify herself and become permissible to her husband. She is therefore considered to be attainable. However, a rebellious wife is not considered attainable although there is a possibility that she will relent; it is therefore forbidden to be secluded with her.[7]]

SIMAN 198

(A) anything, however small. Rebbe Yitzchak[1] states that something that covers most of the body and bothers the woman (that is, it bothers her and she wishes that it were not there[2]), is a *chatzizah* by Torah law. If it covers most of her body but it does not bother her, or if it does not cover most of her body but bothers her, it is not a *chatzizah* by Torah law. But *Chazal* decreed that in both cases this would also be a *chatzizah* to avoid anyone contravening the Torah law. If it does not cover most of her body and also does not bother her, it is not a *chatzizah* even by Rabbinic law, and *Rashi*[3] explains that this is because it becomes like part of her body. Although the *Taz*[4] rules like this in principle, nevertheless both he and the *Rama* write that she must not immerse herself without first removing this minimal *chatzizah*. However where it is essential that she immerse herself and there is

---

5. שו"ת, ח"ב סי׳ קעח
6. ראה תוס׳ יומא יח ע"ב והגר הב"ח שם
7. וראה גם בספר דבר הלכה בשו"ת סי׳ ז בסוף הספר
1. נדה סז ע"ב

2. עיין רש"י עירובין ד ע"ב ד"ה ומקפיד
3. שם ד"ה ושאינו, שבת נז ע"א ד"ה הא
4. ס"ק ד

SIMAN 198: IMMERSION AND CHATZIZAH / §1

usual that people are sometimes concerned about not having a certain thing on their body, it is considered a *chatzizah*, even if at the moment it does not bother her. Moreover, even if such a thing never bothers her, it is still considered a *chatzizah*, if most people would be bothered by it. If it covers most of her body, even if people are not bothered by it, it is still a *chatzizah*.

GLOSS: *She should not immerse herself even if there is something on her body that is not a chatzizah, as a safety measure to prevent her immersing herself when she has something on her that really is a chatzizah.*

NISHMAT AVRAHAM

no alternative (i.e. the *chatzizah* cannot be removed), both the *Chochmat Adam*[5] and *Aruch HaShulchan*[6] rule that she may immerse herself.

Rav Auerbach zt"l wrote to me that if the *chatzizah* covers the whole body, it is a *chatzizah* according to Torah law even if it does not bother her, as stated in the *Gemara*.[7] *Rav Neuwirth shlita* added that this is also the *halachah* if the *chatzizah* covers only all of the hair.

With regard to a *chatzizah* in the *beit hasetarim* (naturally hidden parts of the body, such as the armpits and mouth) the *Tosafot*[8] rule that by Torah law, the water must be able theoretically to come into contact with the area during immersion (even if, in effect, it does not). This is the ruling adopted by the *Avnei Nezer*.[9] However, the *Ramban, Rashba* and *Ritva*[10] rule that this is only a Rabbinic law and this is cited by the *Mishneh LaMelech*.[11] *Rebbe Akiva Eiger*,[12] the *Chatam Sofer*[13] and the *Chazon Ish*[14] also follow this ruling.

The *Chelkat Yoav* writes that if a woman has been told that she must keep an obsorbent-cotton plug in her ear for seven days (or more) it is not considered a *chatzizah*. We rule that a knot tied on *Shabbat* to remain as a knot for less than seven days is not considered a knot at all. However, if the intention is for it to last seven days or more, it is Rabbinically considered a permanent knot and may not be tied. By Torah law one is not culpable unless he wishes the knot to remain tied permanently. Since Rabbinically a knot is only considered permanent if it lasts seven days or more, a *chatzizah* in the *beit hasetarim*, which is only Rabbinically a *chatzizah*, is considered to become a permanent part of her body if it is present for seven days or more, and is therefore not considered a *chatzizah* at all. In the case in question, since she does not change the plug in her ear during the seven days, it is not considered a *chatzizah*.[15]

---

5. כלל קיט סע' ג
6. סע' ט. דוזהו כדיעבד
7. יבמות עח ע"ב
8. קדושין כה ע"א ד"ה כל. וראה גם בסוכה ו ע"ב ד"ה דבר, מנחות יח ע"ב ד"ה ואמר ונדה סו ע"ב ד"ה כל
9. שו"ת, יו"ד סי' רס
10. קדושין שם
11. הל' מקואות פ"א ה"ח
12. פסקים סי' ס
13. שו"ת, יו"ד סי' קצב
14. יו"ד סי' צה ס"ק ג. וראה הסבר הענין שם, ובסדרי טהרה כאן ס"ק כג, תשובת הגר"ב בשו"ת תשובה מאהבה ח"א סי' לט ושו"ת חת"ס יו"ד סי' קצג
15. שו"ת, יו"ד סי' ל

§8 A salve that is put into the eye is not a *chatzizah*, but if it is on the eyelid, it is. If, however, she usually (B)constantly

NISHMAT AVRAHAM

The *Avnei Nezer*[16] disagrees with this ruling and writes that something is not considered to become part of the body unless it is there for six months; if it is there less than six months it is considered a *chatzizah*. Rav Auerbach zt"l told me that the *poskim* accept the ruling of the *Beit Yosef*[17] that a knot that will remain tied for up to a month is accepted as being Rabbinically a permanent knot. Thus if something is present in the body for thirty days it is considered to become part of the body with regard to the *halachah* of *beit hasetarim*.

(B) constantly opens and closes her eyes. The *Noda BiYehudah's* son[18] discusses how a woman with painful eyes, who has been told by her doctor not to allow any water to touch her eyes lest she become blind, should conduct herself regarding immersion. He disagrees with the questioner's advice that she should tie a bandage over her eyes. Rather, he advises that another woman should enter the *mikveh* together with her and stand behind but away from her, to avoid any body contact. This other woman should then wet her hands thoroughly[19] (see later §28) and gently cover the eyes of the patient who then immerses. The patient herself may not use her own hands since water will then not be able to come into contact with the crook of her elbows while she covers her eyes. As to her washing herself in preparation for immersion, he writes that it is sufficient if she washes all her body thoroughly, excluding her eyes. She should examine her eyes well in a mirror or ask another to do so to make sure there is no dirt on them. *The Avnei Nezer*,[20] on the other hand, permits the woman herself to dip her fingers into the *mikveh* and then cover her eyes with them. See also below **L2** p. 155.

1. A GLASS EYE is not a *chatzizah* if the woman is ashamed to remove it in public.[21]

2. CONTACT LENSES should be removed before immersion. If she forgot to remove them before immersion, there are *poskim*[22] who rule that she need not immerse herself again, but the *Minchat Yitzchak*[23] rules that she should. Rav Yonah Emanuel zt"l (editor of the journal, *Ha-Ma'ayan*) pointed out that there are differences in the way people wear contact lenses; there are those who have them on all day and those who wear them only for a few hours a day. It is possible that those *poskim* who rule leniently if she had already immersed herself do not do so for those women who do not wear them all day. On the other hand, those *poskim* who rule strictly if she has already immersed herself would probably agree that if she wears them all day, and forgot to remove them before immersing herself, one could rule leniently. Rav Auerbach zt"l commented to him that, in his opinion, since the lenses are removed at night, they will be a *chatzizah* even for those women who wear them all day. Rav Emanuel zt"l also

---

16. שו"ת, יו"ד סי' רנג ו-רסב וע"ע סי' רסג ס"ק ג
17. או"ח סי' שיז
18. שו"ת שיבת ציון סי' מב מובא בפ"ת ס"ק טו
19. ראה להלן סע' כח ולעיל סי' קב סע' כ ובט"ז וש"ך, אם צריכה להדיח ידה דוקא במי מקוה בתוך המקוה או אפילו במים תלושים. ועיין במטה יהונתן בסי' קב שם
20. שו"ת, יו"ד סי' רסב
21. שו"ת מהרי"י אסאד סי' רכט. שו"ת שו"מ תליתאי ח"ג סי' קח. שו"ת הר צבי יו"ד סי' קסא. שו"ת זכר שמחה סי' קיח. שו"ת אג"מ יו"ד ח"א סי' קד ושו"ת מנחת יצחק ח"ג סי' פב
22. שו"ת שו"מ שם. שו"ת אג"מ שם. שו"ת הר צבי שם
23. שו"ת, ח"ו סי' פט

opens and closes her eyes, then even (C)what is on the eyelid is not considered a *chatzizah*.

§9 (D)Blood that has dried on a sore is a *chatzizah*, but mucus (or pus) is not.

---NISHMAT AVRAHAM---

pointed out that after removal of cataracts and especially when this is done in the young, contact lenses are sometimes implanted. In this case all would agree that they are not a *chatzizah*.

(C) what is on the eyelid. *Rashi*[24] explains that the constant motion of her eyelids thins the salve so that it no longer remains thick enough to prevent the water of the *mikveh* from reaching the skin.

(D) Blood that has dried on a sore. The scab on a wound is not a *chatzizah* once it is dry.[25] The *Chazon Ish*[26] writes that it is possible that one must consider two different kinds of scabs. The first consists of the blood and mucus that appear at the time of the laceration which later congeals on the wound. The second is the scab that comes with healing, covering the healing flesh and finally falling off when the wound has healed. So long as the flesh underneath the scab has not healed, the scab is considered to be like skin and therefore does not become a *chatzizah*. But, once the wound has healed, the scab becomes a *chatzizah*. If a part of the scab spreads beyond the confines of the wound, or the part of the wound under the edges of the scab has healed, or congealed blood or mucus is present outside the wound — all of these are a *chatzizah*.

The *Kitzur Shulchan Aruch*[27] writes that even if a woman finds it painful to remove a scab on a wound she must either remove it before immersion or soften it well in water. However the *Chochmat Adam*[28] writes that if she is able to immerse herself again after removing the salve from around the eye (§8) or the scab over a wound (§9), she should do so. But if she is unable to do this, she may depend on those *poskim* who rule that they are not considered a *chatzizah*. The *She'arim Metzuyanim BaHalachah*[29] writes that she should attempt to remove the scab only if she can do so easily. If, however, it is too painful to do so she need not act strictly. *Rav Neuwirth shlita* also told me that if she cannot remove the scab without pain or bleeding, the wound has not yet healed. The scab is therefore considered part of the body and is not a *chatzizah*. Nevertheless, she should soften it. If the wound has completely healed and the scab is about to fall off, since there is new skin covering the whole wound underneath, and the scab can be removed without pain or bleeding, softening it is still sufficient. However it would be better if she removed the scab before immersion. *Rav Auerbach zt"l* agreed with this ruling of *Rav Neuwirth shlita*.

If she needs to immerse herself on *Shabbat* (Friday night) and forgot to remove the scab before *Shabbat*, she may do so on *Shabbat*. However she must be careful not to cause bleeding.[30] The *Ketsot HaShulchan*[31] writes that the prohibition of the *melachah* of "plucking" is not involved since the scab, although still

---

24. נדה סז ע״א ד״ה פורחות
25. ערוה״ש סע׳ לה
26. יו״ד סי׳ צד ס״ק ד
27. סי׳ קסא סע׳ ג
28. כלל קיט סע׳ ו
29. סי׳ קסא ס״ק ג
30. ראה או״ח סי׳ שכח סע׳ כב
31. סי׳ קלו בבדה״ש ס״ק כב

§10 (E)An adhesive plaster on a wound is a *chatzizah*.

NISHMAT AVRAHAM

attached to the flesh at the moment, will eventually fall off. The situation here is also less problematic than with thin shreds of skin that have almost completely fallen away from the skin surrounding the nails of the hand which may not be removed.[32] In any case, the scab should be removed by hand and not with an instrument.

PEELING SKIN is not a *chatzizah* since it does not prevent water from getting to the body. The base of tags of skin is also not a *chatzizah* since they do not bother anyone enough to cut them off and they are left to fall off on their own. They do not cover most of her body and also do not bother her and thus are not a *chatzizah* according to all opinions.[33]

(E) An adhesive plaster (band-aid) or bandage. This is also the ruling of the *Chochmat Adam*.[34] However other *poskim* rule that it is only a *chatzizah* if it bothers her.[35] Therefore, if it is painful to remove and it must be there for some time, she may immerse herself with it.[36] The *Divrei Malkiel*[37] writes that if she needs the plaster permanently, it will not be a *chatzizah* even though she changes it from time to time. However if the wound will heal and the plaster will then be removed it will be a *chatzizah*. There are those who rule that if the plaster can be removed without too much pain she should do so. But if an attempt to do so will cause her much pain, she may wash around it with hot water as well as possible and immerse herself.[38] This is also the opinion of the *Yabia Omer*[39] who adds, however, that if there are only a few more days before she may remove the plaster, she should wait until then before immersing herself.

The *Mishnah Berurah*[40] discusses situations where hair may be inadvertently plucked from one's body on *Shabbat*. Doing so is forbidden because of the *melachah* of "plucking"; although there is no intention of pulling out hair, it is unavoidable. However, *Rav Ovadiah Yosef shlita*[41] writes that it is permissible when needed. Since removing hair with an instrument is forbidden only Rabbinically, and, since there is no intention to remove hair, many *poskim*[42] permit it, for although it is an unavoidable result it is nevertheless unwanted. The *Shemirat Shabbat KeHilchatah*[43] writes that it is best not to remove a bandage with adhesive tape, since hair will unavoidably be pulled out. However, *Rav Auerbach zt"l*[44] rules that if the bandage bothers her, she may remove it since the hair is pulled out in an indirect manner, it is an act of spoiling and, although unavoidable, it is unwanted. This is also the ruling of the *Mishnah Berurah* in these circumstances.[45] Therefore, a woman who needs

---

32. או"ח סי' שכח סע' לא
33. חכ"א כלל קיט סע' ז
34. כלל קיט סע' ז
35. סדרי טהרה אות כד
36. שו"ת, הר צבי יו"ד סי' קסט
37. שו"ת, ח"ה סי' קח
38. שו"ת ציץ אליעזר ח"ד סי' ט בשם הדברי חיים יו"ד ח"ב סי' סה
39. שו"ת, ח"ג יו"ד סי' יב
40. סי' שיב ס"ק כ, סי' שכח ס"ק קנא וסע' מט ובי"ה"ל

ד"ה לשום
41. לב אברהם ח"א עמ' יב. וראה בשו"ת יביע אומר ח"ה או"ח סי' כז
42. שו"ת באר יצחק סי' טו ובמפתחות. שו"ת בתי כהונה חלק בית דין סי' יח. שו"מ קמא ח"א סי' רי ותליתאה ח"ג סי' ג. שו"ת מהרש"ם ח"ה סי' מח. שו"ת דברי מלביאל יו"ד סי' מב
43. פל"ה סע' כח
44. שם בהערה עג
45. סי' שטו שעה"צ ס"ק יח, סי' שכא שעה"צ ס"ק יח וסי' שלו שעה"צ ס"ק ב. וצ"ע ממה שכותב המ"ב סי' שלו

§11 An arrow or thorn [F]that protrudes from her flesh is a *chatzizah*, but if it is not visible from the outside, it is not a *chatzizah*.

―――――― NISHMAT AVRAHAM ――――――

to immerse herself on *Shabbat* (Friday night) and forgot to remove an adhesive plaster (band-aid) from a hairy area before *Shabbat*, may remove it, even according to the *poskim* who otherwise rule strictly. *Rav Neuwirth shlita* agreed with this.[46]

After the immersion she may put on another adhesive plaster (band-aid). See also *Nishmat Avraham*, vol. 1 *Orach Chaim*, Siman 328 (23A), p. 209.

Rav Neuwirth shlita told me that if the bandage will remain for some months and removing it will cause her discomfort, it is not considered a *chatzizah*.[47] If, however, water can reach the skin through the bandage, and it is difficult for her to remove the bandage, she may immerse herself with it even if it will not remain for a lengthy period.

1. PLASTER CAST. If this cannot be removed without causing great pain and danger to the limb, however minimal, and the cast will remain for some months, she may immerse with it. Since the cast is there for a medical reason, she surely does not wish it to be removed before she is healed.[48] However, if her husband can restrain himself until the plaster cast is removed, she should wait till then.[49] See also below **F**, *Rav Auerbach zt"l's* view with regard to a medical cause of *chatzizah*.

2. INTRAVENOUS CATHETER. Patients are sometimes discharged home to continue receiving intravenous drugs for a period of many weeks or even many months. A special intravenous catheter (peripherally introduced central catheter — PICC) is inserted into a vein in the arm or into a large central vein via the chest wall (Hickman catheter) and can remain there without the need for replacement. The point of entry of the catheter into the body of the patient must be covered with a waterproof dressing to keep it sterile and to allow the patient to bathe, and at the same time keep the non-sterile water from entering the area. The above *halachot* will be relevant to such a female patient. *Rav Neuwirth shlita* told me that if the catheter will remain for less than four weeks, the dressing, which must not be removed, will be a *chatzizah*. However, if the catheter will remain in place for more than four weeks, the dressing will not be considered a *chatzizah*. A *posek* should be consulted in each case.

(F) that protrudes. The *halachah* is the same for sutures, and those sutures that are external are a *chatzizah*.[50] *Rav Auerbach zt"l* told me that although the woman accepts that they are there, this is only because she has no choice and therefore they are considered as something she

―――――――

46. ושמעתי ממו"ר הגרי"י נויבירט שליט"א שלבאורה יש להקשות לשיטות המקילים מהגמ' שבת פא ע"א

47. ראה בשו"ת הר צבי יו"ד סי' קסט

48. שו"ת ציץ אליעזר ח"ד סי' ט

49. שו"ת הר צבי יו"ד סי' קסה

50. ראה סדרי טהרה אות ז. חכ"א כלל קיט סע' ח ושו"ת אג"מ יו"ד ח"ב סי' פז. וראה בש"ך ס"ק טז

מובא בשו"ע סי' שיב סע' ז, ועיין שם במ"ב ס"ק כ ושעה"צ ס"ק כג, שאפילו פס"ר דלא ניח"ל ואינו מכוין ובמקום צער אסור, רצ"ע

§16 (G)Blood that adheres to the skin is a *chatzizah* although it is still wet.

§17 (H)Coloring that a woman puts on her face, hands and hair of her head is not a *chatzizah*. So, too, for one who paints or dyes and her hands are colored, the coloring is not considered a *chatzizah*.

§19 If she has swelling around a nail such that she can neither cut the nail nor clean it, if the swelling is great enough to (I)obscure any dirt which may be under the fingernail, it (the dirt) is not a *chatzizah*.

§23 Jewelry (such as earrings, nose-rings and rings) attached loosely to the body is not a *chatzizah*. However, if it is attached tightly it is a *chatzizah*. The *halachah* is similar with regard to (J)a bandage.

§24 (K)The teeth need to be well brushed so that nothing will act as a *chatzizah*. If she immerses herself and then finds something sticking to them the immersion is nullified.

──────────── NISHMAT AVRAHAM ────────────

minds (see **A** above, p. 144 and **K6** below, p. 154).

(G) Blood that adheres to the skin. This refers to blood that is beginning to dry and stick to the skin. When touched with the finger a thread of blood remains attached to the finger.[51] See also **D** above, p. 147.

(H) Coloring. Ointment on a wound is a *chatzizah* and must be washed off.[52] Rav Neuwirth shlita added that this refers only to a thick ointment.

(I) obsure. The *Beit Yosef* writes that this *halachah* is derived from the *halachah* concerning an arrow (above §11). From this we can further derive that as long as dirt under the nail does not protrude further than the flesh under the nail, it is not a *chatzizah*.[53]

(J) a bandage. See **E** above, p. 148.

(K) The teeth. A number of situations need to be considered:

1. PERMANENT FILLING. The *Chochmat Adam*[54] rules strictly for since the filling is there for a medical reason, it is considered as something which bothers her; she really wishes to remove it but is unable to do so. This is also the opinion of the *Binyan Tzion*[55] who rules that she should not immerse herself.

However, the *Maharsham*[56] permits her to immerse herself since it is impossible for her to remove it. Therefore it is not a *chatzizah*, and, although it was done for a medical reason, nevertheless she would not wish to remove it since the cavity will

---

51. ש"ך ס"ק כ
52. ערוה"ש סע' לב
53. ש"ך ס"ק כד
54. כלל קיט סע' יח ובינת אדם ס"ק יב
55. שו"ת בנין ציון החדשות סי' נז
56. שו"ת, ח"א סי' עט

SIMAN 198: IMMERSION AND CHATZIZAH / §16, 17, 19, 23, 24

NISHMAT AVRAHAM

be unattractive. Although the *Harei Besamim*[57] ruled strictly, he later rescinded his decision[58] ruling that she may immerse herself since it was placed to remain permanently. This is also the ruling of the *Chesed LeAvraham*[59] who includes in his argument the opinion of the *Ritva* and the *Rashba* that the *halachah* of *beit hasetarim* (see above **A**) is Rabbinic and therefore if there is any doubt regarding the *halachah* in such a case, we rule leniently. Although *Tosafot* believe that the *halachah* of *beit hasetarim* is a Torah one, the controversy makes it a matter of doubt; i.e. does it have Torah or Rabbinic force? Add to this matter of doubt the further doubt as to whether a filling is a *chatzizah* anyway, and we have a double doubt, and one may therefore rule leniently. *Rav Neuwirth shlita* also added that *Chazal* ruled strictly only if the *chatzizah* covers most of the area or if she minds it and here neither of these two conditions is present. The *Shach*[60] and *Shevut Yaakov*[61] also write that even if she minds it, if it does not cover most of the area, we again say that the decision is a Rabbinic doubt and therefore rule leniently. Many *acharonim*[62] permit a woman with permanent fillings to immerse herself.

The *Igrot Moshe*[63] writes that everyone, the whole world over, rules leniently and not even those who are very particular in their actions take it into consideration. If not, how can any woman immerse herself? Surely there is no woman nowadays who does not have a permanent filling in at least one tooth. Regarding the *Chochmat Adam's* ruling, the *Igrot Moshe* writes that with modern fillings even the *Chochmat Adam* would have ruled leniently; his ruling was for fillings of wax or lead that covered the cavity to prevent pain, but on which she could not chew. In such a case she would prefer to have a cavity and be able to chew rather than a filled tooth on which she cannot chew. This is also what *Rav Neuwirth shlita* wrote to me.[64]

2. TEMPORARY FILLING. There is disagreement among the *poskim* regarding a temporary filling. Is it considered a *chatzizah* or not? The *Taharat Yisrael*[65] and the *Metsudat David*[66] rule that it is. The *Imrei Yosher*[67] writes that this is a problem involving the *beit hasetarim* and a Rabbinic *chatzizah* — a case of two Rabbinic *halachot* and, moreover, the filling is attached to the tooth and becomes part of it. Nevertheless, since it will be replaced in two weeks with a permanent filling, one should not search for reasons to be lenient. This is also the ruling of the *Levushei Mordechai*[68] who was asked about a filling inserted for two or three days. See **A** above, the opinion of the *Chelkat Yoav* (reference 15).

However, the *Shoel U'Meshiv*[69] rules that it is not a *chatzizah* since the cavity is now filled and the tooth reverts to its for-

---

57. שו״ת, מהד״ק סי׳ קג
58. מהד״ת סי׳ קכח
59. תאומים יו״ד סי׳ מז
60. ס״ק יג. וראה גם בספר דברי שאול סי׳ קצח סע׳ כד ס״ק כג
61. שו״ת, ח״א סי׳ סט
62. שו״ת שו״מ קמא ח״ג סי׳ כז ותניינא ח״ג סי׳ קח. שו״ת לבוש מרדכי יו״ד סי׳ קכח. שו״ת בית יצחק יו״ד ח״ב סי׳ יט. שו״ת אבני נזר יו״ד סי׳ רנח. שו״ת צמח צדק יו״ד סי׳ קסו. שו״ת אמרי יושר ח״ב סי׳ קצג. דרכי תשובה ס״ק עו. טהרת ישראל סע׳ צ. דעת תורה ס״ק כד. בן איש חי שנה ב פ׳ שמיני ס״ק ט ושו״ת רב פעלים ח״ד יו״ד סי׳
63. שו״ת, יו״ד ח״א סי׳ צז ענף ו
64. וז״ל: אצלי ברור שכן כוונת החכ״א, דעיין שם בכלל קיט סע׳ ז לגביה רטיה, וק״ו כאן
65. סע׳ צ
66. על הקיצור שו״ע סי׳ קסא ס״ק יא
67. שו״ת, ח״ב סי׳ קיב
68. שו״ת, ח״ד סי׳ נד
69. שו״ת, מהד״ת ח״ג סי׳ קח

mer state so that the question of it being fit for water to reach it does not apply. In addition, the *Ritva* rules that this is only a Rabbinic requirement. As to whether it bothers her or not, this does not apply to whatever is done for a medical reason.[70] Although the *Sidrei Taharah*[71] is not too happy with this reasoning, for we should be able to say the same for a band-aid or bandage, nevertheless, he leans towards a lenient ruling. One could, however, suggest a difference between a filling and a band-aid or bandage, since the latter are certainly temporary, whereas the filling — first the temporary and then the permanent one — remains and will become part of the tooth. Besides, the filling is in the *beit hasetarim* whereas the band-aid and bandage are not.

The *Darchei Teshuvah*[72] quotes the *Elef Lecha Shlomo*[73] who permits a woman with a temporary filling to immerse herself in a *mikveh* and this is also the ruling of the *Chelkat Yaakov*.[74] The *Har Tzvi*[75] writes that since the cavity will be permanently filled there is no *chatzizah*, although the temporary filling will be replaced by a permanent one. He bases his opinion on a ruling of the *Maharsham*[76] (who discusses an absorbent-cotton plug in the ear), that because she intends to replace the cotton wool plug, this is itself proof that it does not bother her. The *Divrei Malkiel*[77] writes that a band-aid or bandage which will remain permanently does not become a *chatzizah* even though she will change it from time to time. The *Igrot Moshe*[78] also permits a woman with a temporary filling to immerse herself in a *mikveh* since the cavity will be permanently filled, first with a temporary and later with a permanent filling. This is also the ruling of the *Minchat Yitzchak*.[79]

Rav Auerbach zt"l told me, basing his ruling on the opinion of the *Chelkat Yoav* (above reference 15), that he permits a woman with a temporary filling to immerse herself in a *mikveh* provided that it will remain for at least seven days and does not protrude outside the tooth. In this way it is considered part of her body. If, however, it protrudes it does not become part of her body. If she decides that she will wait to return to her dentist only after thirty days (see above, reference 15 what I wrote in the *Rav zt"l's* name) have passed from the time she should have immersed herself, she will be permitted to immerse herself now.[80] Obviously if during this time she has pain and feels that she must return to the dentist for further treatment, she may certainly change her decision.

3. DENTURES and CROWNS. A false tooth or crown that is fixed permanently is not a *chatzizah*.[81] The *Beit Yitzchak*,[82] however, rules strictly writing that since one can have false teeth that are easily removable each time a woman goes to the *mikveh*, she should have this type of tooth.

---

70. וראה שם מהד"ק ח"ג סי' כז. וכן ראה ברמ"א כאן סע' ו
71. סוס"ק יט
72. ס"ק עה
73. שו"ת, ח"ב סי' כו
74. שו"ת, ח"א סי' קלו וח"ב סי' קעג
75. שו"ת, יו"ד סי' קסט
76. שו"ת, ח"א סי' ז
77. שו"ת, ח"ה סי' קח
78. שו"ת, יו"ד ח"א סי' צז
79. שו"ת, ח"ה סי' קיא
80. ועוד שמעתי מהגרשז"א זצ"ל שהמורה הוראה יכול לומר לבעלה מבלי ידיעתה שאם תפסיד את התור או תצטער, תוכל ללכת לרופא להמשך הטיפול, ודאי לא תועיל אם האשה עצמה תחשוב כן בשעת הטבילה. וכן מובא בשמו בספר שערי טבילה סי' לד סוס"ק ד, אך ראה שם שאינו מבדיל בין בולטת ואינו בולטת
81. שו"ת מהר"י אסאד יו"ד סי' רכח. טהרת ישראל כאן סע' פז. עקרי הד"ט סי' כב אות ז. שו"ת בנין ציון החדשות סי' נג. בינת אדם על החכ"א ס"ק יב. שו"ת מהרש"ם ח"א סי' עה. שו"ת אבני נזר יו"ד סי' רנט ושו"ת רב פעלים להבן איש חי ח"ד יו"ד סי' יג
82. שו"ת, יו"ד ח"ב סי' יט

NISHMAT AVRAHAM

For the *Rama* (§1) writes that if she has something on her body that is not a *chatzizah*, she should not immerse herself as a safety measure to prevent her immersing herself when she has something on her that really is a *chatzizah*. True she may immerse herself if, there is pain or suffering in removing it, for one may then consider the situation to be one in which there is no alternative. However, the *Beit Yitzchak* concludes that since in this case there are *poskim* who rule strictly and there is a possibility that it is a *chatzizah*, she must have removable dentures made. The *Avnei Nezer*[83] also rules strictly if most of the teeth are false, since Torah law is involved when a *chatzizah* involves most of the body. For, he rules, not only is the *beit hasetarim* considered a separate entity on its own, but each different *beit hasetarim* is considered a separate entity. However, the *Imrei Yosher*[84] disagrees with this, writing that according to all *poskim* the *beit hasetarim* is not considered an entity separate from the rest of the body and this is also the ruling of the *Sidrei Taharah*.[85]

Removable dentures are a *chatzizah*.[86] I wondered why this is not comparable to a glass eye (above **B**) which is not considered a *chatzizah* since she would be ashamed to remove them in public, and found later that the *Be'er Yitzchak* (see below reference 88) asks the same question. The *Taharat Yisrael*[87] writes that especially nowadays, since the dentures are continuously removed for cleaning, she will need to immerse herself again if she forgot to remove them. However, if a *posek* did rule leniently in a situation where she forgot to remove them before immersing herself, we do not question the decision. The *Be'er Yitzchak*[88] explains that she is really not interested in removing them at all, for were it possible to clean them while they are still attached, she would do so. Besides, she would be ashamed to remove them in public. Therefore, we do not question a lenient ruling if she forgot to remove them before immersing herself. As to her saying the blessing if she immerses herself again, the *Minchat Yitzchak*[89] rules that she should not. He quotes the *Maharsham*[90] who writes that removable dentures are a *chatzizah* only if they are strongly attached to the gums, but if they are not strongly attached so that water could theoretically get to the gums, they are not a *chatzizah*. The *Minchat Yitzchak* rules therefore that although one should not rule leniently and she should immerse herself again, nevertheless, she should not repeat the blessing. Since there is a possibility that they were only loosely attached, and this is commonly so, for food and fluids often find their way between the dentures and the gums, it could have been that there was no *chatzizah* when she immersed herself the first time.[91]

4. LOOSE TOOTH. The *Dovev Mesharim*[92] rules that a loose tooth is not a *chatzizah* even if it is the woman's intention to go to a dentist soon to have it removed. He bases his ruling on the opinion of the *Ritva* (see **K1**) that the ruling that water should theoretically be able to enter a *beit hasetarim* is Rabbinic. In this case the

---

83. שו"ת יו"ד סי' רנט
84. שו"ת, ח"ב סי' קצג
85. סי' קצט בשם הזכרון יוסף
86. שו"ת שו"מ מהד"ק ח"ג סי' כו. שו"ת מהר"י אסאד יו"ד סי' רכט. שו"ת מהרש"ם ח"א סי' עח הגרי"י נויבירט שליט"א באהל שרה הל' חציצה פ"ו סע' י ושו"ת שבט הלוי ח"ג סי' קכח
87. כאן סע' פו
88. ס"ק רסב
89. שו"ת, ח"ה סי' כא וראה גם בתחלת הקדמתו שם
90. שו"ת, ח"א סי' עח
91. ראה גם בשו"ת ציץ אליעזר חי"ב סוסי' סז
92. שו"ת, ח"א סי' פד

§25 If she did not wash the (L)*beit hasetarim* and the folds of her body, and later found that there was something there that is considered a *chatzizah*, the immersion is not valid.

── NISHMAT AVRAHAM ──

tooth that she is anxious to remove only covers a small area and is in a *beit hasetarim*; since the situation is doubly Rabbinic, one may therefore rule leniently. Besides, he quotes the *Noda BiYehudah*[93] that since the tooth is enclosed within the mouth, it is part of the body, and is therefore not a *chatzizah*. The *Avnei Nezer*[94] also rules leniently, even though on the matter of the *beit hasetarim* he rules like *Tosafot* who consider the need for the water to be able theoretically to enter a *beit hasetarim* a Torah law. This is because one tooth is involved and the *halachah* concerning the entry of water to the *beit hasetarim* is not more demanding than that of the *halachah* for non-hidden parts of the body where something covering a small area is not a *chatzizah* from the Torah standpoint. Moreover, although the tooth is loose, it is still part of her body and can be compared to a fingernail which although almost com-pletely separated, is not a *chatzizah*.[95] This is also the ruling of the *Shevet HaLevi*.[96]

5. FIXED ORTHODONTIC APPLIANCE (BRACE). This is used to straighten teeth, and is put in and removed professionally, remaining in place for many months and even years. It is not considered a *chatzizah*.[97] The *Shevet HaLevi*[98] writes that if the brace is put in to treat loose teeth, one may rule leniently since it can only be removed professionally. This is also the ruling of *Badei HaShulchan*.[99] Although there are those who rule strictly,[100] it is not clear to what situation they refer.

6. SUTURES. If temporary sutures, which are visible, were put into the gums, the *Dovev Mesharim*[101] rules that the woman may nevertheless immerse herself. This is because the sutures are in the *beit hasetarim* and to this point we may add the *Ritva's* opinion that two Rabbinic issues are involved (see above **K1**). However, the *Igrot Moshe*[102] rules strictly; since they are visible it is assumed that she is bothered by their presence. Although they are in the *beit hasetarim*, nevertheless they will (theoretically) prevent water from reaching the gums and are therefore a *chatzizah*. However, if they cannot be seen they are not a *chatzizah* since they are enclosed within the body and only become visible if the flesh of the gums is separated with an instrument. *Rav Auerbach zt"l*[103] also rules strictly if they are visible, for since the sutures are only temporary (for less than thirty days[104]), it is best to postpone her immersion.

(L) *beit hasetarim*. There are various other problems of *chatzizah*. In all cases,

---

93. שו"ת, מהד"ק יו"ד סי' סד
94. שו"ת, יו"ד סי' רס
95. ראה שם ס"ק ט
96. שו"ת, ח"א סי' צו
97. שו"ת מנחת יצחק ח"ו סי' פו. שערים מצויינים בהלכה סי' קסא ס"ק ב. שו"ת שבט הלוי יו"ד ח"א סי' צח. הגרי"י נויבירט שליט"א באוהל שרה הלכות חציצה פ"ו סע' טו
98. שו"ת שבט הלוי שם וכן בשיעורי שבט הלוי סי' קצח סע' כד ס"ק ב
99. סי' קצח סוס"ק קעט
100. שו"ת אג"מ יו"ד ח"א סי' צו. שערי טבילה סי' לה ס"ק ד בשם הגרי"ש אלישיב. וכתב לי מו"ר הגרי"י נויבירט שליט"א: יל"ע דהא עומדים לזמן ממושך ומ"ש מאספלנית
101. שו"ת, ח"ג סי' מ, מובא גם בספר שערי טבילה סוסי' לה
102. שו"ת, יו"ד ח"ב סי' פז
103. ספר שערי טבילה שם
104. כן כתב לי הגאון זצ"ל

SIMAN 198: IMMERSION AND CHATZIZAH / §25

NISHMAT AVRAHAM

the treating physician must be consulted first and a ruling obtained from a *posek*.

1. INTRAUTERINE DEVICE (IUD). This does not constitute a *chatzizah*[105] nor does the string attached to it which extends to outside the *cervix*.[106] However *Rav Auerbach zt"l* told me that she should take care that the visible part of the string be as short as possible and that it not be stuck to the walls of the *prozdor*.

2. PESSARY. This is a ring that is put into the *prozdor* to support a prolapsed *uterus*. The *Cheshev HaEphod*[107] writes that it is accepted practice to rule leniently in all cases where the potential *chatzizah* is incorporated into the body for a prolonged period of time even though not permanently. The opinion of the *Chelkat Yoav* (see above 1A) that anything that is incorporated into the body for seven days or more is treated like a permanent situation, is well known. And, although one may argue with this, nevertheless, if there is an additional reason to rule leniently, the accepted practice is to do so. In the case of a *pessary*, it is completely enclosed within the body, and even if this is not so, it is at least in a *beit hasetarim*, and the opinion of the *Ritva* is that this is a situation involving two Rabbinic issues; in such a case we may rely on the *Chelkat Yoav's* opinion. This is also the opinion of the *Maharash Engel*.[108] *Rav Neuwirth shlita* wrote to me adding that the *Chochmat Adam's*[109] tendency to rule leniently with regard to an adhesive plaster (or band-aid) that is impossible to remove at the time, is yet another reason to rule leniently. If she inserts and removes the *pessary* herself from time to time, she should remove it before immersing herself. However, if she forgot to do so and immersed herself, *Rav Neuwirth shlita* told me that she need not immerse herself again.

Nowadays this problem is rare since women who are young enough to be *menstruating* undergo surgery to correct a prolapse rather than use a *pessary*.

3. PERMANENT *COLOSTOMY*. A woman who undergoes surgery on her large intestine and is left with an opening of the intestine protruding through her abdominal wall through which feces is passed, wears a bag, which surrounds the external opening of the *colostomy*, for the feces to pass into. From time to time the bag, and its ring which is glued to the skin, is removed for emptying and the *colostomy* and surrounding skin cleaned. Before immersion she should remove the bag and clean the *colostomy* and surrounding skin thoroughly. She should be the last one to use the *mikveh* before it is cleaned and its water changed.

4. PERMANENT *ILEOSTOMY*. Surgery is on the small intestine and the patient is left with an opening of the small intestine protruding through her abdominal wall. The feces is more fluid and is passed more or less continuously, making it a bigger hygienic problem for her immersion than with a *colostomy*. To prevent soiling of the *mikveh* water while she immerses herself, she may insert a tampon or gauze into the opening of the *ileostomy*, leaving the string of the tampon or part of the gauze outside for easy removal (see above IUD). She should be the last one to use the *mikveh* before it is cleaned and its

---

105. שו"ת נו"ב מהד"ק יו"ד סי' סד. פ"ת ס"ק טז. דרכ"ת ס"ק פז. ערוה"ש סע' נה. שו"ת חת"ס יו"ד סי' קצג. שו"ת בנין ציון סי' עא. שו"ת יד הלוי ח"ב סי' מא. שו"ת זכר שמחה סי' קיט. שו"ת הר צבי יו"ד סי' קנג. שו"ת ציץ אליעזר ח"י סי' כה פ"י או"ק ג וחי"א סי' סג

106. שו"ת ציץ אליעזר חי"א סי' סג. שו"ת מנחת יצחק

107. שו"ת, ח"ב סי' קיח

108. שו"ת ח"ג סי' י. וראה בשו"ת נו"ב מהד"ת סי' קלה. דרכ"ת ס"ק פז. שו"ת הר צבי סי' קנג וערוה"ש סע' נה

109. כלל קיט סע' ז

ח"ו סי' פו

NISHMAT AVRAHAM

water changed. *Rav Auerbach zt"l* told me that she should take care that the gauze or string that is outside the *ileostomy* be loose so that water can theoretically enter there. He added that she obviously must not immerse with the bag and the ring that is stuck onto her skin.

5. PERMANENT *URINARY CATHETER*.
If a woman has a permanent *urinary catheter* inserted into her bladder, she may immerse with it, since the inner end of the catheter is included within the body and the outside end lies on her body only loosely. *Rav Auerbach zt"l* agreed with this.

6. PERMANENT *PERITONEAL DIALYSIS*.
Dialysis may be done through a catheter permanently inserted through the abdominal wall into the abdominal cavity. The area of skin surounding the catheter should be well washed before immersion. There is no problem of *chatzizah* once any sutures that were put in have been removed. The opening of the catheter must be closed with a spigot to prevent any water from entering it.

7. PERMANENT *GASTROSTOMY* AND *JEJUNOSTOMY*.
The patient has a tube inserted through the abdominal wall into the stomach or small intestine respectively for the purpose of feeding. Once the wound has healed, there is no need for a dressing of any kind to cover the area and there is no problem of *chatzizah*.

8. PERMANENT *NEPHROSTOMY*.
A tube is inserted through the back of the patient into the kidney to drain urine. See **6** above as to how this should be treated.

9. COTTON WOOL IN THE EAR.
If a woman has been told by her doctors that she must always have absorbent cotton in her ear, she must put it well in so that the visible part of the ear is not covered. If a thread of absorbent cotton remains outside for easy removal this does not matter and she may immerse herself.[110] If she was told that the only reason for the absorbent cotton is to prevent any water entering her ear she may still immerse herself,[111] but she should preferably put the absorbent cotton in for a whole week before the immersion so that it will be, for her, something which she does not mind.[112] *Rav Auerbach zt"l* told me that this requirement is only if the absorbent cotton is so firmly inserted that water cannot theoretically get there. On the other hand, the *Ben Ish Chai*[113] writes that absorbent cotton in the ear is a *chatzizah*. In his opinion a friend should stand by her in the *mikveh*, wet her finger in the water and then put it into the ear of the woman who is immersing herself. This is also the opinion of the *Maharash Engel*,[114] the *Mahari Shtief*[115] and the *Avnei Nezer*.[116] (See **B** above, p. 146 and **10** below.)

Rav Auerbach zt"l wrote to me that she may put absorbent cotton in her ear, but not firmly, and remove it immediately following the immersion before the water has had a chance to seep through into her ear. Yet, since it is nevertheless theoretically possible for the water to reach her ear, the absorbent cotton is not a *chatzizah*.

10. PERFORATED EARDRUM.
A woman who has been warned by her doctor not to allow any water to enter her ear because of a perforated eardrum or a severe

---

110. דרכ"ת ס"ק י. שו"ת מהרש"ם ח"א סי' ז. שו"ת דובב מישרים ח"א סי' עא. שו"ת אמרי יושר ח"א סי' קצה ו-קצו וח"ב סי' פב. שו"ת אג"מ יו"ד ח"א סי' צח-קג. שו"ת חלקת יעקב ח"א סי' קלח ו-קלט

111. שו"ת אמרי יושר שם. שו"ת מלמד להועיל ח"ב סי' ע

112. שו"ת חלקת יואב ח"א סי' ל. שו"ת הר צבי יו"ד סי' קע

113. שנה ב פ' שמיני סע' י ושו"ת רב פעלים ח"ב סי' כז

114. שו"ת, ח"ב סי' סח

115. שו"ת, סי' מו

116. שו"ת, סי' רסב

NISHMAT AVRAHAM

chronic infection in her outer ear will not be able to immerse herself with cotton wool in her ear since the *mikveh* water entering her ear may cause an infection which could be life threatening.

The *Shulchan Aruch*[117] writes that a woman may immerse herself in whatever originates in water. However, the *Rama*[118] and *Magen Avraham*[119] both write that only if a solid which originated from water is liquefied does it have the *halachah* of water, and the *Shach*,[120] *Divrei Malkiel*[121] and the *Noda BiYehudah's* son[122] all write that immersion in snow that has not been liquefied is not a valid immersion. On the other hand, the *Aruch HaShulchan*[123] writes that this is an unnecessary stringency.[124]

The *Taharat HaMayim*[125] wanted to suggest that a woman who had brain surgery may immerse herself if the operation site is covered with the skin of a fish since it originates in water. However, the *Chazon Ish*[126] wrote that if the skin of a fish is processed to make a garment of some kind, the concept "originating from water" can no longer be applied to it even if it had been first liquefied. Besides, once it has been processed it is a new entity and in the same way as it is no longer a food so no longer can it substitute (as water) for a *mikveh*. Therefore wearing a cap made from the skin of a fish is no solution for this woman who has been forbidden by doctors to have any water come into contact with her skull for the reasons given. See also the *Sha'arei Tevilah* who discusses the problem.[127] The *Taharat HaMayim* concludes that the words of the *Chazon Ish* cannot be easily refuted and certainly not when it comes to an actual practice.

Rav Yechiel Michel Stern shlita[128] discusses whether plastic which is a by-product of petroleum which, in turn, comes from wells in the earth can become *tamei* and therefore be a *chatzizah* or not. He writes that *Rav Eliashiv shlita* told him that it is like something that grows in the sea and therefore does not become *tamei*. However, his uncle *Rav Auerbach zt"l*[129] told him that petroleum does not originate from water but from the earth. Although wells and rivers also originate from the ground and their contents are water, nevertheless, petroleum comes only from the ground and even what is pumped from off-shore wells comes from the ground. Therefore petroleum and any of its by-products (the plastic ear-plug) would constitute a *chatzizah*.[130]

Rav Eliashiv shlita told me that, based on the ruling of the *Chazon Ish* (above), the woman may not immerse herself with a plastic ear-plug even if, as a result, she may no longer be able to live with her husband.

I wondered whether the solution would

---

117. יו"ד סי' רא סע' לג תחלת ברייתו מן המים
The Gemara (*Zevachim* 22a) states that red insects found in water "originate from water" and therefore will not be a *chatzizah*. This does not mean that *Chazal* thought that these insects were created or generated from water, but rather that they came into being in water as opposed to on dry land.

118. או"ח סי' קס סע' י
119. סי' קסב ס"ק יז
120. יו"ד סי' רא ס"ק עא
121. שו"ת, ח"ב סי' נט
122. שו"ת נו"ב מהד"ת או"ח סי' נו
123. או"ח סי' קסב סע' כח
124. וראה בערוך השולחן יו"ד סי' רא סע' קעט ומג"א או"ח סי' קסב ס"ק יז שמקשים על השו"ע יו"ד סי' רא סע' נב
125. סי' נג
126. יו"ד סי' צד ס"ק א
127. סי' ב אות ט
128. מאמר בספר עמק הלכה ח"א עמ' 269
129. ראה מנחת שלמה תנינא סי' עז אות ב
130. והרב שטרן שליט"א מביא ראיה לכך מהתפארת ישראל פי"ג מכלים אות נג

§28 A woman should not hold onto another while the latter is immersing herself unless she does so loosely, allowing water to enter where she is holding her. If, however, (M)she wets her hands before holding the other woman it is permitted, for the water on her hands is joined to the water of the *mikveh*.

──────────── NISHMAT AVRAHAM ────────────

be for another woman to wet a finger in sterile water and insert it loosely into the ear of the woman before the immersion. The woman should then dry the ear canal well with sterile absorbent cotton immediately after the immersion. There is in fact a controversy whether she could wet her fingers in any water[131] or exclusively in the water of a *mikveh*,[132] and, in addition, there is an opinion[133] that the *mikveh* water (on her fingers) must not be separated from the *mikveh* itself. However *Maran*, the *Shulchan Aruch*,[134] did not differentiate, writing only that she must first wet her hand (see below §28).

I spoke to specialists, here and in the USA, who accepted my solution from the medical point of view. There is a recommendation that she should first fill the ear canal with an antibiotic fluid before immersing as above, and she should consult her doctor for his opinion. In addition, they said, the danger is only if the ear remains in contact with water for some time. I then spoke to *Rav Eliashiv shlita* who agreed that this solution is *halachically* permissible.

body there is no *chatzizah* even according to the *poskim* quoted above and below (M) who rule strictly. A religious doctor should make sure, after consultation with a *posek*, that the woman knows exactly what to do. On the one hand, it is imperative that she does not allow **any** water to enter the tube and, on the other, she must not press the flange down hard onto the skin.

11. PERMANENT *TRACHEOSTOMY*. The patient has a tube put via her throat into her *trachea* (windpipe). The tube has a flange which lies on the skin of the throat and is loosely tied behind the neck to keep the tube in place and there is no problem of *chatzizah*. However even a minute amount of water must not be allowed to enter the tube. She should preferably have a well-fitting stopper made, which she puts into the opening of the *tracheostomy* just before immersing herself.[135]

As stated before, in all of the situations mentioned above, the treating physician must be consulted first and a ruling obtained from a *posek*.

(M) she wets her hands. UNABLE TO STAND UNAIDED. This ruling of the *Shulchan Aruch* runs parallel to an earlier ruling regarding the immersion of vessels.[136] It would appear that the *Shulchan Aruch* means that even water from a faucet will suffice, whereas the *Rama*[137] requires water of the *mikveh* and not water which is not from the *mikveh*. The *Taz*[138] rules that water from a faucet may

131. ט"ז יו"ד סי' קב ס"ק ד וסי' קצח ס"ק כח
132. רמ"א יו"ד סי' קב סע' ב. ש"ך סי' קצח ס"ק לז
133. הגהות מטה יונתן על סי' קב סע' ב. וראה בדרכ"ת שם ס"ק לג
134. יו"ד כאן סע' כח וסי' קב סע' ב

135. An alternative is for another woman, standing behind the patient in the *mikveh*, to put her finger on the opening of the tube to close it mo-mentarily but firmly as the patient immerses, making sure, however, not to press the flange down onto the skin. Since there is no contact between the finger and the patient's

136. יו"ד סי' קב סע' ב
137. שם
138. שם ס"ק ד וכאן ס"ק כח

SIMAN 198: IMMERSION AND CHATZIZAH / §28, 40

§40 A female who is at least twelve years and a day old should stand by the *mikveh* to ^(N)see that not even a strand of the woman's hair floats on the water during the immersion.

---NISHMAT AVRAHAM---

be used whereas the *Shach*[139] requires water from the *mikveh*. The *Mateh Yehonatan*[140] interprets the *Shach* to mean that if after wetting her hands in the *mikveh* they are lifted out of the water, this would still be sufficient. However, he writes, this is not so, for what the *Rama* means is that after the hands are dipped into the *mikveh*, they must remain there so that the water on them remains an integral part of the *mikveh*.

This *halachah* is of importance for a woman who is partially or completely paralyzed or has some other medical problem and cannot stand unaided. The *Shach*[141] writes that in such a case she can be immersed with two women holding her arms after they have dipped their hands into the *mikveh*. Rav Neuwirth shlita wrote to me agreeing that this is how she should be immersed. The *Shach* adds that she cannot be put onto a cloth and thus carried into the *mikveh*, for since the cloth itself is something that can become unclean, such an immersion is forbidden.[142]

(N) see. The *Beit She'arim*[143] writes that if the woman whose job it is to oversee a woman immersing, has weak eyes, she may be employed provided that she has been tested that, when wearing glasses, she is able to see even the smallest of objects as well as someone with normal eyesight. Rav Neuwirth shlita wrote to me adding that she should be careful to wipe the condensation from the steam arising from the hot *mikveh* off her glasses before she examines the woman and oversees the immersion.

---

139. כאן ס"ק לז
140. הגהות על השו"ע שם
141. כאן ס"ק לו בשם תשובת משאת בנימין סי' פא
142. ראה בשו"ע כאן סע' לא. וראה במאמרו של הגרי"מ שטרן שליט"א בספר שאלה עמק ח"א עמ' 257
143. שו"ת, יו"ד ח"ב סי' רפו

CHAPTER 19
Laws of Vows

SIMAN 214
ONE NEEDS AN ANNULMENT TO BREAK A CUSTOM

§1 If something is treated as being forbidden even though it is permitted and known to be so, it is as if a vow has been made to prohibit it and it is forbidden to allow it to be done. Therefore if one is accustomed to fast before *Rosh Hashanah* and between *Rosh Hashanah* and *Yom Kippur*, or if one is accustomed to abstain from meat and wine from *Rosh Chodesh Av* or from the seventeeth of *Tammuz*, and he now wishes to change his practice (A)because of ill health, he requires three (Jews) to permit him to do so.

NISHMAT AVRAHAM

SIMAN 214

INTRODUCTION. A vow must be kept by Torah law.[1] Even if one only accepts upon himself to keep a certain custom or to do a good deed on a regular basis, such as going to a regular Torah lesson, giving a certain amount of charity each month or refraining from partaking of certain foods as a mark of piety, it is as if he has taken a vow to do so, even if the intention to do so is not vocalized in terms of a vow. To revert from any of these practices requires a special reason or condition, and it involves a declaration before three Jews (a technical *Beit Din*) at least one of whom must be conversant with the *halachot* involved. If, however, one specifically says, at the time that he took on this custom, that he does not wish his act to have the binding force of a vow, his act is not considered like a vow.

In order to annul a vow there must be "an opening" and "regret." The "opening" is the opportunity that the *Beit Din* puts before the vower for him to have his vow annulled. They ask him whether had he known that there would have been such a change of circumstance in the future, he would have still vowed (see Siman 228 §12). There are, however, many intricate *halachot* concerning the annulment of a vow; sometimes "regret" alone is sufficient to allow the vow to be annulled. The details are mainly dealt with in this Siman.

(A) because of ill health. The *Shach*[2] writes that since he did not specifically think, when he started his *minhag* (custom), that when he would be ill he could not fast, he requires an annulment of the *minhag*. The *Ben Ish Chai*[3] rules that a woman who was accustomed to hear the *shofar* (women are exempt from this mitzvah but have nevertheless accepted it upon

---
1. במדבר ל:ג
2. ס״ק ב
3. שנה א פ׳ נצבים סע׳ יז

SIMAN 228
THE LAW OF ANNULMENT OF A VOW

§12 In order to annul a vow one may present the person who vowed an oppotununity to do so by putting before him a possibility which is (A)commonplace and probable, and

─────────── NISHMAT AVRAHAM ───────────

themselves — author[4]) and could neither go to the synagogue nor have someone come to her home to blow for her, needs to annul the *minhag* on the eve of *Rosh Hashanah*. However, the *Magen Avraham*[5] discusses a situation where the congregation accepted upon themselves a series of fasts. For someone who cannot continue because of some ill health, one may act leniently and not require an annulment, provided that he did not accept upon himself to fast for more than what the congregation accepted. The *Machatzit HaShekel*[6] explains that the congregation did not accept the fasts for those in ill health and he only accepted to fast with them according to their custom. The *Dagul MeRevavah*[7] rejects the *Shach's* explanation and writes that if he felt a little out-of-sorts and wished to eat today but return afterwards to his *minhag* when he is well, he does not require annulment. He says that the *Shulchan Aruch* is discussing one who is ill and does not wish to return later to his *minhag* of fasting; this is why he requires annulment of his *minhag*. This explains the ruling of the *Magen Avraham* (reference 5). The *Mishnah Berurah*[8] writes that one may possibly act leniently in such a situation (*and allow him to eat*) if he cannot find anyone to annul the *minhag* for him, for the *Eliyah Rabbah* and the *Derech HaChaim* both

quote the *Magen Avraham*, and the *Dagul MeRevavah* also upholds his ruling (see also Siman 89A above, p. 35).

SIMAN 228

(A) commonplace and probable. The *Radbaz*,[1] writing about someone who vowed to fast until *Rosh Hashanah*, says that if he vowed to fast for a period of time and then weakened, becoming ill as a result, he is not asked whether had he known that the fast would so weaken him would he have still vowed. However, if there is an "opening" and in addition regret, the vow may be annulled; see the *Rama*[2] and the *Shach*.[3] The *Radbaz* continues that he believes that illness as a result of fasting is not that common, for the non-Jews fast for thirty days and some for forty (*presumably during the day only — author*) and they do not become ill or weak. If he were to become *seriously ill* because of starvation, then even if he has no regrets and there is no "opening" and no one to annul his vow, nothing stands before *pikuach nefesh* and he is fed, but less than the *measure* (which constitutes "eating" in *Halachah*) at a time so as not to abrogate a Torah law. If he must be fed more than the *measure* at a time, then he is fed, for nothing stands before *pikuach nefesh*. If, however, he is *non-seriously ill*, then he may only be fed after the vow has been annulled following regret and an

───────────────────────

8. סי׳ תקפא שעה״צ ס״ק לג

1. שו״ת סי׳ אלף שסב (ח״ד סי׳ רצא) מובא ברעק״א

2. כאן סע׳ יג

3. כאן ס״ק כד

4. See *Nishmat Avraham*, vol. 1 *Orach Chaim*, Siman 585A,C and 589A.

5. סי׳ תקפא ס״ק יב מובא במ״ב ס״ק יט

6. שם

7. כאן

which, had he given it thought, would have stopped him from vowing. One may not do so using a possibility which is not commonplace. Thus, if one took a vow not to benefit from another or not to enter a certain house, and the object of the vow became a great scholar whose services everyone needs or the house became a synagogue, one may not say to the vower, had you known that he would have become a great scholar or the house a synagogue, would you have still taken the vow? For by giving him an opportunity to say: "No, I would not have," the vow is annulled and in this particular instance it cannot be annulled. For since such a circumstance is not commonplace, even if he had thought of the possibility at the time when he vowed, he nevertheless would have made the vow, because the probability of this happening is so rare.

GLOSS. *Similarly,* (B)*the probability that he (the object of the vow) will die is low, but not that of his becoming poor (similarly the probability of a woman becoming pregnant is high).*

§36
If one vows to go to (C)live in the Land of Israel, it may be annulled, the same as any other vow.

NISHMAT AVRAHAM

"opening," for this is a Torah prohibition, as the verse says:[4] "He shall not desecrate his word; according to whatever he said, he shall do." If, however, he is *seriously ill*, and recovered after eating, he must continue to fast the remaining days before *Rosh Hashanah*. Although a vow that has been partially annulled is automatically completely annulled, if it has only been partially postponed it is not automatically completely annulled. However, if he only recovers after *Rosh Hashanah* the vow is completely postponed and he need not fast after *Rosh Hashanah* to make up for the days when he ate.

(B) the probability that he will die.

The *Shach*[5] writes that even were he *seriously ill* it is unusual, for most sick people will live. It would appear though that should he be a *gosses*, death is not unexpected, for most patients who reach this state will die.

(C) live in the Land of Israel. Even if the vow was taken as a public vow, it may be annulled if his wife is pregnant and it would be dangerous for her to travel to Israel.[6]

The *Pitchei Teshuvah*[7] writes that in the opinion of the *Rosh*[8] traveling to *Eretz Yisrael* is not in itself a *mitzvah*; the *mitzvah* is to live there. As the verse says:[9] "And you shall inherit it (*Eretz Yisrael*)

---

4. במדבר ל:ג
5. ס"ק כב
6. תשובת מיימוני פ"ו מהלכות שבועות
7. ס"ק לב בשם הרשב"ש סי' ב
8. תשובת הרא"ש כלל יב אות ז
9. דברים יא:לא

SIMAN 232: VOWS TAKEN UNDER DURESS / §17

§45 GLOSS: *Similarly, if one took a vow* (D)*at a time of trouble, it may not be annulled unless for the purpose of a mitzvah or some great need.*

SIMAN 232
VOWS TAKEN UNDER DURESS

§17 GLOSS: *A wife or husband who vows to their spouse that they will*

---NISHMAT AVRAHAM---

and live there." This is also the opinion of the *Ramban* and the *Rashbetz*. Thus one who vows to travel to *Eretz Yisrael* can have his vow annulled but not if he vows to live there. *Rav Auerbach zt"l* wrote to me that since the interpretation of a vow depends on what people mean to say at a particular time, nowadays, if someone vows to go on *aliyah* to *Eretz Yisrael* and does not specifically say to visit there, he usually means to live there.

The *Chatam Sofer* writes that it is a *mitzvah* to till the land of *Eretz Yisrael*[10] and to build a home there.[11]

How great therefore is the obligation of a physician, who lives in *Eretz Yisrael* and treats the sick of Israel, to acknowledge and thank *Hashem* for this great merit. For there is no greater profession than healing and helping the sick, and if there is no greater *mitzvah* throughout the world, how much greater is it in our Holy Land, the Land of Israel.

(D) at a time of trouble. The *Beit Yosef*[12] quotes the *Ramban*[13] regarding a patient who vowed not to eat cheese as it was bad for his health and now regretted it. He rules that regret is insufficient to allow annulment of the vow unless he also regrets that he vowed at the time he was ill and not only because he is now well. This is certainly not true here for at the time he vowed he did so because it was bad for his health. Now that he fancies the cheese, he wishes to annul the vow. This cannot be done unless there is some other good reason. The *Shach*[14] comments that he is surprised that this *responsum* of the *Ramban* should be quoted here, for what connection is there between the *responsum* and taking a vow at a time of trouble. Many *acharonim* have given examples of "a time of trouble," such as Yaakov Avinu who made a vow when he was fleeing from Esau, or one who vowed that if he would be released from prison he would go to *Eretz Yisrael*, or one who was in great danger at sea who vowed that if he were saved he would go to Jerusalem. This cannot be compared to a patient who vows not to eat cheese because it harms him. A vow taken at a time of trouble cannot be annulled. For, when one vows to do something for a friend who had done him a kindness, the vow cannot be annulled without his friend's knowledge (and permission), as ruled by the *Shulchan Aruch* (§20 in this Siman). How much more so when he vows to *Hashem* Who heard him when he was in trouble; there is no greater kindness than this, and who knows whether *Hashem* agrees to his annulling the vow? The *Shach* concludes that his vow can be annulled since this reason is not relevant to vowing to abstain from cheese when ill.

---

10. על סוכה לו ע"א ד"ה דומה
11. שו"ת, יו"ד סי' קלח. וראה בירושלמי פאה פ"ה ה"ב
12. כאן
13. שו"ת, סי' רנג
14. ס"ק קח. וראה גם בפתחי תשובה ס"ק מב

not remarry after his or her death, or (A)one who vows to a patient, so as to assuage their feelings and prevent them from becoming seriously upset, then these vows are considered as being taken under duress.

SIMAN 234
WHEN MAY A FATHER OR HUSBAND NULLIFY A VOW

§74 (A)A husband cannot nullify a vow taken by his wife to have treatment to conceive.

---NISHMAT AVRAHAM---

SIMAN 232

(A) **one who vows to a patient.** The *Pitchei Teshuvah*[1] quotes the *Shevut Yaakov*[2] who was asked about a husband who vowed to his dying wife that for the year following her death he would bring people to congregate in their home to learn (Torah) together. After she died, he realized that the cost of paying them was too heavy a burden and he asked whether his vow could be annulled. The *Shevut Yaakov* replied that although the husband took the vow because his sick wife implored him to do so, nevertheless it is a vow and is not comparable to the ruling of the *Rama* here. This is because the vow concerns doing a *mitzvah*. Also, since she was involved in the making of the vow, she must acquiesce to the annulment which she can now no longer do. It is also possible that even were the vow to be annulled it would not help since the vow was for the good of her soul.

SIMAN 234

(A) **A husband cannot nullify.** The *Taz*[1] writes that even if the medication will bring her physical hardship and the pregnancy will diminish her beauty, he cannot nullify her vow.[2]

---

1. ס"ק יז
2. שו"ת, ח"ב סי' פא

1. ס"ק סו

2. שו"ת הרשב"א סי' תקס לפי הבאר הגולה. וצ"ל שו"ת הרשב"א חלק ד סימן קכב. וז"ל: ואם מפני שמכחיש יפיה, לא נכנסה זו אצלו אלא לכך שתדל לו. ובעיא חוטרא לידה, ומרא לקבורה

CHAPTER 20
The Laws of Oaths

SIMAN 238
TAKING AN OATH THAT HE WILL NOT EAT

§4 One who takes an oath that he will not eat meat from an animal or bird which has not been ritually slaughtered (*neveilot*) **or cannot** (*because of some blemish*) **be ritually slaughtered** (*treifot*), **and, nevertheless ate such meat, is not culpable for breaking a vow since he is obligated not to eat such food from the** (A)**oath that the Jewish nation took collectively at Mount Sinai to keep the** *mitzvot*.

NISHMAT AVRAHAM

SIMAN 238

INTRODUCTION. An oath applies to the person, obligating or forbidding him to do or not do something, whereas a vow applies to an object obligating or forbidding the person to enjoy or benefit from it.[1] There are *halachic* differences between the two which are discussed at length in this section of the *Shulchan Aruch*.

(A) oath that the Jewish nation took. The *Shach*[2] writes that this *halachah* applies today for a patient who is permitted to eat *neveilot* (meat that has not been ritually slaughtered) and he does not require the annulment of such an oath. This, however, is true only if he took the oath when he was healthy, for then he was forbidden to eat *neveilot* and *treifot* by the general oath (taken at Mount Sinai) and the additional oath does not take effect. But if he took such an oath when he was already (*seriously*) *ill*, since he was then permitted to eat such meat (see Siman 81§7 and 84§17 above), the oath takes effect and will require annulment. However, one could say that even so the oath does not take effect. For since he is permitted to eat these foods because of *pikuach nefesh*, his oath does not take effect because of the oath taken at Mount Sinai which requires him to obey the *mitzvah* of *pikuach nefesh*. Nevertheless, concludes the *Shach*, one should act strictly and his oath should be annulled for him.[3]

---

1 נדרים ב ע"ב
2. ס"ק ה.
3. וראה גם בעצי לבונה בהגהותיו כאן

CHAPTER 21
Honoring Parents

SIMAN 240
WHAT IS CONSIDERED HONORING AND WHAT IS CONSIDERED FEARING AND THEIR LAWS

§4 What is considered honoring? (A)Feeding, giving to drink, dressing and covering, taking them in and out. All this should be done cheerfully for even if the son feeds his parent the best foods every day, if he does so with a sour face, he is punished for it.

---NISHMAT AVRAHAM---

SIMAN 240

◆§ **INTRODUCTION.** The Torah commands us to honor[1] and to fear[2] both our parents; this applies equally to a son and an unmarried daughter. Therefore, whenever a father is mentioned in the following *halachot* this refers equally to a mother. Similarly, both a son and a daughter (see below **B**) are meant whenever a son is mentioned.

(A) Feeding, giving to drink. The *Beit Lechem Yehudah*[3] and the *Aruch Ha-Shulchan*,[4] both quoting the *Sefer Chassidim*,[5] write that a son is not obligated to listen to his sick father who was told by his doctors not to drink water or not to eat a certain food and who asked him to bring him water or that particular food, threatening that if the son refused, he would not forgive him neither in this world nor in the next. However, the *Birkei Yosef*[6] writes that if the water or food will harm the father but not definitely endanger him, the son should do as his father wishes. He notes that the *Sefer Chassidim* writes that if there is a question of danger to the father if he would eat the food, the son should not listen to him; obviously meaning that if there were no danger, the son should do as his father wishes. It would appear, on the other hand, that the *Yad Shaul*[7] rules that even if there is no danger, the son should not listen to his father, for he writes that if one studies the *Shitah Mekubetset*[8] he will see that a son need not listen to his father if the father is not going to derive personal satisfaction or honor from the granting of his request; see also *Tosafot*[9] and *Rashba*.[10] The *Yad*

---

1. שמות כ:יב; The fifth of the Ten Commandments.
2. ויקרא יט:ג.
3. הגהות כאן סע' טו.
4. סע' מא.
5. סי' רלד.
6. כאן ס"ק י.
7. כאן ס"ק יא.
8. ב"מ לב בשם הרא"ש בשם הר"מ.
9. קדושין לב ע"א ד"ה רב.
10. חידושיו על יבמות ו ד"ה מה שכותב דאין עיקר הכבוד אלא במה שיש לו הנאה וכו'. אבל אמר לו לעשות דבר שאין לו בו הנאה של כלום, אין זה כבוד שנטווה עליה, וכבוד כזה אין בו עשה של תורה שידחה אפילו לאו גרידא, עכ"ל. וראה בהגר"א כאן ס"ק לו.

SIMAN 240: HONORING AND FEARING PARENTS / §4, 5

GLOSS: *Alternatively, if he makes his father work on a grindmill, but his intentions are for good, in order to save him from something worse, and he speaks kindly to his father explaining the situation to him so that his father agrees to work the mill, he will inherit the World to Come. He must serve his father in all the ways that a servant serves his master.*

§5 **Whatever he gives his father and mother to eat is paid for by his father so long as he can afford it. If he cannot and the son can, (the *Beit Din*) obligates him to do so in accordance with his means. If the son also cannot afford to do so, he need not go begging from door to door in order to feed his father.**

GLOSS: *There is an opinion that the son need only give his father what he is obligated to give for charity. Nevertheless, if he can afford the expenses for his parent and yet only provides for his*

NISHMAT AVRAHAM

Shaul continues that this is all the more so if the sick father asks his son to give him something that will harm him; the son should not do so, and this is how the *Sefer Chassidim* rules.

I found this a fortiori argument of the *Yad Shaul* difficult to understand, for although the food will harm him, this will only be evident later, whereas now, the father will surely enjoy the food, otherwise why should he specifically ask for it, knowing that it will harm him? Rav Auerbach zt"l wrote to me that it is possible that the *Yad Shaul* meant honoring one's father means giving him something and not causing him a loss. Therefore, since the harm the food will cause him later will be greater than the immediate satisfaction, he is considered to have caused his father to lose more than he gains.

What is the *halachah* for a son whose father demands that he tell him the nature of his illness? The *She'arim Metzuyanim BaHalachah*[11] writes that the *Shach*[12] rules that one may not reveal to a patient that he is *dangerously ill*. From this the *She'arim Metzuyanim BaHalachah* concludes that if the son knows that his father is dangerously ill, he must not tell him so, for fear of diminishing his chances of recovery. He[13] quotes from the *responsa* of *Maharam MeLublin*[14] as proof for his ruling, for the *Maharam MeLublin* writes that one fulfills the *mitzvah* of honoring one's father and mother only if it brings them contentment.[15] In the situation being discussed, what sort of contentment will the father have if he knows the real nature of his illness? Therefore, he should not be told. [However, *if telling him will be for his benefit, he should do so in a manner full of hope and trust; see Siman 338C, p. 298.*]

---

11. סי׳ קצג ס״ק ב
12. סי׳ שלח ס״ק א
13. בקונטרס אחרון שם
14. שו״ת, סי׳ קלו
15. ראה לעיל בשם השיטה מקובצת

CHAPTER 21: HONORING PARENTS

father from the money he has earmarked for charity, he will be cursed. If there are many sons, each one's share is calculated according to his means. If some are poor and others rich, the rich sons alone are obligated (by Beit Din) to pay.

However, he is ^(B)**obligated to honor him physically, even if this will result in him having to discontinue working and then have to beg from door to door.** This is only if the son has enough food for himself that day, but if not he is not obligated to stop work and later beg from door to door.

§7 He is obligated ^(C)to stand up for his father.

§10 A son must try and behave towards a father or mother who has ^(D)become mentally deranged, in the way they

---
NISHMAT AVRAHAM

(B) obligated to honor him physically. A son is obligated to look after his sick father as best he can if he cannot afford to pay for someone who will watch over him. This also applies to an unmarried daughter[16] or to a married daughter whose husband does not object.[17]

(C) to stand. The *Pitchei Teshuvah*[18] rules that a blind person is also obligated to stand up for his parents or for the Rav from whom he has gained most of his Torah knowledge. He brings proof for this ruling from the *Gemara*[19] that Rav Yosef (who was blind) would stand up when he heard the footsteps of his approaching mother, saying: "I will stand before the approaching *Shechinah*." The same *halachah* applies if the father is blind — the son is obligated to stand up for him as we find in the *Gemara*[20] that Rava gave honor to Rav Yosef.[21] (*The halachah of honoring one's Rav is the same as that of honoring one's father. Therefore although Rava was a talmid of Rav Yosef and not his son, we can learn one halachah from the other — author.*) The *Maharit*,[22] however, rules that he must also stand up for any Torah scholar.

(D) become mentally deranged. A scholar asked *Rav Waldenberg shlita*[23] whether it would be permissible for him to tie his mother, who had become mentally deranged and uncontrollable, to a chair since she was greatly affecting the peace of the household, in accordance with the advice given by his doctor. The *Rav shlita* ruled that it was without doubt forbidden for the son to tie her to a chair. Instead, he should give her into someone else's care who would do so since it was unavoidable and, also, since it was being done on medical advice. *Rav Neuwirth shlita* told me that if the mother could come to harm through her uncontrollable actions, the son could tie her down until such time as he could find arrangements for her to be cared for suitably in a home.

---

16. שו"ע סע' יז
17. שם וש"ך ס"ק יט
18. ס"ק ו וראה בהערות נחלת צבי כאן
19. קדושין לא ע"ב
20. יומא נג ע"א
21. שערים מצויינים בהלכה סי' קמג ס"ק ה בשם השו"ת שער אפרים סי' עח
22. מובא בפ"ת ס"ק ו
23. שו"ת ציץ אליעזר חי"ב סי' נט

would wish, until (*Heaven*) has pity on them. If, however, they are so changed that he cannot cope with the situation, he may leave them and get ⁽ᴱ⁾someone else to care for them properly and capably.

SIMAN 241
THE LAWS OF ONE WHO HITS OR CURSES HIS PARENTS

§3 A son may not remove a thorn from his father's flesh lest he injure him in the process. Similarly if he is a doctor he should not draw blood from him nor amputate a limb although he does so for a medical reason.

GLOSS: *This is so* ⁽ᴬ⁾*when there is another who can do this, but if there is no one else and the father is suffering, he may draw blood or operate to the extent that his father permits.*

NISHMAT AVRAHAM

(E) someone else. The *Taz*[24] writes that the *Tur* quotes the *Ra'avad* who disagrees with the ruling of the *Rambam* (the source of this ruling in the *Shulchan Aruch*), for if he were to leave them who would take care of them? The *Ran* and the *Tur*, however, express surprise at the *Ra'avad's* reservation, for the ruling is based on a specific *Gemara*.[25] However, it appears, writes the *Taz*, that the real reservation of the *Ra'avad* is regarding the ruling that he should get someone else to care for them, since this is not mentioned in that *Gemara*. Why did the *Rambam* add this when in any case it will not help, for if he can be looked after why should the son not do so, and, if he cannot, what is the point of getting someone else who will be no more capable than the son? Nowadays, of course, one can certainly differentiate between the care the son, who has no experience, is capable of giving, and the care that a nurse and professional home can provide.

It is worth repeating the words of *Rav Sa'adiah Gaon* as quoted by *Rabbeinu Bachya*.[26] The Torah tells us that the reward for honoring one's parents is longevity, because sometimes the parents live long and become a burden on their children. Therefore, the Torah tells us that the reward for keeping this *mitzvah* is longevity, in other words, you should honor them and thus live (long) with them. If their long lives bother you, know that it is your own life that is at stake.

SIMAN 241

(A) when there is another. The *Minchat Chinuch*[1] writes that when the Torah said that a son who hits a parent deserves punishment, this is only if he does so without the parent's permission. However, if his parent asks him to do so he is not guilty of transgressing the prohibition and is therefore not liable for a sentence of either lashes or death. He writes that

---
24. ס"ק יד
25. קדושין לא ע"ב
26. שמות כ:יב
1. מצוה מח ס"ק ב

NISHMAT AVRAHAM

although he has not found that this is specifically stated, nevertheless he believes that this is so. The *Aruch HaShulchan*[2] also writes that if there is no one else who can do what is needed and his parent is suffering, the son may draw blood or operate if the parent gives him permission to do so. Also, if he is more qualified than another and his father prefers him, he may do so. This is also the ruling of the *Ben Ish Chai*[3] who writes that if another is unavailable the son may draw blood or operate on his father. It would appear from this that he believes that the *Rama* intends to clarify the ruling of the *Mechaber* rather than contradict him. This is also the ruling of the *Minchat Yitzchak*.[4]

The *Gesher HaChaim*[5] also permits a son to give his mother injections, for his being forbidden to give injections, for example, when someone else is available goes beyond the *halachic* requirement (as the *Bach*[6] writes on the basis of the language used by the *Rambam* and others). Moreover, the *Gesher HaChaim* expresses a novel idea, that since the son will do this without payment while another will take money, it is as if there is no one else available. For the son is not obligated to pay for the services of another, since the *halachah* is that the father must pay. Thus, as far as the father is concerned, there is no one else available. This idea is also expressed by the *Chelkat Yaakov*.[7]

However, the *Har Tzvi*[8] writes that although the son is permitted to draw blood from his father, nevertheless he should try and find someone else to do it. He thus avoids inadvertently doing an act (injuring more than absolutely necessary) which, if done purposely, carries the death penalty. And, if this costs money, why should he not be obligated to pay, since this is not, strictly speaking, part of the obligation to honor his parent? He only wishes to make it easier to do the *mitzvah* by using money. This is akin to the father who asks his son, who lives at a distance, to come and feed him. The son finds it difficult to come such a distance on foot. Nevertheless he certainly should spend his money to travel to his father if he does not wish to walk there. For though he is not required to spend his money to honor his father he need not do so; he can walk. This is because the money spent on traveling to his father is not to honor him, but to avoid walking the long distance. Here, too, he is obligated to draw blood from his father, but does not wish to, only to avoid inadvertently injuring his father. That wish involves his private attitude. It does not touch upon the objective obligation to his father; it is like the wish not to go by foot. Therefore, the money he spends to avoid injuring his father is not spent to enable him to fulfill his obligation.

Rav Auerbach zt"l wrote to me that he felt the two situations described by the *Har Tzvi* are not comparable. The fear of not injuring his father more than is absolutely necessary is also part of the *mitzvah* of honoring him. Since, if another is not available to draw blood from his father, he must do so himself without worrying about the possibility of any unnecessary injury, he is not obligated to hire another unless the father pays the expenses.[9] The *Rav zt"l* also told me that if the son

---

2. סע׳ ו
3. שנה ב פ׳ שופטים סע׳ כד. וראה להלן הערה 12 בשם הגרשז״א זצ״ל
4. שו״ת, ח״א סי׳ כו
5. ח״ב פ״א סי׳ א
6. כאן ד״ה הכהן
7. שו״ת, ח״ב סי׳ לט
8. שו״ת, יו״ד סי׳ קצו
9. וראה מאמרו של הגרשז״א זצ״ל במוריה סיון תשל״א ובמנחת שלמה ח״א סי׳ לב

SIMAN 241: HITTING OR CURSING PARENTS / §3

― NISHMAT AVRAHAM ―

cannot reach his father on foot, for example if his father lives overseas, he is not required to pay the expenses. His father must pay for the cheapest possible means of travel, and the son is obligated to get to him in time to fulfill his wish.

The *Gesher HaChaim*[10] quotes *Rav Herzog* who disagrees with his opinion asking, why should the father be permitted to allow the son to do something which may involve a forbidden act, only to avoid paying for another to do it. *Rav Herzog* also disagrees with the opinion of the *Gesher HaChaim* that the son is not obligated to pay the expenses if the father is poor and cannot afford to do so. The son, he argues, is not required to use his own funds only if the father can afford it. However if the father cannot afford it, the son is required to pay for his father's medical expenses. However he later agrees with the ruling on the basis of the *Minchat Chinuch* (quoted above).

Rav Auerbach zt"l also wrote to the *Gesher HaChaim*[11] agreeing with him in the following manner. The *Beit Yosef* ruled like the *Rif* and *Rosh* that although the act is medically indicated, nevertheless because of the severity of causing more injury to his father than necessary, the son is forbidden to do so even if another is not available. Therefore, although the *Rama* disagrees and rules that he may treat his father if another is not available, it is possible that one should act a little more strictly.[12] However, since the *Rambam* and others rule that not permitting the son to treat the father when another is available goes beyond the *halachic* requirement, one may use his other reason to permit him to treat a parent. *Rav Auerbach zt"l* also notes that he found a similar idea to that of the *Gesher HaChaim* in the *Yafe LeLev* (vol. 3 Siman 241) who writes that even if someone else is available for payment, and the son will not charge, the father may choose not to pay.

However, if the parent is *dangerously ill* and the treatment is urgently required to save his life, then, in everyone's opinion, the son must do whatever is necessary, if no one else is available.[13]

A son who injures his father transgresses a prohibition that carries the death penalty, whereas a Jew who injures another transgresses a prohibition that does not carry such a penalty. However, if the action may endanger his life, there is no difference between a son and his father on the one hand and two unrelated Jews on the other. Does the *Halachah* differentiate between these two situations (life threatening and non-life threatening) as to whether a son or someone else should treat the father? For example, if a father requires surgery and wishes his son to operate on him, is there a difference in *Halachah* whether the son or another person who is available does the surgery?

The *Ramban*[14] asks the following question: The *Gemara*[15] asks whether a son may draw blood from his father. And the *Gemara* quotes two *Amora'im* who derive, each from a different verse, that this is permissible. This is, however, followed immediately by the statement that another *Amora* did not allow his son to open an abscess that he had, lest he injure him (*more than necessary*). This would be a serious offense (*even though done uninten-*

---

10. ח"ב עמ' יא
11. ח"ב עמ' טז
12. וכתב לי הגרשז"א זצ"ל נלע"ד הואיל ובשו"ע השמיט הב"י את הבמה דברים אמורים שהוא מפורש בטור, מסתבר שפסק בשו"ע כהרי"ף והרא"ש דאסרו בכל ענין. ואף גם הב"ח הבין כך בדעת הב"י ולא כהבן איש חי (המובא לעיל), עכ"ל
13. שו"ת מנחת יצחק ח"א סי' כח. אך קשה לי לשון המחבר: ולא יחתוך לו אבר, כי לכאורה מדובר בפקו"נ? וצ"ל שאמנם מדובר בפקו"נ, אך לא בדוחפה, ולכן לדעת מרן צריך הבן למצוא אחר שיטפל באביו
14. תורת האדם סוף ענין הסכנה
15. סנהדרין פד ע"ב

NISHMAT AVRAHAM

tionally), for had he done so with intention to harm, he would have been liable for the death penalty. The *Gemara* asks: If this is so why should it be different if a stranger does so? The *Gemara* answers that injuring another (*if done intentionally*) is a transgression of a prohibition (but not one for which there is capital punishment), but injuring a father (*if done intentionally*) is a transgression of a prohibition which carries the death penalty. The *Ramban* wonders that if this is so, how is it possible for a doctor to practice medicine. Should he err (*and cause a patient's death*), this would also be a serious act; for were it done intentionally he would be liable for the death penalty. In addition, he asks, why should there be a difference between treatment by a son or by another. Since drawing blood (*in the quantities taken in those times*[16]) is dangerous, anyone drawing blood may injure the patient. And, finally, if we question the right of a doctor to treat a patient, we should also question the right of the patient to seek treatment. For if he swallows a medicine wrongly prescribed, either because of a mistaken diagnosis or because of a mistaken assessment of what the appropriate treatment should be, the patient has, in effect, killed himself.

The *Ramban* answers that since *Hashem* permitted a doctor to practice medicine and he performs a *mitzvah* in so doing, he need not worry at all, for if he does what he thinks is the right thing to do, all his endeavors become a *mitzvah*. *Hashem* commanded him to heal; he erred unintentionally. However, since someone else is available who can remove the thorn or open the abscess, the son is not permitted to do so to avoid his unintentionally transgressing a commandment which carries the death penalty if done intentionally. A son is, however, permitted to draw blood because the injury itself is part of the treatment and here there is no difference between him and another. Both the son and the other person are performing the same *mitzvah* and both bear the same serious responsibility of a mistake. The *Rif*,[17] however, writes that we conclude that the *Amora* did not allow his son to remove a thorn from his father. Yet the *Ramban* thinks that the *Rif* might agree that injuring someone to heal him is free from punishment and is included within the framework of:[18] "You shall love your fellow as yourself." A son is not allowed to perform such an act lest he cause injury beyond what is medically necessary and fall into the category of a non-intentional transgression of a prohibition which carries a death penalty if done intentionally. But we do not worry that either the son or another may (*inadvertently*) cause the patient's death, for the Torah commanded physicians to heal and there is no treatment that does not carry a risk, for that which may cure one may kill another.

Rav Achai Gaon[19] asks whether if the father requires bloodletting as part of his treatment or needs to have a tooth extracted, his son may do it since he does not intend to cause his father suffering, or since he may sometimes injure his father more than necessary and be guilty of a transgression, he may not do it. The *Ha'amek She'elah*[20] comments that the reason that the *Gaon* chose these two examples was to equate treatment which carries a risk (drawing blood) and one that does not (the extraction of a tooth). If permitted, both are and if not, neither is. This view disagrees with that of the *Ramban* that there is no difference in opinion

---

16. שבת קכ"ט ע"א ורש"י שם ד"ה ומוקי
17. סנהדרין שם
18. ויקרא יט:יח
19. שאילתות פ' משפטים ס
20. על השאילתות, שם ס"ק יא

§9 (B)A *ger* is forbidden to curse, hit or shame his non-Jewish father.

─────────────── NISHMAT AVRAHAM ───────────────

between the *Amoraim* in the above *Gemara*, one discussed drawing blood and the other removing a thorn or opening an abscess. The *Gaon*, however, believes, like the *Rif*, that the *Amoraim* did disagree. In one opinion, the son would not be permitted even to draw blood, for although we do not fear that an error would be fatal (*and there would be no difference between a son and a stranger*), we do fear that an error will cause unnecessary injury (*which is much more serious as far as the son is involved*).

(B) A *ger* is forbidden. Although the *Rambam*[21] writes that he also must honor his father somewhat, the *Mechaber* did not write this. However, the *Igrot Moshe*[22] writes that he believes that the *Mechaber* agrees with the ruling of the *Rambam*. He also writes that a *giyoret* may very occasionally visit her non-Jewish mother, otherwise it would be a sign of ingratitude. But she should not visit her on a regular basis. If the mother took ill and requested that her daughter visit her with her children, she is obligated to visit her with her children because she owes some honor to her mother,[23] and also in order not to cause her shame, as the *Rambam* and *Shulchan Aruch* rule.

---

21. הל' ממרים פ"ה הי"א
22. שו"ת, יו"ד ח"ב סי' קל
23. לבד שמבקרין עכו"ם מפני דרכי שלום - האג"מ שם

CHAPTER 22
The Laws of Honoring a Torah Scholar

SIMAN 244
STANDING UP FOR AND HONORING A TORAH SCHOLAR EVEN THOUGH HE IS NOT HIS TEACHER

§1 It is a positive commandment (A)to stand up for any Torah scholar even if he is not elderly, but young and knowledgeable, and although he is not his teacher (*the only requirement is that he be greater than him and worthy to learn from*). Similarly it is a *mitzvah* to stand up for an elderly person, that is, one who is seventy years old (*or more*) (*even if he is unlearned, provided he is not wicked*).

NISHMAT AVRAHAM

SIMAN 244

(A) to stand up for any Torah scholar. Rav Ovadiah Yosef shlita[1] proves from the *Ran*,[2] the *Torat Chaim*[3] and the *Urim VeTumim*[4] that if one stands up for a Torah scholar in a bus he may not sit down again and leave the scholar standing, but must give him his seat. However if the scholar wishes to forgo the honor, he may do so, and the man may then sit down. Rav Ovadiah Yosef shlita also refers to the *Har Tzvi*[5] and the *Shevet HaLevi*.[6]

Rav Yosef shlita[7] also writes that if the person sitting is ill and cannot remain standing, he need not give the Torah scholar his seat, for *Hashem* forgives one who is compelled by circumstances not to fulfill a *mitzvah*. Rav Auerbach zt"l wrote to me that nevertheless he should fulfill the *mitzvah* of standing up before him for

since he is capable of doing this he is in this respect like a healthy person, and it is considered standing up for the scholar's honor.

The *Chida*[8] writes that the verse:[9] "In the presence of an old person you shall rise and you shall honor the presence of a sage," means that when you see a very old man who is standing with difficulty and you are sitting, stand up and give him your seat. The next part of the verse: "you shall honor the presence of a sage," means that although he is not so old nevertheless honor him by offering him your seat. *Chazal*[10] have said that one who is accustomed to stand up before an old person is granted fear of *Hashem* for the verse says: "In the presence of an old person you shall rise ... and you will fear *Hashem*."

---

1. שו"ת יביע אומר ח"ו סי' כב
2. רפ"ד דשבועות מובא גם בכ"מ הל' סנהדרין פכ"א ה"ג
3. על שבועות ל ע"ב
4. סי' יז אורים ס"ק י
5. שו"ת, או"ח ח"א סי' קז סע' ב
6. שו"ת, ח"ב (יו"ד) סי' קיד
7. שו"ת יביע אומר שם במפתחות
8. נחל קדומים פ' קדושים סי' לב
9. ויקרא יט:לב
10. מובא בספר חרדים פ"ו ממצות עשה סע' ה-ו בשם המדרש רבה והירושלמי

CHAPTER 23
The Laws of Torah Study

SIMAN 245
EVERYONE IS OBLIGATED TO TEACH HIS SON AND TO RAISE DISCIPLES

§15 A teacher should not teach a class of more than twenty-five children. If there are twenty-five to forty children he is given an assistant.

GLOSS: Even if he is hired without the number of children being specified, he may take an assistant, and the town pays his salary. There is an opinion that if the town does not have twenty-five children the community is not obligated to hire a teacher, but there is an opinion that even if there are (A)less than this number they are obligated to do so.

If there are more than forty children, two teachers are hired.

NISHMAT AVRAHAM
SIMAN 245

(A) less than this number. What is the *halachah* regarding mentally handicapped children (such as those with Down syndrome) who can be taught provided the class is kept small? Is the community obliged to pay for extra teachers for these smaller classes? The *Meiri*[1] writes that twenty-five children is an average number. The *Pitchei Teshuvah*[2] quotes the *Emunat Shmuel* who decided in favor of the first opinion (in the *Rama*) but added that the number of twenty-five children was only applicable in the times of the Talmud. For nowadays people are not as they were and one teacher cannot cope with twenty-five children, and would that

he could fulfill his obligations with ten or twelve students. This being so, it is obvious that this number is equivalent to the twenty-five of the Talmud. Therefore in a community with six families totaling ten to twelve children who did not want to pay for a teacher, he ruled that they could force each other to do so.

The *Aruch HaShulchan*[3] expresses surprise at the thought that if there are less than twenty-five children they should be left idle and not be taught. He explains the *Tosafot* and *Rosh*,[4] whom the *Rama* quotes as the first opinion, differently from the ruling of the *Rama*.

However, the *Shulchan Aruch HaRav*[5] writes that one may not force a commu-

---

1. ב״ב כא ע״א
2. כאן ס״ק ח
3. כאן סע׳ כה-כו
4. ב״ב שם
5. הל׳ תלמוד תורה פ״א ה״ג בקונטרס אחרון ס״ק ג

nity to hire a teacher for less than twenty-five children as they did in their days. True that the way we teach today where the main subjects taught are *Mishnah* and *Gemara*, it is impossible to teach such a large class well. Nevertheless, since the obligation to teach in this way was instituted by Yehoshua ben Gamla,[6] we cannot obligate a community to do more than he instituted. The community's obligation is fulfilled when it pays a teacher to teach in the way it was done at that time. Although nowadays the children do not know Hebrew as they did in the past, nevertheless it appears from the *Tur*, the *Shulchan Aruch* and other *poskim* that even though each word must be translated for them, nevertheless it is enough to appoint one teacher for every twenty-five children. Moreover, even though the children then were only taught *Tanach* and not *Mishnah* and *Gemara*, we cannot force the community to pay for a teacher to teach *Mishnah* and *Gemara* since these were taught without any payment and the obligation that Yehoshua ben Gamla instituted was for teaching *Tanach* only.

Rav Moshe Feinstein zt"l[7] writes regarding children who are retarded or are extremely simple that they are certainly obligated to keep *mitzvot* once they have physical signs of adulthood and have reached the age of thirteen (for a boy) or twelve (for a girl) and that their fathers are obligated to teach them whatever is possible as soon as they can begin to understand, each according to his intelligence. Not from the age of six as with other children, but from the time when the father sees that his son is able to comprehend, he is obligated to teach him the *Shema* until he knows the first paragraph by heart. He should then teach him to read Hebrew and teach him the fact that there is a Creator Who creates everything that he eats and drinks and the like. He teaches him that there are foods that are fobidden to eat, that his mother is forbidden to cook on *Shabbat*, and that he must listen to *Kiddush*. Similarly he teaches him other things that the child will understand. Obviously he cannot teach him all this in one day but does so gradually. When the child can read the *Shema* and *Shemoneh Esrei* from a *siddur*, albeit with difficulty, he should start to teach him *Chumash*. Since it is impossible for a father, who is busy with earning his living and learning, to do all this himself, he is obligated, together with others who have the same problem, to hire a teacher who will do so. Since it is obviously impossible for a teacher to teach the same number of these children in a class as he would unaffected children, the fathers are obligated to hire a teacher for a smaller class, the size depending on the capabilities of the children as defined by experts. The class will vary from six, seven or eight children, being two or three times smaller than a normal class and not everyone can afford this without the help of the community.

Seemingly, people could only be obligated to support a single teacher for a class of twenty-five normal children not a class of twenty-five which requires three or even four teachers, from the point of view of charity, were it not that there is a Rabbinic obligation to do so. We do not find that the *Gemara* obligated someone who has no children to pay towards a regular school, since the obligation is on the community to see that each and every city has permanent teachers for its children so that they would not have to be taken to a different city to learn. If indeed it was not so, then possibly each father would have had to pay according to whatever individual agreement he could come to with the

---

6. ב"ב שם. 7. עם התורה מהדורא ב חוברת ב עמ' י

SIMAN 246
EVERYONE IS OBLIGATED TO LEARN TORAH

§1 Every male Jew is obligated to learn Torah, be he poor or rich, healthy or (A)suffering, young or very old. Even if he must beg from door to door, or is married with children, he is obligated to set aside time for learning Torah both by day and by night, as the verse says: "You should contemplate it day and night" (*Joshua* 1:8) (*Under extenuating circumstances, even if he only read the Shema morning and evening,*

---NISHMAT AVRAHAM---

teacher and a poor father would have to beg for money to pay for his son's education. Nevertheless from the wording of the *Gemara* one may deduce that even the person who has no children would have to pay towards the teacher's salary. Besides, since Yehoshua ben Gamla wished to ensure that all children be given an education and not only those who had fathers, he probably was also concerned for those children whose fathers could not afford the fees and those whose fathers did not want to pay. Therefore, the obligation is on the city elders and treasurers who would, in turn, obligate the fathers to pay. We can certainly deduce from this that they can take money from the city's charity funds to pay for the three or four extra teachers necessary for twenty-five mentally handicapped children since *Chazal* did not wish to place this extra burden on the community. It would appear though that everyone would have to contribute the sum that he would normally give to a regular school towards such a special school. It is also possible that it is the city's charity fund that would be obligated to pay all the expenses, since charity must also be given for Torah learning. There is, however, an obligation for the fathers of these children to teach them as much as possible, to hire teachers for the purpose and, if there are many such children, to set up a special school for them. Others

have an obligation to assist with their charity money. Parents of an older child who has a fixed intelligence of only a four- or five-year-old must prevent him, as far as they can, from transgressing any sins. If, however, he has no intelligence whatsoever, even that of a small child, he is considered like a *shoteh*. When these handicapped children come to *shul*, the congregation should receive them well and, even if they cannot be taught, see that they answer Amen and *Kedushah* since just going to *shul* is also a *mitzvah,* and they should be taught to kiss the *Sefer Torah*. Two purposes are served thereby — the child performs whatever *mitzvah* he is capable of doing, and his parents are honored.

However, *Rav Auerbach zt"l* told me that the community is obligated by law to set up small classes appropriate for these children, in the same way that it is obligated to see that a poor sick person gets the treatment he requires but cannot afford. *Rav Eliashiv shlita* also told me that the number of twenty-five children mentioned by the *Gemara* refers only to normal children. With mentally handicapped children there is an obligation to pay for a teacher for the smaller class appropriate for them.

SIMAN 246

(A) **suffering.** See *Nishmat Avraham*, vol. 1 *Orach Chaim*, Siman 155A, p. 75.

the beginning of the verse: "This Book of the Torah shall not depart from your mouth," is applied to him.) **One who cannot learn because he does not know how to learn at all, or because he is very harassed, should make it possible for others to learn.**

GLOSS: *And it will be considered as if he himself has learned.*

§**18** The study of Torah is [B]equivalent to all the *mitzvot*. If he has the choice of either doing a *mitzvah* or learning Torah, he should not cease learning if others can do the *mitzvah*. If no one else can do it, he should do the *mitzvah* and then return to his learning.

──────── NISHMAT AVRAHAM ────────

(B) **equivalent to all the** *mitzvot*. The *Gemara*[1] concludes that studying Torah is greater than saving life. However the *Taz*[2] asks rhetorically that surely nothing stands in the way of *pikuach nefesh*. Therefore, he answers that what the *Gemara* must mean is that the one who studies Torah and has no cause to cease in order to save life has a greater merit than the one who must save life and, in order to do so, must stop studying. He deduces this from what happened to Mordechai, who was more important in the eyes of the Sages before he became involved in saving the Jews than he was afterwards. For to do so he had to forgo studying Torah, and the *Gemara*[3] tells us that, as a result, he was counted lower in the ladder of important sages than before. The *Taz* also expresses surprise at the ruling of the *Derishah* that if one must choose between saving a life and studying Torah, the latter takes precedence, for surely this cannot be.

The *Ben Ish Chai*[4] explains that when the *Gemara* says that studying Torah is greater than saving life, it does not mean saving life literally, for surely nothing stands in the way of saving life. The *Gemara* means the possible saving of life and Mordechai became a governor after the miracle when the Jews had already been saved. But after that there was only a possibility that he might need, because of his high office, to become involved in saving life (*and it would have been better had he remained in Torah study rather than have a position where he might have to spend time saving life instead of studying* — author). The *Or HaChaim*[5] also writes that Mordechai is criticized only because he forsook Torah learning to be in a position to save the Jews again should it become necessary. He really should have returned to studying Torah after the miracle which saved the Jews. Since he did not do so but accepted a high office, although he did so for altruistic reasons, this was the inferior of the two choices. It would have been better had he returned to learning Torah. This is like one who, instead of learning Torah, goes and sits at the crossroads to save people from robbers. But, if someone is in danger, it is obvious that one must forgo studying to save his life for even Sabbath laws (which

---

1. מגילה טז ע"ב
2. סי' רנא ס"ק ו
3. מגילה שם
4. בן יהוידע על מגילה שם
5. ספר ראשון לציון סי' יו"ד סי' רנא סע' יד

SIMAN 246: EVERYONE IS OBLIGATED TO LEARN TORAH / §20

§20 A person should always learn Torah even though he does so (C)only for personal reasons since this will eventually bring him to learn for the sole purpose of fulfilling the *mitzvah*.

---NISHMAT AVRAHAM---

involve both positive and negative commandments) are set aside to save life, how much more so should the study of Torah, which is only a postive commandment, be set aside.

(C) only for personal reasons. What is the *halachah* regarding someone who wishes to submit a paper concerning a research project that he has done in Medical *Halachah*, so that he may win a prize, receive a degree or a grant in order to further his academic career? Is there a problem of ignoring the *Mishnah's* warning[6] not to use the Torah to increase one's own honor or as a source of income? *Rav Auerbach zt"l* told me that if his intention in doing the work is both to learn Torah and also for the purpose of receiving a prize or furthering his career, this would be considered as having learned Torah partly for personal reasons, but would not come under the warning of the *Mishnah*. However if his intentions are entirely for the glory of *Hashem* when doing the research, but afterwards an opportunity presents itself to submit it for a prize or to further his career, this is entirely permissible and he may submit his work for this purpose. *Rav Ovadiah Yosef shlita*[7] writes that it is permissible to learn Torah, to research in it and submit a paper to receive a degree if, at the same time, he also intends to perform the *mitzvah* of learning Torah. Although he does so now for personal reasons, he will eventually come to learn Torah for the sole purpose of fulfilling the *mitzvah*. One may also write and submit a book containing his Torah thoughts to an institution that awards prizes for the best submissions so that he may be a recipient of such a prize. However *Rav Yosef shlita* concludes that he who studies Torah for the sake of the *mitzvah* alone will be happy in this world and have a goodly reward in the next.

The *Mishnah Berurah*[8] writes concerning those who sell *tefillin* and *mezuzot* that they are only considered as being occupied with a *mitzvah* if their main purpose is to provide these articles for those who require them. If, however, their main purpose is to earn money, they are not considered as being occupied with a *mitzvah*. See *Nishmat Avraham*, vol. 1 *Orach Chaim*, Siman 38F, p. 15.

---

6. פרקי אבות פ״ד מ״ה לפי פירוש הרע״ב והתפארת ישראל
7. שו״ת יחוה דעת ח״ג סי׳ עד
8. סי׳ לח ס״ק כד

CHAPTER 24
The Laws of Charity

SIMAN 249
HOW MUCH IS ONE OBLIGATED TO GIVE AND HOW SHOULD IT BE GIVEN

§1 How much charity should one give? If he can afford it he should give as much as the poor require. If he cannot afford to do this, he should give up to a fifth of what he has to fulfill the *mitzvah* in its best way. If he gives a tenth, this is an average sum; less than a tenth is miserly. The fifth of what he has refers to the percentage of his capital the first year. After that he gives a fifth of his profits annually.

GLOSS: *One should not distribute more than a fifth so as not to become dependent himself on others as a consequence. All this applies during his lifetime but on his deathbed a person may give as much as he wishes to charity. The money earmarked for charity may not be used to perform another mitzvah, such as buying lights for the synagogue or* (A)*other mitzvot. He should give it only to the poor.*

NISHMAT AVRAHAM

SIMAN 249

(A) other *mitzvot*. A child requires open-heart surgery that is covered by state insurance and will not cost the parents anything. However if the parents wish the surgery to be performed by a famous expert, they will have to pay him privately. If a family does not have the means to pay for such an expert, will the monies given to them be considered as charity or as an act of loving-kindness. *Rav Auerbach zt"l* told me that if the prognosis will be far better if the surgery is done by such an expert, then the situation is considered to be one of *pikuach nefesh* and the monies given can be considered as fulfilling an obligation to give charity. However, if taking an expert specialist is not really necessary, and medical opinion is that such an operation can be done by a member of the surgical team, the monies given cannot be considered as charity but only as loving-kindness. In such a case he need only give a small amount from the money he has set aside for charity. See also Siman 155H above, p. 72.

Rav Eliashiv shlita told me that if a patient, who did not really need to have his surgery done privately, travels abroad to have his surgery, then if he is medically fit to return home to undergo surgery under state insurance, there is no obligation to give him charity to have the surgery done privately abroad. However if it turns out that he is medically unfit to return, one is obligated to give him charity towards the private surgery.

SIMAN 252
THE LAW OF REDEEMING PRISONERS

§1 (A)The *mitzvah* of redeeming prisoners takes precedence over that of feeding and clothing the poor and there is no greater *mitzvah* than this.

§8 A woman should be redeemed before a man. However, if the captors are homosexuals, the man is redeemed first (and if both are in danger of drowning, (B)the man is saved first).

--- NISHMAT AVRAHAM ---

SIMAN 252

(A) The *mitzvah* of redeeming prisoners. The *Pitchei Teshuvah*[1] writes that it is questionable whether one is obligated to put himself into possible danger in order to save another who is in certain danger, and if he is not obligated to do this, may he do so if he wishes to, out of piety or love for his friend? He answers that the *Beit Yosef*[2] quotes a *Hagahot Maimoniot* that one is obligated to endanger himself in order to save a friend, for his friend is in certain danger whereas his danger is only a possibility. However he writes that one can argue with this ruling and it needs further discussion. (This subject will, with *Hashem's* help, be dealt with more fully in *Nishmat Avraham*, vol. 3 *Choshen Mishpat*, Siman 426.) He continues that if both people involved are equal in stature, for example, if both are Torah scholars or, if both are unlearned, and certainly if the person in danger is unlearned and the other a Torah scholar, the latter may not put himself into even possible danger to save the other who is in certain danger. However, if the one in danger is a Torah scholar and the other also a Torah scholar but of lesser stature, the lesser scholar may put himself into possible danger to save the greater scholar as an act of piety, but he is not obligated to do so.

(B) the man is saved first. TRIAGE. The *Taz*[3] writes that this ruling — that saving a man takes precedence over saving a woman when both their lives are at stake — is based on a *Mishnah*.[4] The reason for this is that a man is obligated to perform more *mitzvot* than a woman (a woman is not obligated to perform most of the mitzvot that are related to time — author). This is also what the *Rambam* and the *Rav MiBartinura*[5] write.

The *Mishnah* says: A man takes precedence over a woman with regard to saving their lives and returning lost property. The woman takes precedence over a man with regard to clothing her and freeing her from prison. However, if both are in danger of sexual assault, saving him takes precedence. A *Cohen* comes before a *Levi*, a *Levi* before a *Yisrael*, a *Yisrael* before a *mamzer*. This, however, is only if they are of equal stature. But, if the *mamzer* is a Torah scholar and the *Cohen*, even if he is the *Cohen Gadol,* is unlearned, the *mamzer* who is a Torah scholar takes precedence over the *Cohen Gadol* who is un-

---

1. ס"ק א בשם היד אליהו סי' מג
2. חו"מ סי' תכו
3. ס"ק ו. וראה להלן סי' שלט סע' א בח' רעק"א וכן
4. הוריות פ"ג מ"ז-ח
5. שם בפירושם על המשנה

באר"ח סי' שלד במג"א סוס"ק ל וביה"ט ס"ק כב

NISHMAT AVRAHAM

learned. See further details in the *Rambam*[6] and the *Shulchan Aruch*.[7]

It should be obvious that the ruling of who takes precedence when lives are at stake applies only when the two patients present themselves simultaneously before the doctor or when the doctor sees them both simultaneously. Since he cannot treat both at one and the same time or if, for example, only one piece of apparatus is available and is essential for both, he treats them as set out by the *Mishnah*, provided that both are equally ill and treating one will automatically lead to the death of the other. However, if one can certainly be saved and the other only possibly, the former takes precedence.[8] [*Rav Auerbach zt"l* wrote to me questioning why I wrote as the *Taz* states "when lives are at stake," for the rules of precedence of the *Mishnah* apply also with regard to returning lost property, giving charity and doing acts of loving-kindness, and are most certainly true with regard to medical attention even if there is no question of danger and both are equally ill.]

The *Igrot Moshe*[9] writes that the doctor must treat the first patient to whom he is called. If, however, the second is sicker than the first, he should go to the second. The decision is a medical one. Moreover, if the doctor knows how to treat the second patient but not the first and goes to the first merely to calm him, he should go on to the second. However the doctor should give much thought to this decision for sometimes the first patient is also ill and, despairing of medical treatment, may become *seriously ill* if not calmed by the doctor. As the doctor of the city, or in a large city where both patients consider him their own doctor, he should consider carefully and without personal considerations what his obligation is. However the *Igrot Moshe* continues that although with regard to the rules of precedence we should follow the *Mishnah*, nevertheless it is difficult in practice to do so without much thought and study. *Rav Auerbach zt"l*[10] also writes that nowadays it is very difficult to follow the rules of the *Mishnah*.

On the other hand, if the doctor is already involved in the treatment of a patient or has already connected him to a machine, and another patient arrives who requires the attention of the doctor or requires to be connected to the same machine, the doctor may not leave the first patient to treat the second, or disconnect the first patient from the machine in order to give it to the second. He may not do this even if it is doubtful whether the first patient will benefit from his treatment or from the machine, whereas the second will certainly benefit. This is also true even if the first patient is an old man and chronically ill and the second an otherwise healthy young man. *Rav Auerbach zt"l* wrote to me that one life may not be set aside for another even if it is to save himself or others. Even if one can save the life of a great Torah scholar and righteous man who is needed by many, at the cost of the life of an ordinary person who is very old or who is deaf and dumb (*considered by Chazal to be equivalent to a shoteh —* author) or a *shoteh,* who is merely a burden on his family, nevertheless one may not do so. The rules of precedence only apply when the doctor, at the outset, must choose between two patients.

---

6. פירושו על המשנה והלכות ענײם פ״ח הט״ז

7. סי׳ רנא סע׳ ט. ולגבי גר ראה בשו״ת הרשב״א מובא בשו״ת מהרי״ק שורש ט מובא בב״י או״ח סי׳ קלה סע׳ ד. וראה באמת ליעקב להגר״י קמנצקי זצ״ל על מס׳ הוריות דף יג ע״א ד״ה ותדע

8. ראה בפמ״ג סי׳ שכח מ״ז ס״ק א ושו״ת ציץ אליעזר ח״ט סי׳ יז פ״י ס״ק ה וסי׳ כח ס״ק ג. שו״ת אג״מ חו״מ ח״ב סי׳ עד אות א וסי׳ עה אות ב

9. שו״ת, חו״מ ח״ב סי׳ עד אות א

10. מנחת שלמה תנינא סי׳ פו אות א

NISHMAT AVRAHAM

The *Gemara*[11] states that the verse:[12] "You shall sanctify him (the *Cohen*)," includes everything that pertains to holiness. And, although *Rashi* explains that this refers only to things that pertain to holiness, the *Ran* and the *Rosh*, on the other hand, explain that this means that he should be given precedence in everything so that it will make him appear greater and holier. For example, he should be the first to speak in any gathering, and when he sits at a meal he should be served first.[13] The *Magen Avraham*[14] asks that if this is so, why do we not take care nowadays to give a *Cohen* precedence in all such things, since it is a Torah requirement? He answers that maybe this is because we are no longer certain of the genealogy of any *Cohen*, as the *Shulchan Aruch* writes.[15] See also *Nishmat Avraham*, vol. 1 *Orach Chaim*, Siman 128, ref. 39.

The *Yavetz*[16] goes even further, and wonders if we should not give precedence to the wife of a *Cohen* or *Levi* over the wife of a Yisrael, for she also has greater holiness. The wife of a *Cohen* eats *terumah* and other gifts given to a *Cohen*, the wife of a *Levi*, *ma'aser*; and the firstborn sons of both are exempt from *Pidyon HaBen*. He points out that the silence of the *poskim* on the issue is something of a proof that the wives do not have precedence. He notes that even the precedence due to a *Cohen* is no longer adhered to today (for the same reason as given by the *Magen Avraham*). The matter, he concludes, remains in doubt. And the *Igrot Moshe*, already quoted above, writes that although with regard to the rules of precedence we should follow the *Mishnah*, nevertheless, in practice, it is difficult to do so without much thought and study. *Rav Auerbach zt"l* wrote,[17] quoting the *Pri Megadim*,[18] that if one of the two patients is definitely *dangerously ill* and the other only possibly so, and only one can be treated, the patient who is definitely *dangerously ill* takes precedence over the one who is only possibly so. Therefore the main criteria that must be considered are the degree of danger to the patient's life and the chances of saving him. The patient's age is of no consequence whatsoever. See the *Mishnah* and *Gemara* at the end of tractate *Horayot* which gives the priorities of who comes first in being freed from captivity and with regard to other issues. See, however, above that both the *Igrot Moshe* (ref. 9) and *Rav Auerbach zt"l* (ref. 10) write that nowadays it is extremely difficult to follow this ruling.

The *Igrot Moshe* (above ref. 9) writes that if the patients do not present themselves simultaneously then they are treated, other things being equal, according to their turn. How does arriving first acquire for one the right to precedence in terms of the *Halachah*? The *Shulchan Aruch*[19] writes that although a *Dayan* must deal with cases in the order of their presentation, nevertheless, he must deal with that of a Torah scholar first even if his were the last. It would appear from this that the order of precedence of the *Mishnah* holds even if the cases did not present themselves at one and the same time.

I found that *Rav Zilberstein shlita*[20] also asks what standing the concept of "in turn" has in *Halachah*? He quotes the *Meiri*[21]

---

11. נדרים סב ע"א
12. ויקרא כא:ח
13. וראה גם בגיטין נט ע"ב ורש"י ותוס' שם
14. סי' רא ס"ק ד מובא גם במ"ב שם ס"ק יג
15. או"ח סי' תנו סע' ב. וראה שם במג"א ס"ק ט ומ"ב ס"ק כב
16. ספר מגדל עוז, אבן בוחן, פנה א ס"ק פט
17. אסיא נט-ס אייר תשנ"ז עמ' 48
18. ריש סי' שכח במש"ז
19. חו"מ סי' טו סע' א ו-ב
20. הלכה ורפואה ח"ג עמ' צא
21. על סנהדרין לב ע"ב

who writes that there are instances when — although not demanded by *Halachah* — one must nevertheless act according to what appears the better of two actions. Thus when two ships meet in a narrow part of a river, the one that is not laden gives precedence to the one that is. Wherever we see that one can better withstand deferment than the other, he should give way — for example, the healthy before the sick. Thus, even with regard to a *Beit Din*, the case involving the orphan is heard before that of the widow, the widow is heard before the Torah scholar, and the Torah scholar before one who is unlearned. A woman takes precedence over a man since her shame (in waiting for her case to be heard) is greater. When they are all of equal standing, the first in turn is seen first. *Rav Zilberstein shlita* writes that we learn from this *Meiri* that the concept of "first come, first served" does not reflect the letter of the law. It is a matter of compromise and stems from the verse:[22] "Righteousness, righteousness shall you pursue." Just as the laden ship is given precedence, so it is only right that the first to come is served first.

Rav Waldenberg shlita[23] wrote to me that the main problem that requires study is the precedence given to a Torah scholar over an unlearned person. The *Sema*[24] writes that when the *Shulchan Aruch*[25] rules that he who arrives first should be heard first, this does not refer to the one who arrived first at the *Beit Din* but rather the one who is the first to stand before the *Dayan* and the *Dayan* is ready to hear the case. Thus with regard to a doctor's office, if someone arrives before the doctor does, his being first then has no meaning in *Halachah*. Only after the doctor arrives and is ready to receive, does this "right to be seen in turn" have meaning. All those who are already present before the doctor is ready are considered as having arrived simultaneously and the doctor may see whomever he wishes to first. Only those who arrive now, after the doctor has started to see patients, should be seen in the order in which they arrive. Thus the accepted practice of "first come first served" is only because everyone has accepted, by default, that this should be so. Thus, although it has no basis in *Halachah*, nevertheless it is binding as is any practice which has been accepted as being for the good of the many. The difference therefore is that this practice is not binding on a doctor who is seeing patients privately, at home or at his office. For him, the patients whom he finds awaiting him on his arrival may be considered as having arrived simultaneously, and he may see whomever he wishes to first.

Rav Waldenberg shlita continues that the ruling of the *Shulchan Aruch* that a Torah scholar takes precedence over an unlearned person is not a universally accepted ruling. The *Mechaber* himself writes in his *Beit Yosef*[26] that *Rashi*, *Rambam* and *Tosafot*[27] all rule that the *halachah* giving precedence to a Torah scholar only applies when he and the unlearned person have arrived together. This being so, one can understand the accepted practice not to give precedence to a Torah scholar who arrives last. For we have before us a double uncertainty: the first, whether a Torah scholar who comes later has priority, and the second, whether for this particular *halachah* the Torah scholar of today is considered a scholar.[28] However this is only so in giving precedence to

---

22. דברים טז:כ
23. שו"ת ציץ אליעזר חי"ח סי' סט. וראה שם סי' א
24. חו"מ סי' טו ס"ק א. וכ"כ הנתיבות המשפט שם
25. שם סע' א
26. יו"ד סי' רמג. וכן בדרישה שם
27. בחד תירוצא
28. ראה ברמ"א יו"ד סי' רמג סע' ב וסע' ז. פ"ת שם ס"ק ב. יד אברהם שם. מ"ב סי' תקמז ס"ק יב. וראה בב"י ע"ב ותוס' שם ד"ה עליונים שאין אנו יודעים לשקול בין התורה והמצוות של יהודי אחד כנגד השני

NISHMAT AVRAHAM

a scholar as against someone who arrived before him after the doctor was ready to receive. But if there were others waiting for the doctor's arrival and the Torah scholar arrived together with the doctor, they are all considered *halachically* to have arrived together. In such a situation the Torah scholar takes precedence and the accepted practice of the world does not have the power to revoke the privilege of the scholar and the *mitzvah* to honor him because of his Torah knowledge. If, however, the Torah scholar came later and others preceded him after the arrival of the doctor, he is seen according to his turn. However a Torah scholar who is famous for his knowledge and good deeds should be given precedence even if he arrives later than others, after the doctor is ready to receive.[29] *Rav Waldenberg shlita* adds that all the above applies also to people making purchases in a shop or to people who come to a Rav with their questions.

Rav Neuwirth shlita wrote to me that all the above applies only if the patients arrive without prior appointment. If they arrive by appointment and the doctor was delayed, each is seen according to his turn as fixed by his appointment.

The *Sefer Chassidim* writes[30] that if an enemy wishes to kill one of two men who are sitting together, should one be a Torah scholar and the other an unlearned person, it would be a *mitzvah* for the unlearned person to volunteer himself to be killed instead of the Torah scholar. This is what Reb Reuben the son of Istrobili did, volunteering himself to be killed instead of Rebbe Akiva since Rebbe Akiva was needed by many. However, the *Igrot Moshe*[31] writes that one is forbidden to sacrifice one's life to save that of another. Even if he is an unlearned person he may not offer his life to save that of a Torah scholar and man of good deeds who is condemned to death (*by the enemy*). And, although the *Gemara*[32] tells us of the brothers Pappus and Lulianus who sacrificed their lives to save the massacre of many (*on a trumped-up charge of having killed the king's daughter*), this is because they saved many Jews by this act.

The *Meshech Chochmah*[33] writes that although all of Israel needed Moshe Rabbeinu to redeem them from Egypt, nevertheless *Hashem* only permitted him to return to Egypt after all those who wished to kill him had died. Also, the Torah[34] tells us that an unintentional murderer may not go outside the walls of a city of refuge, for if he does, the avenger who waits outside can kill him. To this the *Mishnah*[35] adds, even if he (*the murderer*) is the commander-in-chief of the Jewish army, as great as Yoav ben Tseruia (*at the time of King David*), and is needed by all of Israel, he may not leave the city of refuge. *Rav Auerbach zt"l* wrote to me that the *Meshech Chochmah's* intention was to say that although *Hashem* could obviously have saved Moshe Rabbeinu from those who sought to kill him, since there was, in the natural way of things, a danger involved, *Hashem* did not wish to obligate Moshe Rabbeinu to put himself into danger. Therefore he would not, in any case, have been able to save the people of Israel if those seeking to kill him would have done so.[36]

1. HEART TRANSPLANT FROM A DONOR WHO IS A *TREIFAH* OR *GOSSES*. There is no question that this

---

29. ברכי יוסף על חו"מ סי' טו סע' א
30. סי' תרצח
31. שו"ת, יו"ד ח"ב סי' קעד ענף ד
32. תענית יח ע"ב רש"י ד"ה בלודקי ובע"ב י ע"ב רש"י ד"ה הרוגי לוד
33. פ' שמות ד:יט. וראה גם באור שמח הל' רוצח פ"ז ה"ח
34. במדבר לה: כו, כז
35. מכות פ"ב מ"ז
36. ראה בהמעיין ניסן תשמ"ב כרך כב גליון ג עמ' 31

NISHMAT AVRAHAM

is forbidden; one who kills a *gosses* deserves capital punishment;[37] there is no difference between killing him or killing a healthy individual. However, there is a distinction between different types of *gosses*. One who has become a *gosses* through an act of Heaven, such as one who fell ill, has the status of a healthy person, and one who kills him is liable to the death penalty through the *Sanhedrin*. On the other hand, one who kills a person who is a *gosses* due to human action — a victim of an accident, for instance — or a known *treifah* is liable only to Heavenly judgment. The *Sanhedrin* cannot put him to death. Would it be permitted to end the life of a *gosses* of the second type in order to save the life of another, otherwise healthy individual? The *Meiri*[39] writes that if enemies demand that one of a group of Jews be given over to them to be killed, otherwise they would kill all of them, should one of the group be a *treifah*, they may give him over to the enemy to save their own lives (*however, the treifah may not be killed by the Jews themselves — author*).

The *Minchat Chinuch*[40] writes that if one is commanded, on pain of death, to abort a fetus when the pregnancy does not endanger the mother, he is not obligated to refuse to do so and undergo martyrdom, for the fetus is not yet considered a *nefesh*. Similarly, a *treifah* is not considered a *nefesh*. The reason forbidding us to sacrifice one life to save another is because "how do we know whose blood is redder than whose,"[41] that is, whose life ought to be preserved. This does not apply in both these cases, for killing a fetus or a *treifah* does not carry the death penalty.

Nevertheless, the *Minchat Chinuch* concludes that the matter needs further study. And elsewhere,[42] he writes, that he wrote this only to arouse interest but, in practice, the matter requires further deep study.[43] See, however below, the ruling of the *Noda BiYehudah* and of the *poskim* of our day.

The *Beit Yitzchak*[44] writes that although a person who kills a *treifah* is not given the death penalty by the *Sanhedrin*, this is only because there is doubt as to whether the *treifah* would have lived as a result of his defect; if, however, it is known that he would have lived for twelve months or more, in spite of being a *treifah*, his murderer deserves the death penalty.

However, the *Noda BiYehudah*[45] rules differently from the *Minchat Chinuch*, in a reply to *Rav Yeshayah Pick* who expressed surprise at the *Rambam's* explanation as to why a fetus who threatened its mother's life could be aborted. The *Rambam*[46] writes that this is because the fetus is considered a *rodef*, that is, it is trying to kill her. *Rav Yeshayah Pick* wonders why the *Rambam* should say this. Surely even if the fetus is not a *rodef* one could abort it in order to save the mother. For killing it does not carry capital punishment, but the mother has a higher status in terms of the value of her life, since killing her would carry capital punishment. The *Noda BiYehudah* replies that, on the contrary, he is surprised at *Rav Yeshayah Pick's* surprise. For no one ever permitted killing a *treifah* to save someone who is healthy. He never heard of such a thing. Even if killing a *treifah* does not carry the death penalty, in killing him

---

37. רמב"ם הל' רוצח פ"ב ה"ז
38. שם וה"ח
39. סנהדרין עב ע"א ד"ה יראה לי
40. מצוה רצו ד"ה והנה
41. מאי חזית - פסחים כה ע"ב
42. מצוה תר
43. וראה גם בתפארת ישראל סוף"ח דיומא בבועז ועי"ע במאירי נדרים כב ע"א
44. שו"ת, או"ח סי' יח ס"ק טו. וראה גם שם יו"ד ח"ב סי' קסב
45. שו"ת, מהדו"ת חו"מ סי' נט
46. הל' רוצח פ"א ה"ט

SIMAN 252: REDEEMING PRISONERS / §8

NISHMAT AVRAHAM

one actively does that which is forbidden. One must even set aside the very serious Sabbath laws to prolong life for even a short span of time. But if one does not save the healthy person (at the expense of the *treifah*, when it is only possible to save one of them) it is only an act of omission.[47]

The *Igrot Moshe*,[48] *Tzitz Eliezer*,[49] *Minchat Yitzchak*[50] and *Rav Kasher*[51] all rule that it is forbidden to kill a *treifah*, and all the more so a *gosses*,[52] in order to save the life of one who is otherwise healthy. *Rav Auerbach zt"l* also told me that one may not sacrifice one life to save another, not even that of a *treifah* to save one who is not. See also above Siman 157E, p. 82.

2. KIDNEY TRANSPLANT FROM A GOSSES.
Although the kidney is not a vital organ, since a person can live with one of his two kidneys, nevertheless a *gosses* cannot be used as a donor for even one of his two kidneys. This is because in his precarious state the operation itself will kill him. It is also forbidden to prolong the life of a *gosses* by artificial means and prevent him from dying merely in order to obtain a viable kidney from him.[53]

3. PRIORITIES WHEN THERE IS NO PIKUACH NEFESH.
Rav Zilberstein shlita[54] has written about the order or priority when there is no *pikuach nefesh* involved. However, *Rav Auerbach zt"l* wrote to me wondering why *pikuach nefesh* specifically is discussed in this *halachah*. Surely it applies to returning lost property, giving charity, doing acts of loving-kindness and, all the more so, to patients, even if they are not in danger of their lives.

Rav Nebenzahl shlita[55] has written about priorities in the treatment of the elderly.

---

47. אהע"ז סי' מב ס"ק ז ראה גם בחידושי בית הלוי על הרמב"ם שם ובשו"ת תורת חסד
48. שו"ת, יו"ד ח"ב סי' קעד
49. שו"ת, ח"י סי' כה פכ"ה. וראה שם ח"ט סי' יז פ"ו ופ"י ס"ק ה
50. שו"ת, ח"ה סי' ז ו-ט
51. בספרו דברי מנחם חלק התשובות סי' כז
52. רמב"ם הל' רוצח פ"ב ה"ז ו-ח
53. שו"ת אג"מ יו"ד ח"ב סי' קעד ענף ג
54. ספר הלכה ורפואה ח"ג עמ' צא
55. אסיא, חוברת לו, תמוז תשמ"ג

CHAPTER 25

The Laws of Brit Milah (Circumcision)

SIMAN 260

§1 It is a positive *mitzvah* for (A)a father to circumcise (B)his son and this *mitzvah* is greater than other positive *mitzvos*.

──────── NISHMAT AVRAHAM ────────

SIMAN 260

(A) a father. Rav Auerbach zt"l wrote to me that whether or not the father fulfills a (*greater*) *mitzvah* by circumcising his own son (*rather than making a mohel his agent*), even when he will cause greater suffering to the baby, is a matter that needs further study.

A BLIND FATHER. See the *Beit Yosef* and the *Magen Avraham*.[1] The majority of *poskim* rule that a blind person is obligated by the Torah to keep all the *mitzvot* in the same way as a male who is not blind. Therefore he must make certain that his son is circumcised. *Tosafot*[2] believe that the obligation of a blind male to keep the *mitzvot* is only Rabbinic since if he did not keep any *mitzvot*, he would be like a non-Jew[3] (see *Nishmat Avraham*, vol. 1 *Orach Chaim*, Siman 53A, p. 25).

(B) his son. A child born after artificial insemination from a husband to his wife (AIH) (*with permission from a posek*) is considered by most *poskim* to be his son in all respects. However, the *Sefer HaBrit*[4] writes that the *acharonim* have discussed at length what the *Chelkat Mechokek*,[5] the *Beit Shmuel*,[6] the *Bach*[7] and the *Tashbetz*[8] have written regarding whether a child born to a woman who became pregnant from sperm emitted into the bath is considered his father's son in all respects. *Rabbeinu Chananel*[9] writes that if a woman became pregnant in such a fashion, this would be considered a miracle and therefore the verses:[10] "When a woman 'emits' and gives birth to a male, she shall be unclean for seven days ... On the eighth day he shall be circumcised," would not apply to her and such a child may not be circumcised on the Sabbath. However, the *Sefer HaBrit* writes that it is possible that he wrote this only because it would be considered miraculous, and the matter requires further study.

Rav Auerbach zt"l[11] writes that *Rabbeinu Chananel* feels that the juxtaposition of the two verses (*about a woman's impurity after birth and about circumcision*) indicates that impurity and circumcision are related. Since a woman who becomes pregnant in the way described above does not become unclean as a result

---

1. ריש סי' יז
2. ר"ה לג ע"א ד"ה הא וב"ק פג ע"א ד"ה התירו
3. מנחת חינוך סוף מצוה ב ד"ה והנה מילה
4. כאן ס"ק מח וסי' רסב ס"ק צו
5. אהע"ז סי' א ס"ק ח
6. שם ס"ק י
7. יו"ד סי' קצה ד"ה ולא ישב
8. שו"ת תשב"ץ ח"ג סי' רסג
9. חגיגה טז ע"א
10. ויקרא יב:ב-ג
11. נועם כרך א תשי"ח עמ' קנג

SIMAN 261

§1 If a father did not circumcise his son, the *Beit Din* is obligated to do so. If the *Beit Din* do not, the son becomes obligated to do so (A)when he becomes of age (*that is, at thirteen*).

---NISHMAT AVRAHAM---

of giving birth, the baby may not be circumcised on *Shabbat*. *Rav Auerbach zt"l* writes that the same holds true for a baby born as a result of AIH. For the *Gemara*[12] wonders whether a baby born by Caesarian section, whose mother does not become *temei'ah* as a result of giving birth, may be circumcised on *Shabbat* or not, and the *Shulchan Aruch*[13] rules that he may not. We must say that *Rabbeinu Chananel's* real reason is that since the woman (*who became pregnant from sperm in the bath*) did not take part in the emission of her husband's sperm we do not apply to her the verse: "When a woman 'emits'"; also, this is not the normal way of emission as during *coitus*. Both reasons apply to artificial insemination, and the baby should probably not be circumcised on *Shabbat*. On a later occasion, the *Rav zt"l* told me that in any case, why when the Torah uses the word "emits" with regard to a woman it does not refer to ovulation, needs further study. Later still the *Rav zt"l* told me that since the child is considered the father's in every aspect, the father certainly needs to redeem him (*if he is firstborn*) with a blessing. However, with regard to circumcising him on *Shabbat* he is still doubtful as to the *halachah*.

His son *Rav Ezriel Auerbach shlita* told me some ten years ago that his father-in-law, *Rav Eliashiv shlita*, also gave the same ruling when asked about such a baby. However, more recently, he told me that *Rav Eliashiv* has changed his mind and now permits such a baby to be circumcised on *Shabbat* (*when he is born on Shabbat*). *Rav Ovadiah Yosef shlita*[14] wrote to me that since the baby was born normally (*that is, not by Caesarian section*), his circumcision is performed on *Shabbat* (*if he is born on Shabbat*).

I presume that the same difference of opinion will exist regarding a baby born after in-vitro fertilization (IVF), and *Rav Ovadiah Yosef shlita* wrote to me that he rules that such a baby may be circumcised on *Shabbat* for the same reason.

SIMAN 261

(A) when he becomes of age. May an older child or adult who needs to be circumcised be anesthetized? There is an opinion[1] that does not permit even local anesthesia, there are those[2] who permit local anesthesia but forbid general anesthesia and there are those[3] who permit even general anesthesia.

May a local anesthetic cream be used to avoid or lessen pain, even in an eight-day old baby undergoing circumcision? For if *Halachah* permits it and, since the act of circumcision is not affected at all, then perhaps there would even be an obligation to do so. On the other hand, there may be a Kabbalistic reason as to why the baby should be circumcised without any attempt to lessen its pain, in which case it

---

12. שבת קלה ע"ב
13. יו"ד סי' רסו סע' י
14. הערה לנשמת אברהם כרך ד עמ' רכו
1. שו"ת אמרי יושר ח"ב סי' קמ

2. שו"ת שרידי אש ח"ג סי' צו. וכן ראה בשו"ת שבט הלוי ח"ה סי' קמז ס"ק ב שמתיר במקום צערא יתירה

3. שו"ת מהרש"ם ח"ו סי' קח. שו"ת יביע אומר ח"ה יו"ד סי' כב

CHAPTER 25: LAWS OF BRIT MILAH (CIRCUMCISION)

NISHMAT AVRAHAM

would be forbidden to use an anesthetic, unless there was a medical indication.

The *Ollelot Ephraim*[4] writes that those present at the *brit* should pray about their own personal troubles at the time when the baby cries in pain. Since the baby's cry reaches Heaven without any hindrance, their own personal prayers will also be included in it. It is this that the verse refers to, saying:[5] "For *Hashem* has heard my weeping *(that is, the weeping of the baby at circumcision). Hashem* has heard my plea, *Hashem* will accept my prayer." (*I find it difficult to understand that this should be sufficient reason to forbid reducing the baby's suffering — author.*)

The *Imrei Yosher*[6] writes that anesthesia may not be used, for although *Chazal* knew of ways to alleviate pain, we do not find anywhere that it was used during circumcision. It would therefore appear that they believed that the baby's pain should accompany circumcision and Heaven forbid that we introduce new procedures that were never used.

On the other hand, the *Seridei Eish*[7] writes that there are reasons to permit it for we do not find anywhere that there is a *mitzvah* to cause suffering during circumcision. The *Shevet HaLevi*,[8] although permitting the use of anesthesia if there would be great suffering, writes that we find that *Chazal* considered the *mitzvah* of circumcision to include the suffering of the baby and they explain the verse:[9] "Because for Your sake we are killed all the time," to apply to the *mitzvah* of circumcision. He writes that it is obvious that the traditional manner in which the *mitzvah* of circumcision is performed stems from Mount Sinai.

Rav Waldenberg shlita[10] also wrote to me forbidding the use of anesthesia, based on the opinion of the *Imrei Yosher*, the *Ollelot Ephraim* (above) and other *poskim*.[11]

Rav Ovadiah Yosef[12] disagrees with the *Imrei Yosher*, wondering where he found an obligation to suffer at the *brit*. And, if in earlier days suffering was accepted because of the love of the *mitzvah*, as our forefather Avraham accepted it, why should we prevent someone who wishes to find means of alleviating the pain involved in a *brit* from doing so? In such a situation, the onus of bringing a clear proof is on the one who wishes to rule strictly. The truth of the matter is that the lack of suffering does not hinder a *brit*; if the *brit* is done according to the *Halachah*, why should the lack of suffering of the baby be a problem?

Rav Auerbach zt"l told me that, in his opinion, there is no *halachic* reason why anesthesia should not be used. However he did not know whether a Kabbalistic reason might exist and I should attempt to find out. Rav Yosef Winter *shlita* kindly took the trouble to speak at length to *Rav Yaakov Hillel shlita*, the Dean of the Yeshiva of Kabbalists in Jerusalem, who could not find any special reason why the baby has to suffer in the *Zohar* and other Kabbalistic books. *Rav Hillel shlita* himself added an interesting proof to permit the use of anesthesia. The *Zohar* and *Tikkunei HaZohar* write that the suffering of childbirth atones for the sin of Eve. Yet every effort is made to alleviate the pain of childbirth as much as possible, and no one has spoken out against this.

Both *Rav Auerbach zt"l* and *Rav Eliashiv shlita* told me that, provided there is

---

4. סי' תטו, מובא בהגהות הגרא"ג מגרידץ על מסכת שבת קל ע"א
5. תהלים ו:ט-י
6. שו"ת ח"ב סי' קמ
7. שו"ת ח"ג סי' צו
8. שו"ת ח"ה סי' קמז ס"ק ב וראה שם יו"ד ח"א סי' קלב
9. תהלים מד:כג
10. שו"ת ציץ אליעזר ח"כ סי' עג
11. שו"ת ארץ צבי סי' נו. שו"ת מערכי לב סי' נג
12. שו"ת יביע אומר ח"ה יו"ד סי' כב

SIMAN 262
WHEN MAY A HEALTHY OR A SICK CHILD BE CIRCUMCISED

§1 Circumcision may not be performed until after sunrise on (A)the eighth day after the baby's birth (*if it was done after dawn, he has still fulfilled his obligation*). The *milah* is permitted any time during the day, but those who are eager to perform *mitzvot* will do so as early as possible in the morning. A circumcision that had to be postponed till after the eighth day may also only be done during the day.

NISHMAT AVRAHAM

no danger whatsoever in the use of the local anesthetic, one would be permitted, and should therefore be obligated, to use it.

SIMAN 262

(A) the eighth day. It is interesting to note that every baby is born with a normal level of certain *enzymes*, called coagulation factors, which are indispensable for blood coagulation (clotting), having received them from his mother's blood in utero. His own liver, the source of these *enzymes*, is as yet not sufficiently mature to produce normal quantities of these *enzymes*. During the first two to three days after birth, the blood levels of these *enzymes* fall so that every newborn baby at this stage, even though full-term and healthy, has a relative deficiency in the blood levels of these *enzymes*. The liver at this stage begins to function more efficiently, the blood levels of these *enzymes* begin to rise, and reach normal levels by the eighth day.[1] The *Torah Temimah*[2] writes that the *Rambam*[3] wrote that the reason that the Torah set the eighth day as the day for the *brit* was to allow the newborn baby to become stronger. Many have expressed surprise why he should give a reason of his own and not that given by the *Gemara*.[4] However, the *Torah Temimah* answers in the *Rambam's* defense that he did not think up this reason on his own. On the contrary, his reason is specifically stated in the *Midrash*[5] which writes: Why is the baby circumcised on the eighth day? Because *Hashem* has pity on him and gives him time to become stronger. In the opinion of the *Torah Temimah*, the *Rambam* chose this reason over the one given by the *Gemara*, because the reason given by the *Gemara* — that the wife is permitted to her husband on the eighth day after having given birth to a boy — no longer applies today. The Torah (*Leviticus* 12:1-4) gives certain times of uterine bleeding when the wife is nevertheless permitted to her husband; from the eighth day after giving birth to a boy and for thirty-three days following is one such period. This no longer applies today (*and did not apply from the time of the Geonim, before the Rambam*) since we act strictly with regard to all uterine bleeding,

---

1. ראה ספר אסיא כרך ג עמ' 384 רצ"ע קצת מיליד בית ומקנת בית שנימולים באחד, שבת קלה ע"ב
2. ויקרא יב:ג אות כב
3. מורה נבוכים ח"ג סו"פ מט
4. נדה לא ע"ב
5. מדרש רבה ריש פ' תצא

§2 A (B)sick baby may not be circumcised until he (C)recovers

―――――― NISHMAT AVRAHAM ――――――

even with that which the Torah defines as *tahor*.[6] One wonders whether in the *Midrash* quoted above *Chazal* are hinting to the fact that the baby will be well protected from excessive bleeding on the eighth day.

(B) sick baby. The *Maharam Shick*[7] writes that it is obvious that a baby who is a *treifah* must be circumcised and this is also the ruling of the *Chatam Sofer*.[8] This is on condition that specialist physicians feel that the circumcision will not cause him to die earlier. This is also the view of the *Mahari Assad*[9] and the *Zocher HaBrit*.[10] However the *Maharam Shick* was uncertain whether, according to *Rashi*,[11] the circumcision could take place on *Shabbat* if *Shabbat* was the eighth day. However the *Tosfot Rid*[12] and *Shibbolei HaLeket*[13] rule that the *brit* overrides *Shabbat* and this is also the ruling of the *Zocher HaBrit*.[14] The *Chatam Sofer*[15] writes regarding a baby who was given less than three months to live by his physicians that even if the Rabbis believe that the baby is *seriously ill* and has only three months to live, nevertheless if the physicians say that the *brit* will not make him any weaker, he should be circumcised. The *Chatam Sofer* writes that in his opinion, the positive commandment to circumcise a baby on the eighth day applies no less to a *treifah* than to a healthy baby.

(C) recovers. The *Taz*[16] writes that he saw that the *Bedek HaBayit* (written by the *Beit Yosef*) quotes the *Rashba*[17] that in any case the baby (whose brit has been postponed because of illness) should not be circumcised on Thursday. The baby will be suffering on the third day after the *brit*, and this will be *Shabbat* and one should not cause suffering on *Shabbat*. On the basis of this, the *Taz* feels that all the more so one should not circumcise the baby on Friday, for the suffering will be even greater on *Shabbat* as is written later, Siman 266, in the name of the *Rashba* and *Ramban*. However *Rebbe Akiva Eiger*[18] expresses surprise at the *Taz's* statement that a postponed *brit* may not be performed on Friday. For the *Bedek HaBayit* quotes from that same *responsum* of the *Rashba* that a sick baby whose *brit* was postponed and who recovered on Thursday, is circumcised on Friday.

The *Tashbetz*[19] points out that the *Gemara*[20] rules that one may not set sail on a long journey three days before *Shabbat* unless the purpose of the journey is for a *mitzvah*. The *Raza* explains that the reason for this is that he will certainly need to set aside Sabbath laws because of danger. This being so, setting out under these conditions is virtually a statement that he is willing to set aside the Sabbath. Therefore one can learn that the circumcision of a *ger* on Thursday is forbidden so that there will not be a need to set aside Sabbath laws for him on the third day follow-

---

6. רמב"ם הל' איסו"ב פי"א ה"ה-ו. הרא"ש נדה פ"י סי' ו
7. שו"ת, יו"ד סי' רמג
8. שו"ת, ח"ו סי' סד
9. שו"ת, מהר"י אסאד יו"ד סי' רנב
10. סי' י ס"ק לו
11. נדה כג ע"ב ד"ה ושטו נקוב
12. שבת קלו ע"א
13. הל' מילה סי' א
14. סי' ז ס"ק כו
15. שו"ת ח"ו סי' סד
16. ס"ק ג
17. עיין ברכר"י שיש כאן טעות סופר וצ"ל: הרשב"ץ
18. חידושי רעק"א כאן
19. שו"ת ח"א סי' כא הובא בבית יוסף סי' רסח
20. שבת יט ע"א

SIMAN 262: WHEN TO CIRCUMCISE / §2

NISHMAT AVRAHAM

ing his *brit* as the *Gemara*[21] says. This will apply also to a baby whose circumcision must be postponed because of illness and who recovered on Thursday; he should be circumcised on Friday (*and not on Thursday*).

The *Birkei Yosef*[22] also writes that since the third day (*following the brit*) is *Shabbat* and the baby is in danger, (*the father*) may have to set aside *Sabbath* laws for him. This would be like someone who does something before *Shabbat* knowing that he will have to set aside Sabbath laws as a result. Therefore circumcision (*that was postponed from the eighth day*) may not be done on Thursday, since he might, as a result, need to set aside Sabbath laws for the baby who is in danger on the third day. For the same reason the circumcision may not be done on Friday. Since there is an opinion that the danger is present on all of the first three days (*and not just on the third day*), we rule strictly and do not circumcise on Thursday or Friday, following the ruling of the *Knesset HaGedolah*.

The *Maharsham*[23] also ruled that one should act strictly and wait till Sunday to do the *brit*. The *Ben Ish Chai*[24] also writes that a circumcision that has been postponed may not be performed on a Thursday or Friday. See also the *Kaf HaChaim*.[25] The *Zocher HaBrit*[26] writes that he has seen *poskim* who rule that one should wait until Sunday unless the father has a good reason why he cannot wait until then. The *Ikrei HaDat*[27] also writes that a postponed circumcision may not be done on Thursday or on Friday.

The *Yad HaLevi*[28] also rules likewise but adds that if there is doubt whether Thursday is the eighth or ninth day after the birth (*when the baby was born ben hashemashot towards the close of the previous Wednesday*), the *brit* may be done on Thursday. In such a situation there is a double doubt — perhaps the *halachah* is not like the ruling of the *Tashbetz* (ref. 19), and even if it is, perhaps there will not be a need to set aside Sabbath laws. In fact this is how the *Korban Netanel*[29] answers the argument that the *Shach* brings against the *Tashbetz*.

The *Mishnah*[30] states that it sometimes happens that a baby is circumcised on the ninth, tenth, eleventh or twelfth day after his birth. For if *Rosh Hashanah* is on a Sunday and Monday and a baby was born the previous week during *bein hashemashot* on the close of Friday, he may not be circumcised on *Shabbat* (since he may actually have been born on Friday and Shabbat will not be the eighth day). Nor may he be circumcised on the two days of *Rosh Hashanah*. He should be circumcised on Tuesday which is the twelfth day following his birth (if he was really born on Friday and not on *Shabbat*). The *Shach*[31] asks that according to the *Tashbetz* since a baby whose *brit* has been postponed cannot be circumcised on Thursday or Friday, there is a possibility of a *brit* on the fifteenth day after the birth. If *Rosh Hashanah* is on Tuesday and Wednesday and the baby was born at the close of Monday *bein hashemashot*, the twelfth day would be Thursday and the *brit* will be on Sunday on the fifteenth day.[32] The

---

21. שבת פו ע"א
22. כאן
23. שו"ת, ח"ה סי' ז
24. שו"ת, רב פעלים ח"ד יו"ד סי' כח
25. או"ח סי' שלא ס"ק לא
26. סי' ו ס"ק ג
27. או"ח סי' כב ס"ק לה
28. שו"ת, יו"ד סי' קמ
29. על הרא"ש שבת פי"ט סי' ח ס"ק ה
30. שבת פי"ט מ"ה
31. סי' רסו ס"ק יח
32. I wondered whether there is a printing mistake here and "the fifteenth day" should read "fourteenth day," Thursday being, in fact, the eleventh day and not the twelfth.

from his illness. One must wait (D)seven (full) days, each of

NISHMAT AVRAHAM

Korban Netanel answers that since there is a double doubt here (*the bein hashemashot makes it questionable as to whether the baby was born on Monday or Tuesday and it is not certain that there will be a need to set aside the Sabbath laws*), even the *Tashbetz* would agree that the baby may be circumcised on Thursday.

The *Yabia Omer*[33] also rules that a postponed circumcision may not be done on a Thursday or Friday. However if he was born on Wednesday *bein hashemashot* he is circumcised on Thursday.[34]

However there are many *poskim* who rule that it is permitted to perform a postponed *brit* on a Thursday or Friday, and the *mitzvah* should not be delayed. The *Shach*[35] writes that there is no question that the *brit* should be performed on Thursday. On the contrary, he notes that the *Tashbetz's* (ref. 19) proof is from the *Gemara* that forbids sailing three days before *Shabbat*. But the *Gemara* permits such sailing if it is for a *mitzvah*, and what greater *mitzvah* is there than *brit milah*?[36] The *Magen Avraham*[37] also writes that since nowadays it is uncommon that Sabbath laws need to be set aside for a baby who was circumcised on Thursday, one should not be lax in performing the *mitzvah*, and the *brit* should be done on Thursday. This is also the ruling of the *Eliyah Rabbah*,[38] *Noda BiYehudah*[39] and *Chacham Zvi*.[40] However, the *Chacham Zvi's* son, the *Yavetz*,[41] differentiates between the *brit* of a proselyte and that of a baby whose *brit* was postponed because of illness. He writes that the proselyte has no obligation to convert and may change his mind if he so wishes (*before he has converted*). However, every day that a Jewish baby is not circumcised when he should have been, a positive commandment that is punishable by *karet* is set aside. His father, *Beit Din* or all of Israel are obligated to circumcise him; whether or not Sabbath laws will need to be set aside is uncertain and we do not need to take into account the view of the *Tashbetz*. The *Gilyon Maharsha*[42] also rules that he should be circumcised on Thursday, adding that each day that passes without the *mitzvah* having been performed is a transgression and, according to the *Ra'avad*, he is liable for *karet* each day. The *Mishnah Berurah*[43] also rules that the *brit* should be done on Thursday, and *Rav Auerbach zt"l* wrote to me that this is the accepted ruling.

All of the above concerns the possibility of performing a postponed *brit* three days before *Shabbat*. There is, however, no controversy that a postponed *brit* may be performed three days before *Yom Tov*,[44] and the *Chida*[45] writes that one may do this even according to the opinion of the *Tashbetz*, for he forbade it only before *Shabbat*.

(D) seven (full) days, each of *Baruch Hashem*, I found that this is what the *Yavetz* II, 95 and the *Yabia Omer* V Y.D. 23 (3) write.

---

33. שו"ת, ח"ה יו"ד סי' כג
34. שם. וראה בחידושי רעק"א סוסי' רסו
35. סי' רסו ס"ק יח
36. ראה שו"ת יביע אומר שם אות ב שדן בדבר
37. סי' שלא ס"ק ט
38. סי' רמח ס"ק ה וסי' שלא ס"ק י
39. שו"ת, תניינא יו"ד סי' קסו
40. תשובות הנוספות, שאלה ט סי' יד
41. שו"ת, ח"ב סי' צה
42. כאן. עיין ברמב"ם וראב"ד הל' מילה פ"א ה"ב שמדובר על אדם בן י"ג שנה ויום אחד שלא מל את עצמו
43. סי' שלא ס"ק לג
44. זוכר הברית סי' ו ס"ק ה. הבן איש חי בשו"ת רב פעלים ח"ד יו"ד סי' כח. שו"ת יביע אומר ח"ה יו"ד סי' כג
45. ספר מראית העין ליקוטים סי' ח אות ב

SIMAN 262: WHEN TO CIRCUMCISE / §2

twenty-four hours, from the time he recovers from his illness before he may be circumcised. This only applies

─────────────── NISHMAT AVRAHAM ───────────────

twenty-four hours. The *Binyan Tzion*[46] writes that this is a Torah requirement handed down from Sinai to Moshe Rabbeinu. He cites a *Gemara*[47] that quotes a verse[48] from which the *halachah* concerning the *brit* of a sick baby who recovered is derived. Therefore, as with any doubt where a Torah law is concerned, if there arises any uncertainty we act strictly. In any case, he adds, there is a possibility of danger with circumcision,[49] and we have to act strictly.[50] The *Binyan Tzion* rules, therefore, that if he did not wait the mandatory seven days for sickness but circumcised his son on the eight day after his birth which was on *Shabbat*, he is considered to have desecrated the Sabbath.

Rav Auerbach zt"l, commenting on the *Binyan Tzion*'s premise that this *halachah* to wait seven full days of twenty-four hours is of Torah force, wrote to me that this was a surprising statement, particularly since the *Amora* Shmuel ruled that one should wait thirty days.[51] It would rather appear, he wrote, that this is akin to the *halachah* concerning a woman during the three and seven days after she gave birth, with regard to *Shabbat* and *Yom Kippur*.[52] Since there is a possibility that the baby might become dangerously ill if the *brit* is done too close to his recovery, *Chazal* decreed a given time when such a possibility would not exist. This is also similar to their decree that when Sabbath laws need to be set aside for a *seriously ill* patient, they should not be set aside through a non-Jew or a child lest a patient's life be endangered on another occasion (*by wasting valuable time searching unnecessarily for a non-Jew or a child*). The *Rav zt"l* added that since this is a decree of *Chazal*, medical opinion to the contrary is of no consequence, and he refers to what he had written elsewhere.[53]

I wondered, therefore, why there is no obligation to wait seven days after a baby recovers from a simple fever, before carrying out any elective surgery on him, however minor. Did *Chazal* only make their decree regarding circumcision because other surgical procedures were unknown in their day? For, in principle, why should there be a difference between circumcision and any minor surgery? I also wondered whether an adult undergoing circumcision also had to wait seven days after recovering from an illness. *Rav Auerbach zt"l* wrote to me that it is possible that *Chazal* instituted this waiting period in the case of circumcision only, since it is a great *mitzvah*, and in order to avoid any possibility of danger under any circumstance, they instituted it. This would not apply to a surgical procedure. And, if no one differentiates between a baby and an adult, then the waiting period of seven days would indeed also apply to an adult.

See *Nishmat Avraham*, vol. 1 *Orach Chaim*, Siman 213E regarding the blessing of *HaGomel* for an adult or a proselyte after their *brit*.

---

46. שו"ת, ח"א סי' פז
47. יבמות עא ע"א
48. שמות יב:מח
49. רא"ש שבת פי"ט סי' ט
50. וראה בשו"ת מהר"ם שיק יו"ד סי' רמד ד"ה ובתשובה
מובא בנחל הברית סי' לב ס"ק ה
51. ירושלמי פי"ט ה"ה
52. See *Nishmat Avraham*, vol. 1 *Orach Chaim*, Siman 330 §4 and Siman 617 §4.
53. מוריה סיון-תמוז תשל"א עמ' י. מנחת שלמה ח"א סי' ה

when he has (E)recovered from a fever or from (F)a general-

NISHMAT AVRAHAM

(E) recovered from a fever. The *Yerushalmi*[54] writes that a sick baby may not be circumcised until he recovers. Shmuel says that even if he had a fever for a short time the *brit* is postponed. This is also the ruling of the *Rambam*,[55] the *Tur* and the *Shulchan Aruch*. Rav Auerbach zt"l wrote to me pointing out that Shmuel said that one must wait thirty days (after his recovery). It would seem that we do not take the *Yerushalmi* into consideration, although the situation is one of possible *pikuach nefesh*, because, in fact, there really is no controversy between the *Yerushalmi* and the *Bavli*. For Shmuel in the *Bavli* says that one must wait seven days after recovery; one of these statements, therefore, must be a misquotation, and we depend more on the *Bavli* (*there are many different versions in many parts of the Yerushalmi text with numerous printing mistakes — author*).

(F) a generalized illness. The *Rambam's*[56] statement is famous: One may only circumcise a baby who is completely healthy for everything is postponed if there is any danger. It is possible to circumcise later but it is impossible to ever bring back one Jew to life.

I will now discuss a number of possibilities, but the words of the *Aruch HaShulchan*[57] are an important and necessary introduction in this context. He writes that he has seen books on the laws of circumcision that debate whether a particular illness is considered a generalized illness requiring the postponement of the *brit* for seven days after recovery or not. He is amazed at their doubts for it should be obvious that circumcision is delayed if there is any change whatsoever in any part of the baby as a result of illness. If there is also doubt as to whether the illness is generalized or only local the doctor must be consulted, for we always depend on medical opinion with regard to setting aside Sabbath laws or allowing a patient to eat on *Yom Kippur*. It is a clear-cut *halachah* that one must rule leniently when there is any doubt regarding *pikuach nefesh*. Therefore in any uncertainty one must wait seven full days from the time of recovery. So what point is there to go into details? In any case one must ask the doctor.

1. ANEMIA. It is forbidden to circumcise a baby who is anemic, but if no treatment is required, he is circumcised immediately after spontaneous recovery. However, if the anemia is severe enough to require treatment, the *brit* is postponed for a further seven days after recovery.[58]

2. HEART DISEASE. A baby who is *cyanosed* at birth because of a heart condition may not be circumcised until after he has undergone surgery and recovered. If, however, there is no hope of cure, but on the other hand medical opinion is that circumcision will not endanger his life, the *Minchat Yitzchak*[59] writes that it is possible that he may be circumcised on the eighth day. Rav Auerbach zt"l wrote to me expressing surprise at how it is possible to depend on medical opinion in such a situation when the baby is blue and different from a healthy one. It is possible that one should wait until he is thirty days old to be sure that he is viable.

---

54. שבת פ"י ה"ה ויבמות פ"ח ה"א

55. הל' מילה פ"א הט"ז

56. שם הי"ח

57. יו"ד סי' רסג סע' ד

58. שו"ת מנחת יצחק ח"ה סי' יא. וכן אמרו לי הגרש"ז אויערבאך זצ"ל והג"ר בן ציון אבא שאול זצ"ל

59. שם

NISHMAT AVRAHAM

Rav Auerbach *zt"l* wrote to me that a baby that underwent cardiac catheterization without any complications, before he was eight days old, is in the same *halachic* category as a baby with a cardiac condition who did not have this procedure.

3. FEVER. The *brit* of a baby who has fever, from whatever illness, is postponed for seven full days after he has recovered from his illness. How is fever defined for the puposes of this *halachah*? The *Zocher HaBrit*[60] writes that 37.5°C is considered fever sufficient to warrant postponement of the *brit* for seven days after recovery. On the other hand, *poskim* of our generation[61] have ruled that any fever, even less than this, warrants the postponement of the *brit*. Rav Auerbach *zt"l* told me that although the *brit* must be postponed for any fever, one does not need to wait for seven days following recovery unless the temperature reaches 38.0°C. A temperature between 37.5° and 38.0°C places the baby in the category of one who has a local illness and he may be circumcised as soon as he recovers. If, however, in the opinion of a specialist, the baby is not at all ill, and a temperature of less than 38°C in his case is not due to any illness, he may be circumcised on the eighth day. Rav Waldenberg *shlita*[62] writes that if the fever is due to dehydration, either because of a suboptimal intake of fluids or because of an especially hot environment, the baby is not defined as being ill. Since an increase of his fluid intake or removing him to a cooler environment without any additional treatment will immediately normalize his temperature, he may be circumcised on the eighth day. However, Rav Auerbach *zt"l* told me that, in his opinion, such a baby is defined as ill, and, although he may be circumcised immediately after the fever subsides, nevertheless, if his temperature peaked at 38°C, the *brit* is postponed until seven days have passed after the fever has completely subsided.

When does the count of seven days begin for a baby that had a high temperature due to a urinary tract infection whose fever subsided two days after treatment with antibiotics? Does it begin now although he will continue to receive antibiotics for a week or so, or do we wait until treatment has been completed to start counting the seven days? Similarly, with an adult who needs to be circumcised who has abdominal pain due to an acute stomach ulcer, are the seven days counted from when the pains cease or only from when the acute ulcer has completely healed? In both cases, Rav Auerbach *zt"l* told me that the count of seven days starts from when the patient feels well with no symptoms of his disease, and there is no need to wait until the completion of treatment or until the disease has completely disappeared.

4. INCUBATOR. The *Igrot Moshe*[63] and the *Tzitz Eliezer*[64] both rule that a baby who was put into an incubator may not be circumcised until seven days after he is taken out of the incubator. Since he needed the incubator to recover, he is to be considered as one who had a generalized illness. Rav Neuwirth *shlita* told me that if an otherwise healthy baby was put into the incubator with blue light because of physiologic jaundice (see Siman 263A below), only in order to hasten the process of recovery from the jaundice, he may be circumcised on the eighth day if he is no longer jaundiced. See, however, Siman 263A, p. 203.

---

60. סי' י סע' א
61. שו"ת ציץ אליעזר חי"ג סי' פב ס"ק ה. וכן שמעתי מהגרש"ז אבא שאול זצ"ל
62. שו"ת ציץ אליעזר שם
63. שו"ת, יו"ד ח"ב סי' קכא
64. חי"ג סי' פב ס"ק ד

ized illness. However, if he had ^(G)a localized illness, for example ^(H)slightly sore eyes ^(I)or the like, one may

─────────── NISHMAT AVRAHAM ───────────

(G) a localized illness. A few examples will be discussed:

1. HARE-LIP. The *Maharsham*[65] rules that a baby born with a hair-lip severe enough to prevent him from suckling, so that he must be fed manually, should have his *brit* on the eighth day if he is otherwise healthy, and this is also the ruling of the *Zocher HaBrit*.[66]

2. CLEFT PALATE. The baby suckles using a special prosthesis until he undergoes corrective surgery later. *Rav Neuwirth shlita* told me that the *brit* should not be postponed.

3. CONGENITAL DISLOCATION OF HIP. The condition is treated by setting the hip in a special harness (almost in the position that the *mohel* would want him to be held). The *Avnei Nezer*[67] rules that if postponement of the treatment will give rise to an irreversibly crooked leg, the baby should be treated even though this will require postponement of the *brit*. There is no obligation to spend great sums in order to be able to perform a positive commandment;[68] this is especially so to avoid a child becoming maimed. *Rav Auerbach zt"l* wrote to me that perhaps the *Avnei Nezer's* intention was to say that the *brit* should be postponed until the plaster-cast has been removed and they will see that there is no further reason to wait.[69] Orthopedic opinion today is that there is no urgency in initiating treatment for congenital dislocation of the hip or hips, nor is there any reason to post-pone the *brit* (see also *Nishmat Avraham*, vol. 1 *Orach Chaim*, Siman 330R). *Rav Neuwirth shlita* wrote to me agreeing that the *brit* should be done on the eighth day.

4. FRACTURED LEG. The *Yad Yitzchak*[70] rules that a baby whose fractured leg was treated with a plaster-cast may be circumcised on recovery without the necessity of waiting a further seven days. Since he is not obviously suffering and is otherwise healthy, he is considered as having a local illness only, like a baby with a mild eye problem which is not causing suffering and which has no effect on the rest of his body. *Rav Neuwirth shlita* agreed that the *brit* may be performed as soon as the cast was put on and the baby is no longer in pain.

(H) slightly sore eyes. *Rav Waldenberg shlita*[71] writes that if after thorough examination of the baby, the doctor decides that secretion from the eye is due to an external cause and not due to an infection, one need not wait an additional seven days after the baby is cured. There is proof for this ruling from the *Shach*[72] who explains that when the *Rama* writes severe eye pain, he is referring to a pain severe enough to have Sabbath laws set aside. Therefore if the cause is external and temporary, one certainly does not set aside Sabbath laws for it. This ruling of *Rav Waldenberg* is unlike that of the *Da'at Cohen*[73] who rules strictly, requiring a postponement of an additional seven days following recovery from any inflammation

---

65. שו"ת, ח"ה סי' ז
66. סי' י סע' כא
67. שו"ת, יו"ד סי' שכא
68. See *Nishmat Avraham*, vol. 1 *Orach Chaim*, Siman 329B and 656A.
69. וראה גם בשו"ת דברי מלכיאל ח"ה סי' קמח. שו"ת תירוש ויצהר סי' צז וסי' קכו
70. שו"ת, ח"ב סי' רלב
71. שו"ת ציץ אליעזר חי"ג סי' פב ס"ק ז
72. כאן ס"ק ד
73. סי' קלז

NISHMAT AVRAHAM

of the eyes. *Rav Chaim Pinchas Scheinberg shlita*,[74] on the other hand, rules even more leniently than *Rav Waldenberg shlita*. He writes that if the eye inflammation is, according to medical opinon, sterile (allergic) as opposed to infectious, tests have shown that there is no fear of disease, and if the baby behaves and eats normally, the *brit* should not be postponed but performed on the eighth day. In addition, he writes that even if the cause is a bacterial infection, if the doctor feels that the infection is only mild and the baby's suffering slight, he may have the *brit* as soon as he is cured.[75]

BLOCKAGE OF THE TEAR DUCT. The *Minchat Yitzchak*[76] rules that whether the blockage clears spontaneously or is treated surgically, the *brit* must be postponed until after healing. The *Gemara*[77] says that the nerve of the eye is connected to the vessels of the heart, implying that a problem with the eye may affect the heart and must therefore be considered much more seriously. Rav Auerbach zt"l wrote to me, however, that it is possible that it should be considered only as a local problem and there is therefore no need to wait an additional seven days after healing.

(I) or the like. For example:

1. LOW BIRTH WEIGHT. A baby who is born underweight may be circumcised as soon as the doctor agrees.[78]

2. FORCEPS DELIVERY. The *Tzitz Eliezer*[79] writes that following a forceps delivery, a baby may develop a superficial swelling of his head which disappears within a few days or a deeper swelling which may take a month or two to disappear. If the doctor is sure that this is not due to any disease, the baby is not suffering and that the circumcision will not have any adverse effects on the condition, the circumcision may be performed on the eighth day. Otherwise, it should be postponed until the swelling has subsided and the baby no longer suffers because of it. This is also true if, as a result of a difficult birth, there is a transient loss of function of a limb, commonly the hand.

3. *EPISPADIAS* AND *HYPOSPADIAS*. *Epispadias* is a congenital defect whereby the *meatus* (the opening of the *urethra*) is at the upper surface of the *ever* instead of at its tip. *Hypospadias*, on the other hand, is a congenital defect whereby the *meatus* is at the lower surface of the *ever*. The abnormal opening can be at the distal or proximal end of the *ever* or anywhere along its length and, in addition, there may be a curve to the *ever*. In order that the baby and later the adult can urinate and emit semen normally, surgery may be necessary to correct the position of the *meatus*, and if necessary, correct the curve. The surgery, which is usually done when the child is two or three years old, uses the foreskin to correct these defects; circumcision therefore cannot be performed until then. The indications for this surgery are the psychological stress that the child undergoes when he starts school and to avoid the possibility of his being unable to impregnate his future wife.

Hypospadias is a much commoner condition. If the *meatus* is displaced to halfway or more, proximally, that is, it is closer to the child's body, medical opinion is unanimous that the child will require surgical intervention. If, however, the

---

74. מוריה ז תמוז תשמ"ב

75. ראה גם בשו"ת מחזה אברהם ח"ב סי' ד ושו"ת דברי מלכיאל ח"ג סי' קלא

76. שו"ת, ח"ה סי' יא

77. ע"ז כח ע"ב

78. שו"ת אג"מ יו"ד ח"ב סי' קכא. שו"ת ציץ אליעזר חי"ג סי' פב ס"ק ו. וראה במצודת דוד על הקיצור שו"ע סי' קסג סע' ג

79. חי"ג סי' פב ס"ק ה

(J)circumcise him immediately upon his recovery (if, how-

― NISHMAT AVRAHAM ―

meatus is along the more distal half of the ever, there are differences of opinion regarding the necessity for surgery since there is usually no problem with either urination or future fertility. However there may well be cosmetic and psychological problems that require expert advice from an experienced pediatric urologist and a *mohel* before the question is put before the *posek*.[80]

Rav Auerbach zt"l told me that if for whatever reason the circumcision can only be performed at the time of surgery, one must be sure that a *mohel* is present who will remove the foreskin sufficient to expose the *atcrah* and say the appropiate blessing. If this is not possible, the surgeon who will do this must be Jewish and preferably, religious. If none of this is possible and there is no other alternative, it may be enough if *hatafat dam brit* is performed after the surgical wound has healed.[81]

(J) circumcise him immediately. What is the *halachah* regarding a baby who was born on a Friday and on the following Friday (the day on which he should have been circumcised) had a local illness or physiological jaundice (see Siman 263A) which resolved spontaneously late that afternoon before sundown but after the community — and the *mohel* among them — had accepted the Sabbath upon themselves? (*It was, and is, a wide-*

spread custom shared by many communities to start the Sabbath well before nightfall, especially when the Fridays are long, in the summer.) The *Taz*[82] writes that in such a situation where it was not possible to circumcise him earlier, he should be circumcised even though the *mohel* has already recited the prayers accepting *Shabbat* well before sunset. He reasons that the *mohel* did not accept *Shabbat* so early unconditionally and, had he known that such a situation would arise, he would have "brought in" *Shabbat* later. Surely everyone wants to keep the *mitzvot* of *Hashem* and had he known that he would be able to perform this obligatory *mitzvah*, he certainly would not have "brought in" *Shabbat* early. It is similar to a congregation which erred on a cloudy day and brought in *Shabbat* early thinking it was close to sunset; their acceptance of *Shabbat* is not considered an acceptance (see *Orach Chaim*, Siman 263 §14). Here, too, this was a mistake and had the truth been known he would not have "brought in" *Shabbat* so early. The *Shemirat Shabbat KeHilchatah*[83] follows the ruling of the *Taz*. On the other hand, *Rav Ovadiah Yosef shlita*[84] rules that if there is another *mohel* available who did not "bring in" *Shabbat* early, he should circumcise the baby.[85]

However, although the *Shulchan Aruch*[86] rules that an individual who had mistakenly thought that the sun had set

---

80. שו"ת חלקת יעקב ח"ב סי' כ-כא וח"ג סי' לו-לז. שו"ת ציץ אליעזר חי"ח סי' נא. שו"ת לב אריה ח"א סי' מא. ספר הברית ליקוטי הלכות סי' רסא ס"ק קמז-מח ושם מקור וביאור הלכה ס"ק ה. וראה בספר אסיא כרך ג עמ' 389 במאמרו של הרב יוסף דוד ווייסברג זצ"ל

81. ראה סי' רסד סע' א לגבי תינוק שנימול ע"י עכו"ם, וכותב הב"י שם שאפשר לפרש דברי הרמב"ם דמה שכתב אין צריך לחזור ולמול פעם שניה, היינו לומר שאין צריך לחתוך ולחתוך מעט, אבל אין הכי נמי שצריך להטיף ממנו דם ברית דלא עדיף מקטן שנולד כשהוא מהול. אך כותב הגר"א ס"ק י שדעתם של

הרמב"ם ושו"ע הוא שאינו צריך הטפת דם. וכ"כ בשו"ת שאגת אריה סי' נד

82. או"ח סי' תר ס"ק ב

83. פמ"ז סע' טו. וראה גם בשו"ת שואל ומשיב תניינא ח"ב סי' כג

84. לוית חן סי' שלא אות צח עמ' קסה

85. וראה בש"ך יו"ד סי' קצו ס"ק יט. שו"ת שואל ומשיב תניינא ח"ב סי' כג

86. או"ח סי' רסג סע' יד

SIMAN 262: WHEN TO CIRCUMCISE / §3

ever he has (K)*very painful eyes, he is considered as being generally ill).*

§3 An (L)*androgynous*, a baby with two foreskins and a baby

---NISHMAT AVRAHAM---

— because the sky had been overcast — and had prayed *Maariv*, will need to pray *Maariv* again, the *Mishnah Berurah*[87] explains that this is only if he usually prays *Maariv* at its normal time, that is, after nightfall. On this occasion he prayed early only because he mistook a cloudy day for being night.

Rav Auerbach zt"l wrote to me that in the case of the Friday late afternoon *brit* of which the *Taz* wrote, one need not pray *Maariv* again after the *brit*. However, he is only permitted to do the actual circumcision even if he has also recited *Kiddush*, since this is an act permitted on *Shabbat* (when a *brit* is on the eighth day). However Sabbath laws may not be set aside to permit what is only secondary to the *brit*, for example one may not ride to the *brit* in a car for this does not supersede *Shabbat*. However, if the reason is that an illness resolved spontaneously after *Shabbat* was "brought in" before sundown, Sabbath laws may be set aside even for what is secondary to the *brit*; he would also be required to pray *Maariv* again.

(K) very painful eyes. The *Shach*[88] writes that the definition of very painful will apply to any condition for which Sabbath laws are set aside; see *Orach Chaim*, Siman 328 §9 and *Nishmat Avraham* 9A.

What about a *makkah* on the back of the hand or foot? Since the *Shulchan Aruch*[89] rules that it is considered like an internal injury or disease and Sabbath laws are set aside to seek appropriate treatment, does one need to wait seven days after the *makkah* has been cured before circumcising the baby?[90] Rav Neuwirth shlita told me that we are uncertain as to what exactly such a *makkah* is (see *Nishmat Avraham*, vol. 1 Orach Chaim, Siman 328:6A) and, on the other hand, the *Shulchan Aruch* rules[91] that if medical opinion is that one can wait with impunity until after *Shabbat* to treat the condition, it is forbidden to set aside Sabbath laws. Taking this all in all, he rules that the *brit* should not be postponed if medical opinion is that there is no danger to the baby.

(L) androgynous. The *Rambam*[92] defines an *androgynous* as someone who has both male and female genitalia and we are therefore uncertain as to whether he is a male or female. He has no sign, and never will have, by which one may establish whether he is a definite male or a definite female. However, the *Ra'avad*[93] writes that the *androgynous* is not a unique creation but half male. The *Shulchan Aruch*[94] rules like the *Rambam* whereas the *Rama*[95] quotes an opinion that he is a certain male. See also the *Gra*[96] and the *Mishnah Berurah*.[97] Finally, it would appear from the *Magen Avraham*[98] that he alternates between male and female.

Regarding the definition of a *tumtum*, the *Rambam*[99] writes that this is some-

---

87. שם ס"ק נה וביה"ל ד"ה ואם
88. ס"ק ד
89. או"ח סי' שכח סע' ו
90. מלחמת ארי, מובא בספר הברית סי' רסב ס"ק עח
91. שם סע' ד
92. הל' אישות פ"ב הכ"ד
93. הל' שופר פ"ב ה"ב. וראה שם במגיד משנה
94. אהע"ז סי' מד סע' ה
95. שם. וראה באו"ח סי' יז סע' ב בהגה
96. אהע"ז סי' קעב ס"ק יח
97. סי' יז ס"ק ח
98. סי' תקפח ס"ק ב. וראה שם בבאר היטב
99. הל' אישות פ"ב הכ"ה

born by Caesarian section are circumcised on (M)the eighth day.

§4 If a baby is born (N)*bein hashemashot*, we start to count from the night and he is circumcised on the ninth day, which is possibly the eighth day, after his birth. *(Thus, if he was born on Sunday evening, he is circumcised the following week on Monday, which is either the ninth day if he was born on Sunday or the eighth day if he was born on Monday — author.)* **If, however, (O)his head becomes visible outside the *prozdor* during the day, even if he is born much later, the eight days are counted from the day his head became visible.**

──────────── NISHMAT AVRAHAM ────────────

one whose external genitalia are covered so that it is uncertain as to whether he is male or female. If this covering is excised and he is found to be male then he is *halachically* a definite male and if found to be a female, then she is *halachically* a definite female. *Rebbe Akiva Eiger*[100] writes that there is no obligation to excise the covering to ascertain whether he is a male in order to circumcise him. *Rav Auerbach zt"l* wrote to me that *Tosafot*[101] write explicitly that there is no obligation to excise the covering. Since surgery to excise the sac involves pain and danger, there is no obligation to do so.[102]

The *Tzitz Eliezer*[103] writes that the chromosomal diagnosis of sex cannot be used *halachically* to define the sex of the baby; it is the external genitalia that define sex. This is also what I heard from *Rav Neuwirth shlita*.

(M) the eighth day. However, if the eighth day is *Shabbat* or *Yom Tov*,[104] the *brit* is postponed to the first weekday.[105]

(N) *bein hashemashot*. See later Siman 266A.

(O) his head becomes visible. Is the birth of a baby defined from the emergence of the head or forehead? The *Perishah*[106] writes that the *Shulchan Aruch* means most of his forehead. However, *Rav Auerbach zt"l* told me (see Siman 266A) most of his head and certainly this is what the *Shulchan Aruch* writes here. Is this from the *cervix* or into the world? The *Shulchan Aruch*[107] writes that the baby is considered born when his forehead emerges from the *cervix* into the *prozdor* and not when it emerges into the world. And the *Beit Yosef* (*the author of the Shulchan Aruch*) explains that this follows the ruling of the *Rashba* and *Rashi*.[108] The *Sidrei Taharah*[109] writes that although the skull has not yet emerged into the open but is as yet entirely within the *prozdor*, the baby is considered born with regard to its *brit*. *Rav Waldenberg shlita* told me that, following this ruling,

---

100. חידושי רעק״א כאן בשם המהריק״ש
101. פסחים כח ע״ב ד״ה ערל יבמות ע ע״א ד״ה הערל
102. שו״ת פרי יצחק ח״א סי׳ לב. וראה באנציקלופדיה תלמודית כרך יט ערך טומטום עמ׳ קצא
103. שו״ת, חי״א סי׳ עח
104. סי׳ רסו סע׳ ב
105. סי׳ רסו סע׳ י
106. סי׳ קצד סע׳ לה
107. יו״ד סי׳ קצד סע׳ י
108. על נדה מב ע״ב
109. יו״ד סי׳ קצד ס״ק כו

SIMAN 263
A BABY WHO IS RED OR YELLOW; AND ONE WHOSE CHILDREN HAVE DIED AS A RESULT OF CIRCUMCISION

§1 If a (A)baby is yellow, it is a sign that his blood is not yet clear and he may not be circumcised until his blood clears

---
NISHMAT AVRAHAM
---

when most of the baby's head has emerged outside we can be certain that his head is outside the *cervix*.

The *Tur*[110] writes that if a baby is born by breech delivery, birth is the moment when most of his body has emerged. *Rav Auerbach zt"l* and *Rav Abba Shaul zt"l* both told me that this would be when his umbilicus emerged into view.

SIMAN 263

(A) baby is yellow. The *Rambam*[1] writes of a baby who is "very" yellow on the eighth day after his birth etc.; and this is also the wording of the *Chochmat Adam*[2] who adds that he does not know why the *Shulchan Aruch* omitted the word "very." The *Aruch HaShulchan*[3] answers that the *Rambam* rules like all the other *poskim*, but he wrote "very" because a slight redness or yellowness is normal in a newborn baby as everyone knows. The "very" of the *Rambam* indicates more than usual and this is why it is defined as an illness since it is not normal in most babies.

The *Nimukei HaGrib*[4] writes that *Chazal* did not tell us what intensity of yellow or red is dangerous and there are *poskim* who say that a baby with any level of red or yellow coloring may not be circumcised. That is why the *Shulchan Aruch* omitted the word "very" to avoid any possibilty of danger to the baby. But since everyone has the *Chochmat Adam* and he quotes the language of the *Rambam* who does write "very," *mohalim* basing themselves on this "very" will make their own evaluation of the intensity of the coloring, and this leads to the possibility of danger to life. Therefore he finds it necessary to warn the *mohalim* about this.[5]

POST-NATAL JAUNDICE. A newborn baby may be jaundiced for two main reasons:

1. Pathological jaundice. This, by definition, is a sign of disease. Such a baby is considered to have a general illness and his *brit* is postponed to seven full days after he has fully recovered.[6]

2. Physiological jaundice. This is not caused by, or associated with, any disease, but is due to an immature liver which is as yet unable to cope with the excess of the present form of *bilirubin* which is circulating and process it to a different form that will allow it to be excreted by the body. The jaundice resolves itself spontaneously but this process can be hastened by placing the baby under a blue lamp. Usually, no other treatment is required but, if the circulating *bilirubin* level reaches 20mg% or more, exchange blood transfusion may be required. If this happens, the *poskim* are unanimous that

---

110. סי' קצד
1. הל' מילה פ"א הי"ז
2. כלל קמט סע' ד
3. סע' ג
4. הגהות על היו"ד כאן. וכ"כ ה־אש אפרים סי' לח ס"ק לד וס"ק נב והכורת הברית סי' רסג
5. ראה גם בשו"ת ציץ אליעזר חי"ג סי' פב
6. שם סי' פא

the baby's *brit* is postponed until seven full days have passed after full recovery.[7]

The following discussion will be concerned with the majority of those babies who have physiological jaundice and who will recover spontaneously, and includes those who have been placed under a blue lamp (phototherapy). The *Tzitz Eliezer*[8] writes that the baby is not considered ill and may be circumcised on recovery, that is, when the level of jaundice is obviously dropping and medical opinion decides that the circumcision will not be dangerous.

Rav Eliashiv *shlita* rules that the *brit* should be postponed until the *bilirubin* level is normal; if the *bilirubin* level reaches 18mg%, however, he rules that the *brit* can be done only seven full days after the level has returned to normal, even if exchange transfusion is not done. He told me that even if by the accepted medical opinion a baby with physiological jaundice may be safely circumcised, nevertheless we cannot accept their opinion after *Chazal* have ruled that a yellow baby may not be circumcised.

The *Minchat Yitzchak*[9] writes that even if the *bilirubin* level is not very high and the doctor's opinion is that he may be circumcised, we do not listen to his opinion since *Chazal* have told us that it is dangerous to circumcise such a baby. The *brit* may be done only when the yellow color has disappeared and the baby's color is normal. And, even though the *Avnei Nezer* apparently rules leniently if the baby is not too yellow, the (other) *poskim* have ruled strictly even if the jaundice is mild. One cannot ignore the opinion of those who rule strictly, for the *Rambam* and the *Shulchan Aruch* rule that if there is the slightest doubt regarding the health of the baby, the *brit* is postponed, and the

Aruch HaShulchan writes that any change from the normal requires postponement of the *brit*. Rav Neuwirth *shlita* wrote to me that although there are *mohalim* who depend on the laboratory figure of the level of *bilirubin*, we depend on the ruling of our *poskim*, past and present, who rule that if the *mohel* or doctor sees that the baby is jaundiced, the *brit* is postponed and when they see that he is no longer jaundiced, he is circumcised immediately.

I wondered why common practice among *mohalim* was to ask for daily (and sometimes twice daily) measurement of the *bilirubin* level if the baby is obviously yellow. Why would this not be considered inflicting unnecessary injury and suffering on the baby? Rav Auerbach *zt"l* told me that this was done to pick out the baby whose *bilirubin* level has reached 18mg%, for the *brit* would then have to be postponed a further seven days after he is completely normal, even if exchange transfusion was not done. Regarding my second question, he told me that the slight pain that is inflicted on the baby in taking blood is not defined as an injury, since the purpose is to perform the *mitzvah* of the *brit* on the eighth day or as soon as possible after.

Rav Neuwirth *shlita* wrote to me that if the *bilirubin* level reaches 18mg% and one therefore has to wait a further seven days after full recovery, the seven days are counted from the day the level drops below 18mg%. However Rav Auerbach *zt"l* wrote to me that although this is how the *poskim rule*, he does not understand it. If the doctors have defined a level of 18mg% as being an illness then, according to the custom not to circumcise even on the eighth day if the level is greater than

---

7. שו"ת אג"מ יו"ד ח"ב סי' קכא. וראה שם שמדובר על תינוק כחול שזקוק להחלפת דם, רצ"ע מבחינה רפואית כוונתו של הגאון זצ"ל. ואולי אין כוונתו אלא לתינוק צהוב

8. שם סי' פא ו-פג. וראה גם בשו"ת שבט הלוי ח"ב סי' קמב וח"ה סי' קמח ס"ק ב

9. שו"ת, ח"ג סי' קמה, ח"ו סי' צב וח"ח סי' פח

NISHMAT AVRAHAM

12mg%, one should wait until the level drops to 12mg% and then wait a further seven days. I cannot, he wrote, understand the premise that with a level of 18mg% he is ill in his whole body and when the level drops a little below this he is considered immediately healthy. Surely the seven days are counted only after he is completely cured? It is important to try to resolve this problem.

Rav Auerbach zt"l also wrote to me that since there is a minority medical opinion that a baby whose *bilirubin* level reaches 18mg%, in spite of the use of a blue lamp, is considered to be ill, we have to rule strictly and postpone the *brit* until seven days have passed after recovery. He was certain that if the level reaches 18mg% the baby is considered ill and one should postpone the *brit* until he has completely recovered and then wait another seven days. However, if the *bilirubin* level peaked at 15mg% he is not considered ill, but it would not be good to circumcise him.

I asked a further question. The baby can be seen to be yellow when his *bilirubin* level reaches about 6-8mg%. Therefore, according to the *Shulchan Aruch* he should not be circumcised. Why then is a figure of 10-12mg% generally accepted as permitting circumcision even though the baby is still clinically yellow? True this is the figure that a normal baby may reach. However *Chazal* did not measure *bilirubin* but ruled with regard to the color of the baby and this may explain why the *Rambam* writes "very yellow." However the *Shulchan Aruch* writes "yellow." Why then is it permissible to circumcise a baby with a *bilirubin* of 10-12mg%?[10]

Rav Auerbach zt"l. The *Rav's* opinion originally was that the *brit* should be postponed until the jaundice has completely disappeared and that the *bilirubin* level should not be more than 11-12 mg% and the *mohel* does not discern any yellow coloration in the baby, and this is what I wrote in the second volume of the *Nishmat Avraham* published close to twenty years ago.[11] However some time before he died, when told that by universal medical opinion circumcision on the eighth day is not dangerous for an otherwise healthy baby with physiological jaundice, he ruled that this opinion should be heeded. If a specialist, after examining the baby and seeing the laboratory tests, confirmed that the baby has physiological jaundice and is otherwise healthy, the *brit* should be done on the eighth day. He wrote to me that one could say that the ruling of *Chazal* and the *Shulchan Aruch* regarding a baby who is yellow referred to a disease state, which is why it would be forbidden to circumcise him as long as he was yellow. They did not refer to what we now call physiological jaundice when the baby is completely healthy. Therefore, since there is universal agreement among doctors that such a baby may be safely circumcised even while he is yellow, it is possible that it is permitted to do so although he is jaundiced. The *Gemara* and *Shulchan Aruch* refer only to a sick baby. However, if the baby was treated with exchange transfusion, the *brit* is postponed until seven full days have passed after he has completely recovered. The *Rav zt"l* was asked for his ruling regarding a baby whose *bilirubin* had peaked at 19mg% on the third day after his birth and was down to 15mg% by the fifth day. The *Rav zt"l* ruled that he should be circumcised on the eighth day after his birth, without waiting another seven days.

A short while before his death *Rav*

---

10. ראה שו"ת שבט הלוי ח"ה סי' קמח ב"ק ב
11. וכן מובא בשמו בנועם כרך י' עמ' קעח הערה 43 בזה"ל: מ"מ הואיל ולא כל הרופאים הם מומחים ובקל עלולים לטעות ולסכן ח"ו את הולד, לכן נכון יותר לענ"ד לא למול בשום פעם כשהתינוק עדיין ירוק ולא לסמוך בזה על הרופאים

CHAPTER 25: LAWS OF BRIT MILAH (CIRCUMCISION)

and his (B)color becomes normal. Similarly, if (C)he is red, it is a sign that his blood has not yet been sufficiently absorbed into his organs but lies between his skin and his flesh. He may not be circumcised until his blood has been absorbed. One must be extremely careful with these problems for one may not circumcise a baby if there is any possibility that he is ill. Danger to life overrides everything *(except when the three cardinal sins are involved — author)* for it is always possible to circumcise later but never ever possible to bring a single Jew back to life.

§2 A woman who circumcised her first and second sons (D)and both died after the circumcision, is considered as one whose children die from circumcision. This holds true whether they were both from one husband or from

---
NISHMAT AVRAHAM

Auerbach zt"l was invited to a *brit*. When the *mohel* examined the baby just before he was to be brought in for the *brit*, he found that the baby was yellow and wanted to postpone the *brit*. The *Rav zt"l*, who was present, was asked for a ruling. He asked that a doctor examine the baby and if he would pronounce him to be healthy and say that it would be safe to circumcise him, they should do so. The *brit* was done. [I heard this story from the *Rav's* son, Rav Baruch Auerbach *zt"l*, who was also present. I spoke to the father of the baby and the *mohel* who both thought that the baby was "very yellow." I also spoke to the doctor who examined him, and he told me that he estimated the *bilirubin* level to be about 14mg% at least.]

(B) color becomes normal. It would appear from the language of the *Shulchan Aruch* that there is no need to wait a further seven days and this is what the *Chochmat Adam*[12] writes.[13]

(C) he is red. I am not sure what *Cha-* *zal* mean.[14] However, the *Zocher Ha-Brit*[15] in this context describes a bluish-red baby who was breathing with difficulty. It would appear therefore that he is discussing a baby who is suffering from either a lung and/or heart problem, but this is apparently not the problem that the *Shulchan Aruch* discusses.[16]

(D) and both died after the circumcision. HEMOPHILIA. This is a genetic disease caused by the absence of one of the factors essential for clotting. The genetic defect is transmitted via the females of the family but is only clinically apparent in males. The blood in affected males cannot clot normally and therefore bleeding will continue and can reach life-threatening proportions. Such a male can obviously not be circumcised until the defect is (albeit temporarily) treated. Diagnosis of the condition is fairly simple and the baby cannot be circumcised, even if his older brothers have been circumcised without any problem. The missing factor

---

12. כלל קמט סע׳ ד
13. וראה בשו״ת יד הלוי ח״ב יו״ד סי׳ קמא
14. ראה בספר אסיא כרך ד עמ׳ 213
15. סי׳ י ס״ק יז
16. וראה בדעת תורה יו״ד סי׳ לח סע׳ ז

can be injected before and after the *brit* and *Rav Auerbach zt"l* told me that it would be permissible to circumcise such a baby. *Rav Neuwirth shlita* wrote to me asking why this is not considered a disease and, although treatment is available, the disease remains. *Rav Auerbach zt"l* answered that as long as the baby does not bleed unnaturally he is not considered ill.

The treatment before the *brit* (and for that matter before any surgery) consists of the placement of an intravenous catheter into one of the baby's veins and injecting *cryoprecipitate* (the precipitate that is obtained when plasma has been frozen and then thawed; it contains plasma proteins and various factors), which contains the absent factor, just prior to the *brit*. The injections are given twice a day for at least three days after the *brit*. The insertion of this catheter may not be done on *Shabbat* since its insertion is forbidden (by Torah or Rabbinic law) (see *Nishmat Avraham*, vol. 1 *Orach Chaim*, Siman 316B — Injections). Even according to the opinion that it is forbidden only by Rabbinic law, it is nevertheless forbidden to transgress Rabbinic law on *Shabbat* to prepare the baby for circumcision.[17] However, it would possibly be permitted to ask a non-Jewish doctor to put in the catheter.[18] *Rav Auerbach zt"l* agreed with the above and wrote to me that for a *brit* it is permissible to ask a non-Jew even to do something that is forbidden by the Torah for a Jew.

If the baby has an allergic reaction with fever to the injected material, *Rav Auerbach zt"l* told me that it would be forbidden ever to circumcise him.

Nowadays, a genetically engineered factor is available for intravenous injection. A trial of gene therapy has just been reported with a successful but transient (not longer than ten months) effect[19] and two others are underway.[20]

What would the *halachah* be regarding the use of laser to circumcise a baby with *hemophilia* since its use would reduce the amount of bleeding substantially? The *Minchat Yitzchak*[21] was asked regarding a *brit* of a thirteen-year-old boy with *hemophilia*. *Rav Horowitz shlita*, a member of his *Beit Din*, wrote that although the best way to do the *mitzvah* is to use a knife (as the *Rambam* and the *Shulchan Aruch* rule), nevertheless regarding the boy in question who would be in real danger of his life, there is no greater pressing situation than leaving him uncircumcised all his life. Surely in such a situation it should be permissible to excise the foreskin using a laser beam, and although there would be no bleeding whatsoever, he would be completely circumcised. Also, although there is a *mitzvah* that there should be bleeding during the *brit*, again in this situation where it is not possible, it should not prevent the performance of the basic *mitzvah*.[22] Of course, one must be certain that *periah* is done, for without it the *mitzvah* has not been performed. Since *the Rambam* and the *Shulchan Aruch* rule that anything that cuts may be used for a *brit*, a laser beam, which also cuts, may also be used.

The *Minchat Yitzchak*, however, replies that the *Imrei Yosher*[23] rules that a *brit* may not be performed using medication,

---

22. See, however, the *Igrot Moshe* (Y.D. III 99) who rules that the use of an instrument that does not allow any bleeding at all is forbidden. If there is no bleeding at all the *mitzvah* has not been done properly, for bleeding is part of the *mitzvah* of circumcision.

23. שו"ת, ח"ב סי' קמ אות ב הובא במנחת יצחק ח"ה סי' כד אות ב ד"ה וגם

17. או"ח סי' שלא סע' ו
18. או"ח סי' שלא במ"ב ס"ק כד. סי' שז סע' ה ברמ"א ובמ"ב ס"ק כד ועיין בביה"ל סי' שלא שם ד"ה וע"ל
19. NEJM, June 7, '01, p. 1735
20. Ibid., review article, p. 1773
21. שו"ת, ח"ח סי' פט

two. (E)**Her third boy may not be circumcised until** (F)**he is grown and has become strong. The same ruling applies if a man circumcises his two sons and they die as a result of circumcision. His third son may not be circumcised whether his sons were from one wife or from two.** [There

--- NISHMAT AVRAHAM ---

for the word to circumcise means removal with one's hand or cutting with a knife, and not with a medication where the foreskin is passively removed. And although the *Chatam Sofer*[24] and the *Divrei Chaim*[25] explain the word to mean the removal of the foreskin, this is only if the foreskin is actively removed with a knife and not by using a medication. This is also true if the circumcision is done passively and not manually by the *mohel*. One needs to ascertain whether the use of a laser without the hand being involved in the actual cutting is not comparable to the use of medication. Even if we say that the use of laser was unknown to *Chazal* in the times of the *Gemara*, they surely knew of ways to prevent bleeding, such as the use of a "magen clamp" (see later), used by some shallow-minded *mohalim* in the United States. Nevertheless there is no mention in the *Gemara* that a baby whose brothers have died following circumcision should be circumcised by using such a clamp. We must therefore say that *Chazal* preferred that he remain uncircumcised all his life rather than change the way the *mitzvah* is *halachically* performed.

See also the *Igrot Moshe*[26] who writes, in speaking of the use of the "magen clamp," that one may not use any instrument for a *brit* since (the way) the *mitzvah* (is done) must not be changed.

Rav Auerbach zt"l told me that in his opinion also, a laser must not be used for a *brit* since the person wielding the beam does not himself cut the foreskin but merely guides the beam over the line that he wishes to cut; it is the laser beam that does the cutting.

See *Rashi*[27] who explains that piercing the ear of a slave[28] may not be done using a medication for it pierces passively and is not comparable to piercing with an awl, which requires human force.

The *Torah Lishmah*[29] writes regarding twins, one of whom died within eight days of birth, that the other may not be circumcised on the eighth day. One must wait until the surviving baby is more than thirty days old so that there is no longer any fear that he might be a *nefel*. This is also the ruling of the *Nachal HaBrit*,[30] but he adds that he believed that this was not the prevalent custom. However, both the *Chaim BeYad*[31] and the *Mishpetei Uziel*[32] rule that the *brit* should be postponed until he is more than thirty days old.

(E) Her third boy. The *Tashbetz*[33] writes that the *Shulchan Aruch* does not mean specifically the third boy. She may not even circumcise the third or any other son born afterwards.

(F) he is grown and has become strong. The *Pitchei Teshuvah*[34] writes, quoting the *Noda BiYehudah*,[35] about a

---

24. שו"ת, יו"ד סי' רמט
25. שו"ת, ח"ב סי' קיד-קיה
26. שו"ת, יו"ד ח"ג סי' צט
27. קדושין כא ע"ב ד"ה סם
28. שמות כא:ו
29. המיוחס להבן איש חי, סי' שח
30. סי' לב ס"ק ג בשם הרוח חיים והצפיחית דבש
31. סי' עד
32. שו"ת, יו"ד סי' יב
33. שו"ת, ח"ג סוסי' רז מובא בפ"ת ס"ק ג
34. ס"ק ה
35. שו"ת, תניינא סי' קסה

SIMAN 263: A BABY WHO IS RED OR YELLOW / §4

are those who disagree and believe that this is only the case where the woman (had two children who died) and not a man (who had two sons from different wives). Since this is a question of a possible pikuach nefesh we rule leniently and the third baby's circumcision should be postponed in both cases.]

§4 A baby who is (G)born without a foreskin must have (H)*hatafat dam brit* but this must be done gently. He should be well examined using one's hands and eyes, but not with an instrument, so as not to hurt him. One should

--- NISHMAT AVRAHAM ---

three-year-old boy who was as yet uncircumcised, since his brothers had died following circumcision on the eighth day. The *Noda BiYehudah* writes that were it not for the *Rambam*, the *Tur* and the *Nimukei Yosef* who rule that the third boy should not be circumcised on the eighth day but one should wait until he has grown and become strong, he would have wished to rule that the boy should never be circumcised. However since the *Rambam*, the *Nimukei Yosef*, the *Tur* and the *Shulchan Aruch* have given their ruling, who can come afterwards and question their decision? Therefore if the child is seen to be strong and healthy like other children of his age, and his coloring is normal, he may be circumcised. The merit of the circumcision is great enough to protect him from any injury as a result. The *Chatam Sofer*[36] also discusses this problem and concludes that the ruling of the above *poskim* is authoritative.

NAMING THE BABY. If the *brit* is postponed because of illness, there are those who rule that it would be preferable to give him his name before the eighth day.[37] However, others rule that one waits until the *brit* is performed.[38] I wondered whether this would mean waiting even if the *brit* would have to be postponed for a few months or a year or two. *Rav Neuwirth shlita* told me that only if the *brit* will be delayed for two weeks or so, does one wait until then to name the baby.

(G) born without a foreskin. The *Ot Chaim VeShalom*[39] writes that he has never seen a baby who was born completely without a foreskin. Those he saw required the excision of at least a small strip of foreskin that covered all or part of the *atarah*. He writes that this was also the experience of his father (the author of the *Darchei Teshuvah*) who was a famous *mohel*, and also that of other experienced older *mohalim*. This is also what the *Shulchan Gavohah* and the *Koret HaBrit* write. *Rav Gershon ben Rav Yaakov the Mohel* also writes similarly in *Zichron Brit LeRishonim* and *Rav Yosef Weisberg zt"l*, the famous *mohel* of Jerusalem, told me that this was his experience too. However, the *Pachad Yitzchak*[40] tells of babies who were brought to him who were completely without a foreskin.

(H) hatafat dam brit. The *Or Zarua*[41] writes that *hatafat dam brit* should

---

36. שו"ת, סי' רמה

37. ספר הברית עמ' רפא. הגר"י זילברשטיין שליט"א, אסיא לח אלול תשד"מ עמ' 36. הרב ד"ר מרדכי הלפרין שליט"א ספר אסיא כרך ד עמ' 236. וראה גם שם עמ' 243 ו- 244

38. אוצר הברית ח"א פ"ו סי' ב

39. סי' רסג ס"ק ד

40. אות מ ד"ה מילה גר שמל קודם שנתגייר

41. הל' מילה סי' צט

CHAPTER 25: LAWS OF BRIT MILAH (CIRCUMCISION)

examine and be careful about how to circumcise him, but not necessarily on the eighth day, so as not to bring him into any danger.

───────── NISHMAT AVRAHAM ─────────

be done below the *atarah*. On the other hand, the *Ot Chaim VeShalom* [42] quotes the *Koret HaBrit*[43] who, on the basis of the language of the *poskim*, feels that it should be done from the skin of the foreskin that remains on the *atarah* after a *brit* and not, Heaven forbid, from the *glans*. It is, he writes, also obvious that a drop of blood is sufficient. The *Zocher HaBrit*[44] writes of three different situations: (1) If the baby is born completely without a foreskin, it is possible that a foreskin is present but buried in the *atarah*, so that it is not immediately apparent. In such a case the *mohel* cuts slightly into the *atarah* and then searches with his fingernail to discern if a foreskin can be separated out and excised.[45] (2) If the baby is born with some foreskin, the foreskin is then removed as necessary. (3) The baby was circumcised by those who are disqualified from doing a *brit*. In such a case there is no foreskin left. There is no reason whatsoever to say that *hatafat dam brit* should be done from the *atarah*, for why should the *atarah* be involved? The *hatafat dam brit* should be done from the edge of the skin where the foreskin was removed.

The *Chazon Ish*,[46] basing his ruling on the *Or Zarua*, writes that it would appear that *hatafat dam brit* may be done anywhere below the *atarah*. The scratch may be minimal for one does not need to draw blood but only to cause a tiny bruise (*the bruise itself is hatafat dam brit because it is subcutaneous bleeding — author*). He notes that this *halachah* has been forgotten and *hatafat dam brit* is now done from the skin above the *atarah,* which is comparable to the *mohel* drawing blood from the baby's finger. In doing so, he transgresses the negative commandment not to add to suffering. If this is done to a convert, the process of conversion remains incomplete.

However, *Rav Waldenberg shlita*[47] thinks that the *Koret HaBrit* basically insisted that blood not be drawn from the *glans* because such a procedure could endanger the baby. Both the *Ot Chaim VeShalom* and the *Levushei Mordechai*[48] fully support this ruling that *hatafat dam brit* should be done from the skin above the *atarah* and that drawing a single drop of blood is sufficient. The *Avnei Nezer*[49] rules that *hatafat dam brit* should not be done at the *atarah* but at a point where it joins the *glans,* for that is where the baby bleeds when he is circumcised. The *atarah* does not always bleed at circumcision and *hatafat dam brit* must be done where the baby usually bleeds during circumcision. The *Zichron Brit LeRishonim* also writes that it should be done where *periah* is done and not from the *ever* itself. This is also the ruling of *Rav Henkin zt"l*[50] quoting many *rishonim*.

However, the accepted custom is that *hatafat dam brit* is done from the skin above the *atarah*.[51] Nevertheless, *Rav Weisberg zt"l*[52] writes that *Rav Auerbach zt"l* and

---

42. ס"ק ה
43. ס"ק יג
44. סי׳ טז סע׳ יב
45. שם סע׳ א
46. הל׳ מילה סי׳ קנד ס"ק ג והערות למס׳ שבת סי׳ סב ס"ק כז
47. שו"ת ציץ אליעזר ח"ח סי׳ כט אות ד
48. שו"ת, מהד"ת יו"ד סי׳ קסב
49. שו"ת, יו"ד ח"ב סי׳ שלד אות כה ו-כו
50. ירחון קול תורה טבת-שבט תשכ"ג
51. שו"ת אבני נזר יו"ד ח"ב סי׳ שלד אות כו. שו"ת אור לציון ח"א סי׳ יא. וראה גם בשו"ת אחיעזר ח"ג סי׳ כז
52. אוצר הברית ח"ב עמ׳ שמט

§5 A [I]baby who dies before he is eight days old

NISHMAT AVRAHAM

Rav Eliashiv shlita rule that *hatafat dam brit* should be done both from the skin overlying the *atarah* and from the skin above it (that is, towards the baby's body).

Regarding *metzizah* after *hatafat dam brit* see below Siman 264E.

A baby who is born completely without a foreskin only requires *hatafat dam brit* on the eighth day. The *Sdei Chemed*[53] and the *Zocher HaBrit* write that if the baby had a generalized illness before the eighth day we must wait until seven days have passed after recovery just as with a baby requiring circumcision. There is a possibility of danger to his life even with *hatafat dam brit*, and this ruling is clear.[54] The *Maharsham*[55] also writes that *hatafat dam brit* may not be done to a baby who is yellow or red until (seven days) have passed after recovery, since the procedure may curtail his life. This is also the ruling of the *Maharam Shick*[56] and the *Divrei Malkiel*.[57] See also the *Shulchan Aruch*, Siman 265:1.

I found this *halachah* difficult to understand. For it is common practice to draw blood from the veins of a baby who is yellow or who has some other generalized illness for the purpose of diagnosis, sometimes even daily or more. Why is this less dangerous than *hatafat dam brit* where only a single drop of blood is necessary? *Rav Neuwirth shlita* answered me that *Chazal* invested the procedure of *hatafat dam brit* with all the laws of a complete *brit*, for the danger is due to the procedure on the *ever* and is not to be compared with taking blood from a vein. However, *Rav Auerbach zt"l* told me that this is surprising. For on what basis can we introduce the idea that there is danger to the baby by drawing a drop of blood during *hatafat dam brit* if we do not wait until full recovery, when in any case blood is taken from him daily for diagnostic purposes? I also heard this from *Rav Ben Zion Abba Shaul zt"l*.

(I) baby who dies before he is eight days old. This *halachah* is repeated in the *halachot* of mourning.[58] The *Shach*[59] writes that this ruling also applies if the baby died after the age of eight days, but had not been circumcised for some reason or other.[60] The *Tuv Ta'am VeDa'at*[61] writes that there is no difference whether the baby was born alive and died later, was born dead or was removed from his mother after she died; in all cases he is circumcised as above.

At what stage of pregnancy must a baby be buried and be circumcised before his burial? The *Tzitz Eliezer*[62] writes that a *nefel* of five or six months pregnancy needs burial so long as he is whole in all his limbs, and he quotes the *Maharsham*[63] who rules that only if the mother no longer felt the fetus within the first three months of pregnancy is there no need to bury him. *Rav Neuwirth shlita* wrote to me questioning this ruling of the *Maharsham*. For even if the *mitzvah* of burial does not apply to a *fetus* who is less than three months old, nevertheless there is an obligation to bury it to prevent *Cohanim*

---

53. מערכת מ"ם כלל קד אות ו
54. זוכר הברית סי' טז ס"ק יד
55. שו"ת, ח"ד סי' קב
56. שו"ת, סי' רמא
57. שו"ת, ח"ב סי' קלא ס"ק יב
58. סי' שנג סע' ו
59. כאן ס"ק ו
60. וראה בחידושי רעק"א כאן ובפ"ת ס"ק יא
61. שו"ת, מהדורא תליתאי ח"ב סי' צח
62. שו"ת, ח"י סי' כה עמ' קלב
63. שו"ת, ח"ד סוסי' קמו

is (J)**circumcised at his grave using a stone or reed but the blessing is not said. However, he is given a name** (K)**as a remembrance, so that Heaven will have mercy on him and he will merit resurrection.**

GLOSS: *This is not done even on the second day of Yom Tov in the Diaspora since it is* (L)*forbidden to bury a nefel on Yom Tov, for he may not even be moved.*

--- NISHMAT AVRAHAM ---

from becoming inadvertently unclean.

The fetal sac and *placenta* do not require burial so long as the *fetus* is unformed.[64]

(J) circumcised at his grave. The *Gesher HaChaim*[65] writes that every male who was stillborn or who died before he was circumcised, even if he died before he was eight days old, is circumcised at the grave side before being buried. He may be circumcised using anything such as a reed or a stone and not necessarily with a knife. The foreskin is removed but *periah* is not necessary for after death it will not grow to re-cover the *atarah;* he is given a name after the circumcision. However the *Ruach Chaim*[66] writes that the *minhag* is to circumcise him with scissors when the body is being washed. The *Gesher HaChaim*[67] is uncertain as to what the *halachah* is if the baby was born circumcised and *hatafat dam brit* was not done during his lifetime. Must it be done after death, particularly according to those *poskim* who rule that *hatafat dam brit* is a Torah obligation? The *Kol Bo Al Aveilut*[68] quotes the *Koret HaBrit*[69] that this is not necessary.

(K) as a remembrance. The Hebrew word in the *Shulchan Aruch* can be read "male" or "remembrance." The *She'arim Metzuyanim BaHalachah*[70] and the *Sefer HaBrit*[71] point out that it should be read to mean a remembrance, for a baby girl who was a stillbirth or who was not named during life is also given a name at the grave side.

(L) forbidden to bury a *nefel* on Yom Tov. The *Taz*[72] quotes the *Bedek HaBayit* that this ruling applies only if it is certainly known that he was not full-term or if his hair and nails were incomplete. Otherwise he is buried on *Yom Tov*. The *Magen Avraham*[73] writes that there is a *mitzvah* to bury even a *nefel*. However, the *Noda BiYehudah*[74] points out that the *Magen Avraham* did not in fact rule definitively but only raised the view that the *Shulchan Aruch's* ruling requires further study. The *Gesher HaChaim*[75] writes that although the accepted ruling is that there is no positive commandment to bury a *nefel*, and therefore it is not buried on *Yom Tov*,[76] nevertheless we bury it for other reasons. These are either because it is forbidden to have

---

64. שו״ת אג״מ יו״ד ח״ג סוסי׳ קמא. וראה בשו״ת ציץ אליעזר ח״י סי׳ כה
65. ח״א פט״ז סי׳ ג סע׳ ב עמ׳ קמו
66. מובא בספר מנחם אבלים דף לז
67. שם הערה 9
68. פ״ג סי׳ ז סע׳ ז דף 201
69. סי׳ רסג סע׳ יח
70. סי׳ קסג ס״ק כב בשם השו״ת השיב משה סי׳ יג
71. כאן עמ׳ קכח ס״ק מח
72. הגהות הט״ז כאן
73. סי׳ תקכו ס״ק כ
74. שו״ת, מהד״ק או״ח סי׳ טו
75. פט״ז סי׳ ג סע׳ א
76. כמ״ש הגמי״י והב״י או״ח סי׳ תקכו ושם בשו״ע ורמ״א, וביו״ד סי׳ רסג. וכ״כ הב״ח סוסי׳ שנג בשם א״ז - כל זה בגשר החיים

SIMAN 263: A BABY WHO IS RED OR YELLOW / §5

―――――― NISHMAT AVRAHAM ――――――

any benefit from a *nefel*, because of the fear of *tumah* as far as *Cohanim* are concerned, or so that it will merit resurrection. The *Gesher HaChaim*[77] continues that the accepted ruling is not that of the *Magen Avraham,* for his opinion cannot overrule that of our Sages and of the *Shulchan Aruch* and, in any case, his opinion has been strongly opposed by others. However, the *Kol Bo Al Aveilut*[78] writes that although the great *poskim* were divided on the question of whether there is an obligation to bury a *nefel*, virtually all have ruled that there is an obligation to bury it.[79]

The *Mechaber*[80] writes that the *minhag* to remove the foreskin of a *nefel* with a stone or reed is forbidden even on the second day of *Yom Tov*. The *Rama* adds that it is forbidden to bury him on *Yom Tov* and he is not buried until the following day. The *Mishnah Berurah*,[81] commenting on the ruling of the *Mechaber*, writes that it would seem that this does not apply to a *nefel* who is a definite *nefel* since it is forbidden to bury him on *Yom Tov*. The question therefore of removing the foreskin cannot apply to him, for this is done at the grave side, as the *Mechaber* himself states in *Yoreh Deah* 263:5. Thus he must be referring to the *nefel* mentioned by him earlier (§9) who died before he was thirty days old, but was considered as someone who could have lived, in terms of his maturity, since he was born complete with hair and fingernails. Such a baby is buried on *Yom Tov* but, nevertheless, his foreskin is not removed. This is only a *minhag* and not essential to his burial, which is allowed on *Yom Tov*. [The *Mishnah Berurah*[81] wonders why this is not considered an essential part of the burial. Later,[82] he says that since the baby is dead he is merely cutting flesh which is dead and although this is a weekday activity it should be permissible for his honor.] The *Mishnah Berurah*[83] also points out that the *Rama's* ruling is that it would be better to bury even a possible *nefel* after *Yom Tov* so that his foreskin could be removed beforehand. Such a possible *nefel* should be buried on *Yom Tov* only if he died on a *Yom Tov*, following his *brit*, or if the *nefel* was a girl, and this is also the ruling of the *acharonim*. If, however, a baby was not circumcised because of illness and died after he was thirty days old on *Yom Tov*, he should certainly be buried then after excising his foreskin at the grave side. The *Mishnah Berurah* concludes that we should know that there are *acharonim* who rule that it is a *mitzvah* to bury a *nefel* and therefore it is possible that one should permit him to be buried, at least on the second day of *Yom Tov*, by non-Jews.[84]

Rav Auerbach zt"l wrote to me that he had heard in his youth that the *minhag* in Jerusalem was to give the baby an unusual name such as Metushelach or Mahalallel, for there are those who are careful not to call a baby the same name as his deceased brother (*and it is unlikely that the next brother will be called by an uncommon name — author*). He concluded that the matter needs looking into.[85]

---

77. שם הערה ס"ק 8
78. פ"ג סי' ג סע' ב דף 199
79. ראה גם בשדי חמד כללים מערכת הקו"ף כלל מ
80. או"ח סי' תקכו סע' י
81. ס"ק מח
82. שעה"צ ס"ק סד
83. שם ס"ק סז
84. ס"ק מט
85. וראה בחכמת אדם כלל קע סע' ז. ביה"ל ד"ה ואסור. ערוך השולחן או"ח סי' תקכו סע' יט. דעת תורה שם סע' י. מטה אפרים סי' תקצו סע' יג. גשר החיים ח"א פי"ז סי' ב סע' ז

SIMAN 264
WHO IS ELIGIBLE TO CIRCUMCISE, WITH WHAT IS CIRCUMCISION PERFORMED AND HOW IS IT PERFORMED

§1 (A)Every Jew is eligible to perform circumcision, including someone who is himself uncircumcised because his brothers had died as a result of circumcision. If an adult Jewish male is present who knows how to circumcise he takes precedence. However a non-Jew, even if circumcised, may not perform the circumcision under any circumstances. If, however, he did perform a circumcision there is no need to repeat it.

GLOSS: *There are those who say that it is nevertheless obligatory to perform hatafat dam brit and this is the accepted halachah.*

───────── NISHMAT AVRAHAM ─────────

SIMAN 264

(A) Every Jew is eligible. The *Sefer HaBrit*[1] writes that an elderly person whose hands shake and who has poor eyesight is forbidden to circumcise since he may castrate the baby. Furthermore[2] any *mohel* who must wear glasses should also stop circumcising. However, he continues, the *Maharsham*[3] writes concerning ritual slaughter that since we know that nowadays one can see well with glasses, we do not need to worry about this.

The *Sefer HaBrit*[4] writes that if a *brit* was postponed because of illness, and when the baby recovered the father lost a close member of his family for whom he must sit *shivah*, the *brit* may not be postponed until the third day of mourning. Although a *brit* is a joyous occasion, for of circumcision the verse says:[5] "I rejoiced over Your word," nevertheless since the baby is fit for circumcision, every day is considered as being the time for the *mitzvah*. It is forbidden therefore to leave him uncircumcised as *Tosafot*,[6] quoted by the *Magen Avraham*,[7] say.

The *Teshuvah MeAhavah*[8] rules like the *Taz*[9] that a *brit* takes precedence over burying a dead person.[10] Even if the *brit* has been postponed and, on the day that the baby is fit to be circumcised, the father became an *onen*, the baby is circumcised before the dead person is buried. We do not differentiate between a *brit* on the eighth day and one that has been postponed and, on the contrary, the latter is more serious since every hour that passes by after he is pronounced fit to be circumcised is the time for the *mitzvah* and it is

---

1. עמ' קס ס"ק לב בשם ספר כללי המילה לר"ג הגוזר בשם מדרש שכל טוב
2. ספר סוד ד' מובא בספר הברית שם
3. דעת תורה יו"ד סי' א ס"ק נ מובא בספר הברית שם
4. עמ' מג ס"ק מד בשם מהרא"ז מרגלית בחידושיו וביאורים על הל' אבלות אות יב
5. תהלים קיט:קסב
6. מו"ק ח ע"ב ד"ה מפני ביטול פו"ר
7. סי' תקסח ס"ק י
8. שו"ת, ח"א סי' פה
9. יו"ד סוסי' שמא
10. יו"ד סי' שס

§3 (B) How is the *brit* performed? The whole of (C)the fore-

NISHMAT AVRAHAM

forbidden to leave him uncircumcised. But this is not the universal view. There is a controversy among the *poskim* as to which takes precedence, a *brit* or a burial. The *Maharshal*[11] rules that the circumcision is performed before the conclusion of the *Shacharit* prayer in the synagogue and before the burial. On the other hand, the *Rama*[12] rules that the burial is done first since the father would, as an *onen*, be unable to say the blessing over the *brit*. The later *poskim*[13] disagree as to which ruling one should follow. The *Tzitz Eliezer*[14] concludes that since there is no requirement for a *brit* to be held specifically before the end of the *Shacharit* prayer and in the synagogue, the burial should take precedence and there is no difference whether the *brit* is on the eighth day or has been postponed.[15]

(B) How is the *brit* performed? The *Yavetz*[16] writes that there are those who have a long, thick, blunt, silver needle-like instrument which they pass under the opening of the foreskin to feel if it is adherent to the flesh of the *ever* and, if necessary, to separate it from the flesh. This is to take extra care and is not accompanied by damage or too much suffering. The *Ot Chaim VeShalom*,[17] however, writes that he does not understand what good this does. If there is no suffering because the instrument is blunt, it will not separate the thin skin that is sometimes adherent and therefore there is neither benefit nor extra carefulness. And,

if the skin is not adherent, we do not need it or anything similar.

However, I heard in *Rav Eliashiv shlita's* name that one should not use the above instrument before the *brit*, for it causes injury and suffering to the baby and one must not circumcise him then. On the other hand, *Rav Auerbach zt"l* told me that one need not worry about this and it is permissible to use the instrument. He told me that an expert *mohel* had assured him that no injury is caused.

Is it permissible to use the instrument on *Shabbat*? The *Minchat Yitzchak*[18] forbids its use on *Shabbat* for it is a *p'sik resha* (an inevitable forbidden consequence of a permissible action which makes the action itself forbidden), for it inevitably causes a bruise that will bleed. However, *Rav Auerbach zt"l* again told me that he permits it, since expert *mohalim* have told him that this is by no means inevitable. *Rav Ovadiah Yosef shlita*[19] writes that he asked a number of expert *mohalim* who told him that bleeding was not inevitable. Certainly if the procedure is done gently there is no bleeding most of the time. Therefore since it is not done with this intent, it is permissible. Even if it were a *p'sik resha*, continues *Rav Yosef shlita*, it is an unwanted consequence and since the transgression is basically Rabbinic, as such the procedure is permitted. And certainly since in truth there is no intent to draw blood this does not come within the framework of

---

11. שו"ת, סי' ע מובא בט"ז שם
12. כתב יד, מובא בט"ז שם
13. הט"ז שם, הברכ"י סי' שמא ס"ק ח בשם השו"ת בית יהודה ח"ב סי' ע פוסקים כהרמ"א. אך השו"ת חת"ס יו"ד סי' שכה ובח"י סי' לט פוסק כהמהרש"ל. וראה גם בספר בית מאיר הל' מילה סי' רסב סע' כ, שו"ת מהר"ם שיק יו"ד סי' שמ ושו"ת מהר"י אסאד סי' שנו. וראה בזוכר הברית סי' ח סע' לו ובספר הברית עמ' כ ד"ה ובהגהות ל
14. ספר אבן יעקב סי' יח. וראה גם בשו"ת ציץ אליעזר ח"ח סי' לב
15. ראה בפ"ת סי' שמא ס"ק כ בשם התשובה מאהבה ח"א סי' פה
16. סידור בית יעקב אות ברית, הלכות מילה ס"ק סא
17. סי' רסד ס"ק יא
18. שו"ת, ח"ח סי' צ ס"ק א
19. שו"ת יחוה דעת ח"ו סי' נג

CHAPTER 25: LAWS OF BRIT MILAH (CIRCUMCISION)

skin covering the *atarah* is excised until the *atarah* becomes visible. The thin membrane underlying the skin is

--- NISHMAT AVRAHAM ---

the definition of *p'sik resha*.[20]

Rav Auerbach zt"l also wrote to me that if we accept the ruling of the *Maharsham* and the *Sdei Chemed* (see Siman 263 above — *metzizah*) that even to perform only *hatafat dam brit* on a baby who has been ill with a generalized illness one waits until seven days have passed after the baby has recovered, since drawing blood from that area, like a *brit*, will be dangerous, this will be even more true when drawing blood is not in itself a *mitzvah*. Why should anyone think that there is danger specifically only when the drawing of blood is a *mitzvah*? On the contrary, one who performs a *mitzvah* will not come to harm. Also the *Maharam Shick* is quoted as writing that one should avoid causing any suffering to the baby. However it could be that doing this procedure prevents even greater suffering during *periah*.

(C) the foreskin. THE "MAGEN CLAMP." May one use various modern instruments to do the *brit* (apart from the guard and the knife)? The *Igrot Moshe*[21] writes, quoting one of his previous *responsa*,[22] that the spirit of our Sages is not happy with these innovations. The manner in which the *mitzvah* of *brit* is performed must not be altered in any detail from the way it has always been done and, moreover, their use presumably causes more suffering. He writes that he therefore does not attend a *brit* where any instrument is used. However, to use an instrument whose purpose is to prevent any bleeding (such as the "magen clamp") is forbidden, for then the *mitzvah* has not been performed since bleeding is one of

the obligations of a *brit*. He notes that he has already written that no instrument of any kind should be used, for one may not change the way the *mitzvah* is performed. In addition, there is also a transgression involved, for the baby suffers more than with a normal *brit* and it is forbidden to cause him greater suffering than what is inevitable from the *brit*.

An American physician and *mohel* put the following problem before *Rav Waldenberg shlita* and *Rav Auerbach zt"l*. There are parents in the community where he lives who are prepared for their son to have a *brit* according to the *Halachah* but only on condition that a "magen clamp" is used and there is no bleeding. If the *mohel* refuses, they will either dispense completely with a *brit* or will ask someone from the reform clergy to circumcise the baby and he may well do so at a time that is convenient to everyone. Thus the circumcision may be done at night or before the eighth day or even on a *Shabbat* which is not the eighth day after birth. He therefore asked whether he could accede to their request but without closing the clamp tightly so that there would be no bleeding whatsoever, but instead make sure that there is minimal bleeding. Or, would this also be forbidden because of *marit ha'ayin* and for the other reasons mentioned above? *Rav Waldenberg shlita*[23] answered, referring also to one of his previous *responsa*,[24] that he must refuse their request no matter what the consequences of his refusal. This is not only because of *marit ha'ayin* and the additional suffering of the baby, but also because for

---

20. וראה גם בשו"ת שבט הלוי ח"ד סי' קלד ס"ק ה וח"ה סי' קמח ס"ק ג

21. שו"ת, יו"ד ח"ג סי' צט וראה שם בסי' צח

22. שו"ת אג"מ יו"ד ח"ב סי' קיט

23. שו"ת ציץ אליעזר ח"כ סי' נב

24. ציץ אליעזר ח"ה סי' כט וח"י סי' לח

(D) split with the fingernail (*periah*) and turned back on

NISHMAT AVRAHAM

many reasons this is not a proper *brit* even if the clamp would not be fully tightened and there is some bleeding. The *Maharam Shick*[25] already ruled that it is better not to perform a *brit* than to do one without *metzizah*; and so too did the *Ot Chaim VeShalom*[26] in this context. *Rav Waldenberg shlita* concludes that we have a *kal vachomer* to forbid the use of a "magen clamp" for, in addition to the fact that there is no *metzizah*, there are also many severe obstacles and problems with the actual *brit* and *periah*.

However, *Rav Auerbach zt"l* answered that in such circumstances, provided he makes sure that there is some bleeding from the *brit*, he could use the clamp.

(D) split with the fingernail (*periah*). What would be the *halachah* if a baby has surgery, either for a medical indication or for the purposes of circumcision, where the surgeon was a Jew or non-Jew? The surgeon excises both the foreskin and the underlying membrane simultaneously, by first cutting both lengthwise until he reaches the *atarah* and then cutting both around the *atarah* until the latter is exposed. The skin and membrane at the site of the excision beyond the *atarah* (that is closer to the body) is then sutured so that the *atarah* cannot become covered again with time.

The *Shach*,[27] quoting the *Beit Yosef*, writes that both opinions (quoted by him) agree that if the circumcision is not done for the purpose of fulfilling the *mitzvah*, or if it is done by a non-Jewish surgeon, then *hatafat dam brit* will be needed. However the *Sha'agat Aryeh*[28] rules like those *poskim* who do not require *hatafat dam brit*. The *Meiri's*[29] (a *rishon*) ruling supports that of the *Sha'agat Aryeh*. The *Meiri* writes that if a non-Jew circumcised a baby there is no need (for a Jew) to circumcise him again since in any case he is no longer uncircumcised. Moreover, there is no need for *hatafat dam brit* either, for there is no longer a possibility that there is foreskin that is hidden within the *atarah*.

The *Sefer HaBrit*[30] quotes *Rav Hai Gaon* that excising both the foreskin and the underlying membrane simultaneously was an old *minhag* in Bavel. See also *Rashi*[31] who, unlike *Rabbeinu Chananel*[32] and the *Or Zarua*,[33] writes that *periah* means exposing the *atarah* (and this is also attained when the foreskin and the underlying membrane are excised simultaneously — author). The *Igrot Moshe*[34] also rules that if the *mohel* did excise both the foreskin and the underlying membrane simultaneously, he has performed the *mitzvah*. See also the *Maharam Shick*[35] and the *Maharsham*[36] that even if the *mohel* did not split the underlying membrane but only exposed the *atarah*, he has also performed the *mitzvah*. However, the *Binyan Tzion*[37] rules that splitting the underlying membrane with the fingernail is obligatory.

Rav Auerbach zt"l told me that for a baby who had surgery, it would be best to do *hatafat dam brit* in order to fulfill all opinions.

---

25. שו"ת, יו"ד סי' רמד
26. סי' רסד ס"ק יב
27. כאן ס"ק ג
28. שו"ת, סי' נד מובא בפ"ת ס"ק ו
29. ע"ז בו ע"ב ד"ה ישראל שהוא ערל
30. עמ' רז ס"ק ב
31. שבת קלו ע"ב ד"ה פרע
32. שם
33. סי' קו
34. שו"ת, יו"ד ח"א סי' קנה
35. שו"ת, סי' רמ
36. שו"ת, ח"א סי' כז
37. שו"ת, ח"א סי' פח

itself on both sides until the flesh of the *atarah* becomes visible. After this (E)*metzizah* is performed from the *milah* so that blood is sucked from further away thus preventing the baby's life from becoming endangered. A *mohel* that does not do *metzizah* is dismissed (and not allowed to circumcise). After the *metzizah* a bandage, plaster or a powdered medication is put on to stop the bleeding.

NISHMAT AVRAHAM

(E) *metzizah* is performed. What is the reason for *metzizah*? Is it part of the *mitzvah* of circumcision or is it to prevent danger to the baby's life? The *Gemara*[38] and the *Rambam*[39] write that it is to prevent danger to the baby.[40] This is also the ruling of the *Chatam Sofer*,[41] *Shoel U'Meshiv*,[42] *Ketsot HaChoshen*[43] and *Chochmat Adam*.[44]

However, the *Ran*[45] is uncertain as to whether the purpose of *metzizah* is to avoid danger to the baby's life or whether it is also part of the *mitzvah* of circumcision. And the *Chatam Sofer* writes[46] that if indeed it was only to prevent danger to the baby, why should it be allowed on *Shabbat*? Since we know that the circumcision will inevitably endanger the child, why should we not perform the *brit* just before nightfall on *Shabbat* so that the *metzizah* will be done after nightfall on Saturday night without the need to set aside Sabbath laws to do so? The *Mahari Assad*,[47] *Binyan Tzion*[48] and *Maharam Shick*[49] write that *Chazal* did not only demand *metzizah* to avoid danger to the baby but it is possibly also a *halachah* given verbally to Moshe Rabbeinu at Sinai and handed down through the generations. The *Avnei Nezer*[50] also writes that *metzizah* is an integral part of the *mitzvah* of the *brit*; therefore if the *mohel* cannot do so, someone else should, even on *Shabbat*. However, although this does not constitute a desecration of *Shabbat*, it would nevertheless be preferable that the *mohel* does the *metzizah* as well.

Is *metzizah* necessary after *hatafat dam brit*? The *Chavalim BaNe'imim*[51] understands the *Maharil*[52] (who writes that one does *hatafat dam brit* and nothing else), to mean that *metzizah* is unnecessary. However the *Koret HaBrit*[53] writes that *metzizah* is necessary. *Mahari Assad*[54] writes that although there is no *mitzvah* in this case to do *metzizah*, nevertheless not doing so can endanger the baby.

Must the *mohel* do the *metzizah* directly with his mouth or may he use a pipette?

---

38. שבת קלג ע"ב
39. הל' מילה פ"ב ה"ב
40. ראה גם בתפארת ישראל שבת פי"ט מ"ב יכין ס"ק טו ובועז ס"ק א. שדי חמד מילואים לקונטרס המציצה
41. מובא בספר הברית סי' רסד בביאור הלכה סע' ז או"ק ג
42. תנינא ח"ד סי' ז
43. סי' שפב
44. כלל קמט סע' יד
45. חידושי הר"ן שבת קלג ע"ב
46. חידושיו על שבת קן ע"א ד"ה ועוד
47. שו"ת, יו"ד סי' רנח
48. שו"ת, סי' רה
49. שו"ת, יו"ד סי' רמח
50. שו"ת, יו"ד סי' שלח
51. שו"ת, סי' יז
52. מובא בדרכי משה כאן
53. מובא בזוכר הברית סי' טז ס"ק יב
54. שו"ת, סי' רנח

GLOSS: *If the bandage has a (ragged) edge, he should be careful to turn it outward and not inward so that it does not stick to the wound and endanger the baby.*

NISHMAT AVRAHAM

The *Sdei Chemed*[55] deals with the subject at length. The *Yad Eliezer*, a *talmid* of the *Chatam Sofer*, asked him regarding his city where a number of babies who had been circumcised by an expert *mohel* developed a severe skin condition following the circumcision, starting in the area of the *brit* and spreading to cover the whole body. Many of the babies died from it and the doctors came to the conclusion that the source of the disease was the *metzizah*, although when the *mohel* was examined he was found to be clear of any disease. The *Yad Eliezer* asked whether it would be permissible to soak absorbent cotton in wine or water and squeeze it on the circumcision wound. Medically, this would act in the same way as *metzizah*. The *Chatam Sofer*[56] replied that the custom to do *metzizah* directly with the mouth stems from the Kabbalists, but where there is a possibility that it could lead to danger, it need not be done in this way. The root of the word *metzizah* is the same as that of *mitz* (juice) and *Rashi* interprets the word as squeezing, extracting something forcibly.[57] Therefore, we only need to extract blood from a point distant from the wound and this may be done in whatever way one is able to. One should accept the opinion of the experts as to what will act in the same way as *metzizah* by mouth. The *Chatam Sofer* adds that even if the *Talmud* had specifically demanded *metzizah* by mouth, nevertheless it is not a part of the *mitzvah* of *brit milah* but is only meant to prevent danger to the baby. The *mitzvah* of *brit* is completed with the *periah;* the baby, if he is a *Cohen*, can be given *terumah* to eat and his father can now offer up the *Paschal* sacrifice (*both of which are forbidden as long as the baby is uncircumcised — author*). But the baby is now endangered until something is done to draw blood from beyond the wound. The *Talmud*[58] compares *metzizah* to putting on a plaster medicated with cumin;[59] both have the same purpose — to prevent danger to the life of the baby. We do not use cumin at all nowadays, nor the type of plaster mentioned in the *Talmud*. This shows that we may depend on modern forms of medication which are also meant to prevent danger. This would also apply to *metzizah* by mouth. Even if it was specifically stated in the *Talmud*, we may replace it with something else which serves the same purpose. However the expert doctors should be asked whether the sponge will truly act in the same way as *metzizah* by mouth.

The *Maharatz Chayot*[60] also permits *metzizah* to be replaced by medication, and the *Mishnah Berurah*[61] writes that one may use a sponge even on *Shabbat*.

However, the *Binyan Tzion*,[62] *Maharam Shick*,[63] *Beit Yitzchak*[64] and *Mahari*

---

55. ח״ח קונטרס המציצה
56. נדפס בספר כוכב יצחק, מובא בספר הברית כאן בביאור הלכה סע׳ ז ס״ק ג
57. בפסוק וימץ טל מן הגזה (שופטים ו:לח) וכן ברד״ק וראב״ע, ראה מיץ אופים על משלי ל
58. שבת קלג ע״ב
59. ראה משנה דמאי ב:א ותרומות י:ד
60. שו״ת, סי׳ ס
61. סי׳ שלא סע׳ ט בביה״ל ד״ה פורעין. וע״ע בסי׳ תרכא מ״ב ס״ק יא בשם המטה אפרים. ואולי צ״ל שבסי׳ שלא מדובר על מציצה בפה דרך הספוג. גם מה שכתב בסי׳ תרכא "רק יולפו בפה" לבד, צ״ל ביד, ראה במטה אפרים סי׳ תרכא סע׳ ו ובשערי תשובה סי׳ תריב ס״ק ז
62. שו״ת, ח״א סי׳ כג ו-כד
63. שו״ת, או״ח סי׳ קנב ויו״ד סי׳ רמד
64. שו״ת, יו״ד ח״ב סי׳ צח

NISHMAT AVRAHAM

Assad[65] all rule that *metzizah* must only be done directly with the mouth.[66] The *Shevet HaLevi*[67] also writes forcibly against any attempt to change the way the *brit* has been done through the generations.

The *Maharam Shick*,[68] referring to the lenient ruling of the *Chatam Sofer* (above ref. 56) regarding the use of a sponge for *metzizah*, writes that this was because of the fear that there would be a govermental edict against the *brit* because of the possibility of contracting serious disease. His permission to do so was only temporary. Similarly, when the pipette was recommended for use in *metzizah* and was permitted by Rav Yitzchak Elchanan zt"l, the *Sdei Chemed*[69] writes that this permission was only temporary. A disease was rife at the time and the government forbade *metzizah* by mouth. This reason was also given by the *Beit Yitzchak*.[70] The *Divrei Malkiel*[71] writes that a person who deliberately does not do *metzizah* should be suspected of being a potential heretic. A pipette should be allowed only in a situation where if it were forbidden, *metzizah* would be annulled completely by those who consider it irrelevant.

The *Maharam Shick*[72] also writes that the *mohel* should refuse to do a *brit* if he is not allowed to do *metzizah*. Rav Samson Raphael Hirsch zt"l explains that the reason for this is that the *mohel* is not obligated to go against the tradition handed down from our forefathers just because the baby's father will not allow him to do *metzizah*. This is also what the *Ot Chaim*

VeShalom[73] and *Tzitz Eliezer*[74] write. On the other hand, the *Koret HaBrit*[75] writes that if it is not possible to do *metzizah* by mouth, he should accept the *mitzvah* and do *metzizah* with something intervening between his mouth and the bleeding area, for many great *poskim* of the generation have permitted this.

The *Mateh Levi*[76] writes that it is now twelve years since the government wrote to the *Rabbanim* of the area that it intends to abolish *metzizah* because it is dangerous. After one of the *Rabbanim* suggested using a pipette for *metzizah*, the *Rabbanim* voted in favor of its use ruling that it was the same as *metzizah* done directly by mouth. However, he writes, I disagreed with this decision and said that this was not the same as *metzizah* done directly by mouth. Since this was no longer permitted, the *mohalim* should at least do something similar that will suck out the blood. When Rav Yaakov Posner told me that *metzizah* using fluff and absorbent cotton sucks out blood from all corners of the wound, I agreed to this.

The *Har Zvi*,[77] after quoting the *Chatam Sofer* and the *Maharam Shick*, writes that since in our days disease transmitted by *metzizah* is common, if one acts leniently and uses a pipette to do *metzizah* he is not doing anything wrong since he does so for fear of disease. However not everyone knows how to use a pipette and the *mohel* should learn from an expert how to use it effectively.

It should be obvious that it is forbidden for a *mohel* who has a possibly infectious

---

65. שו"ת, סי' ו וסי' רנח
66. וראה גם בשו"ת מנחת יצחק ח"ה סי' כד ס"ק ב וח"ח סי' צא
67. שו"ת, יו"ד ח"א סי' קלב
68. שו"ת, או"ח סי' קנב בשם השו"ת עין הבדולח סי' יג מובא גם בשערים מצויינים בהלכה סי' קסג ס"ק י
69. מערכת המציצה
70. שו"ת, יו"ד ח"ב סי' צח
71. שו"ת, ח"ד סי' פז
72. שו"ת, יו"ד סי' רמד
73. סי' רסד ס"ק יב
74. שו"ת, ח"י סי' לח
75. סי' רסד
76. שו"ת, מטה לוי הורוויץ ח"ב סוסי' ס
77. שו"ת, יו"ד סי' ריד

SIMAN 265
THE ORDER OF THE BLESSINGS AT A *BRIT* AND THE *HALACHAH* PERTAINING TO A *BRIT* WHICH FALLS ON A PUBLIC FAST DAY

§3 A convert to Judaism who had already been circumcised before his conversion and a baby who was born without a foreskin, both require *hatafat dam brit*. However, no blessing is required when this is performed. Similarly no blessing is said when an *androgynous* is circumcised since he does not fall definitely into the category of male.

GLOSS: *If the mohel must* (A)*excise any strands of foreskin which*

--- NISHMAT AVRAHAM ---

disease, for example, jaundice, tuberculosis or any inflammation or sores in his mouth, to do *metzizah* until he is completely well, and the *Binyan Tzion*[78] warns the *mohalim* against this.

Finally, the *Chelkat Yaakov*[79] rules that if the *brit* must be done in a hospital on the eighth day, and *metzizah* is only allowed there if performed via a pipette or sponge, the *brit* should not be postponed to be done elsewhere at a later date when *metzizah* can be done directly by mouth. If, however, the *brit* has been postponed for reasons of health, one may postpone it for a few more days in order to be able to do *metzizah* by mouth.

Nowadays there is a fear of AIDS or *hepatitis* being transmitted if *metzizah* is done directly by mouth. I was present when a *mohel* from the United States asked *Rav Auerbach zt"l* if he were permitted, in those cases where there might be such a possibility, to use a pipette for *metzizah*. The *Rav zt"l* ruled that in a situation where such a possibility could exist, he can use a pipette. Incidentally, my colleagues in Infectious Diseases and in Pediatrics and a search of the literature have not been able to find a single documented case of AIDS or of *hepatitis* (which is much more infectious than AIDS) transmission from *mohel* to baby or vice versa. The American Heart Association's recently published guidelines[80] for *bacterial endocarditis* prophylaxis specifically indicates that babies born with congenital heart disease do not require *bacterial endocarditis* prophylaxis prior to circumcision.

SIMAN 265

(A) **excise any strands of foreskin.** If these were not seen immediately after the *brit* but only later, is it permitted to remove them before the baby has recovered from the pain of the *brit*? The *Mahari Assad*[1] was asked about a baby who was circumcised on the eighth day but for whom it was then impossible to do *periah*. On the third day following the *brit* the *periah* could be done. He was asked whether it is permissible to do the *periah* then or maybe it should not be done since the baby is in danger on the third day after the *brit*. He answered that it was

---

Pediatr. Adolesc. Med. 152: 412, '98.

1. שו"ת, יו"ד סי' רנ

78. שו"ת, ח"א סי' כג
79. שו"ת, ח"ב סי' נג
80. JAMA 277: 1794, '97. See also letter, Arch.

still cover the atarah later (in a normal Jewish baby who was circumcised), without which the brit is still incomplete, the blessings must be repeated.

§13 If there is a *brit* on one of the (B)public fast days which appear in the *Tanach*, the *Selichot* and *Vidui* are said as usual but *Vehu Rachum* is not said and there is no *nefilat apaim*.

―――――――――― NISHMAT AVRAHAM ――――――――――

permitted to do the *periah* then and there is no need to wait until the baby had recovered from the *brit*. There were two reasons: first, a *brit* does not put the baby into the category of the *seriously ill*; second, when *Chazal* ruled that a *brit* is postponed because of ill health they specifically meant the *brit* and not *periah* or *hatafat dam brit*. One cannot compare the *brit* to *periah* or *hatafat dam brit* for there is much more suffering when the foreskin is excised.

The *Maharam Shick*,[2] however, disagrees with the *Mahari Assad*. He expresses surprise at the first reason. For the statement that a baby after his *brit* is not *seriously ill* is not in keeping with the *Gemara*[3] that rules that a baby must be bathed (on *Shabbat*) even on the third day because of *pikuach nefesh*; how can one therefore say that he is not (seriously) ill? The second reason, that it is specifically the *brit* that is postponed because of ill health and not *periah* or *hatafat dam brit*, because there is more suffering with a *brit* than with either *periah* or *hatafat dam brit*, is the correct one. But, even if this is so, and a *brit* is not postponed for some minor illness, here where the baby (after the *brit*) is considered *seriously ill* even the

little extra suffering that will be caused by doing *periah* or *hatafat dam brit* must be avoided. Certainly if the *ever* is swollen and the flesh inflamed, one must not touch it. The *Rambam* has already made the general statement about cases where there is a possibility of danger: One can always circumcise or repair a circumcision later but never ever bring anyone back to life. One must certainly take care in an instance such as this one.

This is also the ruling of other *acharonim*.[4]

(B) public fast days. Regarding *metzizah* for such a *brit*, the *Mishnah Berurah*[5] writes that the *mohel* may do *metzizah* as he normally does, but those who are accustomed to first take some wine into their mouths and then blow it out onto the incision site, should not do so before the *metzizah*. Nor may a sponge be used for this purpose on *Yom Kippur (if this is what they are normally accustomed to do)*, for fear that they may squeeze the sponge. Instead, they should sprinkle the wine on the wound by hand.[6] This is also the ruling of the *Gilyon Maharsha*[7] and *Sha'arei Teshuvah*.[8] The *Ketsei HaMateh*,[9] however, writes that this ruling requires further study. Since the *Yavetz*[10] writes

2. שו"ת, יו"ד סי' רמא
3. שבת קלד ע"ב
4. אות הברית סי' רסד ס"ק יס. כורת הברית סוס"ק כ וסי' רס סוס"ק ח. שו"ת דברי מלכיאל ח"ב סי' קלא ס"ק יב. וראה גם בנחל הברית סי' כח
5. או"ח סי' תרכא ס"ק יא

6. הגרסא במשנה ברורה בפה (ולא ביד) צ"ע - ראה במטה אפרים סי' תרכא סע' ו
7. כאן בתחלת הסימן
8. או"ח סי' תריב ס"ק ז
9. על המטה אפרים שם ס"ק יא
10. בסידורו

SIMAN 266
FOR WHICH CIRCUMCISION ARE THE LAWS OF *SHABBAT* AND *YOM TOV* SET ASIDE

§8 When a baby is born during (A)*bein hashemashot* which does not have a clear status of day or night, the counting of the eight days to a *brit* starts that night and he is circumcised the ninth day which is possibly the eighth day from his birth. If he was born during *bein hashemashot* at the close of a Friday, his *brit* does not take place on *Shabbat* since the laws of *Shabbat* are not set aside by a *brit* when the eighth day is not known with certainty. Similarly, a *brit* does not take place on *Yom Tov*, even on the (B)second day of *Yom Tov*, when the eighth day is in

--- NISHMAT AVRAHAM ---

that *metzizah* with wine is a tried and tested remedy, why should the use of this tested remedy be forbidden on *Tishah B'Av* just because of the rare possibility that the *mohel* might swallow some of the wine? Even if he inadvertently does gulp down some wine, this is not the way one normally drinks wine and would fall into the category of eating or drinking in a way different from the way one normally eats or drinks. This is what the *Torat Chaim*,[11] quoted by the *Pitchei Teshuvah*,[12] writes. True this should be forbidden on *Yom Kippur* since the Torah obligates the fast, and also since the *Sha'agat Aryeh*[13] and other *acharonim* have written that on *Yom Kippur* one is culpable even if he drinks or eats in a manner in which the drink or food is not normally consumed. But why should this be forbidden on *Tishah B'Av*? Furthermore, even if he inadvertently gulps down some wine he is not likely to swallow as much as the *measure* required for transgression. Surely he will swallow only a little and not in the way it is usually drunk. The *Mahari Assad*[14] also rules leniently in this matter on public fast days other than *Yom Kippur*. Therefore the *Ketsei HaMateh* concludes that one should not stray away from the *minhag* of doing *metzizah* with wine. However he refers to the *Maharam Shick*[15] and feels that the matter needs further study.

SIMAN 266

A) ***bein hashemashot***. See below **D**.

B) **second day of *Yom Tov***. This ruling is subject to controversy. The *Rambam*,[1] *Semag*[2] and *Kol Bo*[3] rule that a *brit* which has been postponed may be performed on the second day of *Yom Tov* in the Diaspora (excluding the second day of *Rosh Hashanah*). The *Ritva*[4] rules that

---

11. חולין קב
12. יו"ד סי' קנה ס"ק ו
13. שו"ת, סי' עו
14. שו"ת, יו"ד סוסי' רס וכן הסכים בספר ברית אבות על הל' מילה
15. שו"ת, או"ח סי' שטו

1. הל' מילה פ"א הט"ו
2. עשין כח
3. סי' עג
4. יבמות מו ע"ב

doubt. If (C)only his head appeared in view during *bein hashemashot*, he is not circumcised on *Shabbat*, even though the rest of him emerged on *Shabbat*.

─────────── NISHMAT AVRAHAM ───────────

it does not take place on the second day of *Yom Tov* but quotes the *Ramban* who rules that it does. This is also the ruling of the *Shach*[5] and *Ha'amek She'elah*.[6] On the other hand, the *Rosh*[7] and *Tashbetz*[8] rule that a postponed *brit* may not be done on the second day of *Yom Tov* and this is the ruling of *Maran* here. Since the *Rama* does not contradict *Maran*, one assumes that he also rules like him.

The *Noda BiYehudah*[9] writes that the accepted ruling is that of the *Rosh* that a postponed *brit* may not be done on the second day of *Yom Tov*. Nevertheless if one follows the ruling of the *Shach* who decided in favor of the *Rambam's* ruling there is no need to protest. The *Chatam Sofer*,[10] *Chida*[11] and *Mateh Ephraim*[12] also rule strictly like the *Rosh*. The *Shoel U'Meshiv*[13] writes that he was asked about this but could not find the strength to rule leniently. The *Sdei Chemed*[14] also writes that although the majority rule leniently he fears to rule leniently against the *Rosh* and *Maran* and, by default, probably also the ruling of the *Rama* and the *Levush*.

(C) only his head appeared. The *Shach*[15] writes that both the *Tur* and the *Beit Yosef* write "most of the forehead."

Elsewhere, the *Shach*[16] also writes that we see from the *Shulchan Aruch*[17] that once the forehead has appeared it is as if the whole head has appeared, and this is also the opinion of the *Levush*, *Sema*[18] and *Perishah*.[19]

The *Shach*[20] writes that one has to be extra careful to note the time with a difficult childbirth on Friday close to the beginning of *Shabbat*, for if his head emerged into the outside world on Friday close to the beginning of *Shabbat*, he is not circumcised on *Shabbat* but on Friday. The women in attendance should be questioned as to the exact time this happened and, if they do not know, one follows the *minhag* (see below), and this is also the ruling of the *Kol Bo*.[21]

The *Sidrei Taharah*,[22] however, defines the time of birth (*regarding the brit*) as the moment the baby's head enters the *prozdor* (*similarly, a woman is a niddah when blood from her uterus emerges from the cervix into the prozdor*). The *Pitchei Teshuvah*,[23] on the other hand, defines birth as the moment the head emerged outside. See above Siman 262:4 (**O**). The *Sidrei Taharah*[24] comments that the words of the *Shach*, "one follows the *minhag*," are difficult to understand. He ex-

---

5. כאן ס"ק ח
6. פי' לך לך שאילתא ס"קד. וראה בחי' רעק"א על יו"ד סי' רסו סע' ח
7. שו"ת, כלל כו
8. שו"ת, ח"ג סי' רפד
9. שו"ת, או"ח סי' ל הובא בפ"ת ס"ק ז כאן
10. שו"ת, יו"ד סי' רנו-רנב
11. ברכ"י יו"ד סי' רסו ומחזיק ברכה או"ח סי' שלא סע' ד
12. סי' תקצו סע' יד
13. שו"ת, מהד"ג ח"א סי' תמד
14. מערכת יו"ט סי' א ס"ק י
15. ס"ק י
16. יו"ד סי' יד ס"ק א
17. חו"מ סי' רעז
18. שם ס"ק ו
19. כאן
20. ס"ק ט בשם הסמ"ק
21. סי' עג
22. יו"ד סי' קצד ס"ק כו
23. ס"ק ח בשם הלבושי שרד שכתב בשם מהרי"ע
24. שם ד"ה הש"ך

§9 The (D)length of *bein hashemashot* is a matter of controversy between the *Tanna'im* and between the *Amora'im* at the end of the Chapter *Bameh Madlikin*, and the author of

NISHMAT AVRAHAM

plains them to mean that since the accepted *minhag* is that a baby born at the beginning of Friday night is circumcised the following *Shabbat*, one may be lenient in this case and act according to the *minhag*. However, if one knows that there was a small delay between the emergence of the head and the body, one should act strictly and say that it was then *bein hashemashot*, and the *brit* is delayed to Sunday. This is also the ruling of the *Zocher HaBrit*.[25] See also Siman 305E below.

The *Mishnah Berurah*[26] writes that if one has an accurate watch and he knows without doubt that at this time the previous day it was *halachically* night, that is, three small stars were visible, one may depend on the time shown by the watch, and this is also the ruling of the *Birkei Yosef*.[27]

(D) length of *bein hashemashot*. The *Mishnah Berurah*[28] writes that a baby born during *bein hashemashot*, whether it be on Friday or *Shabbat* evening, is circumcised on Sunday. What is the definition of *bein hashemashot*? There is an opinion that it lasts for fifteen minutes (that is, for the equinox when day and night are equal; appropriate corrections must be made at other times of the year. This has been explained earlier in the *Beur Halachah*.[29]) It is the quarter hour before the appearance of three medium-sized stars; that is the period of doubt. With the lapse of those fifteen minutes, there is no longer any doubt. A baby born after this period on Friday night is circumcised the following *Shabbat*.[30] However there are *poskim* who rule strictly that *bein hashemashot* is the entire period from sunset until the three stars are visible, and the *Birkei Yosef*[31] writes that this is the *minhag* throughout *Eretz Yisrael*. The *Radbaz*[32] rules that even if there is doubt whether the baby was born before or during *bein hashemashot*, he is circumcised on Sunday.

There is in fact an old controversy with respect to the definition of *bein hashemashot*. There are three different opinions — that of *Rabbeinu Tam*, of the *Yerei'im* and of the *Geonim*. *Rabbeinu Tam*[33] rules that after the sun has completely set it is still day in every way for another fifty-eight and a half minutes. *Bein hashemashot* starts after this period and continues for another thirteen and a half minutes; only after that is it night. The *Yerei'im*[34] rules that *bein hashemashot* starts thirteen and a half minutes before sunset and night is immediately after sunset. Finally, the *Geonim*[35] rule that *bein hashemashot* starts immediately after sunset. With respect to the view of the *Geonim* there is another controversy as to the period of time that *bein hashemashot* lasts — one

---

25. סי׳ ה סק״י א. וראה גם באות חיים ושלום סי׳ רסו ס״ק ד
26. סי׳ רצג ס״ק ז.
27. וראה גם במ״ב סי׳ שלא ס״ק יד וביה״ל שם ד״ה ביה״ש ובשו״ת שבט הלוי ח״ד סי׳ קלד ס״ק ג
28. סי׳ שלא ס״ק יד
29. סי׳ רסא בביה״ל ד״ה שהוא
30. מג״א סי׳ שלא ס״ק ב
31. או״ח סי׳ רסא
32. שו״ת, אלף שנג (ח״ד סי׳ רפב). ולא הוי ספק ספיקא ספק יום ספק ביה״ש וביה״ש גופא הוי ספק כמו שכתב הפמ״ג א״א ס״ק ב, דאפשר משום דאוקי אחזקת מעוברת, ועוד אפשר לומר דשם ספק חד הוא - ביה״ל ד״ה ביה״ש
33. שבת לה ע״א ד״ה תרי
34. סוסי׳ רעד הובא בב״ח סי׳ רסא
35. הובא במהר״ם אלשקר סי׳ צו (ביה״ל סי׳ רסא סע׳ ב ד״ה מתחלת)

the *Itur* is uncertain of the *halachah*. Therefore if a baby is born after sunset (*on Friday evening — author*), **there is doubt** (*regarding the day on which he was born - author*) **until the end of *bein hashemashot* as defined by Rebbe Yosi. He is therefore circumcised on the tenth day after his birth. If he was born after sunset on *motza'ei Shabbat* we rule strictly like Rabbah.**

― NISHMAT AVRAHAM ―

opinion is that it lasts thirteen and a half minutes whereas another is that it lasts a full seventy-two minutes. Most *poskim*, *rishonim* and *acharonim*, rule like *Rabbeinu Tam* whether it leads to a lenient ruling (as on *Shabbat* eve) or a strict ruling (as on *motza'ei Shabbat*);[36] this is how the *Chatam Sofer*[37] and the *Torat Chesed*[38] rule.

The *Shulchan Aruch* rules like *Rabbeinu Tam* with regard to *Shabbat*[39] and like the *Geonim* with regard to circumcision.[40] The *Shulchan Aruch HaRav* also rules like *Rabbeinu Tam* with regard to *Shabbat*[41] and like the *Geonim* with regard to circumcision.[42]

The *Chazon Ish* is reported to have said that in *Eretz Yisrael* the time for praying *Maariv* is about forty-five minutes after sunset [on another occasion he said that fifty minutes was definitely enough and there is no need to act more strictly even with regard to (*something which is as serious as — author*) *Shabbat*]. On the other hand, he apparently said that with regard to circumcision on *Shabbat* one may rule a little more leniently and a baby born thirty-five minutes after sunset on Friday may be circumcised on *Shabbat*.[43] *Rav Tukechinsky zt"l*[44] writes that one may work on *motza'ei Shabbat* and eat after *Yom Kippur* thirty-five minutes after sunset. The *Zivchei Tzedek*[45] and *Ben Ish Chai*[46] both rule that one should wait twenty-seven minutes after sunset on *motza'ei Shabbat*. The *Kaf HaChaim*[47] writes that night is about twenty minutes after sunset. *Rav Ezriel Auerbach shlita* told me that his father-in-law *Rav Eliashiv shlita* rules that thirty minutes after sunset is night and a baby born then on Friday night should be circumcised on *Shabbat*. *Rav Auerbach zt"l* told me that all these times were set to act strictly and remove any doubt regarding the circumcision of a baby on *Shabbat* when this was not the eighth day after his birth. But since there were so many variables and

---

וסיעתו) נפרש בלשון השו"ע. ועיק' הדין מבואר באו"ח כי שם ביתו וע"ז סמך מרן שלא הרחיב בזה, והדברים פשוטים וברורים. ועיין שם באות י שבע"ש צריכים להחמיר כדעת הגאונים ולא לעשות מלאכה אחר השקיעה

41. סי' רסא
42. שערים מצויינים בהלכה סי' עה ס"ק א
43. אמרי יושר להרב מאיר גרייננמן בפסקים סע' יז
44. בלוח ארץ ישראל
45. שו"ת, ח"ב יו"ד סי' יז ד"ה ונכתוב
46. שנה ב פ' ויצא סע' א - עש"ים דקות מן המגרב שהוא שבע דקות אחר שקיעת החמה
47. סי' שלא ס"ק לה

36. ראה בביה"ל סי' רסא סע"ב ד"ה המתחלת וד"ה שהוא. The *Zocher HaBrit* 5:3 *Kunteres Bein Hashemashot* enumerates seventy *poskim* who rule like *Rabbeinu Tam*.

37. שו"ת, או"ח סי' פ
38. שו"ת, או"ח סי' טו
39. או"ח סי' רסא סע' ב
40. יו"ד סי' רסו סע' ט. וראה שם בש"ך ס"ק יא. וב"כ השו"ע הרב בסדר הכנסת שבת, מובא בקצות השולחן סוף ח"ג עמ' סט שמרן חזר בו בשו"ע יו"ד הל' מילה. אך הביעי אומר ח"ב או"ח סי' כא אות יד כותב: ואטו משום שהעתיק מרן כלשון הגמרא משתשקע החמה ניקום ונימא דהדר ביה ממ"ש באו"ח, הא ודאי דליתא. ומה שנפרש בלשון הגמרא (דהיינו סוף שקיעה וכמ"ש ר"ת

SIMAN 266: BRIT ON SHABBAT AND YOM TOV / §10, 11

§10 Although the *brit* of a baby who is born without a foreskin, one who has two foreskins, an *androgynous* or one born after (E)Caesarian section takes place on the eighth day, nevertheless it may not be done on *Shabbat*.

§11 A baby born (*on Shabbat*) after seven months of gestation is circumcised on (*the following*) *Shabbat*, even if his (F)hair and nails are as yet incomplete. However if he is born after the (G)eighth month of gestation, he may not be

---
NISHMAT AVRAHAM

rulings, these times are only at the equinox and appropriate corrections must be made for the rest of the year. In every case the exact time that most of the baby's head[48] (and in a breech delivery, most of his body) emerges should be noted, and a *posek* consulted. The *Rav zt"l* told me that twenty-five minutes after sunset was night and *Rav Neuwirth shlita* also told me this in his name.[49]

(E) Caesarian section. See *Nishmat Avraham*, vol. 1 *Orach Chaim*, Siman 331D, p. 233.

A baby born in the Diaspora by Caesarian section who is eight days old on the second day of *Yom Tov* is circumcised the day after the Festival since the laws of *Yom Tov* are not set aside for his *brit*. If a *mohel* from *Eretz Yisrael* is visiting (for whom the second day of *Yom Tov* is a weekday), may he circumcise the baby on the eighth day, that is, on the second day of *Yom Tov*? Or, on the other hand, should he not, for by doing so he may bring those who must keep the second day of *Yom Tov* with all the strictness of the first day, to behave lightly towards it. *Rav Auerbach zt"l* ruled[50] that a baby (*born normally*), who is eight days old on the second day of *Yom Tov*, may not be preferentially circumcised by a visiting *mohel* from *Eretz*

Yisrael (*who only needs to keep one day of Yom Tov*), but should be circumcised by the local *mohel*. If the visiting *mohel* were to perform the circumcision, people will come to treat the second day of *Yom Tov* lightly (*for they would say that were it a full Yom Tov the local mohel would have performed the brit*). With regard to a Caesarian birth, however, he wrote to me that if not everyone is aware of the fact that the baby was born by Caesarian section, he may be circumcised on the second day of *Yom Tov* by the *mohel* who is visiting from *Eretz Yisrael*. See also *Rav Ovadiah Yosef shlita's*[51] discussion whether a *mohel* from the Diaspora who is visiting in *Eretz Yisrael* may circumcise a baby on his second day of *Yom Tov* instead of a local *mohel* for whom it is a weekday.

(F) hair and nails are as yet incomplete. This is a sign that the baby is premature.

(G) eighth month of gestation. *Rav Auerbach zt"l* wrote to me that one may deduce from this that a baby born after eight months of gestation may be circumcised on a weekday even if his hair and nails are incomplete. However, the *Ikrei HaDat*[52] rules that one may not circumcise him under any circumstances until he is thirty days old.

---

48. See above, Siman 262:4(O), p. 202.
49. וכ"כ בשמירת שבת כהלכתה פמ"ו הערה מה. וראה בשולחן שלמה ח"ג עמ' רכ הערה יד
50. יום טוב שני כהלכתו פי"ב הערה ה
51. לוית חן סי' שלא עמ' קסו
52. הל' מילה סי' כח אות ב

circumcised on *Shabbat* unless his hair and nails are complete. This also applies to a baby about whom there is doubt as to whether he was born after seven or eight months of gestation, and he may not be circumcised on *Shabbat* unless his hair and nails are complete.

GLOSS: *There is an opinion that he should be circumcised since he may have been born after seven months of gestation. However in other matters* (H)*Sabbath laws are not set aside for him, and this appears to me to be the halachah.*

NISHMAT AVRAHAM

(H) Sabbath laws are not set aside for him. The *Shach*[53] and *Shevet Ha-Levi*[54] explain why he may be circumcised on the eighth day on *Shabbat* although Sabbath laws are otherwise not set aside for him. Regarding the treatment of a premature baby in general and of a baby born after eight months of gestation in particular, see *Nishmat Avraham*, vol. 1 *Orach Chaim*, Siman 330P,Q, p. 228.

---

53. ס"ק טו

54. שו"ת, ח"ד סי' קלב ד"ה בט"ז

CHAPTER 26
The Laws of Gerim

SIMAN 268
WHAT IS THE PROCESS OF PROSELYTATION

§1 A *ger* who wishes to become part of the People of Israel is (A)obligated to be circumcised first. If he was already circumcised as a non-Jew (*or was born without a foreskin*) he requires *hatafat dam brit*. A blessing is not said.

---NISHMAT AVRAHAM---

SIMAN 268

(A) obligated to be circumcised first. Conversion for a male involves having a *brit* followed by immersion in a *mikveh* after recovery. The conversion process is not completed until both of these obligatory acts have been carried out.

The *Har Tzvi*[1] rules that if circumcision will be dangerous for him, he cannot convert. This is also the ruling of the *Achiezer*,[2] *Seridei Eish*,[3] *Melamed LeHo'il*[4] and *Tzitz Eliezer*.[5] The *Seridei Eish* adds that even if he is willing to risk his life with the circumcision, he may not be accepted.[6]

The *Tzitz Eliezer*[7] rules that if he became *seriously ill* after his *brit*, but before his immersion, whether due to the *brit* or not, Sabbath laws may be set aside for him and this is also the ruling of the *Yesodei Yeshurun*.[8]

Regarding circumcising him on a Thursday or Friday (see Siman 262C above), the *Yavetz*,[9] *Pri Megadim*[10] and *Yabia Omer*[11] all rule that the *brit* should be postponed to Sunday since he has no obligation to convert and can change his mind whenever he so wishes (before he has converted).

See *Nishmat Avraham*, vol. 1 *Orach Chaim*, Siman 219E regarding the blessing of *HaGomel* after he has recovered from his circumcision.

---

1. שו"ת, יו"ד סי' רב
2. שו"ת, ח"ב סי' קג
3. שו"ת, ח"ב סי' קב ו-קג
4. שו"ת, סי' פו
5. שו"ת, חי"ד סי' צב וחט"ו סי' א ס"ק יב
6. לפי שיש בו חילול השם וסכנה לכל ישראל אם ימות מחמת מילה
7. שו"ת, ח"י סי' כה פ"ב, ע"ש שמבדיל בין ג"צ ובין גר בגלל דבר אחר
8. ח"ד עמ' רלו וכן ראה בספרו נחלת צבי עמ' קיח. אך השו"ת אמרי יושר, ח"ב סי' קל, מתיר רק כשהסתכן מחמת מילה וראה בשו"ת מחזה אברהם, ח"א סי' נד, דאם אפשר ע"י עכו"ם יש להתיר
9. שו"ת, ח"ב סי' צה
10. שו"ת מגידות סי' צ
11. שו"ת, ח"ה יו"ד סי' כג

CHAPTER 27
The Laws Concerning the Mezuzah

SIMAN 286
THE PLACES WHICH REQUIRE A *MEZUZAH*

§1 (A)The following places must have a *mezuzah*: The doorways of houses, courtyards, cities and towns, cattle sheds and chicken coops, storerooms of wine and oil, a woman's house and a jointly owned house — all these are obligated to have a *mezuzah*.

─────────── NISHMAT AVRAHAM ───────────

SIMAN 286

(A) The following places must have a *mezuzah*. Every room of a house (with certain exceptions) must have a *mezuzah* affixed to the doorpost on the right, leading into the room.[1] The obligation starts immediately with moving into one's home, be it in *Eretz Yisrael* or in the Diaspora.[2] If the house is rented, one has the obligation to affix a *mezuzah* immediately with one's entry in *Eretz Yisrael* and within thirty days in the Diaspora.[3]

Is there an obligation to have a *mezuzah* affixed on the doorposts of rooms used by the medical staff and patients in hospitals in *Eretz Yisrael* and in the Diaspora? *Rebbe Akiva Eiger*[4] writes that rooms in a prison must have *mezuzot*, for a dwelling place which one is forced to live in is nevertheless considered a dwelling place. On the other hand, he writes that the *Beit Hillel* rules that it is exempt. The *Chida*[5] writes that the *Beit Hillel* exempted a prison because it is not a dignified home. The *Chida* gives another reason to exempt a prison; it is only a temporary dwelling and like cabins in a ship. Thus even a place where one is quarantined for forty days and sometimes two months is exempt from a *mezuzah* although it is a dignified dwelling place. Elsewhere, the *Chida*[6] writes that the cabins in a ship have, in turn, been compared by the *Rambam* to a *succah* which is exempt from a *mezuzah* even in *Eretz Yisrael* where the obligation to fix a *mezuzah* is immediate. Rooms in a ship are exempt even though one knows that they will often be occupied for more than thirty days. And, living in a house in quarantine is worse than living in a borrowed house, since, in the former case, one is forced by the law of the city to live there for a period of time. In addition, the person in charge of the house of quarantine has the right to move him from one room to another. Therefore they are exempt from having *mezuzahs* affixed to the doors. This ruling is also cited in brief by the *Ikrei HaDat*.[7] It would seem from this ruling that a hospital, both in *Eretz Yisrael* and the Diaspora, would also be exempt, for a patient is certainly forced by circum-

---

1. כאן סע׳ יח ורמ״א סי׳ רפו סע׳ ב
2. ע״ז כא ע״א תוסד״ה אף. גליון מהרש״א כאן סע׳ כב
3. כאן סע׳ כב ו-כג
4. חידושי רעק״א כאן בשם שו״ת שער אפרים סי׳ פג
5. ברכי יוסף כאן
6. שו״ת חיים שאל ח״ב סי׳ כב
7. סי׳ לא סע׳ א

SIMAN 286: PLACES REQUIRING A MEZUZAH / §1

――――― NISHMAT AVRAHAM ―――――

stances to be there and he can be moved from one room to another or from one hospital to another. This is the ruling of the *Metzudat David*[8] in the name of the *Chida*. The *Avnei Nezer*[9] also exempts a hospital from the *mitzvah* of *mezuzah* because the patients do not rent rooms there but only pay for being there.

The *Shevet HaLevi*[10] agrees with the reasoning of the *Avnei Nezer*, but writes that it is nevertheless obvious that he only refers to a non-Jewish hospital with Jewish patients.[11] However today in *Eretz Yisrael* where there are Jewish hospitals they cannot be exempted by Torah law since they are owned by Jews and Jews work there. I found this *responsum* difficult to understand for two reasons: first because the *Chida's* ruling is not mentioned; second, what does ownership of a place have to do with the obligation of the occupier to affix *mezuzot*? (*The obligation to affix mezuzot in a house falls on the occupier regardless of who owns it.*[12]) *Rav Neuwirth shlita* agreed with this for in a hospital the patients' rooms are considered as being for temporary occupancy only and the *Chida* and *Pitchei Teshuvah* (quoted above) rule that as such, they are exempt from the *mitzvah* of *mezuzah*. However, *Rav Neuwirth shlita* says there is another reason why the pati-ents' rooms in a Jewish hospital must have *mezuzot* and that is because the beds remain there permanently even if unoccupied and the rooms are therefore in the category of a storeroom because of those who live there permanently. The *mezuzot* should therefore be affixed with the blessing.

As to the rooms used by the hospital personnel, the *Taz*[13] writes that even if they are used daily, they do not require *mezuzot* since they are not used at night. This makes their use temporary and unlike a storehouse which may be used by day or by night. However it appears from the *Pitchei Teshuvah*,[14] *Aruch HaShulchan*[15] and *Kitzur Shulchan Aruch*[16] that they are obligated to have *mezuzot* since they permanently contain various pieces of furniture belonging to the personnel who use the rooms throughout the day. And this also appears to be the opinion of the *Shevet HaLevi* quoted above since the hospital is owned by Jews and Jews work there all the time. The *Chayei Adam*,[17] *Ben Ish Chai*[18] and *Metzudat Tzion*[19] all rule that the *mezuzot* should be affixed without a blessing. However, according to *Rav Neuwirth shlita* (quoted above), since every room contains permanent furniture and equipment belonging to the hospital, there is an obligation to affix *mezuzot* with a blessing.

However, *Rav Auerbach zt"l* wrote to me that it is possible that these rooms cannot be compared to storerooms for storerooms are used only for the purpose of storage. But hospital rooms are not meant for storing beds but for the use of patients and for them the rooms are not defined as a dwelling place that requires a *mezuzah*. This is also true for furniture in

---

8. על הקיצור שו"ע סי' יא סע' יד
9. שו"ת, יו"ד סי' שפ
10. שו"ת, ח"ב יו"ד סי' קנו
11. כתב לי מו"ר הגרי"י נויבירט שליט"א: הלשון לא מובנת, איזה הו"א לחייב דירה של גוי והיהודי במקרה נמצא שם, האם זה שכירות, ובפרט שבדרך כלל גם הגויים שוכבים שם עיין סי' רפו סע' א ברמ"א ועוד. כי אם בביה"ח של גויים ובמקרה היום שוכב יהודי (כמובן שלושים יום) ומחר שוכב גוי וכן הלאה, האם אומרים כל פעם לשים ולהוריד מזוזה. ופעם יהודי שוכב שבוע, שבועיים, ארבע שבועות, והוא יודע שבעוד שבוע
ישוחרר מביה"ח, האם לקבוע עכשיו מזוזה לכמה ימים, היתכן, עכ"ל
12. סי' רצא סע' ב
13. ס"ק י
14. ס"ק י
15. סע' כו
16. סי' יא סע' ד
17. כלל טו סע' יא
18. שנה ב פ' כי תבוא סע' יז
19. על הקיצור שו"ע סי' יא ס"ק כז

the personnel rooms (*it is not stored there*). Besides, patients and personnel are on many occasions moved from one room to another. The *Rav zt"l* told me that this would mean the *mezuzot* should be fixed in all the hospital rooms, but without a blessing. The *Rav zt"l* also wrote to me that the *Halachah* will differentiate between an old-age home and a nursing-care ward in a hospital. In an old-age home everyone is given a permanent room whereas in a nursing-care ward in a hospital he is given only a bed; not only has he no control over which room he has but he can also be moved from room to room; he is like a person who has no home.

If the *mezuzah* in the patient's room is on the inside of the door (which opens outwards),[20] it would best be covered.[21] The *Taz*,[22] quoting the *Semag* and the *Beit Yosef*, writes that if the *mezuzah* is placed higher than ten *tefachim* from floor level it is considered to be resting in a *halachic* domain of its own separate from the room, and this is also quoted by the *Pitchei Teshuvah*.[23] This *Taz* is based on his ruling[24] that even an area that is not four by four *tefachim* is considered a different domain. *Rav Ovadiah Yosef shlita*[25] also writes that a hospital room in which a patient uses a urinal or bedpan is nevertheless required to have a *mezuzah* for, since it is affixed higher than ten *tefachim*, it is considered to be in a different domain from that of the patient. Besides, the *mezuzah* is covered by glass or wrapped in plastic and one does not need to worry at all, and this is also the ruling of the *Zivchei Tzedek*.[26] *Rav Neuwirth shlita* wrote to me that since there are many who disagree with the *Taz* (that anything that is placed higher than ten *tefachim* from floor level is considered to be in a different domain), the *Mishnah Berurah*[27] ruled that one must act strictly. *Rav Auerbach zt"l* wrote to me that if the patient's bed is higher than ten *tefachim* and has an area of four by four *amot*, then even those who disagree with the *Taz* will agree that even if there are uncovered feces in the room, he may pray and learn if he closes his eyes and there is no odor. It would also appear that if there is a partition ten *tefachim* high between him and the feces, it would also be permitted even though the partition is less than four *tefachim* in length, since there is no mention at all for the need to have a partition as well. Only if the person and the feces are in the same room and the bed separates them, is there a requirement (*Orach Chaim* Siman 87) that there should also be a partition that reaches the ground.[28] The *Rav zt"l* concludes, however, that a little further study should be invested on the matter in the *Shulchan Aruch HaRav* Siman 79.

When there are two rooms for the use of the patient, an outer one in which he sleeps and where he uses the bedpan or urinal and an inner one (which is large enough to warrant a *mezuzah*) but which has no exit except through the outer room, the *mezuzah* should be fixed on the doorpost leading into the inner room. However, since it can be seen from the outer room, the question arises whether it should nevertheless be affixed as one would normally do, in spite of the fact that the patient will use the urinal or bedpan in its presence. Or, should it be affixed behind the door leading into the inner room so that when the intervening door is

---

20. כתב לי מו"ר הגרי"י נויבירט שליט"א. וראה בפ"ת ס"ק ז
21. שו"ע כאן סע' ה
22. ס"ק ד
23. ס"ק ח
24. באו"ח סי' עט ס"ק ג
25. אור תורה חוברת ה, שבט תשד"מ
26. ח"ב או"ח סי' לה
27. סי' עט ס"ק יא וסי' רמ סע' ה ביה"ל ד"ה עד
28. See *Nishmat Avraham*, vol. 1 *Orach Chaim*, Siman 87C.

SIMAN 286: PLACES REQUIRING A MEZUZAH / §1

NISHMAT AVRAHAM

closed it cannot be seen? Although the *Shach*[29] and the *Pitchei Teshuvah*[30] rule that the *mezuzah* should be affixed behind the intervening door, *Rav Auerbach zt"l* told me that the *mezuzah* should be affixed as one would normally do, that is, on the side of the doorpost within the outer room. He should then cover the *mezuzah* so that neither the parchment itself nor *Hashem's* Name on the *mezuzah* can be seen. He explained that the ruling of the *Shach* refers to an outer room which is only used as a bedroom for husband and wife or as a bathroom (lavatory).

How should a *mezuzah* be covered? The *Mishnah Berurah*[31] at first quotes the *Derech HaChaim* who rules that *tefillin* (*the same would apply to a mezuzah — author*) need two covers, one inside the other. However he questions this ruling for it is only applicable to a bedroom used by husband and wife (*and a mezuzah that is affixed on the inside of such a bedroom — author*). *Rav Neuwirth shlita* told me that at first sight the *Mishnah Berurah* here seems to contradict what he writes in Siman 43.[32] *Rav Auerbach zt"l* wrote to me that there is no contradiction since Siman 43 discusses a permanent bathroom (lavatory) whereas here the *Mishnah Berurah* is discussing a bedroom where there are *tefillin*.

ELEVATORS. The *Minchat Yitzchak*[33] rules that hospital (and all other) elevators should have a *mezuzah* affixed without a blessing. The *mezuzah* should be affixed to the doorpost of the elevator itself (*going up and down with it*) and not to the doorpost of the entrance to the elevator on each floor. He rules that this should be done even if the floor area of the elevator is less than four by four *amot*. On the other hand, *Rav Zilberstein shlita*[34] writes that it is not the elevator which requires the *mezuzah* but the corridor into which the elevator opens on each floor. Therefore a *mezuzah* should be affixed to the doorpost of the entrance to the corridor on each floor. However, *Rav Auerbach zt"l* wrote to me that it is possible that there is no requirement to affix a *mezuzah* to the doorpost of an elevator, neither to its entrance nor to its exit. Similarly there is probably no requirement to affix one to the elevator itself, since there really is no doorway (*to a room*), for the elevator goes from floor to floor and is not meant to be a home and is therefore exempt even if it were four by four *amot* in area. The corridor is also exempt since there is no true doorway, only a pit, and it is impossible to enter or exit through it except through the elevator. The elevator itself may be compared to a porter who carries a person up and down. As soon as it moves away it leaves behind it a pit, and the frame of the corridor probably cannot be considered a doorway. Neither is it comparable to a permanent ladder leading to a loft, which can be considered a stairway. All that is seen is an elevator that moves electrically, like a horse that carries a box and awaits, at the service of its master, at the entrance to his home, ready to do his wishes at any time, day or night. Nevertheless, the *Rav zt"l* concludes that the Torah writes that a *mezuzah* must be affixed to the doorpost of one's home and does not mention a doorway. Since nowadays it is common that one enters and leaves one's home by an elevator, it would be commendable to affix a *mezuzah*, without a blessing, on the right-hand side of the doorpost leading into the corridor.[35]

---

29. ס"ק ו בשם המעדני מלך
30. ס"ק ו בשם היד קטנה
31. סי' מ סע' ב ס"ק ה ובייה"ל ד"ה אסור
32. ס"ק כב
33. שו"ת, ח"ד סי' צג
34. קונטרס חקרי הלכות והליכות שכנים תשמ"ג עמ' מח
35. ראה מנחת שלמה תנינא סי' ק אות ה

CHAPTER 28
The Laws of Orlah

SIMAN 294
THE LAWS OF *ORLAH*
WHERE DO THEY APPLY AND TO WHOSE PRODUCE

§1 When someone plants a tree for its edible fruit, he counts three years from the time he plants it. It is forever forbidden to have (A)any benefit from the fruits that grow during those three years. This applies to the fruit itself, the seeds and the peels.

--- NISHMAT AVRAHAM ---

SIMAN 294

(A) any benefit from the fruits. The *Radbaz*[1] asks whether the laws of *orlah* apply to a tree that bore fruit within three years of planting and whose fruit are used medicinally. He answers that it would appear that the laws of *orlah* do not apply, for the Torah[2] writes: "When you plant a tree for food." A tree that is planted for its medicinal use is not considered a food tree, even though its medical benefit is derived by eating the fruit, since the healthy do not eat of this fruit. A hint of this can be seen in the words of the prophet Ezekiel[3] who writes: "Its fruit will be for food and its leaves for healing," from which we see that medicine is not a food. Know that regarding *Yom Kippur*, he who eats something that the healthy do not eat (*Rav Neuwirth shlita* wrote to me adding, and it is bitter), has not transgressed Torah law for this is not considered eating. Here also the Torah writes a food tree. If one plants trees as a fence or to use its wood for building, the laws of *orlah* do not apply even though it has edible fruit. It would seem, then, that in our case the laws of *orlah* should certainly not apply at all, and more definitely not in the Diaspora where the laws of *orlah* are not of Torah force. Elsewhere,[4] the *Radbaz* writes that even if there is a minority of healthy people who eat of the fruit of such a tree as a preserve, they do not do so as a food but to protect their health. Such a tree is also not defined as a food tree; the laws of *orlah* do not apply to it and its fruit may be eaten. This ruling is also cited in brief by *Rebbe Akiva Eiger*.[5]

Rav Auerbach zt"l writes, however, that the laws of *orlah* certainly apply to an apple or *etrog* tree that is planted for the smell of its fruits or for their preparation for a medical use. It is the same as an olive tree planted so that its oil be used to give light. This is because the fruits are edible; for it does not seem at all logical to differentiate between the benefit one receives by using the *orlah* fruit for coloring or for lighting, which the Torah forbids, and the

---

1. שו"ת, ח"א סי' תצט
2. ויקרא יט:כג
3. יחזקאל מז:יב
4. שו"ת, ח"א סי' מד
5. חידושי רעק"א על סע' כג כאן

NISHMAT AVRAHAM

benefit one receives from its smell or medicinal properties. True the Torah forbids their use for coloring or lighting but this should not mean that the tree is a food tree. One must therefore say that since they are truly food trees and were planted for their fruit, they cannot be compared to a tree that is planted for a fence or for its wood, which no longer has the name of a food tree. But, a tree planted for the smell or medicinal use of its fruit is still a food tree. This fits in well with what *Rebbe Akiva Eiger* writes, at the end of Siman 294, that a tree that is planted for the aroma of its fruits or whose fruits are not eaten by the healthy but is planted only for its medicinal use, is exempt from the laws of *orlah*. Even when he writes "for its aroma" it would appear that he refers to a tree whose fruits were not really edible and was essentially planted for the smell.[6]

Regarding the *Radbaz's* ruling, *Rav Neuwirth shlita* wrote to me that it needs further study. For how can one say that the laws of *orlah* do not apply to fruit that only the sick eat? They have the taste of fruit. Why should they not be included in the Torah's words "tree for food"? *Rav Auerbach zt"l* wrote to me that the healthy do not eat of these fruits because they do not have a good taste. The sick who eat of them for a cure or to maintain their health do not do so because of their taste. Thus it is not called a "tree for food."

---

6. מנחת שלמה ח"א סי׳ עא סע׳ ד

CHAPTER 29
The Laws of Pidyon HaBen

SIMAN 305
WHO IS OBLIGATED TO REDEEM THE FIRSTBORN MALE, WHEN SHOULD THIS BE DONE AND THE LAWS CONCERNING IT

§2 (A)A woman is not obligated to redeem her firstborn son.

─────────── NISHMAT AVRAHAM ───────────

SIMAN 305

◆§ **INTRODUCTION.** When the first child, born to a woman naturally, is a male, the Torah[1] commands that he be redeemed from a *Cohen* following the thirtieth day after his birth. This law applies only to a woman's first child, and only if it is male. If the first child is a daughter, a subsequent male child is exempt. If she already has a child (male or female) from a former marriage, and now has a son as the first child of her present marriage, he does not need redemption even though he is the firstborn son to his father. If either parent's father is a *Cohen* or a *Levi*, there is no requirement to redeem him. Similarly, there is no requirement to redeem a baby born by Caesarian section. At the ceremony[2] the *Cohen* asks the father: "What would you prefer, your firstborn son or the money that you are obligated to pay to redeem him?" The father answers: "My firstborn son and here is the money for his redemption."

(A) A woman is not obligated. The *Ikrei HaDat*[3] writes that a deaf-mute is not obligated to redeem his firstborn son since he is exempt from all the *mitzvot* of the Torah. May the *Beit Din* redeem him or can only he redeem himself when he reaches the age of thirteen?[4] This depends on whether one rules like the *Shach*[5] or the *Taz*[6] about a firstborn son whose father died before the infant had reached the age of thirty-one days. The *Taz* says *Beit Din* cannot redeem him; the *Shach* rules that *Beit Din* can redeem him, and this is also the opinion of the *Chatam Sofer*.[7] The *Shevet HaLevi*[8] writes that he should be redeemed first by his deaf-mute father and again by the *Beit Din*, both times without the blessings. At the redemption ceremony the father answers the *Cohen* in writing. *Rav Neuwirth shlita* wrote to me asking what his writing accomplishes if *Chazal* have defined him as a *shoteh*? Besides, the *Pitchei Teshuvah*[9] writes that this part of the ceremony is only in order to make the redemption important in the father's eyes, giving him a desire to redeem him. *Rav Auerbach zt"l*, however, wrote to me that the *Shevet Ha-*

---

1. שמות יג:יג
2. רמ"א כאן סע' י
3. סי' לג סע' יא
4. ראה בפ"ת ס"ק כה
5. ס"ק יא
6. ס"ק יא
7. שו"ת, יו"ד סי' רצז
8. שו"ת, יו"ד ח"ב סי' קנב
9. ס"ק טו

§11
The firstborn cannot be redeemed until thirty days have elapsed from his birth. After the thirtieth day he should be (B)redeemed immediately so as not to delay the performance of the *mitzvah*. If the thirty-first day is *Shabbat*, he may not be redeemed on *Shabbat*; one waits until Sunday. (*There are those who say that the Pidyon HaBen may not be done on Chol HaMoed, and there are those who say that it may, and this view is the main one.*)

NISHMAT AVRAHAM

Levi wrote that he should be redeemed by the deaf-mute because possibly today a deaf-mute (*who has been taught*) may not be considered a *shoteh* (see *Nishmat Avraham*, vol. 1 *Orach Chaim*, Siman 38H and 55A). He also explained that the father is asked "What would you prefer" so that he realizes that his son is being redeemed and not that he is only giving the *Cohen* a gift.[10] However one should write this to him in the language that he understands and not in the original Aramaic of the *Gemara*.

SIAMESE TWINS. The *Gemara*[11] tells us that Rebbe Yehudah HaNasi (the compiler of the *Mishnayot*) was asked by a father how much money he should give the *Cohen* to redeem a firstborn son who had two heads — whether the child was one person or two, and double the amount of redemption money should be given. An old sage who was present answered that he had to give double the amount since the Torah[12] writes "per skull." Today such a problem could not arise, for such a child would be delivered by Caesarian section and therefore be exempt. See §12 below. Also see *Nishmat Avraham*, vol. 1 *Orach Chaim*, Siman 27D. As to whether such a person should be considered a *treifah* see the *Chazon Ish*.[13]

(B) redeemed immediately. The *Shach*[14] discusses a firstborn who took ill and could not be circumcised until he was thirty-one days old. Should he be circumcised first or redeemed first? He writes that although this is the time set by the Torah for the *Pidyon HaBen*, nevertheless the *brit* should take precedence. The circumcision is the sign that the baby has been entered into the covenant with *Hashem* and without it there is no obligation whatsoever for the *mitzvah* of *Pidyon HaBen*. This is also the ruling of the *Birkei Yosef*[15] and the *Pitchei Teshuvah*.[16]

If he is still ill when the time comes to redeem him so that he still cannot be circumcised, many *acharonim*[17] rule that he is redeemed on time and circumcised later when he recovers from his illness.

INCUBATOR. A male firstborn who is still in an incubator on the thirty-first experiment to solve the problem.

10. וראה עוד טעמים בפרדס יוסף פ' בא יג אות ב ד"ה וביו"ד ואות יד
11. מנחות לו ע"א
12. במדבר ג:מז ראה שם ברש"י
See *Tosafot* to *Menachot* loc. cit. regarding a genetically affected family and the question that was put before King Solomon whether those with two heads should get a double inheritance or not. And see the *Shitah Mekubetset* there for King Solomon's interesting

13. יו"ד סי' קפג
14. ס"ק יב בשם תשובת ר' אליה ן' חיים סי' עט
15. סי' רסב סע' ב
16. כאן ס"ק כג, וראה גם בעקרי הדת סי' לג סע' ח
17. שיורי ברכה סי' רסב סע' ב. שו"ת הב"ח החדשות סי' נ. שו"ת חתם סופר יו"ד ש. שו"ת מהר"י אסאד יו"ד סי' רסו. שו"ת צמח צדק סי' קפה ושו"ת באר שרים ח"א סי' עה. וראה גם בשו"ת חלקת יעקב ח"ג סי' קט

§12 If a baby died before he was thirty days old, and even if he died on the thirtieth day after birth, or he (C)became a

NISHMAT AVRAHAM

day must be redeemed.[18] The *Chelkat Yaakov*[19] rules that a baby born after eight months of gestation who is still in an incubator on the thirty-first day should have his *Pidyon HaBen* on time. However, *Rav Auerbach zt"l* wrote to me that a premature baby who needs an incubator is as yet a possible *nefel*, and, in particular, if the doctors are not yet sure if he will live. He wrote that it would seem to him that it would be better to wait to redeem him later with the blessings. If he was full term he should be redeemed immediately on the thirty-first day. However if he was born after eight months of gestation and certainly after seven months of gestation, it would be better to wait to redeem him until thirty days after he was taken out of the incubator. It would be as if he had only completed his gestational period then.

A firstborn male was born with a serious congenital defect because of which his doctors were certain that he would not live for more than a few days if untreated. However with intensive care treatment he lived for more than thirty days following his birth. Is there a requirement to redeem such a baby, and do the parents have to formally mourn for him, or do we say that since from the beginning he had no real claim to life he is considered a *nefel* even though he lived for more than thirty days? The *Minchat Yitzchak*[20] ruled that the parents of a baby who was born with-

out a stomach and is therefore considered a *treifah*, are obligated to formally mourn for him if he lived more than thirty days. *Rav Eliashiv shlita* also told me that a baby who is born a *treifah* but nevertheless lives for more than thirty days is exempt from *Pidyon HaBen* and his parents have to formally mourn for him. However, *Rav Auerbach zt"l* wrote to me that in his opinion the parents do not formally mourn for him and he is exempt from *Pidyon HaBen*.[21] He told me that such a baby does not have a status of viability for without medical intervention he would have died before he was thirty days old; therefore although he lived for more than thirty days the parents do not formally mourn for him. See also Siman 374A, p. 366 below.

As to a premature baby that died after having lived for thirty days, the *Tzitz Eliezer*[22] and the *Torat HaYoledet*[23] (quoting *Rav Eliashiv shlita*) rule that there is an obligation to mourn him formally, whereas the *Shevet HaLevi*[24] and *Yalkut Yosef*[25] (quoting his father *Rav Ovadiah Yosef shlita*) disagree, ruling that there is no such obligation.

One does not formally mourn a baby who was killed within thirty days of its birth unless one is certain that it was born at full-term.[26]

(C) became a *treifah*. The *Shach*[27] writes that this *halachah* concerns a baby

---

18. שו"ת חלקת יעקב סי' קו. שו"ת ציץ אליעזר ח"ט סי' כח סוס"ק ח. שו"ת באר משה ח"א סי' סד ושו"ת באר שרים ח"א סי' עה
19. שו"ת, ח"ג סי' קט
20. שו"ת, ח"ט סי' קב
21. וראה בתוס' מנחות לו ע"א סוד"ה שומע. יו"ד כאן סע' יב ושו"ך ס"ק טז
22. שו"ת, ח"ט סי' כח ס"ק ח
23. פרק נז הערה ח
24. שו"ת, ח"ג סי' קמג
25. ח"ז סי' ח הערה ז
26. שבת קלו ע"א ורש"י שב ד"ה נפל. תוס' יבמות לו ע"ב ד"ה הא. וראה גם באהע"ז סי' קנו סע' ד. גשר החיים פי"ט סי' ג סע' ד (עמ' קפב)
27. ס"ק טז

SIMAN 305: WHO IS OBLIGATED TO REDEEM AND WHEN / §12

treifah before thirty days had passed from his birth, there is no requirement to redeem him. If the redemption money was already given to the *Cohen*, it must be returned. (*If he dies after thirty days, there is a requirement to redeem him and a blessing is said over the redemption but without the additional blessing of shehecheyanu.*)

--- NISHMAT AVRAHAM ---

who is definitely a *treifah* and, in such a case, even if he lives a long time there is still no requirement to redeem him. We do not say the rule that a *treifah* does not live for twelve months applies to a definite *treifah* (*and therefore no matter how long he lives there is no requirement to redeem him for he is a treifah — author*). But with respect to a possible but not definite *treifah* there is no obligation to redeem him because it is up to the *Cohen* to bring proof that he must be redeemed and that the father therefore owes him money for the redemption. However, if the baby lives for more than twelve months, there is an obligation to redeem him since by living more than twelve months he removes any doubt that he might have been a *treifah*; see Siman 55:48. However the *Yad Avraham*[28] writes that there is no general agreement to this ruling of the *Shach*, since there are *poskim* who rule that a person who is a *treifah* can live (*for more than twelve months — author*). He refers to *Tosafot*[29] and *Hagahot Mordechai*,[30] and says that he has already proven[31] that this is also the *Rambam's* opinion. Therefore, even if the baby lives for more than a year there is still no obligation to redeem him for the *Cohen* still needs to prove that he is not a *treifah*. (See also Siman 29A above regarding the concept of *treifah* in man.)

The *Yavetz*[32] also disagrees with the *Shach's* ruling that a definite *treifah* is exempt from *Pidyon HaBen* even if he lives a long time. For a baby with two heads is a *treifah* and the Gemara (reference 11, see **A** above) discusses the issue of how much the father needs to pay to redeem him. It says that the Torah uses the word skull with regard to redeeming a firstborn and that there is an obligation to redeem him even though he is a *treifah* because such a *treifah* will live. Certainly therefore, a baby who is externally normal but is a *treifah* and nevertheless lives, or who becomes a *treifah* after his birth and lives is not exempt from *Pidyon HaBen*. The Torah only exempts a *treifah* who has no life in him, for he is then like a *nefel* and we consider him to be without a skull to obligate redemption. Rav Auerbach zt"l wrote to me commenting that the words of the *Yavetz* are very surprising since the *Gemara*[33] specifically states (according to *Tosafot*) that a firstborn who becomes *treifah* before he reaches the age of thirty days is exempt from redemption. Therefore we must say that when the *Gemara* (reference 11) concludes that a firstborn with two heads is obligated to be redeemed, it is because he is not a *treifah*. Rav Chaim of Brisk[34] is also said to have said that since he is one person he is not a *treifah* although he has two heads or, as

---

28. הגהות על השו"ע כאן
29. תוס' בשם ר"ת זבחים קטז ע"א ד"ה דילמא
30. הגהות מרדכי ריש פ"ג דחולין בשם תוס' שאנ"ץ
31. בחיבורו על הרמב"ם הל' איסו"ב פ"י הי"א
32. מגדל עוז, ברכות הורי, פלג א ס"ק ג
33. ב"ק יא ע"ב
34. חידושי הגר"ח ז"ל מבריסק על הש"ס. וראה גם ביעק"ץ מגדל עוז ברכות הורי פלג ג ס"ק יח ושו"ת אבני נזר סי' שצט

NISHMAT AVRAHAM

the *Rambam*[35] rules, a person is not considered a *treifah* until the physicians decide that such an injury has no cure and will eventually kill him if he does not die from something else before then.

There are *rishonim*[36] who rule that only a baby who becomes a *treifah* after his birth is exempt from *Pidyon HaBen*; however if he was a *treifah* at birth, he must be redeemed.

The *Minchat Yitzchak*[37] was asked about a firstborn, less than thirty days old, who had a needle inserted into a chamber of his heart as part of his treatment. He had since recovered and the doctors said that this is a daily occurrence in medical practice.[38] Was a *Pidyon HaBen* required? He replied by quoting the *Yavetz* and *Tosafot* (see above), and felt that since this is a very frequent occurrence in the practice of medicine, he should be redeemed after thirty days without a blessing, based on *Tosafot*.[39] I had difficulty in understanding this ruling since *Rabbeinu Tam*, the *Pleiti* and the *Chazon Ish* (quoted above Siman 29A) all rule that the laws of *treifah* do not apply to humans since they are treatable. Why then should the baby not be redeemed with the blessings? *Rav Neuwirth shlita* agreed with this. *Rav Waldenberg shlita* [40] wrote to me ruling that he should be redeemed with the blessings and that the *Yad Shaul*[41] disagrees with the *Shach* (quoted above, reference 27) ruling that a *treifah* requires

redemption if he can live. He quoted the *Tosfot Rid*,[42] one of the early *rishonim*, who writes that a *treifah*, even though he will not survive, is considered a living person regarding everything. He is obligated to have a *brit*, to be redeemed and must perform all the *mitzvot* of the Torah. Rav Auerbach zt"l also told me that, basing himself on the *Rambam*,[43] he rules that the baby is obligated to be redeemed.

A BABY WHO IS A *GOSSES*. Rebbe Akiva Eiger[44] writes that a *gosses* because of illness is required to have a *Pidyon HaBen*, but as to one who is a *gosses* as a result of human action this needs further study, and he refers to the *Rambam*.[45] However *Tosafot*[46] write that a *gosses* is considered to be alive in every respect (and this is also the ruling of the *Rambam*[47]) and their proof is from the *Gemara*[48] which states that if someone cut both his esophagus and windpipe, or the greater part of each, and he gave a sign indicating that a *get* be written and given to his wife, it should be done although there is no better example than this of a *gosses*. This is also true with regard to the laws of *yibum, chalitzah, terumah*, inheritance, bearing witness, etc.[49] Rav Auerbach zt"l wrote to me that it would appear that a *gosses* as a result of human action is in the same category as a *treifah*, but nevertheless he is considered alive in every respect. However one needs to study further the case of a baby who is

---

35. הל' רוצח פ"ב ה"ח
36. שיטה מקובצת ב"ק יא ע"ב בשם המאירי
37. שו"ת, ח"ז סי' צט
38. I am not too sure as to what was done. On the one hand this is not a description of a cardiac catheterization, and if it was, why should this make the baby a *treifah*? If the needle was inserted via the chest wall, piercing the heart wall to enter a chamber, he would certainly be a *treifah* (see Siman 40:1 and 58:1), but surely such a procedure is not a daily occurrence!
39. ב"ק יא ע"ב ד"ה בכור ומנחות לו ע"א ד"ה שומע
40. שו"ת ציץ אליעזר חט"ז ס"י לב
41. על יו"ד כאן
42. על שבת קלו ע"א ד"ה מאי לאו
43. הל' רוצח פ"ב ה"ח
44. חידושיו כאן בשם היש"ש ב"ק פ"א סי' ל
45. הל' רוצח פ"ב ה"ז שכותב היה גוסס בידי אדם, ההורג אותו אין בית דין ממיתין אותו
46. קדושין עח ע"ב ד"ה לא
47. הל' אבל פ"ד ה"ה
48. גיטין ע"ב
49. וראה גם בשו"ת מהרש"ם ח"ה סי' ע

SIMAN 305: WHO IS OBLIGATED TO REDEEM AND WHEN / §23

§23 The baby boy born after any of the following — (1) a baby after eight months gestation whose head emerged after he died, (2) a discharge of a fetal sac filled with blood, water or with different colors, (3) a discharge of something that looks like any one of different creatures, (4) a ⁽ᴰ⁾miscarriage on the fortieth day of gestation — is a firstborn requiring *Pidyon HaBen*. (*As long as the limbs are not formed it does not exempt the baby that is born later from Pidyon HaBen and we depend on this even nowadays.*)

NISHMAT AVRAHAM

about to die because a stone fell on him. Is there a difference if the stone was thrown by someone or if it fell on him as a result of a strong wind?

(D) miscarriage on the fortieth day of gestation. The *Chida*[50] also rules like the *Rama* that if there is no formation of the flesh and skin, the baby boy born afterwards is redeemed with the blessings. This is also the ruling of the *Noda BiYehudah*[51] and *Yabia Omer*.[52] *Rav Auerbach zt"l* wrote to me that within the forty days of gestation that the *Gemara*[53] considers the fetus to be mere water, one cannot talk of formation of the body. The *Chacham Tzvi*,[54] on the other hand, rules that nowadays a miscarriage of a fetal sac after forty days of conception exempts the next baby from *Pidyon HaBen*. However, if the father wishes to act strictly, he should redeem the baby but he should not say the blessing over the redemption or the *shehecheyanu* blessing. The *Chatam Sofer*[55] writes that if one wishes to take the ruling of the *Chacham Tzvi* into consideration, the father says the blessing of the *Pidyon HaBen* without mentioning *Hashem's* Name and the *Cohen* says the *shehecheyanu* blessing, at the same time exempting the father from the obligation to say it. This is also the ruling of the *Divrei Chaim*[56] and *Avnei Nezer*.[57] The *Zecher Simchah*[58] adds that, if possible, it would be even better if the *shehecheyanu* blessing could be said on a new fruit or garment, but there is no need to take trouble over doing this. Although many *acharonim*[59] have ruled that such a baby is completely exempted from *Pidyon HaBen*, and even if the father wishes to act strictly and misuse his money he should redeem his son without the blessings, *Rav Ovadiah Yosef shlita*[60] rules that he should redeem him with the blessings. This is the *minhag* in Jerusalem and the rule is that although wherever there is a matter of doubt a blessing is not said, this does not apply when a *minhag* is involved.

All the above applies only if the discharge was examined. However if it was not examined or if it was found to contain what looks like flesh, one must take into consideration that there was formation of the fetus and everyone would then agree

---

50. שו"ת חיים שאל ח"ב סי' יו
51. שו"ת, תניינא סי' קפח
52. שו"ת, ח"י יו"ד סי' כו
53. יבמות סט ע"ב
54. שו"ת, סי' קד
55. שו"ת, יו"ד סי' רצט, מובא גם בפ"ת ס"ק כט
56. שו"ת, יו"ד סי' קיג
57. שו"ת, יו"ד סי' שצו
58. שו"ת, סי' קמז
59. שו"ת שבות יעקב ח"א סי' פג. וראה גם בשו"ת חכם צבי שם. שו"ת נו"ב שם. שאילת יעב"ץ ח"א סי' מט. פ"ת ס"ק כט
60. לב אברהם ח"א עמ' יב

§24
A firstborn (E)male born by Caesarian section and the following baby *(boy)* born naturally are both exempt from *Pidyon HaBen*. The first is exempt since he was not born naturally and the second because he was preceded by the first.

NISHMAT AVRAHAM

that the next child should be redeemed without the blessing and the money given to the *Cohen* on condition that he return it.[61] The *shehecheyanu* blessing is also not said.[62]

(E) male born by Caesarian section. The *Taz*[63] writes that although the first baby was not born naturally, and the second was, nevertheless since the second son is not a firstborn in terms of the laws of inheritance,[64] he is also not a firstborn with regard to redemption by a *Cohen*. The *Gemara*[65] states that the first son born naturally who is not the firstborn of the family does not have the *halachah* of a firstborn with regard to *Pidyon HaBen*. Rebbe Akiva Eiger[66] comments that this being so, if the first son (born by Caesarian section) is a *nefel*, the second (born naturally) will require *Pidyon HaBen* since he is also the firstborn with regard to inheritance. This is also the ruling of the *Har Tzvi*.[67] Since the *Taz* rules that the second son (born naturally after the first was born by Caesarian section) is exempt from *Pidyon HaBen* because he is not a firstborn with regard to inheritance, if the first son is a *nefel*, the second son is a firstborn for inheritance.[68] Since he was also born naturally, he requires *Pidyon HaBen*. However, the *Minchat Yitzchak*[69] rules that if the son born by Caesarian section was alive at birth and died after a day, the second son born naturally after him is exempt from *Pidyon HaBen*.

DEFINING THE MOMENT OF BIRTH. The *Cheshev HaEphod*[70] discusses the case of a woman with twins whose first child was in the process of a normal delivery and the doctor saw its head in the *prozdor*. However at this stage the second child's leg also appeared and an emergency Caesarian section was necessary to deliver both. Should the first child be considered as having been born naturally and require *Pidyon HaBen* since the doctor saw his head in the *prozdor*? (see above Siman 266C, p. 224).

The *Cheshev HaEphod* quotes the *Sidrei Taharah*[71] who discusses the definition of the moment of birth — when the baby's head leaves the *prozdor*. This moment is a matter of controversy. Does the *prozdor* include the whole of the birth canal and the baby is only considered born when his head emerges into the world? Or is there an (undefined) boundary between the *cervix* and the *vulva* which is the lower boundary of the *prozdor*, and from there downwards, although still within the birth canal, is considered as being outside the *prozdor*? The baby will then be considered born when he passes this boundary, even though his head is still within the birth

---

61. שו״ת חת״ס שם. שו״ת דברי מלכיאל ח״ו סי׳ כ. שו״ת יד הלוי ח״א סי׳ קצב. שו״ת יביע אומר שם
62. שו״ת יד הלוי שם
63. ס״ק כ. וראה בהגהות נמוקי רי״ב
64. דברים כא:טו
65. בכורות מז ע״ב
66. חידושי רעק״א כאן
67. שו״ת, יו״ד סי׳ רמט
68. חו״מ סי׳ רעה סע׳ ד
69. שו״ת ח״ד סי׳ נ
70. שו״ת, ח״ב סי׳ קנ
71. סי׳ קצד ס״ק כו

SIMAN 305: WHO IS OBLIGATED TO REDEEM AND WHEN / §24 — 243

---NISHMAT AVRAHAM---

canal and has not yet emerged outside.

The *Cheshev HaEphod* continues, quoting the author of the *Ginat Veradim*.[72] He rules that the opinion that defines birth as the moment when the baby's head leaves the *cervix*, although still within the birth canal, applies to the laws about the woman becoming *temei'ah* as a result of giving birth and the calculation of the eight days leading to the *brit*. Both these *halachot* are stated together in the Torah;[73] it is only in this context that the Torah defines birth as outside the *prozdor*. However with regard to the *halachot* of a firstborn, the baby is considered born only when his head emerges into the world. However the sages of his generation[74] disagree with the differentiation made by the *Ginat Veradim* and rule that the baby is considered born when his head emerges outside also with regard to the *halachot* of *tumat ledah* and a *brit* on the eighth day. The *Panim Meirot*[75] agrees with them but the *Sidrei Taharah* (reference 71) and *Chelkat Yoav*[76] agree with the *Ginat Veradim*.[77]

The *Cheshev HaEphod* concludes that since the accepted *halachah* is that the baby is only considered born when it has emerged into the outside world (see Siman 266C above) with respect to all the laws of the Torah without exception, the doubt in the case in question has been resolved. Although the doctor saw the head of the first baby within the birth canal, nevertheless since it had not as yet emerged into the world except after Caesarian section, he is defined as having been born by Caesarian section and he is exempt from *Pidyon HaBen*. See also Siman 194E and 262 (**O**), pp. 124 and 202 above.

Rav Auerbach zt"l[78] writes to the author of the *Kenei Bosem*[79] that birth is defined from the moment the baby's head enters the *prozdor* (*that is, leaves the cervix*). However, the accepted *minhag* about circumcising a baby born at the beginning of *Shabbat* on *Shabbat* is to consider him born if his head has emerged into the world. This is because the time it takes for the baby's head to reach the outside world from the time it enters the *prozdor* is short. However, if it is certain that there was a delay at this stage, he should be circumcised on Sunday. However, the *Rav zt"l* writes that he says this only because he feels uneasy to rule against the *poskim* that the *Kene Bosem* quotes who decide otherwise.

Rav Auerbach zt"l, quoting the *Yad Shaul*,[80] wrote to me that a boy born by Caesarian section is nevertheless considered a firstborn with regard to the fast of the firstborn on the eve of *Pesach* (see *Nishmat Avraham*, vol. 1 *Orach Chaim*, Siman 470 §1).

ECTOPIC PREGNANCY. Sometimes the fertilized egg develops within an *ovary*, *Fallopian tube*, or the abdominal cavity instead of the *uterus*. Such a fetus obviously cannot be viable and must be aborted either medically (it is killed and allowed to become absorbed) or surgically (through the abdominal wall) as soon as the diagnosis is made since it will be dangerous for the mother to continue the pregnancy. The firstborn son after such a pregnancy will require *Pidyon HaBen*.[81] *Rav Neuwirth shlita* also rules similarly.

---

72. קונטרס שמודפס בסוף ספר דרכי נועם לאביו
73. ויקרא יב:ב-ג
74. המה מהר"ם חביב ומהר"י הלוי
75. שו"ת, ח"א סי' ז
76. שו"ת, יו"ד סי' כו
77. וראה גם בפ"ת יו"ד סי' רסב ס"ק ו וסי' רסו ס"ק ח
78. מנחת שלמה תנינא סי' עח
79. שו"ת קנה בשם ח"ב סי' צד
80. על השו"ע כאן
81. שו"ת שבט הלוי ח"ח סי' רלט
ושו"ת דובב מישרים ח"ב סי' לב

―――――― NISHMAT AVRAHAM ――――――

FORCEPS DELIVERY. The *Chelkat Yoav*[82] rules that a baby born by forceps delivery is exempt from *Pidyon HaBen* since the forceps intervene between him and the *uterus*. The *Chelkat Yaakov*[83] rules that he should be redeemed but without the blessings. The *Avnei Nezer*[84] at first ruled that he should be redeemed but later[85] ruled that this should be without the blessings. However these rulings were applicable only in the days when "high forceps delivery" was practiced, the forceps being introduced high up in the *prozdor*. Nowadays, the forceps are only introduced low down in the *prozdor* so that the problem of their being a *chatzizah* between the baby's head and the *uterus* or even the *cervix* does not arise. Therefore such a firstborn requires *Pidyon HaBen*.[86] A child delivered by vacuum also requires *Pidyon HaBen*.

82. שו"ת, סי' כו
83. שו"ת, ח"א סי' מא
84. שו"ת, יו"ד סי' שצא ו-שצג
85. שו"ת, שם סי' שצד
86. שו"ת צפנת פענח סי' ז. מהר"ש ענגיל ח"ד סי' ט. שו"ת לבושי מרדכי ח"ב יו"ד סי' קל. שו"ת שרידי אש ח"ב סי' קיד. שו"ת, דובב מישרים ח"ב סי' לב. זוכר הברית סי' כח ס"ק ה. שו"ת קנה בושם סי' קיז. וראה בשו"ת אג"מ יו"ד ח"ג סי' צו ס"ק ז

CHAPTER 30
The Laws of Challah

SIMAN 322
THE DIFFERENCE BETWEEN *CHALLAH* SET ASIDE IN *ERETZ YISRAEL* AND THE *CHALLAH* SET ASIDE IN THE DIASPORA

§3 There is a Rabbinic obligation to set aside (A)*challah* in the Diaspora so that the Torah commandment to set aside *challah* should not be forgotten.

SIMAN 328
THE LAWS CONCERNING WHO SHOULD SET ASIDE *CHALLAH* AND THE BLESSING BEFORE DOING SO

§2 (A)A blind person may set aside *challah*.

NISHMAT AVRAHAM

SIMAN 322

(A) *challah* in the Diaspora. There is a Torah obligation[1] to set aside a portion of dough belonging to a Jew,[2] and give it to a *Cohen*. This Torah law is applicable to *Eretz Yisrael* only and only when all[3] of Israel are living there. Even in *Eretz Yisrael*, setting aside *challah* is either a Rabbinic or Torah obligation depending on the amount of dough kneaded. It must be done by someone who is ritually clean, and the dough must also be ritually clean. There is then an obligation to give the dough which has been set aside, the *challah*, to a *Cohen* who is also ritually clean, and he can bake and eat it as he wishes. Nowadays the obligation to set aside *challah* is Rabbinic only.[4] Also, since we are all ritually unclean (*tumat met*), the *challah* is burned. If one forgot to set aside *challah* or if he bought bread or cookies from which *challah* had not been set aside, he must set aside *challah* from the baked product.[5] Such a situation may arise with a hospitalized patient who is unsure whether *challah* has been taken from the otherwise kosher bread or cookies that he receives with his meals. The subject will be discussed further in Siman 331G.

SIMAN 328

(A) A blind person. The *Shach*[1] writes that although a blind person may not set aside *terumah* if it can be avoided

---

1. במדבר טו:יז. שו"ע כאן סע' א
2. שו"ע סי' של סע' א
3. כך לשון הרמב"ם הל' תרומות פ"א הכ"ו והל' חלה פ"ה ה"ה. השו"ע יו"ד סי' שכב סע' ב וסי' שלא סע' ב. וכ"כ החינוך מצוה רפד והמנ"ח אות ו(כא) שם. אך ע"ע בחינוך מצוה שפה וערוה"ש סי' יו"ד סי' שכב סע' ט שכתבו כולם דהיינו רובם. וראה בחידושי ר' חיים הל' שמיטה פי"ב הט"ז וקהלות יעקב סי' כו ד"ה אמנם
4. סע' ב
5. סי' שכו סע' ה

1. ס"ק ד

NISHMAT AVRAHAM

(Siman 331 §32), this is because he might inadvertently set aside the poor quality fruit as *terumah* instead of the good fruit. With *challah*, however, there is no difference between the dough that he sets aside and that which remains; the intention to set aside the poorer quality and keep the better does not apply. *Rav Auerbach zt"l* wrote to me that nowadays it is permissible to set aside the poor quality fruit as *terumah* since both *terumah* and *challah* are destroyed and not given to a *Cohen* (*and a blind person may therefore set aside terumah — author*).

CHAPTER 31
The Laws of Terumot and Ma'asrot

SIMAN 331
THE LAWS CONCERNING *TERUMOT* AND *MA'ASROT*, WHERE AND HOW THE *COHEN* RECEIVES THEM AND WHETHER THEY ARE OF TORAH OR RABBINIC ORIGIN

§1 The laws of *terumot* and *ma'asrot* are of Torah origin (A)in *Eretz Yisrael* only, both during and after the times of the Temple. The prophets instituted that it should be obligated even in Bavel since it is close to *Eretz Yisrael* and most Jews travel to and from there. The early Sages ex-

--- NISHMAT AVRAHAM ---

SIMAN 331

INTRODUCTION. All produce of *Eretz Yisrael* is *tevel* and must be tithed before it can be eaten. Nowadays the obligation to set aside tithes is Rabbinic.[1] The first tithe to be set aside is *terumah gedolah* (the great *terumah*) and for this even a tiny amount of the produce fulfills the obligation.[2] Ten percent of the remainder is then set aside as *ma'aser rishon* (the first *ma'aser*) and belongs to the *Levi*.[3] He, in turn, must give a tenth of this *ma'aser rishon* to a *Cohen* (*terumat ma'aser*).[4] A further ten percent of the remainder is then set aside as *ma'aser sheni* (the second *ma'aser*).[5] *Ma'aser sheni* must be brought to, and eaten in, Jerusalem and eaten by its owners (when the Temple stood).[6] However if they are at a distance from Jerusalem, they redeem the *ma'aser sheni* with coinage, take the coins to Jerusalem and use them to buy foodstuffs to be eaten there. The *ma'aser sheni* which has been redeemed may be eaten locally (by anyone). During the third, sixth and seventh years of the seven-year cycle, *ma'aser ani* (*ma'aser* for the poor) is set aside instead of *ma'aser sheni*.[7] The remaining produce is no longer *tevel* and may be eaten by anyone.

(A) in *Eretz Yisrael* only. The *Shemirat Shabbat KeHilchatah* [8] writes that medications made from produce of *Eretz Yisrael* are exempt from *terumot* and *ma'asrot* if they have a bitter taste.[9] However, if they are humanly edible, that is, they can be eaten or drunk and not only swallowed, *terumot* and *ma'asrot* must be set aside from them.[10]

1. כאן סע׳ ב
2. סע׳ יט
3. שם
4. סע׳ כ
5. סע׳ יט
6. סע׳ קלב
7. סע׳ יט
8. פ״מ סע׳ פח
9. ראה חזו״א דמאי סי׳ טו ס״ק א, דטבל שנפסל מאכילת אדם בטל מיניה שם טבל
10. ראה באור שמח פ״ה מהל׳ יסוה״ת סוה״ח

panded this obligation to include Egypt and Transjordan since they border on *Eretz Yisrael*. One who owns fields in Syria is Rabbinically required to give *terumot* and *ma'asrot*. Jews in the rest of the world are exempt.

§19 During the (B)*Shemittah* year everything is considered ownerless and there is therefore no requirement to set aside tithes.

§31 If one (C)sets aside tithes without the owner's permission or picks fruit from a friend's orchard without his permission in order to take them and set aside tithes, they are considered as being tithed provided that the owner said to him afterwards, "Take from the better fruit," and there is better fruit in the orchard. If there was no better fruit, his action is null and void. If the owner picked some more fruit and added it to that which he had already picked, all the fruit picked is considered tithed.

NISHMAT AVRAHAM

(B) *Shemittah* **year.** Every seventh year in *Eretz Yisrael* is a *shemittah* year, when the land must lie fallow. Fruit has a special holiness and may only be eaten and not wasted or used for purposes other than eating. Vegetables may not be eaten.

The *Rambam*[11] writes that one may not use *shemittah* produce to wash with nor may medications be made from them. Rav Neuwirth shlita[12] writes that medications may not be made from *shemittah* produce that is humanly edible. Thus corn (maize) may not be used to make tablets; since it is only for the use of the sick, it is therefore considered as if *shemittah* produce is being destroyed rather than eaten.

(C) sets aside tithes without the owner's permission. The *Gemara*[13] speaks about a *seriously ill* patient who must eat immediately to save his life but only forbidden foods are available. The *Gemara* states that where there is a choice between two degrees of forbidden foods, he is given the lesser of the two (see *Nishmat Avraham*, vol. 1 *Orach Chaim*, Siman 328D). However, when the only two foods available are *terumah* or *tevel*, and if tithes were to be set aside from the *tevel* an insufficient amount of tithed food would be left to save his life, there is a difference of opinion as to whether he should be given the *terumah* or the *tevel* to eat. The *Chacham Tzvi*, quoted by the *Yavetz*[14] and the *Chatam Sofer*,[15] asks why the *Gemara* does not suggest that *terumah* be set aside from the *tevel* and then be mixed back into it. Although it is forbidden to mix a permissible and a forbidden food in order to nullify the forbidden food

---

11. הל' שמיטה ויובל פ"ה ה"י

12. קיצור דיני שמיטת קרקעות, תשמ"ו סע' נט

13. יומא פג ע"א

14. מובא בשאילת יעב"ץ ח"א סי' קלה

15. שו"ת, יו"ד סי' שיט

NISHMAT AVRAHAM

and thus be able to eat the mixture, this is only by Rabbinic law.[16] Furthermore, by Torah law it is sufficient that the quantity of tithed product just be greater than the quantity of *terumah* in order to nullify it, and the ratio of one hundred to one is not required. The *Yavetz* thought that perhaps the *Gemara* considers that when the *terumah* is put back into where it came from, the whole reverts to its original state of *tevel* (see below for *Rav Auerbach zt"l's* comment). He writes that the question of the *Chacham Tzvi* is a profound one, for since the forbidden food, be it *terumah* or *tevel*, is itself permitted to save the patient's life, surely mixing *terumah* with tithed food is a lesser degree of *issur* than eating either *terumah* or *tevel*.

The *Chatam Sofer* notes that even if, as the *Parashat Derachim*[17] would have it, the *Gemara* is discussing a situation where the owners are not present and therefore the tithes cannot be set aside, this itself is a most surprising thought. For if the owners are not in town, how can the patient eat something that does not belong to him? Therefore we must conclude that the patient is permitted to save himself with another's property, provided that he pays for it later (see Siman 157d(1) above). Thus *Hashem* has given him this food to eat and he has the status of an owner. If so, he should set aside tithes from it, for how can we say that he may eat it but may not set aside tithes from it?[18]

However, the *Igrot Moshe*[19] writes that, on the contrary, it is the *Chatam Sofer's* question that is surprising since, although he may eat it to save his life, the food certainly does not become his. It is still technically theft and a thief cannot set aside tithes, even though he is permitted to steal the food and eat it to save his life. Ownership of the fruit, on the other hand, cannot be transferred to him without the owner's consent, and his *pikuach nefesh* has no connection with his acquiring the fruit to become the rightful owner. Therefore he cannot set aside tithes even though he may eat it.

The *Parashat Derachim*, quoted above, also asks why we should not transgress a Rabbinic law (nullify a forbidden food by mixing it with a larger quantity of a similar but permissible food) rather than give the patient food which carries a death penalty from Heaven. For we ritually slaughter an animal (if previously slaughtered meat is not available) for a *seriously ill patient* on *Shabbat*, if he needs to eat meat to save his life, rather than give him *neveilah* to eat.[20] He answers that we have to consider which of two *issurim* is the less severe and give him that to eat. However in the question under discussion, the *issur* of nullifying a forbidden food is not being done for the sake of the patient, since it makes no difference to him if we nullify the forbidden food or not. True we save him from a more serious *issur*, but since this is unnecessary to save his life it remains forbidden. Thus it is better for the patient to eat a forbidden food which, although it is a more serious transgression, is necessary to save his life, rather than that we transgress a lesser *issur* which has no impact on saving his life. However, the *Avnei Miluim*[21] relates to the *Parashat Derachim* and writes that since we are discussing a Rabbinic prohibition, it is better for us to transgress a Rabbinic prohibition rather than that the patient trangress a Torah one. As

---

See *Nishmat Avraham*, vol. 1 *Orach Chaim*, Siman 328 (14A), p. 200.

16. ראה להלן מה שכתבתי בשם האבני מילואים
17. בפרשת דרכים, דרך החיים דרוש תשעה עשר
18. עיין פסחים כט ע"א תוסד"ה בדין הוא
19. שו"ת, יו"ד ח"א סי' ריד
21. שו"ת, סי' יח

§32 (D)A deaf or dumb person, one who is naked or drunk and (E)a blind person should not set aside tithes, but if they did so the fruit is nevertheless tithed. Nowadays since the *terumah* is *temei'ah* and therefore burned, a drunk or

─────────── NISHMAT AVRAHAM ───────────

to the question of setting aside *terumah* and then mixing it again with the fruit from which it had been set aside, the *Avnei Miluim* says that even according to the opinion that nullifying an *issur* is only Rabbinically forbidden, that may be so in general. However in this case it is a Torah prohibition. For the Torah[22] commands us to safeguard *terumah* from becoming destroyed. And, when one nullifies *terumah* by mixing it with permissible food, the *terumah* loses its special status and becomes permissible to all Jews (and not only to *Cohanim*). Thus he has with his own hands destroyed the *terumah*, for it now no longer exists, and the Torah commands us to guard it from loss.

The *Chazon Ish*[23] suggests an answer to the question raised by the *Chacham Tzvi* and the *Parashat Derachim*. If the fruit could not be grated or cut thinly, for by doing so some of the fruit would be lost and then there would not be enough to save the patient's life, nothing would be gained by nullifying the *terumah*. Or, if the patient does not have the strength to grate or cut it — and this must be done before he can remix the *terumah* which has been set aside — in such an instance one cannot speak of nullifying the *terumah*. If, however, he can set aside the *terumah* and then nullify it as above, he should do so. He then must pay a *Cohen* its worth, since the *terumah* belongs to him and the patient surely does not wish to steal from him.

The *Pri Megadim*[24] writes matter of factly that if someone has only a *kezayit* of *matzah* on *seder* night, from which *challah* has not been taken, he should set aside *challah* and then nullify it by mixing it back with the larger portion of *matzah* from which he took it. (*One must presume that the matzah was first crushed before remixing so that the challah cannot be recognized after it was put back — author.*) By doing this, he fulfills his Torah obligation to eat a *kezayit matzah* on *seder* night. If he eats the *matzah* while it is still *tevel* he has not fulfilled the *mitzvah*, even if it is only *tevel* Rabbinically.

Rav Auerbach zt"l wrote to me that he had already wondered why it was not possible to first divide the fruit into two lots, take tithes separately from each and then put the tithes taken from lot A into lot B and those from lot B into lot A. In that way the tithes are not put back to where they came from and each mixture will certainly not revert to its original untithed state. The *Rav zt"l* deals extensively with the subject.[25]

(D) A deaf or dumb person. The blessing over the setting aside of tithes, like all blessings, must be said loud enough to be able to be heard by the person saying it. Since a deaf or dumb person cannot do so, he should not set aside tithes.[26]

(E) a blind person. Since he cannot specifically set aside the best fruit for tithes, he also should not set aside tithes.[27]

───────────

22. במדבר יח:ח. בכורות לד ע"א. וראה ברש"י סוכה לה ע"ב ד"ה שמכשירה

23. דמאי סי' טו ס"ק י

24. או"ח סי' תס מ"ז ס"ק א

25. מנחת שלמה ח"א סי' ס

26. ט"ז ס"ק יז וש"ך ס"ק סא

27. שם

blind person may set aside *terumah* but cannot set aside the (F)*ma'aser* that is for the *Levi*.

§111 (G)Once *Shabbat* sets in fruit is forbidden to be eaten without being tithed, even after *Shabbat*.

──────── NISHMAT AVRAHAM ────────

(F) *ma'aser* that is for the *Levi*. An exact tenth of the produce remaining after the *terumah* has been set aside must be set aside for a *Levi*. Since the drunk and the blind cannot weigh or otherwise set aside an exact tenth, they should not set aside *ma'aser*.[28]

(G) Once *Shabbat* sets in. The following discussion pertains to both the hospitalized patient and to hospital personnel who will be eating food provided by the hospital.

Neither tithes (*terumot* and *ma'asrot*)[29] nor *challah*[30] may be set aside on *Shabbat* or *Yom Tov*. Therefore a hospitalized patient in *Eretz Yisrael* (or in the Diaspora who is given produce of *Eretz Yisrael* to eat), who usually sets aside tithes or *challah* from whatever he eats, should recite a "stipulation" (see later) before *Shabbat* or *Yom Tov*. He may then set them aside on *Shabbat* and *Yom Tov* before eating.[31] Although this "stipulation" is valid only if the fruit is his,[32] Rav Auerbach *zt"l*[33] rules that since most products have already been tithed,[34] and since even with regard to *orlah* which is prohibited by the Torah[35] we say that the fruit before us is from the major part of the total produce which is not *orlah*, certainly with regard to *tevel* which is today of Rabbinic force only, he may rely on the fruit being from the major part of the total produce which has been tithed. And, since the *Yerushalmi*[36] only forbids fruit which is definitely *tevel*, it would appear that one can rule leniently when there is a doubt if the fruit is indeed *tevel*.[37]

THE "STIPULATION." A hospitalized patient may not be able to separate tithes or *challah* on *Shabbat* or *Yom Tov* eve, for he may only receive his food after *Shabbat* or *Yom Tov* has started. Or, even if he receives it earlier, he may be apprehensive that if he cuts the fruit to set aside tithes it may spoil. If he is given two loaves for the *Shabbat* or *Yom Tov* meal he may not wish to set aside *challah* from them, for he wants them to remain whole for *lechem mishneh*. In all of these situations he should make a "stipulation" before *Shabbat* or *Yom Tov* starts to enable him to tithe the fruit and set aside *challah* from the bread on *Shabbat* and *Yom Tov*.

The wording of the "stipulation" is as follows:[38] Whatever there is, over and above the one percent and more that I intend to set aside tomorrow to permit the fruit to be eaten, will be the great *terumah*. This will be on its north side, each piece of fruit for its kind. The remaining one percent and another nine similar portions on the north of the fruit (or bread or cake), each piece of fruit for its kind, will be the *first ma'aser*. The one percent that I designated will be *terumat ma'aser*, each

---

28. ביה"ט ס"ק לא
29. או"ח סי' שלט סע' ד וסי' תקכד סע' א
30. או"ח סי' שלט סע' מ"ב ס"ק כו וסי' תקו סע' ג ומ"ב ס"ק כ-כא
31. ראה חזו"א הל' דמאי סי' ט ס"ק יג בתקנה השלישית
32. חזו"א שם ס"ק יג ו-יט
33. שמירת שבת כהלכתה פי"א הערה צו
34. דומיא דדמאי, ראה ברמב"ם הל' מעשר פ"ט ה"ז
35. יו"ד סי' רצד סע' יז
36. דמאי פ"ז ה"א
37. כל זה בשמירת שבת כהלכתה פי"א הערה צו וראה שם עוד פרטים בדיון
38. שמירת שבת כהלכתה שם סע' כב

piece of fruit for its kind. (Whatever I will later set aside as *challah* will be *challah*.) The *second ma'aser* will be on the south side, each piece of fruit for its kind, and will be redeemed, together with another fifth, by the coin that I have set aside for this purpose. (During the third and sixth years of the seven-year cycle, instead of saying the "*second ma'aser,*" he says "and the *ma'aser* for the poor will be on the south side, each for its own kind of fruit.") On *Shabbat*, before eating he sets aside over one percent of each type of fruit etc. (see above Introduction) and then repeats what he said before *Shabbat,* changing the opening sentence to say: "Whatever there is, over and above the one percent and more that I have set aside now."

If he so wishes, he may use a shortened version as follows: Whatever I may set aside on *Shabbat* (or *Yom Tov*) will be *terumot, ma'asrot* (or *challah*), the redemption being according to the Law.[39] He should add that his intention is that whatever will be set aside later as tithes or *challah* will take effect then at the time he sets them aside.[40] He repeats this on *Shabbat* after setting aside the tithes as above.

There are other ways of carrying out this "stipulation."[41]

The tithes which have been set aside are *muktzeh* and may not be moved.[42] As to *challah*, see below.

If he received only two whole loaves, the *Shemirat Shabbat KeHilchatah*[43] writes that before making the blessing of *hamotzi*, he should decide from which part of a loaf he will set aside the *challah* (the opposite end from where he intends to cut after the blessing of *hamotzi*). He then says the above formula followed by the blessing *hamotzi* and then eats a little of the bread (see below — Setting Aside of *Challah*). He then sets aside the *challah* together with a small part of the remaining bread (so that it is not *muktzeh*). However Rav Auerbach *zt"l* rules that it is not enough to take a small part of the remaining bread; he must take a large piece in addition to the *challah,* for otherwise, according to the *Yerushalmi*,[44] he may not move the *challah* that he has set aside. The *Shemirat Shabbat KeHilchatah* continues that it would be better if he sets aside the *challah* before he says the blessing *hamotzi* so as not to have a break between the blessing of *hamotzi* and eating. Even if he does this the loaf is still considered a complete loaf as far as *lechem mishneh* is concerned.[45]

If the "stipulation" was not made before *Shabbat* or *Yom Tov* started, it is preferable, even for a *non-seriously ill* patient, to set aside tithes or *challah* from the food he receives rather than eat untithed, or possibly untithed, food.[46]

SETTING ASIDE OF *CHALLAH*. Bread and cookies made in *Eretz Yisrael* (that are made from dough kneaded there) may not be eaten until *challah* has first been set aside. Therefore a "stipulation" must be made before *Shabbat* or *Yom Tov* so that they may be eaten on *Shabbat* or *Yom Tov*. On the other hand, if the dough was kneaded in the Diaspora, he may eat the bread (or cookies) and leave a piece from which he later separates out *challah*.[47] The *Rama*[48] rules that he must leave a piece larger than necessary for *challah* from which he later (after *Shabbat* or *Yom Tov*) sets aside *challah* and he should not leave a piece which will

---

39. שם סע' כג
40. שם סע' יח
41. שם סע' כב
42. כתב לי מו"ר הגרי"י נויבירט שליט"א
43. שמירת שבת כהלכתה פי"א הערה עב
44. דמאי פ"ז ה"א
45. ראה גם בשערי תשובה סי' רעד ס"ק א
46. כתב לי מו"ר הגרי"י נויבירט שליט"א
47. סי' שכג סע' א
48. שם

NISHMAT AVRAHAM

all be *challah*. Thus a patient or a hospital worker who receives his bread for his *Shabbat* or *Yom Tov* meal after nightfall, sets aside a piece larger than necessary for *challah* and, after *Shabbat* or *Yom Tov*, sets aside *challah* from that piece.[49] *Rav Neuwirth shlita* told me that he should make sure that this piece of bread is not cleared away to be thrown in the garbage since he has not yet set aside *challah* from it. If it is thrown away before he sets aside *challah* after *Shabbat*, he will have retroactively eaten *tevel*.

Fruits grown and packed in Israel must be tithed even in the Diaspora. One may not eat from them and then set aside tithes after *Shabbat* or *Yom Tov*. He should therefore be careful to either tithe them before *Shabbat* (or *Yom Tov*) or tithe them before eating on *Shabbat* (or *Yom Tov*) having made the "stipulation" the previous afternoon.[50]

---

49. או"ח סי' רסא מ"ב ס"ק ד. וראה בשמירת שבת כהלכתה פל"א סע' מא

50. שמירת שבת כהלכתה שם

CHAPTER 32

The Laws of Bikur Cholim, Medicine, the Dying Patient and the Gosses

SIMAN 335
WHEN SHOULD ONE VISIT A SICK PERSON; WHO SHOULD BE VISITED; HOW DOES ONE PRAY FOR HIM

§1 It is (A)a *mitzvah* to (B)visit the sick. Family and friends

---NISHMAT AVRAHAM---

SIMAN 335

(A) a *mitzvah*. This is part of the *mitzvah* of loving-kindness. The *Gemara*[1] explains the verse:[2] "And you shall make known to them the path in which they should go," as follows: "The path," this is loving-kindness; "they should go," this is to visit the sick. The Sage asked: But *bikur cholim* is part of the *mitzvah* of loving-kindness? The *Gemara* answers that the separate interpretation was necessary to teach us the special *mitzvah* of visiting a patient who is his own age.[3] For the Sage has said that although when one visits a patient who is his own age he will take away one-sixtieth of his illness (*that is, that percentage of the illness will be transferred to the visitor* — author), nevertheless he should still visit him.

The *Tur* and *Beit Yosef* write that when someone falls ill it is a *mitzvah* for everyone to visit him since we find that *Hashem* visits the sick, as *Chazal*[4] have taught us. Rav Chama bar Chanina says: What does the verse:[5] "You shall follow *Hashem*," teach us? That one should follow the virtues and the ways of *Hashem*. Just as He visits the sick as the verse[6] says: "And *Hashem* appeared to him" (to our forefather Avraham after his circumcision), so should you visit the sick.

It is a great *mitzvah* to visit the sick, for by doing so he will pray for mercy on his behalf and this is as if he has given him a new lease on life. Besides, by seeing the patient he inquires into his needs and if he requires anything he will try and supply it for him. He also makes sure that his room is kept clean.[7] The *Beit Yosef*, quoting the *Ramban*, writes that therefore if he visits a patient and does not pray for mercy on his behalf, he has not fulfilled the *mitzvah*. But the *Maharsha*[8] explains that when the *Gemara* (above) deduces the *mitzvah* of visiting the sick from the verse "they should go" it teaches us that merely by going to visit him one does a *mitzvah* even without any further action.

---

1. ב"מ ל ע"ב
2. שמות יח:כ
3. בן גילו - כך פירש רש"י בנדרים לט ע"ב. והרא"ש והר"ן שם פירשו, בן מזלו
4. סוטה יד ע"א
5. דברים יג:ה
6. בראשית יח:א
7. נדרים מ ע"א
8. ב"מ ל ע"ב

SIMAN 335: VISITING THE SICK / §1

NISHMAT AVRAHAM

This would seem to be the point of the *Gemara's* concluding remark that the visitor who is of an age with the patient takes away one-sixtieth of his illness by the very act of visiting him (only).

Rav Moshe Feinstein zt"l[9] deduces from the fact that the Torah[10] says: "And Hashem appeared to him," without describing any prophetic vision during the visit, that *Chazal*[11] learned that *Hashem's* sole purpose was to visit our forefather Abraham when he was ill. From this we can learn that one is obligated to fulfill the *mitzvah* of *bikur cholim* even without the two reasons (mentioned above) — to see to his needs and to pray for him. For *Hashem* has no need to visit the sick to cure; He could cure without causing His Presence to rest on our forefather Abraham's tent. This teaches us that although there are reasons for fulfilling this *mitzvah*, nevertheless the obligation to fulfill it is independent of any reason. The reasons may explain the *mitzvah*, but the *mitzvah* must be fulfilled even when these reasons are not present, because *Hashem* has commanded us to do so. Therefore a person cannot exempt himself from this *mitzvah* with the excuse that the patient does not need his services nor his prayers, since he can pray for himself. *Rav Feinstein zt"l* surmises that perhaps this was why no one visited Rebbe Akiva's disciple (see below); they thought that there was someone (the innkeeper) who would care for him and they prayed for him without going to see him. Even Rebbe Akiva did not visit him because he thought that there was no need to do so. But since there is an obligation to visit the sick in any case, he visited the patient and discovered that there was indeed a need to help him.

The *Perishah*[12] deduces from the language of the *Tur* (above) that the visitor is not himself obligated to clean the sick room but that he must see that the patient's family will do so. A proof for this ruling can be brought from the *She'iltot's*[13] version of the story which is slightly different from that related in the *Gemara*.[14] One of Rebbe Akiva's disciples was ill and dying and Rebbe Akiva came to visit him at the inn where he was staying. When the innkeeper saw this he thought that the patient must be someone important. He immediately boiled water and started to care for him. The next time Rebbe Akiva visited him, he saw that he was recovering. He immediately entered the hall of study and proclaimed that if one does not visit the sick it is as if he has caused his death. The *Gemara's* version is that Rebbe Akiva visited him and because he cleaned and washed the room himself, the patient recovered. The *She'elat Shalom*[15] comments that the *She'iltot* presented the story slightly differently to teach us that it wasn't Rebbe Akiva himself who cleaned and washed the room but the innkeeper.

The *Amora* Reish Lakish asks rhetorically:[16] Where do we find a hint in the Torah for the *mitzvah* of *bikur cholim*? He answers: For it says:[17] "If these (Korach and his followers) die the death of all men and the destiny of all men is visited upon them." How does this verse hint at *bikur cholim*? Rava explained that "die the death of all men" refers to the sick who are in bed and people visit them. The *Maharatz Chayot*[18] comments that the

---

9. דרש משה ריש פ' וירא
10. בראשית יח:א
11. נדרים מ ע"א
12. כאן ס"ק ד
13. פ' אחרי, שאילתא צג
14. נדרים מ ע"א
15. שם ס"ק קיג
16. נדרים לט ע"ב
17. במדבר טז:כט
18. נדרים שם

NISHMAT AVRAHAM

Rambam[19] writes that although Reish Lakish used the term "hint" it does not mean that the *mitzvah* is not really of Torah force, but only Rabbinic. In fact, writes the *Maharatz Chayot*, *bikur cholim* is a Torah *mitzvah*, but the term "hint" was used because it is a *Halachah* that was handed down by *Hashem* to Moshe Rabbeinu on Mount Sinai and not written specifically in the Torah. This is similar to what the *Gemara* asks: Where is there a hint for the obligation to mark graves,[20] and where is there a hint that the *Sanhedrin* was obligated to have two separate graveyards, one for those executed for grave sins and one for those executed for lesser sins?[21] *Rashi* comments that the basis of these rulings is *Halachah* handed down to Moshe Rabbeinu at Sinai; nevertheless, the *Gemara* couches its questions in terms of a "hint" only.

The *Bahag*[22] counts the *mitzvah* of *bikur cholim* as a *mitzvah* of Torah force. *Rav Chaim Palaggi*[23] writes that this is also the ruling of *Rabbeinu Yonah* and of the *Ritva*, who disagree with the opinion of the *Rambam* that this is a Rabbinic *mitzvah*. The *Sdei Chemed*[24] comments that *Rav Palaggi* did not reveal to us where he saw this *Rabbeinu Yonah* and *Ritva* but perhaps he was referring to *Rabbeinu Yonah's* commentary on the *Gemara*[25] where he writes that consoling the bereaved is a Torah law since it is included in the Torah *mitzvah* of practicing loving-kindness, as the *Gemara*[26] says: "The path," this is loving-kindness.

Since the *Gemara* also deduces the *mitzvah* of *bikur cholim* from the same verse, it would appear that, in his opinion, this *mitzvah* is also a Torah law. This is also what the *Machazeh Avraham* Siman 14 writes referring to the same *Rabbeinu Yonah* and pointing out that the *Gemara* only uses the term "hint" because the *mitzvah* is not specifically stated in the Torah. However the *Sdei Chemed* concludes that it might be that *Rabbeinu Yonah's* intention was only to point out that there is indeed a hint to this *mitzvah* in the Torah, but in effect it is a Rabbinic *mitzvah*.

The *Ran*[27] writes that the *Ramban's*[28] opinion is that *bikur cholim* and *nichum aveilim* are Torah obligations and that this is also the opinion of *Rabbeinu Yonah*.

The *Sh'lah*[29] also writes that *bikur cholim* is a Torah obligation. He quotes the *Gemara*[30] as saying Reish Lakish asks: How do we know that *bikur cholim* is a Torah obligation; his version differs from the version we have which states: Where do we find a hint in the Torah.

However, the *Rambam*[31] and *Meiri*[32] both rule that *bikur cholim* is a Rabbinic obligation.

See also the *Shoel U'Meshiv*[33] and the *Mishnah Berurah*.[34]

(B) visit the sick. The *Sh'lah*[35] writes that *bikur cholim* involves using his body, his soul and his money in the performance of the *mitzvah*: with his body — he runs to fulfill all the needs of the patient, to bring him his medication and whatever else he

---

19. ספר המצות שורש ב
20. מו"ק ה ע"א
21. סנהדרין מו ע"א
22. מצות עשה לו
23. ספר חקקי לב ח"ב סי' יז ד"ה עוד
24. מערכת הבי"ת סי' קטז
25. ברכות פ"ג יא ע"א בדפי הרי"ף
26. ב"מ ל ע"ב
27. הגהות ציוני הר"ן על הרמב"ם הל' אבל פי"ד ה"א
28. השגותיו על ספר המצות, שורש השלישי תשובה ג
29. ח"ב מסכת פסחים עמ' כד
30. נדרים לט ע"ב
31. הל' אבל פי"ד ה"א
32. נדרים לט ע"ב
33. שו"ת תליתאה ח"א סי' רמ"ד
34. סי' עב סע' ד ביה"ל ד"ה ביים
35. ח"ב מסכת פסחים עמ' כד

SIMAN 335: VISITING THE SICK / §2

should visit him immediately, and (C)acquaintances after three days. If the illness is sudden, all should visit him immediately.

§2 (D)Even an eminent person should visit one of lesser eminence, even many times a day and even if he is of

---
NISHMAT AVRAHAM
---

needs; with his soul — he pours his soul out in supplication, praying to *Hashem* to send the patient a complete recovery from his illness; with his money — to make sure that the patient has enough money for his needs, for the needs of a patient are many.

The *mitzvah* of *bikur cholim* applies also to a *non-seriously ill* patient. The *Maharil*[36] writes that every illness is grave and he quotes a *Yerushalmi*[37] that in every illness there is a possibility of danger. The *Rama*[38] rules that there is an obligation to visit a patient with any illness.

(C) acquaintances after three days. The *Bach*[39] explains that the reason one should wait is so that the person should not be marked as being ill, thus causing him bad luck, as the *Gemara*[40] says that when Rava took ill he asked that no one be told on the first day. However this does not apply to family and friends who visit him regularly anyway. This is why if the illness is sudden all may visit him immediately.

Rav Waldenberg shlita[41] quotes the *Rambam*,[42] *Ramban*[43] and *Shevet Yehudah* that the intention is not that acquaintances visit after three full days have passed, but that they may visit from the beginning of the third day, as long as they do not visit during the first two days.

(D) Even an eminent person.[44] The *Rosh*[45] writes that a person should visit a sick person even if he does not speak to him at all, for example, if he found him asleep. The patient will nevertheless be pleased when he is later told that he was visited by him and it will raise his spirits.

The *Sefer Chassidim* writes that when there are two patients, one rich and one poor, and the former has many visitors, go and visit the poor patient even if the rich one is a Torah scholar, since there are many who visit the rich patient and no one to visit the poor patient, and the verse says:[46] "Happy is he who visits the needy." However if both a scholar and a poor person need assistance, the honor of the Torah takes precedence (*and visiting the scholar is preferable*). On the other hand, if the poor person is more God-fearing than the scholar, the fear of *Hashem* takes precedence, as it says:[47] "The beginning of wisdom is fear of *Hashem*" (*and the poor man should have first priority*).[48]

The *Aruch HaShulchan*[49] writes that a man may visit a woman or a woman a man, as long as there is no *yichud*, and this is also the ruling of the *Zekan*

---

36. שו״ת, סי׳ קצו (רכד)
37. ברכות פ״ד ה״ד
38. שו״ת, סי׳ יט
39. מובא בט״ז ס״ק א
40. נדרים מ ע״א
41. שו״ת ציץ אליעזר ח״ה קומטרס רמת רחל סי׳ ז
42. הל׳ אבל פי״ד ה״ה
43. תורת האדם ריש שער המיחוש
44. רש״י נדרים לט ע״ב. אהבת חסד ח״ג פ״ג בהגה
45. פירוש על התורה ריש פ׳ וירא
46. תהלים מא:ב ורש״י שם
47. תהלים קיא:י
48. ספר חסידים סי׳ שסא
49. סע׳ יא

NISHMAT AVRAHAM

Aharon.[50] However the *Tzitz Eliezer*[51] wonders what source there is for this ruling and writes that, on the contrary, one should avoid doing so unless the patient is a family member for whom the *issur* of *yichud* does not apply. Rav Auerbach zt"l wrote to me that it is plain to him that just as one may visit a mourner of the opposite sex to offer comfort so one may visit someone of the opposite sex who is sick. However the purpose of the visit must be only in order to pray for her or to see what she needs and help in any way that is (*halachically*) permissible for him to do. The purpose of the visit must not be merely to engage in conversation.

THE LAWS OF A *COHEN* IN A HOSPITAL. A *Cohen* is forbidden by Torah law to touch a dead person or a limb removed from a live or dead person (whether Jew or non-Jew[52]), or be under the same roof as the whole or part of the body of a dead Jew, or with a limb removed from a Jew during life.[53] These rules apply only to a male *Cohen* and do not apply to the wife, daughter or sister of one.[54]

The *Igrot Moshe*[55] writes that in the Diaspora we may assume that the majority of unburied limbs in a hospital (in the Departments of Anatomy or Pathology) are those of non-Jews and according to the accepted *halachah* these do not defile a *Cohen* if he is under the same roof as them. Therefore, in the Diaspora one may permit a *Cohen* to visit a relative if there is great need for it, for example, if the patient is a parent and the son is greatly troubled, or to avoid family strife which might arise if the patient is his wife's relative and he does not visit, and, all the more so, if the patient is his wife. However he should nevertheless do what he can to ascertain that there is no Jewish corpse in the hospital when he visits.[56]

On the other hand, in *Eretz Yisrael*, since the majority of the population, and therefore the majority of patients, are Jewish, any corpse or limb is likely to be from a Jew, and so a *Cohen* should not visit a hospitalized patient[57] unless he is certain that he will not enter or be under the same roof as a corpse, particularly since there are opinions that *bikur cholim* is only a Rabbinic *mitzvah*.

I heard that *Rav Eliashiv shlita* wondered why a *Cohen* not be allowed to enter a hospital even if there is a possibility of a corpse in the building, since the *halachah* is that a possible *tumah* in a public place is considered *tahor*.[58] See also the *Mishneh LaMelech*.[59] However the *Minchat Chinuch*[60] is unsure as to whether this generalization also applies to the prohibition for a *Cohen* to become ritually unclean. Do we say that since the *halachah* rules that it is completely *tahor* the *Cohen* is permitted to enter such a public place where there might be *tumah*? Do we rule the same here as with all Rabbinic ordinances where we rule leniently where there is only a doubtful transgression? Or do we say that indeed the place is *tahor*, but regarding the above prohibition this is like any other Torah commandment and we therefore act strictly even if the transgression is only doubtful? The

---

50. שו"ת, ח"ב סי' עו. וראה גם בשו"ת חלקת יעקב ח"ג סי' לח
51. שו"ת, ח"ה קונטרס רמת רחל סי' טז
52. רמב"ם הל' טומאת מת פ"א הי"ב
53. רמב"ם הל' אבל פ"ג ה"א והל' טומאת מת פ"א ה"א ופ"ב ה"ג ו-ד ולגבי טומאת גוי באהל ראה בטומאת מת פ"א הי"ג
54. הל' אבל פ"ג הי"א
55. שו"ת, יו"ד ח"ב סי' קסו
56. וכ"כ השו"ת תשורת ש"י מובא בכל בו על אבלות עמ' 19
57. שו"ת שבט הלוי ח"ב יו"ד סוסי' רה
58. רמב"ם הל' נזירות פ"ט הס"ז וטומאת מת פ"ב הי"ד
59. הל' אבל פ"ג ה"א
60. מצוה רסג סוף אות יג ד"ה ודנה

SIMAN 335: VISITING THE SICK / §2

NISHMAT AVRAHAM

Tzlach,[61] however, writes that this generalization does not apply to a *Cohen*. For him this is a possible Torah transgression and we therefore rule strictly. The *Har Tzvi*[62] differentiates between two prohibitions: (1) Not to come into contact with a corpse — but if there is a doubt whether he would do so in a public place, he may enter it. (2) Not to enter or be under the same roof as a corpse — this is forbidden in a public place even if its presence is doubtful.[63]

Rav Auerbach zt"l wrote to me that the *Marcheshet*[34] also writes that although a *Cohen* does not transgress the prohibition[65] not to contaminate himself by a corpse (*by entering a public place where there may be one*), nevertheless he transgresses the prohibition[66] not to enter or be (*under the same roof as a corpse — Rashi*). True he is *tahor* because a possible *tumah* in a public place does not cause impurity, but this applies only to the commandment that he shall not contaminate himself. However if he is or enters under the same roof as a corpse, he transgresses he shall not enter, even if the presence of a corpse is a matter of doubt (*as with any doubt regarding a Torah commandment — author*). *Rav Auerbach zt"l* notes that if there is a corpse in the hospital this is known to many. Why then should it be permissible for a *Cohen* to enter under the same roof? He can ask others to first find out if a corpse is present. It is also possible that while he is there he may learn that there is one there and just as it is forbidden to enter a house where there is a *gosses*, so it should be forbidden to enter a hospital where there may be a corpse. Moreover, *Tosafot*[67] write that although a *beit haperas* (*a field containing bones from a plowed grave*) is a public place and should be *tahor* (*since the location of the bones is unknown*), nevertheless, *Chazal* ordained that it has a status of *tamei*, since the *tumah* is permanently there (*unlike a case in which the possible tumah is only there occasionally and by chance — author*). It is possible that large hospitals would be like a *beit haperas*.

The *Rav zt"l* wrote to me later that it is forbidden for a *Cohen* to enter under a roof containing a corpse or even a small part (*kezayit*) of one; that the *tumah* of a corpse spreads into the adjoining rooms if there is an open door or window in the room in which the corpse lies and in the adjoining rooms. Similarly it spreads to all the rooms (and corridors) through which the corpse will eventually be carried out although they are presently closed. It is as if the corpse is already lying in them (*sof tumah latseit*). Therefore a *Cohen* must avoid entering a large hospital in *Eretz Yisrael* for the purpose of performing the *mitzvah* of *bikur cholim*. On the other hand, the *Teshurat Shai* writes that it is permissible for him to enter a hospital since we presume that the patients are still alive. One may also rely on those who rule that the above principle of *sof tumah latseit* is only Rabbinic, as is the principle that *tumah* passes from one room to another (see Siman 372A below). Therefore, *Rav Auerbach zt"l* concludes that if it is impossible for the *Cohen* to ascertain whether there is a corpse or not, he may enter the hospital for the *mitzvah* of *bikur cholim*.[68] As to a *Cohen* who is ill, see Siman 372A, p. 360 below.

---

61. ברכות יט ע"ב ד"ה ורוב ארונות
62. שו"ת, יו"ד סי' רפג בשם הקונטרס נשמת חיים סי' נ
63. וראה גם בהלכה ורפואה ח"ג עמ' קסו
64. שו"ת, סי' ב
65. ויקרא כא:א
66. שם כא:יא. נזיר מב ע"ב. וראה ברמב"ם הל' אבל פ"ג הל' ו-ז וברדב"ז שם הל' ז
67. כתובות כח ע"ב ד"ה בית
68. מנחת שלמה תניינא סי' ק אות ח

(E)**the same age. The more one visits the better, as long as** (F)**it does not trouble the patient.**

GLOSS: *There are those who say that an enemy may visit a sick person but this does not seem to me to be right. On the contrary, he should* (G)*not visit the patient or comfort a mourner who is his enemy, lest the patient or mourner think that he is gloating over his misfortune, thus adding to his suffering.*

§3 **The visitor should not sit on a bed, chair or bench, but he** (H)**should wrap himself and sit before the patient**

NISHMAT AVRAHAM

(E) the same age. *Rashi*[69] explains that the visitor is as young or as old as the patient. Elswhere,[70] however, he writes that this refers to a person who was born at the same hour and under the same star.[71] The *Meiri*[72] writes that a visit from someone of the same age is pleasant to the patient and it is the pleasure he gets from the visit that eases his illness. The *Taz*[73] explains that such a visitor takes one sixtieth of the disease and the second such visitor another one sixtieth of the remainder.[74]

(F) it does not trouble the patient. The *Gesher HaChaim*[75] writes that those who are accustomed to visit a patient and give plentiful advice, for example advising him to bring in a certain physician or to take a certain medication (*in a situation where their advice is unnecessary*), only succeed in confusing and interfering, without the patient deriving any benefit from such advice. On the other hand, the *Mishnah Berurah*[73] writes that one certainly performs a great *mitzvah* if he knows that by visiting the patient he will benefit him since he can advise him regarding his illness (*without contradicting the advice of the treating physician*), and can raise his spirits and give him courage.

(G) not visit the patient. The *Shach*[77] writes that nevertheless it all depends on the reason for the enmity and the degree to which they are enemies. The *Beit Hillel*[78] writes that by his visit they may become friends and this is the custom today that an enemy goes to visit a patient and to comfort a mourner, since this may lead to a reconciliation.

(H) should wrap himself. The *Tzitz Eliezer*[79] writes that he must sit in an appropriately serious fashion and this is specifically stated by the *Meiri*[80] who writes that he must sit or stand before the patient in a subdued fashion with the fear of Heaven upon him, like a man who realizes that he also eventually must face illness and death. In this way the patient

---

69. נדרים לט ע"ב ד"ה ובבן
70. ב"מ כז ע"ב ד"ה בבן
71. וראה במהרש"א נדרים לט ע"ב ד"ה נוטל
72. שם
73. ס"ק ב וראה ברש"י נדרים לט ע"ב ד"ה ליעיילו
74. וכן כתוב בויקרא רבה פ' לד פיסקא א
75. פ"א ס"ק א
76. ביה"ל סי' רפז סוד"ה וכן
77. ס"ק ב
78. הגה על יו"ד סי' שסב סע' ו
79. שו"ת, ח"ה קונטרס רמת רחל סי' י אות ד
80. הגמ' הנ"ל בשבת יב ע"ב בנוגע לביקור חולים כותבת מתעטף ורש"י אינו מוסיף: טלית. אך בברכות נא ע"א לגבי עיטוף בכוס של ברכה מובא שרב פפא מעטף (רש"י מוסיף: בטליתו) ורב אסי פריס סודרא על רישיה. וכן בשבת י ע"א ד"ה דיינין מתעטפין, מוסיף רש"י בטליתן

since ^(I)the *Shechinah* is above the patient's head.

GLOSS: *This applies only when the patient lies on the floor and the visitor therefore sits higher than him. However, if ^(J)the patient lies on a bed the visitor may sit on a chair or bench.*

§4 One should not visit a patient during ^(K)the first three hours of the day since patients feel better in the morning and the visitor may not feel it necessary to pray for mercy on his behalf. Neither should he visit during the last three hours of the day for then the patient is at his worst and the

─────────── NISHMAT AVRAHAM ───────────

will also come to this realization and return to *Hashem* with all his heart. However, the *Tzitz Eliezer* adds that he must be careful not to frighten the patient for this is forbidden.

As to whether wrapping oneself meant covering one's head with a *tallit*,[81] this would refer to the times of *Chazal* when one wore a *tallit* all day and covered his head when in the presence of the *Shechinah* — when praying,[82] sitting in judgment[83] or visiting the sick.

(I) the *Shechinah* is above the patient's head. The *Meiri*[84] writes that the visitor should wrap himself and sit on the floor because then the patient reflects on repentance and will pray to *Hashem* with all his heart. Were he to sit higher up, the patient would despair of prayer. The *Tzitz Eliezer*[85] comments that the *Meiri* is explaining that the *Shechinah* is above the patient's head because it is the way of a sick person to reflect on repentance and to pray with all his heart.

(J) the patient lies on a bed. The *Beit* Hillel writes that it appears from the *Zohar*[86] that it is forbidden to sit at the head of the bed even if he is not higher than the patient and even if they are both at the same level since the *Shechinah* is above the patient's head. He also should not sit by the patient's feet.[87]

(K) the first three hours. The *Rambam*[88] writes that this is because that is when his medical attendants are treating him and the *Radbaz*[89] comments that the *Rambam* gave this additional reason because of his expertise with disease. The *Birkei Yosef*[90] comments that it seems that people follow the reason given by the *Rambam* and therefore do not act according to the rule of the *Shulchan Aruch* here. Since the reason for not visiting is that the patient is being attended to at these times, nowadays when he is attended to in the presence of his visitors, the above ruling is no longer valid. The *Chafetz Chaim*[91] writes that the three hours mentioned are proportional hours.[92] He notes that if the visitor is in a hurry and can

---

81. שבת י ע״א ד״ה דיינים
82. רמב״ם הל׳ תפלה פ״ה ה״ה
83. שם הל׳ סנהדרין פ״ג ה״ז
84. נדרים מ ע״א
85. שו״ת, ח״ה קונטרס רמת רחל סי׳ י אות ה
86. פ׳ פנחס עמ׳ שכט
87. הגהת בית הילל כאן. עיין שם הטעם
88. הל׳ אבל פי״ד ה״ה
89. על הרמב״ם שם
90. ס״ק ב
91. אהבת חסד ח״ג פ״ג
92. A proportional hour is one-twelfth of daytime. There are two opinions as to the definition of daytime: from dawn to nightfall or from sunrise to sunset (see the *Mishnah Berurah* Siman 233:4 and Siman 443:8).

visitor will despair of [L]praying for mercy on his behalf.

— NISHMAT AVRAHAM —

visit only at this time (the first and last three hours of the day), it is better that he visit then rather than not visit at all. Perhaps his visit then will also be of help to the patient in his illness.

VISITING BY TELEPHONE. The *Igrot Moshe*[93] writes that it is clear to him that although one fulfils the *mitzvah* of *bikur cholim* by calling the patient, nevertheless one cannot say that he has fulfilled his obligations since there are matters which are lacking when this is all he does. But the telephone call has a partial merit. For if he cannot visit him in person we do not say that he is exempt from the *mitzvah*. He must at least fulfill the part of his obligation that can be fulfilled on the phone. This can be seen from a ruling in the *Gemara*:[94] If one vowed that he would not benefit from a particular person and the son of that person took ill and is in his father's home, the one who vowed cannot visit the son there since he may not, as a result of his vow, have any benefit from the father or his property. However if he meets the father in the marketplace he may inquire about the son's welfare, for he is still obligated to perform what he can of the *mitzvah*. Besides, when one visits a patient in person as against calling on the telephone, his emotions are more acute and he prays more feelingly for him. Furthermore, there is a greater chance that his prayers there will be accepted, for the *Shechinah* is present with the patient (see §3 above). However even if he cannot visit, either because of personal reasons or because of reasons concerning the patient, he must nevertheless do what he can, and telephoning to ask about him will also fulfill the *mitzvah* in part.[95]

The *Chelkat Yaakov*,[96] *Minchat Yitzchak*,[97] *Tzitz Eliezer*[98] and *Yechaveh Da'at*[99] all rule like the *Igrot Moshe*.[100]

I heard that the *Gra* learned from *Chazal's* explanation of the verse:[101] "They should go" (literally: walk), this is the *mitzvah* of *bikur cholim*, that one receives reward for walking there in addition to the reward for performing the *mitzvah* itself. The *Perishah*[102] writes: Which *mitzvot* does a person perform by walking? The *mitzvot* of visiting the sick and accompanying the corpse on its final journey.

(L) praying for mercy on his behalf. How does one pray for a sick parent or teacher? The *Birkei Yosef*[103] writes that one should not say: "Heal my master, my father," or "my father, my teacher," or "my prince, my master," or any other such title, for King Solomon when speaking to *Hashem* said:[104] "David, my father," and Elisha the prophet said:[105] "the Lord of Elijah." For there are no titles before *Hashem*; Uriah (was guilty of lese majesty and) deserved capital punishment because he said:[106] "My master, Yoav" to King David. However for those whom he is forbidden to call by name (parents and Rav) he may add "my father" or "my teacher" before their name, but no more; see also *Ma'avar Yabok*.[107] The *Knesset*

---

93. שו"ת, יו"ד ח"א סי' רכג
94. נדרים לט ע"א
95. וראה גם בחידושיו של החת"ס על נדרים מ ע"א
96. שו"ת, ח"ב סי' קכח
97. שו"ת, ח"ב סי' פד
98. שו"ת, ח"ה קונטרס רמת רחל סי' ח אות ו
99. שו"ת, ח"ג סי' פג
100. וראה גם בשערים מצויינים בהלכה סי' קצב ס"ק א
101. שמות יח:כ
102. כאן ס"ק ג
103. יו"ד סי' רמ ס"ק ד. וכן בשיורי ברכה שם ס"ק ד
104. מלכים א ב:כד
105. מלכים ב ב:יד
106. שמואל ב יא:יא
107. שפתי צדק פ"ח

(He who visits and (M)*does not ask for mercy on behalf of the patient has not fulfilled the mitzvah.)*

―――――――――― NISHMAT AVRAHAM ――――――――――

HaGedolah quotes the *Sefer Chassidim*[108] who writes in a similar vein.

The *Teshuvah MeAhavah*[109] writes similarly, and *Rebbe Akiva Eiger*,[110] quoting the *Knesset HaGedolah* in the name of the *Sefer Chassidim*, writes that when one prays on behalf of his sick father he should not say: "Heal my father, my master," but just mention his name, as King Solomon said: "David, my father." This is also the ruling of the *Tzitz Eliezer*.[111]

(M) does not ask for mercy on behalf of the patient. *Rav Auerbach zt"l* wrote to me that it is important to remember that one who can ask for mercy on behalf of his friend but does not do so is considered a sinner. And if the prayers are on behalf of a Torah scholar, he should do so until he himself feels ill from his intense prayers.

THE PATIENT'S PRAYERS FOR HIMSELF. The *Midrash*[112] says: Prayers by the patient himself are better than anything else. The *Nefesh HaChaim*[113] writes that although the *halachah* has been laid down by the *Talmud*[114] that an individual may add his own prayer for his needs and suffering in each appropriate paragraph of the *Shemoneh Esrei,*[115] nevertheless, he should not give all his thoughts only to his own suffering for that is not the correct way to behave. It is truly surprising, how one can ever ask and plead before *Hashem* to take away his pain and suffering. For just as in matters of his health, if the physician gives him strong medication or if he is compelled to amputate a limb so that his disease will not spread further, would he plead before the physician not to give him the medication or not to amputate the limb? Surely, the patient himself commissioned him to do just this. In a like manner, how then can he pour out his heart before *Hashem* to remove his suffering? Surely it is meant to atone for his sins. As *Chazal*[116] have said: There is no suffering which is not preceded by sin. If it were not for this suffering, how would the soul find atonement? Therefore, the real purpose of one's prayer before *Hashem* to remove his own suffering is only because *Hashem* (so to speak) suffers along with the supplicant. He should repent and be truly sorry for his sins that caused *Hashem* to suffer and only then will his sufferings disappear.

The *Gra*[117] explains the Gemara that one should turn one's thoughts to his Father in Heaven to mean that one is forbidden when praying the *Shemoneh Esrei* to think of his own needs. But, he should pray for all of Israel to reach perfection here and therefore in Heaven. He should only pray for his own needs when he reaches *Elokai Netsor* (the prayer that is appended to the *Shemoneh Esrei*) for that prayer is meant for the individual.

Rabbeinu Tam[118] writes regarding the verse:[119] "For the rage of man will praise You; You will restrain the remnant of anger": When one is being punished with suffering and with His anger, he will acknowledge You and justify Your Judgment. Then whatever is left over from the anger,

---

108. סי׳ תת
109. שו״ת, ח״ג סי׳ רמ
110. הגהות לאו״ח סי׳ קיט סע׳ א
111. שו״ת, ח״ה קונטרס רמת רחל סי׳ יג
112. בראשית רבה פנ״ג אות יד
113. שער ב פי״א
114. ע״ז ח ע״א
115. או״ח סי׳ קיט סע׳ א
116. שבת נה ע״א
117. שנות אליהו על ברכות פ״ה מ״א
118. ספר הישר סי׳ שצ
119. תהלים ע״ו:י״א

in that You have not (as yet) punished him as fully as he deserves, You will restrain etc. You will not punish him further and exact the remainder which is due, as a reward for his having accepted the suffering with love.

TO PRAY THAT THE PATIENT SHOULD DIE. Rav Dimi said:[120] One who does not visit a sick person in effect does not pray for him — neither to live nor to die (since he does not know his situation — *Rashi*). The *Ran*[121] explains that there are times when one needs to pray for mercy for the patient to die, for instance, if he is suffering greatly from his disease and is in any case dying. We see this from the *Gemara*[122] regarding Rebbe Yehudah HaNasi who was dying and suffering terribly. His maidservant prayed that the Will of Heaven should prevail over the prayers of his disciples who were praying for him to live, and that he should die. That is why Rav Dimi says that the prayers of one who visits a sick person are more acceptable even to preserve his life, for such prayers are more effective. But if one does not visit, not only will his prayers that the patient live not be heeded, but even if the patient will benefit from dying, he will not even be given this small benefit as a result of the visitor's prayers. The words of the *Ran* are also quoted in the *She'arim Metzuyanim BaHalachah*.[123] The *Yerushalmi*[124] also quotes a story of Rav Adda bar Ahavah who prayed that his baby son who became a *patsua daka* (and therefore could not marry — *Korban HaEidah*[125]), should die, and his wish was granted. The *Tiferet Yisrael*[126] rules like the *Ran*, writing that one is permitted to pray that a patient who is suffering greatly will die. The *Tiferet Yaakov*[127] explains that just as one is permitted to pray to *Hashem* to take his own soul, as did the prophets Elijah[128] and Yonah,[129] so too, may he pray similarly for his suffering friend; see the *Gemara*.[130] This is also the ruling of the *Aruch HaShulchan*.[131] See also the *Gemara*[132] regarding Rebbe Yochanan's death and the examples quoted by the *Yerushalmi*.[133] *Rav Moshe Feinstein zt"l*[134] writes that the *Gemara* regarding the death of Rebbe Yehudah HaNasi teaches us that there are times when one needs to pray that one who is suffering should die — one whom medicine cannot help and for whom prayers for his recovery have not been answered; we see this also from Rav Dimi's statement. *Rav Auerbach zt"l* also writes,[135] quoting the *Ran*, that there are times when *halachically* it is a *mitzvah* to pray that a patient who is suffering greatly should die. However the *Tzitz Eliezer*[136] rules that it is forbidden to do so. On the contrary, he writes that the *Gemara* concerning the death of Rebbe Yehudah HaNasi teaches us the opposite, for we see that his disciples, even though they knew his condition, did not desist from praying for mercy that he should live. And, since this *halachah* is not mentioned in the *Tur*, the *Shuchan Aruch* or their commentators, we must rule that it

---

120. נדרים מ ע"א
121. שם
122. כתובות קד ע"א
123. סי' קצד ס"ק ב
124. שבת פי"ט סוה"ב. וראה בבלי שבת קלה ע"א
125. על הירושלמי שם
126. סוף יומא בועז אות ג
127. שם
128. מלכים א יט:ד
129. יונה ד:ג,ח
130. ב"מ פד ע"א
131. יו"ד סי' שלה סע' ג
132. ב"מ פד ע"א
133. שבת פי"ט סוף ה"ב
134. שו"ת אג"מ חו"מ ח"ב סי' עג אות א
135. מנחת שלמה ח"א סי' צא אות כד
136. שו"ת, ח"ה קונטרס רמת רחל סי' ה, ח"ז סי' מט פי"ג וח"ט סי' מז

SIMAN 335: VISITING THE SICK / §5, 6

§5 If the visitor prays for mercy (N)in the presence of the patient, he may do so in any language that he wishes. However, if he prays for him when not in his presence he may do so only in Hebrew.

§6 When praying for a sick person, he should be (O)included among the other sick of Israel. The supplicant should say:

---NISHMAT AVRAHAM---

is forbidden to pray that a patient should die.

The suffering patient himself can pray for his own death as we learn from the prophets, Elijah[137] and Yonah,[138] and from the *Tanna*, Choni the Circle-drawer,[139] who did so.

I should point out that even according to the opinion that one may pray for such a patient to die, this in no way permits euthanasia. Praying to *Hashem* is dependent on *Hashem's* accepting or denying the request and is therefore entirely a spiritual matter. Euthanasia is an active physical action on the part of man and *halachically* is no different from murder, no matter how good and noble one's intentions are. As *Rav Auerbach zt"l* writes:[140] Even while one is praying for a greatly suffering patient to die, one must, nevertheless, simultaneously do everything to prolong his life, even setting aside Torah laws on *Shabbat* to do so.

(N) in the presence of the patient. The *Shach*[141] writes that since the *Shechinah* is present at the patient's bedside, he is praying directly before It. When, however, he prays elsewhere, the angels must, so to speak, convey his prayers to Heaven and they do not understand other languages; see also *Orach Chaim*, Siman 101:4. This is also the ruling of the *Mishnah Berurah*.[142] The *Taz*[143] points out that when the *Shulchan Aruch* writes in the name of the *Rif* (quoted also in *Orach Chaim* Siman 101), that he may pray only in Hebrew (*when not in the presence of the patient*), it would appear that the angels do not understand any other language except Hebrew. However in *Orach Chaim* he writes, in the name of the *Rosh*, that it is only Aramaic that they do not understand. This being so, asks the *Taz*, why did the *Tur*, whose view is brought here, rule against his father (the *Rosh*) insisting that the person pray in Hebrew only? He answers that since the patient is sorely in need of mercy, the *Tur* rules in a way that would be acceptable to both the *Rif* and to the *Rosh*. The *Perishah*[144] answers that he really could pray in any language that he wishes, except Aramaic (a view that is cited in *Orach Chaim*). However here, since he is praying for a patient who sorely needs mercy, it would be best if he prays only in Hebrew since it is the choicest of all languages.

(O) included among the other sick of Israel. By including him with others, one's prayers become more acceptable.[145] The *Yechaveh Da'at*[146] writes that a *ger* may pray for his sick parent since he

---

137. מלכים ב יט:ד
138. יונה ד:ג,ח
139. תענית כג ע"א
140. מנחת שלמה ח"א סי' צא אות כד
141. ש"ך ס"ק ג
142. או"ח סי' קא ס"ק טז
143. כאן ס"ק ד
144. ס"ק יא
145. ש"ך ס"ק ד
146. שו"ת, ח"ז סי' ס

"*Hashem* should have mercy on you together with the other sick of Israel." When (P)praying on *Shabbat* he should say: "Today is *Shabbat* and it is forbidden to cry out in supplication; yet a cure is imminent."

§7 The patient is told to (Q)think about his affairs. Perhaps he lent money to others or has left something in safekeeping with them, or perhaps others have lent him money or given him something for safekeeping. He should not fear death because of this.

§8 One should not visit a patient with (R)diarrhea or other gastro-intestinal disease, illness affecting his eye

―――――――――― NISHMAT AVRAHAM ――――――――――

brought him into the world and he (the son) was found worthy to enter under the wings of the *Shechinah* and inherit eternal life.

(P) praying on *Shabbat*. See *Nishmat Avraham*, vol. 1 *Orach Chaim*, Siman 287D, 288A,B and 301L.

(Q) think about his affairs. The *Tzitz Eliezer*[147] writes that this is only on the third day of his illness, unless, as the *Chayei Adam*[148] and *Ahavat Chesed*[149] write, he is very *seriously ill*.[150]

(R) diarrhea. So that he should not be embarrassed.[151]

INFECTIOUS DISEASE. The *Rama*[152] writes that we do not find anywhere that we differentiate between infectious and non-infectious disease with regard to visiting the sick, except for a particular illness of which the *Gemara*[153] warns that one must not sit in "the shadow of the patient." However, *Rav Chaim Palaggi*[154] writes that there is no obligation for one to put oneself in danger in order to fulfil the *mitzvah* of *bikur cholim*. The *Sefer Chassidim*[155] writes regarding the Torah's admonition[156] not to place a stumbling block before the blind, that a person with an infectious skin disease should not bathe together with another unless he has first told him of his disease, for the Torah says:[157] "You shall love your fellow as yourself," and:[158] "You shall not stand idly by while your fellow's blood is shed."

At first sight the above ruling of the *Rama* seems to contradict his ruling[159] that one should run away from a town that is hit by the plague. *Rebbe Akiva Eiger*[160] writes that *Rabbeinu Bachya*[161] asks why *Hashem* said:[162] "Separate yourselves from amid this assembly." Surely He has the power of life and death without the necessity to first have those who were

147. שו"ת, ח"ה קונטרס רמת רחל סי' טו
148. כלל קנא סע' יא
149. ח"ג פ"ג
150. וראה בהגר"א כאן ס"ק ט
151. ש"ך ס"ק ו
152. שו"ת הרמ"א סי' יט. ובדפוס ווארשא סי' כ. והובא גם בדעת תורה כאן
153. בעל ראתן - כתובות עז ע"ב
154. נשמת כל חי ח"ב חו"מ סי' מט
155. סי' תרעג
156. ויקרא יט:יד
157. שם יט:יח
158. שם יט:טז
159. יו"ד סי' קטז סע' ה
160. חידושי רעק"א שם
161. במדבר טז:כא
162. שם

or (S)head. Similarly one does not visit a patient who is so ill that it is an effort for him to speak. However, one can enter the outer room to ask about him and to inquire if he needs attending to or needs any other help; one listens to his groans and prays for mercy on his behalf.

§10 (T)A man may not attend to a woman patient with diarrhea, but a woman may attend to a man.

---NISHMAT AVRAHAM---

guilty apart. He surely can save one among the many who will be killed. *Chazal*[163] tell us that three may be covered by a single garment, two die and the middle one be saved, as the verse says:[164] "A thousand will die at your side ... and it will not approach you." But since there was going to be a plague, Moshe and Aharon were commanded to separate themselves so as not to be affected by the contaminated atmosphere, as the verse says:[165] "Lot's wife looked back and was turned into a pillar of salt." Or perhaps the reason is that when *Hashem's* attribute of strict justice (as against mercy) prevails, no differentiation is made between the righteous and the wicked.[166] From this statement of *Rabbeinu Bachya* one can possibly answer that there is a difference between a situation where a single patient is involved and one where many are sick, when a town is affected by a plague. *Rav Waldenberg shlita*[167] adds that only the ordinary person should avoid a plague. However a physician, and anyone else whose duty it is to care for the sick, is permitted to endanger himself to do so and, moreover, it is considered a great *mitzvah* on his part. He is not *halachically* bound to do so, but, on the other hand, he must be certain that there is only a possible risk to himself should he treat the patient.[168]

However I wondered why a doctor should not be obligated to treat such a patient who was in a life-theatening situation. Since the doctor, nurse or any other caregiver entered their profession of their own free will, knowing that there would be risks attached to their job, surely they should be obligated to treat such a *seriously* or possibly *seriously ill* patient even if there is a slight risk involved. *Rav Neuwirth shlita* agreed with this and added that if they refused to do so, they would be setting aside the negative commandment:[169] "Do not stand idly by while your fellow's life is in danger." If, however, the risk to the caregiver is very real, he is not obligated to put himself into danger although he may do so if he so wishes. *Rav Wosner shlita*[170] writes that it is forbidden for a doctor to run away if there is a plague, if he can help his patients.

(S) head. Since it is an effort for him to speak.[171]

(T) A man may not attend to a woman patient. See Siman 195F above regarding treating the opposite sex. The

---

163. לא מצאתי את המקור. וראה ברבינו בחיי הוצאת מוסד הרב קוק שם בהערה 5
164. תהלים צא:ז
165. בראשית יט:כו
166. ראה ב״ק ס ע״א וילקוט שמעוני פ' בא רמז רו ד״ה תני רב יוסף
167. שו״ת ציץ אליעזר ח״ט סי' יז פ״ה
168. שו״ת ציץ אליעזר ח״ח סי' טו פ״י ס״ק יג
169. ויקרא יט:טז
170. שו״ת שבט הלוי ח״ח סי' רנא אות ז
171. ש״ך ס״ק ז

GLOSS: *There are those who say that one who has a sick person in his family should* ^(U)*go to the Rav of the town to ask him to pray for mercy on behalf of the patient. There is also a custom* ^(V)*to bless*

--- NISHMAT AVRAHAM ---

Taz[172] writes that the *Darchei Moshe* explains that indecency might occur when a man must clean a woman and perform like tasks. There is a greater risk of this than when a woman must do the same for a man, since the inclinations of a man in such a direction are greater than that of a woman. The *Taz* himself writes that a patient with diarrhea often must be helped to get up to the bathroom. A man who must help a woman do so would come into constant bodily contact with her. This could stimulate him (which is strictly forbidden[173]). This is not so with other illnesses where he does not need to help her get up so often. When a man is ill with diarrhea he is too weak to be stimulated if a woman must help him. *Rav Auerbach zt"l* wrote to me that I should write that this *halachah* applies only to a male patient who is very weak. It does not apply to one who is a cripple or paralyzed.[174] The *Darchei Moshe*, *Bach* and *Derishah*[175] all add that this *halachah* refers specifically to a woman patient with diarrhea since the man helping her to the bathroom will see her exposed.

The *Birkei Yosef*[176] writes that this *halachah* applies only to a patient with diarrhea. With regard to other illnesses, it is permitted for a man to help her even though he may need to help her get up and lie down. The *Terumat HaDeshen*,[177] quoted by the *Shulchan Aruch*,[178] rules that it is forbidden for a husband to help his sick wife who is a *niddah* if it involves physical contact, for example helping her to get up and lie down, in any form of illness. However the situation there is different for since he is familiar with her, his inclinations are stronger.

(U) go to the Rav. The *Gemara*[179] tells us of the time when Rabban Gamliel's son took ill and he sent messengers to Rebbe Chanina ben Dosa to ask him to pray for the boy. The *Ramban*[180] writes that many come to seek his advice and to ask him to pray for their sick ones. This is what happened with the prophets, as the verse says:[181] "Inquire of *Hashem* through the prophet, asking: Will I recover from this illness?" Meaning that the prophet should pray for him to *Hashem* and let him know if his prayers are accepted. The *Tzitz Eliezer*[182] also writes similarly quoting the verse:[183] "At that time Jeroboam's son Abiyah became ill ... and you should go to Shiloh, Achiyah the prophet is there. He shall tell you what will happen to the boy." See also *Nishmat Avraham*, vol. 1 *Orach Chaim*, Siman 301L, p. 150.

(V) to bless a patient in the synagogue. See *Nishmat Avraham*, vol. 1 *Orach Chaim*, Siman 119A and 288B for a discussion of praying in the synagogue for a patient who is in a different town and for praying for him on *Shabbat*.[184] One could ask, what is the point of pray-

---

172. ס"ק ה
173. אהע"ז סי' כג סע' ג
174. וראה גם בש"ך כאן ס"ק ט בשם הב"י
175. כאן
176. כאן
177. שו"ת, סי' רנב
178. יו"ד סי' קצה סע' יז
179. ברכות לד ע"ב
180. פי' יתרו יח:טו
181. מלכים ב ח:ח
182. שו"ת, ח"ה קונטרס רמת רחל סי' יז בשם היפה ללב
183. מלכים א יד:א-ג
184. וראה גם בפ"ת ס"ק ב בשם הבה"ט של המהרי"ט שכתב בשם המהרי"ל

a patient in the synagogue and give him a new name, since changing his name can cause his (Heavenly) sentence to be rescinded. ^(W)*Comforting mourners takes precedence over visiting the sick.*

SIMAN 336
THE LAWS CONCERNING A DOCTOR

───────── NISHMAT AVRAHAM ─────────

ing for a patient when the *Gemara*[185] specifically states that when illness and suffering are sent to afflict a person, they are sworn not to afflict him until a certain day and not to leave him until a certain day and a certain hour? *Tosafot*[186] write that it is ordained when he should take ill but not when he will be cured. The *Yavetz*[187] explains that although they are sworn not to leave the patient before a given day, nevertheless, this is only if there are no prayers on behalf of the patient. Prayers will certainly help to bring forward the date of his recovery. On the other hand, without prayers the length of the illness and suffering is certainly pre-ordained.[188]

(W) Comforting mourners. The *Shach*[189] writes (in effect quoting the *Bach* based on the *Rambam*) that comforting mourners is an act of loving-kindness towards the living and the deceased (*and therefore takes precedence over visiting a patient — author*). He notes that the *Bach* rules that if one cannot fulfill both obligations, he should comfort the mourners. However if he can do both *mitzvot*, visiting the sick comes first so that he can pray for him to live and tend to his needs. The *Da'at Torah*,[190] however, writes that if there is a reason to believe that the patient will benefit from his visit, everyone will agree that *bikur cholim* takes precedence. Not visiting him will then be tantamount to spilling blood, for if he does not visit him, he will not pray for him and tend to his needs. He feels that the *Rama's* ruling concerns one who visits the patient only to honor him.

SIMAN 336
⋠INTRODUCTION

A. "VERAPO YERAPEI." The Torah[1] writes *verapo yerapei* ["and he (the person who caused the injury) shall provide for his healing (of the person injured)"]. Rebbe Yishmael[2] deduces that this tells us that the Torah gives permission to a doctor to heal. This is the basis for the ruling of the *Shulchan Aruch* here. *Rashi*[3] explains that this permission is needed lest we say: *Hashem* has afflicted and he heals? *Tosafot*[4] write that since one might think that a doctor may only treat a person who has been injured by man but to attempt to treat illness that comes from Heaven would seem as if he is attempting to interfere with *Hashem's* decree, therefore the Torah tells us *verapo yerapei*. The *Rashba*[5] also writes that the Torah uses a repetitive phrase, *verapo yerapei*, instead of the single word *yerapei*, lest we think

---

1. שמות כא:יט
2. ברכות ס ע"א. ב"ק פה ע"א
3. ב"ק שם ד"ה נתנה רשות
4. שם ד"ה שניתנה
5. שם

185. ע"ז נה ע"א
186. ר"ה טז ע"א ד"ה כמאן
187. שם
188. ראה במהרש"א ע"ז נה ע"א
189. ס"ק יא
190. כאן

―――――― NISHMAT AVRAHAM ――――――

that one is only permitted to treat injury caused by man but that it would be forbidden to treat illness that comes from Heaven. We should not say that only He who struck shall heal and we may not attempt to treat such a person as it would then appear as if one wishes to nullify Heaven's decree. Therefore the Torah uses a double phrase to emphasize that it is permitted to treat both injury caused by man and Heaven-sent illnesses.

The *Midrash*[6] relates that Rebbe Yishmael and Rebbe Akiva were walking in the streets of Jerusalem and another man was with them. A sick person approached them, asking what he should do to be cured. They answered him: Take such and such and you will be cured. The man walking with them asked: Who struck this man with his illness? They answered: *Hashem*. He said: And you, the Sages, are willing to meddle in something that is not of your concern; He struck and you wish to heal? They asked him: What do you do for a living? He answered: I am a farmer. See, I have my sickle with me. They asked him: Who created the land; who created the vineyard? He answered: *Hashem*. They asked him: Why do you meddle in something that is of no concern of yours? *Hashem* created it and you eat of His fruits? He answered: Don't you see the sickle in my hand? If I would not plow, mow, fertilize and weed, nothing would grow. They answered him: You foolish one, because you are busy with your work you did not learn the meaning of the verse:[7] "Frail man, his days are like grass." Just as the tree does not grow if the earth surrounding it is not fertilized and plowed, and, if it grows, but is not watered and fertilized, it will not live but die, so too the body of man is like a tree, its fertilizer is medication, and its farmer is the doctor.

The *Zohar*[8] writes that one should not say that since *Hashem* ordered a person to be imprisoned, one should not try and release him. King David[9] said: "Praiseworthy is he who contemplates the needy." The patient who lies on his sickbed is the "needy." If the doctor is wise, *Hashem* blesses him to tend to him. That doctor "will discover him in a desert,"[10] lying on his sickbed, because *Hashem* wishes that even though it is as if He imprisoned the sick man, nevertheless one should try to free him. That is why the wise doctor must try to help. If he can cure him of his physical illness, well and good. If he cannot, he should try to cure his soul (*by bringing him to repent for his sins — author*). This is the doctor that *Hashem* will bless, both in this world and in the next.

Chazal[11] tell us that one usually becomes ill through his own fault. Rebbe Acha says that it is up to a person to see that he does not take ill. How do we know this? Rebbe Acha says of the verse:[12] "*Hashem* will turn away every illness from you," that "from you" tells us that not becoming ill depends on you. Rebbe Chanina and Rebbe Natan both say: Ninety-nine out of a hundred deaths are from the cold and one from Heaven.[13] The *Zohar*[14] says that sometimes illness is a result of a punishment decreed on one's property and the patient will not recover until he has spent all the money that he

---

6. מדרש שוחר טוב שמואל ד:א ומובא גם בשו"ת ציץ אליעזר ח"ה קונטרס רמת רחל סי' כ
7. תהלים קג:טו
8. פ' האזינו דף רצט ע"א. ראה בנשמת אברהם כרך א או"ח עמ' 22
9. תהלים מא:ב
10. דברים לב:י
11. ויקרא רבה טז:ח. וראה גם בב"מ קז ע"ב
12. דברים ז:טו
13. ראה גם בתוס' נדה טז ע"ב ד"ה אבל
14. סוף פ' האזינו דף רצט ע"ב מובא בשו"ת ציץ אליעזר ח"ה קונטרס רמת רחל סי' א ס"ק ד

NISHMAT AVRAHAM

was decreed to lose. Only then will *Hashem* send him a cure. The *Ramban*[15] also writes that a door that does not open to *mitzvot* will open to the doctor.

The *Shulchan Aruch* (§1) writes that the Torah gives permission to a doctor to heal and it is a *mitzvah*. The *Taz* asks, if it is a *mitzvah*, why does the *Shulchan Aruch* only say that it is permissible? The author of the *Shoel U'Meshiv*[16] comments that in truth it is a *mitzvah* for a doctor to treat the sick and it concerns *pikuach nefesh*. However had the Torah not given permission it would have appeared as if the doctor wishes to interfere with the work of the Creator. Therefore the Torah gave permission. However the very act of treating the sick is a *mitzvah* and concerns *pikuach nefesh*.

Rav Kook zt"l[17] writes that when *Chazal* said that we learn that the Torah gives us permission to heal from *verapo yerapei*, this teaches us that medicine is an uncertain science. Were it indeed certain, how could one possibly think that there would not be an obligation to treat the sick? On the contrary, would one not abrogate the negative commandment:[18] "You shall not stand idly by while your fellow's blood is shed"? This is why the Torah had to permit the practice of medicine, for there is no alternative available to man.

B. CHARGING FOR TREATMENT.

The *Torah Sheleimah*[19] quotes early *rishonim* who ask why a physician may not heal even without the verse *verapo yerapei*. *Chazal*[20] said that the Torah commandment to return a lost object to its owner also includes returning (restoring) his lost health to him, and the Torah also writes: "You shall not stand idly by while your fellow's blood is shed." They answer that by writing *verapo yerapei* the Torah gives the physician the right to charge for his services, otherwise one might think that this is forbidden. As an alternate possibility they say that we might think that permission is granted only to heal injury or disease caused by man while disease that comes spontaneously may not be treated, as the physician would seem to be attempting to annul a decree of the King. Thus the Torah writes *verapo yerapei*, to tell us that even these diseases may be treated.

Tosafot[21] also ask why the Torah had to write *verapo yerapei* if we already know that the commandment to return lost property to its rightful owner includes returning his health to him. They answer that *verapo yerapei* gives permission to the doctor to bill for his services. Otherwise one would have thought that, since it is a *mitzvah*, it must be done without payment.

I have already quoted *Tosafot* (reference 4 above) who include Heaven-sent disease in the permission to heal. Elsewhere[22] *Tosafot* write that the Torah uses the repetitive phrase *verapo yerapei* to teach us that if one is not helped by one physician he should go to another. One might have thought that since the first physician was unsuccessful in curing the patient, this is a sign that *Hashem* does not wish him to be cured and it would therefore be forbidden to seek further treatment. The Torah therefore writes *verapo yerapei* to tell us that one must continue to search for a cure.

---

15. ויקרא כו:יא
16. דברי שאול יוסף דעת יו"ד סי' שלו. וראה גם בפרישה יו"ד כאן ס"ק ד וכן באנציקלופדיה תלמודית כרך יב ערך חובת מצוה ורשות, עמ' תרנח
17. דעת כהן סי' קמ
18. ויקרא יט:טז
19. תורה שלמה, שמות כא:יט אות שעו בשם התוס' ר"י החסיד בברכות ס ע"א שכך הקשה הר' מאורלייג"ש
20. סנהדרין עג ע"א
21. ספר מושב זקנים, קובץ מפירושי בעלי התוספות על התורה. וראה בתרגום אונקלוס
22. ספר מושב זקנים על התורה פ' שמות כא:יט

NISHMAT AVRAHAM

C. DEPENDING ON MIRACLES. However the Torah does not merely give the physician permission to heal, but it is a *mitzvah* and he is obligated to do so. The *Rambam*[23] writes that the physician is obligated to treat the sick of Israel; this obligation is part of the general obligation to return a lost object, and this includes healing his body. The *Rashba*[24] also writes that it is forbidden to depend on a miracle and everything that may heal is permitted. The *Birkei Yosef*[25] writes that nowadays we may not depend on miracles and the patient is obligated to behave in the way of the world and call a physician to treat him. If he does not do so there is almost an *issur* involved, either of pride or of depending on a miracle.

The *Shevet Yehudah*[26] writes that one is obligated to ask the physician to heal him and this is based on the Torah. It is an important obligation for the patient and his relatives to search for the best specialist physician and the appropriate medications to cure the patient of his disease. He who is lazy or negligent in doing so and does not care to have accepted medical treatment, but rather wishes to depend on a miracle, saying that *Hashem* will send him a cure without cost, is acting strangely and in the manner of a *shoteh*. This is close to being considered as acting with criminal negligence regarding his health and he will have to stand in judgment for this. The *Chovot HaLevavot*[27] also writes that it is forbidden to depend on a miracle for he may not be worthy of one and he thus endangers his life. Even if a miracle does happen to him, it will diminish his credits in the World to Come. Therefore one should act in the way of the world (*and seek medical help*).

D. TREATMENT BY *HASHEM* AND BY MAN. On the verse *verapo yerapei*, *Rabbeinu Bachya*[28] writes that whenever mention is made in the *Tanach* of treatment by man, the verb cure is always written with a *dagesh* (a dot stressing or hardening a consonant) in the letter *pei*. For example, the verse in *Jeremiah*.[29] On the other hand, we find that when mention is made of cure directly from *Hashem*, the consonant is soft, such as in *Jeremiah*,[30] *Psalms*,[31] *Hosea*,[32] *Genesis*[33] and *Exodus*.[34] For treatment by man always involves a certain amount of suffering and trouble and the patient must suffer the side-effects of the medication or of the bitter liquid. However *Hashem* cures with gentleness and there is no suffering at all with it, for:[35] "The blessing of *Hashem* enriches and He does not add sadness to it." The *Chida*[36] writes that at first sight this novel thought of *Rabbeinu Bachya* is difficult to fathom, for there are verses such as:[37] "I have crushed and I will heal," and:[38] "For He has mangled us and He will heal us," and other

---

23. פי' המשניות נדרים פ"ד מ"ד. וראה ברמב"ם הל' נדרים פ"ו ה"ח וכסף משנה שם. וראה בסוטה מב ע"ב למאי נפק"מ ליטרח בנפשיה. ופירש רש"י שם, לבקש לו רפואות. וראה באנציקלופדיה תלמודית כרך יג עמ' רמט (ערך חולה) שמביא בשם הזית רענן (הוא המגן אברהם) על הילקוט שמעוני, שמי שהוא חולה ישבות ממלאכתו ויעסוק ברפואות

24. שו"ת ח"א סי' תיג
25. כאן ס"ק ב
26. סי' שלו, מובא בשו"ת ציץ אליעזר ח"ה קונטרס רמת רחל סי' א ס"ק ד
27. שער הבטחון פ"ד
28. שמות כא:יט
29. רפאנו את בבל ולא נרפתה - ירמיה נא:ט
30. רפאני ד' וארפא - שם יז:יד
31. הרופא לשבורי לב - תהלים קמז:ג
32. ארפא משובתם - הושע יד:ה. וראה בהערה של הרב שעועיאל שליט"א בהוצאת מוסד הרב קוק
33. וירפא את אבימלך - בראשית כ:יז
34. כי אני ד' רופאך - שמות טו:כו
35. משלי י:כב
36. דבש לפי מערכת ר אות חי
37. דברים לב:לט
38. הושע ו:א

SIMAN 336: LAWS CONCERNING A DOCTOR

NISHMAT AVRAHAM

such examples, where a *dagesh* is present. He answers[39] that *Rabbeinu Bachya* was accurate when he wrote that we find that the consonant is soft when healing by *Hashem* is mentioned, since he meant that there are instances when the consonant is soft and he did not mean that it is always soft when *Hashem* is said to heal.

The *Meiri*[40] writes that medical treatment is not pleasant, particularly when the disease is severe and the treatment difficult. But the Torah cures completely, gently and pleasantly — both the body and the soul. The *Tur* explains that in the verse:[41] "For I am *Hashem*, your Healer," the letter *pei* in the Hebrew for Healer (*Rofecha*) is without a *dagesh*, for a Heaven-sent cure comes with ease, whereas a cure dependent on man is difficult, hence the *dagesh* in the letter *pei* of each word of the phrase *verapo yerapei*.

E. HASHAVAT AVEIDAH. (returning another's lost property). The three pillars of definitive *Halachah* — the *Rif*, *Rambam* and *Rosh*, however, do not quote the above *Gemara* (reference 2) regarding the permission to heal from the verse *verapo yerapei*. The *Maharatz Chayot*[42] writes that it is surprising that the *Rambam* should have omitted to write that it is a *mitzvah* for a doctor to heal the sick; he writes[43] that it is a *mitzvah* to cure illness, but he does not give any source for this statement. The *Rambam*, in his *Commentary on Mishnayot*,[44] does quote the verse:[45] "And you shall return it (his lost property) to him," which is quoted in the *Gemara*,[46] but does not quote the verse *verapo yerapei*. (The *Rambam* writes that a doctor is obligated by *Halachah* to treat Jewish patients and this is included in *Chazal's*[47] explanation that returning his lost property also includes his health.) The *Maharatz Chayot* concludes that this omission of the *Rambam* needs looking into. The *Torah Temimah*[48] answers that the *Rambam* did not cite the verse *verapo yerapei* because he believes that this merely gives the doctor permission to heal. The verse: "And you shall return it to him" shows that it is a *mitzvah* according to the *Gemara* (reference 20) which understands "return it to him" to include restoring his health. The *Torah Temimah* then asks that since the Torah teaches us from the verse: "And you shall return it to him" that it is a *mitzvah* to heal, why then should the Torah also write *verapo yerapei*, which merely gives permission to heal? He answers that since this *mitzvah* is not specifically stated in the Torah but is only deduced from the verse by *Chazal*, the Torah also wrote *verapo yerapei*, which specifically mentions medical treatment. He also suggests another answer — that the one who derives treatment from the verse *verapo yerapei* does not derive it from the verse: "And you shall return it to him."

F. THE *RAMBAN'S* VIEW. At first sight it would appear that in the *Ramban's* opinion a patient may not seek medical help whether his disease is Heaven-sent or due to man. He writes[49] that when the majority of the People of Israel are completely free of sin, nature will not in any way affect them, not in their bodies and not in their Land, not the community and not the individual. For *Hashem* will bless their food and water and remove all

---

39. שם בדבש דיבורים
40. בהקדמתו שקודם מס' נדרים עמ' ד (נמצא בהקדמה לבית הבחירה ד"ה ואמר על זה)
41. שמות טו:כו ובעל הטורים שם
42. על ב"ק פה ע"א
43. הל' נדרים פ"ו ה"ח
44. נדרים פ"ד מ"ד
45. דברים כב:ב
46. סנה' עג ע"א
47. ראה ב"ק פא ע"ב
48. שמות כא:יט או"ק קמה
49. ויקרא כו:יא

NISHMAT AVRAHAM

disease from their midst such that they will not need the services of a doctor. They will not even need to guard against disease, as the verse says: "For I am *Hashem*, your Healer." This is how the righteous acted during the era of the prophets, and even if they became ill because of some sin they did not seek the help of a doctor but of the prophet (*who would tell them how they had sinned so that they could repent and mend their ways and thus regain their health — author*). Why mention doctors . . . What role does a doctor have in the home of one who does the Will of *Hashem*? But they sought medical help and *Hashem* left them to the whims of nature. This is what *Chazal* meant when they said that the phrase *verapo yerapei* grants permission to the physician to treat the sick. They did not say that it permitted the sick to seek medical help. However if the patient does seek medical help in the way of the world, and is not part of *Hashem's* flock whose reward is life, the physician is not prohibited from treating him.

Nevertheless, closer examination of the *Ramban's* words show that he was only referring to the righteous and only to the era of the prophets when the people of Israel were free of sin and their affairs were conducted above and beyond the laws of nature. Indeed, *Rav Waldenberg shlita*[50] expresses surprise at this statement of the *Ramban* which, at first sight, contradicts the conclusion of the *Gemara*.[51] The *Gemara* states: Rav Acha says: Before one has blood drawn from him he should say, "May it be Your Will . . .,"[52] for it is not the way that people should act to seek medical help, but they have become accustomed to doing so. (*Rather they ought not to involve themselves in medical treatment but should pray for mercy —*

Rashi). Abaye said: One should not say this for it was taught in Rebbe Yishmael's study hall: *verapo yerapei* — this gives permission to a physician to heal. *Rav Waldenberg shlita* writes that with the phrase *verapo yerapei* specific permission is also given to the patient to seek medical help and the *Ramban* apparently contradicts the *Gemara's* conclusion. Furthermore, it is even more surprising that the *Ramban*[53] himself writes this, adding that this "permission" is actually a *mitzvah* and part of the obligation of *pikuach nefesh*.

Therefore, continues *Rav Waldenberg shlita*, in order to answer this apparent contradiction we must say that the *Ramban's* statement in his commentary on the Torah refers to the basic and original state of affairs of the People of Israel when no outside influences affected them. However circumstances changed and the vast majority of people are no longer at a spiritual level to be worthy of being healed by a Heaven-sent miracle. Thus the permission to heal also includes the permission to the sick to seek medical help and, moreover, this is not just a permitted act but a *mitzvah* and an obligation.

Rav Ovadiah Yosef shlita[54] also writes that the *Ramban* would agree that since nowadays times are different and prophecy has ceased to exist, we must act in accordance with medical advice.

I wondered whether, just possibly, the *Ramban's* opinion that one should depend on *Hashem* and not seek medical help referred to a person who was healthy but sought medical help to prevent illness or to diagnose early disease before it had caused any symptoms, for example today, attending a breast clinic or a clinic for early diagnosis of colonic cancer. Maybe

---

Siman 230:4.

53. תורת האדם ענין הסכנה

54. שו"ת יחוה דעת ח"א סי' סא

50. שו"ת ציץ אליעזר ח"ה רמת רחל סי' כ

51. ברכות ס ע"א

52. See *Nishmat Avraham*, vol. 1 *Orach Chaim*,

SIMAN 336: LAWS CONCERNING A DOCTOR

NISHMAT AVRAHAM

he meant that in such a case one should only pray to *Hashem* and trust in Him to prevent such disease for this would not be considered as if he were depending on a miracle. If he did have early disease it was still unknown to him and therefore a miraculous cure from Heaven would not be an obvious miracle. *Rav Auerbach zt"l*, however, told me that one is permitted to attend such clinics. Since this is the way of the world it is not considered a lack of trust in *Hashem*. *Rav Neuwirth shlita* wrote to me that this is also the opinion of *Rav Moshe Feinstein zt"l*.[55]

G. EXTERNAL AND INTERNAL DISEASE.

In contradiction to all the *poskim* I have quoted above, the *Ibn Ezra*[56] and *Rabbeinu Bachya*[57] differentiate between external and internal disease. They write that the permission to heal was only given for externally visible wounds, for only *Hashem* has the power to cure internal disease.

Rav Yehonatan Eybeschutz zt"l[58] also belongs to this school of thought. He writes that although the Torah gives us permission to heal, this permission is only for injury to a limb, for example, a broken arm, or a wound. It is only in such a case that the physician can make an accurate diagnosis. His knowledge in such matters is comparable to the science of engineering. With internal disease which the physician cannot see, however, the diagnosis is based on the physician's intellect and imagination with only an even chance of being correct. Since the patient's life is at stake, such cases require much composure, patience and other such qualities to prevent mistakes, which unfortunately are not uncommon.

The *Avnei Nezer*[59] rules, based on the *Ibn Ezra* and the *Ramban* (reference 49), that a patient, even if he is *seriously ill*, is permitted to ignore medical advice to eat a forbidden food for his cure, even though he is not known as being particularly righteous. He wonders whether it is at all permitted not to even ask a physician's advice on matters not concerning eating forbidden foods. And he says that since it is so obvious that the physicians are more liable to harm, one may trust in *Hashem* so as not to actively put his life in danger. This is also the ruling of the *Elef Lecha Shlomo*.[60]

On the other hand, the *Shach*[61] writes that a *seriously ill* patient who must eat forbidden foods should do so to save his life, since he had already sworn at Mount Sinai to keep the *mitzvah* of *pikuach nefesh*. And the opinion of the *Ran*[62] is that if he were to act strictly and not eat the forbidden food, this is not an act of piety but of shedding his own blood.[63]

Rav Ovadiah Yosef shlita[64] writes that since the *Ibn Ezra* has a view which is different from the accepted ruling, there is no question that we may not accept his opinion against that of the *poskim*.[65] And, as far as what *Rav Yehonatan Eybeschutz zt"l* and the *Elef Lecha Shlomo* write, their words are surprising, for the *rishonim*[66] have already ruled that a patient is forbidden to act strictly when he is *seriously ill*.

---

55. ספר חול המועד, זכרון שלמה, ס"ק טז, תשובה של בעל האג"מ
56. שמות כא:יט. וראה בדבריו בשמות טו:כו וכג:כה
57. שמות כא:יט
58. כרתי ופלתי סי' קפח ס"ק ה
59. שו"ת, חו"מ סי' קצג
60. אור"ח סי' שנא
61. יו"ד סי' רלח ס"ק ה
62. יומא פב ע"א ד"ה חוץ. וראה בשו"ת יביע אומר ח"ד סי' ו אות ד
63. ראה בלב אברהם ח"ב פ"א סע' ה
64. שו"ת יחוה דעת ח"א סי' סא
65. כמ"ש בשו"ת התשב"ץ ח"א סי' נא שאין לסמוך עליו נגד דעת הפוסקים
66. רמב"ם הל' שבת פ"ב ה"ג. רמב"ן מלחמות, סנה' עד ע"ב ותורת האדם ענין הסכנה. ר"ן יומא פג ע"ב. רבינו יונה איסור והיתר כלל ס דין ח. שו"ת רדב"ז ח"ג סי' תמד (תתפה)

NISHMAT AVRAHAM

H. CURES DEPENDENT ON NATURE AND ON MAN. The *Chochmat Adam*[67] writes that Hashem created vegetation and trees etc. with the natural ability to cure and gave us the permission to use them for this purpose.

The *Chazon Ish*[68] also writes that in his opinion one's natural endeavors to stay healthy are a *mitzvah* and an obligation, and they are part of our obligation to try and be a complete human being. *Hashem* created the world to act in this way. The *Amora'im* also sought medical help from non-Jewish doctors and even from apostates. Much of our vegetation, animals and inanimate objects were created for the purposes of curing illness. Furthermore, the intelligence to think, to observe and to know was given to all.

I. EVERYTHING IS FROM HASHEM. Nevertheless we are obligated to realize that everything comes from *Hashem* and that every cure can come only from Him. Only He decides one's medical fate and not the doctor or a particular treatment.[69] Thus *Chazal* instituted a special prayer to be recited before one undergoes any form of medical or surgical treatment.[70] (*This includes receiving an injection or swallowing a medication and, I believe, even putting on a band-aid, see reference 74 below — author.*) One prays: May it be Your Will, *Hashem*, my Lord, that this endeavor shall cure me, for You are the Healer Who heals gratuitously.[71] After the treatment one says: Blessed is He Who heals the sick.[72] By thus praying he subjugates his heart to Heaven,[73] placing his trust in *Hashem* and asking Him for a cure.[74] One should remember that the doctor and his treatment are only messengers of *Hashem*, as *Chazal* say:[75] When suffering is sent to a person it is sworn not to come upon him except on a certain day and not to leave him except on a certain day and time and only through a certain medication.[76]

The *Gesher HaChaim* writes[77] that the patient who seeks medical help should realize that the doctor is only the messenger of Him Who heals all flesh and Who gave the doctor permission to act as His messenger. The patient is obligated to heed the doctor's instructions, no more and no less than any law of the *Shulchan Aruch* that tells us what is and what is not permitted. This is the *mitzvah* of the Torah which says:[78] "And you shall greatly guard your souls."

J. PROTECTING ONESELF FROM DISEASE. It is generally accepted that the above verse refers to the obligation to guard oneself from all injury or disease. However the *Gemara*[79] tells of a saintly man who was praying *Shemoneh Esrei* at the wayside when a high-ranking official passed by and greeted him. He did not reply. When he had finished praying the official asked him: Why did you not reply to me? Your Torah says:[80] "Only protect yourself and greatly guard your soul," and it says: "And you shall greatly guard your souls." Surely, you realize that I could have beheaded you with impunity. The *Maharsha* points out that this verse refers to guarding oneself from forgetting the

---

67. כלל קנא סע' כה
68. קובץ אגרות ח"א אגרת קלו
69. יד אברהם כאן
70. או"ח סי' רל שעה"צ ס"ק ח
71. See *Orach Chaim* Siman 230:4 and *Nishmat Avraham*, vol. 1 *Orach Chaim*, Siman 230A.
72. Ibid. 230C
73. ראה רש"י פסחים נו ע"א ד"ה וגנז
74. או"ח סי' רל מ"ב ס"ק ו. ומוסיף השעה"צ ס"ק ח שבכל דבר שהאדם עושה צריך לבקש מד' שיהיה לתועלת
75. ע"ז נה ע"א
76. שו"ת ציץ אליעזר ח"ה קונטרס רמת רחל סי' א
77. ח"א פ"א סי' ב ס"ק ב
78. דברים ד:טו
79. ברכות לב ע"ב. וראה בתורה תמימה דברים ד:ט
80. דברים ד:ט

SIMAN 336: LAWS CONCERNING A DOCTOR

―――― NISHMAT AVRAHAM ――――

Torah and has nothing to do with guarding oneself from danger. However the *Rambam*[81] rules: It is a positive *mitzvah* to remove all obstacles that may lead to danger to one's life and to guard oneself well, for the verse says: "Only protect yourself and greatly guard your soul."[82]

The *Minchat Chinuch*[83] questions the *Rambam's* interpretation of the verse, for it warns us to guard ourselves from forgetting *Hashem* and does not refer to protecting one's body from harm. He suggests that the official used the verse wrongly, for the apostates use *Hashem's* Torah for their own purposes, misinterpreting verses to their own liking. But the *Rambam's* interpretation requires understanding, for how does he derive the requirement to protect one's body from this verse which deals with the very basis of our belief? Surely he must have a source for this interpretation that is unknown to us. However, in a later gloss, the *Minchat Chinuch*[84] writes that the *Gemara*,[85] in speaking of one who curses himself, says that he abrogates a negative commandment contained in the verse about guarding oneself. This shows that *Chazal* had a tradition that this verse also refers to the protection of one's body and this is also stated by the *Rambam* elsewhere.[86]

This is also the ruling of *Maran* the *Shulchan Aruch*[87] who writes: Similarly there is a positive commandment to guard and protect oneself well from anything that may lead to danger, for the verse says: "Only protect yourself and greatly guard your soul."

K. THE *NON-SERIOUSLY ILL* PATIENT.
The obligation of the doctor in such a situation stems from the commandment to return lost property to its rightful owner,[88] although according to the *Chovot HaLevavot*[89] it also stems from the verse *verapo yerapei*.[90] *Rav Auerbach zt"l* told me that the obligation of the doctor to treat is not only a positive commandment but also stems from the negative commandment:[91] "You shall not ignore the lost object."

L. MEDICATIONS OF THE *TALMUD*.
The *Midrash*[92] tells us: *Hashem* says there is no illness which cannot be healed; the medication and cure for each and every disease is known. The *Maharsha*[93] writes: One may ask: Why did Ravina and Rav Ashi (the *Amora'im* who compiled the *Talmud*) include the medications mentioned in this and other sections of the *Talmud* (*there are long lists of diseases and their cures, the vast majority of which are unintelligable to us — author*)? On the contrary, the *Talmud*[94] tells that King Hizkiyahu concealed the Book of Cures (*so that people would not be able to cure themselves — author*) so that the sick would pray to *Hashem* for mercy, and *Chazal* praised him for doing so. The *Maharsha* writes that although *Hashem* certainly gave us permission to treat and to discover the cure for every illness, nevertheless the cures should not be made known to everyone because of those who will put their trust in doctors instead of *Hashem*.

---

81. הל' רוצח פי"א ה"ד
82. וראה בכלי יקר שכותב: השמר לך היינו שמירת הגוף ולא הזכיר בו מאד כמו בשמירת הנפש אשר בשמירתה צריך האדם להזהר ביותר מבשמירת הגוף, לכך אמר ושמור נפשך מאד
83. מצוה תקמו
84. קומץ מנחה
85. שבועות לו ע"א
86. סוף הל' סנהדרין
87. חו"מ סי' תכו סע' ח
88. ראה ב"ק פא ע"ב וסנה' עג ע"א
89. שער הבטחון פ"ד מובא במהר"ץ חיות ב"ק פה ע"ב
90. תחומין ג תשמ"ב עמ' 267
91. דברים כב:ג
92. תנחומא פ' יתרו סי' ח
93. גיטין סוף סח ע"ב
94. ברכות י ע"ב

§1 (A)The Torah has (B)given permission to the doctor (C)to

NISHMAT AVRAHAM

However just as it was permitted to write the Oral Law (our *Talmud*) — originally it was forbidden to do so — because of the defective memory of later generations,[95] so too it was permitted to write down the cures for all disease. Because forgetfulness became wide-spread and it was becoming impossible to remember all the cures, permission was given to write them in the *Talmud*, making them available to everyone, so that they would not be forgotten forever. Thus you will see that the Talmud is not lacking in all the wisdoms, since for every illness you will find a complete and certain cure for those who understand the language (*written in code — author*) of *Chazal*. Furthermore, the scoffer cannot say of the Sages of the *Talmud* that they were lacking in their knowledge of medicine.

See also *Nishmat Avraham*, vol. 1 *Orach Chaim*, Siman 4C, p. 5.

M. THE BEST OF DOCTORS. Finally, of all the statements made in the *Talmud* regarding doctors, surely the best known is the cryptic pronouncement:[96] *Tov shebarofe'im legehinnom* — The best of doctors to Hell. This statement cannot obviously be taken literally, for many of our Sages were famous doctors such as the *Amora* Shmuel and, of course, the *Rambam* and the *Ramban*. Many explanations have been given for this statement; see *Rashi* and the *Maharsha*[97] (see also the *Tiferet Yisrael*, quoted below 336F).[98] When I was a medical student, my father, of blessed memory, taught me the following explanation: The elders of the people together with the last of the prophets during the second exile instituted the *Shemoneh Esrei* prayer consisting of eighteen blessings. Each blessing is a specific prayer. If a doctor, even one who keeps the laws of the Torah and its *mitzvot*, prays to and acknowledges *Hashem* in each of the eighteen blessings, except one — *refa'einu Hashem venei'rafei*, Heal us *Hashem* and we will be healed; if he does not take this blessing to heart and does not acknowledge *Hashem's* leading role in his practice of medicine, nor remember that in whatever he does he is only a messenger of *Hashem*, then this *Tov shebarofe'im* — the doctor who only acknowledges *Hashem* in seventeen (the numerical value of the Hebrew word "*tov*") of the eighteen blessings, who believes that it is he alone who brings healing to the sick — surely deserves to go to Hell.

(A) The Torah. The *Birkei Yosef*[1] writes: The real Doctor is the *Shechinah* (the Holy Presence), for the numerical value of *Shechinah* (in Hebrew) is the doctor who treats without fee. The *Yad Avraham*,[2] quoting the *Rashba*,[3] writes that a patient may seek medical help only if he trusts in Heaven and realizes that the true cure comes from *Hashem*. He should not think that everything depends on a particular medication or treatment given by the doctor, as the verse[4] decries: "Asa (a King of Judah), even when he was ill, he did not seek out *Hashem* but only the doctors." The *Taz*[5] writes that the true cure can come only by asking *Hashem* for mercy. Heaven has a cure for him, as the verse[6] says: "I have crushed and I will heal." But for one who does not deserve to

---

95. שם ס ע"א
96. קדושין פב ע"א
97. שם
98. וראה ספר אסיא כרך ב תשמ"א עמ' 21
1. כאן ס"ק א

2. כאן
3. שו"ת, ח"א סי' תיג
4. דברי הימים ב טז:יב
5. ס"ק א
6. דברים לב:לט

SIMAN 336: LAWS CONCERNING A DOCTOR / §1

NISHMAT AVRAHAM

receive it and must be treated in the natural order of things, *Hashem* has permitted this and created medications to be used without the need for miracles.

(B) given permission.

THE STUDY OF MEDICINE. The *Rashba*[7] decreed that one may not study the books of the Greeks concerning the natural sciences. However he writes that his decree does not include the study of medicine although it is taken from the natural sciences, for the Torah gave the doctor permission to treat a patient. The *Rambam*[8] also writes that the practice of medicine is a good introduction to acquiring intellectual and moral values and to attempting to truly succeed in attaining the knowledge of *Hashem*. The study of, and search for, medical knowledge is a great undertaking and not to be compared to the study of weaving or carpentry.

The *Sefer Chassidim*[9] explains the verse:[10] "Do not be overly righteous or excessively wise," by a parable: A father asked his son to study medicine. The son refused, saying that if he would hear of a poor patient and not go to treat him he will have sinned. If he does go and the patient dies he will have killed him. If, however, he would not learn medicine he will not be blameworthy. Those close to him answered: If you knew medicine the sick would live and since you could have learned to treat them but did not do so, it is as if you have killed them.

The *Yavetz*[11] writes that indeed natural science is certainly a permitted and praiseworthy topic for study; it is needed in order to obtain a glimpse of the creations and great works of *Hashem* which are awesome. In particular, the practice of medicine, which brings life to His creations, is a part of this wisdom, and the Torah testifies to its existence and has commanded us to practice it. Even if the researcher into nature only discovers a tiny fraction of its vastness, it will be qualitatively much greater than the other wisdoms. And, if it becomes obvious by trial that his research will help mankind, his reward will be great, now and in the future. It is therefore a worthy pursuit. Similarly, the *Levushei Mordechai*[12] and the *Chelkat Yaakov*[13] write that it is a *mitzvah* to study medicine.

However, the *Igrot Moshe*[14] writes that there is no obligation to study medicine. *Rav Auerbach zt"l* told me that the *mitzvah* was to study Torah. Only if one is going to choose a profession anyway, would it be better to study medicine, if he was capable of doing so. Regarding a *Cohen* studying medicine, see Siman 370B below.

STUDYING MEDICINE ON *SHABBAT*. See *Nishmat Avraham*, vol. 1 *Orach Chaim*, Siman 306C and 307B-D.

(C) to heal. The *Rambam*[15] writes: Take the roots of *Shabbat*, of praise and thanksgiving, of joy and trust; remove from them the seeds of grief and worry; take the flower brimming with knowledge and good sense, the roots of patience and satisfaction. Grind them all in a mortar of lowliness and cook them all in a vessel of humility; knead them with sweet words and dissolve them in the waters of grace and loving-kindness. Give the despairing patient two scoops morning and evening together with three scoops of the waters of

---

7. שו"ת, ח"א סי' תטו
8. פי"ה משמונה פרקים
9. סי' תתרתרסט (הוצאת מקיצי נרדמים)
10. קהלת ז:טז
11. שו"ת, סוסי' מא
12. שו"ת, תליתאה או"ח סי' כט
13. שו"ת, ח"א סי' פד
14. שו"ת, יו"ד ח"ב סי' קנא
15. בהקדמה לספר הנמצא שמיוחס להרמב"ם מובא בספר "רבי משה בן מימון" של הרב י.ל. מימון ז"ל, עמ' קן

heal; it is (D)a *mitzvah* to do so and part of *pikuach nefesh*. If (E)the doctor refuses to do so he is guilty of shedding

─────────── NISHMAT AVRAHAM ───────────

explanation, having first cleansed it all of the refuse of anger and over-strictness and mixed it with a concentrated mixture of the acceptance of the wishes of *Hashem*, the Master to Whom all praise and thanksgiving is due. Give it to the patient to drink in a vessel of praise to the Almighty and he will be comfortable and calmed.

The *Chazon Ish*[16] writes that the endeavor to save life is a *mitzvah*. But one should remember that despite all one's efforts our only hope is that they will arouse the Mercy of Heaven, for everything is dependent on *Hashem*. Although he who prays and unceasingly begs for the patient's recovery does more than he who makes physical attempts, nevertheless if one could save life by one's efforts and instead prays to *Hashem*, he will have abrogated the negative commandment:[17] "Do not stand idly by while your fellow's blood is shed." One who is capable of saving someone who is drowning and instead of doing so stands and prays that he be saved, will have prevented the saving of life.

(D) a *mitzvah* to do so. The *Gemara*[18] rules that if one sees flood waters approaching he should build a dam to stop them. Rava explains that we learn this from the verse in the Torah[19] which commands us to return a lost animal, garment or any other lost object, including real estate. And this is cited by the *Rambam*:[20] One is obligated to build a dam to prevent flood waters from damaging another's house or field, for the verse says: "And any lost object"; this includes real estate. This is also the ruling of the *Shulchan Aruch*.[21] And, indeed, the *Rambam*[22] writes that the Torah commands the doctor to treat the sick of Israel and this obligation is part of the obligation to return to him that which he has lost. Thus, when he sees that he is in danger, he must save him by physical endeavor, his money or his knowledge.

It would seem to me from the above that there is an obligation upon a doctor not only to treat the sick but also to prevent the healthy from becoming sick or injured. And, indeed, the *Rambam*,[23] in his treatise on asthma, writes that the duties of a doctor may be divided into three categories, the first and foremost being to advise one on how he should act to remain healthy.

(E) the doctor refuses. Is a doctor (not on hospital duty) obligated to answer every call by day or by night whether he is eating or sleeping? Would it be considered as shedding blood if he refused to answer each and every call? *Rav Eliashiv shlita*[24] rules that if the doctor lives in a town or area whether there is no shortage of doctors, and the patient can certainly find another doctor to treat him, he is permitted not to accept the patient at a time when he is eating his meal or resting, provided that the patient is not *seriously ill* and does not need urgent attention, for in such a case he who is quick to act is praiseworthy.

───

20. הל' גזילה ואבדה פי"א ה"כ
21. חו"מ סי' רנט סע' ט
22. פיה"מ המשניות, נדרים פ"ד מ"ד
23. במבוא לספר הקצרת
24. ספר הזכרון להגרי"ב זולטי זצ"ל, מוריה תשמ"ז

16. אגרת שנדפסה בקובץ תורני, זכרון יעקב, תשל"ט, ס"ק ו
17. ויקרא יט:טז
18. ב"מ לא ע"א
19. דברים כב:ג

blood, even if there is another who can treat the patient, since the patient is not destined to be cured by any and every one. However, one should not treat a patient unless

---
NISHMAT AVRAHAM

The *Maharsham*[25] was asked if a Rav has delayed the passage of justice if he does not answer a question when he lies down to rest a little during the day. He answered that even in a case involving capital punishment, the concept of delaying justice only applies after the judges have reached their verdict, as *Tosafot*[26] state, proving this from the *Gemara*.[27] Certainly in other matters, when the Rav must deliberate in order to reach a decision, the concept of delaying justice does not apply. The *Pitchei Teshuvah*[28] quotes the *Sh'lah* that in *Rashi's* opinion this concept of delaying justice applies even to rulings concerning *issur v'heter* (what is permissible and what is not) but only when the Rav has reached a definite ruling. The *Rav MiBartinura*[29] also writes that this concept of delaying justice only applies when the judges know to what verdict the case is leading, but delay in pronouncing it. True, *Chazal*[30] tell us that when the two *Tanna'im*, Rabban Shimon ben Gamliel and Rebbe Yishmael, were condemned to death by the Romans, Rebbe Yishmael cried. In reply to Rabban Shimon ben Gamliel who asked why he was crying, he explained that he was crying at the thought that they were to be killed as if they were murderers or had desecrated the Sabbath. Rabban Shimon ben Gamliel answered him that perhaps there had been a time when he was eating his meal or sleeping and a woman had come to ask him to rule on the matter of her being a *niddah*, and his attendant had told her that he was sleeping. And the Torah says:[31] "If you (dare to) cause him (a widow or orphan) pain," and continues:[32] "I shall kill you by the sword."

The *Maharsham* continues that although this particular negative commandment not to cause suffering by making someone wait speaks only of a widow or orphan, it applies to all suffering which one causes another. *Hashem* knows how many times he had warned his family that if anyone came to ask him something while he was eating or sleeping, they should not keep the person waiting but should bring the questioner to him or awaken him, for fear of this statement of *Chazal*. And yet, the conversation between Rabban Shimon ben Gamliel and Rebbe Yishmael was certainly only about behavior of great piety, as the verse says:[33] "His surroundings are exceedingly turbulent." And *Chazal*[34] have interpreted it (*by a play on the Hebrew word for turbulent — author*) to tell us that *Hashem* deals very strictly with those closest to him. For in the case of Rebbe Yishmael, it was his attendant who had sinned and not Rebbe Yishmael who was asleep. Why should he be guilty? We therefore must say that this is because *Hashem* dealt strictly with him; but there is no obligation to cause suffering to oneself for the sake of another. Either these *Tanna'im* ruled like Ben Petura[35] and

---

25. שו"ת, ח"ב סי' רי (השני) בתשובה להגאון האדר"ת
26. סנה' פט ע"א ד"ה ולא בב"ד
27. שם לה ע"א
28. יו"ד סי' רמב ס"ק ט בשם השל"ה והמשנת חכמים
29. פ"ה דאבות מ"ח
30. מסכת שמחות פ"ח מובא שרבי ישמעאל הוא שבכה ור"א שרבן שמעון בכה. וראה גם בילקוט שמעוני פ'
משפטים רמז שמט ד"ה כל
31. שמות כב:כב
32. שם כב:כג
33. תהלים נ:ג
34. יבמות קכא ע"ב. ב"ק נ ע"א
35. ב"מ סב ע"א

he is qualified and there is ^(F)no other doctor who is more competent than he who could treat the patient, for other-

---NISHMAT AVRAHAM---

not like Rebbe Akiva who ruled that one's own life takes precedence over that of another's, or they accepted the judgment of Heaven through their great piety and knowledge that they were being dealt with according to the strictest interpretation of the law.

(F) no other doctor who is more competent. The *Tzitz Eliezer*[36] writes that this *halachah* obviously applies only when the more expert doctor is available to treat the patient. In any case, the less experienced doctor is also obligated to treat patients as long as he is competent. Certainly one may rule leniently when dealing with straightforward diagnoses for which treatment is standard and well known. However the doctor has a duty to be extremely careful in his management of a patient and not to be embarrassed to ask for advice whenever he has the slightest doubt; his profession is a dangerous one and he should always look at himself as if a sword threatens him and purgatory is open beneath him; as the *Ramban*[37] writes: All medications and treatments have their dangers and that which may cure one will kill another. When *Chazal*[38] said: The best of doctors to Hell, they did so as an outcry against their willful and negligent actions. Not that it is a sin to practice medicine, for even though it is a dangerous profession, if a doctor acts as he should, and practices it skillfully and carefully, it will certainly add merit to himself. The *Tiferet Yisrael*[39] writes that this statement of *Chazal* was not meant to be a derogatory one but, on the contrary, it is a statement of praise for the expert doctor. *Chazal* did not say the most "quali-fied" of doctors, but the "best" of doctors, meaning he who considers himself the best among doctors — it is he who is destined for Hell. In his pride, such a doctor will depend solely on his own knowledge, even where he is doubtful of the right course of action, refusing to consult with his colleagues although he wields the power of life and death with his mouth and pen. In his pride, he does not consider that perhaps his self-delusion may cause him to err and he does not consult the textbooks before deciding which medications to give the patient to make sure that they will not harm him. He does not act slowly and surely as one should when considering a matter of life and death. For the *Tanna* did not say, "The best of doctors is evil or will go to Hell," but only, "The best of doctors to Hell," meaning that his profession is one with the potential of bringing him to Hell. However the greater the danger that this may happen, the greater his reward and praise if he conquers this possibility.

The *Tzitz Eliezer* also warns pharmacists not to prescribe medication to patients on the basis of their superficial knowledge of medicine and imaginative assumptions. Besides, they do not examine the patient and do not know how to accurately diagnose his condition. He permits them to prescribe only popular well-known medications for simple conditions such as headache or diarrhea. He writes that the patient also must be very careful not to take medication on his own initiative, other than well-known medicines for simple situations such as a headache. He refers to the *Beit Lechem Yehudah*[40] who

---

36. שו"ת, ח"ה, קונטרס רמת רחל סי' כב
37. תורת האדם
38. קדושין פב ע"א
39. משנה סוף קדושין ס"ק עז
40. ספר בית לחם יהודה על יו"ד סי' שלו ס"ק ב

SIMAN 336: LAWS CONCERNING A DOCTOR / §1

wise he is guilty of shedding blood. If ^(G)he treated a patient without permission from *Beit Din*, he is obligated to pay for damages even if he is qualified. If, however, he has permission from *Beit Din* to treat and ^(H)harmed his pa-

───────── NISHMAT AVRAHAM ─────────

writes that there is a ban forbidding taking medication for any illness unless it is prescribed by an expert doctor, and he who disregards this is like one who commits suicide.

I wish to add to this that there should be an even greater prohibition for a layman to advise a patient to take this or that medication. It is not uncommon for a neighbor or friend to advise a patient or a parent that his sick child take a particular antibiotic or other specialized drug, and even to supply him with some from his own stock. This advice is often based solely on the fact that a doctor once prescribed this "for exactly the same symptoms." One wonders by what right one may do something which the *Shulchan Aruch* (here) specifically prohibits!

(G) he treated a patient without permission from *Beit Din*. The *Chida*[41] writes that nowadays, since no one may practice medicine without permission from a professional body, we may assume that anyone who does is qualified to do so. The *Shulchan Aruch's* ruling applied only to the conditions that existed in his time.

The *Aruch HaShulchan*[42] writes that one is prohibited from practicing medicine unless he is qualified and has permission to do so from the *Beit Din*. Nowadays, he must have legal authorization that he is permitted to treat disease; and there also should not be anyone available who is more expert than he; otherwise, were he to harm the patient, he would be guilty of shedding blood.

The *Shevet HaLevi*[43] also writes that nowadays a doctor, in effect, practices with the permission of *Beit Din*. Since he has received his qualifications from an accredited institution, *Beit Din* accepts this as evidence of his ability to practice medicine competently.

(H) harmed his patient unintentionally. (*The following is only a discussion, and no definitive ruling should be made because of anything that I write here. A posek, expert in these matters, should be consulted before any action whatsoever is taken.*)

1. UNINTENTIONAL INJURY. The *Tzitz Eliezer*[44] writes that there are three different opinions on the problem: (a) The *Ramban*, *Tur* and *Shulchan Aruch* rule that if the doctor inadvertently causes damage and realizes this, he should pay damages in order to be exempt from Heavenly judgment. If the patient dies and the doctor realizes that it was his fault, he should go into exile. The *Bach*,[45] quoting the *Maharshal*, writes that this applies only if the patient died immediately after the treatment given by the doctor. (b) The *Ran*[46] and the author of the *Shoel U'Meshiv*[47] rule that if the patient died the doctor's action is always considered as accidental (*o'ness*) and not just unintentional (*shogeg*); he is therefore exempt from exile. (c) The *Tashbetz* is discussed below.

The *Tosefta*[48] writes that if a qualified

---

41. שיורי ברכה או"ח סי' שכח ס"ק א
42. כאן סע' ב
43. שו"ת, ח"ד סי' קנא
44. שו"ת, ח"ה קונטרס רמת רחל סי' כג
45. כאן
46. על הרי"ף סנהדרין פד ע"ב
47. דברי שאול על יו"ד כאן
48. גיטין פ"ג מי"ג

NISHMAT AVRAHAM

doctor (*rofei uman*) who has the *Beit Din's* permission to practice harms a patient unintentionally, he is not required to pay damages, but if he does so by acting negligently he must pay him, so that society should function properly. If he performs an abortion with *Beit Din's* permission and harms the mother, if he did so unintentionally he is not liable for damages, but if she was harmed as a result of his negligence, he must pay, so that society should function properly. The *Tashbetz*[49] explains this to mean that if a doctor would be liable for damages because of an inadvertent mistake, no one would wish to practice medicine, and the Torah has specifically given permission to heal. He points out that another *Tosefta*[50] writes that a doctor who treats a patient with *Beit Din's* permission and kills him is exiled. And yet, asks the *Tashbetz*, the *Mishnah*[51] states that a teacher who hits his student, a father who hits his son, or the *Beit Din's* messenger who flogs someone on the orders of the *Beit Din*, are all exempt from exile, if, as a result of their action, the person died. What they did was in the course of performing a *mitzvah* and they are therefore exempt. Why should there be a difference? Surely the doctor is also involved in performing the *mitzvah* of restoring the patient's lost health to him, although one could differentiate between the doctor and the others (see the *Yad Avraham*, ref. 60 below).

The *Tashbetz* takes the term *rofei uman* used by the *Tosefta* to mean a surgeon because, like a *mohel* who is called an *uman*, he wields a knife.[52] Any mistake while using a knife may cause injury or death, as the *Gemara*[53] says: Even a needle is capable of killing. On the other hand, a doctor who cures with medications, baths and advice is not called a *rofei uman* but just a *rofei* (doctor). If he inadvertently kills a patient or adds to his suffering while attempting to cure and not to harm, he is not guilty, even in the eyes of Heaven, for he can only act by what his eyes see. However he may not treat a patient where one who has more knowledge than he is available, nor depend on his own experience, for it is regarding this that *Chazal* have stated, "The best of doctors to Hell." But if he treats according to accepted practice, his reward from Heaven will be great for he practices a precarious profession carefully.

This *Tashbetz* is quoted by the *Birkei Yosef*[54] who adds that the *Ramban, Tur* and *Maran* did not differentiate between a physician and a surgeon. However the *Shevet HaLevi*[55] writes that although it would appear from this *Birkei Yosef* that, in his opinion, the *Ramban, Tur* and *Shulchan Aruch* did not accept this distinction of surgeon as against physician, nevertheless it is difficult to contradict this view of the *Tashbetz*. It would be difficult to demand damages from the physician, since he could quote the *Tashbetz* as a support freeing him of any liability, and, particularly since the *Ramban, Tur* and *Shulchan Aruch* do not specifically write to the contrary. On the other hand, the *Shevet HaLevi* notes that with the advent of imaging etc. it would, in many instances, be difficult to uphold the *Tashbetz's* basis for freeing the physician from liability on the grounds that "he can only act by what his eyes see."

At first sight one can question this ruling of the *Tashbetz*, for the *Ramban* rules that a human being is always responsible

---

49. שו"ת, ח"ג סי' פב
50. מכות פ"ב מ"ה השמטה מנוסחאות כ"י
51. מכות פ"א מ"ב
52. שבת קלג ע"ב
53. סנה' עו ע"ב
54. כאן ס"ק ו ו-ז
55. שו"ת, ח"ד סי' קנא

NISHMAT AVRAHAM

for his actions if he causes injury, even if through no fault of his own. However the *Ramban*[56] himself writes that a doctor who inadvertently causes damage to another is not considered a *mazik* (one who causes damage) and is therefore not responsible. Moreover, according to the opinion of the *Ran* and *Shoel U'Meshiv*, he is considered as having had a lack of intention (*o'ness*) and is exempt. And, although the *Shulchan Aruch* does not appear to differentiate between a physician and a surgeon, the *Shulchan Aruch*[57] rules that even if a *dayan* (judge) causes damage, not only by unintentionally coming to a wrong judgment, but even if he, with his own hands, causes damage,[58] he is exempt from paying for the damage. Since he has no intention to harm, if he would be held liable, no one would wish to be a *dayan*.

The *Birkei Yosef*[59] also asks (as did the *Tashbetz*), why there is a difference between, on the one hand, a doctor who errs, and on the other a teacher who hits his student, a father his son or the *Beit Din's* messenger who flogs someone on the orders of the *Beit Din*. The latter are all exempt from exile if the person died but the doctor is not; are they not all equally involved in performing a *mitzvah*? He answers that they struck in the normal fashion and did not err at all. The doctor, on the other hand, who erred by a misdiagnosis or by giving the wrong medication for the disease should have been more careful, since he is dealing with life and death. The *Yad Avraham*,[60] however, does not accept the answer of the *Birkei Yosef*. He writes that the father, and the other examples of the *Gemara*, are considered as having been involved in a *mitzvah* (of teaching Torah or administering a flogging on the orders of Beit Din) at the time when they caused someone's death; see the *Rambam*.[61] On the other hand, if a patient dies, the doctor has not performed any *mitzvah*. The *Yad Avraham* concludes that this is perhaps what the *Tashbetz* meant when he wrote "although one could differentiate between the two situations."

I found it difficult to understand this *Yad Avraham* for the *Tashbetz* himself rejects this possibility when he asks, "But the doctor is also involved in a *mitzvah*?" Rav Auerbach zt"l wrote to me that perhaps the *Yad Avraham* meant a surgeon who operated on a part of the body that he should not have and therefore this was something that should not have been done in the first place. Therefore if, as a result, the patient dies, the doctor deserves exile. On the other hand, the father or messenger of the *Beit Din* did what was necessary but they unintentionally struck beyond the necessary measure, and are therefore exempt. This being so, if they struck unintentionally in a particularly sensitive area of the body where it is dangerous to strike, they would also deserve exile. Thus a doctor who makes a mistake, for instance, by giving too much current in treatment with electricity, would (*like the father and the messenger*) be exempt from exile.

Rav Auerbach zt"l also wrote to me that the doctor is deserving of exile only if the patient dies immediately as a result of the treatment (see above ref. 45). (He referred to the *Rambam*[62] and *Tosafot*.[63]) The Rav zt"l also wrote that if a patient came to a surgeon of his own accord and, although he knows that the surgeon is not always successful, nevertheless comes to

---

56. שטמ"ק ב"מ פב ע"ב
57. חו"מ סי' כה סע' א
58. ע"ש סמ"ע ס"ק ד וש"ך ס"ק ד (ב)
59. ס"ק ו ובשם המעשה רקח
60. הגה כאן
61. הל' רוצח פ"ה ה"ו
62. הל' רוצח פ"ה ה"ב
63. כתובות לג ע"ב ד"ה דלמא

him for treatment, the surgeon will not be liable for any mishap provided that it is not a result of negligence. For it is permitted to operate even though the doctor is in doubt as to whether the operation will succeed, knowing that if it does not the patient may die immediately (see the *Pitchei Teshuvah*[64]). How can one then say to the surgeon, you may operate but if the patient dies you go into exile? Since he is permitted to operate, his action is considered to be under the category of mishap. This is different from all other situations where if one does something wrong thinking that it is right, he would be considered to be close to having done something wrong willfully.

The *Rav zt"l* wrote to me again that it is possible that the ruling that a doctor who caused the death of his patient is exiled does not refer at all to a mistake in judgment on the doctor's part. It refers only to a doctor who intends to give the appropriate medication to the patient and inadvertently gives the wrong one or inadvertently used the wrong instrument — it is in such a case that he would be exiled. It could be that this is also the meaning of the *Gemara* regarding a slave who asks his master, a doctor, to treat his eye; if he blinds by mistake, the slave goes free even though the master's intention was to cure. Although the *Ramban* rules that a person is liable for any injury he causes even if it happens through no fault of his own whatsoever, nevertheless he writes that a doctor who errs in his work is not considered a *mazik*.[65]

If a busy doctor injects the wrong drug (as opposed to prescribing it), the *Tzitz Eliezer*[66] and the *Minchat Yitzchak*[67] both write that this is close to having done something willfully and not unintentionally. However in the opinion of the *Chatam Sofer*[68] this is still considered inadvertent and he requires only some expiation, for if we rule strictly we will stop him from working in the future.

In any event, the *Shach*[69] writes that a doctor should not stop practicing medicine for fear of erring, since his profession is a *mitzvah*. The *Binyan Tzion*[70] asks rhetorically if the sin of possibly killing someone is any worse than the sin of possibly desecrating the Sabbath. For one is permitted to set aside the Sabbath to save the life of a *seriously ill* patient even though it may be in vain and the patient dies, or he might have lived without treatment and the Sabbath would be desecrated needlessly. In spite of this it is permitted to set aside the Sabbath in all situations of *pikuach nefesh*, even though the willful desecration of the Sabbath is otherwise a serious act punishable by stoning (*the most serious form of punishment that the Sanhedrin can give — author*). Certainly one is permitted to do something which may, unintentionally, lead to the death of the patient whose life he is attempting to save, for the crime of murder is punishable by the *Sanhedrin* with death by the sword, a less severe form of execution.

2. NEGLIGENCE. What is a doctor who knows that a colleague has caused a patient harm through negligence to do from the perspective of the *Halachah*? Is he required to reprove him even if he knows that he will be open to revenge by him for doing so? Is he permitted, or required, to tell that doctor's superiors so as to prevent recurrence of such behavior in the future? Is he permitted, or required, to

---

64. יו"ד סי' שלט ס"ק א
65. שטמ"ק ב"מ פב ע"ב
66. שו"ת, ח"ה קונטרס רמת רחל סי' כג
67. שו"ת, ח"ג סי' קה
68. שו"ת, או"ח סי' קעז
69. כאן ס"ק ג
70. שו"ת, סי' קיא

SIMAN 336: LAWS CONCERNING A DOCTOR / §1

─────── NISHMAT AVRAHAM ───────

tell the patient or his family so that he (or they) may receive suitable compensation for the suffering and damage caused?

a. OBLIGATION TO REPROVE. The *Rama*[71] rules that although one is required to reprove someone who sins and, if he does not when he could have done so, he will be held culpable for that same sin, nevertheless he is not required to spend money in doing so. Therefore the custom is to act leniently and not reprove one who sins since we fear that the sinner may harm him in body or in property. The *Mishnah Berurah*[72] writes that it is likely that the ruling of the *Rama* that one is required to reprove one who transgresses what is specifically written in the Torah applies only if he has sinned incidentally. However one is not required to reprove those who have completely discarded the yoke of Heaven, for example, those who publically desecrate the Sabbath or who eat forbidden food in defiance.[73] And *Chazal*[74] tell us that the verse:[75] "You shall reprove your fellow," refers to one who loves you and is your companion with respect to Torah and *mitzvot*. It is he that you have a duty to reprove, but not the sinner who hates you.

See also *Tosafot*,[76] *Rebbe Akiva Eiger*[77] and *Minchat Shlomo*[78] who rule that one may even commit a minor sin in order to prevent possible hatred towards the Torah and religious Jews. See *Nishmat Avraham*, vol. 1 *Orach Chaim*, Siman 163B. The *Chazon Ish*,[79] however, only permits this if otherwise it would certainly cause the sin of hatred.

On the other hand, the *Ritva*[80] quotes an early *Tosafist*[81] that when the *Gemara*[82] says: It is better to allow a fellow Jew to sin unintentionally than to reprove him, for if he will anyway continue to do so, he will now be transgressing willfully — it was only appropriate for that generation. But, in his (the *Ritva's*) generation where people act leniently in many matters, they should enact measures to prevent people from transgressing the Torah itself. And even if they transgress Rabbinic law, whether unknowingly or willfully, they should be reprimanded until they stop doing so. The *Chida*[83] rules according to this opinion although the *Shulchan Aruch* does not. It could be though that the *Ritva* wrote about a situation where the reproof would not engender hatred and revenge. Rav Neuwirth shlita wrote to me that, in addition, the *Ritva* was not discussing those who have thrown off the yoke of Heaven, for there is no obligation to reprove them.

It would therefore perhaps appear that although the doctor is required to reprove, if he feels that this will not only be useless but, on the contrary, will engender hatred and revenge towards him, he is not obligated to do so. In all cases a *posek* must first be consulted before any action is taken.

b. THE OBLIGATION TO REPORT HIM. The *Chafetz Chaim*[84] writes that if one sees another doing wrong to his fellow, for example stealing from him, refusing to pay what is due to him, or harming him, even if he is the only witness, he may

---

71. יו"ד סי' שלד סע' מה
72. או"ח סי' תרח סע' ב בביה"ל ד"ה אבל
73. כי כבר יצא מכלל עמיתך
74. תנא דבי אליהו רבה פי"ח
75. ויקרא יט:יז
76. חגיגה כב ע"א ד"ה כמאן
77. חידושיו על יו"ד סי' קפא סע' ו
78. ח"א סי' לה
79. שביעית סי' יב ס"ק ט
80. שטמ"ק ביצה ל ע"ב
81. בשם רב גדול מאשכנזים שהעיד בשם רבותיו הצרפתים ובכללם ר"י והר"ם מרוטנבורק
82. שבת קמח ע"ב
83. מחזיק ברכה או"ח סי' תרח סע' ב
84. הל' לשון הרע כלל י סע' א

tell others so that they can help the victim, and in order to publicly denounce such acts. However, before he does so, he must be careful that the following seven conditions are met: (1) He himself witnessed what happened. (2) He must be very careful not to decide for himself immediately that what he witnessed was indeed one of the above sins. He should consider carefully if what he saw was *halachically* indeed a sin. (3) He should first reprove the sinner gently, and only if the sinner refuses to listen to him may he publicly proclaim his wrongdoing. (4) He should not exaggerate what he saw. (5) He should only think of the good of the person wronged and not of what pleasure he might derive in blackening the name of the sinner or do what he does because he already feels hatred towards him. (6) If he can help the person wronged in any other way other than by speaking ill about the sinner, it is forbidden for him to tell others. (7) He must be careful that in his attempt to help, the sinner is not harmed more than he would be were he to bear witness against him in a *Beit Din*.

The *Pitchei Teshuvah*[85] writes that many think that it is permitted to flatter someone who has even a little connection with authority, although it is not certain that he has any power to harm him. Thus the Torah is weakened and no one protests if one swallows another alive. But, in fact, this is a terrible mistake, for the *Rama's* ruling (above ref. 71) applies only if it is certain that he will be harmed (as the result of reproving). If you do not report it, you will have completely annulled the negative commandment of the Torah:[86] "You shall not tremble before any man," for surely this refers to a situation where there is something to fear.

We can deduce from the above that one is permitted and required to speak to whoever is senior to the negligent doctor, but only if one is certain, beyond all doubt, that there was indeed negligence on his part and, even then, only after he is sure that he has fulfilled all the seven criteria enumerated by the *Chafetz Chaim*. He is certainly obligated to do so if the doctor continues to act as he did after he reproved him for his conduct.

There is no question that if the doctor's negligence is such that it endangers patients, he is obligated to report him immediately, for the verse says:[87] "You shall not stand idly by while your fellow's blood is shed." This obligation is present even if there is only a reasonable fear of danger to patients, so that the matter can be suitably investigated.

c. TELLING THE PATIENT OR FAMILY. As to whether one may tell the patient or family so that they may demand compensation for the suffering and damage caused, *Rav Neuwirth shlita* told me that if he knows that the patient will take his claim to *Beit Din* he is obligated to tell him. In this way he will receive compensation in accordance with Torah law. This obligation is based on the verse:[87] "You shall not stand idly by while your fellow's blood is shed." However if he thinks that the patient will take his case to the secular courts it is forbidden to tell him. *Rav Auerbach zt"l* told me that the patient may not be told even if he will only take the doctor to *Beit Din*, unless he thinks there is sufficient evidence whereby the patient will benefit if he goes to a *Beit Din*; if there is not, it is forbidden to tell him.

Rav Neuwirth shlita wrote to me that those assisting a doctor or dentist may not do so if they know he carries out unnecessary treatments on his patients, in

---

85. יו"ד סי' שלד ס"ק יט בשם הבכור שור

86. דברים א:יז

87. ויקרא יט:טז

NISHMAT AVRAHAM

order to charge a larger fee. If necessary they must leave the position.

d. NEGLIGENCE BY INACTIVITY. If one does not go to the aid of a *seriously ill* patient is he liable for punishment; can he be fined or is he obligated to compensate the patient or family, and do they have the right to take him to *Beit Din*? The *Tzitz Eliezer*[88] writes that one may not demand compensation from someone who does not fulfill the commandment of returning lost property — including a loss of health. This applies also to the prohibition not to stand idly by while your fellow's blood is shed, since it is a general as opposed to a specific negative commandment, and includes a prohibition not to witness a loss of property and abstain from trying to save it as well.[89] The *Tzitz Eliezer* writes that this is based on the comment of the *Ramban*[90] who writes that two witnesses who can help someone by their evidence but do not wish to do so are guilty in the eyes of Heaven but cannot be charged by man's law. Their Torah obligation to bear witness is because of their obligation to perform acts of lovingkindness. Therefore if one does not wish to take the trouble to save the other, he cannot be made to pay compensation. Moreover, since he does not actively cause damage but only does nothing to prevent it, he cannot be charged for the loss. The *Tzitz Eliezer* therefore writes that although the Torah commands us to save another, if one does not wish to take the trouble to do so, he cannot be charged. Therefore one who refrains from saving life may not be punished by man or forced to compensate the patient or his heirs, but he will be punished by Heaven.

However, *Rav Auerbach zt"l* told me that if a doctor on hospital duty causes damage to a patient by not coming when called during the night, for example, it is possible that if the patient is likely to benefit from taking the doctor to *Beit Din*, he should be told. Even if the negligence was only because of inactivity on the part of the doctor he is at fault, for the patient entered the hospital on the understanding that he would be treated as necessary, by day and by night, and the doctor is on call in order to attend to the patients whenever they need him.

It would seem that this should also apply to a doctor working in a clinic or office if he caused damage to a patient by his negligent inactivity. The *Gemara*[91] says that if one says to another: "See, I am depending on you," he becomes responsible for any loss caused. And the *Shulchan Aruch*[92] writes that if he says: "I am depending on you," or it is obvious that he is depending on him, the one upon whom he is depending is obligated to compensate for loss incurred.

Rav Neuwirth shlita told me that if the matter is a serious one, the hospital is permitted to discharge the doctor.

Rav Eliashiv shlita agreed that if the patient comes to a particular doctor and the doctor was negligent through not attending to him, the patient may demand compensation from him on the strength of the above *Gemara*. If this happens in a hospital, he may sue the hospital.

These halachot are extremely complicated and intricate, and each and every case may only be judged by a Rav who is knowledgeable in this field and who must be consulted from the onset. What I have written is not meant to be taken as a ruling in any given situation.

---

88. שו"ת, חי"ט סי' סג
89. רמב"ם ספר המצוות, לא תעשה רצז
90. חי' הרמב"ן על הש"ס, קונטרס דינא דגרמי
91. ב"ק ק ע"א
92. חו"מ סי' שו סע' ו

tient unintentionally, he is exempt from judgment by man but, nevertheless, will be judged by Heaven. If the patient dies and he realizes that this was due to an error on his part, (I)he goes into exile by his own evidence.

§2 It is (J)forbidden for a doctor to take payment from a patient for his knowledge and advice. He may, however, take (K)payment for his trouble and for (L)refraining from other employment while involved in his care.

─────────────── NISHMAT AVRAHAM ───────────────

(I) **he goes into exile.** The *halachah* of exile does not apply today.[93] *Rav Auerbach zt"l* wrote to me that although the *Shulchan Aruch* mentions it (*the Shulchan Aruch does not deal with rulings that are not applicable today — author*) it is only so that we should realize the enormity of the sin. The *Minchat Yitzchak*[94] writes that in any case in which he would have deserved exile, the doctor must repent in a way which would be sufficient to exonerate himself just as exile would have done.

(J) **forbidden for a doctor.** Since he is engaged in returning lost property, in this case restoring the patient's health, he performs a *mitzvah*.[95] *Hashem* commanded Moshe Rabbeinu:[96] Just as I taught you Torah without taking payment, so must you and all who teach Torah not take payment for teaching others. The *Beit Hillel*[97] says that this rule about teaching Torah without taking payment applies to doing any *mitzvah*. Therefore taking payment for one's knowledge and for advising the patient what he should or should not do is forbidden. This is a *mitzvah*, and with every *mitzvah* we say: Just as I taught you without payment so should you teach others without payment.

(K) **payment for his trouble.** The *Targum Yonatan* on the verse[98] *verapo yerapei* writes: And he must pay the doctor's fees until he is cured, and the *Gemara*[99] states that a doctor who charges nothing is worth nothing. The *Sefer Chassidim*[100] writes that a person should never teach another Torah for payment and he must not even take a fee for treating him. However he may demand his expenses from him and say to him: See for yourself how much I shall spend ... Pay me for my trouble. However if all that is necessary for him to do is to advise the patient how to act, he may not charge for this; see also the *Rav MiBartinura*.[101]

The *Aruch HaShulchan*[102] explains that when the *Shulchan Aruch* writes "For his knowledge and advice," he means, for example, the doctor telling the patient to take a certain medication. However if the doctor visits him he may charge for taking the trouble to do so. Similarly, if he writes a prescription, he may charge the patient for his trouble.

(L) **refraining from other employment (*sechar batalah*).** How is this defined? The *Gemara*[103] states that if one is

---

93. חינוך מצוה תי
94. שו"ת, ח"ג סי' קד
95. ש"ך ס"ק ד
96. נדרים לז ע"א. בכורות כט ע"א
97. הגה על השו"ע כאן
98. שמות כא:יט
99. ב"ק פה ע"א
100. סי' רצה
101. בכורות פ"ד מ"ו
102. סע' ג
103. בכורות כט ע"ב. ועיין שם ברש"י ותוס'

SIMAN 336: LAWS CONCERNING A DOCTOR / §2

NISHMAT AVRAHAM

asked to do a *mitzvah*, for example to sit in judgment or to give evidence, he must be payed for time lost from work. This would therefore apply only to a doctor who is gainfully employed in some other work or profession and treats patients as a sideline.[104] In our days when most doctors are engaged full-time in their profession, how can one define *sechar batalah*? Could this mean that he may charge his patients sufficient for his livelihood so that he can practice his profession only and not need to find other ways of obtaining a livelihood?

The *Rosh*,[105] discussing how *dayanim* (judges of the *Beit Din*) may take payment for sitting in judgment, writes that if one's whole income is derived from this (sitting in judgment) and he has no spare time to earn a living doing something else, one cannot expect him to die of starvation. Therefore one is permitted to charge in order to earn a livelihood. This is also the opinion of *Tosafot*[106] and this is the ruling of the *Shulchan Aruch*.[107]

The *Beit Yosef*[108] writes that the *Rambam*[109] complained bitterly about those *Rabbanim* and students of Torah who were paid for their services — and, although most of the great *Rabbanim* of his time did take payment, he did not refrain from arguing against their reasons for doing so. However the majority, in practice, did not agree with him, and one could refute the proofs that he quoted against them. On the contrary, one can bring proofs to support and encourage the position of the *Rabbanim* who took payment from public funds for their services.

This is how one should act for, otherwise, the Torah would have been forgotten. Only because they are paid enough for their needs can they devote all their time to studying Torah, which is made great and glorious.[110] And he notes that the *Tashbetz*[111] disagreed with the *Rambam* and had brought many proofs from the *Talmud* and *Midrashim* to refute all that he said in this context, and to strengthen the position of the *Rabbanim* and students who take payment from public funds. However it would certainly be an act of piety and a gift from *Hashem* if one can gain a livelihood by a trade and still learn Torah without having to take payment for it. Unfortunately, this is not the usual state of affairs, for not everyone can learn Torah and become knowledgeable in it and simultaneously earn a living by plying a trade.

The *Rama*[112] also writes that if one does not have enough to eat, he may work each day sufficient for his sustenance, and spend the remainder of the day and night studying Torah. However since there are those who rule that for his sustenance one may take from public funds, it has become customary, in all Israel, that the Rav of the city is paid by the community so that he will not need to work publicly and so demean the Torah before the masses. But the *Rama* concludes that this is only if the Rav needs a sustenance; if he is rich he is prohibited from taking a fee.[113]

In truth, the *Tashbetz* does write harshly against the *Rambam* concluding[114] that if he, the *Rambam*, had the good fortune to

---

104. עיין בכתובות קה ע"א במעשה דרב הונא
105. בכורות שם
106. כתובות קה ע"א ד"ה גוזרי
107. יו"ד סי' רמו סע' ה
108. שם אות כא ד"ה ומ"ש כל המשים על לבו שיעסוק בתורה
109. פי' המשניות אבות פ"ד מ"ה. וראה בכסף משנה הל'

תלמוד תורה פ"ג ה"י ורמ"א יו"ד סי' רמו סע' כא וש"ך שם ס"ק כב
110. ישעיה מב:כא
111. שו"ת, סי' קמב-קמח
112. יו"ד סי' רמו סע' כא
113. וראה ההמשך ברמ"א
114. שו"ת, סי' קמז

§3 If one has medication needed by a patient, he is forbidden to charge more than the usual price. Even if the patient agreed to pay a much higher price, since the medication was, temporarily, unavailable elsewhere, he may never-

NISHMAT AVRAHAM

be both close to the ruling body and be very respected because of his practice of medicine and his knowledge, thus not needing to take payment from the community, what should the *Rabbanim* and Sages who have not achieved this stature do? Should they die of starvation or disgrace their honor or throw off the yoke of the Torah? Surely this was neither the intention of the Torah nor that of the *Talmud*.

Rav Auerbach zt"l wrote to me that it is possible that a high salary that a doctor could receive were he to work in another hospital, for example in a non-Jewish hospital (*meaning in the Diaspora, where the earnings are higher — author*), or by doing research, could also be considered as *sechar batalah*. He would then be permitted to take a like salary in a Jewish one (*meaning here in Israel — author*). Similarly, a doctor who is obligated to be on-call in the hospital may also receive a salary for the obligation to be there. However one cannot argue that had he studied for some other profession which commands a higher salary than that of a doctor, he would be earning more and these are grounds to claim the difference as *sechar batalah*. They are not.

There is no question, however, that a doctor who refuses to treat a patient who truly cannot afford his fees is guilty of serious sin and, as *Rashi* writes:[115] It is of him that the *Talmud* exclaims: The best of doctors to Hell. The *Teshuvah MeAhavah*[116] writes that, in such a situation, *Beit Din* can force him to treat the patient without charge. Rav Waldenberg shlita[117] wrote to me that this ruling of the *Teshuvah MeAhavah* is comparable to the *Rama's*[118] ruling about a *mohel*, and indeed, that is the source for the *Teshuvah MeAhavah's* ruling. However if another doctor is available, one may not force either one of them to treat the patient without charge since each of the doctors is no more obligated to do so than the other. In such a situation the *Beit Din* or those responsible in the community must pay the doctor from public funds.

ISSUING A DEATH CERTIFICATE. One may charge a fee for confirming death and issuing a death certificate.[119]

FEES FOR WORK DONE ON *SHABBAT*. Rav Neuwirth shlita told me that a doctor or other member of staff working in a hospital in Israel is permitted to receive payment for doing so on *Shabbat* as part of his monthly salary for the following reasons: (1) The *Mishnah Berurah*[120] rules that a midwife may receive a fee (after *Shabbat*) for attending a delivery on *Shabbat*. This, says the *Rav shlita*, would apply to all those concerned for the patient's welfare, including those who bring him his food and wash the dishes. (2) Besides, the *Mishnah Berurah*[121] writes that since he is paid weekly or monthly, the monies received for *Shabbat* are included within

---

115. קדושין פב ע"א
116. שו"ת, ח"ג יו"ד סי' תח (שלו)
117. לב אברהם ח"ב עמ' כד. שו"ת ציץ אליעזר חי"ד סי' כז ס"ק ב
118. יו"ד סי' רסא רמ"א סוף סע' א
119. שו"ת מהר"ם שיק יו"ד סי' שמג
120. סי' שו ס"ק כד
121. מ"ב שם ס"ק כ בשם השו"ת שבות יעקב ובשעה"צ סי' תקכו ס"ק מא

theless only take its usual price. However, if a doctor demands (M)a high fee as a precondition for treatment, the patient is obligated to pay him since he is, in fact, paying for his knowledge and experience and that has no particular price tag.

GLOSS: *Although it is a mitzvah for the doctor to treat the patient, if he does not wish to do so without receiving a fee, (N)the patient must pay him, since it is a mitzvah required of everyone and not of a particular doctor only.*

──────────── NISHMAT AVRAHAM ────────────

his global salary for the week or month and that is permitted.[122]

(M) a high fee. The *Rama*,[123] writing about the witnesses to a *get* (document of divorce), says that since a condition is made with them that if they spoil the *get* they will have to pay for another, they are permitted to charge a high fee. It would appear to me that this would also apply to a doctor.

(N) the patient must pay him. The *Taz*[124] writes that although it is forbidden to take a fee for his knowledge (see above §2), nevertheless since the doctor accepted the patient on this condition and the patient agreed to his terms, he must pay him as agreed. The *mitzvah* of treating the patient is not only this particular doctor's obligation, for others can also learn medicine. Although one who flees from prison and offers a boatman a large sum of money to take him across the river need only give him his regular fee,[125] that situation is different, since the job is a finite one. On the other hand, the knowledge of medicine has no boundaries and the doctor has no obligation to learn medicine in the first place. Therefore his condition to treat only for a high fee has force. The *Shach*[126] writes, not only is there no question that if the doctor has already received the fee agreed on that *Beit Din* cannot force him to return it, but even if it still has not been payed, the patient must pay him for he agreed to it.

Rebbe Akiva Eiger[127] also writes that even with the ruling of the *Shulchan Aruch* here regarding the pricing of medication, if the patient had already paid for it, he cannot demand that it be returned. The *Be'er HaGolah*[128] writes that the *Rama* referred to above (reference 125), rules that the patient must pay whatever fee was agreed on, because he is paying for the doctor's knowledge of medicine.

Rav Waldenberg shlita[129] writes that the *halachah* regarding the doctor's high fee applies only when other doctors are also available. However, if he is the only doctor available, the patient is not obligated to pay the high fee he agreed upon; see the *Levush*[130] and the *Radbaz*.[131] On the other hand, according to the *Rama*,[132] the patient is obligated to pay since it is

───────────────────────────

122. וראה בשו"ת הרשב"א ח"א סי' ח. דרכי תשובה סי' קנד ס"ק ה ו-ט. ושו"ת חת"ס חו"מ סי' קצד
123. אהע"ז סי' קל
124. ס"ק ג
125. רמ"א חו"מ סי' רסד סע' ז
126. ס"ק ז
127. בהגה
128. חו"מ סי' רסד סע' ז
129. שו"ת ציץ אליעזר ח"ה קונטרס רמת רחל סי' כה
130. כאן
131. שו"ת, ח"ג סי' תקנו
132. חו"מ סי' רסד סע' ז

SIMAN 337
THE LAWS CONCERNING A PATIENT WHEN SOMEONE IN THE FAMILY DIES

§1 If a (A)close family member of (B)a patient dies, (C)he is not

---- NISHMAT AVRAHAM ----

usual to pay highly for this, and so it appears in the *Yam Shel Shlomo*.[133] As long as the patient did not indicate at the time he agreed that he was only doing so under duress, he is not believed if he later says that he did not really mean to accept the condition, and he is therefore obligated to pay in full.

SIMAN 337

INTRODUCTION. A person must mourn for seven close family members — father, mother, brother, sister, son, daughter and spouse. The requirements of the laws of mourning include the tearing of one's clothes, eulogizing the deceased, "sitting *shivah*" and saying *Kaddish* (where appropriate). Following this period, there is a period of mourning of lesser intensity which ends with the thirtieth day after death. In the case of a parent there is a further period, again of lesser intensity, extending for a total of a year from the death. This chapter discusses those laws in relationship to a mourner who is ill and whose condition may be adversely affected by the knowledge of the death or the acts of mourning enumerated above when he knows of the death.

(A) close family member of a patient dies. The *Beit Hillel*[1] writes that even if the deceased is his father or mother and the patient should normally be obligated to say *Kaddish* for them, nevertheless he is not told since it may cause him such grief that it will adversely affect his condition.

(B) a patient. The source of this *halachah* is the *Gemara*[2] and no mention is made of the type of patient under discussion. The *Ramban*[3] writes of this *halachah* in the context of a patient who is dying. Rav Neuwirth shlita told me that the halachah refers to a *seriously ill* patient and not necessarily one who is dying.

(C) he is not informed. If the patient asks about the deceased, he should be told that the person is alive.[4] Rav Auerbach zt"l wrote to me that if a mourner is obligated to visit a very *seriously ill* patient and there is a possibility that if the patient realizes that his visitor is in mourning his condition will worsen, it is obvious that the mourner must do everything necessary to hide the fact that he is in mourning. See also the *Shevut Yaakov*[5] who wrote that a mourner during the seven days of *shivah* after his sister's death may visit his father so that the latter will not suddenly realize that his daughter has died. It would appear, therefore, continues Rav Auerbach zt"l, that he should dress normally and put on leather shoes. However he told me that it would be proper for the mourner to put a little earth inside his shoes if they are made of leather, as mentioned by the *Mishnah Berurah*.[6] If the deceased is a parent, the son or daughter (who is visiting the sick)

---

133. ב"ק פ"י סי' לח.
1. הגה על השו"ע כאן.
2. מו"ק כו ע"ב.
3. תורת האדם, סוף ענין הוידוי עמ' מו ד"ה במס'.
שמחות, בפיסקא על חולה שנוטה למות.
4. כל בו על אבלות עמ' 17 בשם השערי דעה.
5. שו"ת ח"ב סי' צט.
6. סי' תקנד ס"ק לג.

ism 337: WHEN SOMEONE IN THE PATIENT'S FAMILY DIES / §1 295

informed of this since it may (D)cause him great

---NISHMAT AVRAHAM---

is also not obligated to tear his garment after each visit when he leaves the patient's room, since he was *halachically* permitted to wear these clothes (see the *Shach*[7]). However, as soon as he can, he must change back into his mourner's clothes.

(D) cause him great agitation. A patient (who is fully conscious and aware) who knows that a close family member, for whom he is obligated to mourn, has died, and who recovers from his illness within the seven days of mourning, need only sit *shivah* for the remaining days. If he recovers during the thirty-day period, he only needs to fulfill the laws pertaining to this period for the remaining days of the thirty. Since he knew of the death during his illness and did fulfill some of the laws pertaining to the period, his days of illness are like the Sabbath during the week of mourning; it is counted within the seven days for even though all the laws of mourning do not apply to it, some do. This also applies to a woman who has given birth (since she is considered to be *seriously ill;* see *Nishmat Avraham,* vol. 1 *Orach Chaim,* Siman 330I).[8] However, the *Nachalat Shivah*[9] quotes Rav Shapira of Prague that a patient who recovers must observe the laws of mourning for the full seven days after he recovers, if the thirty-day period has not lapsed. The *Chatam Sofer*[10] also quotes him, adding that if there is a *Yom Tov* during this period, this requirement does not apply. For the *Yom Tov* intervenes and stops the seven-day mourning, even if he did not mourn at all before *Yom Tov*. The *Shevut Yaakov*,[11] on the other hand, explains that Rav Shapira was thinking only about a patient who did not know of the death until he had recovered, and not as the *Nachalat Shivah* had understood him. However, *Rav Waldenberg shlita*[12] expresses surprise at the explanation that the *Nachalat Shivah* is discussing a patient who was told about the death while he was ill, when, on the contrary, he specifically writes in a later *responsum*[13] that he is discussing a patient who was not told. The *Aruch HaShulchan*,[14] *Mishnah Berurah*[15] and *Tzitz Eliezer*[16] all rule leniently that a patient who knew that he was a mourner but could not fulfill the acts of mourning during the seven-day period, need not do so even if he recovers during the thirty-day period.

The *Shuchan Aruch*[17] rules that if one did not mourn at all before *Yom Tov* the *Yom Tov* does not cancel his obligation to mourn and he is required to mourn a seven-day period after *Yom Tov*. This applies if he did not mourn intentionally, did not know the *halachah* or was told about the death just before *Yom Tov*, so that there was no time to mourn. However, the *Mishnah Berurah*[18] writes that a woman following childbirth, or a patient who knows about the death but was unable to mourn because of weakness, has no further obligation to mourn for the seven- or thirty-day period should *Yom Tov* occur during the seven- or thirty-day period

---

7. סי' שמ ס"ק כג
8. קיצור שו"ע סי' ריז סע' ג. שו"ת רב פעלים ח"ג יו"ד סי' כח
9. סי' יז
10. שו"ת, יו"ד סי' שמב מובא בפ"ת סי' שצו ס"ק ג
11. שו"ת, ח"א סי' פח
12. שו"ת ציץ אליעזר ח"ה קונטרס רמת רחל סי' כו
13. סי' עג
14. סי' שצו סע' ג
15. שעה"צ סי' תקמח ס"ק לו
16. שו"ת, רמת רחל שם
17. או"ח סי' תקמח סע' ז. וראה שם במ"ב ס"ק כו בשם הפמ"ג
18. סי' תקמח ס"ק נג

agitation. (E)His garment is not torn for him and one does (F)not cry or eulogize the deceased in his presence so as not to (G)break his heart, and comforters are silenced.

NISHMAT AVRAHAM

respectively. This is also the ruling of the *Tzitz Eliezer*.[19]

If, however, the patient did not know of the death while he was ill,[20] or he was told when not in full possession of his faculties and could not observe the *halachot* of mourning,[21] all agree that he must observe the seven-day period when he recovers, if he recovers within thirty days after the death of his relative.

(E) His garment is not torn for him. Not only should he not be told, but even if he were told, we do not tell him to tear his garment for this will increase his sorrow, and this is also the ruling of the *Bach* quoting the *Ran*.[22] The *Birkei Yosef*[23] writes that even if the patient is fast asleep so that he is not aware of what is being done to him, his garment may not be torn lest he will become aware.

Both caregivers and visitors should therefore be extremely careful not to say anything in the presence of an unconscious patient that one would not have said in his presence were he conscious. Perhaps he is not so comatose that he will not hear, and hearing what is being said about him may bring him to despair.

(F) not cry. Even for a deceased who is unrelated to the patient.[24]

(G) break his heart, and comforters are silenced. The *Shach*[25] quotes the *Bach* to explain that when the patient hears of the death of even an unrelated person and sees others crying and eulogizing him, his heart will break from fear that he will also die from his illness. This is why comforters are silenced for they will remind him of the death of that person, bringing him the fear of his own possible death. Even if he knows that a relative has died, one should not cry over or eulogize the deceased in the patient's presence for the same reason.

The *Aruch HaShulchan*[26] writes that it is forbidden for a patient to act strictly and observe those *halachot* of mourning that may harm his health. Even a *non-seriously ill* patient should be careful not to sit on the floor or walk barefooted if this will harm his health. He should only observe those *halachot* that will not affect his well-being.

It is prohibited to cause any suffering to a patient; on the contrary one must make every effort to make him happy.[27] The *Rambam*[28] writes that one should tell him stories that will make him happy, and (Torah) novellae that will make him happy, thus causing him to forget his illness.

---

19. שו"ת, רמת רחל שם, כי באבלות הלוך המיקל
20. ערוה"ש כאן סע' ג
21. ערוה"ש סי' שצו סע' ג
22. ש"ך ס"ק א
23. ס"ק ב
24. ש"ך ס"ק ב
25. שם
26. כאן סע' ג
27. שם סע' ב
28. ספר הנהגת הבריאות, תשובות כ"י בעניני רפואה, מובא בעינים למשפט, נדרים לט ע"ב. וראה ספר אסיא כרך ג עמ' 336

SIMAN 338
A PATIENT SHOULD CONFESS HIS SINS AND HOW HE SHOULD BE TOLD TO DO SO

§1 (A)A dying patient (B)should be told to confess his sins. He is told, "Many have confessed and not died and many who did not confess died. You will live because you confess, and he who confesses will have a portion in the World to Come." If the patient cannot confess verbally he should do

---
NISHMAT AVRAHAM

SIMAN 338

(A) A dying patient. The *Shach*[1] writes that only a dying patient should be told to confess, for any other patient will think that he is *seriously ill* and it will break his heart. Another reason why we do not say this to a patient who is not dying is that there is still time for him to confess. But if he is dying he should be told, lest he die suddenly without having confessed. On the other hand, the *Beit Lechem Yehudah*[2] writes that it is a great *mitzvah* to remind a patient about confessing when he is in a calm state of mind and not wait until he is dying. A person who is always quick to perform *mitzvot* will, when ill, also be quick to confess early and ask *Hashem* for mercy while he still has the strength and composure to do so.

(B) should be told to confess his sins. A patient who sees that his end is near and that he will surely die that day, may confess his sins even if it is *Shabbat*, for if not now, when?[3] Thus, if necessary and there is no alternative, he may confess even if feces or urine are present, but without saying *Hashem*'s Name or refer-

ring to His Kingship.[4] *Rav Auerbach zt"l* added that it would be preferable if he does not contemplate, in this situation, that he is performing a *mitzvah*, just as he should not think that he is performing a *mitzvah* when blowing the *shofar* in the presence of feces or urine (see Siman 19A above and *Nishmat Avraham*, vol. 1 *Orach Chaim*, Siman 588A).

It is not only the patient who is dying who should confess, but any *seriously ill* patient, for example, one who has had a heart attack, however minor; is suffering from pneumonia; or is about to undergo surgery. He should also pray to *Hashem* to send him a full and complete cure. For the prayers of the patient are more acceptable than those of others who pray for him.[5] Confession and repentance for his sins should precede his prayers.[6] *Rav Neuwirth shlita* drew my attention to what the *Ma'avar Yabok*[7] writes: On many occasions, confession by the patient eases his illness for it softens the forces of judgment which are upon him because of his sins. There is no suffering without sin and he therefore needs to sacrifice of himself by being deeply broken in heart and spirit for his sins, as the verse says:[8] "The

---

1. ס"ק א
2. הגה על השו"ע כאן
3. שדי חמד, אסיפת דינים מערכת וא"ו ס"ק ג בשם פתח הדביר
4. שמעתי ממו"ר הגרי"י נויבירט שליט"א מהא דאו"ח

5. רש"י פ' וירא כא:יז. וראה בראשית רבה פנ"ג סי' יט
6. ראה בגשר החיים ח"א פ"א סי' ד (עמ' לג)
7. אמרי שפר פט"ו
8. תהלים נא:יט

סי' תרו שעה"צ ס"ק כב

so in his heart. (*If he does not know how to confess he is told, say: "Let my death be an expiation for all my sins."*) **None of this is said in the presence of an unlearned person, women or children, (C)lest they cry, breaking the patient's heart.**

NISHMAT AVRAHAM
---

sacrifices *Hashem* desires are a broken spirit." And the prophet cries:[9] "Even now, *Hashem* says: Return to Me with all your heart, with fasting, with weeping and with lamentation." And, concludes the *Ma'avar Yabok*, when he confesses his heart breaks.

(C) lest they cry, breaking the patient's heart. Where possible one should not reveal to a relative who is softhearted the true state of the patient, for by his behavior when in the presence of the patient, he might bring him to despair of recovery.[10] *Rav Moshe Feinstein zt"l*[11] rules that it is forbidden to tell the patient that he is *dangerously ill* and that there is no cure for his illness.

There is a view that if a patient is discovered to have cancer, he should not be told this.[12] Today, however, it has become exceedingly difficult to conceal from a patient that he has cancer, particularly since most, if not all, will receive some form of therapy, be it surgery, chemotherapy, radiotherapy or a combination of these. These treatments cannot be given without the patient realizing that he is being treated for cancer. Besides, medicine at present has much more to offer these patients than a decade ago, not only in prolonging life, but even in complete cure. If the patient is not told the truth, or at least part of it, he may not only fear that he has cancer but will also believe the worst, bringing him to unnecessary and unjustified despair. On the other hand, if he is told about his diagnosis, rapport can be established between him and his treating doctor, allowing him to speak his mind and voice his fears freely. The doctor can then encourage him and give him the necessary physiological and psychological support so necessary for his treatment and his ability to withstand its side effects.[13] It would seem to me that when such a diagnosis has been made, a close member or members of the family must be informed of the diagnosis and the true evaluation of the medical team. The patient must then, with their permission and knowledge, be told the diagnosis together with the recommended treatments he should have. Time must be allowed, then and later, for him to voice his thoughts, fears and questions. Answers must be given in a manner full of hope and confidence, particularly regarding prognosis and cure, remembering that we are merely the messengers of *Hashem* and it is only He who can cure him by virtue of the prayers and supplications of the patient and his family.

However if the diagnosis was delayed and the disease is so widespread that nothing can be done other than reduce the patient's suffering, there is surely no room, in the vast majority of situations, to tell the patient either his diagnosis or his serious situation. Most patients will have guessed the truth, but they cling to an element of hope, however tiny this may be. To hear the truth from the doctor will

---

9. יואל ב:יב
10. ש"ך ס"ק א
11. מוריה, אלול תשד"מ עמ' נג. וראה באג"מ חו"מ ח"ב סי' עג אות ב
12. שו"ת בצל החכמה ח"ב סי' נה
13. ראה מכתבו של פרופ' שמעון גליק הי"ו בספר אסיא כרך ג עמ' 497

§2

The confession of a dying person should be: I acknowledge before You, *Hashem*, my God and the God of my fathers, that my cure and my death are in Your Hands. May it be Your Will that You shall cure me completely. If I should die, may my death be an expiation for all the sins which I have sinned in ignorance, those that I committed know-

--- NISHMAT AVRAHAM ---

almost certainly aggravate his condition for the doctor has, in effect, removed the one vestige of hope that the patient may be harboring.

Incidentally, I do not think that what I have written here applies only to a patient with cancer, although most discussions on this subject of informing the patient seem to center on this particular disease. Why should such a patient be any different from one who has advanced heart or lung disease, for whom medicine has nothing further to offer? True, there is a particular fear of cancer among the general public, and its treatment is also complicated and difficult. Nevertheless, in the same way as most doctors do not debate as to whether they should or should not — and most of them do not — tell a patient with terminal heart or lung disease his grim prognosis, I do not see why a patient with terminal untreatable cancer should be told this. However, telling a patient — any patient — to confess when he is dying without at the same time taking away all hope and thus perhaps even hastening his death, is a serious problem. When and how this should be done will obviously depend on the patient and who will be the best person to tell him. Consultation with the family and a Rav is therefore absolutely essential.

On the other hand, even if the doctor thinks that the patient's situation is hopeless, and, under natural circumstances, he cannot possibly recover, he should, nevertheless, not accept this decisively and with absolute certainty. Certainly he should not be so brash as to give a definitive prognosis regarding how long the patient will live. For who knows what medical breakthrough tomorrow can bring, and *Hashem's* salvation can be instantaneous.[14] *Rav Kook zt"l*[15] writes that, in truth, the words of the doctors are only possibilities and not certainties, for even they cannot really believe that what they say is absolute. A theory that many consider to be a basic fact in medicine (and so for all disciplines), and which is accepted as axiomatic will be disdained by a future generation as being nonsense. What one builds, another destroys, and their words are therefore based only on faith and conjectures. And *Chazal's*[16] interpretation of the verse:[17] *verapo yerapei*, "from this we learn that the Torah permits the doctor to heal," is itself a sign that medicine as a science is basically a matter of doubt. Had it been otherwise, how could one possibly think that medical treatment would not have been obligatory? Would the doctor not have transgressed the prohibition:[18] "You shall not stand idly by while your fellow's blood is shed"? But man has no alternative and therefore needs the Torah's permission to practice medicine.

---

14. וראה בשו"ת נצר מטעי סי' ל אות א. מובא בספר אסיא עמ' 339

15. דעת כהן סי' קמ

16. ברכות ס ע"א. ב"ק פה ע"א

17. שמות כא:יט

18. ויקרא יט:טז

ingly, being unable to resist temptation and those that I committed rebelliously. Give me my portion in the Garden of Eden and grant that I be in the World to Come which has been set aside for the righteous. (D)(*If he wishes to say the lengthy confession that is said on Yom Kippur, he may do so.*)

SIMAN 339
THE LAWS CONCERNING A *GOSSES*

§1 (A)A *gosses* is (B)considered to be alive in every respect.

――――――― NISHMAT AVRAHAM ―――――――

(D) If he wishes to say the lengthy confession. The *Gra*[19] writes that this applies even to one who is healthy, as the *Gemara*[20] states. However for a dying patient it would be best to say the lengthy confession for it is better if he enumerates his sins[21] (see *Nishmat Avraham*, vol. 1 *Orach Chaim*, Siman 618L). The *Darchei Moshe*,[22] quoting the *Kol Bo*, writes that if he wishes to say the lengthy confession he should say: My Lord and the Lord of my fathers, may my prayer come before You etc. I have been guilty, I have betrayed etc. (*This is said every day after the Shemoneh Esrei of Shacharit and Minchah by the Sephardi communities and on Yom Kippur by the Ashkenazi communities*[23] — *author.*) It would be good if he enumerates not only his sins but also those occasions when he did resist the temptation to sin, for in this way he may remember other sins that he has forgotten, will regret having done them and thus repent completely.

SIMAN 339

(A) A *gosses*. The *Rambam*,[1] as translated by *Rav Kapach*, defines a *gosses* as one who is breathing his last breaths (the standard translations have: whose death rattle can be heard). The *Rama*[2] defines him as one who, when about to die, brings up sputum into his throat as a result of a tightness in his chest. On the other hand, we find[3] that this period can take up to three days.

There is no accurate modern definition that I know of as to when a dying patient is a *gosses*. A loose, but practical, definition might be: a patient who has reached the terminal stage of his illness and for whom nothing further can be done, and who has been defined, after halachic consultation and ruling, as being in the category of DNR (do not resuscitate). When I asked *Rav Auerbach zt"l* how to define a *gosses*, he answered: You are the doctor. Most doctors and members of burial societies with experience of the dying, sense when a patient becomes a *gosses*. However, although a patient may live for days after senior physicians and nurses have thought that he was a *gosses*, nevertheless the moment this decision is made, various *halachot* apply to him; see C below, p. 318.

---

for the full text.

19. ס"ק ו
20. ע"ז ח ע"א
21. ראה יומא פו ע"ב
22. כאן בשם הכלבו
23. See "The Complete ArtScroll Machzor (*Ashkenaz*) for *Yom Kippur*," pp. 129 and 131

1. פי' המשניות ערכין פ"א מ"ג. וראה שם בתויו"ט
2. אהע"ז סי' קכא סע' ז וחו"מ כי' ריא סע' ב. וראה בפרישה כאן ס"ק ה ואנציקלופדיה תלמודית ערך גוסס כרך ה עמ' שצג
3. יו"ד כאן סע' ב. וראה בפ"ת ס"ק ג

SIMAN 339: THE LAWS CONCERNING A GOSSES / §1

NISHMAT AVRAHAM

(B) considered to be alive in every respect. It is forbidden to hasten his death[4] and, if his condition can be treated, one is obligated to set aside Sabbath laws for him.[5] The *Mishnah Berurah*[6] rules that if he is found alive under rubble, even if his brain is crushed so that he cannot live for more than a while, Sabbath laws are set aside to rescue him. See *Nishmat Avraham*, vol. 1 *Orach Chaim*, Siman 329D. Therefore as long as there is the slightest hope and possibility that a patient is still alive and treatable, every effort must be made to treat him, including full resuscitation where needed.[7]

DEFINING DEATH. The *Mishnah*[8] says: If a building collapses on *Shabbat* and it is uncertain whether someone under the rubble is alive or not ... Sabbath laws are set aside to rescue him so long as there is a chance that he is alive. If he is found dead, he is left where he is until the termination of the Sabbath. The *Gemara*[9] asks: To what extent should the rubble be moved (breaking Sabbath laws) to examine whether he is alive or not? One opinion is, as far as his nostrils, whereas another is, as far as his heart. *Rashi*[10] explains that this refers to one who appears to be dead since he lies motionless. Rav Pappa says that this controversy (as far as his nostrils or as far as his heart) only refers to the situation when the victim's legs are reached first. It is in this situation that one opinion rules that when his heart is reached and can be examined, that is sufficient to detemine whether he is still alive. The other opinion rules that one must continue to clear the rubble until the victim's nostrils are reached, for there are times when his heart is no longer beating perceptibly, although he may still be breathing sufficiently for it to be discerned at his nose (see *Rashi*[11]). But if his head is uncovered first, once his nose can be examined for signs that he is still breathing, no further examination is necessary, for the verse says:[12] "All in whose nostrils was the breath of the spirit of life." This is also the ruling of the *Shulchan Aruch*.[13]

It appears certain to the *Gemara* that there cannot be a beating heart in a person who is not breathing, and at first sight, it would appear from this *Gemara* and *Rashi* that it is sufficient to define death as the cessation of brain function (*Rashi*, reference 10) and breathing alone without any further need to even examine the heart. However, at that time when resuscitation was unknown, it would certainly be immaterial, as far as continuing to desecrate the Sabbath, to examine his heart. Nowadays, however, when there is a possiblity of resuscitating someone who is not breathing or whose heart has stopped beating, or both, one certainly needs to take into consideration all three criteria mentioned in the *Gemara* and *Rashi* (reference 10) — namely that he lies motionless like a stone (*the cessation of brain function*), and is without heartbeat and respiration — before death can be pronounced. Rav Auerbach zt"l wrote to me that since cardio-pulmonary resuscitation (CPR) and other modern measures were unknown then,[14] it is possible that after the patient died "completely" (*that*

---

4. רמ"א כאן וש"ך ס"ק א
5. מנ"ח סוף מוסך השבת ד"ה והנה. ברכ"י או"ח סי' שכט סע' ד. שו"ת שבות יעקב ח"א סי' יג
6. סי' שכט סע' ד בביה"ל ד"ה אלא
7. וראה בספר הלכה ורפואה ח"ב עמ' קפה
8. יומא פ"ח מ"ז
9. שם פה ע"א
10. פה ע"א ד"ה עד היכן
11. שם ד"ה הכי גרסינן
12. בראשית ז:כב
13. או"ח סי' שכט סע' ד
14. אך ראה בילקוט שמעוני פ' שלח לך על הפסוק וישלח אותם משה: צווה בהם תלמי צוחה אחת ונפלו על פניהם ארצה. התחילו מנפחים בפיהם ומנשבים

is, all three criteria are met), he would be considered dead retroactively from the moment he ceased to breathe. Thus we should not think that *Chazal* mistakenly defined a live person (*whose heart was still beating — author*) as dead (*since he was no longer breathing — author*) and thus buried him alive. See also *Nishmat Avraham*, vol. 1 *Orach Chaim*, Siman 329D, p. 219 in *Rav Auerbach zt"l's* name.

The *Mishnah Berurah*, quoted above (reference 6), writes in the name of *rishonim*[15] that Sabbath laws are set aside to rescue someone from under rubble, even if his brain has been crushed to such a degree that he can live only for a short while. At first sight it would appear that such a person is not to be considered dead and Sabbath laws must be set aside for him where necessary, even though he has a crushed brain and, presumably, no brain function. However *Rav Auerbach zt"l* wrote to me that there is no proof from this *Mishnah Berurah*; it could be that his sources refer to cases in which part of the brain is still functioning. *Rav Neuwirth shlita* told me that although the *Mishnah Berurah* says "brain" it could be that the part that was crushed was the skull and not necessarily the brain. See, however, *Rav Eliashiv shlita's* view below, Siman 339D(2), p. 322.

The *Chatam Sofer*[16] rules that when a person lies as still as a stone, there is no heartbeat and he is not breathing, then, and only then, is he defined by our Torah as dead. See also the *Maharsham*[17] and the *Tzitz Eliezer*.[18]

The *Igrot Moshe*[19] writes that the truth of the matter is that if the brain stops functioning this is not a sign of death. As long as a person breathes he is alive. It is just that if the brain has ceased to work, death will follow, for he will stop breathing. There is no mention in *Chazal* or the *poskim* that there should be signs of brain function...[20] However, if there is any evidence of life as evidenced by a cardiogram, he is to be considered absolutely alive even though he is not breathing... There is an obligation to do whatever necessary to treat him, if possible, even on *Shabbat*.

Rav Auerbach zt"l wrote to me that he finds it difficult to believe that one can breathe without there being any brain function.

Until relatively recently, before the advent of the concept of "brain death," the total absence of movement of any part of the body, breathing and heartbeat was the universally accepted definition of death both by the Jewish and the non-Jewish world.

BRAIN DEATH and BRAINSTEM DEATH. These terms will be used interchangeably in this discussion.

1. ANATOMY AND PHYSIOLOGY.

A brief description of basic anatomy and physiology follows, enough to be able to understand the concept of brain death.

(a) Brain. The brain is enclosed by the skull, leaving it through an opening at the base of the skull to become the spinal cord. It consists of a left and right *cerebrum* (*cerebral hemispheres*), and, below them, a left and right *cerebellum*. These link up to the midline *midbrain* containing, among other structures, the *hypothalamus* and *pituitary body* and, lower down, the *pons* and *medulla*. The *midbrain*, *pons* and *medulla* are collectively known as the *brainstem* and contain the *reticular formation* [associated with cortical activity (see *cerebrum*, below) and wakefulness]. The

---

15. בשם האו"ה בשם הסמ"ג וסמ"ק
16. שו"ת, יו"ד סי' שלח
17. שו"ת, ח"ו סי' קכד
18. שו"ת, ח"ט סי' מו וח"י סי' כה פ"ד
19. שו"ת, יו"ד ח"ב סי' קמו
20. רצ"ע מהגמ' ופוסקים הנ"ל

באפס עד שנתיישבה דעתם עליהם. וכותב שם הזית רענן: אנשי כנען היו מנפחים בפיהם כדי להחיותן.

── NISHMAT AVRAHAM ──

respiratory and *cardiac centers* are also situated in the *reticular formation* which lies within, and extends from, the *midbrain* to the lower end of the *medulla*. The *respiratory center* controls the muscles of breathing. The *cardiac center* is responsible for changes in the rate of heartbeat as required, such as occur in anticipation of exercise and stress. The basic heartbeat however is inherent to the heart muscle, which will therefore beat at a fixed rate even when completely severed from the body. The *medulla* becomes the *spinal cord* as it leaves the skull.

(b) The cerebrum or cerebral hemisphere. There are two, one on each side, and each is functionally divided into four main areas. From front to back, these areas are successively called: (1) The *frontal lobes*; they control skilled motor function including speech, mood, and thought. (2) The *parietal lobes*; they interpret sensory information from the rest of the body, such as the sensations of touch and pain, and control body movement. (3) The *temporal lobes*; they are responsible for memory and emotions, and many of the higher functions found only in man. (4) The *occipital lobes*; they interpret the images that the eye sees.

(c) The cerebellum. There are two hemispheres, one on each side. The *cerebellum* is in the main responsible for coordination of movements and maintenance of equilibrium.

(d) The hypothalamus lies at the base of the cerebral hemispheres, together with other structures and subserves three systems: the *autonomic nervous system*, the *endocrine system* and the *limbic system* and functions in the maintenance of *homeostasis*. Thus, it is concerned with temperature regulation, regulating the body's water balance, sleep and wakefulness and controlling metabolism (the rate at which the body burns and utilizes food). By its influence on the nearby *pituitary gland* it also regulates other, distant, glands, such as the *thyroid* and *ovaries*.

(e) Blood supply. The blood supply to the brain comes from the *aorta* which supplies blood to the whole body. Four large vessels, two on each side of the neck, branch off from the *aorta* to bring blood to the brain. Ostensibly, if the blood supply in all four vessels is cut, the whole of the brain will not receive any blood and will therefore die.

2. HISTORY. As stated above, the classical definition of death was the absence of any signs of consciousness and muscular movement, together with cessation of respiration and heartbeat. Since most people died at home, this definition was accepted if a doctor, having examined the patient, confirmed that all these vital signs were indeed absent for a period of at least a minute. No instrumental confirmation, such as a cardiogram, was necessary.

With the advent of transplantation, particularly of the heart, the Harvard Ad Hoc Criteria for brain death was published in '68[21] under the title: A Definition of Irreversible Coma. Its opening sentences state: Our primary purpose is to define irreversible coma as a new criterion for death. There are two reasons why there is a need for a definition: (1) Improvements in resuscitative and supportive measures have led to increased efforts to save those who are desperately injured. Sometimes these efforts have only partial success so that the result is an individual whose heart continues to beat but whose brain is irreversibly damaged. The burden is great on patients who suffer permanent loss of intellect, on their families, on the hospitals and on those in need of hospital beds already oc-

NISHMAT AVRAHAM

cupied by these comatose patients. (2) Obsolete criteria for the definition of death can lead to controversy in obtaining organs for transplantation.

A Presidental Commission set up in '81 formulated its criteria for the definition of death — brain death. It defined brain death as: the irreversible cessation of all functions of the *entire brain* including the brainstem (emphasis mine).[22] The criteria laid down before this diagnosis could be confirmed were: irreversible deep coma not due to external causes such as drugs, *hypothermia*, irreversible cessation of respiration, and neurological confirmation of brain death. Thus brain death could not even be considered in a patient who showed any signs of consciousness or of any brain function, or who had any signs of spontaneous respiration. The fact that the heart was beating spontaneously did not exclude this definition, for, as explained above, it could beat spontaneously even when it lay outside the body. These patients were therefore, by definition, totally dependent on an external form of artificial ventilation — a respirator. In order to be absolutely certain that there was no spontaneous respiration whatsoever, an *apnea test* had to be performed.

Apnea test. The patient is completely disconnected from the respirator for many minutes, and multiple samples of blood are drawn to measure the level of carbon dioxide. If the test is positive, the blood level of carbon dioxide continues to rise, proving that the patient has not breathed at all during the test. He therefore fits the criterion of irreversible (if there were no other factors such as drugs, etc. which could have caused this temporarily) cessation of breathing. However the test is not without its dangers and, in one study,[23] 39% of patients developed marked falls in their blood pressure during its performance and four had to be given pressor drugs to counter this. In another study,[24] a patient had a cardiac arrest.

The neurological definition of brain death requires a full examination by a neurologist, including tests to prove that the *brainstem*, and therefore, indirectly, the *respiratory center*, is not functioning. It is assumed that this would also mean that there is cessation of all functions of the entire brain, and not just that of the *brainstem*.

Cerebral blood flow. Tests to show that there is no evidence of blood supply to the brain are optional in some parts of the United States and obligatory in others. These tests include the injection of a small quantity of radioactive material into tubing (outside the patient's body) that leads to a cannula that was already present in the patient's vein (for the purposes of giving intravenous fluids and medications). Pictures taken of the brain would then show whether any of this radioactive material reached the brain. It should be noted though that although the injection of the radioactive material can be done without touching or moving the patient, "the patient's head has to be positioned against the detector with the chin depressed... A suitably constructed headclamp or masking tape is used to immobilize the head."[25] *Transcranial Doppler ultrasonography* and *cerebral angiography* are also not absolute in their sensitivity or specificity.[26]

A patient who is clinically brain dead,

---

25. Nuclear Medicine Technology and Techniques, Bernier et al., Mosby Co. '81 p. 219
26. Emergency Med. Clinics of N. America 15:713, '97
22. JAMA 246:2184, '81
23. Arch. Neurol. 51:595, '94
24. Neurol. 28:661, '78

therefore, is one who lies motionless in deep coma, not responding to any stimuli, however painful, and who breathes solely by means of a respirator. There is absolutely no medical or surgical treatment that can in any way change this status and he will remain in this situation until his heart stops. Therefore, as a *gosses* for whom nothing can be done, he may not be touched unless for his benefit. Thus he must be given food and fluids artificially, as well as all the nursing care that is necessary. It should therefore be obvious that any of the above tests that are done are done for one purpose and one purpose only — to confirm that he is brain dead so that either the respirator can be legally turned off or, alternatively, so that he can be used as an organ donor.

One can see that the definition of brain death, cessation of all functions of the entire brain — which has remained unchanged today — is confused with brainstem death, since one assumes that if the brainstem is dead, the entire brain must also be dead. In other words, in the comatose patient if his respiratory center is dead, he is considered, by the medical world, as dead.

Do all doctors and medical personnel accept this? I think that we can divide them into three groups: (1) Those, and this is the largest group, whose opinion is unknown. (2) Those who support this definition for the purposes of transplantation. This group can be redivided into two subgroups: (a) Those who believe that the patient is dead, and (b) Those who believe that he is not, or at least are uncertain, but nevertheless will consider it ethical to use him as a donor of vital organs. They believe that since such a patient will never recover (I do not know of any recorded case in an adult), and, in fact most will die soon, he can therefore, both ethically and morally, be used to save the life of another viable person. (3) Those who believe that a brain-dead patient is still alive.

Reasons given by clinicians for supporting the whole brain definition actually imply that these patients are still alive. For example: Their lives are not worth living, their prognosis is hopeless, or they cannot live more than a few days,[27] implies this. A Conference of the Medical Royal Colleges of the United Kingdom '79 concluded that the state of brain death was a state of unsurvivable coma. It stopped short of equating it to death itself. In a letter to the editor on this subject,[28] the following statement appears: Many anesthetists clearly have been very uneasy about the transplant lobby's rather rash assumption that organ donors do not require anesthesia. Many anesthetists do administer an anesthetic to these patients (*who are "dead" — author*), with good reason, as set out in your editorial (see below). It is time that all anesthetists realized that to not administer an anesthetic to a donor is to commit an act of possible barbarous dishonesty. Whatever the effect on donor numbers, one cannot condone such an action. The editorial[29] referred to contains the following passages: The hemodynamic response (increase in blood pressure and heart rate) could be considered to represent an organism in distress and probably occurs at a spinal level although we are unaware of EEG studies during organ collection to confirm this. Faced with the knowledge of the persistence of higher brain and spinal function in some donors, the inability to test the *reticular formation* directly and the dramatic peroperative (*during operation*) hemodynamic changes that occur, sedation and analgesia should be given with muscle relaxation for organ donation. It is imperative that public confidence is maintained in the transplant program. The act of organ donation is a final altruistic one and we should ensure the provision of general anesthesia at least sufficient to prevent the hemodynamic response to surgery.

3. EVIDENCE AGAINST TOTAL BRAIN DEATH IN BRAIN-DEAD PATIENTS.

The editorial quoted above lists the following objective evidence that the *hypothalamus* is still functioning in many patients who fulfill the criteria of brain death. (1) 23% of brain-dead adults did not have *diabetes insipidus* showing that the hormone controlling this is still being secreted by the *hypothalamus*. 23% of clinically brainstem-dead patients had EEG activity — which does not necessarily imply function — but 4% demonstrated sleep-like cortical EEG activity for as long as 7 days (*pointing to functioning of the reticular formation — author*). 27% and 26% of such patients demonstrated *brainstem auditory evoked response* (*showing that part of the brainstem was still functioning — author*) in two separate studies respectively. A third of such patients had perfusion (blood flow) of parts of the brain such as the *basal ganglia*, *thalamus* and/or *brainstem* as measured by *SPECT* (*a method of measuring perfusion to the brain after the injection of a small amount of radioactive material*). In addition, these patients maintain a normal body temperature, even though they have been "dead" for weeks or months.

Persons who meet whole-brain criteria of death, if mechanically ventilated, typically remain normothermic (*have a normal body temperature — author*) ... digest and absorb food, filter blood through both liver and kidneys, urinate and defecate, heal wounds, and may even gestate fetuses.[30] (*This and other such statements are in sharp contrast to those written by others who claim that brain-dead patients typically show sharp variations in body temperature and have to be treated with hormone replacements. However it is precisely this disagreement that adds so much to the uncertainty of what the term brain dead really means and raises the question of how one can be so certain that the patient really is dead medically, let alone halachically.*)

Finally, even patients who are brain dead confirmed by *angiographic studies* (*radio-opaque dye injected into the aorta to fill all four vessels to the brain showing that no blood flows to the brain*) nevertheless retain *hypothalamic* function. It is assumed that a circulation sufficient to prevent necrosis, but too small to be demonstrated by *angiography*, was maintained.[31] Thus, in at least 25% of brain-dead patients, the concept of "physiological decapitation" is meaningless.

HOW MANY OF THESE TESTS ARE DONE? A letter to Dr. Schulman in June '93 from the New York Regional Transplant Program states that their policy pertaining to brain death protocol is to follow hospital protocol in declaring a patient brain dead. In some institutions, they require cerebral blood flow or EEG's plus *apnea* tests as ancillary testing (*implying that in others no ancillary tests — not even the apnea test — are done before a patient is pronounced brain dead — author*). For the 155 donors that they followed, cerebral blood flow studies were not done in 77%, EEG was not done in 64% and *apnea* testing was not performed in 65% of donors. (See below letter by *Rav Auerbach zt"l*, page 310).

A common misconception is that all brain-dead patients will die, that is, the heart will also stop beating, within hours or days[32] of the diagnosis. However a study[33] of 175 brain-dead patients who had survived a week showed that approximately 80 survived at least two weeks, approximately 44 at least four weeks, approximately 20 at least two months and 7 at least six months. An editorial in the same issue comments: The data collected here actually underestimates brain-death survival potential because in one-third of cases (respiratory) support was withdrawn.

In addition, there have been a number of cases of pregnant women who were brain dead and later gave birth to a normal, healthy child by Caesarian section.[34] In one case,[35] a woman was diagnosed as brain dead when she was 15 weeks pregnant. She was fed by naso-gastric tube for 107 days and a live healthy child was delivered by Caesarian section at about 32 weeks. It would appear that these dead women could not only carry through a pregnancy for many weeks, but could even process the food they were given, allowing the fetus to develop and grow normally.

4. DISSENTING VOICES. As I have said above, the majority of physicians who have made their opinion known in the medical literature equate brain death with death. However there are dissenting voices who point out that the whole redefinition of death was only to allow organs to be removed from donors in a legal and socially accepted manner. Thus we find the following statement: The development of organ transplantation required that death be redefined so that physicians who removed organs from patients whose cardiopulmonary function was being supported were not accused of murder.[36] The only purpose served by the concept of brain death is to facilitate the procurement of transplantable organs ... The most difficult challenge ... would be to gain acceptance of the view that killing may sometimes be a justifiable necessity for procuring transplantable organs.[37] See also above 2 (page 303), the Harvard Committee's stated purposes for redefining death.

5. THE *HALACHAH*.

(a) The Chief Rabbinate of Israel. On Nov. 3, '86,[38] the then Chief Rabbinate of Israel published its decision on brain death and heart transplants. It said: The Chief Rabbinate of Israel is prepared to permit heart transplants (from accident victims) to be performed at the Hadassah Medical Center, Jerusalem under the following conditions ... The decision was based on a number of factors, among them that: We have received evidence that even Rabbi M. Feinstein *zt"l* recently permitted a heart transplant procedure in the United States. Further, we know of other leading rabbis (Rabbi Yitzchak Weiss, author of the *Minchat Yitzchak*) who have advised cardiac patients to undergo a transplant.

(b) *Rav Shlomo Zalman Auerbach zt"l*. The following is a summary, presented chronologically, of the *Rav zt"l's* opinion on this problem. The *Rav zt"l* wrote to me[39] that a patient who requires a transplant may not agree to receive it in Israel for by doing so he causes the life of the donor to be shortened. Even if there will

---

32. Neurology 51:1538, '98 quoting a President's Commision '81
33. Neurology 51:1538, '98.
34. Am J Obs Gyn 157:1097, '87. JAMA 248:1089,
   '82. BMJ 290:1237, '85. JAMA 260:816, '88
35. Obs Gyn 74:434 '89
36. JAMA 263:696, '90
37. Hastings Center Report 27:29, '97
38. Assia, Jewish Medical Ethics, 1:2 '89
39. ראה נשמת אברהם כרך ב יו"ד סי' קנז ס"ק ו

Ann. Int. Med 110:814, '89.

be other candidates who will be prepared to commit this sin and be in line for the transplant, it is nevertheless forbidden since the majority of donors in Israel will be Jews (see also above Siman 157E). At the time, the *Rav zt"l* told me that until there is a definitive ruling from the great *poskim* that such a patient is dead, one is obligated to feed and care for him as for any comatose patient. If it were possible that he needed something to be done for him which could only be done by setting aside Sabbath laws, this must be done. However one should not resuscitate him (*were his heart to stop — author*).

In Av 5751 ('90), the *Rav zt"l* told me that since the definition of brainstem death was not to be found in the *Talmud*, we are unable to make a new definition of this kind in our times. Only a *Sanhedrin* will have the power to rule whether brainstem death can be equated with death or not. Until then it is forbidden to remove the patient's heart or any organ as long as his heart is still beating.

That same month, the *Rav zt"l* and *Rav Eliashiv shlita* signed a letter which was published in the local religious press:

> We have been asked to give our opinion, that of the Torah, regarding a heart transplant, or a transplant of other organs, to a *seriously ill* patient. As long as the donor's heart is beating, even if the whole of his brain, including the brainstem, no longer functions, what is known as "braindeath," our opinion nevertheless is that it is not permissible whatsoever to remove any one of his organs, and doing so involves bloodshed.

In Elul 5751(August '91), Rabbi Tendler (Yeshiva University, New York) wrote to both *Rav Auerbach zt"l* and *Rav Eliashiv shlita* explaining in detail his views on the subject. They replied to him briefly: We have received your letter and after studying it closely we see no reason to change our minds. It is not permitted at all to remove organs for the purpose of transplantation as long as the donor's heart is beating, and doing so constitutes shedding blood.

Rav Auerbach zt"l wrote to me: The *Gemara* (*Arachin* 7a) writes that when a pregnant woman dies a natural death, since the life of the fetus is (*more*) fragile, its death precedes that of the mother. Even if it appears that the fetus is still alive, the *Gemara* calls these spontaneous reflex movements like those of a lizard's tail which continues to move even after it has been cut off from the lizard. There is no way that the fetus can live after the death of the mother unless she is already in labor. This is also the meaning of the *Shulchan Aruch Orach Chaim*, Siman 330:5. *Tosafot* (*Chullin* 38b), on the basis of the *Gemara* in *Arachin*, question the possibility of a fetus outliving its mother and say that this can occur only if she was slain and did not die a natural death. Even if occasionally the fetus still lives after the natural death of its mother, this is only if it was delivered soon after the mother's death. Therefore, if (*as in the cases of the pregnant women who were brain dead, mentioned above, page* 307) she can at least receive and digest food and have the fetus grow in her womb (*after brain death — author*), and surely other internal organs must also be involved in this, we have proof that as long as she can be artificially ventilated, she is still alive. We must then say, in a like manner, that when *Chazal* tell us that an old person who breaks his neck or even only his spinal cord (*the cervical portion*), is considered dead, this applies only in their day when they did not have respirators. For in such a person both respiration and heartbeat will immediately stop and he is considered dead even though reflex movements are still present. Today, however, if he is prevented from dying by artificial ventilation, he is considered alive as long as part of him is alive and a heartbeat is present, even though this is only because he is being ventilated. This situation is comparable to the baby born after eight months gestation whom *Chazal* compared to a stone, whereas today, Heaven forbid that we consider him a stone since we can treat him in an incubator. The *Gemara* (see ref. 9) also states that a person who is buried under rubble, if on freeing him he is found not to be breathing, he is considered as dead and it is forbidden to desecrate the Sabbath any further for him. However today one must certainly continue rescue efforts and attempt to resuscitate him. This is so also in the situation of a brain-dead person who is attached to a respirator and thus prevented from dying. One cannot possibly think that the body is merely a host for the passage of food and the growth of the fetus. In this light, whoever removes the heart or liver from the body when the person is attached to a respirator sheds blood. It is possible that even the *Gaon* and righteous man, the author of the *Igrot Moshe* (Y.D. III 132), only meant to rule strictly. (*A patient who does not respond to any stimuli and who has stopped breathing must not be pronounced dead as long as his heart is beating. And if one shows that there is blood flow to the brain he must be artificially ventilated even for a prolonged period.*) But even if we say that he meant to rule leniently (*that if there were no blood flow to the brain, such a patient can be pronounced dead*), this must only be because he was unaware of the possibility that such a woman could digest food and that her fetus could continue to grow. Therefore, since the *Gemara* and *poskim* nowhere state that brain death can be considered death, such a person is considered as still being alive. As long as we have not seen clearly that an artificially ventilated pregnant woman after brain death, or an animal that has been beheaded, can still allow a fetus to grow, we must certainly think that the artificial respiration prevents death, and not that she is already dead. Nevertheless, it would seem to me that if ever it could be absolutely proven that the whole brain and brainstem are destroyed it would be permitted to discontinue the ventilation without moving the patient, since the machine merely prevents him from dying, even if the machine was attached to him originally for his benefit.

Rav Auerbach zt"l wrote to me the following interim summary (italics are mine):

1. Although it would be very important to find, by decapitating a pregnant animal (*whether she will continue with her pregnancy, for if so this will show that continuing pregnancy is not a sign of life, at least in an animal*), nevertheless, it will not solve our doubt with regard to a human being. Even if it will be shown that the body (*of the decapitated animal*) is merely an incubator, we still have to clarify whether a (*brain-dead*) human would not be considered a *gosses* (*we would as yet have no certain proof with regard to a human being and perhaps the brain-dead patient should still be treated not as a corpse but as a gosses*). And even if we do not move him, nevertheless, the injection of material (*to see whether there is blood flow to the brain*) into all his blood vessels — which, of course is not done for his benefit — will hasten his death. (*I, and others, repeatedly told the Rav zt"l that we were talking about a small quantity of fluid, injected into tubing outside the patient's body, but he maintained that an injection into the body of a gosses was more serious than moving his limb.*) We also need to clarify *halachically* whether we may depend on a scientific test and not on the evidence of our eyes and remove organs from him while his heart is still beating.

NISHMAT AVRAHAM

2. Nevertheless, since such a patient is defined as being a *gosses*, and there is no chance that he will ever be cured or breathe spontaneously, it would be permitted to turn off the respirator, which is preventing his soul from leaving the body, in accordance with the ruling of the *Rama* (§1). However this is only on condition that one knows with absolute certainty that there is no flow of blood to the brain which has decayed within the skull.

Letter to Rav Shraga Feivel Cohen (author of the *Badei HaShulchan*): Rav Cohen *shlita* wrote, in Tevet 5752 (Dec. '91), to both *Rav Auerbach zt"l* and *Rav Eliashiv shlita* asking why it should be permissible to receive a transplant in the United States since the recipient would possibly be curtailing the life of another Jew, the donor. *Rav Auerbach zt"l* replied as follows (abridged):[40]

If the doctors will show by the injection of material to the brain that, in their opinion, the patient is certainly dead, and one can show that a pregnant, artificially ventilated sheep without a brain can continue to grow a fetus then the fact that a fetus can continue to live after the death of the mother will invalidate my proof (*see The sheep experiment, below — author*). One must then say that when *Chazal* stated that the fetus always dies first this would only be true if the mother were not artificially ventilated.

In such a situation (*where there is no blood flow to any part of the brain — author*), one can equate such a patient with a decapitated one or with an old person whose spine is broken. In the case in question, where one can certainly follow the rule of the majority that the donor will be a non-Jew, it will certainly be permitted for a Jew to be a recipient. However all the above applies only to the United States and other places where the majority of the population are non-Jews. This does not apply to *Eretz Yisrael*. For here one must carefully consider whether the above test (*injection of material into the donor — author*) may be done. The patient is to be considered a *gosses* and and hastening his death will be murder. And although Rav Tendler writes that the test is done without touching the patient's body, I have heard that it is virtually impossible not to move him. In any case this (*whether the patient's body is moved or not — author*) is a mistake, for the very injection of material that spreads throughout his body is much more serious than moving his body slightly or closing his eyes (*Chazal*[41] have specifically written that anyone who closes the eyes of a *gosses* has shed blood — *author*) and is certainly forbidden (also there are those who are suspect not to carry out this test anyway). And, all these tests are of no benefit whatsoever to the *gosses* (*the donor — author*), but are only for the sake of others.

On the other hand, the above reasoning should also make it forbidden in the Diaspora, since a non-Jew is forbidden to kill another or to hasten the death of a *gosses*. Thus the recipient will have transgressed the prohibition not to place a stumbling block before the blind in a case of bloodshed. However the doctor will in any case remove the organs for someone else, whether or not the Jew puts himself on the waiting list. And, although the patient would not be permitted to put himself on the waiting list in *Eretz Yisrael*, this will nevertheless be permitted in the Diaspora (*since the non-Jewish doctor will, in any case, use the brain-dead patient as a donor for he believes that the patient is dead; see the original letter, reference 40 — author*). However all this is on condition

---

40. ראה בנשמת אברהם כרך ד עמ' קמה את המכתב המלא

41. מסכת שמחות פ"א מ"ד

NISHMAT AVRAHAM

that the blood flow test is done twice (with an interim period of 24 hours), which, in any case they do not do. (*See above* 3, *page* 306 — *author.*) Thus the doubts remain.

However, Professor Abraham has now told me that once the doctors have established that the brainstem is dead, they believe that the patient is certainly dead even without doing this test. Since the doctors are mainly concerned with science and not with the *halachah*, known to every observant Jew, that he who even minimally moves a *gosses* sheds blood, the ruling, based on everything written above, will be that it is permitted to be a recipient in the Diaspora, but forbidden in *Eretz Yisrael*. Signed Shlomo Zalman Auerbach.

The sheep experiment, Shevat 5752 ('92). This experiment was done twice. In each case a full-term pregnant sheep was decapitated after all four of the large vessels to the brain were tied off. The sheep was artificially ventilated throughout the experiment and its heart continued to beat spontaneously throughout. In the first experiment, although the brain was completely sucked out, the sheep's heart continued to beat and the fetus remained alive for some three hours. The sheep was now decapitated but this was followed, some twenty minutes later, by disappearance of the fetal heartbeat. An emergency Caesarian section was done but the fetus was dead. In the second experiment, some twenty-five minutes after the decapitation there were spontaneous contractions of the whole body of the sheep, probably secondary to strong uterine contractions. Caesarian section was then done and a live lamb delivered. Thus, both experiments show that, provided a sheep is artificially ventilated, its fetus can continue to live after the mother was decapitated.

Rav Auerbach zt"l then wrote to me: This disproves what I thought on the basis of the *Gemara*,[42] that the fetus always dies first. We must now say that if the mother is artificially ventilated the fetus can certainly remain alive even after the mother has died. However this does not in any way change my previous conclusion that there is still the fear, nevertheless, of moving a *gosses*. Therefore (*receiving a transplant — author; see letter to Rav Cohen, above*) will be permitted in the Diaspora and forbidden in *Eretz Yisrael*.[43]

In Adar 5752 ('92), at *Rav Auerbach zt"l's* request, three senior and experienced doctors, Robert Schulman of New York (internist/endocrinologist), Jacob Fleischman of Los Angeles (internist/infectious diseases) and Jacob Schacter of New York (cardiologist) wrote to him, in answer to his question, as to how long after a brain-dead patient was disconnected from his respirator would they be willing to define him as dead. They wrote:

After much discussion between ourselves and other doctors, regarding defining the moment of death, we have come to the following conclusion provided two conditions set out below are met. (1) All the tests necessary to show that there is no spontaneous respiration and that the brainstem has been completely and irreversibly damaged have been done. (2) Other tests have also been done to show that there is absolutely no flow of blood to the brain (although these are forbidden by *Halachah*), so that it is absolutely certain that the patient is brain dead (the whole brain including the brainstem). If the respirator is then disconnected so that the patient does not breathe at all, the heart stops beating after some minutes. We believe that 15-20 seconds after the heart has completely stopped, at that mo-

---

42. ערכין ז ע"א.   43. ראה המכתב במלואו בנשמת אברהם כרך ד עמ' קעה.

ment the patient is dead in every way and we would be prepared to sign his death certificate.

The *Rav zt"l* replied to them as follows: Even if the doctors have done all the necessary tests, including cerebral blood flow studies, in a critically ill patient, and they have decided that the whole brain including the brainstem is dead, nevertheless as long as he is being ventilated artificially, he is still considered a possible *gosses* by Torah law, and the law is well known that if one moves a *gosses* it is as if he has shed blood. And it is more certain that one may not take any organ from him, as long as the heart is beating, even if it only does so because the patient is artificially ventilated, nevertheless he is still a possible *gosses* and this is forbidden. In my opinion, if after all the tests of the brain and brainstem have already been done (*against the Halachah — author*) and the doctors have definitely decided that he is dead, the only way in which a person, who keeps the Torah, can definitely find out whether the patient is dead, is to disconnect the respirator and then, if the heart is not beating at all and the patient lies like a stone, only then can he be considered dead. All this is in accord with what I have been told by expert doctors who are also Torah observant that they would be willing to sign a death certificate in such a case, thirty seconds after the heartbeat has completely ceased.

Therefore, in the Diaspora, where the majority of doctors and patients are non-Jews who depend on medical science and do not fear moving a *gosses*, and, after doing all the tests regarding the brainstem they consider the patient to be dead, even though he is still being ventilated artificially and his heart is beating, only there (*in the Diaspora — author*) will it be permitted to be a recipient of an organ transplant, but not in *Eretz Yisrael* where the majority of both patients and doctors are Jews who are bound by all the laws of the Torah.

All this I have written according to my humble opinion although I know that there are those who think differently.

Signed with trembling, with the honor of the Torah and with great respect, Shlomo Zalman Auerbach.

In a letter addressed to Rabbi Tendler, dated Nissan 5752 ('92), *Rav Auerbach zt"l* also writes (in part):[44] After the doctors have established that the patient's brainstem is dead, it would still be permissible for them to continue to perform other tests, if in their opinion, they will be for the patient's benefit. They may not perform tests for any other reason, for one may not actively hasten the death of a *gosses* even to save another's life. My heart tells me that whatever is done within the patient's body or in his blood, is worse than moving him slightly, and is forbidden.

With the growing evidence that there were still parts of the brain, such as the *hypothalamus* and *pituitary body*, that remain functional after brain death is diagnosed, the *Rav zt"l* wrote me the following letter in Av 5753 (July '93):[45]

However lately I have been told that it is possible that even with a patient such as I have spoken about, whose heart has stopped for thirty seconds, that the part of the brain known as the hypothalamus, that influences all the parts of the body, is still functional. If the patient were reconnected to the respirator and the heart could be restarted, it would continue to function for many days. Therefore, I am not certain that *halachically* the thirty-second wait can be still be considered suf-

---

44. המכתב במלואו פורסם במנחת שלמה ח"ב סי' פג אות ו(ב) עמ' שכה 45. נשמת אברהם ח"ה עמ' צז

SIMAN 399: THE LAWS CONCERNING A GOSSES / §1

NISHMAT AVRAHAM

ficient; one would have to wait until it is a certainty that this part of the brain has also died, since an important part of the brain might still be alive and functional. If so, although it would be permissible to write a death certificate after the thirty-second wait, one should not remove any organs. Therefore I am writing to you explicitly that I retract from what I have previously written and it is as if I have not said anything.

In the spring of '94, *Tradition*[46] published a letter to the editor on brain death. In the last paragraph of the letter the authors write:

All Rabbinic authorities agree that the classic definition of death in Judaism is the absence of spontaneous respiration in a patient with no other signs of life. A brief waiting period of a few minutes to a half-hour after breathing has ceased is also required. Brain death is a criterion for confirming death in a patient who already has irreversible absence of spontaneous respiration. The situation of decapitation, where immediate death is assumed even if the heart may still be briefly beating, is certainly equated with organismal death, classic Jewish sources, as well as the responsa of Rabbi Moshe Feinstein, *z"l*. This view is now supported by more and more rabbis including Rabbi Shlomo Zalman Auerbach, the Israeli Chief Rabbinate, Rabbi Feinstein's sons David and Reuben, and seemingly, Rabbi Eliezer Y. Waldenberg.

As a result of the above letter, Dr. Robert Schulman of New York[47] wrote to both *Rav Auerbach zt"l* and to *Rav Waldenberg shlita* asking them whether they had indeed changed their ruling regarding brain death. *Rav Auerbach zt"l*[48] answered (in a letter dated 10th Kislev 5755 — 13 Nov '94 — text as in *Tradition*):

I received your letter and I am informing you that I have not changed my mind from what I had originally written to you in '92 as published in *Assia* [Elul 5754 (August '94) pp. 26-28]. I still believe that a person who is brain dead has the status of a *gosses* according to the law of our Holy Torah. When a person moves a *gosses* it is as if he has spilled blood, and, obviously, one cannot remove any organ from him. I have written this same statement to Prof. Avraham (ibid. p. 28), (*letter above page 312: However, lately I have been told — author*) and this too was published in *Assia* (August '94) and was explained in the article of Dr. Steinberg (ibid. pp. 10-16).

See below for *Rav Waldenberg shlita's* reply.

Rav Neuwirth shlita,[49] eulogizing *Rav Auerbach zt"l*, writes: The letter caused *Maran zt"l* much pain and anguish ... And I add that this opinion is not only that of *Maran zt"l* but all the great of Israel unanimously concur with him, for example, *Rav Eliashiv shlita*, *Rav Ovadiah Yosef shlita* and *Rav Waldenberg shlita*.

(c) *Rav Yosef Shalom Eliashiv shlita*. When I first spoke to *Rav Eliashiv shlita* on this subject many years ago, I pointed out to him that, with the majority of these patients (considered brain dead), the heart would also stop beating within forty-eight hours. He answered that I had convinced him that most of these patients would die in an extremely short time, but that there was no evidence that they were now dead. Therefore, as long as the heart is beating, it is forbidden to do anything to hasten his death. I later asked *Rav Eliashiv shlita* how such a patient should be defined if he did live for many months. He answered me that he would be defined as a possible *gosses*.

The *Dayanim* of the *Beit Din* of London

---

46. 28:94, Spring '94

47. אסיא חוברת נו תשרי תשנ"ו עמ' 121

48. נשמת אברהם ח"ה עמ' צט. אסיא שם עמ' 122
See *Tradition* 28:102, Spring '94.

49. המעין כרך לה ניסן תשנ"ה עמ' 3

and Great Britain asked *Rav Eliashiv shlita* whether they were permitted to allow Jews to sign an organ-donation card since they feared that Jews would not receive transplants if they refused to be donors. The *Rav shlita* ruled that there was no basis for this fear, and that the signing of such cards is not permitted.[50]

In a reply to Rav Shraga Feivel Cohen *shlita* (see above) *Rav Eliashiv shlita* wrote,[51] dealing at length with the *halachic* ramifications of a *gosses* and the rule of the majority. He concluded that in this case one may depend on who the majority of the population are (*regarding the donor — author*).

(d) Rav Eliezer Yehudah Waldenberg shlita. *Rav Waldenberg shlita*[52] rules that a patient who is brain dead is considered to be alive in every respect.

Following the letter to the editor in *Tradition* mentioned above, *Rav Waldenberg shlita*[53] replied to Dr. Schulman on the 25th Cheshvan 5755 (Oct. 30 '94 — text as in *Tradition*):

I received your letter today and I hasten to reply. I was amazed to read in your letter that I have reversed my *p'sak* forbidding transplanting a heart or any other organ for a seriously ill patient where the heart of the donor beats, even if his brain, including the brain stem, is not working at all, which is called brain death. I publicly inform you that as my opinion was then, my opinion is now: to forbid such a thing according to the halakha, and with great emphasis. I have not reversed my opinion and have already repeated this and have again published my opinion to forbid this in my book *Tzitz Eliezer* (volume 19). To strengthen my position, I wrote an addendum in the back of the book in which I published the opinion of my friends, the Gaon Rabbi Shlomo Zalman Auerbach and the Gaon Rabbi Eliashiv, who also forbid this. I am puzzled! How is it possible for a living person to contradict another living person? In this matter I state publicly that the letter which was published in *Tradition* regarding my opinion has no basis in fact at all.

(e) Other *gedolei hador* who do not accept brain death as a definition of death. *Rav Yitzchak Weiss zt"l*,[54] *Rav Wosner shlita*,[55] *Rav Ovadiah Yosef shlita*,[56] *Rav Shach zt"l*, and *Rav Kulitz shlita* (the Ashkenazi Chief Rabbi of Jerusalem)[57] all agree that such a patient is not dead.

(f) Rav Moshe Feinstein zt"l. Four *responsa* were published in the *Igrot Moshe* during the Rav *zt"l's* lifetime — two dealing with the criteria of death and two with transplantation. A fifth *responsum* came to light posthumously.

(1) Criteria of death. In the first,[58] 5730 ('70) he writes: In truth, it is certain that the absence of brain function does not mean that he is dead. For as long as he breathes he is alive. It is only that if the brain has ceased to function this will lead to death, for he will cease to breathe. It is possible that there are medications that are either known, or even those that are as yet unknown, that will restore the brain's function. Besides, one may pray to *Hashem* to cure him for he is still considered alive, though dangerously ill, and one may pray for him; he is not dead

---

See *Tradition* 28:102, Spring '94.

50. ראה בנשמת אברהם כרך ד עמי קלח
51. ראה בנשמת אברהם כרך ד עמי קמח את המכתב המלא
52. שו"ת ציץ אליעזר חי"ז סי' סו וחי"ט סי' נג בסוף. אסיא חוברת מד-מה בסלו תש"ן, עמי קטו. וראה גם בשו"ת ציץ אליעזר ח"ט סי' מו וח"י סי' כה פ"ד
53. שו"ת ציץ אליעזר חכ"א סי' כח. נשמת אברהם כרך ה עמי צח. אסיא חוברת נו תשרי תשנ"ו עמי 122
54. מובא בשו"ת ציץ אליעזר חי"ז סי' סו
55. שו"ת שבט הלוי ח"ז סי' רלה
56. בהרצעה פומבית לפני כמה שנים
57. מובאים ע"י הרב דוד בליץ שליט"א באור המזרח תשרי תשכ"ח
58. שו"ת אג"מ יו"ד ח"ב סי' קמו

―――――― NISHMAT AVRAHAM ――――――

which would make it forbidden to pray for him since that would be a prayer in vain. Therefore one who kills him is plainly a murderer ... There is no mention in the *Gemara* or *poskim* that there should be a sign of life in the brain and the premise that nature has changed is unapplicable here. For in the times of *Chazal* the brain functioned as it does now and from it came all the vitality of the body. Nevertheless, a person was not considered dead because his brain had stopped functioning and this is clearly so even today. And, regarding your discussion to decide leniently, that even if the doctors see evidence of the heartbeat in a cardiogram ... that this is not meaningful, and he should be considered dead once he has stopped breathing ... this, in my opinion, is not so ... Therefore, it is forbidden to establish that such a person (*is dead — author*) and, on the contrary, everything that is possible to do to treat him must be done, including treatment on *Shabbat*.

In a second *responsum*[59] 5736 ('76) *Rav Feinstein zt"l* writes: Patients who cannot breathe and are artificially ventilated ... with regard to other signs of life he does not feel anything ... as long as the respirator is working it is forbidden to disconnect it from the patient for he might still be alive and disconnecting him will kill him. However, when the respirator stops, because its supply of oxygen is finished, it should not be reconnected to him for a period of about a quarter of an hour. If he is no longer alive, he will have stopped breathing and one will know that he is dead ... however those who are injured in traffic accidents ... even if they can no longer breathe spontaneously, and there are no other signs of life, it is still possible that they are still alive. Since you say that there is now a possibility of injecting a substance that will tell us whether the connection between the brain and the rest of the body has been severed and also since the brain is already completely necrotic, it is as if he has been decapitated ... even though he is not breathing spontaneously at all, death must not be established until this test has been done. If they see that there is still a link between the brain and the body, even though he is not breathing, he should be ventilated artificially even for a long period of time. Only if they see, by this test, that there is no connection between the brain and the body, may death be established since he is not breathing.

The above two *responsa* concern the establishment of death, and the problem of transplantation is not dealt with. Although the test for cerebral blood flow is mentioned in the second responsum, *Rav Feinstein zt"l* rules that it must be used as an even stricter criterion of death in a post-accident artificially ventilated patient. Second, the Rav *zt"l* was told that a patient in whom the test shows no connection between brain and body, the brain is completely necrotic and it is as if he has been decapitated, and his ruling is based on this information. We now know this to be incorrect in many brain dead patients (see 3 page 306).

(2) Transplantation. The first *responsum*[60] concerning transplantation was written in 5728 ('68): Regarding heart transplantation that a few doctors have started performing, I do not wish to write at length with proofs, theories and discussions ... Therefore I will write a practical reply which will be clear and absolute and will not lead to any discussion on it. Heart transplants that the doctors have started to do recently is absolutely the murder of two souls. They actively kill the donor since he is still alive ... and also the recipient since most have died within hours of

---

59. שם יו"ד ח"ג סי' קלב.

60. שם יו"ד ח"ב סי' קעד.

the transplant and a few within days.

In a second *responsum*[61] in 5738 ('78) Rav Feinstein zt"l writes: I have already sent you a telegram that this is forbidden and will be considered as the active murder of two souls, as I have already written in 5728 ('68) and published in my work *Igrot Moshe Y.D.* II, Siman 174 (reference 60 above), and, as I wrote then, one should not discuss the subject at length lest people make a mistake and think that there may be some latitude to possibly permit it ... I have gone into the matter ... and know that there has not been any change for the better since the advent of transplantation and no recipient has lived for some years. Even the months that they have lived have been a life of suffering and pain...

A third letter, dated 5745 ('85) and written to Dr. Bondi, appeared in the summer of 5752 ('92)[62] and concerns the ruling of the State of New York to accept brain death as the definition of death. It states: As I have heard from my son-in-law ... they have only accepted what is right in *Halachah*, the definition known as the "Harvard criteria," by which the patient is considered exactly as if "he has been decapitated" and his brain completely necrotic. Therefore, although the heart may still beat for some days, nevertheless if the patient can no longer breathe spontaneously, he is considered to be dead, as I have stated in my *responsum* in *Igrot Moshe Y.D.* III, Siman 132.

If one looks at this letter, as it stands, Rav Feinstein zt"l accepted brain death as the death of the person. But, as he clearly writes, this is based on the Harvard criteria by which, he was told, "the patient is considered exactly as if he has been decapitated and his brain completely necrotic." As I have written above (see 3 page 306), this assumption is far from true in many patients, since a "decapitated brain" cannot allow the continuing growth of a fetus or, for that matter, keep the body temperature at 37°C or control the influence of hormones in the person. In addition, in a postmortem study of 503 patients, the authors write:[63] It was not possible to verify that a diagnosis made prior to cardiac arrest by any set or subset of criteria would invariably correlate with a diffusely destroyed brain. (*That is to say that whatever criteria was used to define a patient as being brain dead — that is "his brain was completely necrotic," postmortem examination of the brain would not invariably confirm this and, in some patients, parts of the brain were still intact — author.*)

Rav Auerbach zt"l, in response to this last letter of *Rav Feinstein zt"l*, writes:[64] As to the transplantation of organs from a person who is (*brain*) dead to a *dangerously ill* patient, in hospitals in the Diaspora the majority of doctors and patients are non-Jews, who act only in accordance with medical science and the law of the land. Therefore, if according to this law the patient is considered dead, they will immediately remove the organs that are required for transplantation from him. In my opinion, it will be permitted there, even for a Jew who is observant of Torah and *mitzvot*, to place himself on the waiting list to be a recipient. However in *Eretz Yisrael*, where they (*the population who are mainly Jews — author*) are bound to act in accordance with the Laws of the Holy Torah and the *Halachah*, even if it is shown by the tests that we have today that the brain is completely dead, an artificially ventilated patient is still consid-

---

63. Quoted in Crit. Care Med. 20:1705, '92.

64. ראה נשמת אברהם כרך ה עמ' צה

61. שם חו"מ ח"ב סי' עב

62. אסיא חוברת נג אלול תשנ"ד עמ' 24

ered as a possible *gosses* and cannot be a donor for a transplant. Nevertheless, since he can be shown over many hours not to have any spontaneous respiration, and since it was the doctors who put him on a respirator, it may be regarded as prolonging the end of the period of *gesisah*, preventing the soul from leaving the body. Therefore it will be permitted to disconnect the patient from it. And, although this is also stated in the *Igrot Moshe Y.D.* III, Siman 132, nevertheless one could, with difficulty, explain it differently. Therefore I was pleased to see the Gaon's letter to Dr. Bondi where he writes this clearly and explicitly. However although he wrote "right in *Halachah*," "as if he has been decapitated" and "although the heart may still beat for some days," nevertheless, I think that all these phrases only show that he intended to rule that "it is permitted to disconnect the patient from the respirator." The letter was written in Kislev 5745 when the whole Torah world was discussing the question of whether transplantation was permissible or not. If he had thought that such a patient was considered dead even with regard to being a donor and his organs could be removed, it is astonishing that he did not mention that there is also a *mitzvah* to take organs from him to save the lives of *seriously ill* patients. And, although the Gaon zt"l wrote plainly in *Igrot Moshe* in the year 5738 (reference 61) that a heart transplant murders two souls, nevertheless in the present letter, written years later, in 5745, when he already knew about the important test (*cerebral bloodflow — author*), he certainly should have mentioned that it is permitted to remove the organs. Therefore, I think that he did not want at all to depend on this test to perform a positive act and remove organs from the patient.[65] [*This letter was written before Rav Auerbach zt"l's letter to me in July '93; see above, page 312 — author.*]

6. SUMMARY. The consensus of opinion of the *gedolei hador* is that a brain-dead patient is not dead and he cannot be used as a donor, even to save the life of a *seriously ill* patient. As the *halachah* stands, it is forbidden to be either a donor or a recipient of organs in *Eretz Yisrael* from a brain-dead patient, but it is permitted to be a recipient in the Diaspora. The view of *Rav Moshe Feinstein zt"l* has been discussed.

7. THE NAME GAME. In the search for suitable donors two other groups of patients have been suggested. Although they do not fit the present criteria of brain death, it has been suggested that the criteria be extended so that they can also be labeled dead and thus be used as donors for transplantation. Thus definitions can be changed to suit the demands.

(1) Chronic vegetative state. This state has been defined as chronic wakefulness without awareness.[66] It is a chronic neurologic condition characterized by lack of awareness of external stimuli with preservation of vital vegetative functions such as cardiac activity, respiration and maintenance of blood pressure.[67] These patients are generally able to breathe without mechanical support and their cardiovascular, gastro-intestinal and renal functions are usually sound.[68] Should they be used as donors? We find the following statement in a medical journal: If the legal definition of death were to be changed to include comprehensive irreversible loss of higher brain function, it would be possible to take the life of a patient (or more accurately to stop the heart,

---

65. ראה שם להמשך המכתב בו הרב זצ"ל חוזר וכותב
על הענין של המתנת חצי דקה
66. JAMA 263, 426 '90

67. Ann. Neurol. 33:386, '93
68. Lancet 350:795, '97
69. Lancet 350:1320, '97

§1 (CONTINUED): For (C)one who closes the eyes of a *gosses* when he is about to die has shed blood.

───── NISHMAT AVRAHAM ─────

since the patient would be defined as dead) by a "lethal" injection, and then to remove the organs needed for transplantation, subject to the usual criteria for consent. Another approach would be not to declare such individuals legally dead, but rather to exempt them from the normal legal prohibition against "killing" in the way that was considered for anencephalic infants.[69]

(2) Anencephalic infants. These infants are born without an upper brain but have a normally functioning brainstem and breathe spontaneously. They will usually die shortly after birth. It has been proposed that the definition of brain death be widened to include them; that is, the absence of higher brain function should be enough to define them as dead at a time that they are breathing spontaneously and have a normal heartbeat.[70]

In the context of changing the name (that is, the definition of death), when the situation demands it, the following sentence in a medical paper[71] nicely characterizes it: The Neur tribe viewed defective newborns as non-human "hippopotamuses" who were mistakenly born to human parents and who would be put in the river, which was viewed as their natural habitat.

(C) one who closes the eyes of a *gosses*. And he who touches him sheds blood. For Rebbe Meir used to say: It is like a light that is about to go out; the moment one touches it he extinguishes it.[72] This is also the ruling in the *Gemara*,[73] *Rif*[74] and the *Rambam*.[75] Rebbe Akiva Eiger[76] writes that nevertheless if the house where the *gosses* lies is on fire, he may be moved out; that is, if it is for his benefit, the *gosses* may be moved. Rav Neuwirth shlita agreed with me that this is true even if the *gosses* is unconscious since he might regain consciousness or, alternatively, he was only mistakenly thought to be completely unconscious. There is no question that a doctor, or anyone else for that matter, who wishes to treat, help or save him, may touch or move him as is necessary. Moreover, he is obligated to do so if he thinks he can save his life. Even a *Cohen*, who is forbidden to enter a room containing a *gosses*,[77] is required to do so if he thinks that he may save his life. Even if there is doubt whether the patient has already died or not, he must enter, for even the smallest possibility of saving life sets aside that which is forbidden (unless the three cardinal sins are involved — see Siman 157 §1 above).[78] Moreover, even if a non-*Cohen* is present who is also capable of treating the patient, the *Cohen* must enter and help to treat,[79] for it is not by everyone that a patient is destined to be cured.[80] See also Siman 370:2 below.

However if nothing more can be done to save him, one must be very careful, particularly in a hospital, that routine taking

---

70. NEJM 321:388, '89; NEJM 322:669, '90; JAMA 259:2284, '88
71. Arch. Neurol. 49:570, '92
72. אבל רבתי, מסכת שמחות פ"א ה"ד
73. שבת קנא ע"ב
74. דף סה ע"ב מדפי הרי"ף
75. הל' אבל פ"ד ה"ה. וראה ש"ך ס"ק ה
76. חידושיו כאן
77. יו"ד סי' שע
78. שו"ת חת"ס יו"ד סי' שלח. גשר החיים ח"א פ"ב ס"ק ב
79. פ"ת יו"ד סי' שע ס"ק א
80. יו"ד סי' רבא סע' ד ט"ז וש"ך ס"ק כ

SIMAN 399: THE LAWS CONCERNING A GOSSES / §1

GLOSS: *It is also* **(D)***forbidden to hasten his death, for example,*

─────────────── NISHMAT AVRAHAM ───────────────

of temperature, pulse and blood pressure should no longer be carried out nor should blood be drawn for laboratory tests. In such a situation, since the results of these actions will not change his treatment, they should not be done since they involve moving him. If, however, the patient is conscious, and will realize that these routine actions have been stopped, and the knowledge and its resultant despair and hopelessness may aggravate his condition, they may be done carefully. However all nursing care that is necessary for his physical and mental comfort, such as washing, cleaning him and changing the bed linen must be done. *Rav Neuwirth shlita* agreed with all this.

On the other hand, *Rav Auerbach zt"l* was asked whether it was permissible to move a *gosses* in the emergency room whose bed, or one of his limbs, was in such a position that it was impossible to move another *seriously ill* patient to where he could receive appropriate treatment (for example, to move him to the intensive care unit or to connect him to a respirator). The *Rav zt"l* answered: As to moving a *gosses* so that another's life may be saved, since there is a great need to try and save life, one may move the arm of a *gosses* carefully or his bed even though moving him would involve much effort. For since this will be done carefully and it is only a possibility that his death will be hastened, it is permitted. This is not like removing an instrument from his mouth or from his body for use in another patient, which is forbidden.[81]

The *Rav zt"l* explained to *Rav Neuwirth shlita* and myself that the ruling of the *Shulchan Aruch* refers to moving him for no reason or for the benefit of a non-seriously ill patient. But if, in order to save a *seriously ill* patient, the *gosses* must be moved, part of his body or his bed may be moved. He also told us that it would be permitted to stroke the hand of a *gosses* who was frightened so as to calm him. However, if the *gosses* is a child, his mother would not be permitted to take him into her arms in order to hug him although she does so to calm him. He added that the permission to move a *gosses* had nothing in common with the injection of a substance into the body of a *gosses* (even if he were to do it without touching him) to ascertain whether his brain was dead.

Rav Wosner shlita[82] was also asked the above question. He wrote: The *halachah* that it is forbidden to touch or move a *gosses* refers to touching his body, for example, closing his eyes or moving an arm that is hanging over the bed. In our situation, his body is not touched but his bed is moved ... It is obvious to me that *Chazal* ruled strictly (by Torah law) with regard to touching a *gosses* for fear of hastening his death. It is also well known that, in reality, even if one does move a *gosses*, he will not necessarily definitely die sooner ... Besides, the experts know that there are many uncertainties as to when the process of *gesisah* begins. In any case, in this situation there is only a remote chance that very carefully moving the bed in which the *gosses* lies will hasten his death, but by doing so it will be possible to save someone who can certainly be saved. In such an instance the Torah ruling would be that one ought to do so.

(D) forbidden to hasten his death. PROLONGING THE LIFE OF A GOSSES AND OF ONE WHO IS SUFFERING. EUTHANASIA. The *Minchat*

---

83. מצוה לד

81. אסיא חוברת נ"ה טבת תשנ"ה עמ' 43
82. שם עמ' 44, שו"ת שבט הלוי ח"ט סי' רמה

NISHMAT AVRAHAM

Chinuch[83] writes: Even if the prophet Elijah were to say that a person would live only for another hour or minute, nevertheless the Torah does not differentiate between killing a child who has many years to live and killing an aged person of one hundred. The killer is always guilty; even if the victim was marked to die in a minute, he is guilty for the minute of life that was still left to him. The *Gesher HaChaim*[84] explains that since there is neither a measure nor a boundary to the worth of a life, one cannot differentiate between a tiny fraction of life and a period one hundred million times greater. Therefore in Torah law there is no difference between killing a young healthy individual and killing a *gosses* who is one hundred years old. *Rav Jakobovits zt"l*[85] writes: The worth of a person's life is immeasurable and therefore cannot be divided; each and every fraction of it is infinite. Therefore, seventy years of life have exactly the same value as thirty years or a year, an hour or even a second. This exacting definition of the sanctity of the life of a person is not only based on pure mathematics or logic, but is based, to no lesser extent, on moral values. If the value of a human life is lessened because his end is near, the life of man will lose all of its absolute value, being replaced by a relative one — relative to his life expectancy, the state of his health, his value to society, or any other arbitrary index. It will then be necessary to grade people, and no two people will ever have the same worth. Once we curtail the life of a dying patient because it is no longer of value, we are in fact curtailing the infinite worth of each and every individual's life, assigning them limited boundaries.[86]

Rav Jakobovits zt"l[87] continues: The sanctity of life therefore is such that under no circumstances will it be permissible to curtail life because of pain and suffering, even if by a second. Even if death's victory in a short time is absolutely obvious, the patient's life remains of infinite value and killing him is no less a crime than killing a perfectly healthy person.

Even if the patient is suffering and is in severe pain, we have no right to kill him or to bring about his death to put an end to his suffering. On the contrary his suffering is for his benefit, as the *Gemara*[88] and the *Rambam*[89] write: The *(final)* punishment of a *sotah* who has merits ... will be postponed so that she does not die immediately *(on drinking the bitter waters — author)*. Instead, she wastes away, being afflicted with severe illnesses until she dies a year or two or three later depending on her merits, dying eventually with swelling of her abdomen and the falling (wasting) away of her limbs.

1. RAV AUERBACH zt"l. The *Rav zt"l* told me that one must differentiate between treatments that fulfill the natural needs of a patient or those which are routine and conventional on the one hand and those which are not routine. Thus, one may neither stop nor desist from giving a patient who, for instance, has widespread cancer in his body and is close to death, oxygen, food or nutritional fluids as needed, even if he is suffering and is in severe pain. If he is a diabetic, one may not stop his insulin so as to hasten his death. One may not stop a blood transfusion or any other medication, such as antibiotics, that are needed for his treatment. One must not desist from giving him any of the above, with the purpose of causing

---

84. ח"א פ"ב סע' ב הערה 3

85. הרפואה והיהדות עמ' 152

86. וראה בדעת זקנים מבעלי התוס' בראשית ט:ה, מובא בב"י יו"ד סי' קנז

87. הרפואה והיהדות שם

88. סוטה כ ע"א

89. הל' סוטה פ"ג ה"כ

SIMAN 399: THE LAWS CONCERNING A GOSSES / §1

NISHMAT AVRAHAM

his earlier death. On the other hand, there is no obligation to actively treat such a patient, when the treatment itself will cause him suffering over and above his present suffering, and when the treatment is unconventional, if there is no expectation of curing his underlying illness but merely of prolonging his life a little. This is certainly so if the patient does not wish to receive such treatment because of the severe pain and terrible suffering.

The *Rav zt"l* also told me that narcotics such as morphine may be given to a patient who is terminally ill when this is necessary to alleviate his pain, even if there is a possibility that this might hasten his death, provided that the morphine is given only in order to alleviate his pain and suffering and not with any ulterior motive of shortening his life. If each dose on its own will not certainly curtail his life, then although many repeated doses will do so, he should be treated. However a patient for whom even a single dose will cause respiratory arrest, may not receive a single dose, even if he is suffering agonizing pain, unless he will be artificially ventilated should he stop breathing.[90] See also the *Tzitz Eliezer*[91] and *Rav Nebenzahl shlita's* comment.[92]

I should point out in this context that expert advice must be sought, from a specialist in treating pain, at an early stage in the treatment of painful disease. The advice of a psychiatrist must also be sought for treating depression and other psychiatric conditions in these suffering patients.

Rav Auerbach zt"l writes:[93] Although it is obviously clear that the lives of those who are paralyzed are not really "lives" in our simplistic way of thinking, and the suffering of the patient and his family is great, nevertheless we are commanded and required to actively do what we can to prolong their lives. If he takes ill we are bound to hasten to save him and, if necessary, set aside Sabbath laws for him. For we have no yardstick by which to measure life, its value and importance, even in terms of Torah and *mitzvot*. We must set aside Sabbath laws even for an elderly patient smitten with a repulsive disease although he is deaf and dumb and a complete *shoteh*, and is incapable of performing any *mitzvah*. His life is merely a burden on, and causes great suffering for, the family, prevents them from studying Torah and keeping *mitzvot*, and, in addition to their great suffering, is a strain on their resources. In spite of all this, it is a *mitzvah* for even the great of Israel to try and do what they can to save him and set aside Sabbath laws if necessary. Moreover, even if the patient has such great suffering that the *Halachah* would permit one to pray that he die, as the *Ran* rules,[94] and this is also the opinion of some *poskim*,[95] nevertheless at the same time as one prays and asks *Hashem* that the patient die, he is obligated to do what he can to save him and set aside Sabbath laws on his behalf repeatedly... However, since the lives of those who are paralyzed are painful and bitter, and there are those who would prefer death, therefore in the case in question, where the success of surgery on the spine is not certain and may, in fact, leave the patient paralyzed all her life, there is no obligation to actively treat her by operation, particularly since, in her case, the success of the surgery is

---

90. וראה מנחת שלמה תנינא סי' פו אות ב
91. שו"ת, חי"ג סי' פז
92. אסיא חוברת כה, סיון תש"מ עמ' 39
93. מנחת שלמה ח"א סי' צא אות כד
94. נדרים מ ע"א
95. ערוה"ש יו"ד שלה סע' ג. שו"ת אג"מ חו"מ ח"ב סי' עג ס"ק א. וע"ע בשו"ת ציץ אליעזר ח"ה רמת רחל סי' הוח"ט סי' מז
See Siman 335M, p. 264 above (to pray that the patient shoud die).

NISHMAT AVRAHAM

itself doubtful.

The *Rav zt"l* told me that there is no obligation to do anything to a terminally ill patient that will cause him severe pain even if the patient is comatose and not evidently suffering. The *Rav zt"l* was of the opinion that a comatose patient who could not respond to pain should be considered as if he were in pain.

Many years ago I spoke to the *Rav zt"l* regarding a patient with a spreading muscle paralysis (ALS). This disease causes complete paralysis of all the muscles of the body, usually starting at the periphery of the body and spreading, over an unpredictable time, to involve the chest muscles, so that eventually the patient will die, unless he is artificially ventilated. In some cases, the disease is accompanied by extreme sensitivity of the skin and muscles of the body so that every slight touch causes severe pain. The patient is completely conscious, hears, understands and is aware of everything that is going on, but, as he cannot speak, his only means of communication is with an up-down or side-to-side movement of his eyes. Because of weakening of the chest muscles, he is prone to recurrent attacks of pneumonia. There is as yet no known treatment for the disease. I asked the *Rav zt"l* whether, when the time came that he needed to be artificially ventilated to keep him alive, there would be an obligation to do so. The *Rav zt"l* answered me that it would be permissible not to connect him to a respirator. I asked him whether when the patient was terminal, it would be permitted not to treat yet another attack of pneumonia with antibiotics, in view of his great suffering, both physical and mental. The *Rav zt"l* wrote to me that one would be required to treat him with oral antibiotics. As to intravenous antibiotics, if this involved additional pain as a result of muliple injections, the patient should be asked whether he would want to be treated. If he wished to reject treatment, one possibly should respect his wishes. In any case Sabbath laws should not be set aside for the purpose (see below *Rav Eliashiv shlita's* ruling).

The *Rav zt"l*[96] writes: There are many who have difficulty with the problem of treating a *gosses*. Some think that just as we set aside Sabbath laws (even) for *chayei sha'ah* (a short span of life), so we must force a *gosses* to receive treatment since he does not own himself to be able to concede even a moment of his life. However it would appear that if the patient is suffering great pain and torment, or even severe mental distress, although we must give him food and oxygen, even against his will, we may nevertheless desist from giving him medication that will cause him suffering, if this is his wish. If, however, the patient is Heaven-fearing and has not become deranged, it would be most desirable to explain to him that an hour of repentance in this world is better than all of the World to Come. This is what the *Gemara*[97] means when it says that it is a privilege to suffer for seven years rather than die quickly.

2. RAV ELIASHIV shlita. The Rav *shlita* rules that a doctor must do everything he can to prolong the life of a patient even if there is no treatment for his basic disease as long as the patient has not become a *gosses*. However if the patient is suffering greatly and asks that his life not be prolonged with such treatments, it is permitted to passively let him die. One must do everything for a patient who is comatose including a full resuscitation, even if he has been defined as brain dead, as long as it is not obvious that he is suffering,

---

96. מנחת שלמה סי׳ צא אות כד

97. סוטה כ ע״א

NISHMAT AVRAHAM

even if the treatment is only meant to prolong his life. As proof the *Rav shlita* quotes the *Mishnah Berurah*[98] who rules in the name of *rishonim* that if someone is found buried under rubble on *Shabbat*, even if his brain is crushed and he only has a short while to live, nevertheless, one rescues him so that he may live a little longer. (I have already noted in 339B above that *Rav Auerbach zt"l* wrote to me concerning this *Mishnah Berurah* that it could be that part of the brain was still functioning. *Rav Neuwirth shlita* told me that it could be that the part that was crushed was the skull and not necessarily the brain.)

Rav Eliashiv shlita was asked about a patient with ALS (see above) who asked not to be connected to a respirator. In a *responsum* (written in his name by Rav Yosef Ephrati *shlita*) the Rav *shlita* rules: A patient who is beyond cure, and all that medical science can offer him is a prolongation of *chayei sha'ah* at the cost of additional suffering due to the treatment itself, may refuse the treatment. If, however, the treatment is not accompanied by additional suffering, it is forbidden to listen to him. I also heard this personally from *Rav Eliashiv shlita*.

In a recent (August '01) conversation that I had with *Rav Eliashiv shlita* concerning a terminal patient, he ruled that since the patient was conscious and suffering, one was permitted to desist from intubating him or dialyzing him since these measures would only serve to prolong his *chayei sha'ah*. However the patient, who himself was a great sage, should be given the choice to decide what he wished his doctors to do. I asked him whether this ruling would change if the patient lost consciousness and he answered: No, there would be nothing to gain by any further treatment such as artificial ventilation or dialysis.

3. RAV WALDENBERG shlita. The Rav *shlita* writes[99] that as long as the patient has any spontaneous life even though he is a *gosses*, the majority of whom will certainly die, he is nevertheless given blood, antibiotics, oxygen and intravenous nourishment, just in case he will be revived, since a minority may live. Even if this will only prolong his independent life, this must be done. It is forbidden to stop any of the above and the doctor is obligated to continue to treat him with whatever treatment is necessary to prolong his independent life except at the time when his soul leaves his body.

4. RAV MOSHE FEINSTEIN zt"l. The Rav *zt"l* writes:[100] It is certainly forbidden to do anything to prolong the *chayei sha'ah* of a patient when this is accompanied by suffering. In another *responsum*,[101] the Rav *zt"l* writes: If the doctors have no further means to cure the patient or even to lessen his suffering, but only to prolong, by a little, his life of suffering, they should not give such a treatment ... There are wicked people who say that a patient who is a *shoteh*, or was comatose because of injury and is lacking "quality of life" should not be treated. This is not so. There is an obligation to treat someone who is so mentally affected that some insensitive people call him a "vegetable," and say that he need not be treated if he becomes ill without suffering and can be cured to continue to live a long life. However it should be obvious and clear that if he were to become physically ill, one is obligated to do everything necessary to save him, regardless of his wisdom or intelligence.

---

98. סי' שבט סע' ד ביה"ל ד"ה אלא
99. שו"ת ציץ אליעזר חי"ד סי' פ וראה גם שם סי' פא. וראה גם בחי"ג סי' פט אות יא
100. אג"מ יו"ד ח"ב סי' קעד ענף ג
101. אג"מ חו"מ ח"ב סי' עד אות א

NISHMAT AVRAHAM

The Rav *zt"l* also discusses a patient whose basic illness is uncurable but medication can be given to prolong his life with its suffering, even for many years but not for a normal lifespan. He writes:[102] If he now becomes *seriously ill* with a second disease, which does not cause additional suffering, he must be treated for it, even against his will, although he will still be left with the original disease and its suffering. However if the (second) illness causes additional suffering and neither it nor its suffering can be treated, so that people would prefer death rather than living a life of such suffering, it would appear that there is no obligation to treat him, if he does not wish such treatment which will merely prolong a life of suffering. And even if the patient's wishes are unknown, one may assume that he would not want it and there would not be an obligation to treat. The Rav *zt"l* also writes:[103] A *seriously ill* patient whom the doctors think will live only seven days or less, who becomes ill with another life-threatening illness, such as pneumonia, must be treated as necessary, even though there is no cure for the underlying disease.

In yet another *responsum*,[104] the Rav *zt"l* was asked whether there is an obligation to treat a patient with incurable cancer who would then only live a life of suffering for a few months. The Rav *zt"l* replies that if there was no alternative treatment, the patient should be told this and asked if he wishes to have the treatment. For if he prefers to live with suffering rather than die, he must be given the treatment, but if he does not wish to live with suffering the treatment must not be given, unless this is done to gain time so as to give the doctors an opportunity to bring in specialists.

5. SUMMARIZING THE ABOVE

(where differences of opinion exist *Rav Auerbach zt"l*'s opinion is quoted):

(1) Every patient must be fed and given fluids, oxygen and anything else, such as blood and insulin, as necessary, since these are intrinsic and natural requirements of every human being. If these can only be given artificially, for example, oxygen by mask or nasal cannula, food by *naso-gastric tube* or even *gastrostomy*, fluids intravenously, this must be done. Antibiotics and all routine treatments must be given as necessary. *Rav Auerbach zt"l* told me that if the patient was a *gosses* and would die from his disease before he would die from lack of the above, if he rigorously refused to have them given, one could desist from doing so. However treatment, once started, cannot be discontinued, if doing so will hasten his death.

(2) A patient with a chronic, incapacitating but non-terminal disease should be treated as any other patient, including the administration of full resuscitation if necessary even if only for *chayei sha'ah*. Thus the very aged and senile, someone with advanced *Alzheimer's disease* or a *shoteh* must all be treated like any young robust and healthy individual.

(3) A terminally ill patient should receive all that is enumerated in the first section of the summary. However if he requires extraordinary treatments — for example surgery, intubation and cardiac massage — for complications of his underlying disease, which will only prolong his *chayei sha'ah* but at the cost of additional pain and suffering to what he already has, one may desist from such treatments.

(4) A DNR (Do not resuscitate) decision can be made only if **all** the following three conditions have been met: (a) the patient is terminally ill with a non-treatable disease; (b) he is suffering greatly, physically

---

104. שם אות א

102. שם אות ב
103. שם סי' עה אות ד

or mentally; and (c) any further treatment will only prolong his *chayei sha'ah* and add to his suffering.

(5) The suffering of the family must never ever be a part of the decision making process.

(6) All nursing care necessary for his comfort must be given.

Remember! The decision "Do not resuscitate (DNR)" does not mean "Do not treat."

No decision to withhold treatment of any kind should be made without consultation with a *posek* who must be made aware, in detail, of the patient's condition and of the pros and cons of the treatment concerned.

Finally, in all situations, the patient must be given much TLC — Tender, Loving Care.

CONCLUSION. In conclusion, I cannot emphasize strongly enough that these are life and death decisions that can be made only by a *posek* who must be made fully aware of the medical facts as decided by a full team of medical experts. Although allowing a patient to die is not the same as actively killing him, it is nevertheless a very serious sin. Unlike the world at large that is more and more coming to believe that there is no difference between withholding and stopping nourishment, oxygen and treatment in a terminal — and even not so terminal — patient, and that both are permissible, *Halachah* clearly differentiates between the two. Stopping is never permissible and withholding may be, but only in very particular circumstances, and then only with the express ruling of a recognized and medically informed *posek*. No two patients and no two circumstances are exactly alike and only a *posek* can decide when one may allow a patient to die and when one must continue to fight even for a few more moments of life, even if only artificially maintained. As physicians, we should approach these very difficult problems of life and death with humility and realize our fallibility and lack of absolute knowledge. We must accept completely the tenets of our Torah as expounded by our Sages, with the readiness to listen to, and put into practice, what they tell us. We must be willing to control our emotions, including those of pity and compassion, within the boundaries set by the Torah. We, who hold life and death in our hands, must therefore continually remind ourselves that the Almighty only gave us permission to treat.

See also *Nishmat Avraham*, vol. 1 *Orach Chaim*, Siman 330Q and *Assia*, "Jewish Medical Ethics," vol.1 p. 38, May '89.

6. LIVING WILL. It is quite commonplace in Western society for people to sign, or be asked to sign, a living will. The purpose of such a will is to let those treating the patient know what he wishes them to do or not do for him in the event of illness, if he is unconscious or unable to communicate with them because of the loss of his mental faculties, such as occurs in advanced *Alzheimer's disease*. These wills may allow even detailed advanced directives, for example, being given food and fluids by artificial means, dialysis, intubation, resuscitation. They may include directives as to when the doctors should desist from or stop anything that will prolong his life. He may also appoint a member of his family, a friend or his lawyer to act on his behalf. He may also be asked to donate his organs for medical research or for transplantation.

However, *Halachah* lays down quite clearly that one does not have any jurisdiction over or ownership of, one's body, be it in life or after death.[105] Therefore

---

105. רמב״ם הל׳ חובל ומזיק פ״ה ה״א והל׳ רוצח פ״א ה״ד. רדב״ז על הרמב״ם הל׳ סנה׳ פי״ח ה״ו. שו״ע הרב הל׳ נזקי גוף ונפש סע׳ ד. שו״ת אג״מ יו״ד ח״ב סי׳ קמ״ז. וכך שמעתי מהגרש״ז אויערבאך זצ״ל

when the period of dying is long drawn out, (E)it is forbidden to remove the pillow or cushion from under him because it is said that the feathers of certain fowl cause a prolongation of dying. Similarly, he should not be moved from where he is lying. How-

---NISHMAT AVRAHAM---

one does not have the power to decide what may or may not be done to him when he is ill, certainly in decisions of life and death, and certainly not with regard to whether his life should be prolonged or curtailed, even if this is only done passively (that is by desisting from feeding or treating, for example). Neither may one donate any of his organs after death (however defined) without prior consultation with a recognized Orthodox *posek* whose views are those of *gedolei Yisrael*.[106] Therefore, if one does wish to write such a will, it must contain only the statement that:

> In the event of my being unable to participate in decisions of life and death concerning myself, I appoint Rabbi ... who will make all such decisions for me and who must be consulted at each step of my illness and for each separate decision, and his decision will be binding on all my caregivers as if they were mine. If Rabbi ... is not available, Rabbi ... should be consulted in his absence.

The Rabbis chosen must be recognized as those whose *halachic* outlook and decisions are based on those of *gedolei Yisrael* and who will consult with them in these difficult decisions. They must be consulted at the time that the will is prepared.

(E) it is forbidden to remove the pillow or cushion from under him.

The *Aruch HaShulchan*[107] explains that the *Shulchan Aruch* first tells us that it is forbidden to do anything that will hasten the patient's death, for example, removing the pillow from under his head. Even if one thinks that it is a *mitzvah* to hasten his death for his benefit, for instance, if he is a *gosses* for a long time and is obviously suffering greatly, nevertheless it is forbidden to do so, for this is *Hashem*'s Will. Moreover, not only is it forbidden to pull the pillow away from under his head, thus moving his head a substantial distance, but even to move him a little is forbidden. And, even if one does not move him at all but does something that will hasten his death, this is also forbidden. Any of these will lead to an earlier death even if it is not done to him directly. On the other hand, if something prevents his soul from leaving his body, it may be removed, for since the impediment is external and not intrinsic to the patient, why should he suffer?

The *Gemara*[108] tells of the elderly inhabitants of the town of Luz (where no one ever died) who, when they tired of living, walked outside the walls of the town and died. This is not considered like committing suicide, or doing something that is suicidal, for their action only led, indirectly, to death by "natural causes." See also the *Gemara*[109] that tells us of the martyrdom of the *Tanna*, Rabbi Chanina ben Teradyon. The *Yalkut Shimoni*[110]

---

106. שמעתי מהגרש"ז אויערבאך זצ"ל. וראה גם בשו"ת אג"מ יו"ד ח"א סי' קכט ענף ה ויו"ד ח"ג סי' קמ

107. סע' ד

108. סוטה מו ע"ב. אך עיין בבראשית רבה פ' ויצא סו"פ סט שהגירסא שם היא "מוציאים אותם"

109. ע"ז יח ע"א. וראה בשו"ת אג"מ יו"ד ח"ב סי' קעד

ענף ג (עמ' רצ), וחו"מ ח"ב סי' עג (עמ' שה) וסי' עד (עמ' שיב). חי' בית הלוי על הרמב"ם הל' רוצח פ"ב ה"ז ו-ח. שו"ת תורת חסד אהע"ז סי' מב סי' קה. שו"ת ציץ אליעזר ח"ט סי' יז פ"י ופ"י ס"ק ה

110. פ' עקב סי' תתעא ומשלי סי' תתקמג

ever if there is something external to the patient or on his body that prevents his soul from leaving him, (F)*it may be removed, since by doing so one does not do a positive action to shorten his life, but merely removes an impediment to his dying.*

§4 A dying patient (G)must not be left alone to die. (*It is a*

───────────── NISHMAT AVRAHAM ─────────────

relates the story of a very elderly woman who came to Rebbe Yosi ben Chalafta complaining that she was tired of living a life bereft of pleasure since she could no longer taste food or drink. On questioning her as to what *mitzvah* she was careful to keep each day, she answered that even when she had something she wanted to do she would forgo it in order to go early to *shul* every morning. He told her not to do so for three days. She did as she was told and on the third day she took ill and died.

None of these examples should be mistaken for permission to take life or to hasten death, whether it be one's own or someone else's. They are all examples where an action, although premeditated and certain to lead to death, nevertheless only leads to an entirely natural death, and not one directly caused by man.

(F) it may be removed...but merely removes an impediment to his dying. A patient was admitted with an acute myocardial infarction (heart attack) and cardiac arrest requiring cardiac resuscitation and artificial respiration. Two days later his heart stopped again requiring another resuscitation that left him comatose. He went into kidney failure and stopped passing urine. His blood pressure was extremely low and he required intravenous drugs to raise it to normal, and to keep him alive. After this situation continued for another half day, and when all expert advice was unanimous that there was no hope of recovery because of the extensive cardiac damage with the consequent complications, he was defined as a *gosses*. Every time that the bag containing the drug that kept his blood pressure up to normal was changed, his pressure fell immediately and it was obvious that he was being artificially and "cosmetically" kept alive. The family asked me to ask *Rav Auerbach zt"l* how long they were obligated to let this situation continue, prolonging his dying and his *gesisah*. The Rav *zt"l* answered that, in this particular situation, there was no longer an obligation to change the bag when the present one ran out, for this would come under the category of "removing the impediment to dying."

(G) must not be left alone. The *Taz*[111] writes that this is because the soul becomes desolate upon leaving the body. The *Beit Lechem Yehudah*[112] writes that if one is with a dying patient, and there is no one else present who can decide when the patient has died in order to straighten his limbs, close his eyes and do whatever else is necessary, he must not leave him even if he will miss the opportunity to pray.

Rav Auerbach zt"l wrote to me that if a *Cohen* is alone with a patient who is a *gosses*, he must leave the place (*not be under the same roof — author*). However, *Rav Neuwirth shlita* told me that this ruling needs further study for there is a controversy as to whether it is permissible or

───────────────────────────────────────

111. ס"ק ג 112. על השו"ע כאן

NISHMAT AVRAHAM

forbidden for a *Cohen* to enter a house where there is a *gosses*[113] and the *Rama* rules that it would be "best to act strictly." And, although the *Shach*[114] quotes the *Bach's* ruling that the *halachah* is that the *Cohen* must be careful not to enter, the *Shach* himself rules that if the *Cohen* was sleeping, there would be no need to awaken him so that he should leave. (*If a corpse were there, then the Cohen must be awakened so that he can leave immediately — author.*) If the *Cohen* is told and he is completely undressed, he may get dressed before leaving. Moreover, it would be possibly true to say that there is no obligation for the *Cohen* to leave. The language of the *Shulchan Aruch* is that it is forbidden for a *Cohen* to enter, meaning that it is only specifically entering such a room that is forbidden. However it would be proper to act strictly and leave the room, since other *poskim* have not differentiated between entering the room and remaining there (end of quote from *Rav Neuwirth shlita*).

Rav Auerbach *zt"l* wrote to me again: But there are *poskim* who rule according to the opinion in the *Gemara*[115] that a *Cohen* is forbidden by the Torah to be in the same room as a *gosses*. Therefore, although we rule according to the opinion that this is not forbidden by Torah law, nevertheless we should be concerned that the *Cohen* may come to set aside Torah law (*if the gosses dies while he is still in the room — author*). Thus the *Shach* rules that it would be right for him to act strictly and leave.

On the other hand, *Rav Auerbach zt"l* told me that if the *gosses* is conscious and afraid to be left alone, and there is a possibility that were he to be left alone this fear would hasten his death, it is forbidden for the *Cohen* to leave him.

The *Pitchei Teshuvah*[116] writes that a doctor who is a *Cohen* may enter the place where there is a *gosses* in order to treat him, even if another doctor who is not a *Cohen* is already present. The *Chatam Sofer*[117] also writes that it is obvious, even according to those *poskim* who rule that a *Cohen* may not enter a place where there is a *gosses*, nevertheless, a Cohen who is a doctor may, since in this case there is a possibility of *pikuach nefesh*. The *Cohen*-doctor should enter and help to treat, if he is needed. Moreover, even after the patient was thought to have died, if any slight movement is discerned, the *Cohen*-doctor must hurry in even though there is only a remote possibility of saving his life. And, concludes the *Pitchei Teshuvah*, although the *Chatam Sofer* was uncertain as to the ruling about the *Cohen*-doctor treating a *gosses* if another non-*Cohen* doctor was present, he should help in treating the *gosses*, for the patient may not be worthy to be cured by everyone.

Incidentally, *Rav Auerbach zt"l* told me that when Rabban Shimon ben Gamliel was beheaded by the Romans,[118] Rebbe Yishmael, the *Cohen Gadol*, who was next in line for execution, took the head in his lap and cried bitterly. The *Rav zt"l* asked rhetorically: How could he do this, he was a *Cohen* and forbidden (by Torah law) to defile himself by touching the dead? (*He could have wept without touching the corpse — author.*) The *Rav zt"l* answered that it is obvious that he asked, and received permission, to do so. In this way his execution was delayed by a few more moments and it was permissible to do this to gain a few more moments of life.[119]

---

113. יו"ד סי' שע סע' א
114. ס"ק ד
115. נזיר מג ע"א
116. סי' שע ס"ק א. ועיין שם בנחלת צבי
117. שו"ת, יו"ד סי' שלח
118. אבות דרבי נתן פל"ח ה"ג
119. וראה באג"מ או"ח ח"ד סי'סט אות ח

mitzvah to stand by him at the time (H)*his soul leaves the body as it says: "Can one live eternally, never to see the pit? Though he sees that wise men die..." [Psalms 49:10].)*

NISHMAT AVRAHAM

(H) his soul leaves the body. ARTIFICIAL RESPIRATION. Mouth-to-mouth (in adults) or mouth-to-nose (in children) respiration has been known to modern medicine for about forty years. Many think that the first description of this is to be found in the *Tanach*, in the stories of the prophets Elijah[120] and Elisha,[121] each of whom revived a dead child in this way. However the text shows that this is not true. Elijah prayed to *Hashem* after having stretched himself over the boy three times. Elisha came some time after the boy had died. He also prayed to *Hashem*, lay upon the boy, placing his mouth upon his mouth, his eyes upon his eyes and his palms upon his palms. He stretched himself out over him and warmed the boy's flesh. He then walked up and down and again stretched himself out over the boy's body until the boy sneezed seven times and opened his eyes. In both cases no mention is made of mouth-to-mouth breathing and, in any event, in the natural way of things, lying on someone who is not breathing would hardly be conducive to a successful resuscitation. According to most of our Sages,[122] in both cases the boys were dead and what the prophets did was to pray to *Hashem* to resurrect them. However a source for mouth-to-mouth and mouth-to-nose respiration can be found in *Chazal*.[123] We are told that when the spies came to Hebron, Talmy the King yelled (*in surprise at these grasshoppers who looked like men*[124] — *author*) and the spies fell on their faces to the ground. They (the inhabitants) started to puff into their mouths and blow into their noses (in order to resuscitate them[125]) until they revived.

Incidentally, the practice of intubation — whereby a hollow tube is inserted into the windpipe of a non-breathing patient so that he can be ventilated artificially, either by manually operating a balloon connected to the tube or by connecting the tube to a respirator — is also only known to medicine during the last one hundred years or so. However the *Tur*, who lived some seven hundred years ago, writes[126] that when a baby was born dead, the midwife would take a hollow reed (*shefoferet*), place it in the baby's throat and then puff into it, thus reviving him. The name Shifra (*who, Chazal tell, us was Moshe Rabbeinu's mother Yocheved and was one of the two midwives in Egypt some 3400 years ago — author*) comes from the word *shefoferet*.

---

120. מלכים א י״ז:י״ז-כב
121. מלכים ב ד:י״ח-לה
122. ראה נשמת אברהם כרך ד יו״ד סי׳ שלט ס״ק ה (עמ׳ קנט)
123. ילקוט שמעוני רמז תשמב פ׳ שלח לך על הפסוק וישלח אותם משה
124. ראה במדבר יג:לג
125. זית רענן שם
126. בעל הטורים שמות א:טו

CHAPTER 33
The Laws of Keri'ah
(Tearing One's Garments for a Person Who Has Just Died)

SIMAN 340
LAWS CONCERNING *KERI'AH*:
THE LENGTH (of the tear), WHERE (the tear is made), FOR (the death of) WHOM AND WHEN SHOULD IT BE DONE

§5 (A)Whoever is present (B)at the death of a Jew or Jewess is required to perform *keri'ah*, even if the deceased sometimes committed a sin, because he was unable to conquer his desire, or even if he did not do a *mitzvah* because of the bother.

―――― NISHMAT AVRAHAM ――――

SIMAN 340

Everyone (male or female) must tear his garments (*keri'ah*) on hearing of the death of one of his seven close relatives. These are his father, mother, son, daughter, brother, sister and spouse. However if one is in the presence of a Jew (male or female) when he or she dies, one must perform *keri'ah* even though he is not related.

(A) Whoever is present. The *Radbaz*[1] writes that even if his face is averted at the moment of death, he is nevertheless obligated to perform *keri'ah* since he could have seen it had he not turned away. However, if one is unable to see the patient at the moment he dies, even if he is in the same house, he is not required to perform *keri'ah*. Therefore, writes the *Sdei Chemed*,[2] a blind person, even if he feels and realizes that the patient in his presence has just died, is not obligated to perform *keri'ah*. Rav Neuwirth shlita wrote to me that the blind person must obviously perform *keri'ah* if the patient is one of the seven close relatives.

(B) at the death. Are doctors, nurses and other caregivers who are present when a Jewish patient dies obligated to tear *keri'ah*? Rav Waldenberg shlita[3] wrote to me: As is well known, those who are present when someone dies do not tear *keri'ah* at all, not religious doctors, other caregivers or members of the burial society. What is the source for this leniency? It is worthwhile to copy, with regard to this, what the *Shulchan Gavoha*[4] says, as we find that he throws light on this issue. "It is difficult to understand why it is not customary to tear *keri'ah* when in

---

1. שו"ת, ח"ב סי' תתלח, הובא בפ"ת כאן ס"ק ג
2. מערכת אבלות סי' קעב בשם הצפיחית דבש
3. לב אברהם ח"א עמ' כא. שו"ת ציץ אליעזר חי"ג סי' לה ס"ק ד
4. על יו"ד כאן ס"ק טות מובא בכף החיים או"ח סי' תקמז ס"ק כה

NISHMAT AVRAHAM

the presence of someone when he dies. I have heard it said that if this were not so (*that is, if people were to tear keri'ah*), no one would wish to be at the side of a person when he dies and this is the reason why the members of the *bikur cholim* society in Jerusalem do not tear *keri'ah*. It would appear that everyone relies on the *Rama's* statement at the end of §7 that: 'There is an opinion that *keri'ah* is only done when one is present at the death of a Torah scholar who is also his Rav and it is the custom to act leniently in these countries.' And, although the *halachah* of *keri'ah* for a Torah scholar is plainly stated in the *Talmud* and *poskim*, nevertheless it has become customary to act leniently, for otherwise there would be no end to the matter, since there is no town or place where there is no Torah scholar. If we would have to tear *keri'ah* on every Torah scholar, we would not be left with any (whole) garments for a cold day."

Rav Waldenberg shlita adds that this is also written in *Nahar Mitzrayim*, the Laws of Mourning 17. However, continues the *Rav shlita*, the proof that the *Shulchan Gavohah* brings from the ruling of the *Rama* is not sufficient, for the *Rama's* ruling regarding *keri'ah* for a Torah scholar is that it must be done even if one is not in his presence at the time of death. But one must say, regarding this question, that the main reason for the lenient custom is for the benefit of the deceased, so that it will not be difficult to find those who will be willing to be by him when he dies. As to the doctors and nurses in a hospital, there is another reason for leniency; the outer garment that they wear is not theirs but belongs to the hospital and it was not given to them do be torn — see this Siman, §34 and the *Shach*,[5] and this is the custom.

This is also the ruling of *Rav Ovadiah Yosef shlita*.[6] However *Rav Moshe Feinstein zt"l* rules[7] that one must tear *keri'ah*. *Rav Neuwirth shlita* wrote to me, regarding *Rav Waldenberg's* observation that the outer garment belongs to the hospital, that the *halachah* is not clear cut that it is specifically the outer garment that must be torn to fulfill the obligation of *keri'ah*. There is an opinion that if one tore an inner garment, one has also fulfilled his obligation; see *Rebbe Akiva Eiger* on §9, the *Pitchei Teshuvah*[8] and the *Gilyon Maharsha*. In addition, it is also possible that a hospital coat is not considered a garment regarding this *halachah*.

Rav Auerbach zt"l wrote to me that if one tore a hospital coat for one of his seven close relatives who had died, he will not have fulfilled his obligation.

If this happens on *Shabbat* or *Yom Tov*, those standing by the bedside, who are not one of the seven close relatives, are exempt from tearing *keri'ah* after *Shabbat* or *Yom Tov*.[9]

Regarding the obligation of a patient to perform *keri'ah* for a relative who has died, see Siman 337C above and Siman 396 below.

---

5. ס"ק נ
6. שו"ת יביע אומר ח"ד סי' לה ס"ק ט
7. מוריה אלול תשד"מ עמ' סא. שו"ת אג"מ חו"מ ח"ב סי' עג אות י
8. ס"ק ח
9. שו"ת רדב"ז ח"ב סי' תתלח. שו"ת חת"ס יו"ד סי' שכג. הגרש"ז אויערבאך זצ"ל, לב אברהם ח"א עמ' יח

CHAPTER 34
The Laws of Aninut

SIMAN 341
THE LAWS CONCERNING ONE WHOSE RELATIVE IS AWAITING BURIAL. THE LAWS OF AN *ONEN*.

§1 If a close relative for whom one is required to mourn has died, the mourner must eat in a room other than where the deceased is lying. If there is no other room he should eat in the house of a friend. If this is also unavailable, he should put up a partition between himself and the deceased, so that he may eat. If he does not have the wherewithal to make a partition ⁽ᴬ⁾he should turn away from the deceased to eat.

──────── NISHMAT AVRAHAM ────────

SIMAN 341

(A) he should turn away from the deceased. The *Shulchan Aruch*[1] rules that one may not be within four *cubits* of a deceased while wearing *tefillin* because of *loeg larash* (mocking the deceased because you can perform the *mitzvah* and he cannot). In many hospitals men visit to help patients put on *tefillin* or to offer a patient, who would not otherwise put on *tefillin*, the opportunity to perform the *mitzvah*. What would the *halachah* be for a bedridden patient who wishes to put on *tefillin* with the help of such a visitor, but whose bed is next to one in which a deceased patient is lying, if the visitor cannot wait until the deceased has been taken away? The question arises for a bedridden patient who cannot leave the room and, if he does not put on *tefillin* now, he will miss doing so on that day. Is the curtain between the two beds sufficient to prevent *loeg larash* or will it be necessary to have a curtain with specific dimensions (see *Nishmat Avraham,* vol. 1 *Orach Chaim,* Siman 87C) to permit this? Rav Ezriel Auerbach *shlita* told me that his father-in-law, Rav Eliashiv *shlita*, told him that although he has no specific proof, it would nevertheless seem to him that in a situation such as this, where a *mitzvah* will be lost, one may use an ordinary curtain although it does not have the necessary dimensions, and this is how he ruled when he was asked in a specific case. For the *Gemara*[2] writes that if a close relative for whom one is required to mourn has died, the mourner must eat in a room other than where the deceased is lying ... and, if he does not have the means to make a partition, he turns away from the deceased to eat. *Rashi* explains that he must eat in another room for otherwise it would appear as if he is mocking the deceased. The *Shulchan Aruch* (above) rules that a relative cannot eat in

1. או"ח סי' מה סע' א ויו"ד סי' שסו סע' ב   2. ברכות יז ע"ב

SIMAN 341 / §1

―――― NISHMAT AVRAHAM ――――

the presence of the deceased and the *Shach*[3] comments that eating in the presence of the deceased mocks the deceased. The *Pitchei Teshuvah*[4] explains that in the *Shach's* opinion it is forbidden even for a non-relative to eat in the presence of the deceased and he concludes that one should act strictly according to the *Shach's* ruling.[5] (Thus, one should not perform a *mitzvah* in his presence without at least drawing the curtain.)

Rav Auerbach zt"l wrote to me that since the *Shulchan Aruch*[6] rules that it is permissible to be in the presence of a deceased if the *tefillin* are covered, then surely it must be permissible if the deceased is behind a curtain.

The *Da'at Kedoshim*[7] writes that although the *Shulchan Aruch* requires a fixed partition that will not be moved by normal winds, nevertheless if this is not possible, it would be sufficient if the deceased is covered by something other than his shrouds. This is no worse than his turning away from the deceased, which is permitted.

Rav Auerbach zt"l wrote to me that this ruling requires further study, for if the deceased is covered only with a sheet and it is obvious that the sheet covers a dead person, it would be forbidden. On the other hand, to cover him completely in such a way that one cannot discern that there is a deceased present would be disgracing him. Nevertheless, a dividing curtain would certainly be permitted.

---

3. ס"ק ג
4. ס"ק ב
5. וראה בערוך השולחן סע' ז ו-ח שמדובר רק במי שחייב להתאבל על המת, וחולק על הפ"ת
6. יו"ד סי' שסז סע' ב
7. על סי' שסז

CHAPTER 35
The Laws of Mourning

SIMAN 345
THE LAWS CONCERNING ONE WHO HAS COMMITTED SUICIDE

§2 Who is defined as (A)having committed suicide? For example, if one says that he is going up to the roof and he is seen to do so immediately in anger or distress and then fell and died, he is considered as having committed suicide.

---NISHMAT AVRAHAM---

SIMAN 345

A person who commits suicide is denied certain rites of burial and mourning; see the *Shulchan Aruch* here §1.

(A) having committed suicide. The *Ben Ish Chai*[1] writes that all three conditions of the *Shulchan Aruch* must be fulfilled before he is considered to have committed suicide: (1) That he was heard to say that he is going up to the roof; (2) he goes up immediately and falls; and (3) he does so in anger or distress. This also applies to other such situations. The *Ben Ish Chai* himself adds another condition — that we do not know if he did not repent. Thus he concludes that it is extremely rare to be able to find someone who fulfills all of these conditions. The *Darchei Moshe*[2] writes that he is defined as having committed suicide only if he was warned not to go up to the roof just before he did. The *Birkei Yosef*[3] writes that a child or *shoteh* (*and this includes anyone suffering from a psychiatric illness that can lead to suicide — author*) cannot be said to have committed suicide; see §3. The *Yad Avraham*[4] adds to this one who commits suicide to absolve himself of his sins or one who does so for fear of torture.[5]

Although the *Minchat Chinuch*[6] writes that it is possible that the verse:[7] "Do not stand idly by while your fellow's blood is shed," does not obligate one to try and save someone who is attempting suicide even if one could do so, nevertheless the *Margaliot HaYam*[8] quotes a proof[9] that one must try to prevent it. The *Gemara*[10] applies the verse:[11] "You shall lend the poor man whatever he requires," not only to someone who does not have means and does not wish employment, but even if he has means but does not want to use them, one is obligated to give him a loan (and claim payment from his possessions after

---

1. שו״ת רב פעלים ח״ג יו״ד סי׳ כט. וראה גם שם סי׳ ל
2. יו״ד כאן. וראה גם בספר חסידים סי׳ תרעז
3. ס״ק ב
4. על היו״ד כאן
5. ראה בפ״ת ס״ק ב. שו״ת שואל ומשיב מהד״ק ח״ג סי׳ ריז. שו״ת מהרש״ם ח״י יו״ד סי׳ קכג. שו״ת חיים שאל ח״א סי׳ מו. שו״ת חתם סופר יו״ד סי׳ שכו ואהע״ז ח״א
6. קומץ למנחה מצוה רלו
7. ויקרא יט:טז
8. על סנהדרין עג ע״א או״ק יב
9. בשם ספר עין אליהו
10. ב״מ לא ע״ב
11. דברים טו:ח

SIMAN 349
IT IS FORBIDDEN TO BENEFIT FROM A CORPSE OR FROM ITS SHROUDS

§1 It is forbidden to benefit from the shrouds of a corpse, (A)whether the corpse is that of a Jew or a non-Jew.

NISHMAT AVRAHAM
---

he dies — *Rashi*). Rebbe Shimon says that if he has the means, one ignores him. But even according to Rebbe Shimon's view, he is only ignored since he has the means to provide for himself. However one is required to save someone who threw himself into the sea and is then unable to save himself. This is the meaning of the verse:[12] "You shall return it (his lost property) to him"; even if he tries to kill himself you should return his life to him.[13] And, even if he shouts, "Do not save me," one ignores his wishes.[14] The *Radbaz*[15] rules that a person has no jurisdiction over his soul, which belongs to *Hashem* only, as the verse says:[16] "The souls are mine."[17]

One sets aside Sabbath laws for an attempted suicide who is *seriously ill*.[18] Similarly, one may set aside Sabbath laws for someone who knowingly puts himself in danger.[19] The *Orchot Chaim*,[20] however, writes that Sabbath laws may only be set aside for him if he is *seriously ill*. If he is *non-seriously ill*, however, even Rab-

binic laws may not be set aside for him.

See *Nishmat Avraham*, vol. 1 *Orach Chaim*, Siman 219I regarding the thanksgiving blessing of a person who recovers after attempting suicide.

SIMAN 349

(A) whether the corpse is that of a Jew.

1. AUTOPSIES (postmortem) FOR THE PURPOSE OF LEARNING MEDICINE.

The *poskim* prohibit an autopsy (when it is not done to possibly save the life of a patient who is present — see below) because of:

a. Disrespect of the corpse. This is forbidden by the Torah[1] which forbids delaying burial, even of one who was killed by the *Sanhedrin*, because of desecration and disrespect.[2] The *Gemara*[3] also prohibits an autopsy for this reason.[4] This reason for prohibiting an autopsy is also given by the *Sha'agat Aryeh*,[5] *Noda BiYehudah*,[6] *Chatam Sofer*[7] and *Ketav Sofer*.[8]

---

12. שם כב:ב
13. ספרי פ׳ תצא על הפסוק והשיבותו לו
14. מרגליות הים שם בשם תשובת מהר"ם בן ברוך סי׳ לט
15. על הרמב"ם הל׳ סנה׳ פי"ח ה"ז
16. יחזקאל יח:ד
17. כל זה במרגליות הים שם
18. ארחות חיים סי׳ שכח סע׳ יטף. שו"ת חלקת יעקב ח"א סי׳ עב. שו"ת אגרות משה או"ח ח"א סי׳ קכו. שו"ת ציץ אליעזר ח"ח סי׳ טו פ"ד וח"י סי׳ יז פ"ב אות ו. וראה ביומא לה ע"ב במעשה של הלל ובעיון יעקב ופתח עינים להרב חיד"א שם
19. שו"ת אגרות משה שם ושו"ת ציץ אליעזר ח"ח סי׳ טו פ"ז. וראה במ"ב סי׳ רמח ס"ק כו
20. סי׳ שכח ס"ק יט בשם החקר הלכה ח"ב דף ו. וכתב שכן יש ללמוד מדברי המג"א סי׳ תרמ ס"ק ד

1. דברים כא:כג
2. רמב"ן שם כא:כב
3. חולין יא ע"ב
4. וכותב הגר"י אריאלי זצ"ל, תורה שבעל פה תשכ"ד עמ׳ מ, הרי מה שצוותה תורה להרוג את הרוצח הוא דוקא לאחר שיבדקו את הנרצח אם אינו טרפה, ואעפ"כ אמרו לא לבדקו משום דמנוול, ע"כ שניוול המת אסור מן התורה
5. שו"ת, סי׳ ו
6. שו"ת, מהד"ת יו"ד סי׳ רי
7. שו"ת, יו"ד סי׳ שלו
8. שו"ת, יו"ד סי׳ קעד

NISHMAT AVRAHAM

b. Benefiting from the corpse. According to most of the *poskim* this is also prohibited by Torah law.[9] *Rav Auerbach zt"l*[10] writes that this includes watching an autopsy in order to learn medicine.

c. Delaying or abrogating the *mitzvah* to bury the dead. There is a controversy as to whether the *mitzvah* to bury the dead is of Torah[11] or Rabbinic[12] origin. According to many *poskim*[13] this *mitzvah* also applies to parts of a corpse.

d. The sanctity of the corpse. *Chazal* compare the sanctity of a corpse to that of a Torah scroll.[14]

e. It is difficult for the departed soul to see the desecration of its body.[15]

For all of these reasons the vast majority of *poskim* prohibit an autopsy on a Jewish corpse if performed to learn medicine. These include the *Noda BiYehudah*,[16] *Yavetz*,[17] *Chatam Sofer*,[18] *Maharam Shick*,[19] *Binyan Tzion*,[20] *Chazon Ish*,[21] *Kol Bo Al Aveilut*,[22] *Gesher HaChaim*,[23] *Seridei Eish*,[24] *Igrot Moshe*,[25] *Minchat Yitzchak*,[26] *Yabia Omer*[27] and *Tzitz Eliezer*.[28] See also the extensive list of *poskim* quoted by others.[29]

The *Mishpetei Uziel*[30] is one of the few well-known *poskim* who does permit an autopsy which is meant only for the study of medicine. In his opinion, the study of medicine includes *pikuach nefesh*, for if autopsies were not done, one could not learn medicine.[31] However he also rules strictly that the autopsy must be done with respect and not disdainfully and lightly. One must be very careful that every part of the corpse is then buried with honor and no part of it, however small, remains unburied.

Today, with the different forms of imaging, needle biopsies and simulation that are available, the necessity to perform autopsies to learn medicine is no longer valid, and medical schools in the United States now grant recognition to departments of medicine or surgery without demanding a minimum quota of autopsies per year. There is also no evidence that the standard of knowledge of medical students or physicians or the level of patient

---

9. רש"י סנהדרין מז ע"ב ד"ה פינחס. ר"ת שם מח ע"א ד"ה משמשין. רמב"ן מובא במגיד משנה הל' מאכ"א פ"ב ה"ג. יראים סי' שי. ש"ך יו"ד סי' עט ס"ק ג. שו"ת חת"ס יו"ד סי' שלו. אך לדעת היעב"ץ שו"ת סי' מא האיסור הוא מדרבנן

10. מנחת שלמה תנינא סי' צו בסוף

11. הרמב"ם ספר המצוות, עשה רלא והל' אבל פי"ב ה"א גשר החיים ח"ב פי"ב בדעת

12. שו"ת יביע אומר ח"ג יו"ד סי' כב בדעת הרמב"ם

13. מהתויו"ט, שבת פ"י מ"ה, משמע שמצות הקבורה חלה על כל כזית מן המת, ודעת הנו"ב, מהר"ק יו"ד סי' צ, והמנחת חינוך שיש לחייב קבורה אף לכל חלק אפילו פחות מכזית. וכן כותבים השו"ת משפטי עוזיאל יו"ד סי' כח-כט הקצות השולחן בבדי השולחן סי' קלח סוס"ק יח. וראה להלן דעת פוסקי דורנו. לעומתם המל"מ, הל' אבל פי"ד הכ"א סובר שאין מצות קבורה חלה אלא על ראשו ורובו

14. גופו של אדם הוא לא רק נרתיק של קדושה ששימש לנשמה העילאית אלא שהוא עצמו נתקדש גם בקדושה עצמית, בדומה לספר תורה (ברכות יח ע"א) - גשר החיים ח"א פ"ה סע' א ס"ק א. ועיין גם בשו"ת חת"ס יו"ד סי' שלו

15. שו"ת הרשב"א ח"א סי' שסט. ספר חסידים סי' תתשסג. תויו"ט אבות פ"ב מ"ז

16. שו"ת, מה"ת יו"ד סי' רי

17. שאילת יעב"ץ

18. שו"ת, יו"ד סי' שלו

19. שו"ת, יו"ד סי' שמד ו-שמז

20. שו"ת, סי' קע ו-קעא

21. אהלות סי' כב ס"ק לב

22. ח"א סי' ג סע' יב

23. ח"א פ"ה ס"ק ו

24. שו"ת, ח"ב סי' קיט

25. שו"ת, יו"ד ח"א סי' קנא

26. שו"ת, ח"ה סי' ט

27. שו"ת, ח"ג סי' גב אות כו

28. שו"ת, ח"ד סי' יד

29. הגר"ק כהנא זצ"ל, המעין כ-ך ז תשכ"ז. וכן ראה בספר אסיא כרך ד עמ' 32

30. שו"ת, יו"ד סי' כח-כט

31. וראה מה שכתב החת"ס בחי' על ע"ז לא ע"ב ד"ה איידי והבן איש חי בספרו בן יהוידע על פסחים מט ע"ב בד"ה ודע

NISHMAT AVRAHAM

care is any different whether autopsies are performed or not.

2. AUTOPSIES TO SAVE LIFE. If a *seriously ill* patient is present in the same department or hospital where someone else, with the same symptoms, has just died, and it is reasonable to expect that by performing an autopsy on the deceased the life of the other may be saved, autopsy is permitted if this is the only way to arrive at a firm diagnosis. Similarly, if other, even at present healthy, members of the family or contacts may be harboring the same undefined disease and may soon become *seriously ill*, an autopsy may be done if this is the only way to arrive at a firm diagnosis. This would apply to infectious disease and familial disease.[32] However, if the patient is not present now but such a patient may present himself in the future, autopsy is forbidden.[33] Although, these days, one can virtually instantly transmit information to the whole world and thereby inform those interested in the results of the autopsy, thus saving the lives of patients in other medical centers, this has never been done. Even the most important and far-reaching breakthroughs are only accepted by the medical profession after they have been published in peer-reviewed articles in a well-known medical journal, a process that can take many months at least.

The *Chazon Ish*,[34] quoting the *Noda BiYehudah* and *Chatam Sofer*,[35] writes that an autopsy may be performed to save the life of a *seriously ill* patient who is present in the same hospital. If such a patient is not present there, the autopsy is forbidden. However this difference between whether the patient is present on the spot or not applies only if the disease is not prevalent. *Rav Auerbach zt"l* explained to me that the *Chazon Ish* meant that even if the *seriously ill* patient was not actually present, if the disease was so prevalent that a similar patient was certain to be present elsewhere and could immediately be helped by the autopsy, it would be permitted.[36]

However the *Aruch LaNer*[37] forbids an autopsy to be performed even if it would save the life of another *seriously ill* patient present at the time in the same hospital.

3. DONATES OR SELLS HIS BODY TO SCIENCE. There is a controversy between the *poskim* whether it is permitted[38] or forbidden[39] to perform an autopsy on the donor. However even according to those who permit an autopsy to be performed, every single part of him must be buried the same day. *Rav Auerbach zt"l* wrote to me that it is, however, forbidden to sell or donate one's body for this purpose.

The *Igrot Moshe*[40] writes that by Torah law which *Chazal* received, generation after generation, going back to Moshe Rabbeinu on Mount Sinai, no one has any rights over his body that he may tell others what they may do with it or any part of it, not even to advance the knowledge of medicine. His children and relatives certainly have no ownership rights over his body. Even without this reason, it is forbidden to have any benefit from the corpse or even from any part of it. They

---

32. כל בו על אבלות ח"א סי' ג סע' יב ס"ק 10. הגר"י אריאלי זצ"ל, תורה שבעל פה תשכ"ד עמ' מ, ע"פ הפוסקים המובאים לעיל

33. הגר"י אריאלי זצ"ל, תורה שבעל פה שם

34. אהלות סי' כב סוסע' לב

35. מובאים בפת"ש סי' שסג ס"ק ה

36. ראה גם במנחת שלמה תנינא סי' פו אות ה

37. שו"ת בנין ציון סי' קע ו-קעא

38. שו"ת בנין ציון סי' קע. שו"ת ציץ אליעזר ח"ד סי' יד. וראה גם בשו"ת חלקת יעקב ח"ד סי' לט ובשו"ת חת"ס או"ח סי' קמד

39. שו"ת חת"ס יו"ד סי' שלו. שו"ת מהר"ם שיק יו"ד סי' שמז

40. שו"ת, יו"ד ח"ג סי' קמ

have an obligation to bury him as soon as possible on the very day of death, intact. It is forbidden to make even a single incision into the body, but he should be buried complete just as when he died. Even if it is not possible to bury him the day he died, but only after some days, or if the corpse is to be transported elsewhere for burial, he must still be buried complete as he was when he died.

4. AUTOPSY ON AN ABORTED FETUS. This is also forbidden if it is performed for the purpose of studying medicine.[41] *Rav Neuwirth shlita* told me that the autopsy is forbidden only if the woman had miscarried more than forty days after conception, but if it was less than this, autopsy of the fetus would be permitted. He also told me that if a woman had recurrent miscarriages and there is a possibility that an autopsy could prevent her from aborting in a future pregnancy, autopsy would be permitted even if she miscarried more than forty days after conception. *Rav Auerbach zt"l* told me that this would also apply to a baby who died less than thirty days after birth. Such a baby is a possible *nefel* and besides, by performing an autopsy, one may prevent the likelihood of danger to the mother from giving birth in the future to such children (*nefalim*). See also the *Shulchan Aruch*,[42] *Magen Avraham*,[43] *Binyan Tzion*,[44] *Gesher HaChaim*[45] and *Tzitz Eliezer*[46] as to whether there is an obligation to bury the fetus.

5. WATCHING AN AUTOPSY. Although it is, as stated above, forbidden to perform an autopsy to learn medicine, there are those who permit[47] the autopsy to be observed; others[48] forbid it. *Rav Auerbach zt"l* writes[49] that he is surprised at those who permit watching an autopsy because, in their opinion, merely observing an autopsy is not considered having benefit from the corpse and is comparable to an act of hearing and observing which is only Rabbinically forbidden. He quotes the *Mishneh LaMelech*[50] who writes that the accepted ruling that hearing and observing is only Rabbinically forbidden applies only if, for example, a sanctified wick is lit for a permitted reason and one benefits from its light. However if one takes a sanctified wick and lights it, there is surely no greater abuse of a sanctified object than this. In our case, continues the *Rav zt"l*, the corpse is cut with a knife and there is no doubt that this is forbidden by Torah law, see the *Or Same'ach*;[51] therefore it is necessary to emphasize this for many have written incorrectly about this.

6. NEEDLE BIOPSY. *Rav Auerbach zt"l* told me that it is permissible to take blood samples, samples of fluid that are present in body cavities and needle biopsies from a corpse even if this is done only to increase one's knowledge of medicine. This is also the ruling of the *Igrot Moshe* who writes that this is not a desecration of the corpse.[52] *Rav Auerbach zt"l* also told me that this is not included in the prohibition against benefiting from a corpse. Since the benefit obtained is to increase one's practical experience so as to be able to

---

41. הגר"י אריאלי, תודה שבעל פה, שם. וראה גם בשו"ת בנין ציון סי' קיט ושו"ת מהר"ם שיק יו"ד סי' שמד
42. יו"ד סי' רסג סע' ה
43. סי' תקכו ס"ק כ
44. שו"ת, סי' קיג
45. ח"א פט"ז סע' ג
46. שו"ת, ח"י סי' כה פ"ח או"ק ז
47. שאילת יעב"ץ סי' מא. חזו"א יו"ד סי' רח ס"ק ז. שו"ת הר צבי יו"ד סי' רעה וראה שם במילואים
48. שו"ת מהר"ם שיק יו"ד סי' שמד. שו"ת חלקת יעקב ח"א סי' פד אף שמלמד זכות על המתירים. כל בו על אבלות ח"א סי' ג סע' יב ס"ק 3
49. מנחת שלמה תנינא סי' צז בסוף
50. כלי מקדש פ"ח ה"ו
51. אור שמח שבת פ"א ה"ח
52. שו"ת, יו"ד ח"ב סוסי' קנא

treat a future patient better, this is not considered forbidden benefit. It is also permissible to take needle biopsies from a *nefel* for the same reason;[53] *Rav Auerbach zt"l* wrote to me to add: since this may be beneficial to others. (*These procedures are minor ones with a minimal cut or hole in the body of the deceased and not therefore to be compared with an autopsy — author.*)

Rav Auerbach zt"l also told me that one may practice procedures such as intubation on a corpse in order to be able to save the life of a future patient.

A needle biopsy may also be done on *Shabbat* provided that a *seriously ill* patient is present at the time and may be helped by the results. *Rav Auerbach zt"l* wrote to me that there is no *melachah* since all one does is to cut into flesh[54] and it is possible that there is no prohibition of *muktzeh* either (both the needle and the biopsy specimen may be handled) since it is permitted to move something that is *muktzeh* to avoid loss (*in this case, the ability to possibly help a seriously ill patient — author*). In addition, the prohibition of *muktzeh* is lighter than other Rabbinic prohibitions since one is also permitted to move an object that is *muktzeh* in an unusual manner. On the other hand, this may be considered making use of an object that is *muktzeh,* which is a more serious matter than moving it. However it is forbidden to take blood samples unless it is for the benefit of a *seriously ill* patient. The *Rav zt"l* added, in another letter to me, that since the blood is enclosed in the vein, the *Rambam*[55] rules that removing a *measure* of blood (the volume of a dried fig) would be a *melachah*. This is not to be compared with salting meat to remove the blood, which is akin to squeezing fruit which is not meant to be squeezed for juice, as explained by the *Minchat Chinuch*.[56] (*Squeezing grapes or olives for their juice on Shabbat is prohibited by Torah law since this is common practice. On the other hand, squeezing any other fruit for its juice is only prohibited by Rabbinic law since this was not common practice at the time of Chazal — author.*)

A Jew may not put the biopsy specimen into formalin (as is usually done to preserve it before it can be processed) on *Shabbat*, since this involves a *melachah*,[57] unless the biopsy is done to help a *seriously ill* patient who is present at the time.[58]

7. AUTOPSY TO SAVE THE LIMB OF A *NON-SERIOUSLY ILL* PATIENT.

The *Shach*[59] rules that one may set aside all Torah prohibitions to save the limb of a *non-seriously ill* patient, but the *Pri Megadim*[60] adds that this does not include the prohibition of desecrating the Sabbath by *melachah*. However, the *Pri Megadim* also writes that although it is permissible to eat Rabbinically forbidden foods if there is danger to a limb, he is uncertain whether this also applies to that which the Torah forbids to eat or have benefit from. The *Chavot Yair*[61] was asked about the case of a soldier who threatened to cut off a Jew's ear if he did not drink wine that had been used as libation for idol worship. He replied that if the threat was just empty words and exaggerated talk, he should not comply easily. However if he was truly frightened that the soldier would, in his anger at being

---

53. שבילין, מרחשון תשכ"ג עמ' לג

54. אין כאן מלאכה של דש, ראה שבת קלו ע"א

55. הל' שבת פ"ח ה"זו-ח. וראה בפמ"ג פתיחה כוללת, הל' שבת ד"ה וראיתי להפני יהושע וכן בפמ"ג א"א סי' שטז ס"ק טו

56. מצוה לב במוסך השבת מלאכת הדש [ה] (הוצאת מכון ירושלים) ד"ה והנה המל"מ

57. מלאכת עיבוד, ראה חיי אדם כלל לג סע' יב

58. שמעתי ממו"ר הגרי"י נויבירט שליט"א והסכים אתו הגרש"ז אויערבאך זצ"ל

59. יו"ד סי' קנו ס"ק ג

60. או"ח סי' שכח מ"ז ס"ק ז

61. שו"ת, סי' קפג, מוזכר בחידושי רעק"א על יו"ד סי' קנז

§2 It is also forbidden to benefit from (B)adornments that are attached to the corpse, such as a wig and the like. (*This is*

---NISHMAT AVRAHAM---

refused, actually carry out his threat, he does not commit a sin by drinking the wine. One should not think that because losing an ear (lobe) will not affect his hearing, it is not as serious as a *danger to a limb,* for its loss is numbered among those injuries by which a slave is freed. Also, any blow with a sword is dangerous and permits Sabbath laws to be set aside to treat the person injured.

The *Yabia Omer,*[62] in discussing the question of corneal transplants, writes that there is room to rule leniently, following the ruling of the *Shach* and *Pri Megadim* (reference 59 and 60).

With regard to a corneal transplant from a corpse, *Rav Eliashiv shlita* in a written *responsum* rules that since there is an obligation to bury even a small part of a corpse,[63] this would be forbidden in a situation where there was no danger to life. *Rav Auerbach zt"l* wrote to me that this needs further discussion since this is comparable to saving oneself at the expense of another's money (property). And although the *Tosafot*[64] permit this, they only do so in the context of danger to life and this is the ruling of the *Shulchan Aruch.*[65] [See below **(B) 2(a) CORNEA.**]

Therefore, someone who has a burn on his hand requiring a skin graft may not have this done using skin from a skin bank in order to permit normal functioning of the hand, if there is no danger to life. This would also be the ruling with regard to a bone transplant from a bone bank if there is no danger to the patient's life as in hip replacement surgery for osteoarthritis. Although, at first sight, both these transplants should be permissible according to the *Shach* that all Torah prohibitions may be set aside if there is danger to a limb, *Rav Neuwirth shlita* told me that this would not be applicable here. The recipient would be continuously obligated to bury the part of the deceased that was transplanted into him and would therefore be continuously setting aside both a negative[66] and a positive commandment[67] — according to *Rav Eliashiv shlita's* opinion — and would be guilty of stealing and not returning someone else's property (the transplanted part of the deceased's body) — according to *Rav Auerbach zt"l.* [See below **(B) 2(b) SKIN.**]

8. **NON-JEWISH CORPSE.** If the family of a non-Jew either demand or permit an autopsy to be performed for medical reasons on the corpse of that non-Jew, the *Igrot Moshe,*[68] based on the opinion of many *rishonim* and *acharonim,*[69] and *Rav Auerbach zt"l*[70] both rule that this is allowed.

(B) adornments that are attached to the corpse.

1. **REMOVAL OF A PACEMAKER FROM A CORPSE.** May an implanted internal pacemaker be removed from a corpse? The battery which runs the pacemaker is usually surgically implanted subcutaneously in the upper part of the patient's chest and the pacemaker attached to it is inserted into an internal

---

62. שו"ת, ח"ג יו"ד סי' כג אות ל
63. קצות השולחן סי' קלח בבדה"ש סוס"ק יח
64. מצוה תקלב
65. חו"מ שפח סע' ב וראה שם בהגר"א ס"ק כה וסי' שנט סע' ד
66. לא תלין נבלתו - דברים כא:כג
67. קבור תקברנו - שם
68. שו"ת, יו"ד ח"א סי' רכט ענף ו וחו"מ ח"ב סי' עג אות ו
69. ראה בשדי חמד דברי חכמים סי' נב ושו"ת יביע אומר ח"ג סי' כ-כג. נשמת אברהם כאן באריכות
70. שמעתי מפיו

only if they are tied to the hairs of the body, but if they are not tied, it is permitted to benefit from them. Thus rings and the like may be removed.) **This is only true if the person did not say any-**

─────────────── NISHMAT AVRAHAM ───────────────

vein and passed into the heart.

The *Tzitz Eliezer*[71] rules that it may be removed. He writes that although the *Shulchan Aruch* rules that an adornment that is tied to the hairs of the corpse cannot be removed even if this was the express wish of the person, nevertheless the *Shach*,[72] quoting the *Rambam*[73] and *Semag*, disagrees with this ruling.[74] In addition, since this involves a large loss of money for the hospital that provided the pacemaker and it can be reused to save another's life, one can certainly depend on the ruling of those who believe that whatever is attached or tied to the corpse is not considered part of the corpse and it is not forbidden to benefit from it. As to desecrating the corpse (an incision must be made to remove the battery), this is also permitted for one can see from the *Gemara*[75] that a corpse may be desecrated to prevent monetary loss, and this is the ruling of the *Rambam*[76] and the *Shulchan Aruch*.[77] The *Shoel U'Meshiv*[78] also rules that if this is not done to desecrate the corpse but in order to prevent monetary loss it is not considered desecration of the corpse. Therefore, in this case, since it is the hospital authorities, and not the relatives, that demand the return of the pacemaker because of the substantial monetary loss involved — for the pacemaker was only lent to the patient — it is permissible to cut into the corpse to remove it. However this must be done with appropriate respect to the corpse, cutting only to the extent necessary to remove the pacemaker and no more, and being careful to suture the wound immediately afterwards. However in order to act according to all opinions and to avoid all uncertainties, it would be better, continues the *Tzitz Eliezer*, if the patient were asked to sign a document, before receiving the pacemaker, stating that since the hospital is only lending it to him for the duration of his life, he wills that the pacemaker be removed from his body after his death and returned to the hospital. If the patient refuses to sign and, should he not receive the pacemaker his life will be put in danger, the pacemaker must be inserted, and after his death the hospital may rely on the lenient ruling stated above to get it back. Obviously if the patient pays for the pacemaker, it may not be removed from his corpse without express permission from him during his lifetime.

Rav Auerbach zt"l also told me that since the pacemaker is not an integral part of the patient's body and, in addition, he certainly would have agreed to such surgery in his lifetime (had it been necessary), then removing it from him after his death is not a desecration of his body. The *Rav zt"l* also wrote to me that it is possible that a pacemaker is not the same as

───────────────

he was a minor at the time of the sale and the sale was therefore invalid. The buyer claims that he was not and demands that the body be exhumed so that it can be examined for external signs of puberty.

71. שו״ת, חי״ד סי׳ פב
72. נקודת הכסף כאן
73. הל׳ אבל פי״ד הכ״א
74. וראה גם בפ״ת ס״ק ד
75. ב״ב קנד ע״ב

The Gemara discusses the case of a young person who sold property inherited from his father to another and then died. The relatives claim that

76. הל׳ מכירה פכ״ט הט״ז
77. חו״מ סי׳ רלה סע׳ יג ויו״ד סי׳ שסג סע׳ ז
78. מהד״ק ח״א סי׳ רלא

objects which are part of a person's body, such as a permanently fixed false tooth, or a wig which has been attached to the person and looked upon as his hair. The same applies to the other examples which the *poskim* have forbidden to be removed from a corpse, for all of these do not need any outside help or assistance, and can therefore, to some extent, be considered as part of his body. The pacemaker, however, is an instrument that is driven by a battery that requires changing from time to time and must therefore be viewed as an electrically driven instrument permanently installed under the skin which cannot be compared to an artifical heart or to an adornment to the body. It is more comparable to a respirator which is attached to the body. It is only that a respirator lies outside the body of the patient and it is established beforehand that it will be attached to him only as long as he requires it, whereas the pacemaker is within his body for a long period of time. Thus, after the pacemaker is no longer of use, it becomes a foreign body which is no longer a part of the body. One may assume therefore that the patient would prefer that the foreign body be removed from him to be used for someone else. I also believe, continues *Rav Auerbach zt"l*, that this is not a desecration of the corpse since only the battery is removed and not the pacemaker which has been inserted into the heart and this is also exactly the same procedure that is done when the battery needs changing. And since it would seem that the ruling of the *Aruch LaNer* (who forbids autopsies even if done to save life — see above reference 37) is not accepted, and also since there is no fear that this is forbidden by the Torah, it is possible that with Rabbinic law one can add the argument given and arrive at a lenient ruling.

2. TRANSPLANTATION FROM A DEAD DONOR. The discussion does not include a patient who is brain dead but only one who has no brain function and permanent and complete cessation of respiration and heartbeat.

a. Cornea. Although according to most *poskim* benefiting from a corpse is forbidden by Torah law (see reference 9), *Rav Unterman zt"l* writes[79] that there is no problem whatsoever of benefiting from a corpse, since an organ that is transplanted into a living body comes back to life. Therefore the laws pertaining to a corpse (or part of one) no longer apply to it and the benefit obtained from it is benefit from the living.

The *Har Tzvi*[80] also rules that this is permissible, since a cornea is less than a *kezayit*.[81] This is certainly so, if we say that the benefit is obtained in an unusual manner. The opinion of the *Radbaz*[82] and the *Shivat Tzion*[83] is that benefiting from a corpse in a manner that is not the usual one is not forbidden by the Torah. However, *Rebbe Akiva Eiger*[84] quotes the *Ginat Veradim* who disagrees with the *Radbaz* and rules that benefit from a corpse is forbidden even if it is obtained in an unusual manner. And this is also the ruling of the *Igrot Moshe*.[85] See also the *Minchat Shlomo* quoted above (reference 49).

Rav Eliashiv shlita, in a written *responsum,* rules that this approach needs clarification. For when a part of a corpse is transplanted into a living person, even though it is accepted and not rejected by the recipient's body, nevertheless it does not become alive but merely remains attached

---

83. סוטה סב
84. חידושי רעק"א כאן
85. שו"ת, יו"ד ח"א סי' רכט ענף ג. וראה שם בענף ה מה נקרא כדרך הנאה

79. שו"ת שבט מיהודה עמ' שיד
80. שו"ת, יו"ד סי' רעז
81. וחצי שיעור אינו ראוי לאצטרופי
82. שו"ת, ח"ג סי' תקמח (תתקעט)

to a living person. Therefore, if there was a *mitzvah* to bury it before, this does not disappear following transplantation. And since, according to the *Minchat Chinuch*,[86] the *mitzvah* of burial applies even to a *kezayit* of a corpse, the Torah commandment has been set aside in a situation not involving *pikuach nefesh*.

The *Yabia Omer*[87] discusses desecration of the corpse with relation to corneal transplants. He quotes the *Shoel U'Meshiv*[88] and the *Maharil*[89] who both rule that the *issur* to desecrate a corpse only applies when it is done for no purpose. But, if, for example, the desecration is done to free an *agunah* to marry, it is permitted. In the case of a corneal transplant, bringing light to a blind person and freeing him from his prison of darkness is surely a great need. *Chazal*[90] have compared a blind person to a dead one and surely one may tip the scales to permit this. And, continues the *Yabia Omer*, even for one who is only blind in one eye, since this is considered a defect and he has much suffering and shame as a result, "great is the honor of a human being that one may set aside a prohibition of the Torah for it."[91] (*The Torah injunction not to deviate from the words of Chazal*[92] — *which in effect means that one may set aside Rabbinic law in order not to cause dishonor to a person* — *author.*) As to the issue of denying burial to the corpse, the *Yabia Omer*[93] notes that according to the *Rambam*[94] and the *Chavot Yair*[95] the obligation to bury the dead is only Rabbinic and, according to the *Tosfot Yom Tov*,[96] there is possibly no obligation at all if the part involved is less than a *kezayit in size*. (Although the *Rambam* writes[97] that there is a Torah obligation to bury the dead, there are those[98] who explain this to refer only to the relatives who are required to mourn; however the obligation on others is only Rabbinic.)

Rav Neuwirth shlita wrote to me that according to *Rav Unterman zt"l* (above) who feels that the cornea comes back to life, there is no *mitzvah* of burial anyway. Rav Auerbach zt"l wrote to me that were we to say that there is an obligation to bury the dead, it is possible that even afterwards when it comes back to life and there is no benefit derived from the dead, nevertheless the obligation to bury it once rested upon it. How then can we say that it is permitted to nullify the *mitzvah* to bury it because it is attached to another person? This is not to be compared to one who is brought back to life since, in that instance, it is the very body that was dead that comes back to life and there is no connection whatsoever in this case with bringing a dead person back to life.

The *Yabia Omer* concludes that if a person who is blind in both eyes were to ask whether he may undergo a corneal transplant when the donor is unknown to us, he may do so even in a city where the majority of the inhabitants are Jews.[99] This is because there are two interlocking

---

86. מצוה תקלב
87. שו"ת, ח"ג יו"ד סי' כג
88. שו"ת, מהד"ק ח"א סי' רלא
89. שו"ת, יו"ד סי' לא
90. נדרים סד ע"ב
91. ברכות יט ע"ב
92. דברים יז:יא
93. שם סי' כב
94. הל' אבל פי"ד ה"א
95. שו"ת, סי' קלט
96. שבת פי"ם מ"ה
97. ספר המצות, מצוה רלא
98. ארעא דרבנן בספר עפרא דארעא אות תקמו. וראה בנשר החיים ח"ב פי"ג שכתב שגם להרמב"ם מצות קבורה דאורייתא. אך כותב היביע אומר דעכ"פ הואיל ולא יצא דבר זה מכלל מחלוקת, חזי לאצטרופי הך סברה דרבנ"ד חי הוא ולא מת, ואין בזה מצות קבורה כלל
99. וכותב הרב שליט"א: וכ"ש במקום שמצווים שם גוים שיש לתלות שקרומי העין הם ממתי עכו"ם (וזה רק לפי הפוסקים שמת עכו"ם מותר בהנאה מן התורה)

―――――――――――――― NISHMAT AVRAHAM ――――――――――――――

uncertainties, the combination of which would tend to permit it. First, perhaps this is not considered having benefit from the dead since the cornea returns to life; and second, even if the cornea is not considered as coming to life, perhaps the *halachah* is according to the opinion that having benefit in an unusual manner is permitted. As to the annuling of the *mitzvah* of burial we need not have qualms, for since the cornea comes back to life, there is no longer an obligation to bury it. Regarding desecration, this was already done (for the cornea is taken from an eye bank). One may add to this the opinion of those who rule that a blind person is considered in danger with regard to setting aside all prohibitions for him apart from those involving *Shabbat* (see above references 59 and 60).

However, the *Yabi Omer* continues that if a religious doctor asks whether he is permitted to remove the corneas from a corpse for transplanting, he is not permitted to do so particularly because of the prohibition of desecrating the corpse. If, on the other hand, the person willed his corneas for this purpose, one may rely on the *poskim* who permit it when sorely needed.[100]

The *Seridei Eish*[101] also permits corneal transplants, but only for someone who is blind in both eyes.

On the other hand, the *Minchat Yitzchak*[102] reasons that a corpse has no obligation whatsoever to do *mitzvot* and we cannot forgive, in his name, the insult to his honor. For these reasons there are *poskim* who forbid an autopsy even if done to save the life of a patient who is present at the time. Certainly in such an instance of great disrespect — disrespect both to the dead and the living — there is no obligation on the family to forgo the respect due to themselves and to the deceased, nor must they exacerbate their suffering, even according to those who permit autopsies to save life.

This is also the ruling of the *Tzitz Eliezer*[103] who writes that the living have a Torah obligation to fully perform the *mitzvah* of burial. However elsewhere[104] the *Tzitz Eliezer* writes that if the deceased has been buried and his cornea sent to an eye bank, even if we know that it has been taken from a Jew who willed it while alive, nevertheless it can be transplanted even into a patient who is in danger of being blind in only one eye.

The *Shevet HaLevi*[105] writes that it is difficult to permit the removal of the eye from a deceased who has so willed, for the fact that he wished this does not permit it. He has no right to allow this because of the disrespect caused to the living and because of the obligation to bury the dead. The only time it is permitted is according to the *Noda BiYehudah*[106] (who only permits an autopsy to save life). Our Rabbis, continues the *Shevet HaLevi*, only permitted an autopsy when the seriously ill person is before us; permission to remove and send the cornea to a bank remains completely doubtful. And, if to this we add the matter of possible *pikuach nefesh*, then we may come to a situation where the eyes of all deceased will be removed and sent to an eye bank. We can permit only what our Rabbis have permitted and no more.

The *Igrot Moshe* (reference 85), *Rav Auerbach zt"l* (reference 49) and *Rav Elia-*

---

100. כותב היביע אומר: באופן שקשה מאד להשיג זאת ממתי עכו"ם, אבל אם אפשר לעשות כן מקרומי עכו"ם אין להתיר כלל להשתמש בקרומי עיני מתי ישראל

101. שו"ת, ח"ב סי' קב

102. שו"ת, ח"ה סי' ח

103. שו"ת, חי"ג סי' צא

104. שו"ת ציץ אליעזר חי"ד סי' פד. וראה גם שם חט"ו סי' יג ס"ק ב

105. שו"ת, יו"ד ח"א סי' ריא

106. שו"ת, מה"ת יו"ד סי' רי

NISHMAT AVRAHAM

shiv shlita (p. 340) appear to forbid the transplantation of any part of a corpse, even if taken from a bank, unless this is to save life.

b. SKIN. The *Yabia Omer*[107] discusses the problem. Although the *Tosafot* [108] and the *Piskei Tosafot*[109] both rule that it is not forbidden to have benefit from the skin of a corpse, most *poskim*[110] disagree and rule that it is forbidden.

It would appear that the controversy regarding corneal transplant (above) will also apply here. The *Igrot Moshe*[111] forbids the taking of skin for grafting to a *non-seriously ill* patient even if it has already been removed from the deceased (for example, from a skin bank; see **A7** above). *Rav Auerbach zt"l* wrote to me that if a patient has large burns which threaten his life it is permissible to take skin from a corpse for grafting, since we do not follow the ruling of the *Aruch LaNer* (reference 37 above).

3. TRANSPLANTATION FROM A LIVING, HEALTHY DONOR. Whether such transplantation is permitted or not depends on whether a person is permitted, obligated or forbidden to put his life into possible danger to save the life of another who is in certain danger.[112]

The *Beit Yosef*,[113] quoting the *Yerushalmi*,[114] writes that a person should put himself into possible danger in order to save his fellow who is in certain danger. However, both the *Beit Yosef* and the *Rama* do not bring this ruling in the *Shulchan Aruch*. The *Sema*[115] says that since the *Rif*, *Rambam*, *Rosh* and *Tur* all omit this *Yerushalmi*, the *Shulchan Aruch* and the *Rama* did the same. The *Pitchei Teshuvah*[116] explains that these major *poskim* omitted it because they believe that the *Talmud Bavli*[117] disagrees with this ruling. See also the *Pitchei Teshuvah*[118] in *Yoreh Deah* and the *Minchat Chinuch*.[119]

The *Radbaz*[120] was asked by someone who was given the choice by a non-Jewish ruler of either agreeing to have his hand cut off or seeing his friend killed, what he should do. The *Radbaz*, in discussing the case, writes that even if there is the likelihood of a little danger to the rescuer, he is nevertheless obligated to save the one who is in real danger, for example, one who is drowning. However, if the possible danger to the rescuer is close to being a real one (that is, more than 50%), he is not obligated to put himself into such danger to save another. Even if the danger is close to this there is no obligation. However if the chances of success are greater and the danger to himself negligible, and he does not attempt to save him, he has set aside the Torah commandment:[121] "Do not stand idly by while your fellow's blood is shed."[122]

---

107. שו"ת, ח"ג יו"ד סי' כ ו-כא
108. נדה נה ע"א ד"ה שמא. זבחים עא ע"ב ד"ה ובטריפה
109. נדה סי' צו
110. ר"ת סנה' מח ע"א ד"ה משמשין. רשב"א שו"ת סי' שסה. רמב"ן חי' לחולין קכב ע"א וכתובות ס ע"א. הרא"ה והריטב"א בחי' הריטב"א נגה נה ע"א. רמב"ם טומאת מת פ"ג הי"א ואבל פי"ד הכ"א. ר"ן תוס' הראש והמאירי נדה נה ע"א. והחת"ס, בחי' לע"ז כט ע"ב, כתב שלדעת הרמב"ם האיסור הוא מן התורה, אך הוא עצמו פוסק שהאיסור הוא מדרבנן - כל זה ביביע אומר
111. שו"ת, יו"ד ח"א סי' קכט
112. ראה המעין תשמ"ב עמ' 31
113. חו"מ סי' תכו
114. תרומות סוף פ"ח
115. חו"מ סי' תכו ס"ק ב
116. חו"מ שם ס"ק ב בשם ספר אגודת אזוב
117. נדה סא ע"א וסנהדרין עג ע"א. ערוך לנר שם. ראה במהר"ם שיק על המצוות, מצוה רלח. שו"ת ציץ אליעזר ח"ט סי' מה
118. יו"ד סי' רנב ס"ק א
119. מצוה רלז ס"ק ב
120. ללשונות הרמב"ם סי' אלף תקפב (ריח)
121. ויקרא יט:טז
122. וראה גם בשו"ת ציץ אליעזר ח"ח סי' טו פ"י ס"ק יג

NISHMAT AVRAHAM

However the *Chatam Sofer*[123] expresses surprise at this ruling of the *Radbaz* believing that the *Gemara* rules that one is obligated to endanger oneself to save another. However he later differentiates between having one's hand cut off with a sword, in which he agrees with the *Radbaz's* ruling (and so does the *Shach*[124]), and having it amputated by drugs (in which case he is unsure of the ruling). The *Radbaz* himself writes elsewhere[125] that putting himself into real danger to save another is foolish piety.

The *Pitchei Teshuvah*[126] quoted above continues that nevertheless one needs to weigh the situation carefully before deciding that there is definitely a possible danger. One should not be overly cautious, as the *Gemara*[127] says that he who is overly cautious in these situations will one day find himself in a similar predicament, and the *Shulchan Aruch*[128] writes in the same manner. The *Aruch HaShulchan*[129] writes in a similar vein: Everything depends on the circumstances; one must weigh the situation well and not be too concerned about oneself. It is about this that the verse says:[130] "I will show him the salvation of *Hashem*," referring to one "who finds the right path," for whoever saves a single Jew is like one who has saved the whole world.[131] See also **c.** below.

a. BLOOD. The *Igrot Moshe*[132] was asked whether one could donate blood to a blood bank if he was paid for it and needed the money, when one does not know whether this blood will be given to a patient for whom Torah prohibitions may be set aside. He writes that there is a good reason for not forbidding it; for we find that in earlier ages it was customary to draw blood for relief; see the *Gemara*.[133] Therefore, even though times have changed since then, as in the *Rambam's* times,[134] and even more so in our day where this is no longer practiced, nevertheless, there must be even today some benefit in doing so, for the change cannot be so extreme. Besides, today blood is withdrawn practically without any pain; therefore, it is possible that it is not forbidden to undergo the wound caused by the procedure and one who wishes to act leniently should not be prevented from doing so.

However, *Rav Neuwirth shlita* wrote to me wondering how the *Igrot Moshe* could compare the drawing of blood at the time of *Chazal* to donating blood to a blood bank for money. He also wondered what proof there is in the source that he quotes from the *Gemara* that the blood was drawn for relief only and not for disease.

Rav Auerbach zt"l wrote to me that he also permits donating blood to the blood bank in Israel, for the donor performs a *mitzvah* of saving a Jewish life, even if he does so only for the money.

b. BONE MARROW. This involves multiple aspirations from the hip bones of the donor and must be done under general anesthesia. *Rav Auerbach zt"l* told me that it is a *mitzvah* to be a donor to save a Jewish life. Today more and more marrow transplants are done using *stem cells* obtained from the umbilical cord and placenta, directly after delivery of the baby

---

123. חידושיו על כתובות סא ע"ב ד"ה מ"ט סמכת אניסא
124. יו"ד סי' קנז סוס"ק ג - דהיינו שסכנת אבר דומה לסכנת נפשות
125. שו"ת, סי' אלף נב (תרכז)
126. חו"מ סי' תכו ס"ק ב
127. ב"מ לג ע"א
128. חו"מ סי' רסד סע' א
129. חו"מ סי' תכו סע' ד
130. תהלים נ:כג
131. סנהדרין לז ע"א
132. שו"ת, חו"מ ח"א סי' קג
133. שבת קכט ע"א וע"ב
134. הל' חובל ומזיק פ"ה ה"א

SIMAN 349: BENEFIT FROM A CORPSE IS FORBIDDEN / §2

thing in his lifetime, but if he bequeathed such adornments to his son or daughter or said that they be used for any other purpose, they may be used. His hair, however, may not be used even (C)if he bequeathed it.

NISHMAT AVRAHAM

(and stored in banks for future use) or by separating *stem cells* from blood drawn from a donor. Thus, the risk of a general anesthetic, and the pain involved in obtaining bone marrow from the donor, is avoided. In addition, the procedure is also safer for the recipient.[135]

c. KIDNEY. The *Igrot Moshe*[136] writes that although one may not obligate someone to put himself into possible danger to save another from certain danger, one is, however, permitted to put himself into possible danger to save the life of another who is in certain danger, since a Jewish life will be saved. The *Tzitz Eliezer*[137] writes that if there is a good possibility that he will not come to harm one may volunteer to be a donor of an organ to save another who is *seriously ill* and he performs a great *mitzvah* of saving a Jewish life by so doing. Therefore it is permitted for a healthy person to donate a kidney if the doctors are sure that there will be no danger to him.[138] In yet another *responsum*, the *Tzitz Eliezer*[139] rules that a person may volunteer himself for experiments which are for the good of a patient and that he performs a *mitzvah* by doing so. However this is conditional on medical advice that there is no danger to himself. *Rav Ovadiah Yosef shlita*[140] also rules that one may give one's kidney to save the life of another.

However, the *Minchat Yitzchak*[141] writes that there is the risk of the operation to the donor and also a future risk in having only one kidney. Also the controversy seems to be whether one is obligated to be a donor or not; however, if one wishes, he is permitted to do so. All of these hold true only if he definitely will save the life of the recipient by putting himself into possible danger. These points must be clarified and he only raises the issues as of the moment.

Rav Auerbach zt"l wrote to me that if the *seriously ill* patient is present (*and known to him, as clarified to me later by the Rav zt"l*) it is certainly permissible for a person to even undergo much suffering, for example, by donating his kidney, to save the life of the patient.

d. BONE. Bone that was removed from a patient undergoing orthopedic surgery may be taken from a bone bank and used to transplant into another patient, even if he is undergoing surgery for a non-life threatening condition. There is no *mitzvah* to bury it and neither is it forbidden to benefit from it (see Siman 362A below).[142]

e. HUMAN EXPERIMENTATION. See Siman 28B and Siman 155B and B(3) above.

(C) if he bequeathed it. See **A3** above regarding one who donates or sells his body to science.

---

140. שו״ת יחוה דעת ח״ג סי׳ פד
141. שו״ת, ח״ו סי׳ קג. וכותב לעיין בספר כלי חמדה על התורה פ׳ תצא דף קצב מדפי הספר
142. שמעתי ממו״ר הגרי״י נויבירט שליט״א

135. Edit. BMJ 323:60, '01
136. שו״ת, יו״ד ח״ב סי׳ קעד ענף ד
137. שו״ת ציץ אליעזר ח״י סי׳ כה פ״ז
138. שם ח״ט סי׳ מה
139. שם חי״ג סי׳ קא

SIMAN 362
THE DECEASED MUST BE BURIED IN THE GROUND

§1 If one leaves his deceased relative in a coffin and (A)does not bury him in the ground he transgresses the prohibition to leave a corpse unburied. If he puts the corpse in a coffin and buries it in the ground he does not violate the commandment. However it is best to actually bury him (without a coffin) in the ground, even in the Diaspora.

NISHMAT AVRAHAM

SIMAN 362

(A) does not bury him. The *Pitchei Teshuvah*[1] quotes the *Shevut Yaakov*,[2] who was asked about someone who had to have his leg amputated, whether he was obligated to arrange that it be buried. The *Shevut Yaakov* answered that although it would appear from the *Gemara*[3] that the leg should be buried, nevertheless this is not because there an obligation to do so. However it must be put somewhere where a *Cohen* will not enter, since a limb taken from a living person also ritually defiles a *Cohen* who is under the same roof as the limb. See Siman 369B below.

The *Maharil Diskin*[4] also writes that from the laws of burial (Siman 374) it would appear that burial does not apply to a single limb (taken from a live person). Nevertheless, the *Gemara*[5] writes that it is customary to bury it and it would appear from *Rashi* that this was only to avoid ritual defilement. It would therefore appear that one may also benefit from it for otherwise there would have been an obligation to bury it. There is certainly no positive Torah commandment to bury it.

The *Noda BiYehudah*[6] also writes that there is no *mitzvah* to bury a limb taken from a living person and the reason that it is buried is only to avoid ritual defilement. This is also the opinion of the *Melamed LeHo'il*,[7] *Kol Bo Al Aveilut*,[8] *Gesher HaChaim*[9] and *Yabia Omer*.[10]

The *Igrot Moshe*[11] rules that flesh removed from a living person may be used for experimentation, provided that any left over is buried. In another *responsum*[12] he writes that a limb that contains flesh, tendons and bone (*as opposed to organs that do not contain all three elements — author*) no matter how small, requires burial even if some of the bone is missing. However this does not apply to the intestines, kidneys, spleen, or an embryo or placenta before the fetus has been formed (*that is, before forty days have passed from the time of conception — author*). The *Tzitz Eliezer*[13] writes that one may benefit from a limb that has been taken from a live person and doctors may use it to study medicine. However it must not be thrown away afterwards in a disrespect-

---

1. ס"ק א
2. שו"ת, סי' קא
3. כתובות כ ע"ב
4. שו"ת, בקו"א אות קפח
5. כתובות שם
6. שו"ת, מהד"ת יו"ד כי' רט
7. שו"ת, יו"ד סי' קיח
8. עמ' 184
9. ח"א פט"ז סי' ב סע' ב
10. שו"ת, ח"ג יו"ד סי' כב אות ב
11. שו"ת, יו"ד ח"א סי' רלב
12. שם ח"ג סי' קמא
13. שו"ת, ח"י סי' כה פ"ח

SIMAN 364
IT IS FORBIDDEN TO HAVE BENEFIT FROM A GRAVE

§4 If (A)a Jew is found slain, he is buried as he is without shrouds. No clothes are removed from him, not even his shoes.

GLOSS: *The same is done to a woman who died in childbirth or to one who fell from a height and died. There are those who say that shrouds are put over his clothes. The custom is not to make them shrouds as with other corpses, but they are buried in their clothes with a sheet to cover them as with other corpses.*

──────── NISHMAT AVRAHAM ────────

ful manner, but must either be stored away or buried. The *Gesher HaChaim*[14] also writes that it is not forbidden to benefit from a limb taken from a live person.

SIMAN 364

(A) a Jew is found slain. See the *Taz*[1] and *Shach*[2] about someone who falls from a roof and dies. The *Chochmat Adam*[3] writes that if a Jew falls (from a roof) and dies and has bled from his injuries there is a possibility that his life's blood (all the blood that comes forth as a jet[4]) has been absorbed into his clothes and shoes. He is not ritually cleansed but is buried in his clothes and shoes with a sheet wrapped around him. All the earth around him into which he has bled is collected and buried with him. This only applies to the clothes that he is wearing, but blood that was spilled on other clothes or blood which he bled into the sheets on which he was lying, need not be buried with him. They must be well washed to remove every trace of blood and the water containing the blood is poured on his grave.

The *Gesher HaChaim*[5] writes that this applies to blood absorbed into his clothes, but blood that dripped from one who was killed, from a woman who died in childbirth, or one who died on the operating table need not be collected for burial. If a woman who died in childbirth stopped bleeding before she died then she is like any other deceased and is ritually cleansed before burial. If she continued to bleed at the time she died, there are those whose custom is not to ritually cleanse her but to bury her in her clothes and shoes the same as one who died accidentally. However, here, in Jerusalem the custom is like that of the *Shach*[6] — to ritually cleanse every woman who died in childbirth and to bury her in shrouds. If she bled at the time of death, her bloodstained clothes are put on over the shrouds, and she is then wrapped in a sheet. If she was only put into shrouds the bloodstained clothes are buried with her. A person who died a natural death and bled from his nostrils or gut, either before, or even at the time of death, this blood does not need burial provided he did not

---

14. ח"א פט"ז סי' ב סע' ב
1. ס"ק ג
2. ס"ק יא
3. כלל קנז סע' י
4. ראה אנציקלופדיה תלמודית כרך ז עמ' תכג-תכד

שיש מחלקות תנאים ואמוראים בהגדרת דם שהנשמה יוצאה בה. ופוסק הרמב"ם הל' מאכלות אסורות פ"ו ה"ג: כל זמן שמקלח

5. ח"א פי"א סע' ה-ז
6. סוס"ק יא

SIMAN 369
WHICH *TUMAH* IS PROHIBITED TO A *COHEN*

§1 (A)A *Cohen* is forbidden to become ritually defiled by a corpse or by any *tumah* that is emitted by its body, or from

---NISHMAT AVRAHAM---

die as a result of the bleeding. He is ritually cleansed in the usual manner. However if his illness and death was the result of hemorrhage, he is like a woman who dies in childbirth and the ruling above applies to him also.

Rav Auerbach zt"l wrote to me that if he bled at the time of death why should we not be concerned that this was possibly his life's blood?

The *Tzitz Eliezer*[7] writes that even if a patient dies after surgery, but before the bloodstained operating-room clothes have been taken off him, we need not worry about this blood and the clothes may be removed from him if the doctors are sure that he did not die of hemorrhage. The corpse can then be ritually cleansed, put in shrouds and buried. However, *Rav Auerbach zt"l* wrote to me that this ruling also needs further study. Why should we not think that this blood is his life's blood?[8]

SIMAN 369

(A) A *Cohen* is forbidden to become ritually defiled. The *Gesher HaChaim*[1] writes: A *Cohen* is forbidden to become defiled either by a corpse or by entering or being under the same roof as the corpse as the verse says:[2] "He shall not defile himself to a (dead) person." This is a prohibition of itself and the reason is not that it causes him to become ritually unclean. It therefore applies even today and therefore according to most *poskim* is in force even if the *Cohen* is already in a state of uncleanliness. However in the *Ra'avad's*[3] opinion the prohibition nowadays is only Rabbinic since all *Cohanim* (and all of *Am Yisrael*) are in a state of ritual uncleanliness; see the *Minchat Chinuch*[4] and *Mishneh LaMelech*.[5] See also the *Pitchei Teshuvah*,[6] *Dagul MeRevavah*[7] and the *Chatam Sofer*.[8]

However the *Ra'avad*[9] changed his opinion, and ruled like the *Rambam*, so that it is universally accepted that even today there is a Torah prohibition for a *Cohen* to become ritually defiled.

1. STUDYING MEDICINE. A *Cohen* is forbidden to become defiled by a corpse, a limb or even a tiny piece of bone of one; he may not enter or be under the same roof as a corpse or even a *kezayit* of flesh from one.[10] Therefore, he may not study medicine if he will be required, as part of his studies, to become defiled in any one of the ways enumerated above.[11] The corpse of a non-Jew also causes defilement.[12] The *Tur* and *Shulchan Aruch*[13] rule that it is also proper for a *Cohen* to

---

7. שו"ת, חיי"א סע' ע
8. וראה גם בשו"ת מהרש"ם ח"ד סי' קיב ושו"ת שבט הלוי ח"א סי' קלד וח"ה סי' קעט
1. ח"ב פכ"ח סע' א
2. ויקרא כא:א
3. הל' נזיר פ"ה הט"ו. וראה בשו"ת חת"ס יו"ד סי' שלט
4. מצוה רכג
5. הל' אבל ריש פ"ג
6. סי' שעב ס"ק ט

7. שם
8. שו"ת, יו"ד סי' שלח ו-שלט
9. תמים דעים סי' רלו. מובא בפ"ת סי' שעב ס"ק ט
10. אהלות פ"ב מ"א. רמב"ם טומאת מת פ"א ה"א ו-ב
11. כל בו על אבלות עמ' 81. גשר החיים ח"א פ"ז סע' א ס"ק ד
12. וי"א שהוא מן התורה - גשר החיים שם סע' ג
13. יו"ד סי' שעב סע' ב. ראה מה שכתב לי הגרש"ז אויערבאך זצ"ל, לב אברהם ח"ב עמ' כא

SIMAN 369: TUMAH PROHIBITED TO A COHEN / §1

NISHMAT AVRAHAM

avoid entering or being under the same roof as the corpse of a non-Jew.

The *Igrot Moshe*[14] writes that since it is obvious and clear and known to everyone that it is forbidden for a *Cohen* to defile himself from a corpse, even if the great sages of the world were to come and state that one may act leniently, one does not heed them. The *Gemara*[15] tells us that even if the prophet Elijah himself would tell us to act strictly against established custom he is not heeded. Most certainly, there is no way that we can rely on the ruling of anyone who says that since he is already in a state of defilement, a *Cohen* can act leniently. It is therefore forbidden for a *Cohen* to study medicine if he will need to become defiled by a corpse. He may not take our teachers, the *rishonim*, who were both *Cohanim* and doctors, as an example; for they, in their greatness, learned everything there was to know about medicine by word of mouth only, without even looking at a corpse. They never ever touched a corpse or were under the same roof as one. Since, in our day, this is impossible, it is certainly forbidden for a *Cohen* to study medicine. And, even if there would not be a single doctor in the whole world, there would be no obligation to study medicine, because of *pikuach nefesh*. The obligation to save life (*pikuach nefesh*) is incumbent on everyone; each person must save another as best he can; if he is a doctor, he is required to save a patient from his illness. However there is no obligation to study medicine in order to do so. There is no room for the mistake of thinking that one may give up learning Torah to study medicine for the acts of *pikuach nefesh* which he will perform. On the contrary, learning a trade in order to earn a living is, as the *Gemara*[16] says, an acceptable excuse for giving up the study of Torah for ordinary people. But, there is no excuse for not learning Torah if the reason is *pikuach nefesh*, since there is no lack of doctors in the world. Besides, he should consider the risk involved that he may even harm patients by misdiagnoses.

See Siman 336B above with regard to a non-*Cohen* studying medicine.

The *Shulchan Aruch*[17] rules that it is forbidden to give a *Cohen* who willfully defiles himself from a corpse, the honor due to his elevated standing as a *Cohen*, unless he agrees to stop doing so. This will obviously apply to a *Cohen* who insists on studying medicine. This is also the ruling of the *Mahari Assad*[18] and the *Ketav Sofer*.[19] However, the *Mahari Assad* does add that a *Cohen* who studies medicine and becomes defiled should be considered as doing so unintentionally for perhaps he thinks that since this knowledge will allow him to cure others it is permissible. Or perhaps he thinks that a non-Jewish corpse does not defile one.[20] He says that there is a *mitzvah* and an obligation to speak to him quietly and show him the *halachah* which is plainly stated in the *Shulchan Aruch* so that he should realize that being a *Cohen* is an honor given to him by *Hashem* and that he should accept it upon himself before the *Beit Din* that he will no longer defile himself. The *Melamed LeHo'il*[21] writes that if we know that he continues to daily defile himself and we nevertheless call him up to the reading of the Torah, we are encouraging him to continue in his mistaken way. It is therefore a *mitzvah* not to call him up. However the

---

14. שו״ת, יו״ד ח״ג סי׳ קנה
15. יבמות קב ע״א
16. מנחות צט ע״ב וראה שם בתוסד״ה לא
17. או״ח סי׳ קכח סע׳ מא
18. שו״ת, סי׳ מז
19. שו״ת, סי׳ טז
20. כדעת הירא״ם סי׳ שיא, אף שכל הפוסקים חולקים עליו. וראה בשו״ת חת״ס יו״ד סי׳ שלט
21. שו״ת, ח״א סי׳ לא

its grave and tombstone or from (B)a limb that has been removed from a live person.

─────────── NISHMAT AVRAHAM ───────────

Melamed LeHo'il quotes the *Aruch La-Ner*[22] who in turn quotes the *Sh'lah* that if the *Cohen* refuses to admit that he is committing a sin, there is a *mitzvah* not to reprove one who will ignore the reproval. This is what all the sinners of our generation do — they find questionable permission for what they do.[23]

A *Cohen* may not go up to recite the priestly blessing as long as he continues to willfully defile himself in the study of medicine.[24]

If, however, the *Cohen* can avoid defiling himself in any way, then he may study medicine although he may later as a doctor become defiled once in a while[25] (see, however, 2 below).

2. A *COHEN* WHO IS A DOCTOR, NURSE OR OTHER CAREGIVER.

May he work in a hospital where he will very likely become defiled? The *Tuv Taam VeDa'at*[26] writes that where the sick need him in a situation where there is no other like him, or if he needs the livelihood badly, one may permit him to work in a hospital. If there is a corpse, but at the same time there is *pikuach nefesh* for another patient, he may remain to treat him. However, the *Igrot Moshe*[27] writes that a *Cohen* may not accept a position in a hospital, if he will not be able to leave the hospital when someone dies there because of his obligation to treat other patients; even though he is able to be in a separate room (but under the same roof as the corpse) with his patients. However if he can make it a condition of his employment that if there is a Jewish corpse he will be permitted to leave the building, and if the hospital is one where Jewish patients are not common and there is no Jewish corpse over many days, we can rely on the fact that most patients will live. Not only if a Jew does die must he leave the building, but even when he knows that there is a Jewish *gosses* in the building, he must leave it.

Rav Neuwirth shlita wrote to me that perhaps if the *Cohen* is in a separate room, which according to the *Shach* only involves Rabbinic *tumah*, there is place to rule leniently for the sake of the patients who need his help. *Rav Auerbach zt"l* wrote to me that one may possibly also add that it is not definitely certain that the *Cohanim* of our day are truly *Cohanim*. In the opinion of the *Ra'avad*, nowadays since the *Cohanim* are, in any case, in a state of defilement with respect to the impurity of a corpse, the prohibition against becoming further defiled is only Rabbinic. We may also add to this that in the opinion of the *Shach*, if the *Cohen* is in a different room than the corpse (although under the same roof) the prohibition is only Rabbinic.

Regarding a *Cohen* who is hospitalized, see below Siman 372A.

(B) a limb that has been removed from a live person. The *Rambam*[28] writes that a limb, or part of it, no matter how small,[29] that was amputated from a living person defiles one if touched, carried (without being touched) or if it is under the same roof as he, just as a corpse does. This is only if it contains flesh, si-

---

22. יבמות סה ע"ב
23. ראה גם בשו"ת שבות יעקב ח"ב סי' ב
24. או"ח סי' קכח סע' מא ומ"ב ס"ק קן. שו"ת חת"ס יו"ד סי' שלח
25. שו"ת שבט הלוי יו"ד ח"ב סי' קסד
26. שו"ת, מהד"ג ח"ב סי' ריב
27. שו"ת, יו"ד ח"א סי' רמח
28. טומאת מת פ"ב ה"ג. ראה שם פרטי דינים
29. שם ה"ז

SIMAN 369: TUMAH PROHIBITED TO A COHEN / §1

NISHMAT AVRAHAM

news and bone, even if these are incomplete. However, organs such as the kidney and the tongue are like flesh[30] removed from a living person and do not cause ritual defilement.

The *Pitchei Teshuvah*[31] quotes the *Noda BiYehudah*[32] who rules that a *Cohen* whose leg was amputated may not keep it to show what was done to him in order to gain sympathy. He is forbidden to become ritually defiled even from his own amputated leg. However if the leg is not whole it does not cause defilement.[33]

May a surgeon attempt to rejoin a *Cohen's* finger that has been traumatically amputated although the *Cohen* will become ritually defiled by the finger until it is rejoined to his body? *Rav Waldenberg shlita*[34] wrote to me that that it cannot be permitted. One cannot argue that since the finger will be rejoined to its stump and then will no longer defile the *Cohen*, it should not defile him until then. In addition to the *Noda BiYehudah's* ruling quoted above, it would appear from the *Gemara*[35] that even though Elisha the prophet brought the child back to life,[36] before he was revived his corpse nevertheless caused defilement; see also *Rashi*[37] and the *Chatam Sofer*.[38] And though the prophet Elijah (who was a *Cohen*) did defile himself from the corpse of the Tsarphatit's son,[39] that does not furnish proof because it involved *pikuach nefesh*.[40] Nevertheless, since the *Shach*[41] writes

that when there is danger to a limb (*even without danger to the person — author*), one may act leniently, one can rule permissively in our case. For the *Shach* rules that one may set aside prohibitions of the Torah when there is danger to a limb. This is also the ruling of the *Pri Megadim*[42] who says, however, that since Sabbath prohibitions are much stricter, they are not set aside. Therefore, relying on the rulings of the *Shach* and the *Pri Megadim*, we may permit a *Cohen* to set aside the prohibition against defilement so that he may be treated and his finger restored to life. See too the *Igrot Moshe*.[43]

See *Nishmat Avraham*, vol. 1 *Orach Chaim*, Siman 328 (17D) regarding the definition of danger to a limb.

Rav Auerbach zt"l wrote to me that it is possible that it would be permitted to rejoin an amputated hand or finger even on *Shabbat*. Since Sabbath laws must be set aside anyway to prevent infection of the stump and the like, the patient will be categorized as *seriously ill*. It will therefore be incumbent upon us to save him with the same best possible treatment that would have been given him on a weekday since, in any case, Sabbath laws must be set aside. And, although rejoining a limb involves doing many more *melachot*, nevertheless everything the doctor does falls within the framework of *pikuach nefesh*. The *Mabit's*[44] opinion that we set aside commandments in order of

---

Rav Auerbach zt"l wrote to me commenting that there is no *pikuach nefesh* involved in attempting to resuscitate a corpse, and many explanations have been given on this matter. See also below Siman 370A.

41. יו"ד סי' קנו ס"ק ג וראה שו"ת ריב"ש סי' שכו (צ"ל שפז) ושו"ע או"ח סי' שכח סע' יז

42. או"ח סי' שכח מ"ז ס"ק ז

43. שו"ת, יו"ד ח"א סי' רל

44. קרית ספר סוף פי"ד ממאכלות אסורות See *Nishmat Avraham*, vol. 1 *Orach Chaim*, Siman 328 (12D).

30. שם ה"ו
31. כאן ס"ק ג
32. שו"ת, תניינא יו"ד סי' רט
33. בשם הספר הר אבל ריש ענף יח
34. שו"ת ציץ אליעזר חי"ג סי' צ
35. נדה ע ע"ב
36. מלכים ב ד:לב-לה
37. שם ד"ה בן השונמית
38. שו"ת, יו"ד סי' שלו
39. מלכים א יז:יט-כא
40. ב"מ קיד ע"ב ד"ה אמר

CHAPTER 35: LAWS OF MOURNING

SIMAN 370
WHO IS CONSIDERED AS DEAD EVEN THOUGH HE IS STILL ALIVE

§1 (A)A person whose neck has been broken and who has lost most of the surrounding flesh at the same time, and one who is torn open at the back, lengthwise, just as a fish is cut open, is considered *halachically* dead and causes ritual defilement although still alive. On the other hand, a

---
NISHMAT AVRAHAM
---

the less strict commandment first, is Rabbinic. Thus, by Torah law one may kindle a light on *Shabbat* for a *seriously ill* patient and there is no obligation to give one's own lamp which is lit to the patient rather than perform the *melachah* of kindling. This needs further study.

SIMAN 370

(A) A person whose neck has been broken. The *Igrot Moshe*[1] writes that someone who is decapitated but whose body still has convulsions causes defilement according to the *Rambam*.[2] This does not contradict what the *Rambam*[3] writes that one whose *esophagus* and *trachea* have been cut does not cause defilement until he dies. When the *esophagus* and *trachea* are cut, he is alive as long as there are signs of life, as the *Gemara*[4] writes. However, if the neck and spine have been cut from behind, even if most of the surrounding flesh remains and the *esophagus* and *trachea* have not been cut, he is considered *halachically* dead and he causes defilement as a corpse. Therefore, if one is decapitated, even if there are convulsions, he is considered as dead. And, even if, theoretically, it would be possible to reattach his head to his body and bring him back to life, there is no obligation to do so. Since there is no obligation to revive the dead even on a weekday, it would certainly be forbidden to bring one back to life on *Shabbat*. The Torah only obligates us to treat the ill and even to set aside Sabbath laws (*for a seriously ill patient — author*), but not to revive the dead. *Tosafot*[5] ask how did the prophet Elijah, who was a *Cohen*, revive the son of the Tsarphatit and their answer is that this was permitted because of *pikuach nefesh*. We must explain that they did not mean the *pikuach nefesh* of the dead boy but the *pikuach nefesh* of the mother.[6] She was greatly perturbed that her son had died, in spite of the great *mitzvah* that she had done and her belief in *Hashem* and his prophets, in feeding and giving a home to Elijah. Scripture expressly speaks of this complaint of hers.

But, when a *gosses* is found with a crushed skull, although he may have only a short while to live he is nevertheless still alive and there is an obligation to do everything possible to treat him, even to set aside Sabbath laws for the purpose.[7]

---

1. שו"ת, יו"ד ח"ב סי' קעד ענף א
2. טומאת מת פ"א הט"ו
3. שם
4. גיטין ע ע"ב וחולין ל ע"א
5. ב"מ קיד ע"ב ד"ה אמר
6. ועיין ברבינו בחיי פ' פנחס כה:י"א. העמק שאלה שאילתא קסז אות יז. שו"ת יביע אומר ח"א יו"ד בהערה. שמירת שבת כהלכתה פמ"א הערה ח בשם הגרש"ז אויערבאך זצ"ל
7. ראה גם בשו"ת מהרש"ם ח"ו סי' קכד

SIMAN 370: WHO IS CONSIDERED AS DEAD / §1

gosses, or one whose *esophagus* and *trachea* have both been cut, or one with multiple wounds does not cause defilement until he dies. Nevertheless it is forbidden for a *Cohen* to enter a house where a *gosses* is lying (*there are those who permit this but* (B)*it is best to act strictly*).

──────── NISHMAT AVRAHAM ────────

I found it difficult to understand why someone whose (cervical) spine is broken should be considered *halachically* dead more so than one whose *esophagus* and *trachea* have been cut, and why someone who is torn open at the back is *halachically* dead more so than one who has been torn open from the front.[8] There is ample evidence, from those injured in traffic accidents and war, that one can live for years after suffering traumatic severance of the cervical spine, even when artificial ventilation is required. As to *Rav Moshe Feinstein zt"l's* contention that were it possible to reattach a severed head to the body and revive the patient there would not be any obligation to do so since he is *halachically* dead, why is that different from the obligation to treat a baby born after eight months of gestation who is also considered *halachically* dead[9] and yet for whom Sabbath laws may be set aside?

Rav Auerbach zt"l wrote to me that only *Hashem* can revive the dead. Therefore were it possible for us to reattach a severed head and the patient lived, it would be considered *pikuach nefesh* and one would even need to set aside Sabbath laws to do so. He noted that he had already written to me that in instances when they did not know how to treat the patient and he died, he would be considered dead earlier, before he died, just as one who was buried under rubble in earlier times was considered as dead from the moment he stopped breathing because he could not be treated, as no means of saving him was known (*artificial respiration was as yet unknown* — *author*).

(B) it is best to act strictly. The *Pitchei Teshuvah*[10] writes that everyone agrees that a *Cohen* may enter a room in which a *gosses* is lying in order to treat him, even if another non-*Cohen* doctor is already present. He quotes the *Chatam Sofer*[11] to the effect that it is obvious that even according to the *poskim* who rule that a *Cohen* is forbidden by Torah law to enter a room where there is a *gosses*, nevertheless if there is a question of *pikuach nefesh*, it is permissible. Moreover, if the patient is confirmed dead and later found to have any sign of life, the *Cohen* should enter quickly because of the faintest possibility of *pikuach nefesh*. But if another doctor who is not a *Cohen* is present, the *Chatam Sofer* is uncertain, for everyone agrees that *pikuach nefesh* does not nullify all Torah laws but only overrides them (see the *Rosh*[12]). The *Pitchei Teshuvah*, however, questions this indecision of the *Chatam Sofer* who did not mention the *Shulchan Aruch*[13] which says that this is not dependent on whether Torah laws are nullified or overridden but rather on the premise that the patient does not have the fortune to be cured by everyone.

The *Machazeh Avraham*[14] and *Gesher*

---

8. ש"ך ס"ק ב
9. See *Nishmat Avraham*, vol. 1 *Orach Chaim*, Siman 328 (2B).
10. ס"ק א
11. שו"ת, יו"ד סי' שלח
12. פ' יוהכ"פ סי' ד
13. יו"ד סי' רכא סע' ד. ראה שם בט"ז ובש"ך ס"ק כ
14. שו"ת, ח"ב יו"ד סי' יט

SIMAN 371
THE LAWS CONCERNING A ROOF AND HOW IT CAUSES *TUMAH*

§1 A *Cohen* is forbidden to enter (A)under the same roof as a corpse even if the space under the roof is very big. He may not enter a room in the same or upper story if there is an opening measuring one *tefach* by one *tefach* between his room and the room containing the corpse.

§4 If a corpse is in a room which shares a common roof with other rooms, all the other rooms whose doors are open become ritually unclean (*if they open to a common stairwell or corridor — author*).

─────────── NISHMAT AVRAHAM ───────────

HaChaim[15] agree with the *Pitchei Teshuvah*. However, the *Shevet HaLevi*[16] writes that one may not permit the nullification of a *Cohen's* holiness and allow the possibility that he will be defiled, if there is another doctor, as competent as the *Cohen*, who is also present; one may not allow this on the premise that the patient does not have the fortune to be saved by everyone. On the other hand, if there is the possibility that the *Cohen* is slightly more competent than the non-*Cohen* and he is more capable and experienced than the others present, it is obvious that he is permitted and it is a *mitzvah* for him to enter to treat the seriously ill patient.

The *Pitchei Teshuvah* also quotes the *Chatam Sofer*, regarding a town where the doctor was a *Cohen*, and by law a deceased could not be buried without first being examined and confirmed dead by a doctor. The *Chatam Sofer* was asked whether the doctor could examine him to confirm death. The *Chatam Sofer* at first ruled that there was no way this could be permitted. However he realized that it was not the said doctor who asked guidance, for in any case, he did not keep the laws of the Torah. The question was asked by those who did keep the *mitzvot* who wanted to know whether they could call the doctor to examine the deceased or whether, by calling him, they would transgress the prohibition not to place a stumbling block before the blind[17] and help him to do that which was prohibited. In such a situation, the *Chatam Sofer* ruled that if they could remove him completely from his position, they should do so. If they could not, and the deceased would be lying shamefully, unable to be buried, he would then be a *met mitzvah* who has no one to bury him (or to authorize his burial). In such a case a *Cohen* is permitted to defile himself in order to bury the deceased.

SIMAN 371

(A) under the same roof. See *Nishmat Avraham*, vol. 1 *Orach Chaim*, Siman 343A, p. 246 regarding the pregnant wife of a *Cohen*.

---

15. ח"א פ"ב ס"ק ב (ב).
16. שו"ת, ח"ג יו"ד סי' קסד.
17. ויקרא יט:יד.

GLOSS: Cohanim ^(B)may not force the family of a deceased to remove him from his home so that they may enter their own homes.

SIMAN 372
TUMAH WHICH IS PERMITTED IN THE CONTEXT OF A MITZVAH

§1 A *Cohen* may enter and pass through an area of Rabbinic *tumah* in order to perform a *mitzvah* such as marrying or learning Torah, if there is no alternative route that he can take.

GLOSS: *A Cohen who is lying naked in a room without realizing that there is* ^(A)*a corpse in the room need not be told this directly. Instead he should be called to come out so that he will dress himself before coming out. However, if he is told, he must leave the room immediately without waiting to dress himself.*

―――― NISHMAT AVRAHAM ――――

(B) may not force the family of a deceased. If the doors or windows of the houses open under a common roof, such as in an apartment block, the *tumah* enters from the apartment of the deceased to the other apartments. Moreover, since the deceased will be taken out through the common stairwell or corridor, *tumah* will enter another apartment if there is an opening from it into the stairwell or corridor even if the door to the deceased is still closed (see below Siman 372A). Hence the situation discussed by the Gloss.

Rebbe Akiva Eiger writes,[1] quoting the *Chacham Tzvi*[2] and the *Magen Avraham*,[3] that the *Cohen* may not force the family of the deceased to remove him unless the *Cohen* is ill and cannot leave his house because of the *tumah*. In such a case the deceased is removed so that the *Cohen* does not have to transgress Torah law in order to leave his home. However, if the *Cohen* is a minor the *halachah* needs further study. The *Pitchei Teshuvah*,[4] on the other hand, writes that the *halachah* is the same whether the *Cohen* is a child or an adult for *Beit Din* is obligated to prevent a child who is a *Cohen* from becoming defiled by a corpse. The *Magen Avraham*[5] rules that this applies only to a child who has reached the age of understanding. *Rav Auerbach zt"l* wrote to me that to take a *kezayit* of a corpse into a house where there is a *Cohen* who is a child is forbidden in any case.

SIMAN 372

(A) a corpse in the room. What is the *halachah* concerning the rooms on a hospital floor when there is a corpse in one of them? The *Shach*[1] rules regarding two separate issues that ritual uncleanliness can spread from a room containing a corpse into adjacent areas or rooms:

1. An adjacent room (*with an opening*

---

1. חידושיו כאן
2. שו"ת, סי' נט
3. או"ח סי' שיא ס"ק יד
4. ס"ק יב
5. או"ח סי' שמג ס"ק ב
1. ס"ק ב

―――――― NISHMAT AVRAHAM ――――――

measuring one tefach by one tefach between the rooms — author), will also be ritually unclean (see above Siman 371:4), nevertheless this is only by Rabbinic law according to the *Tur (he refers to the Beit Yosef)* and *poskim*.

2. If the room containing the corpse is completely closed on all sides, the common corridor or stairwell also becomes ritually unclean. Since the corpse will later be taken out through the corridor or stairwell, by Rabbinic law they are already unclean now. Thus, if the door to one of the other rooms off the corridor or stairwell is opened, the *tumah* will spread into it although the room containing the corpse is closed. Therefore, if a *Cohen* is in one of the other rooms he must keep the door closed until the deceased has been taken away to avoid becoming ritually unclean by Rabbinic law. This is also the ruling of the *Pnei Yehoshua*[2] and the *Yad Avraham*.[3]

The *Magen Avraham*,[4] however, writes that if there is an opening between the two rooms the *tumah* is in both by Torah law, as specifically noted by the *Beit Yosef* (*Yoreh Deah*, Siman 369) quoting the *Rambam*. The *Avnei Nezer*[5] writes that he has always been troubled that such a mistake should be found in the *Shach*, a central pillar upon which all the House of Israel rests. Although he had always tried to justify his rulings since he comes from his lineage, here he finds this impossible. However he is very pleased to have just seen that the *Chatam Sofer*[6] writes that the *Shach* did not say that the impurity was Rabbinic. The *Chatam Sofer* writes that there is a printing error in the *Shach* and what the *Shach* actually wrote was that even if the room containing the corpse was completely closed on all sides, nevertheless the other room would also become ritually unclean, but, in this case only, this would be by Rabbinic rule. The *Chatam Sofer* then continues that there is no need for this explanation, for the *Shach* was referring to another room which, although completely separated from the room of the deceased, will now be Rabbinically unclean if the deceased will later be taken through it or through a common corridor.

The *Chatam Sofer*, *Chochmat Adam*[7] and *Shevut Yaakov*[8] all rule that the *tumah* enters another room through an opening from the room containing a corpse and that this is a Torah law. However the *Shoel U'Meshiv*[9] writes that the ruling of most *poskim* is like that of the *Shach*.

Rav Auerbach zt"l wrote to me that when there is a common stairwell or corridor through which the deceased will be taken out, the *tumah* will enter the other rooms as well, if their doors are opened into the corridor even if the door to the room of the deceased is closed, or alternatively, if the door to the room containing the deceased is opened even if the doors to the other rooms remain closed. The *tumah*, according to the *Shach*, is Rabbinic. This is because although the door of an adjacent room is opened, it is nevertheless considered closed by Torah law. Since the opening of the door is narrower than the total length of its walls, that is, the walled part of the room is greater in length than its entrance, the room is considered to be closed by Torah law even when the door is open. Hence the *tumah* does not spread into it by Torah law, only by Rabbinic law.

Rav Neuwirth shlita told me that if a

---

2. סוכה כא ע״א ד״ה והנלע״ד
3. הגהות כאן
4. או״ח סי׳ שיא ס״ק י׳ וסי׳ שמג ס״ק ב
5. שו״ת, יו״ד סי׳ תסח
6. שו״ת, יו״ד סי׳ שמ
7. כלל קנט סע׳ ה ו-ח
8. שו״ת, ח״א סי׳ פה
9. שו״ת, מהד״ג ח״ג סי׳ כו

SIMAN 372: TUMAH PERMITTED FOR A MITZVAH / §1

NISHMAT AVRAHAM

deceased is present in one of the apartments in an apartment building and a *Cohen* lives in another, the door to his apartment may not be opened and he may not go out into the common stairwell. Since the deceased will be taken out through the stairwell, the area is already *tamei*, even if the door leading to the apartment containing the deceased is closed, and, when the door to the *Cohen's* apartment is opened, the *tumah* will enter it and he will become ritually impure. He must remain in his apartment until the deceased is removed from the building. Even if the *Cohen* must go out to perform a Torah *mitzvah* such as listening to the *shofar* on Rosh Hashanah, he may not do so. Since there is a controversy among both the *rishonim* and the *acharonim*[10] whether this is a Torah or Rabbinic *halachah*, the *Cohen* must act strictly. If he and his sons are in a room of his apartment with the door of the room closed, the female members of the family may leave and enter the apartment. *Rav Auerbach zt"l* wrote to me that just as one may not set aside a Rabbinic law in order to perform a Torah commandment such as *shofar* or *lulav*, here, too, he may not set aside the Rabbinic prohibition against becoming *tamei* and then perform the Torah commandment. *Rav Neuwirth shlita* wrote to me adding that even were he to perform the Torah commandment at the same time as he would set aside Rabbinic law (*since the halachah is that a positive commandment overrides a negative one if in performing the positive one he simultaneously sets aside a negative one — author*), in this instance he may not do so. For the *halachah* concerning the ritual defilment of a *Cohen* consists of both a positive and negative commandment and a positive commandment cannot override a negative and a positive commandment combined.

A corpse is *muktzeh* and cannot be moved on *Shabbat*. Under special circumstances it may be moved if an object that is not *muktzeh* is placed on it.[11] The *Rama*[12] writes that it may not be moved even in this way, if the purpose is to prevent a *Cohen* from becoming defiled, but there are those who permit the corpse to be moved by a non-Jew. The *Mishnah Berurah*[13] adds that this is permitted only if the family agrees but they cannot be forced to do so. Even if there is a *shul* in the apartment building and *Cohanim* cannot pray there because of the presence of the corpse, the family cannot be forced to remove him from his apartment since it is an honor to the deceased that he is ritually cleansed in his own home (*after Shabbat*). However, if the custom is to take the deceased elsewhere to cleanse him ritually, the family can be forced to move him immediately in one of the ways stated by the *Shulchan Aruch*. Similarly, if the deceased is a *nefel*, there are those who rule that the family can be forced to have it removed to prevent a *Cohen* from becoming defiled.

The *Taz*[14] and *Shach*[15] disagree as to whether a closed door prevents *tumah* from entering a room if the door hinges are made of metal.[16] *Rav Neuwirth shlita* wrote to me that the custom is to rule leniently. The *She'arim Metzuyanim Ba-Halachah*[17] writes that a glass window in a door bars the *tumah* from passing

---

10. ראה ביד אברהם כאן ס"ק א ובמג"א סי' שיא ס"ק יד וסי' שמג ס"ק ב
11. או"ח סי' שיא סע' א
12. שם סע' ב
See *Nishmat Avraham*, vol. 1 *Orach Chaim*, Siman 311A.
13. ס"ק יג
14. יו"ד סי' שעא ס"ק ג
15. נקודות הכסף שם על הט"ז ס"ק ג
16. ראה גם בפ"ת שם ס"ק ט
17. סי' רב ס"ק יא. שם מדובר בדלת עם חלון וכותב דכלי זכוכית פשוטין הן טהורין, רמב"ם כלים פ"ב ה"ה, וגם היא מחוברת להדלת שהיא מחוברת לקרקע

NISHMAT AVRAHAM

through because it is attached to the door which is attached to the ground. *Rav Neuwirth shlita* explained that he means that since the glass was fashioned with the intention to attach it to the ground it does not become defiled. A metal door or hinges would, then, fall into the same category.

◆§ THE *COHEN* AS A PATIENT

Minor illness. If a Cohen has a *minor illness* he is forbidden to enter a hospital to receive treatment even if there is no one deceased in the hospital at the time of entering.

A *non-seriously ill Cohen.* In view of the above *Shach* and the fact that most *poskim* rule like him, the *Chelkat Yaakov*[18] writes that the *Cohen* may act leniently in the Diaspora, for since the majority of patients in a hospital are non-Jews it is likely that a deceased patient will be a non-Jew. The *She'arim Metzuyanim BaHalachah*[19] writes that since the *Mechaber*[20] writes that it is "proper to be careful" and the *Rama* adds that "it is proper to act strictly" we see that this is only a question of acting strictly and with care. Since Rabbinic *tumah* is set aside when there is a *mitzvah* to perform,[21] certainly if the *Cohen* is ill he may be hospitalized, for the *Machatzit HaShekel*[22] writes that seeking cure is more important than a *mitzvah*. See also the *Maharsham*,[23] *Maharash Engel*[24] and *Seridei Eish*.[25]

In the hospitals in *Eretz Yisrael*, however, where the majority of patients and therefore deceased are Jews, it would appear that a *Cohen* may not attend a clinic, laboratory or department of radiology if these are within the hospital building, even if he is a *non-seriously ill* patient. If such a patient requires hospitalization, he may not enter a hospital where the wards are not completely separated from the department of pathology. If, however, the wards are separated from the department of pathology, and the *non-seriously ill Cohen* can only be treated as an inpatient, he may be hospitalized there, provided that there is no one deceased at the time he enters the hospital building. The *She'arim Metzuyanim BaHalachah*[26] writes that in such a situation we can rely on the *Shach's* opinion that the *tumah* moves from one room to another (*if a corpse is present later in a different room — author*) by Rabbinic law. One is not obligated to spend all of his money to avoid setting aside Rabbinic law.[27] It should follow, all the more so, that it be set aside to treat illness, even if *non-serious*, for health is more important than money; such is the comment of the *Binyan Shlomo*[28] basing himself on a *Gemara*.[29]

However, the *Chelkat Yaakov*[30] rules that a *non-seriously ill Cohen* is forbidden to enter a hospital for treatment. And, although I have noted, just above, that there is a view that one need not spend all of his money to avoid setting aside Rabbinic law, the *Chafetz Chaim*[31] cites rulings to the contrary, that one must give up all of his wealth to avoid setting aside even Rabbinic law.

It is clear that a *seriously ill Cohen* or

---

18. שו"ת, ח"א סי' כז
19. סי' רב ס"ק ו
20. כאן סע' ב
21. שו"ע כאן
22. או"ח סי' שלח ס"ק א
23. שו"ת, ח"ב סי' רלג
24. שו"ת, ח"ג סי' כז
25. שו"ת, ח"ב סי' קלד
26. סי' רב ס"ק ו
27. שו"ת שבות יעקב ח"א סי' צח. וראה בפ"ת יו"ד סי' קנז ס"ק ד
28. שו"ת, סי' מז
29. ב"ק צג ע"א. וראה גם בהלכה ירפואה ח"ג עמ' קסז
30. שו"ת, ח"א סי' כז
31. ספר חפץ חיים הל' לשון הרע כלל א באר מים חיים ס"ק א והל' איסורי רכילות באר מים חיים ס"ק יב

SIMAN 372: TUMAH PERMITTED FOR A MITZVAH / §1

NISHMAT AVRAHAM

one who is only possibly *seriously ill*, is permitted to enter a hospital to receive treatment, even if the body of a deceased patient is known to be present under the same roof, if he requires treatment urgently and it cannot wait until the deceased has been removed.

A hospitalized *Cohen* (in *Eretz Yisrael*) should try to see that the door to his room is always closed and only opened for medical reasons or to bring him food, and the like. He is forbidden to leave his room merely to walk around. I wondered whether he is allowed to leave his room (when there is no one deceased under the same roof) in order to go to the hospital *shul* to pray with a *minyan* or to perform a Torah commandment such as hearing the *shofar* on *Rosh Hashanah*. He entered the corridors and *shul* when there was no *tumah*, and in remaining there he is halachically passive and not active (*shev v'al ta'aseh*).[32] See also the *Igrot Moshe*[33] quoted above Siman 369A (2), p. 352 and the *Shevet HaLevi*.[34]

Rav Waldenberg shlita[35] wrote to me that the *Cohen* is permitted to go to the *shul*, not only to perform a Torah commandment but even to pray with a *minyan* which is Rabbinic. The door to the *shul* should remain closed in case a patient dies elsewhere in the hospital while he is in the *shul*. Although most of the patients will be Jews, nevertheless he gives many reasons for permitting this. We can rely on a combined picture of the following: (a) The opinion of the *Shach* that the *tumah* spreads from room to room only by Rabbinic law and most *poskim* do not differentiate between an opening into the room of only one *tefach* by one *tefach* and one of three *tefachim* by three or more. (b) The opinion of the *Ra'avad* that today a *Cohen* is not punishable with lashes for deliberately becoming defiled. Many *poskim* explain that he means that a *Cohen* is not forbidden to become defiled today by Torah law, only by Rabbinic law.[36] (c) The opinion of *Rabbeinu Tam*[37] (and others[38]) that a *Cohen* is not forbidden by Torah law to become defiled if he has already become defiled that day. Since today a *Cohen* is in a constant state of ritual uncleanliness, for in the absence of the ashes of a red heifer he cannot become ritually clean, he is viewed as having become defiled on that day (see the *Maharsham*[39]). (d) The opinion of the *Derishah*, the *Shach* and others that the *tumah* cannot enter a room whose door is closed; and, the *Mishnah Berurah*[40] who rules that if the doors and windows of the *shul* are closed, it is only by Rabbinic law that the *tumah* enters the room. Therefore the *Cohen* can remain in *shul*, even if he is aware that there is a corpse in a nearby room, until after he has performed *birkat Cohanim*, since it is a Torah *mitzvah* and the *tumah* involved is only Rabbinic. There is further evidence from the *Teshurat Shai*[41] who permits a *Cohen* to visit the sick in a large hospital even though hardly a day passes in which at least one deceased Jew cannot be found there. The *Tuv Ta'am VeDa'at*[42] permits a *Cohen* to work in a hospital and the *Maharash Engel*[43] permits a *Cohen* to be hospitalized. On the basis of all the above

---

32. וראה גם בפ"ת כאן ס"ק ד וביד אברהם כאן
33. שו"ת, יו"ד ח"א סי' רמח
34. שו"ת, ח"ה סי' קפד
35. שו"ת ציץ אליעזר חט"ז סי' לג
36. עייו גשר החיים ח"ב פכ"ה סע' א
37. הובא ברא"ש הל' טומאת כהנים סי' ו. וכן הוא דעת היראים סי' שיא
38. ראה בשו"ת חת"ס יו"ד סי' שלט
39. שו"ת, ח"ב סי' רלג
40. סי' קכח ס"ק ח
41. שו"ת, ח"א סי' תקנט
42. שו"ת, מהד"ג ח"ב סי' ריב
43. שו"ת, ח"ג סי' כו

SIMAN 373
WHICH *COHEN* IS OBLIGATED TO AVOID DEFILEMENT; TO WHICH DEAD MUST HE ALLOW HIMSELF TO BE DEFILED; AND UNTIL WHEN IS HE ALLOWED TO BE DEFILED BY THEM

§2 Even if (A)a *Cohen* has a blemish he is forbidden to allow himself to become defiled. However, a *chalal* and a daughter of a *Cohen* may defile themselves by contact with a corpse.

---NISHMAT AVRAHAM---

and other reasons, *Rav Waldenberg shlita* rules that a *Cohen* may rely on the fact that most patients will live and, even in a large hospital where most patients are Jewish, leave his room to go to *shul*, if he has ascertained that there is no one deceased under the same roof at the time he leaves his room.

Rav Auerbach zt"l also told me that the *Cohen* is permitted to go to the hospital *shul* if there is no one deceased at the time. However if afterwards he becomes aware that there is a deceased patient in the hospital, he must immediately leave the *shul* and closet himself in the nearest room until the deceased has been removed.

Rav Scheinberg shlita[44] rules that a *Cohen* may bring his young son for treatment to a hospital, where most patients are Jewish, but only up to the entrance of the hospital. From there it is best that a non-Jew take him to the doctor's clinic.[45] If the child is frightened, then he may be taken by another (older) child, and if this is not possible, by an adult Jew who is not a *Cohen*. It is forbidden for his father or adult brothers to accompany him into the hospital. However, if there is a possibility that he is *seriously ill*, this is permitted.

SIMAN 373

(A) a *Cohen* has a blemish. May a *Cohen* who is *not seriously ill* have surgery which will leave him with a blemish which will disqualify him from service in the Temple?[1] The *Chavalim BaNe'imim*[2] writes that even if we say that this is comparable to disqualifying a sacrificial offering by blemishing the animal, which, according to the *Rambam*,[3] is forbidden by the Torah even today, nevertheless his is a single opinion. All other *rishonim* rule that nowadays (*when there is no Temple service — author*) this is only Rabbinically forbidden. This is seen from the *Gemara*,[4] *Tosafot*,[5] *Rosh*,[6] and *Darchei Moshe*.[7]

45. There are two separate prohibitions involved:
1. A *Cohen*, no matter how young, must not become defiled by a corpse, and 2. One may not cause a *Cohen* to become defiled by a corpse. Therefore the child cannot be brought under the same roof as a corpse by his mother (who, herself is permitted to become defiled even if she is a *Cohenet* — that is, the daughter of a *Cohen* and not merely the wife of one — in her own right) or by another Jew who is not a

Cohen. See also *Nishmat Avraham*, vol. 1 *Orach Chaim*, Siman 343A.

1. ראה בכורות מג ע"א. רמב"ם ביאת מקדש פ"ז
2. שו"ת, ח"ה סי' כג
3. איסורי מזבח פ"א ה"ז
4. ע"ז יג ע"ב
5. בכורות לג ע"ב ד"ה בעל מום ומנחות נו ע"ב ד"ה אלא
6. ב"מ פ"ז סי' ו
7. יו"ד סי' שיג בשם הגה"מ

44. מוריה, אלול תשד"מ עמ' 60

SIMAN 373: WHEN A COHEN MAY OR MAY NOT BE DEFILED / §2, 3, 5

§3 It is a *mitzvah* for a *Cohen* (male or female) to defile himself (with respect) to those (B)deceased relatives (C)mentioned in the Torah. If he (or she) refuses to do so he (or she) is made to do so.

§5 He must defile himself to the relatives mentioned even if (D)there is no need to do so, but there are those who rule that this is only permitted where this is necessary.

GLOSS: *According to the first opinion even if the relative died on Shabbat when he cannot be buried, the Cohen is permitted to defile himself to the corpse and guard him so that he is not left to lie disrespectfully. It is right to rule strictly like the second opinion and not to defile himself except if this is necessary in order to bury him or to bring him a coffin and shrouds.*

NISHMAT AVRAHAM

See also the *Minchat Chinuch*[8] and *Chatam Sofer*.[9] Therefore a *Cohen* who is *non-seriously ill* may undergo such surgery. The *Beit Yosef*[10] explicitly writes of a case where for necessary (non-medical) reasons, permission was granted to amputate the fingertips of a *Cohen*. The same ruling should apply where there is a medical reason, even for a *non-seriously* ill *Cohen*. This should be obvious, for it is a *mitzvah* to receive treatment. For all these reasons the *Chavalim BaNe'imim* permits such surgery.

The *Shoel U'Meshiv*[11] also permitted the amputation of a sixth finger growing from the thumb of a young *Cohen*.

(B) deceased relatives. These include a baby born at term or one who is more than thirty days old.[12] The *Shach*[13] writes that a *Cohen* must not defile himself to his newly born relative who is a possible *nefel*.

(C) mentioned in the Torah. A *Cohen* is obligated[14] to defile himself to the corpse of his father, mother, son, daughter, brother, virgin sister and wife.[15]

(D) there is no need to do so. The *Nekudot HaKesef*[16] writes that the first opinion in the *Shulchan Aruch* is the main one and this is the accepted custom. The *Pitchei Teshuvah*[17] writes that certainly on a weekday it is permissible for the *Cohen* to be in the same room as the deceased (one of his seven close relatives) for it is a *mitzvah* for him to defile himself even if there are others who are attending to the corpse. Nevertheless he should be there since it is possible that they might need him for something regarding the coffin, shrouds, and the like. Since these are necessary for the burial, he is permitted to be there. *Rav Neuwirth shlita* and *Rav Ovadiah Yosef shlita* told me that when a *Cohen* dies his son is obligated to attend to

---

8. מצוה רפו אות ג
9. שו"ת, יו"ד סי' שו ו-שיח
10. אהע"ז סי' ו ד"ה מ"ש וכל קול שלא הוחזק בב"ד, בשם תשובה לגאון
11. שו"ת, מהד"ק ח"ג סי' טז
12. כאן סע' ד
13. ס"ק ז. וראה גם במגן אברהם סי' תקכו סוס"ק כ
14. יו"ד כאן סע' ג
15. ויקרא כא:ב,ג. כאן סע' ד. וראה שם פרטי דינים
16. כאן
17. ס"ק ד בשם הגאון מליסא בסדור תפלה שלו

CHAPTER 35: LAWS OF MOURNING

NISHMAT AVRAHAM

him and guard the corpse. If the father dies in a hospital, the son must accompany the corpse to the room where it will lie until burial. All of this is for the honor of his father, even if there are others (non-*Cohanim*) present to do this.

The *Gesher HaChaim*[18] writes that the mourning *Cohen* whose deceased relative lies before him is permitted to defile himself in order to guard him. There are those who permit this even on *Shabbat* even though he cannot be buried then.

The *Shemirat Shabbat KeHilchatah*[19] writes that it is proper for a *Cohen* to act strictly on *Shabbat* and not defile himself to a relative; similarly he should act strictly on *Yom Tov* unless the deceased is to be buried then. If the *Cohen* needs to guard his relative to prevent his dishonor, we may depend on the ruling of the *Nekudot HaKesef* that the first opinion is the main one, particularly since it receives support from *Chazal*.[20] See also the *Minchat Chinuch*,[21] that even the second opinion will permit guarding the deceased as long as this is done for his honor. And, the *Shemirat Shabbat KeHilchatah* continues[22] that he heard from *Rav Auerbach zt"l* that *Cohanim* enter the room where their deceased relative lies in order to recite Psalms in his honor, since the *Nekudot HaKesef* and others have ruled that the first opinion in the *Shulchan Aruch*, that a *Cohen* may defile himself to his close relatives, even if it is not necessary for their burial, is the main one. And, although the *Rama* appears to disagree with the *Mechaber*, the *Aruch HaShulchan* writes that the *Rama's* position is very surprising. Nevertheless, *Rav Auerbach zt"l* felt it is best to act strictly (see the

Minchat Chinuch[23]). However, if there happens to be another deceased (who is not a relative) in the same room, the *Cohen* must be careful not to touch him; but he need not worry about being under the same roof as the other deceased. (*It would appear that the Rav zt"l made this differentiation since a Cohen is permitted to be in the same room as his deceased relative for the express purpose of honoring him. However touching the other deceased is in no way related to honoring his relative and is therefore forbidden. Rav Neuwirth shlita agreed with this.*)

The *Shevut Yaakov*[24] was asked about a *Cohen* whose deceased son's body was still at home. His wife had given birth to another son whose *brit milah* was to be that day. The question was whether the baby (a *Cohen*) could be brought back home from the *shul* after his circumcision while the body of his deceased brother was still there (see *Nishmat Avraham*, vol. 1 *Orach Chaim*, Siman 343A). The *Shevut Yaakov* quotes the *Gemara*[25] and *Rambam*[26] that adults are forbidden to defile a *Cohen*, no matter how young, to the body of a deceased. He then notes that in this case, the deceased is the baby's brother and is one of the seven relatives to whom a *Cohen* is permitted to become defiled. However, according to one opinion in the *Shulchan Aruch*, such defilement is only permitted when there is good reason and the *Rama* rules that it is proper to act strictly and this is the accepted ruling. Defiling the baby cannot be considered as necessary for the burial of the child. But since the baby has not as yet reached the age of education, one need not act strictly and the baby can be brought back home.

---

18. פ"ה סע' ד ס"ק ג
19. פס"ד סע' ו
20. אבל רבתי, ראה בהגר"א ס"ק יג
21. הוצאת מכון ירושלים, מצוה רסד ס"ק ד
22. שם הערה לא
23. שם הערה יב
24. שו"ת, ח"ג סי' צב
25. יבמות קיד ע"א
26. הל' אבל פ"ג הי"ב

§9

A *Cohen* is not permitted to defile himself (see above §3) (E)**by a limb or by a bone, etc. that was removed from his father while his father was alive. When his father dies, he is not permitted to defile himself to the corpse if it is not whole. This is so even if only a small part of the body has been removed, or is not attached to the body, even if it is present by the corpse. There is, however, an opinion that this applies only if the part was removed after death, but**

---NISHMAT AVRAHAM---

For a *brit* is performed publicly in *shul* to honor the *mitzvah* of circumcision. However, if possible, the deceased should be taken away before the baby is brought back home.

The *Pitchei Teshuvah*[27] quotes the *Magen Avraham*[28] who writes that if a sick *Cohen* cannot leave his home and the body of a deceased person is there, the relatives are forced to remove the deceased from the house so that the *Cohen* not transgress the prohibition against becoming defiled (see *Nishmat Avraham*, vol. 1 *Orach Chaim*, Siman 311A). For this he relates[29] the case of a baby *Cohen* whose *brit milah* was due on *Shabbat* and whose father was a *mohel*. That Friday night a neighbor living in the same building died. The ruling was that the relatives could be forced to take the deceased out of the building,[30] for the *halachah*[31] is that *Beit Din* is required to prevent a child who is a *Cohen* from becoming defiled by a corpse and the baby is like the sick adult (in the case quoted by the *Magen Avraham*) who cannot leave his home and because of whom the relatives can be forced to take the deceased out. And there is another reason, besides. The father of the baby is a *mohel*, and it is first and foremost the *mitzvah* of the father to circumcise his son. He may not perform the circumcision at home, if the deceased is not moved. The *brit* would, then, take place in the *shul* and it would be forbidden to bring the baby back home to his mother. Bringing him home again would be tantamount to actively defiling him which is forbidden according to all opinions. Since, however, it is important for the baby to be brought home to his mother, the relatives may be pressured (see *Nishmat Avraham*, vol. 1 *Orach Chaim*, Siman 343A).

See also the *Minchat Chinuch*,[32] *Pitchei Teshuvah*,[33] *Achiezer*,[34] *Mishnah Berurah*[35] and *Gesher HaChaim*.[36]

(E) by a limb. See above Siman 369B. A limb which is whole, that is, which consists of bone, sinew and skin as it did when it was created, also causes defilement when it is (found) under the same roof as a *Cohen*, even without direct contact.[37] Therefore not only may a *Cohen* not enter a hospital if there is a corpse there, but he may also not enter if he will be under the same roof as a limb, even a finger, that has been surgically or traumatically amputated.

---

27. יו״ד סי׳ שעא ס״ק יב
28. סי׳ שיא ס״ק יד
29. בשם שו״ת דת אש סי׳ ח
30. ע״י ככר או תימוק, או ע״י גוי, אבל בלא״ה אסור - שמעתי ממו״ר הגרי״י נויבירט שליט״א
31. טור סי׳ שעג
32. מצוה רסד
33. יו״ד סי׳ שעג ס״ק א
34. שו״ת, ח״ב סי׳ פא ס״ק ו
35. סי׳ שמב ס״ק ג
36. ח״א פ״ו ס״ק י
37. רמב״ם הל׳ טומאת מת פ״ב ה״ג

if (F)it was removed while his father was alive, the son defiles himself to the corpse even if it is not whole.

SIMAN 374
FOR WHOM MUST ONE MOURN

§8 The laws of mourning do not apply to (A)a newborn baby who dies during the first thirty days of his life including the thirtieth day, even if his hair and nails are fully

--- NISHMAT AVRAHAM ---

(F) it was removed while his father was alive. See above Siman 369B. The *Igrot Moshe*[38] follows the second opinion of the *Shulchan Aruch*, that a *Cohen* defiles himself to one of the relatives enumerated above (C) even if a limb or internal organ had been removed from the relative during his lifetime. This is also the ruling of the *Gesher HaChaim*[39] quoting the *Chochmat Adam*. As to an organ that was removed from the relative at autopsy, the *Igrot Moshe*[40] rules that it is permitted for a *Cohen* to defile himself if one can see that no part of the body is missing externally. This is also the ruling of the *Tzitz Eliezer*[41] quoting the *Maharam Shick*.[42]

However, the *Shemirat Shabbat KeHilchatah*[43] writes that a *Cohen* may not defile himself to a relative unless the body is complete; if a tiny part is missing he may not defile himself to the corpse. He notes that although the *Igrot Moshe* rules that a missing internal organ does not render the body incomplete, nevertheless this is not the ruling of the *Chazon Ish*,[44] and this controversy will be of importance with respect to someone who had an autopsy. Thus, according to this view, *Cohanim* who are close relatives are forbidden to defile themselves to the corpse following an autopsy. However, the *Shemirat Shabbat KeHilchatah* continues that if a limb was removed while he was alive, there are those who permit *Cohanim* who are close relatives to defile themselves; see the *Shulchan Aruch* and the *Kol Bo Al Aveilut*[45] who writes that this is the accepted ruling.

SIMAN 374

(A) a newborn baby. See above Siman 305B regarding the laws of mourning for a baby born with a severe congenital defect who dies after thirty days of life and regarding a healthy baby who was killed within thirty days of birth.

The *Levushei Mordechai*[1] writes that a baby born after eight months of gestation who was treated in an incubator and fed intravenously and who died when he was six months old, is still considered a *nefel*;[2] see also the *Kol Bo Al Aveilut*.[3] The *Tzitz Eliezer*,[4] however, quotes the *Da'at*

---

38. שו"ת, יו"ד ח"א סי' רנא
39. פ"ו סע' ה ס"ק ב
40. שם ח"ב סי' קסה
41. שו"ת, ח"ט סי' כ"ח
42. שו"ת, יו"ד סי' שנט
43. פס"ד סע' ו* והערה לא*
44. יו"ד סי' רי ס"ק סו סוד"ה בב"י לא משמע הכי. וכ"כ שו"ת שבט הלוי, ח"ב (יו"ד) סי' קסא. וראה גם בחזו"א אהלות סי' כב ס"ק לה דלענין נקב שיש בו חסרון בלב או

בושט מיפשט פשיטא ליה דהוי חסרון אע"ג דהוא מבפנים
45. עמ' 69 הערה 6
1. שו"ת, תליתאי או"ח סי' יד ס"ק ב
2. ראיתיו מהגמ' יבמות פ ע"א אמר ר"א בן שמונה אין עושין בו מעשה עד כ' שנה. וא"כ לא מהני כלל כ' שנים דאז נתברר שהוא בן קיימא, כ' פ' התוס' שם ד"ה והא
3. עמ' 141
4. שו"ת, ח"ט סי' כח ס"ק ח

formed. After the thirty-first day he is mourned unless it is known that he was born after (*only*) eight months of gestation.

SIMAN 376
THE CUSTOM OF THE CONSOLERS

§1 The consolers are not permitted to speak until the mourner speaks. The mourner sits at the head (*of those present — author*). When he nods his head to intimate that they are free to leave, they may no longer sit by him. (*A mourner or* (A)*sick person is not required to stand, as a sign of honor, even before a head of state.*)

SIMAN 380
THINGS FORBIDDEN TO A MOURNER

§2 A mourner may not have others run his business for him (*even a non-Jew*), unless there will otherwise (A)be a monetary loss. Only if there will be a loss to the mourner as a result of his not working may the work be done for him by

--- NISHMAT AVRAHAM ---

Sofer[5] who rules that a baby born after seven months of gestation who died after three months is to be considered like any other child to whom the laws of mourning apply, if he has lived for thirty days after birth, even if we do not know whether or not he was full term. Moreover, the *Yad Yitzchak* rules that even if his hair and nails are not fully formed, the laws of mourning apply to him if he lived for thirty days. *Rav Auerbach zt"l* wrote to me that even a baby who was born after five months of gestation is redeemed with a blessing and the laws of mourning apply to him, if he lives for thirty days after being removed from the incubator. This is because we depend on the fact that the baby matures in the warmth of the incubator as he would in his mother's womb; this is more certainly so for a baby born after eight months of gestation who has nails and hair; see the *Maggid Mishneh*.[6]

SIMAN 376

(A) **sick person.** See *Nishmat Avraham*, vol. 1 *Orach Chaim*, Siman 559A.

SIMAN 380

(A) **be a monetary loss.** The *Pitchei Teshuvah*[1] writes that a mourner may work even to prevent loss to another person and not just to himself. Hence if a doctor who is in mourning is called to see someone who is very ill, he may go to visit the patient even though it is during his (the doctor's) *shivah*. The *Shevut Yaakov*[2] writes that he saw his teachers permit a

---

1. ס"ק א בשם ספר חמודי דניאל
2. שו"ת, ח"א סי' פו הובא בשדי חמד מערכת אבלות סי' מד

5. שו"ת, סי' קיד
6. יבום וחליצה פ"א ה"ה וכן בלחם משנה שם. וראה גם במנחת שלמה תנינא סי' צט אות א

others. Even work that is normally forbidden on *Chol HaMoed* because of the effort involved is permitted, and even if it is the work of a professional.

NISHMAT AVRAHAM

doctor to visit a patient during his (the doctor's) *shivah*, since treating a patient whose life may be in danger and doing a *mitzvah* are not barred in the decree forbidding a mourner to work. This is permitted even if there is another doctor available since a person does not merit being cured by everyone. It is possible that he may even be payed for his services, for "a doctor who treats for nothing is worth nothing."[3] Nevertheless, the doctor should be careful not to accept payment, if he can afford not to do so. He must also continue to observe the laws of mourning about not wearing leather shoes, as enumerated in the *Shulchan Aruch*, Siman 382.

It would appear from this that a doctor in mourning would not be allowed to leave his home to visit a *non-seriously ill* patient. Rav Auerbach zt"l wrote to me that this is indeed surprising since it is certainly a *mitzvah* of great importance to cure even a *non-seriously ill* patient and the doctor is permitted to go out to treat the patient even if he only has *discomfort*.

It would also appear from the *Shevut Yaakov* that the doctor should be careful not to take a fee for services rendered during his *shivah* even after it is over. Rav Auerbach zt"l wrote to me that one may not make a profit from work done during the *shivah* and he may only take payment for any expenses that he incurred. Although *Chazal*[4] permitted a mourner who is a barber, or in charge of public baths to work before a Festival (*since he is needed by the public — author*), and he could also charge for his services, nevertheless when a doctor does a *mitzvah* (of treating a patient), he is not allowed to receive money, even on the basis of the use of his time (*sechar batalah*), let alone for his medical services. For we see that although his wife and children who are dependent on him and are not mourners are permitted to work, nevertheless they may not earn money for him.[5]

Rebbe Akiva Eiger[6] writes that it is customary not to take anything during the *shivah* from a house of mourning.[7] However the *Gesher HaChaim*[8] writes that there is no need to be particular about this and this is also the ruling of the *Yabia Omer*.[9] Rav Palaggi[10] writes that this worldwide custom is a mistake. Rav Waldenberg shlita[11] adds that this is the custom only if the deceased died in the house where the mourners are sitting, but if he died elsewhere, this certainly does not apply.

Is a doctor, therefore, permitted to take a fee for visiting a patient in a house of mourning? Rav Auerbach zt"l[12] wrote to me that since there is an opinion that this custom is a mistaken one,[13] one may act leniently and only be careful not to take something that is particularly used in the mourner's home. This does not apply to money and it may certainly be taken as

---

3. ב"ק פה ע"א
4. מו"ק יא ע"ב
5. ראה מנחת שלמה תנינא סי' צט אות ג
6. חידושיו על סימן שעו. וכן כותב הבית לחם יהודה שם, הובא בערוה"ש שם סע' יא
7. כי רוח הטומאה שורה עליו כל ז'
8. ח"א פ"כ סי' ה כ"ק יב בשם היוסף אומץ והערך שי
9. שו"ת, ח"ד יו"ד סי' לה ס"ק ד
10. ספר חיים ביד סי' קכה סע' טו"ב
11. ספר אבן יעקב סי' מד ס"ק ג
12. ראה מנחת שלמה תנינא סי' צט אות ב
13. כפי שכתב בספר יוסף אומץ דף קסב ששמע ממורו הגאון מוהר"ר סגל ז"ל

SIMAN 381
A MOURNER IS FORBIDDEN TO WASH HIMSELF

§3 A woman in mourning who (A)has given birth and needs to wash herself, may do so.

SIMAN 382
A MOURNER IS FORBIDDEN TO WEAR (LEATHER) SHOES

§2 A woman in mourning who has (A)given birth may wear (leather) shoes during the thirty days after having given birth, since the cold is harmful to her.

SIMAN 384
A MOURNER IS FORBIDDEN TO STUDY TORAH

§2 If the mourner is a *Cohen* and there is no other *Cohen* in the *shul* he is nevertheless forbidden to be called up (A)to the Torah.

NISHMAT AVRAHAM

pay by a worker, be given to charity or be used to pay a debt. There are no grounds for concern and "he who performs a *mitzvah* will not come to harm."[14] Rav Neuwirth shlita told me that the mourner may pay for food, even when there is no *mitzvah* involved.

The *Taz*[15] writes that a mourner may have blood drawn. It would appear that this is permitted even if he is healthy[16] and it is done prophylactically, and is certainly permitted as treatment even though he has only a minor illness.[17]

SIMAN 381

(A) **has given birth.** The *Shach*[1] writes that this is permitted even on the first day of mourning. However, if the need is not great she should not do so on the first day.

SIMAN 382

(A) **given birth.** This also applies to one who is ill or who has a wound on his foot.[1]

SIMAN 384

(A) **to the Torah.** The *Sdei Chemed*[1] writes that a patient who recovered during his period of mourning must say the *Birkat HaGomel* (see *Nishmat Avraham*, vol. 1 *Orach Chaim*, Siman 219) before a *minyan*, but without being called up to the Torah.

The *Ran*[2] writes that a doctor in mourning may not study medicine from a text if he does not need that particular piece of information at the time. Although he is not doing work, he is nevertheless

---

Siman 532A.

14. קהלת ח:ה
15. בשם הרש"ל בשם האגודה
16. מהא דמאירי מו"ק י ע"א ד"ה מקיזין, לגבי רפואה במועד
17. See *Nishmat Avraham*, vol. 1 *Orach Chaim*.

1. ס"ק ב
1. ש"ך ס"ק א. כי הצנה קשה להם - או"ח סי' תריד מ"ב ס"ק י

1. מערכת אבלות סי' נב
2. מו"ק י"א ע"ב בשם הרב ר' יהושעיה ז"ל

SIMAN 385
GREETING A MOURNER

§1 A mourner is forbidden to (A)greet others.

SIMAN 396
THE LAWS CONCERNING A MOURNER WHO DID NOT MOURN DURING THE WHOLE OF THE *SHIVAH*

§1 A mourner who did not mourn during the seven days (*following the burial — author*) whether knowingly or unknowingly, must make it up during the thirty-day period of mourning. However, (A)he does not need to tear his garments since if he did not do so at the time his relative died or at the burial, he only needs to do so during the first seven days, unless he mourns for a parent. Then he must tear his garments even after the first seven days of mourning have passed.

--- NISHMAT AVRAHAM ---

gaining knowledge. It would appear to me that the reason is so that he does not take his mind off the fact that he is in mourning. The *Aruch HaShulchan*[3] writes that it is clear that a mourner may not study anything so as not to take his mind off his mourning.

SIMAN 385

(A) greet others. May a woman who has given birth who is in mourning be greeted with "*mazal tov*"? The *Gesher HaChaim*[1] writes that one may bless a mourner with blessings such as "long life," "*refuah sheleimah*" (a complete cure), and the like; no evidence has been found that it is forbidden to wish "*mazal tov*." It is only forbidden to greet a mourner with "*shalom*."[2] Not only is he permitted to bless others, but others may also bless him with a blessing other than "*shalom*." This is also the opinion of the *Chazon LaMoed*[3] and this is also the ruling for *Tishah B'Av*.[4]

SIMAN 396

(A) he does not need to tear his garments. The *Shach*,[1] quoting the *Bach*, writes that if he did not tear his garments because of the force of circumstances, for example, if he was *seriously ill* and could not tear his garments, or if he was in a confused state of mind and recovered only after the seven days of mourning, it is as if the deceased died now, and he must tear his garments. He is not like one who did not tear his garments, either knowingly or unknowingly, when he should have done so. For since he was healthy when he heard that a relative had died, he was

SIMAN 397
LAWS OF EYEWITNESS STATEMENTS WHICH REQUIRE ONE TO MOURN

§2 If two witnesses say that a relative has died and two that he has not, (A)he does not mourn.

NISHMAT AVRAHAM
---

required to tear his garments then. However the *Taz*[2] distinguishes between one who did not tear his garments when he was *seriously ill* upon hearing of the death of his relative but was of stable mind, and one who was not of clear mind. He of stable mind does not tear his garments if he recovers after the *shivah*; the one who was not of clear mind does tear his garments when he comes to himself even if the *shivah* has elapsed. This is the way the *Nachalat Tzvi*[3] understood the *Taz*, but see the *Ba'er Heitev*[4] who understood the *Taz* differently.

See Siman 337A and B regarding mourning and also Siman 337C regarding a mourner visiting a *seriously ill* patient.

SIMAN 397

(A) he does not mourn. Every year following the death of a parent, the anniversary of the death (*yahrzeit*) is commemorated by the sons saying *Kaddish*, learning *Mishnayot* and the like, for the soul of the deceased.[1]

If someone was seen alive some hours before sunset and found dead some hours after nightfall, which day should be commemorated as his *yahrzeit*? It would appear that this will depend on the controversy between the *Taz*[2] and the *Maharam Mintz*.[3] The *Taz's* opinion is that since he was found dead we assume he died just after he was seen alive, whereas the *Maharam Mintz's* opinion is that he died just before he was found. The *Shach*,[4] however, disagrees with the *Taz* arguing against all his proofs. See also the *Pitchei Teshuvah*[5] and *Gilyon Maharsha*.[6] The *Chatam Sofer*[7] also writes that we may not rule like this *Taz*. The *Chochmat Adam*[8] writes that even if we know the month in which a person died but do not know the day, we assume that he was alive until the last day of the month. The *Da'at Torah*[9] quotes a *Maharashdam*[10] who also rules like the *Maharam Mintz*. The *Da'at Torah himself* brings a proof from the *Beit Yosef*[11] quoting the *Terumat HaDeshen* that if an *eruv* of a *mavoi* is found to be down on *Shabbat* (in a walled city) and it is not known whether it came down before *Shabbat* or on *Shabbat*, we assume that it came down just before it was found, and one may therefore continue to carry on that *Shabbat*. The subject is discussed in great detail by the *Sdei Chemed*.[12]

---

2. ס"ק א
3. כאן
4. ס"ק א
1. סי' תב סע' יב ברמ"א ועיין פרטי דינים בט"ז ס"ק ט וש"ך ס"ק י
2. ס"ק ב
3. שו"ת, סי' צה, מובא בט"ז
4. בנקודות הכסף כאן
5. ס"ק א
6. כאן
7. שו"ת, יו"ד סי' שמא ד"ה ואל תשיבני
8. כלל קעא סע' יא
9. כאן
10. שו"ת, יו"ד סי' רא
11. או"ח סוסי' שסה
12. אסיפת דינים מערכת אבילות אות יג

NISHMAT AVRAHAM

The *Igrot Moshe*[13] writes that if a corpse is found and it is not known when the person died, we presume that he died at the latest time that it was still possible that he was alive. Regarding his *yahrzeit*, even the *Taz* would agree that it will be the anniversary of the day he was found for then he was certainly dead. If one was found dead at the end of twilight and was probably alive at the beginning of twilight, he is considered to have died at the time he was found.

However, the *Gesher HaChaim*[14] writes that if it is uncertain as to whether a person's *yahrzeit* should be today or tomorrow or if he died at twilight (*and then there is uncertainty as to whether the moment he died was part of yesterday or today — author*), if there are no other mourners in *shul*, the relative leads the prayers and says *Kaddish* both days. (*This applies to a congregation where only one person is permitted to say Kaddish at a time. If there is another mourner in shul whose relative definitely died on that date he takes precedence over one who is uncertain as to whether his relative died on that date or not — author.*) If there are other mourners on both days he presumes that the *yahrzeit* of his relative is on the earlier date. Certainly with regard to fasting and visiting the grave, he should do so on the earlier date.

The *Chatam Sofer*[15] was asked by someone who was uncertain as to whether his father died on the fourth or the fifth of the month, what he should do regarding the customs of the *yahrzeit* — saying *Kaddish*, lighting a candle and fasting. He answered that he should keep the customs on both days since the benefit to his father's soul will be only on the real *yahrzeit*. But, since it is very difficult to expect someone to fast two consecutive days, he should fast on the fourth of the month and increase his usual Torah study and service of *Hashem* on the fifth. This responsum of the *Chatam Sofer* apparently is in contrast to his previous ruling (see reference 7). It is possible that in the latter ruling there were witnesses who knew that the father had died on the fourth and the son later had doubts about the true date.[16]

The *Igrot Moshe*[17] also answers the apparent contradiction in the *Chatam Sofer* in the above fashion adding that in such a situation he should keep both days. However if the doubt can never be resolved, which happens if he died during twilight, then the second day only should be kept.

Rav Auerbach zt"l wrote to me regarding someone who was alive on *Shabbat* but was found dead during twilight at the end of *Shabbat*. Even if it was definitely known that he died during twilight, there is much controversy as to when his relative should observe the *yahrzeit*, and whichever day he chooses to keep is acceptable in *Halachah*. Nevertheless, in this case there is a double uncertainty (*did he die on Shabbat or during twilight, and if we say twilight there is doubt in Halachah as to which day he should observe — author*). It would appear that all would agree that he should observe the *yahrzeit* on the anniversary of the date of *Shabbat*. Moreover, even if he certainly died during twilight, the *Chazon LaMoed*[18] says that the *yahrzeit* should be observed on the date of *Shabbat*, because all Israel still observes *Shabbat* during twilight.

This ruling of the *Chazon LaMoed* only

---

13. שו"ת, יו"ד ח"ג סי' קנט

14. ח"א פל"ב סע' יב

15. שו"ת, או"ח סי' קסא

16. ראה בספר ליקוטי הערות על החת"ס בשם התורת חיים והשו"ת מחנה חיים

17. שו"ת, יו"ד ח"ג סי' קנט

18. סי' כח הערה ד

SIMAN 402
THE LAWS CONCERNING ONE WHO HEARS OF THE DEATH OF A RELATIVE

§12 There is (A)no obligation to tell someone of the death of a relative even if it is a father or mother who has died. It is of this that the verse (*Proverbs* 10:18) says: "One who utters

―――――― NISHMAT AVRAHAM ――――――

applies to this specific case of someone who dies during twilight at the end of *Shabbat*. However, if one dies during twilight during the week, the *Chazon La-Moed*[19] writes that there are those who say that it is more correct if the relative leads the congregation in prayer on the anniversary of the second day, whereas others say he should do so on the anniversary of the first day. If there are no other mourners in *shul* he should do so on both days. As fasting, he[20] writes that he may fast on either day.

If the deceased was a *gosses* during twilight, the *Kol Bo Al Aveilut*[21] writes that in such a case one cannot assume that he was alive until he was found dead, particularly since *gesisah* is close to or the beginning of death. Nevertheless, the controversy remains and many have ruled that even in such a case the *yahrzeit* should be observed on the anniversary of the second day with regard to leading the congregation in prayer and fasting, though if he wishes to fast on the first day he may do so. However he should say *Kaddish* on both days.

Rav Neuwirth shlita told me that both with regard to a patient or a *gosses* who was seen alive before twilight, even many hours before, and was then found dead after twilight, he is presumed to have been alive until he was found dead. The *yahrzeit* is therefore observed, with all its customs, on the anniversary of the day the deceased was found dead.

SIMAN 402

(A) **no obligation to tell someone.** What is the *halachah* regarding a doctor or nurse who must inform a family that the hospitalized patient has died? The *Kitzur Shulchan Aruch*[1] writes that "one must not tell" rather than "there is no obligation to tell." The *Maharam Shick*[2] writes that a brother must not be informed of the death of a sister, for although he will continue to pray for her recovery in the *Shemoneh Esrei* prayer giving rise to the problem of a prayer in vain,[3] nevertheless one does not tell someone to sin by relating bad news so that another should not say a prayer in vain. However, *Rav Chaim Palaggi*[4] writes that since in any case he will eventually hear the news, this is not considered speaking evil and why should one be prevented from saying *Kaddish*?

The *Rama* writes that a son should be informed that his father has died so that he can say *Kaddish*, but not the daughters. However, the *Chavot Yair*[5] writes that it

---

19. שם סע׳ ט
20. פכ״ט סע׳ כ
21. פ״ה סי׳ ד סע׳ ב (עמ׳ 390)
1. סי׳ רו סע׳ ט
2. שו״ת, או״ח סי׳ כו
3. ראה במחצית השקל או״ח סי׳ רפח ס״ק יד בשם המהרי״ל
4. שו״ת חיים ביד חיו״ד סי׳ קג
5. שו״ת, סי׳ רא

slander is a fool." Nevertheless, if asked ^(B)he must not lie by saying that he is alive, for the verse (*Exodus* 23:7) says: "Put yourself at a distance from falsehood."

GLOSS: *If, however, a father dies it is customary to inform the sons so that they may say Kaddish. There is no custom at all to inform the daughters.*

NISHMAT AVRAHAM

is customary to inform the daughters as well, for people say that it is befitting for the parents that their children should mourn them.[6]

It would therefore appear from the above that a doctor or nurse may, as part of his or her duty, inform a relative of the death of the patient. *Rav Auerbach zt"l* told me that hospital staff must inform the family of the death of the patient so that they may make the arrangements to bury him and there is no sin involved in doing so. *Rav Neuwirth shlita* wrote to me that a son should not inform a parent of the death of a relative for he will cause him pain and violate the *mitzvah* of honoring one's parents.

It should be obvious that one must be very careful how a relative is informed to avoid shock and even death from the news. We find that our matriach Sarah[7] died upon hearing that her son Yitzchak was offered up for a sacrifice (before she could be told that he was, in fact, alive) and Eli the high priest[8] fell back and died on hearing that the Ark of *Hashem* had been captured by the Philistines. The family should not be informed by telephone that the patient has died, but rather they should be asked to come "because of his condition." Only when they arrive should they be informed personally and gradually, particularly if the patient died unexpectedly. If he died on *Shabbat*, one may, if one wishes to act strictly, not inform them even through a non-Jew, but wait for them at the entrance of the ward to tell them the news. However *Rav Neuwirth shlita* told me that because a member of the family might come in unexpectedly and suddenly discover that the patient has died and this could give rise to possibly tragic consequences, the family should be informed through a non-Jew.

See also above Siman 337A,D that a *seriously ill* patient should not be informed of the death of a relative for fear of aggravating his condition.

(B) he must not lie. The *Taz*[9] writes that it would appear that he should answer in a fashion that could also be interpreted to mean that the person is alive. As proof he quotes the *Gemara*[10] and *Tosafot*.[11] Also, we are told[12] that while Rebbe Meir was teaching one *Shabbat* afternoon at the *Beit HaMidrash*, his two sons, who were home, died unexpectedly. His wife placed them both on a bed and covered them with a sheet. When Rebbe Meir returned home after *Shabbat* and asked his wife where they were, she answered that they had gone to the *Beit HaMidrash* (which could also mean that they went to the Heavenly *Beit HaMidrash*). (*It was only after she had given him wine to*

---

6. ראה בהלכה ורפואה ח"א עמ' שנג
7. רש"י בראשית כג:ב
8. שמואל א ד:יב
9. ס"ק ח
10. מו"ק כ ע"א
11. ד"ה אייבו
12. ילקו"ש משלי רמז תתקסד. וראה במג"א סי' רצ ובשעה"צ ס"ק ה

SIMAN 402: ONE WHO HEARS OF A RELATIVE'S DEATH / §12

――― NISHMAT AVRAHAM ―――

recite Havdalah and given him to eat that she gradually prepared him for what he would find in the bedroom — author.) See also the *Shevut Yaakov*,[13] *Beit Lechem Yehudah*,[14] *Pitchei Teshuvah*[15] and *Gilyon Maharsha*.[16]

BLESSED BE HE WHO GIVES STRENGTH TO THE WEARY

---

13. שו"ת, ח"ב סי' צט
14. יו"ד סי' שצג סע' ד
15. כאן ס"ק א
16. כאן

GLOSSARY

HEBREW AND *HALACHIC* TERMS

acharonim — Rabbinic authorities contemporary with or after the time of *Rav Yosef Karo,* the author of the *Shulchan Aruch* (16th century)

achshevei — elevating that which is not considered edible to the status of food by eating it (literally: giving it importance)

agunah — a married woman whose husband's whereabouts are unknown. She cannot remarry without proof that he is dead

aliyah — coming to live in Israel

Am Yisrael — the Jewish people

amirah lenochri — asking a non-Jew to do whatever a Jew may not do

Amora (pl. ***Amora'im***) — sage(s) from the Talmudic period, 3rd-6th century

amot — cubits; each cubit is equivalent to six *tefachim,* that is, 48 cm. (60 cm. according to the *Chazon Ish*)

androgynous — hermaphrodite; one who has something of both male and female physical attributes

aninut — the period of mourning from the time of death until the burial. The *halachot* of this period are not identical to those of the period of mourning which follows burial; see *onen*

arayot — see *gilui arayot*

atarah — see *corona* (Medical Terms)

bediavad — after the event. The *halachah* often differentiates between forbidding an act before the deed is done (*lechatechilah*) and accepting it if it has already been done (*bediavad*)

bein hashemashot — the period of transition from *halachic* day to *halachic* night

Beit Din — a rabbinical court consisting of three judges

Beit HaMikdash — the Temple of *Hashem* on the Temple Mount in Jerusalem

beit haperas — a field containing a grave that was plowed over such that the crushed bones are scattered and their exact location unknown. A person entering such a field will become *tamei*

beit hasetarim — naturally hidden parts of the body such as the mouth and armpits

berachah acharonah — a blessing made after eating or drinking

berachah rishonah — a blessing made before eating or drinking

Beraitot — statements made by *Tanna'im* but not included in the *Mishnah* which was compiled by *Rebbe Yehudah HaNasi*

bikur cholim — visiting the sick; it is a *mitzvah*

birkat Cohanim — the priestly blessing; recited by the *Cohanim*

birkat erusin — the first two blessings said at the marriage ceremony

birkat hagomel — thanksgiving blessing; see *Nishmat Avraham,* vol. 1 *Orach Chaim,* p. 93

birkat hamazon — the grace after meals

birkat hamitzvah (pl. ***mitzvot***) — a blessing(s) made before performing a *mitzvah*

birkat hanehenin — a blessing recited before enjoying physical pleasure such as that derived from eating food and smelling fragrant odors

borei peri hagafen — the blessing made before drinking wine

brit or ***brit milah*** — Jewish ritual circumcision

bulimos — acute, ravenous, life-threatening hunger; not to be confused with bulimia, a non-life-threatening mental health disorder characterized by self-induced vomiting after eating

carmelit — an area which does not fit the definition of either a *private* or *public domain* but may be confused with either of them. The prohibition of carrying in a *carmelit* on *Shabbat* is Rabbinical

Chachamim — literally: wise men; Sages of the *Mishnah* and *Gemara*

chadash — grain from the seed of the five species (wheat, spelt, barley, oats and rye) which was planted after the fall harvest and grew before *Pesach* may not be eaten until after the *Omer* sacrifice is brought on the second day of *Pesach.* See *Leviticus 23:9-14.* Since the destruction of the *Beit HaMikdash, chadash* may not be eaten until after the second day of *Pesach* in Israel and after the third day of *Pesach* in the Diaspora

chalal — one who has lost his priestly status; the son of a *Cohen* who marries a woman forbidden to him by Torah law, see *Leviticus 21:15*

challah — the portion of the dough set aside as the *Cohen's* share; the term is also used for bread baked for the Sabbath and Festival meals

chalitzah — if there are valid reasons against a *yibum,* the *mitzvah* of *chalitzah* is performed to release a childless widow and allow her to remarry at will. Part of the *chalitzah* ceremony involves the widow untying the shoelaces and removing a shoe, made specially for this purpose, from the foot of her brother-in-law

chametz — flour of the five types of grain (wheat, spelt, barley, oats and rye) which has come into contact with water and become leavened; it and whatever is produced from it is forbidden on *Pesach*

chatzizah — that which stands between and does not allow direct contact between two entities

chayei olam — a full life span

chayei sha'ah — a life span of less than a year

Chazal — an abbreviation for *chachameinu zichronam livrachah* — our Sages of blessed memory (of the *Mishnah* and *Gemara*)

chesed — loving-kindness

Chol HaMoed — the intermediate days of the Festivals of *Pesach* and *Succot*

Chumash — each of the five Books of Moses

Cohen (pl. ***Cohanim***) — Priest(s); direct descendants of Aharon — the first High Priest — along the male line

Cohen Gadol — High Priest

cubit — 48 cm. (60 cm. according to the *Chazon Ish*)

GLOSSARY

danger to a limb — for a definition see *Nishmat Avraham*, vol. 1 *Orach Chaim*, Introduction to Siman 328

dangerously ill patient — see *seriously ill patient*

Dayan — Rabbinical Judge

discomfort — for definition see *Nishmat Avraham*, vol. 1 *Orach Chaim*, Introduction to Chapter 328

Eretz Yisrael — the Land of Israel

eruv — a "*halachic* wall" constructed to enclose a city or part of it to enable carrying on *Shabbat*

ever — male organ of reproduction and urination

Gaon (***Geonim***) — highest *halachic* authorities from about the 6th-11th century; the term is also used for outstanding Torah personalities of later generations

Gedolei Hador — the Torah leaders of the generation

Gemara — Talmud

ger, (pl. ***gerim***), (f. ***giyoret***) — convert to Judaism

gesisah — dying

gilui arayot — illicit sexual relationships, including forbidden bodily contacts

gloss — annotation on the *Shulchan Aruch* by the *Rama*

gosses — one who is dying

HaGomel — an individual's blessing of thanksgiving — see *Birkat HaGomel*

halachah (pl. ***halachot***) — Jewish law(s)

hamotzi — the blessing recited over bread

hargashah — a feeling of the uterus opening or of some other internal awareness of the start of menstruation

hashavat aveidah — the *mitzvah* to return another's lost property

Hashem — God

hatafat dam brit — if, for example, a baby is born without any foreskin, and a *Brit* cannot be done, the *corona* is scratched slightly, just sufficiently for it to bleed a minute amount

Havdalah — the ceremony which marks the formal close of the Sabbath and Festivals

hefseik taharah — an internal examination performed by a woman at the end of the obligatory preliminary five-day period (or any subsequent day when she has stopped bleeding) following the beginning of menstruation. Its purpose is to establish that all bleeding and staining have completely stopped. See Siman 196 §1 for details

issur (pl. ***issurim***) — that which is forbidden

issur v'heter — a term which includes the laws concerning forbidden and permissible foods, *shechitah*, *kashrut*, *niddah*, and others covered in the *Yoreh Deah* section of the *Shulchan Aruch*

Kabbalah — Jewish mysticism

Kaddish — prayer said by the cantor or by mourners in praise of *Hashem*

karet — the "cutting off" of the soul

karut shofcha — a person whose male organ has been severed

kasher — to *halachically* cleanse and purge a vessel of the absorption of any forbidden food, including *chametz*

Kedushah — verses sanctifying *Hashem*, recited by the congregation during the repetition of the *Shemoneh Esrei*

keli rishon — literally: first vessel; a receptacle containing food which was on the fire and is as yet hot

keli sheni — literally: second vessel; a receptacle into which food from a *keli rishon* was poured

keri'ah — tearing; the obligation to tear one's garment on the demise of a close relative

ketem — bloodstain found on a woman's body, garments or bedlinen

kezayit — a measurement equivalent to the volume of an olive, 27-30 grams

Kiddush — the blessing sanctifying the Sabbath and Festivals recited over a cup of wine

kiddushin — bethrothal under the *chupah* canopy; it is the first stage of the marriage ceremony

kila'im — sowing or growing heterogenous plants in the same field, hybridization or using animals of different species that are harnessed together (*Leviticus* 19:19 and *Deuteronomy* 22:11). See also *sha'atnez*

kippah — skullcap

kosher — halachically permissible; usually refers to permissible food

lechem mishneh — two loaves of bread which are required for each of the Sabbath and Festival meals

Levi — one of the twelve sons of our forefather, Jacob. The tribe of Levi served in the Temple and had special privileges granted to them

lifnei iveir — literally: (placing a stumbling block) before the blind. However, the verse is interpreted as referring not only to physical blindness, but also includes causing another to sin

loeg larash — literally: mocking the poor; performing a *mitzvah* in the presence of a deceased. This shows disrespect for the deceased who is "poor" in that he cannot perform *mitzvot*

lulav — a palm branch; one of the four species held together on the Festival of *Succot*. The term is also used to denote all four species together

Ma'ariv — the evening prayer service

ma'aser (pl. *ma'asrot*) — after *terumah* has been set aside from produce grown in Israel, a further 10 percent of the rest is set aside and given to a *Levi*

makkah — injury, disease or growth (benign or cancerous). In the context of the laws of *niddah* it refers to bleeding from the *uterus* or *cervix* which is not due to *menstruation*

malkot — lashes. Some negative commandments carry the punishment of lashes. This, like capital punishment, is only applicable when there is a *Sanhedrin*

mamzer — bastard; child born out of certain forbidden unions

Maran — literally: the Master; the title usually reserved for the *Mechaber*

marit ha'ayin — an act is forbidden if it looks like a transgression to the eye of an onlooker even though it really is not

mavoi — cul-de-sac. An example of a *carmelit*. If an *eruv* is constructed at its opening into the road, one may carry within the *mavoi* on *Shabbat*

measure — generally accepted to be between 27 and 30 grams of solid food or 40 to 45 cc. of fluid, consumed within 9 minutes

Mechaber — *Maran* Yosef Karo, author of the *Shulchan Aruch*

melachah (pl. *melachot*) — an activity forbidden on *Shabbat* and *Yom Tov* by Torah law

met mitzvah — a deceased that has no one to arrange his burial; everyone is obliged to bury him

GLOSSARY

metzizah — the procedure of sucking out a little blood from the wound immediately after circumcision

mezuzah (pl. ***mezuzot***) — parchment upon which is written the first two paragraphs of the *Shema*; it is affixed to a doorpost

Midrash — includes many different homiletic and *halachic* expositions on the Torah, gathered from 400 to1200 CE

mikveh — pool for ritual immersion and purification

milah — Jewish ritual circumcision

minhag — a custom that a person or congregation has accepted upon itself over and above what is demanded by *Halachah*

minor illness — for the definition see *Nishmat Avraham*, vol. 1 *Orach Chaim*, Introduction to Chapter 328

minyan — a quorum of ten adult male Jews — the minimum required for communal prayer

Mishnah (***Mishnayot***) — code of basic Jewish law, enunciated by the *Tanna'im* and arranged by Rebbe Yehudah HaNasi, about 200 CE

mitzvah (pl. ***mitzvot***) — Torah or Rabbinical commandment

moch dachuk — examination cloth that is inserted into the *prozdor* immediately after the *hefseik taharah* showed that she had stopped bleeding. It is then left in until after nightfall

mohel (pl. ***mohalim***) — a qualified practitioner of Jewish circumcision

motza'ei Shabbat — after the termination of Shabbat

muktzeh — that which may not be moved on the Sabbath or Festivals

nefel — a stillborn or a baby which dies within thirty days of birth

nefesh — a person (as opposed to a fetus) with a normal life expectancy

neveilah (pl. ***nevelot***) — the corpse of an animal or bird which has not been killed by ritual slaughter

nichum aveilim — comforting mourners

niddah — a woman in a ritually impure state which lasts from the beginning of her menses, or other hormonal uterine bleeding, until after she has immersed herself in a *mikveh* at the appropriate time

non-seriously ill patient — for definition see *Nishmat Avraham*, vol. 1 *Orach Chaim*, Introduction to Chapter 328

Omer sacrifice — barley offering brought on the second day of *Pesach* see *Lev.* 23:10-13

onah benonit — it is assumed that the average menstrual cycle is thirty (or thirty-one) days; thus if *menstruation* has not started on that day, she must abstain from marital relationships on that day

onen — the term for a mourner who has lost a relative for whom he must mourn before the body has been buried; see *aninut*

o'ness — duress; that which is accidental or unavoidable — a lack of a willful act

Orach Chaim — the first of the four parts of the *Shulchan Aruch*

orlah — the fruits produced by a tree during the first three years after its planting. It is forbidden by Torah law to eat them or to have any benefit from them if the tree is planted in Israel. In the Diaspora, the *Halachah* is much more lenient

Paschal lamb — sacrifice brought on the eve of *Pesach* and eaten at the *seder* service

patsua daka — a person whose genitalia have been injured

pe'ot — the hair at the top of the sideburns, at the bottom of the cheeks and the end of the chin are called *pe'ot* (literally: the ends). Shaving each of them is a transgression of a negative commandment. Shaving all of them is a trangression of five negative commandments, each punishable by thirty-nine lashes

periah — after the foreskin has been removed, the underlying membrane is split and then turned back on itself so as to completely expose the *corona*

Pesach — the Festival of Passover celebrating the Exodus from Egypt

petichat hakever — the opening of the uterus (that is, the cervical canal)

Pidyon HaBen — redemption of a firstborn male

pikuach nefesh — life-threatening situation

posek (pl. ***poskim***) — an authoritative Torah scholar who gives rulings in matters of Jewish law

private domain — enclosed area, such as a house, courtyard or car, at least 4 *tefachim* square surrounded by partitions at least 10 *tefachim* high. Carrying to and from this to a public domain on *Shabbat* is prohibited by Torah law

proportional hour — one-twelfth of daytime. There are two opinions as to the definition of daytime — from dawn to nightfall or from sunrise to sunset (see the *Mishnah Berurah* Siman 233:4 and Siman 443:8)

prozdor — vagina (birth canal)

p'sak — *halachic* ruling

p'sik resha — an inevitable forbidden consequence of a permissible action which makes the action itself forbidden

public domain — street, highway or public square with a minimum width of 16 *cubits*, open at both ends and unroofed. According to many *poskim* a *public domain* must, in addition, be frequented by 600,000 people each day. Carrying to and from this to a *private domain* or a distance of four *amot* or more within it on *Shabbat* is prohibited by Torah law

Rabbeinu — our teacher; first used for Moses and also usually reserved for some of the *rishonim*

responsum (pl. ***responsa***) — written response by a *posek* to a question on Jewish law

rishon (pl. ***rishonim***) — Rabbinic authorities who lived from after the period of the *geonim* until the time of the *Shulchan Aruch*; 11th to 16th century

rodef — one who is attempting to take the life of another

Rosh Chodesh Av — the first day of the Jewish month of Av (about July/August)

Rosh Hashanah — the Jewish New Year

sandak — the person who holds the baby on his knees during the *brit milah*

Sanhedrin — a high court of Jewish law; it is composed of twenty-three judges. The Great Sanhedrin was made up of seventy-one judges

sechar batalah — payment for loss of earnings incurred during the performance of a *mitzvah*

seder — the order of the *Pesach* night ceremony recalling the Exodus from Egypt and the liberation from Egyptian bondage

Sefer Torah — the Scroll of the Law. It contains the five Books of the Torah which Moses received on Mount Sinai and transmitted to the Jewish people

Selichot — prayers of repentance and supplication

Sephardi(m) — Jews of Spanish or Middle Eastern origin

seriously ill patient — for definition see *Nishmat Avraham*, vol. 1 *Orach Chaim*, Introduction to Chapter 328

GLOSSARY

Shabbat — the Sabbath

Shacharit — the morning service

shatnez — a mixture of wool and linen. The Torah fobids one to wear or cover oneself with a garment containing such a mixture (*Leviticus* 19:19 and *Deuteronomy* 22:11). For details see *Rambam, Kila'im* Ch. 10 and *Shulchan Aruch, Yoreh Deah*, Siman 298-304. See also *kila'im*

Shechinah — the Holy Presence

shechitah — ritual slaughtering of an animal or bird

shehakol — a general blessing made before eating or drinking foods and drinks that have no specific blessing

shehecheyanu — blessing made on new fruits and garments, on Festivals and on other joyous occasions

Shema — "Hear " (*Deuteronomy* 6:5), the opening word of the fundamental prayer in which a Jew proclaims twice daily the unity of *Hashem* and the acceptance of Heavenly kingship

Shemittah — the seventh year of a seven-year cycle. The Torah commands that the Land of Israel remain fallow in that year and forbids plowing, sowing and other acts of agriculture. Since the exile, the obligation to keep *Shemittah* is Rabbinic

Shemoneh Esrei — the eighteen blessings; the principal prayer said silently three times daily; also known as the *Amidah*

sheretz (pl. *sheratzim*) — loosely translated as a creepy or teeming creature. There are water *sheratzim*, such as crabs, eels and worms; there are those found on land, such as toads, rodents, lizards, snails, ants and worms; and there are those that fly such as flies and bees. See *Leviticus* Chapter 11

shevut — Rabbinic decree forbidding an act on *Shabbat* (or *Yom Tov*) which is permitted by the Torah

shivah — the seven-day mourning period following the death of a close relative

shlita — a Hebrew acronym for *sheyichyeh l'yamim tovim ve'aruchim*, meaning: may he live a good and long life; it is used after mentioning the name of a living Torah scholar

shochet — ritual slaughterer

shofar — ram's horn, sounded on *Rosh Hashanah*

shogeg — a person who commits an act of transgression because he has forgotten that it is prohibited

shoteh — someone who is so mentally impaired as to be irresponsible for his actions. He is exempt from all *mitzvot*

shul — synagogue

softumah latseit — if a corpse is in a room, anyone in the room or entering it becomes *tamei* by Torah law. In addition, all the rooms and corridors through which the body will be taken on the way to burial will also have the same *halachah* as the room even if the doors and windows are presently closed, since he is destined to pass through them.

sotah — a woman who is suspected of adultery

stam yenam — any wine that was made or touched by a non-Jew even if part of it has not been poured as a libation

Succot — the Festival of Tabernacles

tahor — ritually clean

tallit — prayer shawl with four fringes

tamei (f. *temei'ah*) — ritually unclean

Tammuz — the eighth Jewish month (about July)

Tanach — the Books of the Torah, Prophets and Sacred Writings

Tanna (pl. ***Tanna'im***) — Sage(s) from the *Mishnaic* period

tefach (pl. ***tefachim***) — a measurement of 8 cm. (9.6 cm. according to the *Chazon Ish*)

tefillin — phylacteries — worn on the arm and the head during the weekday morning service

terumah — tithe set aside from all produce grown in Israel and given to a *Cohen*

tevel — untithed produce of the Land of Israel

Tishah B'Av — the ninth of the month of Av (about August), the day on which both Temples were destroyed

Tosefta — collection of *Beraitot* arranged according to the order of the *Mishnah*

treifah (pl. ***treifot***) — a bird or animal that may not be eaten because of a blemish. The term is applied also to a person with a severe internal injury or disease who is expected to live less than a year

tumah — ritual uncleanliness

tumat Cohen — ritual uncleanliness caused to a *Cohen* who touches or is under the same roof as a corpse

tumat ledah — ritual uncleanliness due to childbirth, even if there is no bleeding

tumat met — ritual uncleanliness caused by a corpse

tumtum — baby whose external genitalia are covered by a sac so that its sex is indeterminate until the sac is excised

verapo yerapei — "And he shall surely heal" (*Exodus* 21:19)

Vidui — confession of one's sins

yad soledet — heat from which the hand would recoil

yahrzeit — anniversary of the death of a close relative

yibum — the *mitzvah* of Levirate marriage. The Torah commands one to marry the widow of his brother who passed away childless

yichud — seclusion of a man with a woman who is not his mother, wife, daughter or sister; the transgression applies to both the man and the woman

Yom Kippur — the Day of Atonement

Yom Tov — Jewish Festival

zt"l — a Hebrew acronym: *zecher tzaddik levrachah,* meaning: may the memory of a righteous person be for a blessing

MEDICAL TERMS

aorta — main artery of the body
angiography — see *cerebral angiography*
anus — external opening of the *rectum*
apnea — complete cessation of breathing
bacterial endocarditis — bacterial infection of one or more valves of the heart causing serious disease and even death. In certain situations where bacteria may, as a result of some medical procedure, enter the bloodstream and infect the heart valves, prophylactic antibiotic treatment is given
basal ganglia — are part of the brain; they lie at the base of the *cerebrum* and help smooth out movements
bilirubin — pigment produced when the liver processes certain waste products. A high level causes *jaundice*, a yellow discoloration of the skin
brainstem auditory evoked response — an objective test of electrical functioning of the brainstem
cerebral angiography — a test in which radio-opaque dye is injected into the *aorta* to fill all four vessels to the brain to show the blood flow to the brain
cerebrum — largest part of the brain; it consists of two halves, the right and left cerebral hemispheres, and is responsible for all the higher brain functions
cervical canal — a narrow canal within the *cervix* with an internal diameter of about three millimeters
cervical cerclage — a procedure to close an incompetent *cervix* with stitches to prevent a miscarriage
cervical spine — that part of the spine that lies in the neck
cervix — neck of the *uterus*, it extends and opens into the *vagina*
cholecystostomy — the procedure whereby a tube is inserted to drain the contents of the gall bladder to outside the body
coitus — intercourse
colostomy — artificial opening of the large intestine onto the abdominal wall; see also *ostomy*
contrast medium — a radio-opaque substance that allows radiographic visualization of a structure, for example, the coronary arteries, the *renal* and *gastro-intestinal tracts* or the *uterus* and *fallopian tubes*
corona — base of the *glans*; before circumcision, the foreskin extends from the *corona* to cover the *glans*
corpus luteum — formed from a *follicle* after it has released its egg; see *follicles*
cyanosed — blue discoloration of the skin due to a lack of oxygen
DNR — do not resuscitate
diabetes insipidus — a disease characterized by the excessive production of urine due

to the inadequate production of the antidiuretic hormone or to the failure of the kidneys to respond to it. The hormone is formed in the *hypothalamus* and stored in, and subsequently released by, the *pituitary gland*

EEG (*electroencephalogram*) — a diagnostic test which measures the electrical activity of the brain (brain waves) using highly sensitive recording equipment attached to the scalp

endometrium — inner lining of the *uterus*; it is shed and replaced at each menstrual cycle

enzyme — a protein molecule produced by living organisms that catalyses (speeds up) chemical reactions

epispadias — a congenital defect whereby the *meatus* is at the upper surface of the male organ

esophagus — gullet

fallopian tubes — two tubes, each attached to one side of the upper part of the *uterus*, into which the egg is released from the *ovary* at *ovulation*

fibrillate — a disorganised chaotic contraction of the ventricle of the heart preventing effective ejection of blood from it to the rest of the body

fibroid — fibro-muscular growth in the *uterus*

follicles — fluid-filled cavities in the *ovary*, each containing an egg. At *ovulation*, one of these ruptures, releasing the egg into the *fallopian tube,* then closes to form the *corpus luteum*

gastro-intestinal — pertaining to the stomach and intestines

gastrostomy — the procedure whereby a tube is put through the abdominal wall into the stomach, for artificial feeding (see also *PEG*, below)

glans — cone shaped end of the male organ

hematuria — bloody urine

hemorrhoids — piles

hepatitis — viral infection of the liver

homeostasis — the tendency of biological systems to maintain relatively constant conditions in the body while continuously interacting with and adjusting to changes originating within or without the system

hymen — membrane that partially covers the opening into the *vagina* in the virgin

hypospadias — a congenital defect whereby the *meatus* is at the undersurface of the male organ

hypothermia — body temperature below 35 degrees centigrade

hysterectomy — surgical removal of the *uterus*. **Total hysterectomy** — removal of body of *uterus* together with the *cervix*. **Subtotal hysterectomy** — removal of body of *uterus* only

hysterosalpingography — X-ray examination of the *uterus* and *fallopian tubes* after injection of a *contrast medium* via the *cervix*

hysteroscopy — examination of the uterine cavity through a thin instrument, about one-third of an inch (about 8-9mm) in diameter, inserted via the *cervix*

ileostomy — artificial opening of the small intestine onto the abdominal wall; see also *ostomy*

jaundice — see *bilirubin*

jejunostomy — the procedure whereby a tube is put through the abdominal wall into the beginning of the small intestine (the jejunum), for artificial feeding

GLOSSARY

lactation — secretion of milk

limbic system — collective term denoting an array of structures near the edge (limbus) of the *cerebral hemisphere*, connected to the *hypothalamus*. Exerts an important influence upon the endocrine and autonomic motor systems

meatus — opening of the *urethra* at the tip of the male organ

menarche — beginning of menstrual function

menorrhagia — excessive uterine bleeding during *menstruation*; the period of flow is of greater than the usual duration

menses — menstrual bleeding

menstruation — cyclic, physiologic, monthly *uterine* bleeding caused by the sloughing off of the *endometrium*

myoma — see *fibroid*

naso-gastric tube — tube put into the stomach via the nose, for artificial feeding

nephrostomy — insertion of tube through the patient's back into the kidney; urine can then drain from the kidney to the outside

ostomy — operation to create an opening from an area inside the body to the outside

ovary — female organ which contains the eggs

ovulation — the release of an egg from the *ovary* into the *fallopian tube*

Pap smear — brush sampling from the birth canal, *cervix* and *cervical canal*

PEG — percutaneous entero-gastrostomy — the insertion of a feeding tube via the abdominal wall into the stomach or small intestine (see also *gastrostomy*)

penis — male organ

pessary — an instrument placed in the *vagina* to support the *uterus* or *rectum*

phlebotomy — bloodletting

pituitary gland — an endocrine gland lying within the skull at the base of the brain. It stores and releases the antidiuretic hormone, among its other functions

placebo — a dummy treatment administered to the control group in a controlled clinical trial so that the specific and nonspecific effects of the experimental treatment can be distinguished; the experimental treatment must produce better results than the placebo in order to be considered effective

rectum — the last section of the large intestine; it opens into the *anus*

sonography — ultrasound

SPECT scan — single photon emission computed tomography. A test which creates very clear three-dimensional pictures of a major organ such as the brain. It can be used to see how blood flows in certain regions of the brain

stem cells — the first cells in the new embryo; they have the ability to both replicate and differentiate, and thus produce specialized cells for all the tissues and organs in the body

tenaculum — a type of forceps used to hold the *cervix* in place

thalamus — it lies at the base of the *cerebrum* and organizes sensory messages to and from the *cerebral cortex* (of the brain)

trachea — windpipe

tracheostomy — insertion of a tube into the *trachea* to enable the patient to breathe

transcranial Doppler ultrasonography — a non-invasive procedure that enables the viewing of blood flow to the brain

triage — sorting out and classification of casualties of war or other disaster, to determine priority of need and proper place of treatment

uterus — womb

urethra — a tube leading from the bladder to the outside through which urine is voided. In a woman it runs from the bladder to the *vulva*. In males it runs from the bladder to the *meatus*

urinary catheter — tube inserted into the bladder to enable urination

vagina — female organ of sexual intercourse; birth canal

vulva — the external area of the female genitalia into which the birth canal and *urethra* open

BIBLIOGRAPHY

Achiezer — Rav Chaim Ozer Grodzinsky, d. 1940
Ahavat Chesed — see *Mishnah Berurah*
Ari z"l — Rav Yitzchak Luria, d. 1572
Aruch HaShulchan — Rav Yechiel Michel Epstein, d.1908
Aruch LaNer — see *Binyan Tzion*
Atsei HaLevanon — Rav Yehudah Leib Tziralson, d. 1941
Atsei Levonah — Rav Nissan Aronson, 19th century
Avnei Miluim — see *Ketsot HaChoshen*
Avnei Nezer — also *Eglei Tal;* Rav Avraham Bornstein, d. 1910
Bach (Bayit Chadash) — Rav Yoel Sirkes, d. 1640
Badei HaShulchan — Rav Shraga Feivel Cohen, contemporary
Ba'er Heitev — Rav Yehudah Ashkenazi, d. 1748
Bahag (Ba'al Halachot Gedolot) — the author of the *Halachot Gedolot;* identity unknown. According to various *rishonim*, between the 6th and 10th centuries
Bavli — the Babylonian Talmud, compiled by Ravina and Rav Ashi, 5th century
Bedek HaBayit — see *Shulchan Aruch*
Be'er Esek — Rav Shabtai Be'er, 17th century
Be'er HaGolah — Rav Moshe Rivkesh, d. 1671
Be'er Moshe — Rav Moshe Stern, contemporary
Be'er Sheva — Rav Yisachar Eilenberg, d. 1623
Beit Hillel — Rav Hillel bar Naftali Hertz, d. 1690
Beit Lechem Yehudah — Rav Tzvi Hersh, 18th century
Beit Meir — Rav Meir Posner, d. 1807
Beit She'arim — Rav Amram Blum, d. 1906
Beit Shmuel — Rav Shmuel Faivish, d. 1694
Beit Yitzchak — Rav Yitzchak Yehudah Shmulkes, d. 1906
Beit Yosef — commentary on the *Tur* by the author of the *Shulchan Aruch*, Maran Yosef Karo, d. 1575
Ben Ish Chai — also *responsa Rav Pe'alim;* Rav Yosef Chaim of Baghdad, d. 1909
Beur Halachah — see *Mishnah Berurah*
Binyan Shlomo — Rav Shlomo HaCohen of Vilna, printed 1889
Binyan Tzion — also *Aruch LaNer;* Rav Yaakov Ettlinger, d. 1871
Birkei Yosef — see *Chida*
Chacham Tzvi — Rav Tzvi Hirsch Ashkenazi, d. 1718
Chafetz Chaim — see *Mishnah Berurah*
Chaim BeYad — Rav Chaim Palaggi, d. 1869
Chatam Sofer — Rav Moshe Sofer Shreiber, d. 1839

Chavalim BaNe'imim — Rav Yehudah Leib Graubart, d. 1938
Chavot Da'at — also *Derech HaChaim;* Rav Yaakov Lorberbaum, d. 1832
Chavot Yair — Rav Yair Chaim Bacharach, d. 1702
Chayei Adam — also *Chochmat Adam* and *Nishmat Adam;* Rav Avraham Danzig, d. 1820
Chazon Ish — Rav Avraham Yeshayah Karelitz, d. 1953
Chazon LaMoed — Rav Chanoch Zundel Grossberg, d. 1977
Chazon Yechezkel — Rav Yechezkel Abramsky, d. 1975
Chelkat Mechokek — Rav Moshe Lima, d. 1658
Chelkat Yaakov — Rav Mordechai Yaakov Breish, d. 1977
Chelkat Yoav — Rav Yoav Yehoshua Weingarten, d. 1923
Chesed LeAvraham — Rav Avraham Teomim, d. 1877
Cheshev HaEphod — Rav Chanoch Dov Padwa, d. 2000
Chida — also *Birkei Yosef;* Rav Chaim Yosef David Azulai, d. 1806
Chikrei Lev — Rav Yosef Refael Chazzan, d. 1820
Chinuch — author unknown; probably 13th century
Chochmat Adam — see *Chayei Adam*
Chochmat Shlomo — also *Elef Lecha Shlomo, Tuv Taam VeDa'at* and *Mei Niddah;* Rav Shlomo Kluger, d. 1869
Chok Yaakov — also *Minchat Yaakov, Shevut Yaakov, Torat HaShelamim*; Rav Yaakov Reisher, d. 1733
Choshen Mishpat — the fourth of the four parts of the *Shulchan Aruch*
Chovot HaLevavot — Rabbeinu Bachyei beRav Yosef Ibn Pakuda, d. 1161
Da'at Sofer — Rav Akiva Sofer, d. 1959
Da'at Kedoshim — Rav Avraham David Werman of Butasht, d. 1841
Da'at Torah — see *Maharsham*
Dagul MeRevavah — see *Noda BiYehudah*
Darchei Moshe — see *Rama*
Darchei Teshuvah — Rav Zvi Hirsch Shapira of Munkatsch, d. 1913
Derech HaChaim — also *Chavot Da'at;* Rav Yaakov Lorberbaum of Lissa, 19th century
Derishah — Rav Yehoshua Falk, d. 1614
Dina DeChayei — see *Knesset HaGedolah*
Divrei Chaim — Rav Chaim Halberstam of Sanz, d. 1875
Divrei Chamudot — also *Tosfot YomTov* and *Ma'adanei Yom Tov;* Rav Yom Tov Lipman Heller, d. 1654
Divrei Malkiel — Rav Malkiel Tzvi HaLevi Tennenbaum, d. 1910
Dovev Mesharim — Rav Dov Berish Weidenfeld, d. 1966
D'var Shmuel — Rav Shmuel Abohav, d. 1694
D'var Yehoshua — Rav Yehoshua Menachem Mendel Ahrenberg, d. 1975
Eglei Tal — see *Avnei Nezer*
Elef HaMagen — Rav Meshulam Finkelstein, early-20th century
Elef Lecha Shlomo — also *Chochmat Shlomo, Tuv Taam VeDa'at* and *Mei Niddah*; Rav Shlomo Kluger, d. 1869
Eliyah Rabbah — Rav Eliyahu Shapira, d. 1712

BIBLIOGRAPHY

Encyclopedia Talmudit — Talmudic Encyclopedia, digest of *halachic* literature and Jewish law from the *Tannaitic* period to the present time. Published by Yad HaRav Herzog, Jerusalem
Even HaEzer — third volume of the *Shulchan Aruch*
Gaon of Tshubin — see *Dovev Mesharim*
Gesher HaChaim — Rav Yechiel Michel Tukechinsky, d. 1951
Gilyon Maharsha — Rav Shlomo Eiger (the son of *Rav Akiva Eiger*), d. 1852
Ginat Veradim — Rav Avraham HaLevi, d. 1730
Gra — Rav Eliyahu ben Shlomo Zalman, the Gaon of Vilna, d. 1797
Ha'amek She'elah — Rav Naftali Tzvi Yehudah Berlin (Netziv), d. 1892
HaEshkol — Rabbeinu Avraham ben Rabbeinu Yitzchak of Narbona, d. 1159
Hafla'ah — Rav Pinchas HaLevi Ish Horowitz, d. 1805
Hagahot Maimoniot — Rabbeinu Meir HaCohen, a student of the Maharam of Rotenberg (who also had the same name), d. 1298
Hagahot Mordechai — author unknown; probably 14th century
Halachos Niddah — Rav Shimon Eider, contemporary
Halachot Ketanot — Rav Yaakov Chagiz, d. 1764
Har Tzvi — Rav Tzvi Pesach Frank, d. 1960
Harei Besamim — Rav Aryeh Leibish Horowitz, d.1909
Ibn Ezra — Rabbeinu Avraham ibn Ezra, d. 1164
Igrot Moshe — see *Rav Moshe Feinstein*
Ikrei HaDat — Rav Daniel Terni, late-18th early-19th century
Imrei Yosher — Rav Meir Arik, d. 1926
Issur VeHeter — Rabbeinu Yonah Ashkenazi, d. 1504
Itur — Rabbeinu Yitzchak ben Abba Mari, d. 1193
Kaf HaChaim — Rav Yaakov Chaim Sofer, d. 1938
Kalkelet Shabbat — see *Tiferet Yisrael*
Kapot Temarim — see *Tosefet Yom HaKippurim*
Kenei Bosem — Rav Meir Brandsdorfer, contemporary
Kesef Mishneh — see *Shulchan Aruch*
Ketav Sofer — Rav Avraham Shmuel Binyamin Sofer, d. 1872
Ketsei HaMateh — Rav Chaim Tzvi Ehrenreich, d. 1937
Ketsot HaChoshen — also *Avnei Miluim*; Rav Aryeh Leib HaCohen Heller, d. 1813
Ketsot HaShulchan — Rav Avraham Chaim Na'eh, d. 1954
Kitzur Shulchan Aruch — Rav Shlomo Ganzfried, d. 1885
Knesset HaGedolah — Rav Chaim Benveniste, d. 1673
Kol Bo — Rabbeinu Aaron ben Yaakov HaCohen from Luneil, d. 1334
Kol Bo Al Aveilut — Rav Yekutiel Yehudah Greenwald, d. 1955
Korban HaEidah — Rav David Frenkel, d. 1762
Korban Netanel — Rav Netanel Weil, d. 1769
Koret HaBrit — Rav Eliyahu Posek, 20th century
Kovetz He'arot — see *Rav Wasserman*
Kreiti U'Pleiti — Rav Yehonatan Eybeschutz, d. 1764
Lechem VeSimlah — see *Kitzur Shulchan Aruch*

Lev Aryeh — Rav Aryeh Lev Grossnass, d. 1997
Levush — Rav Mordechai Yaffe, d. 1612
Levush Mordechai — Rav Moshe Mordechai Epstein, d. 1944
Levushei Mordechai — Rav Mordechai Leib Winkler, d. 1932
Ma'adanei Yom Tov — also *Tosfot YomTov* and *Divrei Chamudot*; Rav Yom Tov Lipman Heller, d. 1654
Ma'avar Yabok — Rav Aharon Berechya, d. 1639
Mabit — Rav Moshe Mitrani, d. 1580
Machatzit HaShekel — Rav Shmuel Nata HaLevy Kolin, d. 1807
Machazeh Avraham — Rav Avraham Menachem HaLevi Steinberg, d. 1928
Machazeh Eliyahu — Rav Pesach Eliyahu Falk, contemporary
Magen Avraham — Rav Avraham Abele Gombiner, d. 1682
Maggid Mishneh — Rabbeinu Vidal de Tolosha, d. mid-14th century
Maharam MeLublin — Rav Meir of Lublin, d. 1616
Maharam Mintz — Rabbeinu Moshe Mintz, d. 1473
Maharam Shick — Rav Moshe Shick, d. 1879
Maharash Engel — Rav Shmuel Engel, d. 1934
Maharatz Chayot — Rav Tzvi Hirsch Chajes, d. 1855
Mahari Assad — Rav Yehudah Assad, d. 1865
Mahari Shtief — Rav Yonatan Shtief, d. 1958
Maharik — Rabbeinu Yosef Kolon, d. 1480
Maharil — Rav Yaakov ben Moshe Mulin HaLevy, d. 1427
Maharil Diskin — Rav Yehoshua Yehudah Leib Diskin, d. 1898
Maharashdam — Rav Shmuel Di Modina, mid-16th century
Maharsha — Rav Shmuel Eliezer Eidels, d. 1631
Maharshal — also *Yam Shel Shlomo*; Rav Shlomo Luria, d. 1573
Maharsham — also *Da'at Torah*; Rav Shalom Mordechai HaCohen Shwadron, d. 1911
Marcheshet — Rav Chanoch Henoch Eigish, d. 20th century
Margaliot HaYam — Rav Reuven Margoliot, d. 1971
Mateh Ephraim — Rav Ephraim Zalman Margoliot, d. 1828
Mateh Levi — Rav Mordechai HaLevi Horowitz, d. late-19th century
Mateh Yehonatan — also *Urim veTumin, Kreiti U'Pleiti*; Rav Yehonatan Eybeschutz, d. 1764
Mei Niddah — also *Chochmat Shlomo, Tuv Taam VeDa'at* and *Elef Lecha Shlomo*; Rav Shlomo Kluger, d. 1869
Meiri — Rabbeinu Menachem ben Rabbeinu Shlomo, d. 1315
Mekor Mayim Chaim — Rav Yaakov Meir Padwa of Brisk, d. 1851
Melamed LeHo'il — Rav David Tzvi Hoffman, d. 1922
Meshech Chochmah — also *Or Same'ach*; Rav Meir Simchah HaCohen of Dvinsk, d. 1925
Metzudat David — Rav David Feldman, commentary on the *Kitsur Shulchan Aruch*, d. 1886
Metzudat Tsion — Rav David Feldman, commentary on the *Kitsur Shulchan Aruch*, d. 1886
Midrash — expositions on the Torah

Minchat Chinuch — Rav Yosef Babad, d. 1877
Minchat Elazar — Rav Chaim Elazar Shapira of Munkatsch, d. 1937
Minchat Shlomo — Rav Shlomo Zalman Auerbach, d. 1995. There are two different editions of volumes two and three. The תנינא edition has vols. 2 and 3 bound together; the other has vols. 2 and 3 each bound separately.
Minchat Yaakov — also *ChokYaakov*, *Shevut Yaakov*, *Torat HaShelamim*; Rav Yaakov Reisher, d. 1733
Minchat Yitzchak — Rav Yitzchak Yaakov Weiss, d. 1989
Mishkenot Yaakov — Rav Yaakov of Karlin, d. 1845
Mishnah — code of laws transmitted orally through the generations until arranged in its present form by *Rebbe Yehudah HaNasi* about 200 CE
Mishnah Berurah — also *Ahavat Chesed*, *Beur Halachah*, *Chafetz Chaim;* Rav Yisrael Meir HaCohen, d. 1933
Mishnah Rishonah — Rav Ephraim Yitzchak, d. 1843
Mishneh LaMelech — also *Parashat Derachim*; Rav Yehudah Rozanis, d. 1727
Mishpetei Uziel — Rav Ben Zion Meir Chai Uziel, d. 1953
Mordechai — Rabbeinu Mordechai HaCohen Ashkenazi, d. 1298
Nachal Eshkol — Rav Tzvi Binyamin Auerbach, d. 1778
Nachal HaBrit — Rav Asher Inshel Katz, 20th century
Nachalat Shivah — Rav Shmuel HaLevy, d. 1681
Nachalat Tzvi — see *Pitchei Teshuvah*
Nahar Mitzrayim — Rav Rafael Aharon, d. 1929
Nefesh HaChaim — Rav Chaim of Volozhin, d. 1821
Nekudot HaKesef — see *Shach*
Nimukei HaGrib — Rav Yehudah Bachrach, d. 1846
Nimukei Yosef — Rabbeinu Yosef Chaviva, d. 1400
Nishmat Adam — see *Chayei Adam*
Noda BiYehudah — also *Dagul MeRevavah* and *Tzlach*; Rav Yechezkel HaLevi Segal Landau, d. 1793
Ollelot Ephraim — Rav Shlomo Ephraim Luntshitz, d. 1619
Oneg Yom Tov — Rav Refael Yom Tov Lipman Halperin, d. 1878
Or HaChaim — Rav Chaim ibn Atar, d. 1743
Or Same'ach — see *Meshech Chochmah*
Or Zarua — Rabbeinu Itzchak ben Moshe, d. 1260
Orach Chaim — the first of the four parts of the *Shulchan Aruch*
Orach Mishor — Rav Yochanan Karmanitsar, 20th century
Orchot Chaim — Rav Nachman Kahana of Spinka, d. 1900 and Rav Shalom Mordechai HaCohen Shwadron, d. 1911
Ot Chaim VeShalom — see *Minchat Elazar*
Otzar HaPoskim — contemporary compendium of *responsa* on *Shulchan Aruch Even HaEzer*
Pachad Yitzchak — Rav Yitzchak Lamperonti, Rabbi and physician, d. 1755
Panim Meirot — Rav Meir Eisenstadt, d. 1744
Parashat Derachim — see *Mishneh LaMelech*
Perishah — Rav Yehoshua Falk, d. 1614

Petach HaDevir — Rav Chaim Binyamin Pontremoli, late-19th century
Piskei Tosafot — author either the *Rosh* or his son the *Tur*
Pitchei Teshuvah — Rav Avraham Tzvi Hirsch Eisenstadt, d. 1868
Pleiti — *Kreiti U'Pleiti,* also *Mateh Yehonatan, Urim VeTumin*; Rav Yehonatan Eybeschutz, d. 1764
Pnei Moshe — Rav Moshe Margaliot, d. 1781
Pnei Yehoshua — *responsa*, Rav Yehoshua of Cracow, d. 1647 (grandfather of the *Pnei Yehoshua* below)
Pnei Yehoshua — commentary on the *Talmud*; Rav Yaakov Yehoshua Falk, d. 1756
Pri Chadash — Rav Hizkeya ben David DiSilva, d. 1698
Pri Megadim — Rav Yosef Teomim, 1792
Ra'ah — Rabbeinu Aharon ben Yosef HaLevi, d. 1300
Ra'avad — Rabbeinu Avraham ben David, d. 1198
Rabbeinu Bachya — Rabbeinu Bachya ben Asher Ibn Halawa, d. 1338
Rabbeinu Chananel — d. 1053
Rabbeinu Tam — Rabbeinu Yaakov ben Meir, d. 1171
Rabbeinu Yonah — Rabbeinu Yonah ben Avraham Girondi, d. 1263
Radbaz — Rabbeinu David ben Shlomo ibn Zimra, d. 1574
Rama — also *Darchei Moshe*; Rav Moshe Isserles, author of the *glosses* on the *Shulchan Aruch*, d. 1572
Ramatz — Rav Meir Tzvi Veitmeir, d. 1874
Rambam — Rabbeinu Moshe ben Maimon (Maimonides), d. 1204
Ramban — Rabbeinu Moshe ben Nachman (Nachmanides), d. 1270
Ran — Rabbeinu Nissim ben Reuven Gerondi, d. 1380
Rashba — Rabbeinu Shlomo ben Avraham Adereth, d. 1310
Rashbetz — Rabbeinu Shimon ben Tsemach Duran, author of *responsa Tashbetz*, d. 1443
Rashi — Rabbeinu Shlomo Yitzchaki, d. 1105
Rav Shlomo Zalman Auerbach — author *Minchat Shlomo*, d. 1995
Rav MiBartinura — Rav Ovadiah of Bartinura, d.1528
Rav Chaim of Brisk — Rav Chaim HaLevi Soloveitchik, the Brisker Rav, d. 1918
Rav Chaim of Volozhin — d. 1821
Rav Yehonatan Eybeschutz — also *Mateh Yonatan, Urim VeTumin, Kreiti U'Pleiti;* d. 1764
Rav Eider — Rav Shimon Eider, contemporary
Rav Eliashiv — Rav Yosef Shalom Eliashiv, contemporary
Rav Yonah Emanuel — d. 2002
Rav Moshe Feinstein — author *Igrot Moshe*, d. 1986
Rav Achai Gaon — one of the early *geonim*, author of the *She'iltot*, d. 752
Rav Hai Gaon — one of the *geonim*, d.1038
Rav Natronai Gaon — one of the early *geonim*, 8th century
Rav Sa'adiah Gaon — one of the *geonim*, d. 942
Rav Chaim Ozer Grodzinsky — see *Achiezer*
Rav Aryeh Lev Grossnass — author of *responsa Lev Aryeh*, d. 1997
Rav Henkin — Rav Yosef Eliyahu Henkin, d. 1973

BIBLIOGRAPHY ❏ 395

Rav Herzog — Rav Yitzchak Isaac HaLevy Herzog, first Chief Rabbi of Israel, d. 1959
Rav Samson Rafael Hirsch — d. 1888
Rav Jakobovits — Lord Immanuel Jakobovits, Chief Rabbi of Great Britain and the Commonwealth, d. 2000
Rav Kanievsky — Rav Shemaryahu Yosef Chaim Kanievsky, contemporary
Rav Kapach — Rav Yosef Kapach, d. 2000
Rav Kasher — Rav Menachem Kasher, d. 1983
Rav Shlomo Kluger — see *Chochmat Shlomo*
Rav Kook — Rav Avraham Yitzchak HaCohen Kook, former Chief Rabbi of Palestine under the British Mandate, d. 1935
Rav Nebenzahl — Rav Avigdor HaLevi Nebenzahl, contemporary
Rav Yehoshua Y. Neuwirth — contemporary, author of *Shemirat Shabbat KeHilchatah*
Rav Chaim Palaggi — d. 1869
Rav Pe'alim — *responsa*, see *Ben Ish Chai*
Rav Yeshayah Pick — contemporary of the *Noda BiYehudah*, 18th century
Rav Ben Tzion Abba Shaul — d. 1996
Rav Scheinberg — Rav Chaim Pinchas Scheinberg, contemporary
Rav Tukechinsky — Rav Yechiel Michel Tukechinsky, d. 1954
Rav Unterman — Rav Isser Yehudah Unterman, former Chief Rabbi of Israel, d. 1976
Rav Waldenberg — Rav Eliezer Yehudah Waldenberg, contemporary
Rav Elchanan Wasserman — killed by the Nazis, 1940
Rav Weiss — see *Minchat Yitzchak*
Rav Wosner — see *Shevet HaLevi*
Rav Ovadiah Yosef — contemporary
Rav Zilberstein — Rav Yitzchak Zilberstein, contemporary
Raza — Rabbeinu Zerachiah Gerondi, d. 1186
Rebbe — Rebbe Yehudah HaNasi (the prince) the compiler of the *Mishnah*; lived about 200 CE
Rebbe Akiva Eiger — d. 1838
Rif — Rabbeinu Yitzchak HaCohen Alfasi, d. 1103
Ritva — Rabbeinu Yom Tov Ashbili, d. mid-14th century
Rivash — Rabbeinu Yitzchak ben Sheshet, d. 1407
Rosh — Rabbeinu Asher ben Yechiel, d. 1327
Ruach Chaim — Rav Chaim Palachi, d. 1869
Sdei Chemed — Rav Chaim Chizkiah HaLevi Medini, d. 1904
Sefer Chassidim — Rabbeinu Yehudah ben Shmuel HaChasid, d. 1217
Sefer HaBrit — Rav Moshe Bunim Pirutinsky, contemporary
Sefer HaKovetz — Rav Menachem Nachum Trebitsch, d. 1847
Sefer HaMachriya — see *Tosfot Rid*
Sema (Sefer Meirot Einayim) — Rav Yehoshua Falk Katz, d. 1614
Semag (Sefer Mitzvot Gadol) — Rabbeinu Moshe of Coucy, one of the early *Tosafot*, early-13th century
Seridei Eish — Rav Yechiel Yaakov Weinberg, d. 1965
Sha'agat Aryeh — Rav Aryeh Lev Ginsburg, d. 1785
Sha'ar Mishpat — Rav Yisrael Iser Wolff, d. early-19th century

Sha'arei Teshuvah — Rav Chaim Mordechai Margolis, d. 1820
Sha'arei Tevilah — Rav Yechiel Michal Stern, contemporary
Shach — Rav Shabbtai HaCohen, d. 1662
She'arim Metzuyanim BaHalachah — Rav Shlomo Zalman Braun, d. 1995
She'elat Shalom — Rav Yeshaya Pick-Berlin, d. 1799
She'elat Yavetz — see *Yavetz*
She'iltot — Rav Achai Gaon of Shabcha, d. 752
Shemirat Shabbat KeHilchatah — Rav Yehoshua Y. Neuwirth, contemporary
Shevet HaLevi — Rav Shmuel HaLevi Wosner, contemporary
Shevet Yehudah — Rav Yehudah Eiyash, 18th century
Shevut Yaakov — also *Minchat Yaakov, Chok Yaakov, Torat HaShelamim*; Rav Yaakov Reisher, d. 1733
Shibbolei HaLeket — Rabbeinu Zidkiyahu ben R' Avraham the physician, 13th century
Shitah Mekubetset — Rav Betzalel ben Avraham Ashkenazi, d. 1564
Shiurei Knesset HaGedolah — also *Knesset HaGedolah*; Rav Chaim Benveniste, d. 1673
Shivat Tzion — Rav Shmuel Landau, d. 1832
Sh'lah — Rav Yeshaya HaLevy Horowitz, d. 1630
Shoel U'Meshiv — Rav Yosef Shaul HaLevi Natanson, d. 1875
Shulchan Aruch — *The Code of Jewish Law* by *Maran* Yosef Karo, d. 1575
Shulchan Aruch HaRav — Rav Shneur Zalman of Liadi, d. 1813
Shulchan Gavohah — Rav Yosef Molcho, printed 1764
Sidrei Taharah — Rav Elchanan Ashkenazi, late-18th century
Taharat HaBayit — also *Yabia Omer* and *Yechaveh Da'at*; Rav Ovadiah Yosef, contemporary
Taharat HaMayim — Rav Nisan Talushkin, 20th century
Taharat Yisrael — Rav Yisrael Yitzchak, mid-19th century
Talmud Bavli — the Oral Law, as it appears in the work compiled by Ravina and Rav Ashi, in the 5th century in Bavel
Talmud Yerushalmi — the Oral Law, as it appears in the work compiled by Rebbe Yochanan, in the 4th century in *Eretz Yisrael*
Tashbetz — *responsa*; Rabbeinu Shimon ben Tsemach Duran, d. 1443
Taz — Rav David HaLevi, d. 1667
Tehillah LeDavid — Rav David Ortenberg, d. 1910
Teshurat Shai — Rav Shlomo Yehudah Tabak, d. 1908
Teshuvah MeAhavah — Rav Elazar Flaklish, d. 1825
Tevilat Keilim — Rav Tzvi Cohen, contemporary
Tiferet Yaakov — Rav Yaakov Tzvi Shapira, early-20th century
Tiferet Yisrael — Rav Yisrael Lipshitz, d. 1866
Tirosh VeYitzhar — Rav Tzvi Yechezkel Michalzon, killed in Holocaust
Torah Lishmah — probably by the *Ben Ish Chai*
Torah Sheleimah — Rav Menachem Kasher, d. 1983
Torah Temimah — Rav Baruch HaLevi Epstein (son of the *Aruch HaShulchan*), killed by the Nazis, 1942

BIBLIOGRAPHY

Torat Chesed — Rav Shneur Zalman, Lublin, d. 1902
Torat HaShelamim — also *Minchat Yaakov, Shevut Yaakov, Chok Yaakov*; Rav Yaakov Reisher, d. 1733
Torat HaYoledet — Rav Yitzchak Zilberstein, contemporary
Tosafot — 12-13th century glosses on the Talmud
Tosefet Yom HaKippurim — also *Kapot Temarim*; Rav Moshe ibn Habib, d. 1696
Tosefta — supplements to the *Mishnah*
Tosfot HaRosh — see *Rosh*
Tosfot Rid — Rabbeinu Yeshayah ben Mali d'Trani the elder, 13th century
Tosfot Yom Tov — also *Divrei Chamudot* and *Ma'adanei Yom Tov*; Rav Yom Tov Lipman Heller, d. 1654
Terumat HaDeshen — Rabbeinu Yisrael Isserlin, d. 1460
Tur — Rabbeinu Yaakov ben Asher Ashkenazi, d. 1340
Tuv Taam VeDa'at — also *Chochmat Shlomo, Mei Niddah* and *Elef Lecha Shlomo*; Rav Shlomo Kluger, d. 1869
Tzlach — see *Noda BiYehudah*
Tzitz Eliezer — Rav Eliezer Yehudah Waldenberg, contemporary
Urim VeTumim — also *Mateh Yehonatan*; Rav Yehonatan Eybeschutz, d. 1769
VeShav HaCohen — Rav Refael HaCohen, d. 1804
Yabia Omer — also *Taharat HaBayit* and *Yechaveh Da'at*; Rav Ovadiah Yosef, contemporary
Yad Avraham — Rav Avraham ben Rav Yehudah Leib, d. 1847
Yad HaChazakah — also known as the *Mishneh Torah*; the Code of Law written by the *Rambam*
Yad HaLevi — Rav Yitzchak Dov HaLevi Bamberger, d. 1879
Yad Shaul — see *Shoel U'Meshiv*
Yad Yitzchak — Rav Avraham Yitzchak Glick, 19th/20th century
Yalkut Lekach Tov — Rav Yaakov Yisrael HaCohen Beifuss, contemporary
Yalkut Shimoni — Rav Shimon Ashkenazi Darshan, 13th century
Yalkut Yosef — Rav Yitzchak Yosef, contemporary (a son of *Rav Ovadiah Yosef*)
Yam Shel Shlomo — Maharshal, Rav Shlomo Luria, d. 1573
Yavetz — *She'elat Yavetz*; Rav Yaakov Emden, d. 1776
Yechaveh Da'at — also *Yabia Omer* and *Taharat HaBayit*; Rav Ovadiah Yosef, contemporary
Yefei To'ar — Rav Shmuel Yafe Ashkenazi, 16th century
Yerei'im — Rabbeinu Eliezer of Metz, one of the *Tosafot*, d. 1198
Yerushalmi — the Jerusalem Talmud, compiled by Rebbe Yochanan, 4th century
Yeshuot Yaakov — Rav Yaakov Meshulam Orenstein, d. 1840
Yesodei Yeshurun — Rav Gedaliah Felder, d. 1991
Yoreh Deah — the second of the four parts of the *Shulchan Aruch*
Zecher Simchah — Rav Simchah Bamberger, d. 1896
Zekan Aharon — Rav Aharon Walkin, 20th century
Zer Zahav — commentary on the *Issur VeHeter*; Rav Avraham Bruin
Zera Emet — Rav Yishmael HaCohen, d. 1811
Zichron Brit LeRishonim — Rav Yaakov Gelsberg, 19th century

Zichron Yosef — Rav Yosef Shteinhart, d. 1776
Zivchei Tzedek — Rav Abdallah Somech, d. 1900
Zocher HaBrit — Rav Asher Enshel Greenwald, 20th century
Zohar — major and central work on Jewish mysticism (Kabbalah), by Rebbe Shimon bar Yochai, 3rd century

INDEX

References are to the page number of either the **Shulchan Aruch** or the **Nishmat Avraham**

A

abortion
- needle biopsy of the fetus — 338
- or martyrdom — 186
- postmortem of the fetus — 338
- the woman's transgression — 93

addiction
- narcotic drugs — 41

adhesive tape — see **band-aid**

adoption
- handicapped child — 22

aiding and abetting another to sin — 82, 83

AIDS
- *brit milah* — 221
- obligation to treat — 266

AIH — see **artificial insemination**

ALS
- obligation to treat — 322, 323

Alzheimer's disease
- parent — 168, 169
- treating him if he takes ill — 324, 325

amputee — see **limb**

amulet
- wearing on *Shabbat* — 90

androgynous
- *brit milah* on *Shabbat* — 202
- chromosomal diagnosis — 202
- definition — 201
- features of — 201

anemia
- *brit milah* — 196

anencephalic baby
- donor for organ transplant — 318

anesthesia
- *brit milah* — 189

animal
- blood — 16
- castration, indirect — 10
- cruelty to — 10
- experimentation — 10
- fat, use of — 42
- killing — 10
- hunting — 10

aninut — see **onen**

annulment of a vow — see **vow**

anointing
- compared to drinking — 42

apnea test
- to determine brain death — 304
- in what percentage of donors is actually done — 306

apostate — 49

arm — see **limb**

armpits
- shaving hair — 92

artificial eye
- *chatzizah* — 146

artificial feeding
- definition of eating — 36
- feeding meat with milk — 38

artificial insemination from husband (AIH)
- *brit milah* on *Shabbat* — 188
- during "seven clean days" — 143
- *pidyon haben* — 189
- status of the child — 188

artificial respiration
- source in *Chazal* — 329

ashamed
- to be seen in public — 92

assisting another to do wrong — 288

attempted suicide — see **suicide**

autopsy
- aborted fetus — 338
- blood samples — 338
- body fluids — 338
- *Cohen* present at — 350
- corneal transplant — 340, 342
- donating one's body to science — 337
- father of a *Cohen* who had an autopsy — 366
- fetus — 338
- necessity today — 336
- needle biopsy — 338
- non-Jewish corpse — 340
- ownership of one's body — 12, 337
- partial — 337
- practicing procedures — 338, 339
- reasons that it is usually prohibited — 335
- recurrent miscarriage — 338
- removal of
  - bone — 340
  - cornea — 340, 342
  - pacemaker — 340
  - skin — 340, 345
- *Shabbat* — 339
- to learn medicine — 335, 338
- to save another's life — 337
- to save another's limb — 339

INDEX

watching one 338
when permitted 337
who owns the body 12, 337

B

baby
  born circumcised 207
  burial 211, 212
  chromosome examination
    to define its sex 201
  circumcision see **brit milah**
  died before he was eight days old 211, 212
  elective surgery after recovery
    from illness 195
  gosses 240
  jaundice and *brit milah* 201
  mother eats non-kosher food 21
  mourning for baby who
    received intensive care
      treatment 238, 366
    was born a *treifah* 238
    was born prematurely 238, 366
    was killed within
      thirty days of birth 238
  naming him if the *brit* is postponed 209
  naming him or her at burial 212, 213
  nefel 211, 212, 238, 366
  passing from husband to *niddah* wife 126
  phototherapy for jaundice 201
  premature with serious
    congenital defects 13
  setting aside Sabbath laws 12
  stillborn 212
  treifah 240
baby carriage
  carrying together with a *niddah* wife 127
bacterial endocarditis
  metzizah 221
band-aid
  chatzizah 148, 152
  prayer before using 276
  removing hair on *Shabbat* 148
bandage
  chatzizah 148, 152
baths
  miracle 64
beard
  dyeing 94
  shaving 93
bed-bound patient
  bowing before a crucifix or statue 53
  corpse in the same room 332
  performing *mitzvot* 9
bein hashemashot
  brit milah 202, 225
  definition 223

yahrzeit, day of death unknown 371
Beit Din
  their permission to practice medicine 283
beit hasetarim 145, 150-154
benedictions see ***birkat***, **blessing**
best of doctors to Hell 278, 282, 292
bestiality
  the transgression 134
bikur cholim
  advising the patient 260
  asking a Rav to pray for him 268
  asking for mercy on his behalf 263
  behavior of the visitor 260
  calling by telephone 262
  Cohen and *tumat met* 364
  Cohen visiting a patient 258
  comforting a mourner
    which takes precedence 271
  diarrhea 266, 268
  euthanasia 265
  ger 265
  giving advice 260
  how is it performed 256, 257, 260, 261
  infectious disease 266
  non-seriously ill patient 257
  opposite sex 257, 267
  patient
    an enemy 260
    asleep 257
    his own prayers 263
    if he has pleasure from the visit 260
    prayers in the synagogue 268
    praying for himself 263
    praying for his recovery 262-266
    praying that he die 264
    suffering from diarrhea 266
  praying
    for the patient 262, 263
    in his presence 264
    in the synagogue 268
    that the patient should die 264
    on *Shabbat* 266
  Shechinah above the patient's head 261
  sitting at the head of the bed 261
  sitting by the patient 260
  telephone visit 262
  the *mitzvah* 254
  tumah of a corpse 258
  visiting hours 261
  walking to visit 262
  when should one visit 257, 261
  which of two patients should one visit 257
  yichud during the visit 257
biopsy
  from a corpse 338
  Shabbat 339
birkat see also **blessing**

INDEX

HaGomel	see **HaGomel**	by *niddah* wife	132
hamitzvot	4, 47	by son	171
hanehenin	4	for a mourner	369
birth	see **childbirth**	from a corpse on *Shabbat*	339
birth control pills		dried and immersion in a *mikveh*	147
seven clean days	138	examining for with dipsticks	110
bleeding		in urine	111, 113
after first coitus	116	life's blood, definition	349
at coitus	100, 102	*shechitah*, covering it	5, 9
at ovulation	100	sucking a bleeding wound	16
birth control pills	138	**blood transfusion**	
breast-feeding	107	donation to a blood bank	346
bride	114	from one who eats non-kosher foods	22
due to a *makkah*	101, 123-125	**blue baby**	
fibroids	102	*brit milah*	196, 206
following hysterectomy	106	**bodek**	
hemophilia	206	weak eyesight	6
ketem, using tablets to decide whether		**boiled wine**	
blood or other stain	110	*Kiddush* or *Havdalah*	47
myoma	102	**bone marrow**	
pregnancy	108	donor	346
surgery on hymen	115	**bone transplant**	
uncertain whether from hemorrhoids	110	donor	347
urine	111, 113	recipient	340
vaginal (*prozdor*)	100, 106	**borrowing with interest**	
wound	16	to save life	83
blemish		**brace, orthodontic**	
that comes with age	95	*chatzizah*	154
blessing	see also **birkat**	**brain**	
before *shechitah*	4, 8	anatomy and physiology	302
person who is dumb	4	circulation	303, 304
said before doing a *mitzvah*	4	crushed	301, 323
saying it for someone else	4	**brain death**	
unclean place	8	anatomy and physiology	302
blind person		apnea test	304
child, standing up for parent	168	cerebral blood flow, tests	
doubt as to whether he is	3		304, 309, 310, 312
husband or wife and laws		classical definition of death	301
of *niddah*	125, 141	definition, presidential commission	304
keri'ah	330	description of blood supply	303
obligation to perform *mitzvot*	7, 188	dissenting medical opinion	307
parent, standing up for him	168	evidence against total brain death	306
placing a stumbling block before him	82, 83	evidence for residual circulation	306
separating *challah*	246	*Halachah*, views	
separating *terumah*	245, 250	Chief Rabbinate of Israel	307
shochet	3, 6	other *gedolei hador*	314
standing up for parent or Rav	168	Rav Auerbach	307
weak eyesight	3, 6	Rav Eliashiv	313
woman, examination cloth	141	Rav Feinstein	314
blood		Rav Waldenberg	314
bleeding wound	16	Harvard criteria	303
clotting	191	historical review	303
consuming it	16	how long do these patients live	306
donating	337	hypothalamus	303, 306, 312
drawing		injecting radioactive material	
Abba Umna	134		304, 309, 310, 312
by medical students	62	name game	317

organ donation card	325	dehydration	197
pregnancy	307	Diaspora	223, 227
reasons given for supporting		died before he was eight days old	211
brain death	305	dislocation of hip	198
sheep experiment	311	drawing blood for laboratory	211
summary	317	eight days and *bein hashemashot*	223
testing for, what percentage of donors		epispadias	199
actually have tests	306	exchange transfusion	201
views of the medical profession	303	eye	
brainstem		blockage of tear duct	199
description and function	302	inflammation or infection	198, 201
brainstem death	see **brain death**	fast day	223
breakthrough bleeding		father an *onen*	215
birth control pills	138	father sitting *shivah*	214
bride	114	fever	196, 197
breast-feeding		first time	63
bleeding from an IUD	123	forceps delivery	199
menstruation during the period of	107	foreskin	
mother eats non-kosher food	21	removal at burial	211, 212
breech delivery		removing strands	221
moment of birth	123, 202	separating it from the flesh	215
bride		fracture	198
bleeding after first coitus	115	generalized illness	196, 207
does not bleed after first coitus	116	*ger*	194
preparation before marriage	140	hare-lip	198
surgery of hymen	115	*hatafat dam brit*	209, 217, 218, 221, 222
taking tablets to prevent menstruation	114	*hatafat dam brit* after death	212
brit milah		heart disease	196
adult	189, 197	hemophilia	206
AIDS	221	hepatitis	221
AIH	188	how long must one wait after	
allergic reaction	207	recovery from illness	196
androgynous	201	hypospadias	199
anemia	196	incubator	197
anesthesia	189	infection	197, 198, 201
at burial	211, 212	innovations	216
bein hashemashot	202, 223, 225	IVF	189
bilirubin levels	202	jaundice	197, 201, 209
birth, definition of	124, 224	laser, use of	207
blood clotting	191	limb, transient loss of function	199
born		localized illness	198
after artificial insemination	188	loss of function of limb	199
bein hashemashot	202, 223, 225	magen clamp, use of	208, 216
circumcised	209	*makkah* on back of hand	201
IVF	189	medical opinion	195, 202
breech delivery	202	medication to remove the foreskin	207
brit or burial, which takes precedent	214	*metzizah*	
brothers died following circumcision	209	AIDS	221
Caesarian section	227	brit in hospital	221
cardiac catheterization	197	following *hatafat dam brit*	218
causing unnecessary suffering		hepatitis	221
	188, 189, 202, 215	infection from	219
cleft palate	198	public fast day	222
clotting factors	191, 206	reason for doing	218
completion of treatment	197	*Tishah B'Av*	222
convert	194	using a pipette	218
cyanosed baby	196, 204	with magen clamp	216

INDEX

Yom Kippur	222
modern innovations	216
mohel	
brought in *Shabbat* early	200
first circumcision	63
poor eyesight	214
shaking hands	214
wears spectacles	214
who is eligible	214
moment of birth, definition	202
naming the baby	209, 212, 213
nefel	208, 211, 212
nerve injury	199
obligation of blind father	188
obligation to cause bleeding	216
or burial, which takes precedent	215
performed by the father	188
periah	
after death	212
circumcised by surgeon	217
procedure	215
removing the foreskin with the underlying membrane	217
three days later	221
with magen clamp	216
phototherapy	201
pipette, use of	218
plaster cast	198
postponed	
pidyon haben	238
second day of *Yom Tov*	223, 227
three days before *Yom Tov*	194
Thursday or Friday	192
premature	227, 228
procedure	215
public fast day	222
removing the foreskin together with the underlying membrane	217
second day of *Yom Tov*	223, 227
separating the foreskin from the flesh	215
seriously ill baby	192
"seven days" after illness	
generalized illness	196, 204
when does the count start	197
Shabbat	63, 192, 215, 227, 228
sick baby	192
stillborn	211
swelling of head	199
temperature	196, 197
Tishah B'Av	222
treifah	192
tumtum	201
twins, one of whom died before he was eight days old	208
unnecessary suffering	188, 189, 202, 215
use of various instruments	215, 216
weight, low at birth	199
why the eighth day	191
Yom Kippur	222
Yom Tov	
born by Caesarian section	227
postponed *brit*	192, 223
second day	227
bulimos	
eating forbidden food	78, 88
burial	
baby that died before he was eight days old	208, 211, 212
circumcision before	21, 212
died during surgery or childbirth	349
fetal sac	212
found killed	349
life's blood	349
limb	348
naming at burial	212, 213
nefel	208, 211, 212
or *brit milah*, which takes precedent	215
placenta	212
busy with one's duties	134(ref. 92)

C

C section	see **Caesarian**
CPR	301
Caesarian section	
brit milah	227, 242
fast of the firstborn	243
pidyon haben	242
prearranged date	125
cardiac catheterization	
brit milah	197
cardinal sins	
causing another to sin	80
martyrdom	52, 73-75, 88, 131
offshoots	47, 53, 79, 88, 129, 131, 135
perverting justice	80
robbing	75
shaming another publicly	79
signing to a falsehood	78
torture	81
cardiopulmonary resuscitation (CPR)	301
caregiver	see **paramedical staff**
carrying	
baby carriage together with *niddah* wife	127
cast, plaster	see **plaster cast**
catheter, urinary	
chatzizah	156
catheter, venous	
chatzizah	149
placement on *Shabbat*	207
causing another to sin	70, 82, 84
cerebellum	
description	303

INDEX

cerebral blood flow
   brain-dead patient   304, 309, 310, 312
cerebrum
   description   302
cervical cerclage
   to prevent a miscarriage   119
cervical culture
   bleeding following the procedure   122
cervical spine
   traumatic severance   354
cervix
   bleeding after surgery   142
   culture   122
   dilatation during labor   119
   incompetence during pregnancy   119
   normal opening   119
chadash
   when the Israelites entered the Land of Israel   48
challah
   blind person   245
   Diaspora   245, 251, 252
   laws concerning   245
   separating on *Shabbat*   251, 252
chametz
   searching for while wearing spectacles   6
charity
   for child that requires heart surgery   180
   for other *mitzvot*   72
   for surgery done abroad privately   180
   for unconventional treatment   72
   how much is one obligated to give   180
charms
   use of for patient   87, 89, 90
chatzizah   see also ***mikveh***
   absorbent cotton in ear   145, 156
   adhesive tape   148, 152
   artificial eye   146
   band-aid   148, 152
   bandage   148, 152
   beit hasetarim   145, 150-154
   blood, dried   147, 150
   brace   154
   cannot stand   158
   catheter
      Hickman   149
      PIC   149
      urinary   156
      venous   149
   coloring   150
   colostomy   155
   contact lenses   146
   covering part of herself with her fingers   146, 158
   crown of tooth   152
   danger of blindness   146
   definition   144
   dentures   152
   dialysis   156
   dirt under the nail   150
   ear-plug   157
   eardrum, perforated   156
   fingers, use of to protect   146, 158
   gastrostomy   156
   glass eye   146
   Hickman catheter   149
   ileostomy   155
   intrauterine device   155
   intravenous catheter   149
   jejunostomy   156
   nephrostomy   156
   ointment   150
   originates in water   157
   otitis   157
   painful eyes   146
   paralysis   158
   peeling skin   148
   perforated eardrum   156
   peritoneal dialysis   156
   pessary   139, 155
   PIC catheter   149
   plaster, adhesive   148
   plaster cast   149
   plastic ear-plug   157
   salve on eye   146, 147
   scab   147
   seven days or more   145
   supported by another woman   158
   sutures   149, 154
   swelling round a nail   150
   teeth
      brace   154
      crowns   152
      dentures   152
      false   152
      loose tooth   153
      orthodontic appliance   154
      permanent filling   150
      sutures   154
      temporary filling   151
   tracheostomy   158
   urinary catheter   157
   venous catheter   149
   woman who oversees   158
chayei sha'ah
   and *chayei olam*   56
   patient refuses treatment   57
   prolongation of   319
chemical change
   non-kosher food   30
chemist   see **pharmacist**
child   see also **mentally handicapped**
   blind, hospitalization   23

INDEX

Cohen
    causing him to become *tamei*   364
    needs to attend a hospital clinic   362
    Down syndrome   25, 176
    eating non-kosher foods   21, 22
    facilitated communication   28
    forbidden foods   21, 22
    giving up for adoption   25
    handicapped   25
    institutional care   25
    low intelligence   25
    mentally handicapped   25, 176
    non-kosher foods   21, 22
    obligation to perform *mitzvot*   26
    psychotherapy   87
    research   11
    shoteh   25
childbirth
    after eight months gestation   309
    at what stage does she
        become *niddah*   117
    breakage of water   117
    breech delivery   122, 202
    Caesarean section   see **Caesarean section**
    cessation of contractions   118
    danger of   124
    definition   124, 202, 224, 242
    died during and burial   349, 350
    dilatation of cervix   119
    "dry"   119
    forceps delivery   199
    greeting the mother *mazal tov* if she
        is in mourning   370
    husband present   127
    induction of labor   124
    lessening the pain   189
    mother in mourning   370
    mucus plug before   118
    premature   227, 228
    presence of husband   127
    psychological stress   127
    ritual uncleanliness following   118-120
    setting aside Sabbath laws   117
    without bleeding   119
chromosomes
    to define sex   202
chronic vegetative state
    donors for organ transplants   317
circumcision   see **brit milah**
cleft palate
    brit milah   198
Cohen
    amputated limb   353
    amputation of extra finger   362
    baby and *tumah*   364
    caregiver   352
    causing his baby son to become *tamei*   364

certifying death   356
child and *tumah*   357
child who needs to attend
    a hospital clinic   362
corridor and stairwell rooms
    under the same roof   357, 357
daughter of a *Cohen*   362
deceased in another apartment   357, 359
deceased relatives   363
defilement
    by a corpse   258, 350, 327
    by a limb   350, 361, 365
    Ra'avad's opinion   350
defiling himself for a *nefel*   363
defiling himself for a relative
    following an autopsy   366
    Shabbat   365
    weekday   363
    who had a limb removed   366
defiling himself to perform a
    Torah *mitzvah*   359
defilement, two prohibitions   362(ref.45)
doctor   352
Elijah and revival of dead child   354
entering a hospital   258
entering the room of a *gosses*   318, 355
giving him precedence   181
giving his wife precedence   183
his wife   258, 362
honoring one who defiles himself   351
hospital corridors   357
hospital rooms   357
hospital synagogue   361, 362
in hospital   258, 352, 357, 365
insists on studying medicine   350
met mitzvah   356
minor illness   360
non-Jewish corpse   350
non-seriously ill   360
nurse (male)   352
patient in hospital   357
pregnant wife, in hospital   356
Ra'avad's opinion   350
rejoining amputated finger   353
sick, corpse in the same house   363
seriously ill   360
setting aside Rabbinic *tumah* to perform
    a Torah commandment   360
spread of *tumah*   357
studying medicine   350
surgery that will leave him
    with a blemish   362
surgery to rejoin a limb   353
treating a *gosses*   318, 327, 355
tumah
    of a corpse   258
    of a limb   352

INDEX

two separate prohibitions regarding
    defilement   362(ref.45)
  visiting a patient   258
  wife of a *Cohen*   258, 362
  writing a death certificate   356
colored underwear
  niddah   110
colostomy
  mikveh   155
comatose patient   see **unconscious patient**
computers
  communication with mentally disabled   28
confession of sins
  enumerating them   300
  in the presence of excreta   297
  mitzvah to remind him   297
  nature of the confession   299
  no suffering without sin   297
  on *Shabbat*   297
  when should he do so   297
confused
  parent   168, 169
congenital defects
  baby, setting aside Sabbath laws   13
  brit milah   196, 198, 199, 201, 206
  requires surgery   179
consent
  research   11
contact lenses   see also **glasses**
  immersion in a *mikveh*   146
contagious disease   see **infectious disease**
contraceptives
  pills and bleeding   114
controlling one's inclinations   134
convert
  blessing of *HaGomel* after his *brit*   194
  brit
    on Thursday or Friday   192, 229
    three days before *Yom Tov*   194
  hatafat dam brit   229
  honoring parents   173
  obligation to be circumcised   229
  praying for a sick parent   262, 265
  visiting parents   173
cornea, transplant
  from a corpse   340, 342
corpse   see also **autopsy**
  benefiting from h m   335, 336
  biopsy   338
  blood samples   338
  burial of even smallest part of one   336, 340
  body fluids   338
  donor for organ transplantation
    bone   340
    cornea   342
    skin   345

  learning to intubate   339
  loeg larash   332
  muktzeh   359
  needle biopsy   338
  nefel, needle biopsy   338
  obligation to bury even the
    smallest part   337, 340
  obligation to bury it   337, 340
  postmortem   see **autopsy**
  putting on *tefillin* in its presence   332
  removal of pacemaker   340
  Shabbat, biopsy   338
  who owns the body   337
cosmetic surgery
  is it permitted   60
covering
  the blood spilt during *shechitah*   5, 9
CPR   301
critically ill patient   see **seriously ill**
crown of tooth
  chatzizah   152
crotch
  shaving hair   93
cruelty
  to animals   10
custom, praiseworthy
  force of a vow   35

D

D and C   125
DNR (do not resuscitate)   320, 322, 324, 327
dairy after meat   see **meat with milk**
danger to a limb
  autopsy of a corpse   339
  compared to danger to one's life
    or danger to one's money   75
  non-kosher food   70
  setting aside Sabbath laws   75, 339
danger to life   see also **saving life**
  causing another to sin   80-82
  chayei sha'ah and *chayei olam*   56
  endangering oneself to save another   181, 185
  giving up another to be tortured   81
  illness brought on by sin   52
  illness brought on willfully   70
  infectious disease, treating   266
  robbery   75
  shaming another publicly   79
  three cardinal sins   53, 73, 75
dangerously ill patient   see **seriously ill**
daughter
  treating a parent   168
dead person
  how did Eliyahu resuscitate him   354
  mitzvah to revive   354

INDEX

deaf
  separating tithes   4
  saying a blessing   250
  shochet   4
deaf-mute
  doubt as to whether he is   3
  examination regarding *niddah*   141
  pidyon haben of his son   236
  setting aside Sabbath laws for him   321
  sacrificing him to save one who is not   182
  shechitah   2
  status in *Halachah*   141
  treating him   321
death   see also **brain death**
  charging for issuing a
    death certificate   292
  definition   311
  examination by a *Cohen*   356
  examination to determine   311
  obligation to tell a relative   373
  pikuach nefesh of a relative   354
  probability of   162
deathbed   see **confession**
decapitation
  if possible to reattach the
    severed head   355
deceased   see **corpse**
defilement   see **ritual defilement**
dehydration
  brit milah   197
delaying justice   281
dental treatment
  chatzizah   150-154
dentist
  assisting him in doing wrong   288
  charging wrongly   288
  extracting a tooth from a parent   172
dentures
  chatzizah   152
  kashering   36
dialysis
  mikveh   156
diaphragm
  seven clean days   138
diarrhea
  bikur cholim   266
  caring for a *niddah* wife   129
Diaspora
  challah   245, 252
  Cohen in hospital   258
  mezuzah   230
  second day of *Yom Tov*
    born by Caesarian section   227
    postponed *brit*   192, 223
    removal of foreskin before burial   212
  tithes   252
dilatation and curretage   123

dipsticks
  examination of blood stain   110
disabled   see **handicapped**
disclosure of information to
  the family that a colleague was
    negligent   288
  a relative of a death   373
  the patient of his illness   167, 298
divinations
  when permitted to a patient   86
do not resuscitate   320, 322, 324, 327
doctor
  Abba Umna   134
  acknowledging *Hashem*   276, 278
  annuling a decree of *Hashem*   269-271
  assisting him to do wrong   288
  at the time of the prophets   274
  best of doctors to Hell   278, 282, 292
  billing a patient   271
  "busy with his work"   134 (ref.92)
  caring for wife   129
  causes damage to patient   169, 283, 286
  causing suffering   202, 281
  charging
    charges nothing, worth nothing   290
    for issuing death certificate   292
    for *Shabbat* call   292
    for treatment   271
    high fee   293
    obligation to pay him   290, 293
    wrongly   288
  Cohen and a *gosses*   318, 327, 355
  Cohen   352
  consultation with colleagues   282
  credibility of his opinion in
    Halachah   99, 101
  cures in nature   276
  diagnosing internal disease   102
  did not attend to patient   289
  disclosing information to
    the family that a colleague
      was negligent   288
    a relative of a death   373
    the patient of his illness   167, 298
  does not take a fee   270
  duty to answer all calls   280, 289
  endangering himself   266, 345
  error in judgment   283
  examining a woman   74, 132
  exile   283
  experimental treatment   11, 12
  external and internal disease   104, 275
  fear of making a mistake
    170, 279, 282, 283
  forced treatment   57, 322
  giving
    a prognosis   298

precedence to one patient over
    an other   181
   the patient hope and confidence   298
graduation cloak   85
gynecological
   examination   74
   instrumentation   121-123
hashavat aveidah   273
high fees   293
in mourning   367
infectious disease, treating   266
informing
   a family that a colleague
      was negligent   288
   a relative of a death   373
   the patient of his illness   167, 298
injury to patient   169, 283, 286
keri'ah, present at patient's death   330
less experienced   282
liability for damages   283
license to practice   54
messenger of *Hashem*   276, 298
misdiagnosis   283
mitzvah
   of saving life   279
   to practice medicine   172
negligence   286, 289
niddah wife   129
non-Jew   276
non-seriously ill patient
   obligation to treat   277
obligation to
   answer calls at all times   289
   report a colleague for negligence   287
   reprove a colleague   287
   tell a family of a colleague's
      negligence   288
   treat   279
obligation to inform a relative of a death
   Shabbat   374
   weekday   373
obstetrician, attending to his
   sister-in-law   74
patients waiting to see him   184
permission to treat
   by *Beit Din*   283
   by the Torah   269, 273
   in spite of risks   59, 60
physician different from surgeon
   regarding liability   284
practicing medicine in *Eretz Yisrael*   162
praising his treatment   52
praying to *Hashem*   280
preventive medicine   274, 276, 280
pride   282
priority in treatment   181
putting himself in danger   266, 345

qualification   284
Rambam's formula for treatment   279
Ramban's view   273
refuses to treat without a fee   292
reporting a colleague   287
reproving a colleague   287
research   see **research**
returning his lost health
   to the patient   273
risk to himself   181, 183, 266, 345
sechar batalah   290
self control   134
Shabbat fees   292
shivah, seeing a patient   367
side-effects of treatment   58, 59
speaking about a comatose patient
   in his presence   296
surgeon who erred   284
taking a fee
   for services   271, 290
   from a house of mourning   368
   Shabbat call   292
   to confirm death   292
   to issue a death certificate   292
telling the patient his diagnosis   298
the best of doctors to Hell   278, 282, 292
the right to charge a fee   271, 290
tov shebarofe'im   278, 282, 292
training   62
treating a parent   169
treating his *niddah* wife   129
treatment
   by *Hashem* and by man   272
   of infectious disease   266
   of opposite sex   132
   unnecessarily, for fee   288
triage   181
unintentional harm   283
vaginal examination   73
verapo yerapei   269
whom to treat first   181
wife a *niddah*   129
wine for *Kiddush* and *Havdalah*   47
working in Israel   163
worth nothing if charges nothing   290
worthy of *Hashem's* blessing   270
donor for organ transplantation
after death   342
anencephalic baby   318
brain dead   see **brain dead**
card   325
chronic vegetative state patient   317
corpse
   bone   347
   cornea   342
   skin   345
gosses   181, 185, 302

INDEX

healthy
    bone   347
    bone marrow and stem cells   346, 347
    kidney   347
    putting one's life in danger
        to save another   345
    organ donation card   325
douching
    niddah   137
Down syndrome (trisomy 21)
    abandoning the baby   25
    care of child with   25
    facilitated communication   25
    institutional care   25
    obligation to keep *mitzvot*   25
dressing
    as one of opposite sex   94
drop attacks
    shochet   2
drug abuse
    Halachic view   41
    Rashi's definition   42
drug store
    prescribing medication   282
duchanning
    Cohen studying medicine   352
dumb
    covering the blood of *shechitah*   4
    saying a blessing   4, 250
    shochet   4
dying patient
    Cohen in his room   318, 327
    confession of sins   297-300
    "cosmetic" treatment   327
    DNR   320, 322, 324, 327
    leaving him alone   327
    passive euthanasia   320, 322, 324, 327
    removing an impediment to death   327

E

ears
    absorbent cotton and *chatzizah*   145, 156
    perforated eardrum and *chatzizah*   156
eating
    definition   38
ectopic pregnancy
    niddah   120
    pidyon haben   120, 243
elastoplast   see **band-aid**
elderly
    patient   321
    shochet   3, 5
    woman who was tired of living   327
electric lamp
    moving it for a non-seriously ill patient   70
elevator

mezuzah   233
Elijah
    revival of dead child   354
epilepsy
    category of illness   29
    shochet   2
epispadias
    brit milah   199
Eretz Yisrael
    challah   245, 251, 252
    practicing medicine   163
    tithes   247-253
    travelling there, is it a *mitzvah*   162
    vows to live there   162
euthanasia
    citizens of Luz   326
    Halachic views
        Rav Auerbach   320
        Rav Eliashiv   322
        Rav Waldenberg   323
        Rav Feinstein   323
        summary   324
    narcotics for pain   321
    passive   320, 322, 324, 327
    praying that a patient die   264
    removing an impediment
        to death   326, 327
    sanctity of life   320
    severe pain and suffering   322
    worth of a life   321
examination
    female patient by male doctor   74
    gynecological, by a male doctor   74
examination cloth
    absorbent cotton   140
    showing to husband   141
exchange transfusion
    brit milah   201
experimental treatment
    seriously ill patient   11, 12
experimentation   see **research**
eye, inflammation
    brit milah   198, 201
eye drops
    niddah wife   132
eyesight
    wearing spectacles
        bodek   6
        mohel   212
        searching for *chametz*   6
        shochet   3, 6
        woman in charge of the *mikveh*   159

F

facilitated communication
    by mentally retarded children   28

INDEX

fallopian tubes
   ectopic pregnancy   120
   insufflation   122
false teeth   see **dentures**
fast
   of the firstborn   243
father   see also **parents**
   ownership rights over his daughter   12
female organs of reproduction   98
fetus
   sonography to discover its sex   109
fever
   brit milah   196, 197
fibroids
   bleeding   102
finger
   protecting herself during immersion   146, 158
first come, first served
   in *Halachah*   184
firstborn
   fasting on *Pesach* eve   243
fish oil (non-kosher)
   non-seriously ill patient   30(ref. 26), 65(ref. 100)
fish with milk   33
flesh (human)
   research   348
forbidden food
   eating to save life   24
   nullifying it for a seriously ill patient   248
   underwent chemical change   30
forceps delivery
   brit milah   199
   pidyon haben   244
foreskin
   removal before burial   211, 212
   separating it from the underlying flesh   215
foster care
   handicapped child   25

G

gastrostomy
   feeding meat with milk   38
   mikveh   156
   seriously ill patient   324
Gemara
   medications mentioned   277
ger   see **convert**
gilui arayot
   definition   134
   martyrdom   74, 134
   passive   88
   unmarried girl   134
giving precedence
   first come, first served in *Halachah*   184

   in any medical situation   187
   patients waiting to be seen by doctor   184
   to one of many patients   185
   who should be given precedence   181
glasses   see also **contact lenses**
   bodek   6
   mikveh woman   159
   mohel   212
   searching for *chametz*   6
   shechitah   3, 6
gosses
   baby   240
   blocking the path of another patient from receiving treatment   319
   blood tests   318
   Cohen, entering his room   318, 327, 355
   comatose   296, 322
   considered to be alive in every respect   240
   cosmetic treatment   327
   crushed skull   354
   definition of   300
   disconnecting him from a respirator for another patient   319
   donor for heart transplant   185
   donor for kidney transplant   187
   forced feeding   320, 322, 323, 324
   forced treatment   322, 324
   hastening his death   319, 326
   Heaven-fearing patient   322, 323
   hugging a dying child   319
   injecting radioactive material to confirm brain death   304, 309, 310, 312
   killing him   185
   leaving him alone   327
   moving him   60, 319, 326
   nursing care   319, 325
   oxygen   320, 324
   pidyon haben   240
   prevents treatment of another patient   319
   probability of dying   162
   prolonging life   319
   quality of life   321, 323
   removing an impediment to dying   327
   removing his respirator for another patient   319
   routine measurements of pulse, temperature and blood pressure   318
   sacrificing him to save one who is not   186
   setting aside Sabbath laws   301, 321
   stroking his hand   319
   touching him   318
   treating him   301, 318, 321
   treating him forcibly   322, 323, 324
   treatment by a *Cohen*   318, 355
   unconscious   322, 323

INDEX

value of life	321
graduation gowns	
shatnez	85
grape juice	see **wine**
gums	
bleeding, *Shabbat*	17
sutures, *chatzizah*	154
gynecological examination	
by a male physician	74
instrumentation	121-123

H

HaGomel **blessing**	
attempted suicide	335
convert, after his *brit milah*	194
patient in mourning	369
treifah	15
hair	
dyeing black	94
removing on *Shabbat*	148
shaving beard	93
shaving body hair	94
wig or toupee in a man	97
Halachic **rulings**	
concerning one's wife	141
handicapped	see **mentally handicapped**
hands, trembling	
and *brit milah*	214
and *shechitah*	5
harelip	
brit milah	198
Harvard criteria	
brain death	303
Hashem	
everything is from Him	276
follow Him with perfect faith	86, 89
His protection and the *mitzvah* of procreation	124
putting one's entire trust in Him	86, 89
thanking Him for the merit of living in *Eretz Yisrael*	163
the Decider of one's fate	276
the True Doctor	276, 278
treatment from Him	276
treats without fee	278
hatafat dam brit	
after illness	221
circumcised by non-Jew	217
circumcised by surgeon	217
drawing blood for laboratory	211
generalized illness	210
jaundice	210
metzizah following	218
where and how is it done	209
Havdalah	

boiled wine	50
pasteurized wine	50
stam yenam	46
wine touched by Jew who desecrates *Shabbat*	49
heart	
bypass surgery	58
insensitivity of	21
mechanical	58
transplant	82, 185
unable to restart the heart after surgery	58
heart transplant	see also **brain death**
causing the death of the donor	82
from a *treifah* or *gosses*	185
recipient	82
hefsek taharah	
birth control pills	138
diaphragm	138
difficulty with examination	140
IUD	139
medically forbidden to her husband	137, 143
procedure	136
use of absorbent cotton	140
uterine pessary	139
vaginal suppository	138
virgin bride	140
hematuria	
niddah	111, 113
hemiplegia	
when wife is a *niddah*	132
hemophilia	
brit milah	206
hemorrhoids	
attributing a *ketem* to them	108
hepatitis	
brit milah	221
hermaphrodite	see **androgynous**
Hickman catheter	
chatzizah	149
hospital	
bed-bound patient	53
Cohen	258, 352
corridors and *tumat Cohen*	357
eating from vessels that have not been immersed	44
metzizah during *brit milah*	218
mezuzah	230
missionary	64
praising the care received	53
rooms and *tumat Cohen*	357
rooms, *mezuzah*	230
separating tithes and *challah*	251, 252
human experimentation	11
hunting	
cruelty to animals	10

husband
  caring for ill wife ... 129
  forbidden to have coitus ... 143
  making *Halachic* rulings regarding his wife ... 141
  nullifying a vow made by his wife ... 164
  present at childbirth ... 127
  wife vowed to take treatment to conceive ... 164
hymen
  bride, after first coitus ... 115
  surgical removal ... 115
hypnosis
  as treatment ... 87
hypospadias
  brit milah ... 199
hypothalamus
  description and function ... 303
  in brain death ... 306, 312
hysterectomy
  bleeding following surgery ... 104
hysterosalpingography
  bleeding following the procedure ... 121
hysteroscopy
  bleeding following the procedure ... 122

I

IUD ... see **intrauterine device**
IVF ... see **invitro fertilization**
idolater ... see also **non-Jew**
  living in Israel ... 54
  medical treatment ... 54
  praising his deeds ... 53
  wine libation ... 46
ileostomy
  mikveh ... 155
illicit relationships ... see *gilui arayot*
illness
  brit milah ... 196-198, 209
  brought upon himself ... 52
  preordained ... 268
  shochet ... 5
  spiritual ... 89
immersion ... see *mikveh*
inciting another to sin
  to save life ... 80, 82, 83
incubator
  for jaundice ... 197
  pidyon haben ... 237
induction of labor
  prearranged date ... 124
infant ... see **baby**
infectious disease
  bikur cholim ... 266
  metzizah ... 219
  mohel ... 220
  physician endangering himself ... 266
  town with plague ... 266
  visiting a patient ... 266
infertility
  short menstrual cycle ... 137
informing
  patient of death of relative ... 294
  patient of his illness ... 167, 298
  relative of death of patient ... 373
injections
  niddah wife ... 132
  parents ... 170
injury
  minimizing ... 62
  parent ... 169
  patient ... 172
  surgery ... 60
institutional care
  handicapped child ... 22
  shoteh ... 22
instrumentation and *niddah*
  bleeding after ... 121-123
  petichat hakever ... see *petichat hakever*
interest, for loans
  medical instruments ... 84
  to save life ... 83
internal examination ... see **gynecological examination**
intoxicated
  considered a *shoteh* ... 5
intrauterine device
  bleeding ... 122, 139
  breast-feeding ... 123
  mikveh ... 155
intubation
  practicing on a corpse ... 339
  source in *Chazal* ... 329
IUD ... see **intrauterine device**
invitro fertilization (IVF)
  brit milah on *Shabbat* ... 189
  pidyon haben ... 189

J

jaundice
  brit milah ... 197
  phototherapy ... 201
jejunostomy
  mikveh ... 156
Jew
  collective responsibility ... 4
  found killed, burial ... 349
  willfully desecrates the Sabbath ... 49
justice, perverting
  to save life ... 80

INDEX

K

Kaddish
  informing a sick son of his
    father's death   375
  seriously ill patient   296
  yahrzeit, doubtful date   373

kashering
  utensils bought from a non-Jew   44

keri'ah
  coat belonging to the hospital   330
  for who is one obligated   330
  obligation of blind person   330
  obligation of medical staff   330
  obligation when in proximity of patient
    who just died   330
  seriously ill patient   296
  Shabbat   331
  which garment   331
  who is obligated   330
  Yom Tov   331

ketem
  blood in urine   111, 113
  elderly woman   113
  hemorrhoids   110
  nylon underwear   113
  toilet paper   112
  using tablets or dipsticks to decide
    whether blood or stain   110
  wearing colored underwear   110

Kiddush
  boiled wine   50
  pasteurized wine   50
  stam yenam   47
  wine touched by Jew who desecrates
    Shabbat   49

kidney transplant
  healthy donor   347

kila'im   see also **shatnez**
  eating or benefiting from   63

killing
  any living creature   11

knot, tying
  definition regarding *Shabbat*   145

L

labor   see **childbirth**

Land of Israel
  living there   162
  practicing medicine   163
  visiting   163

laser, use of
  brit milah   207

leather shoes
  Yom Kippur   96

life   see also **saving life**
  curtailing   see **euthanasia**
  gaining a few more moments   328
  its worth   321, 323
  quality of   321, 323
  sacrificing one's life for another   181, 183

life, danger to   see **danger to life**

life's blood
  definition   349

lifnei iveir   see **placing a stumbling block**

lift
  mezuzah   233

limb
  burial   348
  danger to   62, 70, 75, 339, 353
  definition   348
  rejoining on *Shabbat*   62, 353
  removed from a living person
    part of it   352
    research   348
    ritual defilement   352
  setting aside Torah law to save it   75, 339
  transient loss of function and *brit milah*   199
  traumatic amputation   62, 353

living person carries himself   126

living will
  organ-donor card   325
  what it should say   326

loan with interest
  saving life   83

loeg larash   332

Lou Gehrig disease (ALS)
  obligation to treat   322, 323

low-salt diet
  salting meat   18

Luz
  inhabitants of   326

lying
  about the death of a relative   374
  to a patient about his disease   298

M

Maariv
  prayed early by mistake   200
  time for praying   226

ma'asrot   see **tithes**

magen clamp
  use in *brit milah*   208, 216

man
  attended to by a woman   268
  bikur cholim by a woman   257
  dressing as a woman   94
  wearing a wig or toupee   97

marit ha'ayin
  danger to life   52

man wearing a wig	97
of idolatory	52
sucking a bleeding finger	16
using a magen clamp	216
martyrdom	
abortion to save the life of the surgeon	186
acts which are offshoots of one of the three cardinal sins	47, 53, 79, 88, 129, 131, 135
cardinal sins	see **cardinal sins**
causing another to sin	80, 82
gilui arayot	see ***gilui arayot***
giving up another to be tortured	80
illicit relationships	see ***gilui arayot***
illness brought on by sin	52
performing an abortion to save one's life	186
perverting justice	80
Rabban Shimon ben Gamliel and Rebbe Yishmael	281
robbery	75
shaming another publicly	79
signing to a falsehood	78
three cardinal sins	see **cardinal sins**
torture	81
uttering a charm	87
when is it not obligatory	73
when the reason for the decree is not to cause the Jew to sin	88
matzot	
forgot to take *challah*	250
made from *chadash* when the Israelites entered the Land of Israel	48
meat, salting	see **salting**
meat with milk	
chewing meat for a baby	36
clear meat soup	39
cooking	32
domesticated animals	33
eating	32
false teeth	36
feeding by naso-gastric tube or gastrostomy	38
having benefit from	32
minimal waiting time between meat and diary products	34, 39
non-meat non-dairy food	39
reason for the prohibition	36
tasting a meat dish	36
three Torah transgressions	32
mechanical heart	58
medical instruments	
renting out	84
medical opinion	
credibility in *Halachah*	101, 103, 133, 271, 275, 298
regarding *brit milah*	195, 202

medical student	
Cohen	350
drawing blood	62
mitzvah to study medicine	279
permission to study medicine	134
medication	
cures in nature	276
gelatine capsules	31
ma'asrot	247, 251
of the Talmud	277
orlah fruit	234
prayer before taking	276
prescribing by lay person	283
Shemittah	248
side-effects	59, 60
terumah	247
medicine	
an uncertain science	271, 275
medicine, study of	
Cohen	350
obligation to	279, 293
permission to	134
Shabbat	279
shivah week	369
treating someone of the opposite sex	132
menorrhagia	102, 121
menstrual cycle	
physiology	98, 137
short	137
menstruation	
during the period of breast-feeding	107
during pregnancy	108
heavy	102
physiology	98, 137
preventing	114
short cycle	137
mental anguish	see also **psychological stress**
prolonging life	57
mental illness	
parent	168, 169
suicide	334
mental retardation	see ***shoteh***, **mentally handicapped**
mentally confused	
parent	168, 169
mentally handicapped	see also ***shoteh***
abandoning	26
child or adult	25
facilitated communication	28
foster care	25
giving up for adoption	25
institutional care	22, 25
non-kosher food	21
obligation to keep *mitzvot*	26, 176
size of classroom	175
teaching him	175

INDEX

mercy killing   see **euthanasia**
met mitzvah
    and a *Cohen*   356
metzizah
    AIDS   221
    bacterial endocarditis   221
    brit in hospital   221
    following *hatafat dam brit*   218
    hepatitis   221
    infection from   219
    public fast day   222
    reason for doing   214
    Tishah B'Av   222
    using a pipette   218
    with magen clamp   216
    Yom Kippur   222
mezuzah
    Diaspora   230
    elevator   233
    Eretz Yisrael   230
    hospital rooms   230
    inside of the door   232
    lift   233
    nursing care ward   232
    old-age home   232
    prison   231
    which rooms must have one   230
Midrash
    as a source of *Halachah*   79
mikveh, immersion in
    beit hasetarim   145, 150-154
    chatzizah   see ***chatzizah***
    for physical contact only   143
    Friday night   147
    husband or wife forbidden to have coitus   143
    procedure   144
    utensils made by a non-Jew   44
milah   see ***brit milah***
milk
    from mother who eats non-kosher foods   21
    with fish   33
    with meat   see **meat with milk**
minhag
    and annulment of a vow   160, 161
minor
    doubt as to whether he is   3
minor illness
    Cohen   360
mirror
    use of by male   96
miscarriage
    ectopic pregnancy   120
    incompetence of cervix   119
    niddah and *tumat ledah*   119, 120
    pidyon haben for the boy born next   241
    within forty days of conception   118, 241

missionary
    treatment   64
mitzvot
    bikur cholim   254
    blessing before   4
    blind person's obligation   6, 188
    child   25
    low intelligence   25, 176
    performing in an unclean place   8
    performing without charge   290
    saving life   280
    shoteh   22
    to keep healthy   280
moch dachuk
    procedure   136
    uterine pessary   139
modern innovations
    in the performance of a *brit milah*   216
mohel
    brought in *Shabbat* early   200
    first circumcision   62
    has infectious disease   219
    not permitted to do *metzizah*   220, 221
    poor eyesight   214
    shaking hands   214
    visiting in the Diaspora   227
    visiting Israel   227
    wears spectacles   214
    who is eligible   214
mother   see also **parent**
    after childbirth, wishing her *mazal tov*
        if she is sitting *shivah*   370
    nursing, eats non-kosher food   21
mourning
    bathing   369
    birkat HaGomel   369
    childbirth   370
    comforting mourners   268
    doctor
        in mourning   367, 368
        studying medicine   369
        taking a fee from a house of mourning   368
    for baby who
        received intensive care treatment   238
        was born a *treifah*   238
        was born prematurely   238, 366
        was born with a severe congenital defect   238
        was killed within thirty days of birth   238
    greeting her *mazal tov* if she has given birth   370
    Halachot of   294
    monetary loss   367
    mourner or patient, who takes precedence   269

INDEX

patient whose parent died 294
seriously ill patient
    another mourner visiting him 294
    asks about the deceased 294
    crying in his presence 296
    did not mourn because of his state 370
    eulogizing the deceased in his presence 296
    HaGomel blessing 369
    Kaddish 294
    observing its *Halachot* 296
    recovers during the *shivah* week 295
    seven close family members 294
    silencing comforters 296
    tearing his garments 296, 370
    telling him 294
    visited by another mourner 294
seven close family members 294
shivah see ***shivah* week**
studying medicine 369
treifah 238
visiting a patient 367
wearing leather shoes 369
wishing her *mazal tov* if she has given birth 370
yahrzeit, day of death unknown 371
mucus plug
    niddah 118
muktzeh
    food for a non-seriously ill patient 68
    medication 69
    moving it for a patient 69
myoma
    bleeding 102

N

narcotic drugs
    Halachic view 41
naso-gastric tube
    feeding meat with milk 38
    seriously ill patient 324
nature
    change in 14, 33, 108, 315
    study of 279
neck
    broken 354
needle biopsy
    from a corpse 338
    from a *nefel* 338
nefel
    autopsy 338
    burial 211, 212
    burial on *Yom Tov* 212
    mourning for him 238, 366
    needle biopsy 338
    removal of foreskin 211, 212

negligent treatment 286
nephrostomy
    mikveh 156
neveilah
    definition 165
niddah
    accepting medical opinion as to source of bleeding 101, 103
    after first coitus, reason 115
    birth control pills 138
    bleeding
        at ovulation 100
        birth control pills 114, 138
        bride 114
        due to a *makkah* 101, 121-123
        during breast-feeding 107
        during pregnancy 108
        fibroids 102
        following hysterectomy 106
        hemorrhoids 110
        hymen 115
        instrumentation 121-123
        myoma 102
        polypectomy 122
        surgery on hymen 115
        urine 111, 113
        vaginal (*prozdor*) 100, 106, 121
    bleeding at coitus 100, 102
    blind husband or wife 125, 141
    blood in urine 111, 113
    bride, taking tablets to prevent menstruation 114
    caring for sick husband 128
    carrying a baby carriage with husband 127
    cervical culture 122
    childbirth 117-120, 224
    credibility of medical opinion 101, 103
    definition 98-100, 136
    diaphragm, use of 138
    diarrhea 132
    difficulty with examination 140
    douching 137
    drawing blood 132
    ectopic pregnancy 120
    eye drops 132
    fibroids 102
    hefsek taharah
        difficulty with examination 140
        medically forbidden to her husband 137
        procedure 136, 139
        use of absorbent cotton 140
        uterine pessary 139
        virgin bride 140
    helping husband to put on *tefillin* 126
    hematuria 111, 113
    hemiplegia 132

INDEX

hemorrhoids	110
hymen, removed surgically	115
hysterectomy	106
ill, cared for by husband	129, 131, 268
injections	132
instrumentation	121-123
intrauterine device	139
introduction to its laws,	
life span of an egg	99
life span of the sperm	99
menstrual cycle, description	98
Rambam's description of the anatomy	99
reproductive organs, anatomy	98
when does she become *niddah*	100
ketem,	
found on toilet paper or nylon cloth	112
using tablets to decide whether blood or other stain	110
wearing colored underwear	110
makkah, definition	101
martyrdom	134
menorrhagia	102
mikveh, immersion in	136
miscarriage	119, 120
moch dachuk	136, 139
mucus plug before labor	118
myoma	102
non-Jewish doctor	101, 103, 107
non-observant Jewish doctor	105, 106
ovulatory bleeding	100
Pap. Smear	122
passing something to her husband	126
pessary	139
physical contact with husband when ill	see **physical contact**
pressure sores	132
prolapse of uterus	106
ritual purification	136
"seven clean days"	see **seven clean days**
sick husband	126, 128
treatment by her husband	129
underwear, colored	110
unmarried woman	134
urinating with blood	111, 113
uterine bleeding	98, 100-102
uterine prolapse	108
vaginal	
bleeding	100, 106
laceration	140
suppository, use of	138
virgin bride	114
washing a sick husband	128, 129
what is forbidden	125
non-Jew(ess)	see also **idolater**
asking him to do what a Jew may not	207
corpse and a *Cohen*	350
doctor	276
following their customs	96
food cooked by him	68
nursing a Jewish baby	21
performed circumcision	217
research on *Shabbat* and *Yom Tov*	12
non-Jewish hospital	
mezuzah	230
missionary	64
non-kosher food	51, 65, 71
non-kosher food	
blessing before and after eating it	47
bread and cookies from which *challah* has not been separated	245, 251, 252
chametz on or after *Pesach*	67
child	22
danger to a limb	70
eating less than a *measure*	67
fish oil	30 (ref. 26), 66 (ref. 100)
gelatine capsules	31
muktzeh, eating and moving it	69, 70
nullifying it	29, 30, 48
non-seriously ill patient	46, 65
nursing mother	21
pronounced kosher by *Sanhedrin*	26
research on *Shabbat*	13
seriously ill patient	24
shoteh	22, 24
soap	42
tablets and capsules	30, 66
undergone chemical change	30
untithed food	247, 248, 251
non-seriously ill patient	
bikur cholim	257
brought his illness upon himself	70
chametz on or after *Pesach*	67
eating less than a "measure"	67
electric lamp, moving it	70
food cooked by non-Jew	68
forbidden food	65
gelatine capsules	31
hazardous treatment	54, 55
kosher food cooked on *Shabbat* by a non-Jew	46, 68
may become seriously ill	47
medication made from forbidden food	30
mitzvah to treat him	368
niddah and treatment by husband	129
non-kosher fish oil	30 (ref. 26), 66 (ref. 100)
non-kosher food	46, 65, 71
obligation of the doctor to treat	277
Shabbat	67, 69
shaving hair of armpits or crotch	94
stam yenam	46
surgery	59
treatment, hazardous	54, 55

nullification of forbidden food
    attaining any special status of the
        kosher food   48
    eaten by a patient   29, 30, 246
    matzah from which *challah* was not
        separated   251
    undergone chemical change   30

nurse
    Cohen   352
    keri'ah   330
    nursing care for a *gosses*   319, 325
    obligation to inform a relative of a death
        Shabbat   374
        weekday   373
    speaking about an unconscious patient
        in his presence   296
    treating a patient of the opposite sex
        132, 267
    treating a patient with infectious
        disease   266
    wine for *Kiddush* and *Havdalah*   47

nursing mother
    eats non-kosher foods   21

nylon underwear
    ketem   110

O

oath   see also **vow**
    difference from a vow   165
    taken by all Israel at Mount Sinai   165
    taken by a patient   165

ointment
    chatzizah   150

onen
    brit milah for son   214
    laws concerning   332

one's body
    donating to science   337
    ownership rights   12, 337

operations   see **surgery**
organ donation   see **donor**
organ transplants   see **transplantation**

orlah fruit
    to save life   88
    use as medicine   234

orthodontic appliance
    chatzizah   154

ovary
    life span of an egg   99
    ovulation and bleeding   98
    physiology   98

ovulation
    problems of pregnancy   137

ownership rights
    over one's body   12, 337
    over one's children   12

P

pacemaker
    removal from corpse   340

pain
    comatose patient   322, 323
    suffering, to save life   80

Pap. smear
    bleeding following   122

paper
    ketem   112

paralysis
    baby, *brit milah*   199
    helped by person and his *niddah* wife   126
    immersion in a *mikveh*   158
    niddah, helped by her husband   129
    value of life   321

paramedical staff
    Cohen   352
    keri'ah   330
    treating a patient with infectious
        disease   266
    treating someone of the opposite sex   132
    wine for *Kiddush* and *Havdalah*   47

parent
    blind, standing up for him   168
    blind child, standing up for parent   168
    caring for a sick parent   168, 169
    confused   168, 169
    daughter's obligation   168
    demands to be told the nature of his
        illness   167
    drawing blood   170
    extracting a tooth   172
    giving them something that is
        medically harmful   166
    honoring and fearing them   166
    injections   170
    injury   169
    listening to their demands against
        medical advice   166
    medical expenses   167, 169
    mentally deranged   168, 169
    non-Jewish   173
    nursing home   169
    ownership rights over their children   12
    paying for expenses   167, 170
    praying for him   262
    professional care   169
    punishment for injuring   169, 171
    reward for the *mitzvah*   169
    standing up for him   168
    surgery   171
    telling them the nature of their illness   167
    treating a sick parent   168, 169
    treatment by *Hashem* and by man   272

INDEX

tying down when confused	168
unable to care for them	169
unnecessary injury	169
who pays the expenses	167, 169
paschal lambs	
whose skins have become mixed	48
passive euthanasia	
when permitted	321, 323, 324, 327
pasteurized wine	
Kiddush or *Havdalah*	50
patient	
annuling a vow	35, 160, 163
bed-bound	9, 53
bowing before crucifix or statue	53
causing him unnecessary suffering	296
compensation for injury	283
confession of sins	see **confession of sins**
cures in nature	276
depending on miracles	272
diarrhea	267
experimental treatment	11, 12
external and internal disease	275
forced treatment	57, 321
healing by Heaven	274, 278
Heaven-fearing	322
helped by *niddah* wife	125, 127
hypnosis for treatment	87
illness brought on by sin	52
illness, preordained	268
infectious disease	266
informing him of death of relative	294
making him happy	296
mental anguish	57
mi sheberach	268
milk after meat	34
minor illness	39
mitzvah to keep healthy	276
mourner, who takes precedence to visit	269
mourning	see **seriously ill**
niddah wife	125, 128, 129, 268
non-seriously ill	see **non-seriously ill**
obligation to pay doctor's fees	293
obligation to seek treatment	272
offering a Torah scholar or and an elderly person his seat in a bus	174
paralyzed	126
partition to separate him from a corpse	332
permission to continue to seek cure	271
permission to seek medical care	269, 273
praying	
asking the Rav to do so	268
before any treatment	276
by a *ger*	265
confession of sins	297-300
for himself	263, 297
for his recovery	262-266, 297
for mercy	278
in the synagogue	268
including the patient among the sick of Israel	265
mi sheberach	268
reciting Psalms	89
Shabbat	266
that he die	264
which language	265
preventive medicine	274, 276, 280
psychotherapy	87
responsible for his illness	270
salt-free diet	18
saving his limb	339
seeking treatment	271
seriously ill	see **seriously ill**
settling his affairs	266
shaving body hair	92
stam yenam	46
standing up for Torah scholar	174
suffering and prolonging life	57
suffering with diarrhea	267
taking medicine on his own initiative	283
tefillin, helped by *niddah* wife	126
telling a parent the nature of his illness	167, 298
took an oath	165
treatment by *Hashem*	272
trusting in Heaven	278
unclean surroundings	8
uttering a charm	87
"vegetable"	323
visiting him	see **bikur cholim**
vows taken	35, 160, 163
washing by someone of the opposite sex	267
wine for *Kiddush* and *Havdalah*	47
woman, helped by a man	267
pe'ot	
shaving	92, 93
periah	
after death	210
circumcised by surgeon	217
procedure	215
removing the foreskin with the underlying membrane	217
three days later	221
with magen clamp	216
peritoneal dialysis	
chatzizah	156
perverting justice	
to save life	80
Pesach	
drinking from the Kinneret	67(ref. 107)
eating Rabbinically forbidden *chametz*	67
fast of the firstborn	243

pessary	
going out on *Shabbat*	139
ritual purification	139, 155
petichat hakever	
breakage of water	117
breast-feeding	117
cessation of contractions	118
childbirth	117-120
definition	117, 120
"dry childbirth"	119
how much	117, 119
instrumentation	121-123
natural or instrument	120
pregnancy	117
without bleeding	118
pharmacist	
prescribing medication	282
phlebotomy	see **blood, drawing**
phototherapy	
for jaundice	202
physical contact with husband when *niddah*	
blind husband or wife	125
carrying baby carriage together	127
drawing blood	132
helping paralyzed person together	126
hemiplegia	132
husband tending to ill wife	129
in health	125
injections	132
passing baby from one to another	126
putting in eye drops	132
putting *tefillin* on husband	126
tending to ill husband	128
throwing objects from one to another	126
wife has diarrhea	132
physician	see **doctor**
PIC catheter	
chatzizah	149
pidyon haben	
after ectopic pregnancy	120, 243
after IVF	189
baby born	
after a miscarriage	241
after an ectopic pregnancy	243
by AIH	188
by Caesarian section	242
by forceps delivery	244
by vacuum delivery	244
baby in incubator	237
baby with two heads	237, 239
Caesarian section	242
circumcision postponed till the thirty-first day	237
definition of childbirth	124, 224, 242
ectopic pregnancy	120, 243
father a deaf-mute	236
father died before the baby was	
eligible	236
following a miscarriage	241
gosses	240
ill baby	237
incubator	237
inheritance	242
intensive care treatment	238
nefel	237
premature baby	238, 366
redeeming himself	236
Siamese twins	237
treifah	236, 238
who is obligated	236
pikuach nefesh	see also **seriously ill**
of a relative of the deceased	354
pills	
birth control	114
placebo controlled trials	
conditions	12
Shabbat and *Yom Tov*	12
placing a stumbling block before the blind	
causing another to sin	24(ref. 30), 80, 82, 83, 356
infectious disease	266
paying interest for a loan	83
to save life	83
plaster cast	
chatzizah	149
plastic ear-plug	
chatzizah	157
plastic surgery	
when permitted	60
polypectomy	
bleeding after	122
postmaturity	
induction of labor	124
postmortem	see **autopsy**
pots and pans made by a non-Jew	
drinking at a kiosk or restaurant	44
food cooked in it	45
hospitalized patient	45
immersion in a *mikveh*	44
pram	
carrying together with *niddah* wife	127
prayer	
asking the Rav to do so	268
before any treatment	276
by a *ger*	265
confession of sins	297-300
feces in the room	232
for a parent or Rav	262
for himself	263, 297
for his recovery	262-266, 297
for mercy	278
in the synagogue	268
including the patient among the sick of Israel	265

INDEX

its purpose	263
mi sheberach	268
partition to permit	232
reciting Psalms	89
Shabbat	266
that he die	264
which language	265
while someone drowns	280
pregnancy	
breakage of water	117
Caesarian section	see **Caesarian section**
cervical cerclage	119
cessation of contractions	118
danger of	124
diagnosis of	108
ectopic	120
incompetence of the cervix	119
induction of labor	124
menstruation during	108
postmaturity	124
sex of fetus	109
sonography during	109
prescribing medication	
layman	283
pharmacist	282
Rambam's prescription	279
prescription for a patient	279
pressure sores	
niddah wife	132
preventive medicine	274, 276, 280
priority	see **giving precedence**
procreation	
danger to the woman	124
prolapsed uterus	
bleeding from	106
pessary	139, 153
proselyte	see **convert**
Psalms	
reciting for patient	89
psychiatric illness	
suicide	334
psychological stress	
childbirth	127
discussed in *Yerushalmi*	128
support for a dying patient	298
psychotherapy	
when permitted	87
purification from *niddah* state	
	see **ritual purification**
putting a stumbling block before the blind	
	see **placing**
putting one's life in danger	
bikur cholim	266
donor for transplantation	
bone marrow	346
kidney	347
to save another	266, 345

Q

quality of life	
resuscitation	321, 323

R

Ra'avad	
his opinion regarding the *tumah* of a *Cohen*	350
Rabbi	
making *Halachic* rulings regarding himself or his wife	141
praying for patient	268
pronounced non-kosher food kosher	26(ref 40)
Rabbinic law	
deriving one from another	65
setting aside to perform a Torah commandment	359
***Rambam's* prescription**	279
Rebbe Yishmael and Rabban Gamliel	281, 328
redemption of the firstborn	
	see ***pidyon haben***
renting out medical instruments	
taking interest	84
research	
animal	10
healthy volunteer	11
patient	
adult	11
child	11
flesh taken from living person	348
limb taken from living person	348
placebo controlled	12
Shabbat and *Yom Tov*	12
resident doctor	
negligent in answering a call	289
performing surgery	62
respiratory center	
description	303
resuscitation	
DNR	320, 322, 324, 326
intubation, source in *Chazal*	329
mouth to mouth respiration, source in *Chazal*	329
of the dead	354
quality of life	321, 326
risking one's life	
to save another	181, 185, 266, 345
ritual defilement	
broken spine	354
Cohen	258, 350, 352, 365
decapitated person who is convulsing	354
internal organs	353

INDEX

limb
  from a corpse   258, 350
  from a living person   352, 365
ritual immersion   see *chatzizah, mikveh*
ritual purification
  birth control pills   138
  absorbent cotton, use of   140
  diaphragm   138
  difficulty with examination   140
  IUD   122, 139
  procedure   136
  Shabbat   139
  uterine pessary   139
  vaginal suppository   138
  virgin bride   138
ritual slaughter   see *shechitah*
robbing
  to save life   75, 249
Rosh Hashanah
  fasting before and vow   162
  woman and *shofar*   160

S

Sabbath
  autopsy   339
  baby with serious congenital defects   13
  biopsy from corpse   339
  bleeding gums or teeth   17
  brit milah   62, 192
  brought his illness on himself   70
  brought in early and *brit milah*   200
  buried under rubble   301
  challah, separating   252
  charging fees   290
  childbirth   117, 224
  circumcision   62, 227, 228
  confession of sins   297
  corpse   301, 359
  covering blood spilt during *shechitah*   10
  danger to a limb   75
  desecration
    to prevent another being shamed   80
    willfully   49
  difficult childbirth   224
  elective surgery   88
  experimental treatment   12
  food cooked by non-Jew   65, 68
  found dead   301
  gosses   301, 321
  illness brought on willfully   70
  induction of labor   124
  keri'ah   331
  Kiddush and *Havdalah* with
    stam yenam   47
  knot, definition   145
  melachot

    plucking   148
    removing body hair   148
    tying a knot   145
  moch dachuk   139
  muktzeh   67, 252
  needle biopsy from corpse   338
  non-seriously ill patient
    see **non-seriously ill**
  one who willfully desecrates *Shabbat*   49
  pessary   139
  placebo controlled trials   12
  postponed *brit* to Thursday or Friday   192
  prayed *Maariv* early   200
  praying for a patient   262, 266
  premature baby   13
  psik resha   216
  pulling out hair   148
  rejoining amputated limb   353
  research   12
  scab, removing before *mikveh*   147
  separating
    challah   251, 252
    the foreskin from the underlying
      flesh   217
    tithes   251, 252
  seriously ill patient   see **seriously ill**
  setting aside
    for a deaf-mute   321
    for a patient with ALS   322
    for a *shoteh*   321
    for a *treifah*   15
    for an elderly patient   321
    needlessly   12
    to prevent another being shamed
      publicly   79
  shechitah   10
  "stipulation" for tithes   221
  studying medicine   279
  sucking a bleeding wound   16
  tithes, separating   251, 252
  treifah, treating him   15
  vaginal pessary   139
  willful desecration   49
  writing on one's skin   89
sacrificing one life to save another
  aborting a fetus   186
  can only treat one of two patients   15, 182
  heart transplant from a *treifah* or
    from a *gosses*   185
  kidney transplant from a *gosses*   187
  treifah, concept in man   13
Sages of today
  does the Torah commandment: "You
    shall not deviate from what they
    tell you" refer to them   26(ref 40)
salt-free diet
  salting meat   18

INDEX

salting meat
  minimum time the salt should remain
    on the meat   19
  patient   18, 19
  procedure   18, 19
  using dietetic salt   19
  using sugar   18
Sanhedrin
  death penalty when the victim is a
    treifah   103
  pronounced non-kosher food, kosher
    26(ref 40)
saving life   see also **danger to life**
  at risk to oneself   181, 185, 266, 345
  at the expense of another   15, 60, 182
  borrowing with interest   83
  bulimos   78, 88
  by
    damaging property   75
    eating forbidden food   24, 88
    inciting another to sin   82, 83
    perverting justice   80
    robbery   75, 249
    shaming another publicly   79
    signing to a falsehood   78
  cardinal sins   53, 73
  eating *orlah* fruit   88
  illness brought on by sin   52
  one flask of water between two   77
  reciting Psalms   89
  sacrificing one's life to save another   182
  signing falsehood   78
  transgressing a negative commandment   87
  triage   181
  undergoing suffering to save life   80
scab
  chatzizah   147
  removing on *Shabbat*   147
sechar batalah   290
seriously ill patient
  blessings when eating forbidden foods   48
  brought his illness upon himself   70
  bulimos   78, 88
  cancer, telling the patient   298
  cardinal sins   53, 73
  causing him unnecessary suffering   294
  charms, use of   87-90
  chayei sha'ah and *chayei olam*   55
  chemotherapy   298
  Cohen, treating the patient   355
  coma   296, 322, 323
  confession of sins,
    enumerating his sins   300
    in the presence of excreta   297
    mitzvah to remind him   297
    nature of the confession   299
    no suffering without sin   297

    on *Shabbat*   297
    when should he do so   297
  DNR   320, 322, 324, 327
  dangerous treatment   54, 55
  dangerously ill, telling the patient   298
  deaf-mute   321
  do not resuscitate   320, 322, 324, 327
  dying patient   298
  eating
    non-kosher foods willfully   24
    orlah fruit   88
    tevel or *terumah*, which is the
      lesser sin   248
  elderly   321
  epileptic   29
  experimental treatment   11, 12
  forced treatment   57, 321, 322, 323
  giving a definitive prognosis   298
  Heaven-fearing   322
  high risk treatment to save his life   54, 55
  hypnosis   87
  illness
    brought on by sin   52
    preordained   268
  informing him of his illness   298
  Kiddush or *Havdalah* with *stam yenam*   48
  medication of known efficacy   71
  mother who must eat non-kosher foods   21
  mourning
    another mourner visiting him   294
    asks about the deceased   294
    crying in his presence   296
    did not mourn because of his state   370
    eulogizing the deceased in his
      presence   296
    Halachot of   294
    Kaddish   294
    observing its *Halachot*   296
    recovers during the *shivah* week   295
    seven close family members   294
    silencing comforters   296
    tearing his garments   296, 370
    telling him   294
    visited by another mourner   294
    which type of patient   294
  nasogastric tube   324
  niddah and treatment by husband   129
  non-kosher food   22, 71
  non-religious   88
  prayer
    asking the Rav to do so   268
    before any treatment   276
    confession of sins   297-300
    for himself   263
    for his recovery   262-266, 297
    for mercy   278
    in the synagogue   268

mi sheberach	268	shatnez	see also **kila'im**
reciting Psalms	89	graduation gowns	85
that he die	264	**shaving**	
probability of dying	162	armpits or crotch	94
psychological effects	72	body hair	94
psychological support for a dying patient	298	for medical reason	94
		pe'ot	93
psychotherapy	87	the prohibition	91
radiotherapy	298	**shechitah**	see also **shochet**
reciting Psalms	89	blessing before	4
settling his affairs	266	covering the spilt blood	5, 9
shoteh	22, 321	is it a *mitzvah*	4
sorcery	86	knife used for	2 (ref. 3)
suffering	see **suffering**	*Shabbat*	10
suicide	334	while confined to a chair	5
telling a parent the nature of his illness	167	while sitting	5
telling a patient that he is dangerously ill	298	*Yom Tov*	9
		Shemittah	
terminal disease, telling him	298	medications	248
thinking about his affairs	266	**Shemoneh Esrei**	
took an oath	165	bed-bound patient	53
transgressing a negative commandment	87	***sheretz***	
treatment		seriously ill patient	29
experimental	11, 12	***shevut***	
hazardous	54, 55	deriving one from another	65
treifah	13	**shivah week**	
unconscious patient		bathing	369
pain and suffering	322, 323	*brit milah* for son	214
speaking in his presence	296	doctor	367, 369
unconventional treatment	72	*Halachot* of	294, 296
undergoing suffering to save him	80	*Kaddish*	294
unproven treatment	29, 72	monetary loss	367
"vegetable" — patient	323	patient	294-296, 370
visiting him	254	tearing garments	296, 370
vowed to fast	161	wishing the mourner *mazal tov*	370
vowed to him	163	wishing the mourner *shalom*	370
waiting for kosher food	73	**shochet**	see also **shechitah**
wife who is a *niddah*	129	blind	3, 6
"seven clean days"		confined to a chair	5
artificial insemination during	143	covering the spilt blood	5, 9
birth control pills	138	deaf	4
ceased to be aware	142	deaf-mute	2
counting	136, 142	drop attacks	2
diaphragm	138	dumb	4
douching	137	elderly	3, 5
intrauterine device	139	epileptic	2
pessary	139	ill	5
Shabbat	139	knife, examination	2 (ref. 3)
surgery during	142	minor	3
vaginal suppository	138	*shoteh*	2
severed head		unsteady hands	5
if possible to rejoin	354	weak	3
Shabbat	see **Sabbath**	weak eyesight	3, 6
shaming another publicly		wears spectacles	6
akin to murder	79	**shofar**	
desecrating *Shabbat* to prevent it	80	unclean place	9
to save life	79	woman who cannot go to hear it	160

INDEX

shoteh
   child   21, 25
   definition   2
   doubt as to whether he is   3
   facilitated communication   28
   institutional care   22
   obligation to *mitzvot*   23
   sacrificing him to save one who is not   182
   setting aside Sabbath laws   26, 321
   shochet   2
   signs of   2
   treating him   26, 321, 323

Siamese twins
   pidyon haben   237

side-effects of medication
   why is it permitted to treat   60, 61

sin
   between man and his fellow   63
   between man and Heaven   63
   causing another to   see **placing a stumbling block**
   injury to parent   62
   lack of intention to harm   63

sinful thoughts
   control of   134

skin
   graft   340, 345

soap made from non-kosher fat   42

sodomy   134

sof tumah latseit   259

son
   treating his parent   166

sonography
   during pregnancy   107

sorcery
   for treatment   86

soul
   harmed by non-kosher food   22

spectacles   see **glasses, contact lenses**

sperm
   life span   99

springs
   miraculous powers   64

stam yenam
   boiled wine   50
   Kiddush or *Havdalah*   47
   non-seriously ill patient   46
   one who willfully desecrates *Shabbat*   49
   pasteurized wine   50
   seriously ill patient   47
   what is prohibited   46

stealing
   to save life   75, 249

stem cell donation
   for patient who requires a bone marrow transplant   347

stew in one's own juice   84

"stipulation"
   for separating tithes   251

stomach tube   see **gastrostomy, naso-gastric tube**

study of medicine
   Cohen   350
   examination of the opposite sex   132
   obligation to   279, 293
   permission to   134
   shivah week   369

study of nature
   obligation   279

suffering
   ALS   322, 323
   animals   10
   ashamed to go out in public   92
   causing unnecessary suffering
      brit milah   188, 189, 202, 215
      patient   296
   comatose patient   321, 322, 323
   do not resuscitate   320, 322, 324, 327
   euthanasia   319, 327
   forced treatment   321, 322, 323
   increased by treatment   322, 324
   merit   322
   narcotics   321
   nasogastric tube   324
   obligation to undergo suffering to save life   80
   praying that the patient die   264, 321
   prolonging life   319
   standard requirements such as food, fluids, oxygen   324
   value of life   321, 323

suicide
   absolution of sins   334
   definition in *Halachah*   334
   fear of torture   334
   HaGomel blessing   335
   obligation to save his life   335
   preventing it   334
   psychiatric illness   334
   Shabbat   335

suppositories
   vaginal   138

surgeon   see **doctor**

surgery
   Caesarian section   see **Caesarian section**
   cervix and bleeding   142
   charity for private surgeon   180
   cosmetic   60
   died during and burial   349
   doctor in training   62
   elective on *Shabbat*   88
   hemophilia   206

hymenectomy	115
hysterectomy and bleeding	106
laser for *brit milah*	206
non-seriously Il patient	59
parent	171
plastic	60

rejoining amputated finger
Cohen	353
Shabbat	353
sick parent	169

sutures and *chatzizah*
gums	154
skin	149

T

tablets
birth control	114

Talmud
medications mentioned	277

tattooing
the prohibition	91
writing on one's skin	91

teaching Torah
for free	290

teeth
bleeding, *Shabbat*	17
dental treatment and *chatzizah*	150-154
extraction by a son	172

false
chatzizah	152
kashering	36

tefillin
helped by wife who is a *niddah*	126
putting on in the presence of a corpse	332
unclean place	8

telling a patient
about the death of a relative	374
he is seriously ill	167, 296

temperature see **fever**

terminally ill patient see also **gosses**
"cosmetic" treatment	327
DNR	320, 322, 324, 327
euthanasia	327
narcotics for pain	321
treatment causing pain	321

terumah see **tithes**

tests for brain death
in what percentage of donors are they done	306

tevel see **tithes**

Tishah B'Av
metzizah	222
wishing *Shalom*	370

tithes
blessing over	250
definition of *tevel*	247
Diaspora	251, 252
fruit grown in Israel	251, 252
laws concerning	247, 251
ma'asrot	247, 251
medications	247
nullifying *terumah*	248

separation
blind person	245, 250, 251
deaf person	4, 250
dumb person	4, 250
on *Shabbat*	251
without permission	238
seriously ill patient	238
Shabbat	251
"stipulation"	251
terumah	245, 247
tevel	247

which is the lesser sin —
eating *tevel* or *terumah*	248

toilet paper
blood stains	112

Torah law
setting aside to save life	26
setting aside to save a limb	75, 339

Torah scholar
offering him one's seat in a bus	174
one who is too ill to remain standing	174
standing up for him	174
today	185

Torah study
equivalent to all the *mitzvot*	178
greater than saving life	178
research project	179
teaching for free	290
to cure illness	89
to further one's career	179
who is obligated	177

torture, undergoing
to save life	81

toupee see **wig**

tov shebarofe'im
the best of doctors	278, 282, 292

tracheostomy
chatzizah	158

transplantation

from a corpse
bone	340
cornea	340, 342
skin	340, 345
from anencephalic babies	318
from chronic vegetative state patients	317

healthy donor
bone	347
bone marrow	346
kidney	347

putting one's life in danger
to save another	345

INDEX

stem cells	347
when permitted	345
mechanical heart	58
treatment	
annuling Heaven's decree	269
by Heaven	272, 276
charms	87, 90
depending on miracles	272
doctor's fees	271
experimental treatment	11, 12
external and internal disease	275
forced	57, 321, 323
hashavat aveidah	271
hazardous for non-seriously ill	59
high risk to save life	54, 55
hypnosis	87
infectious disease see **infectious disease**	
medicines of the Talmud	277
missionary hospital	64
nature and man	276
niddah wife	129
obligation to seek	272
opposite sex	132, 267
parent	170
patient refuses	57
preventive	274, 276
priorities	181
psychotherapy	87
Ramban's view	273
side-effects	59, 60
sorcery	86
risk to doctor	267
triage	181
unconventional	72
unproven efficacy	29, 72
unsuccessful	271
verapo yerapei	269
which is the more serious problem, treating one's *niddah* wife or another's wife	132
whom to treat first	181
treifah (ot)	
baby	240
birkat HaGomel	15
circumcision on *Shabbat*	192
concept in man	13
death penalty for killing him	105, 185
definition	165
difference between man and animals	13
donor for heart transplant	185
eight types	13
mourning for him	240
pidyon haben	236, 238
Sabbath laws	15, 186
sacrificing him to save the life of another	15, 185
triage	
already involved in treating a patient	182
setting aside one life for another	181, 185
two patients, one machine	182
two patients present simultaneously	182
who should be saved first	181
trisomy 21 see **Down syndrome**	
tubal patency	
bleeding following the examination	122
tubal pregnancy	120
tumat Cohen	
baby	364
decapitated person	354
deceased in another apartment	357, 359
door with metal hinges	359
limb	350
of a corpse	258, 350
setting aside Rabbinic *tumah* to perform Torah commandment	359
spread of *tumah*	357
tumat ledah	
"dry childbirth"	119
ectopic pregnancy	120
tumtum	
brit milah on *Shabbat*	201
features of	201
twilight see ***bein hashemashot***	
twins	
one of whom died before he was eight days old	208
tzedakah see **charity**	

U

ultrasound see **sonography**	
unclean place	
performance of *mitzvot*	8
praying	9
shechitah	8
shofar	9
tefillin	9
thinking words of a blessing	9
thinking words of Torah	9
unconscious patient	
pain and suffering	322, 323
prolonging life	319
speaking about him in his presence	296
unconventional treatment	
charity for	72
seriously ill patient	72
undergoing suffering	
to save life	80
underwear	
colored and a *ketem*	110
untithed produce see **tithes**	
urine	
blood in	111, 113

U

utensils
  bought from a non-Jew   44
uterus   see also **niddah**
  bleeding following hysterectomy   106
  fibroids   102
  pessary   139, 155
  prolapsed   106

V

vacuum delivery
  pidyon haben   244
vaginal bleeding   see **niddah**
vaginal examination
  by a male physician   74
  suppository   138
"vegetable"
  patient   323
verapo yerapei   269
visiting the sick   see ***bikur cholim***
volunteer
  research   11
vow
  accepting a custom on oneself   160
  annulment of   35, 160, 163
  custom to fast   35, 160, 161
  difference from an oath   165
  minhag   35, 161
  nullify by husband   164
  procedure to annul a vow   161
  regular Torah lesson   160
  seriously ill   161
  taken under duress   164
  taken when ill   35, 160, 163
  to a friend   163
  to a patient   164
  to live in Israel   162
  to take treatment to conceive   164
  woman and *shofar*   160

W

washing off mud
  Yom Kippur   96
wearing
  a woman's coat   96
wheelchair
  shochet   6
wife
  caring for ill husband   128
  forbidden to have coitus   137, 143
  refuses to cohabit with husband   143
  vowed to take treatment to conceive   164
wig worn by a man
  does he need to wear a *kippah*   97
  marit ha'ayin   97
  mentioning *Hashem's* Name   97
  tefillin   97
will
  living   325
wine
  boiled   50
  Kiddush and *Havdalah*   47
  pasteurized   50
  stam yenam   47
  touched by Jew who desecrates
    Shabbat   49
woman
  bikur cholim by a man   258
  blind, examination cloth   141
  breast-feeding and menstruation   105
  Caesarian section   see **Caesarian section**
  cared for by a man   267
  caring for a sick parent   168
  colored underwear   110
  daughter of *Cohen*   362
  difficulty with self-examination   140
  dressing as a man   94
  examination by male   74, 132
  forbidden to have coitus   137, 143
  gilui arayot   134
  gynecological examination by male
    physician   73, 132
  in charge of *mikveh*   159
  marital obligation   137, 143
  medically forbidden to her husband   137, 143
  mitzvah of *shofar* and annuling a vow   160
  obligation to perform *mitzvot*   6
  physical contact with husband when ill   129, 131, 267
  refuses to cohabit with husband   143
  reproductive organs   98
  tended to by a man   267
  treatment by male   132
  unmarried, *niddah*   134
  wearing colored underwear   110
  who cannot have coitus and *yichud*   143
  who oversees the process of immersion   159
  wife of *Cohen*   362
wound
  sucking it   16
writing
  on one's skin   89

X

X-Ray
  uterus   121

INDEX

Y

yad soledet
    definition   36
    temperature   38
yahrzeit
    day of death unknown   371
yichud
    bikur cholim   257
    when coitus is forbidden   143
Yom Kippur
    leather shoes (Torah law)   94
    metzizah   222
    washing off mud   96

Yom Tov
    burying a *nefel*   221, 212
    covering blood spilt during *shechitah*   9
    keri'ah   321
    postponed *brit milah*   192
    research   12
    second day
        born by Caesarian section   227
        postponed *brit milah*   192, 223
        removal of foreskin before burial   210
    separating tithes or *challah*   251
    seriously ill *patient* and mourning   295
    shechitah   9

About the Author

Abraham S. Abraham is Emeritus Professor of Medicine, Hebrew University and Hadassah Medical School, and has very recently retired from his position as Director of the Department of Medicine B at the Shaare Zedek Medical Center, Jerusalem, Israel.

He studied medicine at the Leeds School of Medicine, England, receiving his medical degree of Bachelor of Medicine and Surgery (MB, ChB) in 1960. His residency training in Internal Medicine included specialist training in Gastroenterology. He completed his Boards in 1964 (MRCP — Member of the Royal College of Physicians, London). He then went on to specialist training in Cardio-Pulmonology at the Queen Elizabeth Hospital, Birmingham, England receiving his MD (equivalent to a medical Ph.D.) from the University of Birmingham in 1968 for his pioneering work on the effects of oxygen in the treatment of patients with chronic bronchitis and emphysema. For this work he was awarded the annual prize of the American Heart Association / British Heart Foundation — to spend a year of research in the United States, which he did at the Johns Hopkins School of Medicine, Baltimore 1968/9. In recognition of his achievements in and contributions to the field of medicine, he was elected a Fellow of the Royal College of Physicians, London (FRCP) in 1977.

Abraham returned to his birthplace, Jerusalem, Israel in 1970 where he has practiced medicine for the last thirty years. For many years he has been the Director of the Department of Medicine B at the Shaare Zedek Medical Center and a teacher at the Hebrew University-Hadassah Medical School, becoming a Professor of Medicine at the latter institution, a member of the Senate of the Hebrew University, an examiner for the Israel Board in Internal Medicine and has served on a variety of national and local committees. He has published over eighty articles on cardio-pulmonary medicine, trace elements in cardiovascular disease and other subjects, in prestigious international medical journals including the New England Journal of Medicine and has, on many occasions, been included in the list of outstanding teachers at the Hadassah Medical School.

Professor Abraham has also published extensively in the field of Medical Halachah: *Lev Avraham* (2 volumes, Hebrew) and its English translation, *Medical Halachah for Everyone,* followed later by an updated and more extensive volume, *The Comprehensive Guide to Medical Halachah.* His magnum opus, the six-volume *Nishmat Avraham* (Hebrew), based on the four sections of the *Shulchan Aruch* (*Orach Chaim, Yoreh Deah, Even HaEzer* and *Choshen Mishpat*), is today the classical text for health-care personnel, laymen and Rabbis alike, encompassing medico-halachic problems and their solutions in all branches of medicine, surgery, gynecology and obstetrics. He has also published two pocket-books (both in Hebrew and in English) dealing specifically with medico-halachic problems on the Sabbath, Festivals and Yom Kippur, for health-care personnel and patient respectively.

The present book is his edited translation of the *Yoreh Deah* section of *Nishmat Avraham,* and is taken from volumes two, four and five.

This volume is part of
THE ARTSCROLL SERIES®
an ongoing project of
translations, commentaries and expositions
on Scripture, Mishnah, Talmud, Halachah,
liturgy, history, the classic Rabbinic writings,
biographies and thought.

For a brochure of current publications
visit your local Hebrew bookseller
or contact the publisher:

Mesorah Publications, ltd
4401 Second Avenue
Brooklyn, New York 11232
(718) 921-9000
www.artscroll.com